# FELICIA HEMANS

This portrait, engraved by Edward Smith from a miniature painted by Edward
Robertson in Dublin, autumn 1831, displays the blend of beauty and melancholy
that became Felicia Hemans's hallmark. With her signature underneath, it was
the frontispiece for Chorley's *Memorials of Mrs. Hemans* London: Saunders and
Otley, 1836). Chorley called it "a faithful and graceful likeness" (*Memorials* 2.253).

# FELICIA HEMANS

*Selected Poems, Letters, Reception Materials*

EDITED BY
SUSAN J. WOLFSON

PRINCETON UNIVERSITY PRESS
PRINCETON AND OXFORD

*Library of Congress Cataloging in Publication Data*
Hemans, Felicia Dorothea Browne, 1793–1835.
[Selections. 2000]
Felicia Hemans : selected poems, letters, reception materials /
edited by Susan J. Wolfson.
p.   cm.
Includes bibliographical references and indexes.
ISBN 0-691-05029-5 (alk. paper)
1. Hemans, Felicia Dorothea Browne, 1793–1835—Correspondence.
2. Hemans, Felicia Dorothea Browne, 1793–1835—Criticism and
interpretation.   3. Hemans, Felicia Dorothea Browne, 1793–1835—Appreciation.
4. Poets, English—19th century—Correspondence.
I. Wolfson, Susan J., 1948–   II. Title.
PR4780.A4 2000
821'.7—dc21
[B]      00-039146

This book has been composed in Adobe Caslon
Designed by Jan Lilly
Composed by Gretchen Oberfranc

The paper used in this publication meets
the minimum requirements of
ANSI/NISO Z39.48-1992 (R 1997)
(*Permanence of Paper*)

www.pup.princeton.edu

Printed in the United States of America

1   3   5   7   9   10   8   6   4   2

# CONTENTS

# ACKNOWLEDGMENTS

THIS EDITION of the works of Felicia Hemans was made possible by a subvention from the Princeton University Committee on Research in the Humanities and Social Sciences, which also sustained my work on Hemans with other grants. I am also grateful for substantial material support from the Department of English.

My preparation of this edition is indebted to several libraries and archives, as my list of permissions indicates. My primary resource has been Firestone Library, Princeton University. For generously sharing expertise and information, I thank Simone Balayé, Fred Burwick, David Damrosch, Paula Feldman, Denise Gigante, Erik Gray, Tom Hothem, John Claiborne Isbell, Nicholas Jones, Uli Knoepflmacher, Jonathan Lamb, David Latané, Ron Levao, Albert Levine, John Logan, Peter Manning, Richard Matlak, Carol McGuirk, Anne Mellor, Mark Olsen, Morton Paley, David Quint, Susan Reilley, Daniel Riess, Susan Scheckel, English Showalter, Jeffrey Skoblow, Nan Sweet, Ted Underwood, Elena Urebi, and Duncan Wu. A detailed correspondence with Gary Kelly during 1997 helped sharpen and clarify my interests. For research advice, I was lucky to enlist Duncan Wu (again), Christopher Rovee, Gayle Barkley, Peter Cochran, Philip Dundas, Joanna Knowles, and most especially Libby Fay, for a meticulous review of *The Siege of Valencia* manuscript. For sustained research and technological assistance, I was fortunate in Laura Struve's care and dedication, and most especially grateful for Andrew Krull's resourcefully persistent intelligence and sheer energy. Paula Feldman provided steady encouragement, information and advice, and a valuable prepublication review. For general support and advice, I thank friends and colleagues Isobel Armstrong, Stephen Behrendt, Claudia Johnson, Angela Leighton, Harriet Linkin, Peter Manning, Anne Mellor, Michael Wood, Duncan Wu; for timely professional counsel, Richard Levao and, especially, Melissa Klipp. For her steady support for this project, I am grateful to Mary Murrell of Princeton University Press.

For support, advice, encouragement, practical assistance, and much more beyond naming, I am, as always, unendingly grateful to Ronald Levao.

THIS EDITION reflects several kind and generous grants of permissions to use materials under copyright. Details (e.g., MS identification codes, texts, shelfmarks, folio numbers, etc.) will appear with each text, where appropriate.

The Berg Collection of English and American Literature, The New York Public Library, Astor, Lenox and Tilden Foundations for excerpt from MS letter from Joanna Baillie to Hemans.

The Bodleian Library, University of Oxford: MS letter from P. B. Shelley to Felicia Dorothea Browne.

British Library Board of the British Library: MS letters from Robert Peel to Hemans, from Hemans to Samuel Butler, James Simpson, and William Jacob.

Camden Local Studies and Archives Center: excerpts from MS letters from Joanna Baillie to Hemans.

Harry Ransom Humanities Research Center, University of Texas at Austin: MS letter from Joanna Baillie to Hemans.

Houghton Library, Harvard University: MS letter from Joanna Baillie to Andrews Norton, and citations of the MS of *The Siege of Valencia*.

The Huntington Library, San Marino, California: MS letters from Hemans to B. P. Wagner, W. Atherton, T. Cadell, C. Graves, and Anne Grant; and from Andrews Norton to Hemans.

Liverpool Libraries and Information Services: Hemans's MS of *The Forest Sanctuary*; MS letters to Matthew Nicholson from Felicia Dorothea Browne and from Felicity Browne (mother), and from Hemans to William S. Roscoe and to Mary R. Mitford.

John Murray (Publishers), Ltd. excerpts from *Byron's Letters and Journals*, ed. Leslie A. Marchand (London, 1977); MS letters from Hemans to Murray.

Trustees of the National Library of Scotland: MS correspondence between Hemans and William Blackwood, and letters from Joanna Baillie to Walter Scott.

Excerpts from *The Letters of William and Dorothy Wordsworth: The Later Years, 1821–1850*, ed. Ernest de Selincourt; 2d ed., revised, arranged, and edited by Allan G. Hill (Clarendon Press, 1979) appear by permission of Oxford University Press.

Princeton University Library, Department of Rare Books and Special Collections, the Manuscript Division: MS letters from Hemans to W. H. Ainsworth and to Fanny Luxmore; MS of *The Broken Chain*; excerpts from Rose Lawrence, *The Last Autumn, With Recollections of Mrs. Hemans*.

The President and Council of the Royal College of Surgeons of England, for Joanna Baillie's letters to William Sotheby.

# INTRODUCTION

## *Felicia Dorothea Browne Hemans*

### 1793–1835

#### HEMANS'S FAME

By the late 1820s, beset by budding poets seeking advice and support, by fans seeking autographs, inscriptions for their albums, or just a glimpse of the famous "poetess," Felicia Hemans was waxing wry and rueful about "the dust of celebrity," with more than a few of her letters and poems sighing of "the nothingness of Fame, at least to woman."[1] This weariness was the consequence of a remarkable career. In the United States and Britain, she was one of the best-selling poets of her century and one of the first women to make a living by writing verse. Between 1808 and 1835 nineteen volumes of her works appeared, some in multiple editions. By the 1820s, with increasingly appreciative reviews in the establishment press and a regular presence in popular magazines and ornate annuals, "Mrs. Hemans" had emerged as England's premier "poetess," celebrated as its epitome of "feminine" excellence. This icon sentimentalized a success born of industry and facility, business acumen and alertness to the literary market, as well as talent. Adept in a range of genres and verse forms (sonnet, ode, heroic verse, ballad, epistle, narrative, monologue, drama, lyric, didactic), literate, imaginative, and intellectually appetitive, Hemans fashioned popular themes with a transhistorical, international range of subjects, drawing on literatures past and present, English and Continental. Well into the century, her work was admired by a wide readership, including men and women of letters. Her books were cherished gifts and prizes; many poems were public favorites, memorized and anthologized, illustrated and set to music. *Casabianca* ("The boy stood on the burning deck") became a standard at recitals; Americans took *The Landing of the Pilgrim Fathers* ("The breaking waves dashed high") to heart, while *The Homes of England* and *England's Dead* became virtual national anthems for the British.[2]

It was with such pieces that "Mrs. Hemans" became the "undisputed representative poet of Victorian imperial and domestic ideology."[3] But as the title lost luster, this sifting of her works was further thinned by late-century anthologizers, and then cast out altogether as pretty pieties. If Wordsworth advanced the "Poet" as a man speaking to men, "poetess" Hemans seemed a woman speaking only to nineteenth-century sentimental culture, and not even all women. By 1880, A. Mary F. Robinson, a young scholar and poet who might have embraced Hemans as a predecessor, wanted only to dissociate herself. "Fifty years ago few poets were more popular than Mrs. Hemans; her verses were familiar to all hearts," she began her headnote for T. H. Ward's *English Poets*. This anthology offered just one dirge, one ballad, and *Casabianca*. "These simple, chivalrous, pathetic" domestic lyrics, "sprung from a talent expressive but not creative, [. . .] stamped with feminine qualities," were Hemans's "claim to remembrance," and even then it seemed weakening, her poems "chiefly forgotten, and without injustice" (4.334–35). Although Hemans was still popular in the 1880s, her prestige in canonical estimations was slipping. Robinson's view was not unusual, and it was predictive. Eighty years later, Ellen Moers's compendious *Literary Women: The Great Writers* (1963) had even less to say of Hemans, citing her only as a cautionary example of "precocious" yet ultimately "facile" talent.[4] The bicentennial of her birth, in 1993, passed without the parade of conferences, exhibits, special issues of journals, anthologies of essays, and new editions that have been marking other bicentennial milestones of the "Romantic" era.

But Hemans was gradually, then emphatically, being rediscovered as new historicism and feminism began to reshape the landscape of Romantic studies.[5] Her work was attracting interest not as a historical curiosity from the shop of outworn tastes, but for its currency, for its sounding of dissonances in nineteenth-century cultural ideals. Her perspectives, moreover, seemed to cast in new lights the traditional canon of male "Romantic" poets (an early twentieth-century construction that, with minor adjustments, held up through the 1980s).[6] Emerging from a complex social and political vision, Hemans's career of writing and its erratic reception history—from polite discouragement, to emerging appreciation, to celebrity, to condescension, to obscurity, to critical and scholarly recovery, to renewed classroom interest—cut to the core of a number of our current critical concerns: how women's poetry is shaped in a gendered culture; how aesthetic value is determined in a given historical setting; how we represent the Romantic era of poetry; and (as the Victorian "Mrs. Hemans" suggests) how we represent Hemans herself. Her celebrity in her own day became her curse in literary history, and the modern recovery, in no small part, has been a project of rescuing her from the terms of her nineteenth-century popularity.

I first heard of Hemans in Wordsworth's *Extempore Effusion* (1836), where a reverential elegiac stanza is matched by an affectionate headnote that still managed to voice discomfort about her ignorance of household skills. Then I found Byron, in a letter of 1820 to John Murray (also Hemans's publisher), jibing at "your feminine *He-Man*" and "Mrs. Hewoman's"—the punning and insistent misspelling of her surname aimed at her intellectual pretensions. Like many male poets, Byron preferred women in their place, not his. "I do not despise Mrs. Heman—but if [she] knit blue stockings instead of wearing them it would be better," he said to Murray. In 1977 editor Leslie Marchand identified Byron's reference: "a popular poetess of the day" (7.158). Wanting to know more about a poet able to put Byron and Wordsworth on such rare common ground, I opened Ian Jack's *English Literature, 1815–1832* (1963), only to find, under the rubric of "other minor and minimus poets of the period," one page of condescension, which included the following slam: "She took the pulse of her time, and helped to prevent it from quickening. [. . .] The general level of her work is high, but unfortunately it almost always stops short of memorable poetry. Many of her better things [. . .] might be the work of a poetical committee. For her, we feel, poetry was a feminine accomplishment more difficult than piano-playing and embroidery [. . .] We read her, we commend, and we forget" (168). Forget we did. It was not until the 1970s that a coordinated recovery of women's writing took shape,[7] and even then Hemans was no immediate beneficiary. Many critics, female as well as male, continued to dismiss her as "a popular versifier" and a defender of "obsolete ideologies."[8] Even some of the newer anthologies settled for short lyrics easily dismissed as "chauvinistic, sentimental, and derivative."[9] In 1993 the influential *Norton Anthology of English Literature* (6th ed.) cast her with minor "lyric poets" (863) and presented a Victorian sampler: *Casabianca, Pilgrim Fathers* and *England's Dead.* The durability of this "Hemans" is reflected in Germaine Greer's cursory glance, as late as 1995, at her as a poet of "quaintness and insipidity," remembered only "if at all" for *Casabianca.*[10]

The difficulty of reviving Hemans is felt even by readers who take her seriously, such as Stuart Curran. In his pioneering essay of 1988 he hoped to identify a complicated poet, arguing that while Hemans's contemporaries made her "synonymous with the notion of a poetess, celebrating hearth and home, God and country in mellifluous verse that relished the sentimental and seldom teased anyone into thought," there were "other and darker strains"—"a focus on exile and failure, a celebration of female genius frustrated, a haunting omnipresence of death—that seem to subvert the role [she] claimed and invite a sophisticated reconsideration." But five years on, Curran took another measure, here not against the icon of "poetess" but against Wollstonecraft. This time, he was arrested by a definitive mode of Hemans-restraint by which she "became, above all, the creator and enforcer of [an] ideological control masking itself as praise for feminine instinct and female duty," indeed, became "the major figure" in a cosmopolitan "bourgeois literary culture" that "she exemplified and may in some sense be said to have forged." Curran does concede that the scene of this forging was "a trap of cultural contradiction," and other critics have continued to be fascinated by this circumstance. In one of the first sustained rereadings of Hemans, Marlon Ross proposed that her poetry was distorted by being held to a hypostasized "Romanticism" formed on a male canon; he resituated her in relation to a community of writers both male and female, and in relation to the reading public who made her famous. Norma Clarke saw "Felicia" exploiting conventional images of "femininity" (passivity, helplessness, suffering, and retreat into domesticity from the conflicts of worldly life) as "a defence against personal unhappiness which had significant general implications." (Even Greer sensed the terms, if not the argument, when she sneered at Hemans as one of those women who, straining off from their writing the rage and bitterness of an enforced self-discipline, took pride in "the pure mush that they were then able to offer the complacent public, whose certainties they were endorsing at such secret and unremitting cost to themselves.") Cora Kaplan interpreted the "normative morality" and "the emerging Victorian stereotype of the pure, long-suffering female" in Hemans's work as a symbolic discipline that turned anger inward and romanced death as the only resolution: "bitter, feminine but pre-feminist consciousness is disguised by proper sentiments." Isobel Armstrong discerned in Hemans an emerging tradition of women's poetry defined by such doubleness: "an affective mode, often simple, often pious, often conventional" turns out to be "subjected to investigation, questioned, or used for unexpected purposes"; "the simpler the surface of the poem, the more likely it is that a second and more difficult poem will exist beneath it." Tricia Lootens shifted this surface-and-depth paradigm sideways, describing a "body of work whose development often seems more centrifugal than linear and whose force seems to derive from its erratic course among and through contradictions." Complex and illuminating readings continue to be offered by such major critics as Anne Mellor and Jerome McGann.[11]

Not only are Hemans's more troubling works, which Victorian anthologizers ignored, now returning to light, but even the old anthology favorites are presenting more problematic aspects. The supposed patriotic celebrations for which Hemans is famous prove on closer reading to betray a death-haunted consciousness. *England's Dead* asks readers to ponder the empire, not as a realm on which the sun never sets, but as a global graveyard: "*There* slumber England's dead!" More than a few such poems come trailing dark clouds of "glory." To nineteenth-century eyes, *Casabianca* was a tribute to a youthful war martyr to weep over (or, in mocking temper, parody). Yet a French boy's futile call to his dead father ("unconscious of his son") for release from his post is no "simple, chivalrous" poetry, but a grim meditation on patriotic and patriarchal obligations.[12] Hemans's exotic historical or cultural displacements (a French family, ancient Carthage, medieval Valencia, Renaissance Italy, Tudor England, the American West) may seem strategically distancing and derealizing, but their fictionality allows disturbingly familiar issues to emerge, with the foreign scene returning a sign of a universal condition.[13] Hers is an imagination repeatedly drawn to the latent tensions in cherished ideologies. Living in an era dominated for nearly a quarter century by warfare against Revolutionary and then Napoleonic France— warfare that involved her brothers and a husband-to-be—Hemans may seem at one with the romance of patriotism that idolized military leaders such as Nelson and Wellington. But her poetry also addresses a public that had mixed feelings about war—a public that was quick to memorize a dirge that concluded in a rhyme of "gory" and "glory": Charles Wolfe's *The Burial of Sir John Moore at Corunna* (1817) (one of her brothers was there). This is the same culture that responded to Byron's mordant critiques of military glory in *Childe Harold's Pilgrimage, A Romaunt* (1812) and *Don Juan Canto VII* (published the same year as Hemans's *Siege of Valencia*, 1823). Hemans's poetry reflects this cultural ambivalence and is more remarkable for this quality than for its famed pieties. She insists that readers confront the violence of war, its child martyrs, its female victims, its devastation of domestic affections, and the hollowness of its "glory" and "fame."

Hemans could tap into these conflicting currents precisely because she was so adept in the mainstream—a complexity that also ripples through those famed "feminine qualities." Her references to male-authored traditions and texts could pay homage, or they could turn oppositional and ironic, reworking subjects from the perspective of women's lives, desires and dissatisfactions. Her signal achievement was a genre she would eventually call "Records of Woman," featuring women as historical figures, as repositories of cultural values (heroines of "domestic affection"), as interpreters (herself included) of history and social structure, and (not the least) as perpetual victims of men's rivalries, political contentions, and wars. Gender was the haunt and main region of her song: she wrote of woman's social fate in a man's world, her sufferings and love-longings, her abandonments, desperate suicides and infanticides, her release only through death. Alternating with celebrations of the paradise of home and all its loves, Hemans limned the oppressions and devastations of domestic life. She wrote in an intensely personal way of socially specific conflicts: between being an artist and being a woman; between affection and ambition, between family and fame. That she was not always (or even fundamentally) a poet of sweetness and light was noted even in her own day. But in their imaginary investments, most nineteenth-century readers found ways to contain her challenges, ascribing the shadows to a hyper-susceptible "female melancholy," or celebrating a "feminine" heroic of forbearance and patience, faith and martyrdom.[14] In the post-Wollstonecraft, revolution-anxious 1820s, Hemans's contemporaries did not want to hear in her repeated connections of the political to the personal, and of private life to the public world, any emerging critique of the ideology of "feminine" virtue or "universal" female fate.

Reviewing the poetry that comprised, then compromised, Hemans's literary stature, we have recovered her crosscurrents. We have noticed that the central conflicts of her most powerful narratives, and even some unlikely suspects (*The Domestic Affections*), remain spectacularly unresolved, not just on a predictable sociohistorical level (that's life), but on the level where some critical schools tell us resolutions should take shape and perform their mystifying work: the level of aesthetic harmony (that's art). As Lootens remarks, Hemans's poetry "is never simply Victorian," and where "most Victorian, [. . .] perhaps least simple" (239). With historical distance and close reading, we are seeing a poetry more apt to be strained by rhetorical effects and thematic configurations that tap into and voice a cultural unconscious of fragmented, contradictory awarenesses.

## THE FAME OF "MRS. HEMANS"

To appreciate the recovery of Hemans from Victorian constructions, we need to look more fully at the constituent parts of the figure so easily, and until quite recently, so persistently adopted. One thing that Greer's flawed representation, for example, does make clear is the systematic selectivity and distortion that Hemans's canon underwent in order to conform to a fundamentally negative sense of female capacities. Sharing the fate of several other powerful and intelligent women writers, Hemans was reduced to a few pieces, a process that purified, by bleaching out, the fabric of her most intellectually ambitious and most politically sharpened poetry. Whether in idealization or in disparagement, she was taken as the epitome of the "feminine," her poetry a primer of the domestic affections, of religious and patriotic piety, and of the "female" (more particularly, maternal) responsibility for binding these sensibilities together. "Critics and casual readers have united in pronouncing her poetry to be essentially feminine," Lydia Sigourney (a poet known as "the American Hemans") summed her praises in 1840; "The whole sweet circle of the domestic affections,—the hallowed ministries of woman, at the cradle, the hearth-stone, and the death-bed, were its chosen themes," all sites of "the disinterested, self-sacrificing virtues of her sex" (xv). When *Edinburgh Monthly Review* said in 1820, on the cusp of Hemans's fame, that she "never ceases to be strictly *feminine* in the whole current of her thought and feeling," it meant that she displayed "the delicacy which belongs to the sex, and the tenderness and enthusiasm which form its finest characteristic" (3.374).

This admiration is often contingent on assumed incapacities. Take the encomium that Hemans's friend Henry Chorley issued in his *Memorials* to this "essentially womanly" character, and the poems so inspired: "Their love is without selfishness—their passion pure from sensual coarseness—their high heroism [. . .] unsullied by any base alloy of ambition. In their religion, too, she is essentially womanly—fervent, trustful, unquestioning, 'hoping on, hoping ever'—in spite of a painfully acute consciousness of the peculiar trials of her sex" (1.138). This well-meaning praise presents the "essentially feminine" as a perfection through negations: "without selfishness," "unsullied" by ambition, "unquestioning" of contradictory awarenesses. So, too, the premier critic of the age, Francis Jeffrey, writing in 1829 at the height of her fame, called "the poetry of Mrs Hemans a fine exemplification of Female Poetry." The fineness was keyed to negative verdicts: "Women, we fear cannot do every thing; not even every thing they attempt," he begins this influential essay.[15] The rest of its paragraph is a parade of negative incapabilities:

> They cannot [. . .] represent naturally the fierce and sullen passions of men—nor their coarser vices—nor even scenes of actual business or contention—and the mixed motives, and strong and faulty characters, by which affairs of moment are usually conducted on the great theatre of the world. For much of this they are disqualified by the delicacy of their training and habits, and the still more disabling delicacy which pervades their conceptions and feelings; and [. . .] by their actual inexperience, [. . .] by their substantial and incurable ignorance of business—of the way in which serious affairs are actually managed—and the true nature of the agents and impulses that give movement and direction to the stronger currents of ordinary life. Perhaps they are also incapable of long moral or political investigations, where many complex and indeterminate elements are to be taken into account, and a variety of opposite probabilities to be weighed. [. . .] They rarely succeed in long works, [. . .] their natural training rendering them equally averse to long doubt and long labour. (*Edinburgh Review* 50.32)

Hemans often represents public and private in dialectical formation, but Jeffrey insists on a dichotomy: Women's "proper and natural business" is "private life." Their "delicacy" amounts to faint praise; Jeffrey himself says "disabling." He concludes by urging Hemans to respect that "tenderness and loftiness of feeling, and an ethereal purity of sentiment, which could only emanate from the soul of a woman." This means, among other things, that this woman ought to stick to "occasional verses" and not "venture again on any thing so long as The Forest Sanctuary" (47), a work Hemans herself regarded as "almost, if not altogether, [her] best" (*CM* 1.123).

Jeffrey's occasion was the publication of second editions of this poem and *Records of Woman*, but he does not note the many ways these works contest the terms of his praise. *The Forest Sanctuary* opens with a lurid *auto-da-fé* during the Spanish Inquisition; the latter is a universalizing chronicle of war, blood feuds, torture, murders, suicides, infanticide, betrayal, and fatal heartbreak. Subsequent praise of Hemans observed Jeffrey's strictures and prescriptions more closely than had Hemans. When in 1848 Frederic Rowton edited *The Female Poets of Great Britain*, he celebrated her ability "to represent and unite as purely and completely as any other writer in our literature the peculiar and specific qualities of the female mind. Her works are [. . .] a perfect embodiment of woman's soul: [. . .] *intensely* feminine. The delicacy, the softness, the pureness, the quick observant vision, the ready sensibility, the devotedness, the faith of woman's nature find in Mrs. Hemans their ultra representative" (407). Echoing the consensus, Rowton uses "representative" not just in the sense of being "representative of" but also of "representing to," as in conveying a conservative gender prescription. This is the story he tells in his "Introductory Chapter":

> Man is bold, enterprising, and strong; woman cautious, prudent, and steadfast. Man is self-relying and self-possessed; woman timid, clinging, and dependent. Man is suspicious and secret; woman confiding. Man is fearless; woman apprehensive. Man arrives at truth by long and tedious study; woman by intuition. He thinks; she feels. He reasons; she sympathises. He has courage; she patience. He soon despairs; she always hopes. The strong passions are his; [. . .] The mild affections are hers; [. . .] Intellect is his; heart is hers. [. . .] Female Intellect seem[s] to be rather negative than positive: [. . .] fitted more for passive endurance than for aggressive exertion. (xxiv-xxv)

Rowton goes on to say that his selections will "amply illustrate and fully prove the[se] distinctions," but he has selected precisely those works that seem to exhibit these "she" capacities. A different selection might show Hemans equally endowed with the capacities ascribed to "Man."

If Rowton and Jeffrey allow themselves to beg the question, they (like Chorley) assumed the benevolence of their motives. A self-confessed champion of "Female Intellect" and "the poetical productions of the British Female mind" (xvii), Rowton even goes so far as to echo Wollstonecraft in blaming any apparent deficiencies in woman's intellectual capacity on "our system of educating females," and to ask whether "such a word as Poet*ess*" should not be replaced by "Female Poet" (xviii). But as his anatomy of gender suggests, this nicety is a distinction without a difference. In the culture of letters, "poetess" operates as signal differential, and it is no coincidence that in the 1820s the term adhered to women, such as Hemans and Landon, who were presenting the female poet as a professional calling.[16] Chorley meant only to be descriptive when he wrote, at the conclusion of *Memorials*, that "the woman and the poetess were in [Hemans] too inseparably united to admit of their being considered apart from each other" (2.355), but such compounding easily served Rowton's oppositions. Alluding to the etymology of "poet," George Gilfillan (another admirer, writing just before Rowton) decided that "in its highest sense, the name of poet" had to be denied Hemans: "A *maker* she is not." To the degree that she exemplifies the "feminine" she loses credit: "Mrs. Hemans's poems are strictly effusions. And not a little of their charm springs from their unstudied and extempore character [. . .] in fine keeping with the sex." Having been fit into the mold, Hemans becomes the mold: "we consider her by far the most feminine writer of the age. [. . .] You could not [. . .] open a page of her writings without feeling this is written by a lady" (*Tait's* n.s. 14.360–61). W. M. Rossetti's *Prefatory Notice* to his later Victorian edition of Hemans follows suit. Having already indicated "the deficiency which she, merely as a woman, was almost certain to evince" for the higher genres (16), he gallantly accords "Mrs. Hemans [. . .] a very honorable rank among poetesses" (24).

The nineteenth-century honors to Hemans as "most feminine" always imply a double-negative, "not un-feminine"—not, that is, of the Jacobin sorority lambasted in 1798 by Tory Reverend Richard Polwhele in *The Unsex'd Females* (neutered by entering the public sphere of speech an action).

> Survey with me, what ne'er our fathers saw,
> A female band despising NATURE's law,
> As "proud defiance" flashes from their arms,
> And vengeance smothers all their softer charms.
>    *I* shudder at the new unpictur'd scene,
> Where unsex'd woman vaunts the imperious mien.
>
>                           (11–16)[17]

In the double negatives of this cultural grammar, what Hemans was "not" was an unfilial, defiant, denatured, Amazonian, unpatriotic, immodest spawn of Wollstonecraft; she was strictly "feminine, according to the masculine acceptation of the word," so Wollstonecraft herself satirized the term in *Vindication of the Rights of Woman* (1792). In an age in recoil from such polemics, Hemans seemed to idealize "essentially feminine" as essentially "domestic" and "self-sacrificing." In 1820 *Edinburgh Monthly Review* warmly praised "the modesty of Mrs. Hemans, for whose gentle hands the auxiliary club of political warfare, and the sharp lash of personal satire are equally unsuited," and admired her for "scrupulously abstaining from all that may betray unfeminine temerity" (374–75). Warne's Chandos Classics edition of her work (1889) urged "lady readers" to study Jeffrey's review (from which it quotes lavishly) "in its entirety": "it commences with an estimate of womanly powers which appears to us to answer many of the vexed questions of the present day" (xxiii–xiv). Warne's later Albion edition (1900) amplifies the advice by way of elegy: the waning popularity of Hemans's "essentially feminine" genius seems due to a "lamentable change in the tone of modern society. The age [the 1890s] that gave birth to the cry of 'Women's Rights,' and to the unfeminine imitators of masculine habits, was not likely to appreciate the voice of the *true* woman that spoke in Felicia Hemans" (xv–xvi).

This is not to say that Hemans's nineteenth-century admirers did not notice her wide reading and intelligence, but rather that they saw such accomplishments tempered by "feminine" propriety. Writing in 1820 with the 1790s in mind, William Gifford, infamous for his satires of Della Cruscan women, could accept Hemans's obvious "reflection and study," because "talent and learning have not produced the ill effects so often attributed to them; her faculties seem to sit meekly on her" (*Quarterly* 24.130–31). "You are saved the ludicrous image of a double-dyed Blue, in papers and morning wrapper, sweating at some stupendous treatise or tragedy," Gilfillan chimed in the 1840s. He applauded the lack of "pedantry": "the authoress appears only the lady in *flower*" (*Tait's* n.s. 14.361). This florid romance of the "exquisitely feminine" was so immune to Blue stigma that it could absorb such stark contradictions as the eponym of *The Wife of Asdrubal*, taking revenge on a husband turned traitor both to his family and his country: "sternly beauteous in terrific ire . . . / She might be deem'd a Pythia," Hemans writes, in a figure that apparently escaped Robinson's notice ("no Pythian enthusiasm fills the poet and compels us to forget her womanhood," she sighed [*Ward's* 4.334–35]). Hemans's longest and most ambitious poems (*War and Peace*, all of the *Tales, and Historic Scenes*, *The Siege of Valencia*, *The Forest Sanctuary*, almost all of the *Records of Woman*) pulse with domestic and political strife, violence and warfare, an aesthetics of equivocation, or voices of protest and latent critique. Victorian reports tend to elide these stories and voices, as well as the circumstances of Hemans's life unsuited to their cherished image of "Mrs. Hemans": her education, her failed marriage, the assistance she had with domestic obligations and, not the least, her professionalism.

## Hemans's Life

Born in Liverpool in 1793, the same year that England launched nearly a quarter of a century of war against France, Felicia Browne lived in this bustling city until 1800, when her merchant father, suffering business reversals, closed up shop and moved the family to a coastal village in North Wales. If its beauty and serenity were an important influence on the young girl, so too was her mother, whose devoted care included encouraging her to use the large home library. She read avidly, memorized poetry, studied music and art, and learned French, Portuguese, Spanish, and Italian from her mother, Latin from the local vicar, and later, German. Felicia Browne began to write poetry (her first subjects were her mother and Shakespeare) and by age fourteen, with her mother's management, published a handsome illustrated quarto, *Poems* (1808), undertaken to help pay for her education. It was sold by subscription, and on its list appeared Captain Alfred Hemans (an army friend of her brothers, who were in Spain fighting against Napoleon) and Thomas Medwin. Medwin reported the poet's talents and beauty to his teenage cousin Percy Shelley, who ventured a correspondence.

Though Mrs. Browne intervened in this correspondence (saving her daughter from the chance fate of Shelley's other infatuations), one of Shelley's better impulses was to offer sympathy to the poet in the wake of the disappointing reviews of *Poems* (see the headnote to "Reception: Lifetime"). The poet was stung, but she was persistent. *England and Spain, or, Valour and Patriotism* appeared in 1809 (to no sales and no notice) and she was finishing another long poem, *War and Peace*, an impassioned plea for peace in an age of war. She fell in love with Captain Hemans when they met in 1809. In 1810, her father left the family behind to seek a fresh start in Canada, where he died two years later. Captain Hemans returned to England in 1811, weakened and scarred from war, and the couple married in 1812, the year she turned nineteen and her third volume, *The Domestic Affections &c* (including *War and Peace*) appeared, the same year Byron changed the literary landscape with his epic of alienation, *Childe Harold's Pilgrimage*. Hemans's volume, assembled by a family friend, did not attract notice, and when the Captain's postwar appointment ended in a discharge without pay, they and their baby boy joined her mother's household in Wales. Hemans kept writing, and her first genuine success came with a poem keyed to Britain's triumphant emergence as world power after the fall of Napoleon. This was her topical poem, *The Restoration of the Works of Art to Italy* (1816), which Byron praised and his publisher Murray purchased for a second edition. Soon after, Murray published *Modern Greece* (1817) and a volume of translations and original poetry (1818). There were four boys by this point, and Hemans was pregnant again. In 1818, just before the birth of their fifth son, the Captain left for Italy. The reasons were unclear; the "story" was his health, but Hemans's friend Maria Jewsbury suggested that he was uncomfortable living off his wife's income (see "Egeria"), and a later memoir reports his complaint that "it was the curse of having a literary wife that he could never get a pair of stockings mended" (echoing Byron's crack about bluestockings).[18] The marriage never mended either (repeating her father's desertion). The idealism of hearth and home for which "Mrs. Hemans" would become famous was haunted by these desertions, even as the Captain's departure strengthened her determination to support her family with her writing.

If the marketplace was a challenge, so was home, despite all the advantages Hemans enjoyed. In 1822 this mother of five boys, ages three to ten, wrote to a friend that she felt herself in "the melancholy situation of Lord Byron's 'scorpion girt by fire'—'Her circle narrowing as she goes,' for I have been pursued by the household troops through every room successively, and begin to think of establishing my *métier* in the cellar." All that "talk of tranquillity and a quiet home" made her "stare about in wonder, having almost lost the recollection of such things, and the hope that they may probably be regained." Yet there were enough practical advantages—a sister, a mother, and brothers to help, no husband to press for wifely service and obedience—that Hemans had time to read, study, and write, and her career took off. *Tales, and Historic Scenes* (1819), a wide-ranging critical view of politics and culture, was well reviewed and commercially successful. By 1820 she was winning prize competitions and further favor with the public and the reviewers. In rapid succession she produced *Wallace's Invocation to Bruce, The Sceptic, Stanzas to the Memory of the Late King* (which expressed sympathy for the suffering of George III), *Dartmoor*, and *Welsh Melodies*. New venues for publishing poetry opened with the founding of *Blackwood's Edinburgh Magazine* in 1817, and the inauguration of the annuals fad with the publication of *Forget Me Not* in 1822. Hemans quickly grasped the importance of these venues, especially for women's poetry. As sensitive as she was to the value of performing "the feminine" in mainstream British culture and its male-managed literary institutions, she was also alert to women's power as purchasers and readers. Throughout the 1820s she sold her work to magazines and annuals, then gathered many of these pieces for volumes from Murray and then William Blackwood. Her fame was clinched with *The Forest Sanctuary &c* (1825 and 1829), *Records of Woman &c* (1828, with several subsequent editions), and *Songs of the Affections &c* (1830).

Amidst this acclaim, her family life also bestowed, paradoxically, an important public advantage: the installment of "Mrs. Hemans" as a poet not only *of* home but sited *at* home, under "the maternal wing" (a phrase used throughout the nineteenth-century biographies). The professional who would dismay Wordsworth (also a poet at home, whose work was materially enabled by the labor of the women of his household) by seeming "totally ignorant of housewifery" thus avoided the stigma of "unfeminine" independence. A dyspeptic W. M. Rossetti manages to be warmest to this "admired and popular poetess" when he can speak of her as a "loving daughter" and a "deeply affectionate, tender, and vigilant mother" (15). The death of her own mother in 1827 was a devastating loss, deepened by the relentless breakup of the household, as older sons left for school and siblings married or moved away. To escape the emptiness, Hemans moved with her younger sons to a village near Liverpool, where she found schooling for them and literary and musical society for herself: Chorley, the poets Rose Lawrence and Mary Howitt, the vivacious writer Maria Jane Jewsbury, and a charming young musician, John Lodge, with whom she flirted and who arranged musical settings for her poems (see her lively letters to him in the summer of 1830). She met Wordsworth and Scott and enjoyed summer sojourns with each. But her health was weakening from emotional and physical stress, and in 1831 she sent her two oldest boys, Arthur and George, to their father in Italy and moved to Dublin, to be near her brother George and his wife. Although she again found good society and continued to write and publish, the Irish climate proved a disaster. She became very ill and bed-ridden in 1834, and died a few months before her forty-second birthday, in 1835, only eight years after her mother—and with regrets about the poetry she never realized: "My wish ever was to concentrate all my mental energy in the production of some more noble and complete work" (letter to Rose Lawrence, 13 February 1835).

Chorley, in his *Memorials*, was unsure how to evaluate the effects of Hemans's domestic situation on her poetic sensibility. While "the peculiar circumstances" of her being "in a household, as a member and not as its head, excused her from many of those small cares of domestic life," he wondered whether this relief liberated a "search for knowledge" or removed a defense against "melancholy." He understood the larger bearing of this question on the lives of intelligent and ambitious literary women but left his speculation about Hemans at the level of personal psychology: her tendency to dwell "a little too exclusively upon the farewells and regrets of life—upon the finer natures broken in pieces by contact with a mercenary and scornful world" (*CM* 1.43–44). Yet it is a combination of social and psychological forces that produced in Hemans's poetry a distinctive self-consciousness about female artistic careers. Two late, self-reflecting poems, *Corinna at the Capitol* and *Woman and Fame*, both first published in the annuals marketed chiefly to women, advise domestic humility but wind up contradicting such advice with the energies of aesthetic elaboration. *Corinna* takes as its subject a poet of antiquity and the modern version of her created by Germaine de Staël in the wildly popular novel *Corinne, ou l'Italie* (1807). "Corinna" (the eponym of the poem as published in *The Literary Souvenir*, 1827) was the most renowned Boeotian poet of Greek antiquity after Pindar, and was said to have won five victories over him for the lyric prize. Alluding to this prototype, Staël's heroine is also accomplished and famous, but pays dearly: she dies of a broken heart, rejected by the Englishman who was initially enchanted by her, against his standards of social propriety. Hemans's poem forces the glory of Corinna/ Corinne into this larger economy, imposing a frame of moralizing instruction with an admonitory epigraph and these final lines:

> Happier, happier far, than thou
> With the laurel on thy brow,
> She that makes the humblest hearth
> Lovely but to one on earth!
>
> (*Literary Souvenir*, 191)

Her epigraph is from Staël herself: "Les femmes doivent penser qu'il est dans cette carrière bien peu de sorts qui puissent valoir la plus obscure vie d'une femme aimée et d'une mère heureuse."[19] The French synonymy of *woman* and *wife* (*femme*) is to the point: this is the essentialized cultural prescription.

Yet between this epigraph and the concluding lines falls not the shadow, but the electric brilliance, of Corinne's performance. When Hemans republished the poem in *Songs of Affections &c*, she retitled it *Corinne at the Capitol*, matching the title to book 2 of Staël's *Corinne*. There Staël presents the heroine for the first time, celebrated in her glory, and elaborates her triumph, giving the text of "Corinne's Improvisation" and concluding in an apotheosis: "No longer a fearful woman, she was an inspired priestess, joyously devoting herself to the cult of genius." Hemans represents the "Improvisation" in 42$^1/_2$ lines of present-tense drama punctuated by repeated "now"s and swelling with a radiant lexicon: *fires, Joyously, festal, triumphs, glory bright, golden light, ascending, freedom, proudly, gemlike, summit, rich music, victorious notes, proud harmony, thrilling power, tide of rapture, flush,* "the joy of kindled thought / And the burning words of song." By contrast, the moralizing coda can't sustain more than 5$^1/_2$ lines, and thus the poem becomes a text of subversive disproportions—a characteristic of Hemans's representations of insoluble conflicts in all spheres, from the personal and domestic, to the social and patriotic, to the religious and metaphysical.

*Woman and Fame* (1829) is linked to Corinne in theme, drawing its epigraph from the last four lines of the earlier poem. It repeats the fundamental and unresolvable conflict by which Hemans and many of her contemporaries saw female fame as a purchase against female happiness. Its argument disparages woman's fame against the durable nurture of "home-born love." Yet this proves to be another poem at war with its lesson, a war again waged by the pressures of its aesthetic elaborations:

> Thou hast a voice, whose thrilling tone
>   Can bid each life-pulse beat,
> As when a trumpet's note hath blown,
>   Calling the brave to meet:
> But mine, let mine—a woman's breast,
> By words of home-born love be bless'd.

> *(Amulet,* 90)

The paradox is clear: Hemans's imagery, if not her argument, associates artistic achievement with the thrill of life itself, only to force a turn at the couplet (this turn shapes the structure of each of the poem's first three stanzas) back into a domestic sphere—one she argues is "bless'd" but which she can imagine only in opposition to the life-pulse to which her own talents beat.

Out of such contrary pressures—intelligence, ambition, insecurity, domestic affection, and material necessity—emerges a keenly tuned critical capacity, neither absorbed in complacent pieties nor polemically oppositional, but one whose necessary placement in the mainstream culture made Hemans especially alert to the crosscurrents. Her close friend Rose Lawrence described her, at the height of her celebrity, in terms strikingly at odds with the icon of "feminine" propriety established by the reviews: "In the world, as it is called, [. . .] it fared with her as it has done with all other women of genius, from Madame de Stael, downward: she was frequently accused of heresy and schism, and several times regularly convicted of contumacy and non-conformity," among the provocations, the way "her brilliant conversation rose above the level and conventional tone of society. Her pleasantry was not always genuine or happy" (*Recollections* 316–17). The poetry that Hemans developed for, in, and against this "world" is often unpredictable, courageous, filled with unexpected surprises and juxtapositions. The conflicts that appear in and across her work more directly reflect the complexity of the period—its international politics, its views of war, its attitude toward domestic and gendered life—than the orthodoxies into which her critics, for a variety of ideological motivations, have tried to place her.

## THIS EDITION

Whatever our view of Hemans, informed discussion needs more accessible sources and better scholarly resources than have been available, notwithstanding the interventions of recent anthologies. The compendious nineteenth-century volumes are long out of print, as are the lifetime volumes (except for a few facsimile reprints, some of them now out of print, too). The best of the big posthumous volumes, by Blackwood, retain Hemans's copious textual notes and embellish with excerpts from reviews and memoirs—a form popularized in Murray's landmark edition of Byron in the 1830s. But the last volume of Hemans was Oxford University Press's severely reduced edition of 1914, which remained in print for a couple of decades. Despite its University Press imprint, it is far less adequate than the best of Blackwood's: printing corrupt texts, shearing off Hemans's notes (as essential to her textual display as Byron's or T. S. Eliot's notes to theirs), excluding plays, not supplying any essays or letters, and unmarked by any help beyond line numbers, Oxford's is no resource for scholars, even if it could be had. The memoirs of the 1830s (Chorley and Hughes) include some letters, but excerpted and edited to accord with "feminine" propriety, while some of Hemans's most interesting correspondence—her business dealings, for instance—has languished in archives. In the absence of a standard edition, citations in critical discussion have been hodgepodge, often relying on corrupt texts. The best recent anthology selections suffer from some of these same problems, as well as restraints of space and classroom-oriented annotation.[20]

   Building on the recent recovery of Hemans, I developed this edition in order to meet the need for substantial, professionally prepared materials on which informed discussion may develop. As such, this publication is meant both as a contribution to literary study, making the work of this important writer available, and as an intervention in a scholarly enterprise that has been in want of a common, reliable reference. While it is a selection (in advance, I hope, of a complete edition of her poems and letters), it is ample and wide-ranging, representing both the poetry that fostered Hemans's fame and the texts that the nineteenth century winnowed away. Contents range from her third volume, *The Domestic Affections* (1812), up to the work she published in the mid-1830s. Five major works appear entire: *The Restoration of the Works of Art to Italy*; *Modern Greece*; *Tales, and Historic Scenes*; *The Forest Sanctuary*; and *The Siege of Valencia*—as well as an entire subgroup, *Records of Woman*, in which the aggregate, like that of *Tales*, is an important macrotext. There is also a sample of her essay writing, one on the relation of poetry and contemporary politics. Many letters appear here for the first time since the 1830s, many for the first time ever—presenting Hemans's views of her contemporaries, her negotiations with her publishers, and her reflections on her writing and her emerging celebrity. The "Chronology" gives a detailed account her life in the context of her career, the contemporary literary culture it engaged, and key historical events. The section titled "Reception" spans the nineteenth century: along with some newly published letters, I include samples of major reviews that appeared in her lifetime, widely published elegies, and landmark memoirs, prefaces, and literary biographies. The "Bibliography," moving into this century, is both a reference and a demonstration. Its first section lists Hemans's chief lifetime publications, with information on the magazines where she most frequently appeared. A list of other important nineteenth-century commentaries, memoirs, and critical essays supplements the "Reception" section, and a list of editions provides a resource and a story, the nineteenth-century volumes reflecting Hemans's formation in the culture of the annuals, the twentieth-century anthologies showing both the sway of Victorian canons and the emergence of revisionary interests. The bibliography of modern resources includes critical essays on Hemans, Web sites, and general studies illuminating her situation as a woman writer in the Romantic era—those decades marked by war and political unrest, by commercial bustle and empire, and wending toward the Victorian culture that would find its lights, and try to avoid seeing its shadows, in Felicia Hemans.

## NOTES

[1] Letter to Rose Lawrence, summer 1830; another from early 1831. Among the poems, *Woman and Fame, Properzia Rossi, Corinne at the Capitol.*

[2] For an account of Hemans's durability on publishers' lists, see Paula Feldman, "Endurance and Forgetting" 14–17. Feldman notes that when most of Hemans's work went out of copyright in the 1870s there was a surge of new editions, including volumes in Edward Moxon's various series: Popular Poets in the 1870s (selling well into the 1880s), Standard Poets, and Library Poets. In 1914, Hemans joined the 53-volume Oxford Editions of Standard Authors.

[3] Norma Clarke, *Ambitious Heights* 45. Here and throughout, brief references signal an item listed in the Bibliography, with complete publication information.

[4] (Rpt. Garden City: Anchor/Doubleday, 1977) 301. Moers's study, it should be noted, generally slights poets, and all Romantic-era ones. It would not not be until the 1980s that a recovery would emerge as a wide-scale project. Hemans has only a very minor place in such canon-defining collections as Ward's nineteenth-century anthology, *English Poets*, and the 1906 *Oxford Book of English Verse*, and no place at all in Francis Palgrave's *Golden Treasury* (1860s to 1880s), William Stanley Braithwaite's *Book of Georgian Verse* (1908), or Geoffrey Grigson's *The Romantics, An Anthology* (1942).

[5] Important forces in and heralds of this recovery were Stuart Curran's "The 'I' Altered" (1988), Marlon Ross's *The Contours of Masculine Desire: Romanticism and the Rise of Women's Poetry* (1989), and Norma Clarke's *Ambitious Heights* (1990).

[6] For the tenacity of this canon (Blake, Wordsworth, Coleridge, Byron, P. Shelley, Keats), one need only note that in 1985, it still defined the MLA's authoritative bibliography, *The English Romantic Poets* (4th edition, edited by Frank Jordan).

[7] Following Moers were Patricia Spacks, *The Female Imagination* (New York: Knopf, 1975), Elaine Showalter, *A Literature of Their Own* (Princeton: Princeton UP, 1977), and Sandra Gilbert and Susan Gubar, *The Madwoman in the Attic* (1979). Favoring novelists, these studies had several related projects: fresh discussions of the few women in the received canon; attention to lost or neglected writers; analyses of women's rhetorical strategies for representing their

experience, and a comparison of these practices to the representations of women and gender dynamics by canonical male writers. For my review of this history and its consequences for the study of Romantic-era women writers, see *British Literature: Discipline Analysis*.

[8] In 1985 Alan Hill's footnote identified her merely as "popular versifier" (*Letters of Dorothy Wordsworth* [Oxford: Clarendon], 175). In 1991 Virgil Nemoianu cites her to chasten the canon liberalizers of the 1980s, warning us that once popular, now marginalized writing was "*par excellence* the domain of conservatism," replete "with acquiescence, formalized harmonies, and translations of obsolete ideologies" ("Literary Canons and Social Value Options," *The Hospitable Canon: Essays on Literary Play, Scholarly Choice, and Popular Pressures*, ed. Virgil Nemoianu and Robert Royal [Philadelphia and Amsterdam: John Benjamins], 240).

[9] Jennifer Breen, *Women Romantic Poets, 1785–1832* (London: J. M. Dent, 1992), 160. Meant to remedy "long-neglected achievements" (back cover), this anthology mentions Hemans only once in passing, in the introduction (xii), ridicules her in the notes ("She was an admirer of William Wordsworth's poetry but he did not reciprocate this admiration" [160]), and represents her with two of her duller poems: *Dirge*, a short piece of conventional pieties on the death of a child, and a reverential *To Wordsworth* (147–48). Both the attitude and the selection recall Ward's *English Poets* and the 1906 *Oxford Book of English Verse*.

[10] Greer, *Slip-Shod Sibyls* 60. Innocent of most recent discussions of Hemans, Greer was also unembarrassed by factual mistakes, ignorance of her canon (e.g., 144; and 262, 509, where volume titles are incorrectly cited), and research no more ambitious than a single Victorian preface (92–94)—a regrettable and ironic slip-shodiness. Norton's 7th edition does a bit better, releasing her from the dubious category of "minor lyric poet," and supplying two more poems, the anthology favorite, *The Homes of England*, and one of Hemans's own favorites, *A Spirit's Return*.

[11] Curran, "The 'I' Altered" 189 and "Women Readers" 190, 194; Ross, *Contours*; Clarke, *Ambitious Heights* 76; Kaplan, *Salt and Bitter and Good* 93–95; Armstrong, "A Music" (ed. Leighton) 251; Lootens, "Hemans and Home" 241. Mellor notes how often the celebration of "the enduring value of the domestic affections, the glory and beauty of maternal love, and the lasting commitment of a woman to her chosen mate" evokes "the fragility of the very domestic ideology it endorses" (*Romanticism & Gender* 124); and McGann summed up the poetry as "haunted by death and insubstantiality" ("Literary History, Romanticism, and Felicia Hemans," *Poetics of Sensibility* 187).

[12] For revisionary discussions, see Armstrong, *ibid* 258–59, and Lootens, *ibid* 241.

[13] See my "Domestic Affections and the Spear of Minerva," and more generally, my essay on the reception of *The Siege of Valencia* ("Revolving Doors of Reception").

[14] See Angela Leighton, *Writing Against the Heart* 11–12.

[15] The essay became canonical by force of lavish quotation in *1839*. The preface to Warne's Chandos Classic (ca. 1889) is still quoting it generously (xxiii).

[16] See Leighton, *Writing Against*: the mystique of the woman poet that emerges in the 1820s, especially in the celebrity of Hemans and L.E.L., "offers to subsequent generations of women both an enthusiastic incentive to write and a subtly determining myth of what being a woman poet means" (2). Mellor tracks the cult and culture of the "poetess" into twentieth-century accounts, which shift only tonally; that is, they do not condescend to the category. She does not read Hemans in the counter-tradition she calls the "Female Poet" ("The Female Poet and the Poetess" 261–62).

[17] Polwhele gives this footnote for the quoted phrase: "'A troop came next, who crowns and armour wore, / And proud defiance in their looks they bore.' Pope. The Amazonian band—the female Quixotes of the new philosophy, are, here, too justly characterised." Pope's verse is from *The Temple of Fame* (1711) 342–43; the troop is answering "the direful trump of Slander." In Charlotte Lennox's popular novel, *The Female Quixote* (1752), the heroine lives in a fantasy-world constructed from her reading of French romances.

[18] By this time, Byron's letter to Murray had been published in Moore's *Life* (with asterisks replacing Hemans's name). For the Captain's grumble, see *A Short Sketch* (1835) 489. For

Jewsbury's hunch, see *The History of a Nonchalant*. Peter Cochran is right to note that "whatever the case, he had the power, as a man, to leave" (13).

[19] *LS* 189. See the notes to *Corinne* for the translation and source. For the Corinne myth, see Moers, ch. 9, and for Hemans and Corinne, Leighton, *Writing Against* 32–34.

[20] A welcome development is Paula Feldman's edition of *Records of Woman, With Other Poems*.

# TEXTS, FORMATS,
# EDITORIAL PRINCIPLES,
# ABBREVIATIONS

COPYTEXTS are listed in the Table of Contents of headnotes, with full information in the Bibliography. Except for the annuals and a few magazine pieces, I use the first volume edition, and note prior and sometimes later publications, listing the most significant substantive variants. I retain original spelling, punctuation, capitals, and italics, with these exceptions: I delete stanza numbers in the shorter poems; checking against other texts, I silently emend printers' errata; I modernize a few nineteenth-century conventions of punctuation (e.g., I delete quotation marks at the beginning of stanzas where there has been no change of speaker; I move semicolons outside of terminal quotation marks; I replace Hemans's long dashes with ellipses).

My headnotes comment (variously) on textual issues, literary traditions, historical situations and references, and biographical circumstances. My endnotes clarify allusions, echoes, and references, gloss obscure phrasing or words, and offer other relevant information. For major names (such as Hemans's contemporaries), the most informative note is usually with the most significant event in relation to Hemans: Mary Tighe, for instance, with the notes to *The Grave of a Poetess*, Germaine de Staël with *Corinne at the Capitol*, Joanna Baillie with the dedication page to *Records of Woman*, Maria Jane Jewsbury with her essay on Hemans for the *Athenæum*. The index gives all references, with the chief one in boldface. The "Bibliography" gives full information on items identified in headnotes and footnotes by short title.

Hemans herself wrote headnotes, footnotes, and endnotes, their texts often substantial and their foreign-language passages untranslated. For the efficiency of my own annotation and for my readers' convenience, I place her footnotes and endnotes in sequence with my endnotes, appending [FH] to hers; where, in the same note, I supply commentary, this follows in a separate paragraph. Punctuation and styling are hers, except for brackets, in which I indicate an important variance from a source she is quoting. In the pre-photocopy era, inexact transcription was not unusual. I comment only on major elisions, conflations, or rewordings, and silently emend minor errors and slips. Translations are my own, unless otherwise credited.

The following abbreviations are used throughout:

| | | | |
|---|---|---|---|
| *CM* | Chorley's *Memorials* | FDB | Felicia Dorothea Browne |
| f / ff | folio / folios (pages of a | FH | Felicia Hemans |
| | manuscript) | *HM* | Hughes's *Memoir* |

| | | | |
|---|---|---|---|
| *LS* | *The Literary Souvenir* | *NMM* | *The New Monthly Magazine* |
| | (an annual) | *1839* | *The Works of Mrs. Hemans* |
| *MM* | *The Monthly Magazine, or* | | (Blackwood, 1839) |
| | *British Register, of* | *&c* | *and Other Poems / With Other* |
| | *Literature, Sciences,* | | *Poems* (full titles of volumes) |
| | *and the Belles-Lettres* | &c | and other publishing partners |

In addition, these abbreviations are relevant to correspondence to, from, and about Hemans:

| | | | |
|---|---|---|---|
| ALS | Autograph letter, signed | HL | Huntington Library |
| BA | Blackwood Archives, National | LL | Liverpool Libraries |
| | Library of Scotland (NLS) | MA | John Murray Archives |
| BL | British Library | | |

Professional journals cited by abbreviations:

| | | | |
|---|---|---|---|
| *ERR* | *European Romantic Review* | *PMLA* | *Publications of the Modern* |
| *KSJ* | *Keats–Shelley Journal* | | *Language Association of* |
| *MLQ* | *Modern Language Quarterly* | | *America* |
| *NCC* | *Nineteenth-Century Contexts* | *SiR* | *Studies in Romanticism* |

# CHRONOLOGY

## *The Life of Felicia Dorothea Browne Hemans in Context*

[In addition to primary sources, information is from the National Union Catalogue, Chorley, Hughes, Trinder, Feldman (*KSJ*), Nicholson, and Sweet's "Bibliography."]

1793    25 September, FDB (the fifth of seven children) born in Liverpool to George Browne, a well-to-do merchant of aristocratic Irish descent, and Felicity Dorothea Wagner, daughter of the Consul at Liverpool for Austria and Tuscany, whose lineage includes Venetian doges. The family's fortunes suffer in the financial panic of that year.
        Louis XVI and Marie Antoinette executed; Reign of Terror; Britain and France declare war.

1794    FDB's brother Claude Scott born.
        Danton and Robespierre executed.

1795    Famine in England; Napoleon invades Italy.

1796    Spain shifts allegiance, taking France's side against England.
        Mary Robinson, *Sappho and Phaon*; Southey, *Joan of Arc*; Staël, *De l'influence des passions*.

1798    FDB's sister and future memoirist Harriett-Mary born (d. 1858).
        *Lyrical Ballads* (Wordsworth and Coleridge); the Edgeworths, *Practical Education*; Joanna Baillie, *Plays on the Passions* (vol. 1); William Godwin, *Memoir of Wollstonecraft*.
        Irish Rebellion; Napoleon invades Egypt; the Battle of the Nile (Nelson's first great victory) claims the lives of French admiral Louis de Casabianca and his son.

1799    His finances suffering, FDB's father closes his Liverpool business; the family moves to a large house named Gwrych, near the coastal town of Abergele, North Wales, where they reside for nine years.
        Mary Hays, *Victim of Prejudice*; Hannah More, *Strictures on Female Education*.
        Religious Tract Society formed; Napoleon's coup d'état.

1800    FDB's first poems, including *Lines on her Mother's Birthday*.
        *Lyrical Ballads*, 2d edition, with Preface; Mary Robinson, *Lyrical Tales*; Coleridge's translations of Schiller's *Piccolomini*, *Death of Wallenstein*.
        Act of Union with Ireland.

1801    Pitt resigns after George III refuses Catholic Emancipation.

1802    Baillie, *Plays*, vol. 2; Scott, *Minstrelsy of the Scottish Border*; Staël, *Delphine*.
        Founded: *Edinburgh Review*; Society for the Suppression of Vice.
        Peace of Amiens between England and France; France reoccupies Switzerland; Napoleon made First Consul for life.

1803    FDB's elder sister Eliza dies.
        War resumes with France; British capture Delhi, India.

1804    FDB writes a poem on Shakespeare, spends the winter in London with her parents.
        Baillie, *Miscellaneous Plays*; Schiller, *Wilhelm Tell*.

Napoleon becomes Emperor and prepares to invade Britain; Britain declares war on Spain.

1805 FDB spends another winter in London.

Scott, *The Lay of the Last Minstrel.*

Nelson dies in the victory at Trafalgar; French victory over Austria and Russia.

1806 FDB's brother Thomas Henry (1787–1855) enlists as subaltern in the 23d Regiment, the Royal Welsh Fusiliers, and would distinguish himself and be wounded in the war.

Amelia Opie, *Simple Tales*; Scott, *Ballads and Lyrical Pieces*, *Marmion*; Sydney Owenson, *Wild Irish Girl*; Byron, *Fugitive Pieces.*

End of the Holy Roman Empire; Napoleon closes Continental ports to British ships and defeats Prussia at Jena.

1807 Wordsworth, *Poems*; Owenson, *Lays of an Irish Harp*; Byron, *Hours of Idleness.* Staël's *Corinne* achieves international success.

France invades Spain and Portugal.

1808 FDB's *Poems*, dedicated to the Prince of Wales, published in handsome quarto. It has almost 1,000 subscribers, including royalty (Prince of Wales, Duke of Gloucester, Princess Sophia of Gloucester), aristocracy, John Wilson Croker, Reginald Heber. Captain Alfred Hemans of the 4th or King's Own Regiment orders three copies. Thomas Medwin shows it to his cousin Percy Shelley, reporting FDB's "beauty," "grace," "charm," "simplicity," and "naiveté"; Shelley initiates a correspondence.

Thomas Moore, *Irish Melodies*; Southey, *Chronicle of the Cid.*

Anti-French uprisings in Spain; British land in Portugal; the Convention of Cintra (August) supervises French withdrawal from Portugal.

1809 Evicted from Gwrych for nonpayment of rent, in March the Brownes move to Bronwylfa, a house in St. Asaph, North Wales. FDB contracts scarlet fever and completes *England and Spain; or Valour and Patriotism* (in praise of the war against Napoleon), which Cadell & Davies publish but let languish, to no sales and no reviews. She studies French, Italian, Spanish, and Portuguese and begins German; she and Captain Hemans (whom she met through her brothers) pledge their love before he returns to Spain. Her brother George returns from the wars wounded and disillusioned.

John Murray founds the *Quarterly Review*; edited by William Gifford, it becomes the chief Tory-establishment journal. Byron, *English Bards and Scotch Reviewers*; Wordsworth, *Convention of Cintra*; Campbell, *Gertrude of Wyoming* (which "much pleased" FDB).

Sir John Moore (under whom one of the Browne brothers serves) dies in the retreat at Coruña in Spain; Joseph Bonaparte coronated in Madrid; Wellesley in command in Portugal; Napoleon takes Vienna.

1810 FDB's father leaves for Quebec "on business," never to return (d. ca. 1812). Scott, *The Lady of the Lake* (this "delighted" FDB); Jane Porter, *The Scottish Chiefs* (this also delighted her). Death of Mary Tighe, author of *Psyche; or the Legend of Love.*

George III's mental health declines; London riots as recession worsens; Napoleon annexes Holland, besieges Lisbon.

1811 Captain Hemans returns. Reginald Heber reads and praises *War and Peace.* FDB rendering translations of Italian poets. May: George Browne in the battle of

Albuera (of nearly 60,000 troops, 13,000 were killed). FDB spends summer weeks in Conway.

Tighe's *Psyche* (privately printed, 1805) published with other poems; Austen, *Sense and Sensibility*; Charlotte Dacre, *The Passions*; P. Shelley, *The Necessity of Atheism*. George III is deemed incompetent; the Prince of Wales named Regent; Luddite riots in the Midlands, against mechanical weaving frames.

1812   Matthew Nicholson surprises FDB with the publication of *The Domestic Affections &c* published (but no success). FDB intensely studying Spanish. Shelley writes again to her, praising her talents but not liking her enthusiasm for "fatal sanguinary war"; her mother terminates the correspondence. George Browne recovers and re-enlists. 30 July: FDB and Captain Hemans marry and take up residence in the small market town of Daventry, where he is adjutant to the Northamptonshire Militia.

Anna Barbauld, *Eighteen Hundred and Eleven*; Baillie, *Plays on the Passions*, vol. 3; Byron, *Childe Harold's Pilgrimage I-II*, an overnight sensation.

Britain declares war on the U.S.; Napoleon invades Russia in June and retreats in October, with catastrophic losses; Luddite riots provoke the Frame-Breaking Bill (prescribing capital punishment for offenders); Sarah Siddons retires from the stage.

1813   Arthur Hemans born. FH is unhappy in Daventry and longs for Wales; when Captain Hemans is discharged, they move to Bronwylfa, joining her mother's household.

Byron, *The Giaour* and *The Bride of Abydos*, both sensations; Southey, *Life of Nelson*; Shelley, *Queen Mab*; Coleridge, *Remorse*; Austen, *Pride and Prejudice*; Mary Russell Mitford, *Narrative Poems on the Female Character*, and "Our Village" sketches in *Lady's Magazine*, with great success for sales and circulation. Southey becomes Poet Laureate (after Scott declines); Wordsworth gets a government patronage position; Staël visits England and *De l'Allemagne* (suppressed by Napoleon in 1810) is published by Murray; Leigh Hunt imprisoned until 1815 for libelling the Prince Regent.

Massive Luddite trial in York, with many sentenced to death or transportation; Napoleon defeated at Leipzig, retreats from Spain, Holland, Italy, and Switzerland; Austria joins the Alliance against France; East India Company monopoly in India is ended.

1814   Byron, *The Corsair* (10,000 copies sell at once) and *Lara*; Wordsworth, *The Excursion*; Scott, *Waverley*; Austen, *Mansfield Park*; Edgeworth, *Patronage*; Henry Cary's translation of *The Divine Comedy*; *New Monthly Magazine* founded. The Allies invade France and Paris falls; Napoleon abdicates and is exiled to Elba; the Bourbon restoration brings Louis XVIII to the throne. Treaty of Ghent ends Britain's war with the U.S.

1815   FH sends Scott a poem inspired by an episode in *Waverley*, which he publishes in the *Edinburgh Annual Register*. Son George Willoughby born (?).

Scott, *Guy Mannering*; Wordsworth, *White Doe of Rylstone, Poems*; Byron, *Hebrew Melodies*.

Napoleon escapes Elba, enters France, is defeated at Waterloo, and exiled to St. Helena; restoration of European monarchies.

1816   Son Claude Lewis born. FH works on *Tales, and Historic Scenes*. May: *The Restoration of the Works of Art to Italy*, "by a Lady," published; Murray issues a second expanded edition under her name, FH's first critical and popular success, with modest profits.

Byron, *The Siege of Corinth*, *The Prisoner of Chillon &c*, *Childe Harold III*; Shelley, *Alastor*; Austen, *Emma*. Byron and Lady Byron separate, and in the wake of the scandal, he leaves England forever.

Elgin Marbles displayed in British Museum; economic depression.

1817    Son Henry William born; June: *Modern Greece* published anonymously by Murray. Byron, *Manfred*, *Lament of Tasso*; Coleridge, *Biographia Literaria*, *Sibylline Leaves*, *Zapolya*; Moore, *Lalla Rookh*; Scott, *Rob Roy*. *Blackwood's Edinburgh Magazine* founded; deaths of Austen and Staël.

Princess Charlotte dies delivering a stillborn child and is widely lamented.

1818    April: FH's debut in *Blackwood's* with *Stanzas on the Death of the Princess Charlotte* (written 23 December 1817), signed "F. D. H., Brownwhyfla" [*sic*]; Murray publishes *Translations from Camoens &c*. September: Captain Hemans departs for Rome for "his health," never returns, and ceases to support his wife and sons; after he leaves, FH gives birth to their fifth son, Charles Lloyd, and remains in her mother's household, which she supports by writing.

Byron, *Beppo*, *Childe Harold IV*; Keats, *Endymion*; "Z.'"'s articles on the "Cockney School" in *Blackwood's* attack Hunt, Keats, and eventually P. B. Shelley; a scathing review of Keats's *Endymion* in the *Quarterly*.

1819    May: *Tales, and Historic Scenes* published by Murray, profit-sharing (about £120 by 1821); it is well reviewed. In a competition that included James Hogg, FH wins a £50 prize for *The Meeting of Wallace and Bruce on the Banks of the Carron*; when it appears in *Blackwood's* (September), it receives a warm notice from John Wilson, who places her in a female pantheon: "Scotland has her Baillie—Ireland her Tighe—England her Hemans." It is republished in London and Edinburgh (by Blackwood) as *Wallace's Invocation to Bruce*. November: FH sends Gifford, Murray's literary advisor and editor, *The Sceptic*.

John Gibson Lockhart, *Peter's Letters to His Kinfolk*; Byron, *Mazeppa*, *Ode to Venice*, *Don Juan I–II*, *Childe Harold's Pilgrimage I–IV*; Scott, *Bride of Lammermoor*; Thomas Hope, *Anastasius*. August: Peterloo Massacre (a violent suppression of a peaceful working-class demonstration).

December: Six Acts (against political unions and freedom of the press). Birth of Queen Victoria; William Parry's Arctic expedition.

1820    January: Murray publishes FH's 16-pg. *Stanzas to the Memory of the Late King* (George III). In a profit-splitting agreement, he publishes *The Sceptic;* it is admired by Rev. Reginald Heber, a hymn writer and later Bishop of Calcutta, who was soon, with his brother Richard, to become a close friend of FH. Encouraged by Rev. Heber, FH begins a project "contrasting the spirit and tenets of Paganism with those of Christianity" (*HM* 40), provisionally titled *Superstition and Revelation*. April: *Wallace's Invocation to Bruce* (five hundred copies published by Blackwood in Edinburgh and Cadell & Davies in London). Summer: Byron ridicules FH to Murray; October: Gifford gives a warm retrospective review to several of FH's volumes in Murray's *Quarterly*, helping to boost sales of *The Sceptic*. FH writes articles on Italian literature for *Edinburgh Monthly* (–1821).

P. Shelley, *Prometheus Unbound &c*, *The Cenci*; Keats, *Lamia* volume; Elizabeth Barrett, *The Battle of Marathon*; Scott, *Ivanhoe*, *The Abbott*, *The Monastery*; Bernard Barton, *Poems*. *London Magazine* and *John Bull* founded.

Prince Regent becomes George IV; Queen Caroline tried for adultery (FH's brother Thomas is one of George IV's legion of spies); Scott is knighted. First iron steamship. Revolutions in Spain, Portugal, and Naples; royalist reactions across Europe.

1821 June: *Superstition and Error*; FH wins a prize of fifty guineas (£52.50, a year's income for many at the time) from the Royal Society of Literature for *Dartmoor*, soon published; second editions (from Murray) of *The Sceptic, Stanzas to the Memory of the Late King*, and *Modern Greece*, bound together. FH begins to contribute to *NMM* and *Blackwood's*; writes *The Vespers of Palermo*; extends her study of German; corresponds with poets Henry Hart Milman and George Croly. Brother Claude dies in Canada.
De Quincey, *Confessions of an English Opium Eater* (*London Magazine*); Morgan (Sidney Owenson) *Italy*; Byron, *Sardanapalus, Marino Faliero, Don Juan III–V, Cain, The Two Foscari*; Baillie, *Metrical Legends of Exalted Characters*; L.E.L. [Landon], *The Fate of Adelaide*; Scott, *Kenilworth. Manchester Guardian* founded.
Deaths of Napoleon, Queen Caroline, and Keats; Greek War of Independence.

1822 FH's *Songs of the Cid* in *NMM*; John Parry sets her *Welsh Melodies* to music.
Samuel Rogers, *Italy* (–1828); P. Shelley, *Hellas*; Caroline Bowles, *The Widow's Tale &c*; Byron, *The Vision of Judgment*. Death of P. Shelley.

1823 Hereafter, FH's annual earnings average over £200. June: *The Siege of Valencia &c* published by Murray, one thousand copies; gives FH £210 for the copyright for *The Vespers of Palermo*, a verse tragedy about the "Sicilian Vespers" insurrection against French rule in 1282 (it is published in November). Though not meant for the stage, Heber and Milman recommend it to Covent Garden; with Charles Kemble as the tormented hero, and featuring Charles Young, the play opens on 12 December but fails immediately, Fanny Kelley's inept acting blamed. FH begins contributing regularly to *NMM*.
Mitford's *Julian* staged, with Macready in the title role. Byron, *Don Juan VI–XIV*; Scott, *Quentin Durward*; M. Shelley, *Valperga* (inspired by Sismondi); Mary and William Howitt, *The Forest Minstrel &c*. Rudolf Ackermann produces *Forget Me Not*, the first of the English literary annuals.
French intervention in Spain, to suppress anti-Royalist rebellion.

1824 Baillie persuades Scott to approach Sarah Siddons about staging *Vespers* in Edinburgh; April: with Mrs. Henry Siddons acting and a new epilogue by Scott recited by Sarah Siddons, it is favorably reviewed. June: responding to a request by the principal of the University of Edinburgh to contribute to a new hymnal for the Scottish Church, FH writes *Christ's Agony in the Garden* and *Christ Stilling the Tempest*; studies German (Schiller, Herder, and Goethe, Körner); *Lays of Many Lands* appears in *NMM*; begins *De Chatillon, or, The Crusaders* and *The Forest Sanctuary*; *Hymns for Childhood* published in America, second edition of *Tales, and Historic Scenes*.
Scott, *Redgauntlet*; P. Shelley, *Posthumous Poems*; Byron, *Don Juan XV–XVI*; Mitford, *Our Village* (–1832); L.E.L., *The Improvisatrice*. Alaric Watts introduces his annual, *The Literary Souvenir*; progressive *Westminster Review* founded. Death of Byron. National Gallery opens in London.

1825 After FH's brother marries, she, her three youngest sons, her mother, and her sister Harriett move to Rhyllon, a house near St. Asaph; returning from Canada, her second brother and his wife join the household. *The Forest Sanctuary &c* (several previously published poems) is issued by a somewhat cautious Murray in a run of 750; FH earns £34 (enough to support her family for several months). An American edition of her poems, managed by Professor Andrews Norton, is very successful. FH declines an invitation to edit a periodical in Boston—a sinecure with an annual stipend of $1,500; enters the lucrative annuals market with two poems in *LS*.

Scott, *The Talisman, Tales of the Crusaders*; L.E.L., *The Troubadour*; M. J. Jewsbury, *Phantasmagoria; or Sketches of Life and Literature*; Banim brothers, *Tales of the O'Hara Family*; Carlyle, *Life of Schiller*; Christopher North's report in *Blackwood's* of Jewsbury's stay with the Wordsworths.

Major financial crash; Catholic relief bill defeated in the House of Lords.

1825–35    FH gets "continual overtures" from the annuals; "the number and urgency of these applications was already beginning to be half tormenting, half amusing"; across this decade, FH publishes almost a hundred poems in "the *annual* fever" (*HM* 82).

1826    Mother's health begins to fail; *Casabianca* and *The Landing of the Pilgrim Fathers* published; *Evening Prayer at a Girls' School* appears in *Forget Me Not* (other contributions from L.E.L., Mitford, Hester Lynch Piozzi, Thomas Hood, M. Shelley). Andrews Norton edits FH's poems, four volumes (1826–28), and she profits from the American market.

Mitford's *Foscari* staged with Charles Kemble. C. Bowles, *Solitary Hours*; Cooper, *The Last of the Mohicans*; Scott, *Woodstock*. Financial crash and failure of Scott's publisher.

Liverpool's ministry fails; new elections; Reform bills defeated; new Luddite riots.

1827    FH's mother dies, 11 January; FH's offer to join her husband is rejected (Lawrence 297). *Corinna at the Capitol* published in *LS*. At Rhyllon, FH sits for three portraits by William West, commissioned by Alaric Watts, editor of *LS*, for a gallery of famous living British poets. FH asks Baillie for permission to dedicate *Records of Woman* to her and begins a correspondence with her and other women writers: Mitford, Bowles, Howitt, Jewsbury. "She had a genuine womanly sympathy for those of her own sex, whom she esteemed as authors, and not manufacturers of prose or rhyme" (Chorley, *Athenæum* 402: 529). *Hymns on the Works of Nature, for the Use of Children* and *The Forest Sanctuary* published in Boston, edited by Norton. When Murray loses over £26,000 on a new newspaper, he backs off from the chancy publication of poetry; FH realizes she will need a new publisher. *The Homes of England* appears in *Blackwood's*; invited to contribute regularly, FH negotiates a payment of over £1 per page of poetry—more than Hood and Scott received. She begins to have serious health problems.

Scott admits authorship of *Waverly* novels. Scott, *Life of Napoleon*; Alfred and Charles Tennyson, *Poems by Two Brothers*; Reginald Heber, *Hymns*.

Greek independence; death of Blake and Canning; Wellington becomes Prime Minister.

1828    FH's sister marries and her brother moves to Dublin. In poor health, FH moves to Wavertree, a village near Liverpool, to seek medical care and situations for her younger sons, to be near friends (especially Lawrence), and to have access to cultural life; meets Henry Chorley (future memoirist), Mary Howitt, whose works she had long admired, and M. J. Jewsbury, soon to be a close friend. Andrews Norton visits. May: *Records of Woman*, dedicated to Baillie and with an epigraph from Wordsworth, published by Cadell in London, Blackwood in Edinburgh (one thousand copies), and pirated in New York. With help from Norton, it is also published in Boston, along with a fifth edition of her collected poems. "Christopher North" praises her in "Noctes Ambrosianae," in *Blackwood's*, to which FH now contributes regularly. By midsummer she earns £75 for *Records* and Blackwood publishes a second edition in October. When she suggests a second, expanded edition of *The Forest Sanctuary &c*, he advances her £150. Jewsbury, *Letters to the Young*; Leigh Hunt, *Lord Byron and Some of His Contemporaries*; Mitford's *Rienzi* at Drury Lane, admired by FH.

1829    FH is paid at least £45 for *The Broken Chain*, published in *The Keepsake*, along with pieces by Wordsworth (£105), Scott (£500), Coleridge (£50), Southey (£50), L.E.L., T. Moore, M. Shelley, P. Shelley (posthumous). *Woman and Fame* appears in *The Amulet* (verses by "Mrs. Hemans" on its title page), along with Coleridge, L.E.L., M. Howitt, W. Howitt, Lucy Aikin, Hood, Mitford, Clare, Barbauld, and Opie. *Casabianca* is republished in 2d edition of *The Forest Sanctuary*, a volume so successful that Blackwood henceforth pays FH £100 advances. July: visits Scotland and spends time with Scott at Abbotsford; in Edinburgh meets Blackwood, Jeffrey, and others of the literary community; sits for a bust by Angus Fletcher. October: Jeffrey's praises in *Edinburgh Review*. Jewsbury dedicates *Lays of Leisure Hours* to FH.
         Catholic Emancipation Act (granting full civil and political rights).

1830    June: 3d edition of *Records*. FH and her younger sons stay with the Wordsworths at Rydal Mount, then spend several summer weeks at a cottage on Lake Windermere. They enjoy Jewsbury's company. Family leaves mid-August to revisit Scotland; returns to Wales via Dublin and Holyhead. *Songs of the Affections &c* published in Edinburgh and London; sells well.
         Jewsbury, *The Three Histories*, with two characters based on FH; Tennyson, *Poems, Chiefly Lyrical*; Scott, *Tales of a Grandfather*; Moore, *Life of Byron, with Letters and Journals*. *Fraser's Magazine* founded.

1831–33  Cholera epidemic in London.

1831    FH sends her two oldest sons to live with their father in Italy, leaves England for Dublin to be near her brother, George Browne, Commissioner of the City Police, and befriends liberal Anglicans (Archbishop Whately, Joseph Blanco White) and renowned mathematician William Rowan Hamilton; visits Tighe's grave; her health worsens. FH now receiving more than £2 per page from Blackwood, its highest rate.
         Jewsbury contributing to and reviewing for *Athenæum*; essay on FH (February). Mary Shelley, *Frankenstein* (revised, with "Author's Introduction"); Mrs. Sandford, *Woman, In Her Social and Domestic Character* (2d ed., 1832); L.E.L., *Romance and Reality*.
         First Reform Bill; dissolution of Parliament; general election; second Reform Bill rejected by the Lords; final Reform Bill introduced.

1832    FH earns over £100 from *Blackwood's* (–1833).
         Cholera epidemic in Dublin; Reform Act; Jewsbury marries Rev. W. K. Fletcher, East India Company chaplain, and departs for India.
         *Tait's Edinburgh Magazine* founded. Anna Jameson, *Characteristics of Women*; Scott, *Tales of My Landlord*; Tennyson, *Poems*. Death of Scott.

1833    FH writes *Songs of Captivity*, *Songs for Summer Hours*, *Sonnets Devotional and Memorial*, and many of the *Scenes and Hymns of Life*; toward the year's end, she begins to translate passages from German authors; *Hymns for Childhood* republished in London. As her health worsens, she is devastated by Jewsbury's death in cholera epidemic in India. Son Claude departs for America to make his living. June: fourth edition of *Records*.

1834    *Hymns for Childhood* published in Dublin, as is *National Lyrics and Songs for Music* (dedicated to Rose Lawrence); FH's last lifetime volume, *Scenes and Hymns of Life &c* (dedicated to Wordsworth), published by Blackwood and Cadell, to disappointing reviews. May: essay on Goethe's *Tasso* in *NMM*. April–June: *Records of the Spring 1834*. Illness prevents a summer in the Lakes and reunion there with her sister and brother-in-law. July: FH goes to Wicklow, Ireland, for her health but contracts scarlet fever; upon poor medical advice to spend time outdoors in the cold Dublin fogs, her health worsens. October–November: composes *Records of the Autumn 1834*, *Despondency and Aspiration*, *The Huguenot's Farewell*, *Antique Greek Lament*.
Deaths of Lamb, Coleridge, and William Blackwood.

1835    February: P. M. Robert Peel gives FH £100 and arranges a clerkship in the Customs at £80 a year for son Charles. Second edition of *Songs of the Affections*, third edition of *The Forest Sanctuary*. American editions of *Songs of the Affections* and *Lays of Many Lands*. FH dictates a sonnet series, *Thoughts During Sickness* (published in *NMM*, March) and her last poem, *Sabbath Sonnet* (26 April), to Charles.
16 May: death of FH.
July: *Sabbath Sonnet*, appears in *Blackwood's* with Δ's (D. M. Moir) essay on FH. L.E.L.'s memorial verses and essay in *NMM*; Chorley's "Personal Recollections" in *Athenæum* (13 and 27 June, 11 July).

1836    *Poetical Works* (Philadelphia), *Collected Works* (Dublin), *Poetical Remains* (Edinburgh and London). January: Norton's thirty-page monograph, *On the Poetry of Mrs. Hemans*, in *Christian Examiner*. Lawrence's *Recollections of Mrs. Hemans* and Chorley's *Memorials* published in England and America.

1837    5th edition of *Records of Woman*. In the latest edition of his collected poems, Wordsworth adds a stanza on Hemans to *Extempore Effusion on the Death of James Hogg*, as well as recollections of her in a lengthy headnote.
Accession of Queen Victoria.

1838    L.E.L., "Felicia Hemans," in *Fisher's Drawing Room Scrapbook* (a lavish annual).

1839    *The Works of Mrs. Hemans, with a Memoir of Her Life, by Her Sister* 7 vols. (London and Edinburgh); like the American edition, this includes excerpts of critical reviews and reprints of appreciations: Δ (*Blackwood's*, July 1835), "Miss Landon" (L.E.L., *NMM*, August 1835), H. F. Chorley (*Athenæum*), and Norton's monograph, in *Christian Examiner* (January 1836).

1840    *Early Blossoms; a Collections of Poems Written Between Eight and Fifteen Years of Age, With a Life of the Authoress* (London).

1844    *De Chatillon; or, The Crusades* (Edinburgh and London).

# WORKS

# From *The Domestic Affections and Other Poems*

### (1812)

———⟪∞⟫———

## *The Statue of the Dying Gladiator*[1]

Commanding pow'r! whose hand with plastic art
Bids the rude stone to grace and being start;
Swell to the waving line the polish'd form,
And only want Promethean fire to warm;[2]—
Sculpture, exult! thy triumph proudly see,
The Roman slave immortalized by thee!
No suppliant sighs, no terrors round him wait,
But vanquish'd valor soars above his fate!
In that fix'd eye still proud defiance low'rs,
In that stern look indignant grandeur tow'rs!                        10
He sees e'en death, with javelin barb'd in pain,
A foe *but* worthy of sublime disdain!
Too firm, too lofty, for one parting tear,
A quiv'ring pulse, a struggle, or a fear!

   Oh! fire of soul! by servitude disgrac'd,
   Perverted courage! energy debas'd!
   Lost Rome! thy slave, expiring in the dust,
   Tow'rs far above Patrician rank, august!
   While that proud rank, insatiate, could survey
   Pageants that stain'd with blood each festal day!                20

Oh! had that arm, which grac'd thy deathful show,
With many a daring feat and nervous blow,
Wav'd the keen sword and rear'd the patriot-shield,
Firm in thy cause, on Glory's laureate field;
Then, like the marble form, from age to age,
His *name* had liv'd in history's brightest page;
While death had but secur'd the victor's crown,
And seal'd the suffrage of deserv'd renown!
That gen'rous pride, that spirit unsubdu'd,
That soul, with honor's high-wrought sense imbu'd,                  30

Had shone, recorded in the song of fame,
A *beam*, as now, a *blemish*, on thy name!

Yet here, so well has art majestic wrought,
Sublimed expression, and ennobled thought;
A dying *Hero* we behold, alone,
And *Mind's bright grandeur* animates the stone!
'Tis not th' Arena's venal champion bleeds,
No! 'tis some warrior, fam'd for matchless deeds!
Admiring rapture kindles into flame,
Nature and art the palm divided claim!                          40
Nature (exulting in her spirit's pow'r,
To rise victorious in the dreaded hour,)
Triumphs, that death and all his shadowy train,
Assail a mortal's constancy—in vain!
And Art, rejoicing in the work sublime,
Unhurt by all the sacrilege of time,
Smiles o'er the marble, her divine control
Moulded to symmetry, and fir'd with soul!

[1] Not collected in *1839*. Composed July 1810. The heroic couplets celebrate this famous statue in Rome's Capitoline Museum, thought to be a marble copy of a bronze original by Ctesilaus. The William Roscoes (father and son) "expressed great admiration" (Nicholson 23–24). The statue also inspired Byron, *Childe Harold's Pilgrimage IV*, cxl-cxlii (1818).

[2] Prometheus created man from clay and then, in pity for Zeus's mistreatment of his creation, stole fire from heaven and gave it to humanity.

---

## The *Domestic Affections*

[The crowning poem of *The Domestic Affections and Other Poems* (1812) begins as a celebration of home and its "feminine" value—the ideals for which the nineteenth century would esteem "Mrs. Hemans": "full of calm sweet pictures of most gentle and refining tendency," says Rowton (386). But this iconic poem betrays a precociously dark intuition: an economy of female self-sacrifice that, however heroic, may leave women without nurture or hope in a world perpetually at war—an ambivalence that saturates the volume's longest poem, *War and Peace—A Poem. Written at the age of Fifteen*. That poem was in heroic couplets—the measure here, too, but with greater frequency of "romance" forms such as enjambment and feminine rhyme. *1839* did not include *War and Peace* and put *The Domestic Affections* in an appendix of "Juvenile Poems" (7.330–60; cf. Gall and Inglis's *Poetical Works* [1876]), with none of these "curiosities" in the title index. In the wake of her reception thus far, FDB told her sponsor, Matthew Nicholson, "as I have no sanguine expectations from readers or critics, [. . .] their censure will not disappoint me, and I have so little of the passion for fame which renders authors so acutely sensible to the public opinion, that I am secured from much anxiety respecting the reviewers" (25 April 1812; Nicholson 36).]

Whence are those tranquil joys, in mercy giv'n,
To light the wilderness with beams of Heav'n?
To sooth our cares, and thro' the cloud diffuse,
Their temper'd sun-shine, and celestial hues?
Those pure delights, ordain'd on life to throw
Gleams of the bliss ethereal natures know?
Say, do they grace Ambition's regal throne,
When kneeling myriads call the world his own?
Or dwell with luxury, in th' enchanted bow'rs,
Where taste and wealth exert *creative* pow'rs?          10

Favor'd of Heav'n! O Genius! are they thine,
When round thy brow the wreaths of glory shine;
While rapture gazes on thy radiant way,
'Midst the bright realms of clear and mental day?
No! sacred joys! 'tis yours to dwell enshrin'd,
Most fondly cherish'd, in the purest mind;
To twine with flowers, those lov'd, endearing ties,
On earth so sweet,—so perfect in the skies!

Nurs'd on the lap of solitude and shade,
The violet smiles, embosom'd in the glade;          20
There sheds her spirit on the lonely gale,
Gem of seclusion! treasure of the vale![1]
Thus, far retir'd from life's tumultuous road,
Domestic bliss has fix'd her calm abode,
Where hallow'd innocence and sweet repose
May strew her shadowy path with many a rose:
As, when dread thunder shakes the troubled sky,
The cherub, infancy, can close its eye,
And sweetly smile, unconscious of a tear,
While viewless angels wave their pinions near;          30
Thus, while around the storms of discord roll,
Borne on resistless wing, from pole to pole;
While war's red lightnings desolate the ball,
And thrones and empires in destruction fall;
Then, calm as evening on the silvery wave,
When the wind slumbers in the ocean-cave,
She dwells, unruffled, in her bow'r of rest,
*Her* empire, home!—her throne, affection's breast!

For her, sweet nature wears her loveliest blooms,
And softer sun-shine ev'ry scene illumes.          40
When spring awakes the spirit of the breeze,
Whose light wing undulates the sleeping seas;

When summer, waving her creative wand,
Bids verdure smile, and glowing life expand;
Or autumn's pencil sheds, with magic trace,
O'er fading loveliness, a moon-light grace;
Oh! still for her, thro' Nature's boundless reign,
No charm is lost, no beauty blooms in vain;
While mental peace, o'er ev'ry prospect bright,
Throws mellowing tints, and harmonizing light!          50
Lo! borne on clouds, in rushing might sublime,
Stern winter, bursting from the polar clime,
Triumphant waves his signal-torch on high,
The blood-red meteor of the northern sky!
And high thro' darkness rears his giant-form,
His throne, the billow!—and his flag, the storm!

Yet then, when bloom and sun-shine are no more,
And the wild surges foam along the shore;
Domestic bliss! *thy* heaven is still serene,
Thy star, unclouded, and thy myrtle, green!          60
Thy fane of rest *no* raging storms invade,
Sweet peace is thine, the seraph of the shade!
Clear thro' the day, her light around thee glows,
And gilds the midnight of thy deep repose!
Hail, sacred home! where soft Affection's hand,
With flow'rs of Eden twines her magic band!
Where pure and bright, the social ardors rise,
Concentring all their holiest energies!
When wasting toil has dimm'd the vital flame,
And ev'ry power deserts the sinking frame;          70
Exhausted nature still from sleep implores
The charm that lulls, the manna that restores![2]
Thus, when oppress'd with rude tumultuous cares,
To thee, sweet home! the fainting mind repairs;
Still to thy breast, a wearied pilgrim, flies,
Her ark of refuge from uncertain skies!

Bower of repose! when torn from all we love,
Thro' toil we struggle, or thro' distance rove;
To *thee* we turn, still faithful, from afar,
Thee, our bright vista! thee, our magnet-star!          80
And from the martial field, the troubled sea,
Unfetter'd thought still roves to bliss and thee!

When ocean-sounds in awful slumber die,
No wave to murmur, and no gale to sigh;

Wide o'er the world, when peace and midnight reign,
And the moon trembles on the sleeping main;
At that still hour, the sailor wakes to keep,
'Midst the dead calm, the vigil of the deep!
No gleaming shores his dim horizon bound,
All heaven—and sea—and solitude—around! 90
Then, from the lonely deck, the silent helm,
From the wide grandeur of the shadowy realm;
Still homeward borne, his fancy unconfin'd,
Leaving the worlds of ocean far behind,
Wings like a meteor-flash her swift career,
To the lov'd scene, so distant, and so dear!

Lo! the rude whirlwind rushes from its cave,
And danger frowns—the monarch of the wave!
Lo! rocks and storms the striving bark repel,
And death and shipwreck ride the foaming swell! 100

Child of the ocean! is thy bier the surge,
Thy grave the billow, and the wind thy dirge?
Yes! thy long toils, thy weary conflicts o'er,
No storm shall wake, no perils rouse thee more!
Yet in *that* solemn hour, that awful strife,
The struggling agony for death or life;
E'en *then*, thy mind, embitt'ring ev'ry pain,
Retrac'd the image so belov'd—in vain!
Still to sweet home, thy *last* regrets were true,
Life's parting sigh—the murmur of adieu! 110

Can war's dread scenes the hallow'd ties efface,
Each tender thought, each fond remembrance chase?
Can fields of carnage, days of toil, destroy
The lov'd impressions of domestic joy?

Ye day-light dreams! that cheer the soldier's breast,
In hostile climes, with spells benign and blest;
Sooth his brave heart, and shed your glowing ray,
O'er the long march, thro' desolation's way;
Oh! still ye bear him from th' ensanguin'd plain,
Armour's bright flash, and victory's choral strain; 120
To that lov'd home, where pure affection glows,
That shrine of bliss! asylum of repose!
When all is hush'd—the rage of combat past,
And no dread war-note swells the moaning blast;
When the warm throb of many a heart is o'er,
And many an eye is clos'd—to wake no more;

Lull'd by the night-wind, pillow'd on the ground,
(The dewy death-bed of his comrades round!)
While o'er the slain the tears of midnight weep,
Faint with fatigue, he sinks in slumbers deep!                                    130
E'en then, soft visions, hov'ring round, portray,
The cherish'd forms that o'er his bosom sway!
He sees fond transport light each beaming face,
Meets the warm tear-drop, and the long embrace!
While the sweet welcome vibrates thro' his heart,
"Hail, weary soldier!—never more to part!"

And, lo! at last, releas'd from ev'ry toil,
He comes! the wanderer views his native soil!
Then the bright raptures, words can *never* speak,
Flash in his eye, and mantle o'er his cheek!                                       140
Then love and friendship, whose unceasing pray'r,
Implor'd for him, each guardian-spirit's care;
Who, for his fate, thro' sorrow's lingering year,
Had prov'd each thrilling pulse of hope and fear;
In that blest moment, all the past forget,
Hours of suspense! and vigils of regret!

And, oh! for him, the child of rude alarms,
Rear'd by stern danger, in the school of arms;
How sweet to change the war-song's pealing note,
For woodland-sounds, in summer-air that float!                                     150
Thro' vales of peace, o'er mountain-wilds to roam,
And breathe his native gales,° that whisper—"Home!"          *breezes*

Hail! sweet endearments of domestic ties,
Charms of existence! angel-sympathies!
Tho' pleasure smile, a soft, Circassian queen![3]
And guide her votaries thro' a fairy scene;
Where sylphid forms beguile their vernal hours,
With mirth and music, in Arcadian bow'rs;[4]
Tho' gazing nations hail the fiery car,
That bears the son of conquest from afar;                                          160
While Fame's loud Pæan bids his heart rejoice,
And ev'ry life-pulse vibrates to her voice;
Yet from your source *alone*, in mazes bright,
Flows the full current of serene delight!

On Freedom's wing, that ev'ry wild explores,
Thro' realms of space, th' aspiring eagle soars!
Darts o'er the clouds, exulting to admire,
Meridian glory—on her throne of fire!

Bird of the sun! his keen, unwearied gaze,
Hails the full noon, and triumphs in the blaze!                    170
But soon, descending from his height sublime,
Day's burning fount, and light's empyreal clime;
Once more he speeds to joys more calmly blest,
'Midst the dear inmates of his lonely nest!

Thus Genius, mounting on his bright career,
Thro' the wide regions of the mental sphere;
And proudly waving, in his gifted hand,
O'er Fancy's worlds, Invention's plastic⁵ wand;
Fearless and firm, with lightning-eye surveys
The clearest heav'n of intellectual rays!                          180
Yet, on his course tho' loftiest hopes attend,
And kindling raptures aid him to ascend;
(While in his mind, with high-born grandeur fraught,
Dilate the noblest energies of thought;)
Still, from the bliss, ethereal and refin'd,
Which crowns the soarings of triumphant mind,
At length he flies, to that serene retreat,
Where calm and pure, the mild affections meet;
Embosom'd there, to feel and to impart,
The softer pleasures of the social heart!                          190

Ah! weep for those, deserted and forlorn,
From ev'ry tie, by fate relentless torn!
See, on the barren coast, the lonely isle,
Mark'd with no step, uncheer'd by human smile;
Heart-sick and faint, the shipwreck'd wanderer stand,
Raise the dim eye, and lift the suppliant hand!
Explore with fruitless gaze the billowy main,
And weep—and pray—and linger!—but in vain!

Thence, roving wild thro' many a depth of shade!
Where voice ne'er echo'd, footstep never stray'd;                  200
He fondly seeks, o'er cliffs and deserts rude,
Haunts of mankind, 'midst realms of solitude!
And pauses oft, and sadly hears alone,
The wood's deep sigh, the surge's distant moan!
All else is hush'd! so silent, so profound,
As if some viewless power, presiding round,
With mystic spell, unbroken by a breath,
Had spread for ages the repose of death!
Ah! still the wanderer, by the boundless deep,
Lives but to watch,—and watches but to weep!                       210

He sees no sail in faint perspective rise,
His the dread loneliness of sea and skies!
Far from his cherish'd friends, his native shore,
Banish'd from being—to return no more;
There must he die!—within that circling wave,
That lonely isle—his prison and his grave!

Lo! thro' the waste, the wilderness of snows,
With fainting step, Siberia's exile goes![6]
Homeless and sad, o'er many a polar wild,
Where beam, or flower, or verdure, never smil'd;          220
Where frost and silence hold their despot-reign,
And bind existence in eternal chain!
Child of the desert! pilgrim of the gloom!
Dark is the path which leads thee to the tomb!
While on thy faded cheek, the arctic air
Congeals the bitter tear-drop of despair!
Yet not, that fate condemns thy closing day.
In that stern clime, to shed its parting ray;
Not that fair Nature's loveliness and light,
No more shall beam enchantment on thy sight;          230
Ah! not for *this*, far, far beyond relief,
Deep in thy bosom dwells the hopeless grief;
But that no friend of kindred heart is there,
Thy woes to meliorate, thy toils to share;
That no mild soother fondly shall assuage
The stormy trials of thy lingering age;
No smile of tenderness, with angel-power,
Lull the dread pangs of dissolution's hour;
For this alone, despair, a withering guest,
Sits on thy brow, and cankers in thy breast!          240

Yes! there, e'en there, in that tremendous clime,
Where desert-grandeur frowns, in pomp sublime;
Where winter triumphs, thro' the polar night,
In all his wild magnificence of might;
E'en *there*, Affection's hallow'd spell might pour,
The light of heav'n around th' inclement shore!
And, like the vales with bloom and sun-shine grac'd,
That smile, by circling Pyrenees embrac'd,
Teach the pure heart, with vital fires to glow,
E'en 'midst the world of solitude and snow!          250
The Halcyon's charm, thus dreaming fictions feign,
With mystic power, could tranquilize the main;[7]

Bid the loud wind, the mountain-billow sleep,
And peace and silence brood upon the deep!

And thus, Affection, can *thy* voice compose
The stormy tide of passions and of woes;
Bid every throb of wild emotion cease,
And lull misfortune in the arms of peace!

Oh! mark yon drooping form, of aged mien,
Wan, yet resign'd, and hopeless, yet serene! 260
Long ere victorious time had sought to chase
The bloom, the smile, that once illum'd his face;
That faded eye was dimm'd with many a care,
Those waving locks were silver'd by despair!
Yet filial love can pour the sovereign balm,
Assuage his pangs, his wounded spirit calm!
He, a sad emigrant! condemn'd to roam
In life's pale autumn from his ruin'd home;
Has borne the shock of peril's darkest wave,
Where joy—and hope—and fortune—found a grave! 270
'Twas his, to see destruction's fiercest band,
Rush, like a TYPHON, on his native land,
And roll, triumphant, on their blasted way,
In fire and blood—the deluge of dismay![8]
Unequal combat rag'd on many a plain,
And patriot-valour wav'd the sword—in vain!
Ah! gallant exile! nobly, long, he bled,
Long brav'd the tempest gath'ring o'er his head!
Till all was lost! and horror's darkening eye,
Rous'd the stern spirit of despair—to die! 280

Ah! gallant exile! in the storm that roll'd
Far o'er his country, rushing uncontroll'd;
The flowers that grac'd his path with loveliest bloom,
Torn by the blast—were scatter'd on the tomb!
When carnage burst, exulting in the strife,
The bosom ties that bound his soul to life;
Yet one was spar'd! and she, whose filial smile,
Can sooth his wanderings, and his tears beguile,
E'en *then*, could temper, with divine relief,
The wild delirium of unbounded grief; 290
And whisp'ring peace, conceal, with duteous art,
Her own deep sorrows in her inmost heart!
And now, tho' time, subduing ev'ry trace,
Has *mellow'd* all, he *never* can *erase*;

Oft will the wanderer's tears in silence flow,
Still sadly faithful to remember'd woe!
Then she, who feels a father's pang alone,
(Still fondly struggling to suppress *her own*;)
With anxious tenderness is ever nigh,
To chase the image that awakes the sigh!                      300
Her angel-voice his fainting soul can raise
To brighter visions of celestial days!
And speak of realms, where virtue's wing shall soar
On eagle-plume—to wonder and adore!
And friends, divided here, shall meet at last,
Unite their kindred souls—and smile on all the past!

Yes! we may hope, that Nature's deathless ties,
Renew'd, refin'd—shall triumph in the skies!
Heart-soothing thought! whose lov'd, consoling pow'r,
With seraph-dreams can gild reflection's hour;                310
Oh! still be near! and bright'ning thro' the gloom,
Beam and ascend! the day-star of the tomb!
And smile for those, in sternest ordeals prov'd,
Those lonely hearts, bereft of all they lov'd!

Lo! by the couch, where pain and chill disease,
In ev'ry vein the ebbing life-blood freeze;
Where youth is taught, by stealing, slow decay,
Life's closing lesson—in its dawning day;
Where beauty's rose is with'ring ere its prime,
Unchang'd by sorrow—and unsoil'd by time;                    320
There, bending still, with fix'd and sleepless eye,
There, from her child, the mother learns—to die!
Explores, with fearful gaze, each mournful trace
Of ling'ring sickness in the faded face;
Thro' the sad night, when ev'ry hope is fled,
Keeps her lone vigil by the suff'rer's bed;
And starts each morn, as deeper marks declare
The spoiler's hand—the blight of death—is there!
He comes! now feebly in th' exhausted frame,
Slow, languid, quiv'ring, burns the vital flame!             330
From the glaz'd eye-ball sheds its parting ray,
Dim, transient spark! that flutt'ring, fades away!
Faint beats the hov'ring pulse, the trembling heart,
Yet fond existence lingers—ere she part!

'Tis past! the struggle and the pang are o'er,
And life shall throb with agony no more!
While o'er the wasted form, the features pale,

Death's awful shadows throw their silvery veil!
Departed spirit! on this earthly sphere,
Tho' poignant suff'ring mark'd thy short career;                    340
Still could maternal love beguile thy woes,
And hush thy sighs—an angel of repose!

But who may charm *her* sleepless pang to rest,
Or draw the thorn that rankles in her breast?
And while she bends in silence o'er thy bier,
Assuage the grief, too heart-sick for a tear?
Visions of hope! in loveliest hues array'd,
Fair scenes of bliss! by Fancy's hand portray'd;
And were ye doom'd, with false, illusive smile,
With flatt'ring promise, to enchant awhile?                    350
And are ye vanish'd, never to return,
Set in the darkness of the mouldering urn?
Will no bright hour departed joys restore?
Shall the sad parent meet her child no more;
Behold no more the soul-illumin'd face,
Th' expressive smile, the animated grace?
Must the fair blossom, wither'd in the tomb,
Revive no more in loveliness and bloom?—
Descend, blest Faith! dispel the hopeless care,
And chase the gathering phantoms of despair!                    360
Tell, that the flow'r, transplanted in its morn,
Enjoys bright Eden, freed from every thorn;
Expands to milder suns, and softer dews;
The full perfection of immortal hues!
Tell, that when mounting to her native skies,
By death releas'd, the parent-spirit flies;
There shall the child, in anguish mourn'd so long,
With rapture hail her, 'midst the cherub-throng;
And guide her pinion, on exulting flight,
Thro' glory's boundless realms, and worlds of living light![9]                    370

Ye gentle spirits of departed friends!
If e'er on earth your buoyant wing descends;
If, with benignant care, ye linger near,
To guard the objects in existence dear;
If hov'ring o'er, ethereal band! ye view
The tender sorrows, to *your* memory true;
Oh! in the musing hour, at midnight deep,
While for your loss Affection wakes to weep;
While ev'ry sound in hallow'd stillness lies,
But the low murmur of her plaintive sighs;                    380
Oh! then, amidst that holy calm, be near!

Breathe your light whisper softly in her ear!
With secret spells, her wounded mind compose,
And chase the faithful tear—for you that flows!
Be near! when moon-light spreads the charm you lov'd,
O'er scenes where once your *earthly* footstep rov'd!
Then, while she wanders o'er the sparkling dew,
Thro' glens, and wood-paths, once endear'd by you;
And fondly lingers, in your fav'rite bow'rs,
And pauses oft, recalling former hours;                     390
Then wave your pinion o'er each well-known vale,
Float in the moon-beam, sigh upon the gale!
Bid your wild symphonies remotely swell,
Borne by the summer-wind, from grot and dell;
And touch your viewless harps, and sooth her soul,
With soft enchantments and divine control!
Be near! sweet guardians! watch her sacred rest,
When slumber folds her in his magic vest!
Around her, smiling, let your forms arise
Return'd in dreams, to bless her mental eyes!               400
Efface the mem'ry of your last farewell,
Of glowing joys, of radiant prospects, tell!
The sweet communion of the past, renew,
Reviving former scenes, array'd in softer hue!

Be near, when death, in virtue's brightest hour,
Calls up each pang, and summons all his pow'r!
Oh! then, transcending Fancy's loveliest dream,
Then let your forms, unveil'd, around her beam!
Then waft the vision of unclouded light,
A burst of glory, on her closing sight!                     410
Wake from the harp of heav'n th' immortal strain,
To hush the final agonies of pain!
With rapture's flame, the parting soul illume,
And smile triumphant thro' the shadowy gloom!

Oh! still be near! when, darting into day,
Th' exulting spirit leaves her bonds of clay;
Be yours to guide her flutt'ring wing on high,
O'er many a world, ascending to the sky!
There let your presence, once her earthly joy,
Tho' dimm'd with tears, and clouded with alloy;             420
Now form her bliss on that celestial shore,
Were death shall sever kindred hearts no more!

Yes! in the noon of that Elysian clime,
Beyond the sphere of anguish, death, or time;

Where mind's bright eye, with renovated fire,
Shall beam on glories—never to expire;
Oh! there, th' illumin'd soul may fondly trust,
More pure, more perfect, rising from the dust;
Those mild affections, whose consoling light
Sheds the soft moon-beam on terrestrial night;                    430
Sublim'd, ennobled, shall for ever glow,
Exalting rapture—not assuaging woe!

[1] An echo of Wordsworth's *Song* ("She dwelt among th'untrodden ways") (1800).

[2] See Exodus 16.35.

[3] Girls from Circassia, on the Black Sea's northeast coast, were often bred for harems. In ch. 5 of his influential novel *Émile* (1762), Rousseau states that he "would have a young maid cultivate her agreeable talents, in order to please her future husband, with as much care and assiduity as a young Circassian cultivates hers, to fit her for the haram of an Eastern bashaw"— provoking caustic responses from Macaulay (*Letters on Education*, no. 23) and Wollstonecraft (*Vindication of the Rights of Woman*, ch. 5). The Ottoman in Byron's *The Giaour* (1813) swoons over harem-slave Leila as "Circassia's daughter" (505), glossed by the *Quarterly* (1814) as "a beautiful Circassian slave, highly seducing, and like most slaves, easily seduced."

[4] The darker sense of Death's pronouncement, *Et in Arcadia ego* (inscribed on a shepherd's tomb in two famous seventeenth-century paintings, by Guercino and by Poussin), is here suppressed but later emerges. FH's *And I too in Arcadia* (*NMM*, 1824) appears in *1839* (7.36– 38) with a headnote: "A celebrated picture of Poussin represents a band of shepherd youths and maidens suddenly checked in their wanderings, and affected with various emotions, by the sight of a tomb which bears this inscription—'*Et in Arcadia ego.*'"

[5] With shaping power, a term from aesthetic theory used thus by Mark Akenside, Alexander Gerard and Abraham Tucker, and later in Coleridge's *Biographia Literaria* (1817), ch. 9.

[6] *Elisabeth; ou, Les Exilés de Sibérie* (. . . or the Exiles of Siberia), a popular sentimental novel by Marie-Sophie Risteau Cottin (1770–1807), was published in 1806.

[7] In the Greek myth (retold in Ovid's *Metamorphoses*), Halcyone, in grief over her husband's drowning, threw herself into the sea. In pity, the gods changed them both into kingfishers (halcyons) and calmed the winds for seven days around the winter solstice so that they could nest. Halcyon days are any magical interim of peace and tranquility.

[8] In Greek myth, the fierce monster Typhon sired Cerebus, Hydra, Sphinx, and Chimera; fearing his power, Zeus set him afire and buried him under Mount Etna (*typhon*, Greek for *whirlwind*, yields *typhoon*; cf. 1.97). In 1812 the Napoleonic wars still raged over Europe; storms and hurricanes were frequent images for the cataclysms (cf. Felicia Browne's *Wreath of Loyalty* 45). Several poems of "patriot-valour" appear in the *The Domestic Affections &c*: *War-Song of the Spanish Patriots*, *The Bards to the Soldiers of Caractacus*, *The Call of Liberty*, and the poem just prior to *The Domestic Affections*: *To My Eldest Brother, with the British Army in Portugal*.

[9] The image inspires a hypermetrical line.

# Epitaph on Mr. W——,
## a Celebrated Mineralogist

### (ca. 1814–16)

———〜〜〜———

[First published in *CM*, then *HM*, these verses show a side of Hemans not suspected in the cult of "feminine delicacy." "As may easily be supposed, they were never intended for publication," Hughes says (21); "merely a *jeu d'esprit* of the moment, in good-humoured raillery," they earned no place in the canon proper. The playful pentameter couplets— peppered with nearly hudibrastic rhymes (*about them / without them*; *by his side / petrified*; *hostile actions / petrifactions*)—and parodies of elegiac conventions and tropes ("Stop, passenger!"; "Weep not for him! but envied be his doom"; "O ye rocks!") are not treating the subject indelicately, however. C. Pleydell N. Wilton, later to hold clerical posts in New South Wales and Newcastle, was very much alive when she wrote his "epitaph." But his zeal for research could be risky: "during one of those 'mountain rambles' so delightfully enlivened by the wit & good humour of Mrs. Hemans, in the neighbourhood of Dyganwy" (in Wales), he "unfortunately fell off a rock, whilst in the act of exclaiming '*Ocular demonstration*'" (NLS; MS 4090, f. 193). Hemans presented the poem to him on the morning of his departure from North Wales for St. John's College, Cambridge; "at the end of the piece M^rs Hemans has written 'Conway 12 Oct 1816' F. H." (f. 194), though Hughes, who was with her on this visit, recalls the date as 1814–15 (*HM* 18–20). Text: *CM* 1.48–50; variants from the copy of Wilton's MS (ibid.).]

> Stop, passenger! a wondrous tale to list—
> Here lies a famous mineralogist!
> Famous, indeed,—such traces of his power,
> He's left from Penmanbach to Penmanmawr,—
> Such caves, and chasms, and fissures in the rocks,
> His works resemble those of earthquake shocks;
> And future ages very much may wonder
> What mighty giant rent the hills[1] asunder;
> Or whether Lucifer himself had ne'er
> Gone with his crew to play at foot-ball there.          10
>
> His fossils, flints, and spars, of every hue,[2]
> With him, good reader, here lie buried too!
> Sweet specimens, which, toiling to obtain,
> He split huge cliffs, like so much wood, in twain:
> We knew, so great the fuss he made about them,
> Alive or dead, he ne'er would rest without them;

So, to secure soft slumber to his bones,
We paved his grave with all his favourite stones.

His much-loved hammer's resting[3] by his side,
Each hand contains a shell-fish petrified;                    20
His mouth a piece of pudding-stone incloses,
And at his feet a lump of coal reposes:
Sure he was born beneath some lucky planet,
His very coffin-plate is made of granite!

Weep not, good reader! he is truly blest
Amidst chalcedony and quartz to rest—
Weep not for him! but envied be his doom,
Whose tomb,[4] though small, for all he loved had room:—
And, O ye rocks! schist, gneiss,[5] whate'er ye be,
Ye varied strata, names too hard for me,                    30
Sing, "O be joyful!" for your direst foe,
By death's fell hammer[6] is at length laid low.
Ne'er on your spoils again shall —————— riot.
Shut up your cloudy brows, and rest in quiet![7]
He sleeps—no longer planning hostile actions,—
As cold as any of his petrifactions;
Enshrined in specimens of every hue,
Too tranquil[8] e'en to dream, ye rocks! of you.

---

[1] MS] sent *such* hills
[2] MS] green, red & blue
[3] MS] rusting
[4] MS] grave
[5] MS] quartz
[6] Taking revenge on the research tool (see 19); on this same visit FH composed *Epitaph on the Hammer of the Aforesaid Mineralogist* (*HM* 21–22; MS 4090, f. 193).
[7] *HM*] Clear up
  Again, a comic reversal, "Rest in Peace" being a common inscription on gravestones.
[8] MS] quiet

# The Restoration of the
# Works of Art to Italy: A Poem

## (1816)

—◁◯◯◯▷—

[In the course of his conquests, Napoleon plundered about 5,000 artworks for removal to Paris to enhance the prestige of his empire. After his fall in 1815 and "the restoration of the monarchies," nations demanded "the restoration" of their art treasures. Hemans's title touches both senses. *Edinburgh Monthly Review* admired her "fine and deep enthusiasm" for "the rescue of the immortal monuments of Italian art from the den of Gallic plunder" (April 1820: 875). In heroic couplets, a form associated with public poetry, she manages a "feminine" subject, aesthetics, on the example of Staël's popular novel *Corinne* (1807), whose heroine evokes the spirit of an independent Italy and its past glories as she describes its scenery, art, and antiquities. "The best guide or rather companion which the traveller can take with him, is *Corinne ou l'Italie*, a work of singular ingenuity and eloquence," said Rev. J. C. Eustace (whose *Classical Tour* supplies Hemans's headnote); it "describes the climate, the beauties, the monuments of that privileged country with glowing animation" (30–31n). Following the pattern of Austen's signature for *Sense and Sensibility* (1811), Hemans signed the first edition of *Restoration* "BY A LADY." Affording a fresh start for the unevenly reviewed poet as well as modesty, the anonymity still announced a female point of view, in a mode of gentility distinguishable from Wollstonecrafted "Woman." The title-page of the first edition bears this epigraph:

AS IF FOR GODS A DWELLING PLACE.

BYRON.

—a description from *The Giaour* (1813) of the Greek Isles: "Strange—that where Nature loved to trace, / As if for Gods, a dwelling place, / And every charm and grace hath mix'd / Within the paradise she fix'd / There man, enamour'd of distress, / Should mar it into wilderness, / And trample, brute-like, o'er each flower" (46–52). Murray paid Hemans £70 for the copyright and issued a second edition of one thousand—now signed "By FELICIA HEMANS"—to which she added six notes and much new verse, doubling the length. Byron praised the poem to Murray, also his publisher (letter, 30 September 1816). The poem was favorably noticed by *British Critic*, *Monthly Review*, *Blackwood's*, and other journals, but Murray did not break even on it until the end of 1828. Text: 2d ed.; the new verse is in brackets.]

*Italia, Italia! O tu cui feo la sorte*
*Dono infelice di bellezza, ond'hai*
*Funesta dote d'infiniti guai,*
*Che'n fronte scritte per gran doglia porte;*
*Deh, fossi tu men bella, o almen piu forte.*

FILICAJA.[1]

*"The French, who in every invasion have been the scourge of Italy, and have rivalled or rather surpassed the rapacity of the Goths and Vandals, laid their sacri-*

*legious hands on the unparalleled collection of the Vatican, tore its Masterpieces*
*from their pedestals, and dragging them from their temples of marble, transported*
*them to Paris, and consigned them to the dull sullen halls, or rather stables, of*
*the* Louvre. . . . *But the joy of discovery was short, and the triumph of taste*
*transitory!"*

          —*Eustace's Classical Tour through Italy*, vol. ii. p. 60.[2]

Land of departed fame! whose classic plains,
Have proudly echoed to immortal strains;
Whose hallow'd soil hath given the great and brave,
Day-stars of life, a birth-place and a grave;
Home of the Arts! where glory's faded smile,
Sheds ling'ring light o'er many a mould'ring pile;
Proud wreck of vanish'd power, of splendor fled,
Majestic temple of the mighty dead!
Whose grandeur, yet contending with decay,
Gleams thro' the twilight of thy glorious day;          10
Tho' dimm'd thy brightness, rivetted thy chain,
Yet, fallen Italy! rejoice again!
Lost, lovely Realm! once more 'tis thine to gaze
On the rich relics of sublimer days.[3]

  Awake, ye Muses of Etrurian shades,
Or sacred Tivoli's romantic glades;[4]
Wake, ye that slumber in the bowery gloom,
Where the wild ivy shadows Virgil's tomb;
Or ye, whose voice, by Sorga's lonely wave,
Swell'd the deep echoes of the fountain's cave,[5]          20
[Or thrill'd the soul in Tasso's numbers high,
Those magic strains of love and chivalry;
If yet by classic streams ye fondly rove,
Haunting the myrtle-vale, the laurel-grove;[6]]
Oh! rouse once more the daring soul of song,
Seize with bold hands the harp, forgot so long,
And hail, with wonted pride, those works rever'd,
Hallow'd by time, by absence more endear'd.

  [And breathe to Those the strain, whose warrior-might
Each danger stemm'd, prevail'd in every fight;          30
Souls of unyielding power, to storms inured,
Sublim'd by peril, and by toil matured.
Sing of that Leader,° whose ascendant mind,          *Wellington*
Could rouse the slumb'ring spirit of mankind;
Whose banners track'd the vanquish'd Eagle's flight
O'er many a plain, and dark Sierra's height;
Who bade once more the wild, heroic lay,

Record the deeds of Roncesvalles' day;
Who, thro' each mountain-pass of rock and snow,
An Alpine Huntsman, chas'd the fear-struck foe;      40
Waved his proud standard to the balmy gales,
Rich Languedoc! that fan thy glowing vales,
And 'midst those scenes renew'd th' achievements high,
Bequeath'd to fame by England's ancestry.[7]

Yet, when the storm seem'd hushed, the conflict past,
One strife remained—the mightiest and the last!°      *Waterloo*
Nerved for the struggle, in that fateful hour,
Untamed Ambition summon'd all his power;
Vengeance and Pride, to frenzy rous'd, were there,
And the stern might of resolute Despair.      50
    Isle of the free! 'twas then thy champions[8] stood,
    Breasting unmov'd the combat's wildest flood,
    Sunbeam of Battle, then thy spirit shone,
    Glow'd in each breast, and sunk with life alone.

Oh hearts devoted!° whose illustrious doom,      *doomed; consecrated*
Gave there at once your triumph and your tomb,
Ye, firm and faithful, in th' ordeal tried
Of that dread strife, by Freedom sanctified;
Shrin'd, not entomb'd, ye rest in sacred earth,
Hallow'd by deeds of more than mortal worth.      60
What tho' to mark where sleeps heroic dust,
No sculptur'd trophy rise, or breathing bust,
Yours, on the scene where valour's race was run,
A prouder sepulchre—the field ye won!
There every mead, each cabin's lowly name,
Shall live a watch-word blended with your fame;[9]
And well may flowers suffice those graves to crown,
That ask no urn to blazon their renown.
There shall the Bard in future ages tread,
And bless each wreath that blossoms o'er the dead;      70
Revere each tree, whose sheltering branches wave
O'er the low mounds, the altars of the brave;
Pause o'er each Warrior's grass-grown bed, and hear
In every breeze, some name to glory dear,
And as the shades of twilight close around,
With martial pageants people all the ground.
Thither unborn descendants of the slain,
Shall throng, as pilgrim's to some holy fane,[10]
While, as they trace each spot, whose records tell,
Where fought their fathers, and prevail'd, and fell,      80
Warm in their souls shall loftiest feelings glow,

Claiming proud kindred with the dust below!
And many an age shall see the brave repair,
To learn the Hero's bright devotion there.

And well, Ausonia!° may that field of fame,                    *Italy*
From thee one song of echoing triumph claim.
Land of the lyre! 'twas there th' avenging sword,
Won the bright treasures to thy fanes restored;
Those precious trophies o'er thy realms that throw
A veil of radiance, hiding half thy woe,                       90
And bid the stranger for awhile forget
How deep thy fall, and deem thee glorious yet.]

Yes! fair creations, to perfection wrought,
Embodied visions of ascending thought!
Forms of sublimity! by Genius traced,
In tints that vindicate adoring taste;
Whose bright originals, to earth unknown,
Live in the spheres encircling glory's throne;
Models of art, to deathless fame consign'd,
Stamp'd with the high-born majesty of mind;                    100
Yes, matchless works! your presence shall restore
One beam of splendor to your native shore,
And her sad scenes of lost renown illume,
As the bright Sunset gilds some Hero's tomb.

Oh! ne'er, in other climes, tho' many an eye,
Dwelt on your charms in beaming ecstasy;
Ne'er was it yours to bid the soul expand
With thoughts so mighty, dreams so boldly grand,
As in that realm, where each faint breeze's moan,
Seems a low dirge for glorious ages gone;                      110
Where 'midst the ruin'd shrines of many a vale,
E'en Desolation tells a haughty tale,
[And scarce a fountain flows, a rock ascends,
But its proud name with song eternal blends!]

Yes! in those scenes, where every ancient stream,
Bids memory kindle o'er some lofty theme;
[Where every marble deeds of fame records,
Each ruin tells of Earth's departed lords;][11]
And the deep tones of inspiration swell,
From each wild Olive-wood, and Alpine dell;                    120
Where heroes slumber, on their battle plains,
'Midst prostrate altars, and deserted fanes,
And Fancy communes, in each lonely spot,
With shades of those who ne'er shall be forgot;

*There* was your home, and there your power imprest,
With tenfold awe, the pilgrim's glowing breast;
And, as the wind's deep thrills, and mystic sighs,
Wake the wild harp to loftiest harmonies,
Thus at your influence, starting from repose,
Thought, Feeling, Fancy, into grandeur rose.                    130

 Fair Florence! Queen of Arno's lovely vale![12]
Justice and Truth indignant heard thy tale,
And sternly smil'd, in retribution's hour,
To wrest thy treasures from the Spoiler's power.
Too long the spirits of thy noble dead
Mourned o'er the domes they rear'd in ages fled.
Those classic scenes their pride so richly graced,
Temples of genius, palaces of taste,
Too long, with sad and desolated mien,
Revealed where conquest's lawless track had been;              140
Reft of each form with brighter life imbued,
Lonely they frown'd, a desert solitude.
 Florence! th' Oppressor's noon of pride is o'er,
 Rise in thy pomp again, and weep no more!

 As one, who, starting at the dawn of day,
From dark illusions, phantoms of dismay,
With transport heighten'd by those ills of night,
Hails the rich glories of expanding light;
E'en thus, awak'ning from thy dream of woe,
While Heaven's own hues in [radiance round thee][13] glow,      150
With warmer ecstasy 'tis thine to trace
Each tint of beauty, and each line of grace;
More bright, more priz'd, more precious, since deplored,°   *lamented*
As lov'd, lost relics, ne'er to be restored,
Thy grief as hopeless as the tear-drop shed,
By fond affection bending o'er the dead.

 Athens of Italy! once more are thine,
Those matchless gems of Art's exhaustless mine.
For thee bright Genius darts his living beam,
Warm o'er thy shrines the tints of Glory stream,               160
And forms august as natives of the sky,
Rise round each fane in faultless majesty,
So chastely perfect, so serenely grand,
They seem creations of no mortal hand.

 Ye, at whose voice fair Art, with eagle glance,
Burst in full splendor from her deathlike trance;

Whose rallying call bade slumb'ring nations wake,
And daring Intellect his bondage break;
Beneath whose eye the Lords of song arose,
And snatch'd the Tuscan lyre from long repose,                    170
And bade its pealing energies resound,
With power electric, through the realms around;
Oh! high in thought, magnificent in soul!
Born to inspire, enlighten, and control;
Cosmo, Lorenzo! view your reign once more,[14]
The shrine where nations mingle to adore!
Again th' Enthusiast there, with ardent gaze,
Shall hail the mighty of departed days:
Those sovereign spirits, whose commanding mind,
Seems in the marble's breathing mould enshrined;                    180
Still, with ascendant power, the world to awe,
Still the deep homage of the heart to draw;
To breathe some spell of holiness around,
Bid all the scene be consecrated ground,
And from the stone, by Inspiration wrought,
Dart the pure lightnings of exalted thought.

There thou, fair offspring of immortal Mind!
Love's radiant Goddess, Idol of mankind![15]
Once the bright object of Devotion's vow,
Shalt claim from taste a kindred worship now.                    190
Oh! who can tell what beams of heavenly light,
Flash'd o'er the sculptor's intellectual sight,
How many a glimpse, reveal'd to him alone,
Made brighter beings, nobler worlds his own;
Ere, like some vision sent the earth to bless,
Burst into life thy pomp of loveliness!

Young Genius there, while dwells his kindling eye
On forms, instinct with[16] bright divinity,
While new-born powers, dilating in his heart,
Embrace the full magnificence of Art;                    200
From scenes, by Raphael's gifted hand arrayed,
From dreams of heaven, by Angelo° pourtrayed;                    *Michelangelo*
From each fair work of Grecian skill sublime,
Seal'd with perfection, "sanctified by time";[17]
Shall catch a kindred glow, and proudly feel
His spirit burn with emulative zeal,
Buoyant with loftier hopes, his soul shall rise,
Imbued at once with nobler energies;
O'er [life's dim scenes on rapid pinion][18] soar,

And worlds of visionary grace explore,                        210
Till his bold hand give glory's day-dreams birth,
And with new wonders charm admiring earth.

    Venice exult! and o'er thy moonlight seas,
Swell with gay strains each Adriatic breeze!
What tho' long fled those years of martial fame,
That shed romantic lustre o'er thy name;
[Tho' to the winds thy streamers idly play,
And the wild waves another Queen° obey;]                        *Britain*
Tho' quench'd the spirit of thine ancient race,
And power and freedom scarce have left a trace;[19]              220
Yet still shall Art her splendors round thee cast,
And gild the wreck of years for ever past.
Again thy fanes may boast a Titian's dyes,
Whose clear soft brilliance emulates thy skies,
And scenes that glow in colouring's richest bloom,
With life's warm flush Palladian halls illume.[20]
From thy [rich] dome again th' unrivalled steed
Starts to existence, rushes into speed,
Still for Lysippus claims that wreath of fame,
Panting with ardour, vivified with flame.[21]                   230

    [Proud Racers of the Sun! to fancy's thought,
Burning with spirit, from his essence caught,
No mortal birth ye seem—but formed to bear
Heaven's car of triumph° thro' the realms of air;     *chariot of the sun*
To range uncurb'd the pathless fields of space,
The winds your rivals in the glorious race;
Traverse empyreal spheres with buoyant feet,
Free as the zephyr, as the shot-star° fleet;              *meteor*
And waft thro' worlds unknown the vital ray,
The flame that wakes creations into day.                        240
Creatures of fire and ether! winged with light,
To track the regions of the Infinite!
From purer elements whose life was drawn,
Sprung from the sunbeam, offspring of the dawn.
What years on years, in silence gliding by,
Have spar'd those forms of perfect symmetry!
Moulded by Art to dignify alone,
Her own bright deity's resplendent throne,
Since first her skill their fiery grace bestowed,
Meet for such lofty fate, such high abode,                      250
How many a race, whose tales of glory seem
An echo's voice—the music of a dream,
Whose records feebly from oblivion save,

A few bright traces of the wise and brave;
How many a state, whose pillar'd strength sublime,
Defied the storms of war, the waves of time,
Towering o'er earth majestic and alone,
Fortress of power—has flourished and is gone!
And they, from clime to clime by conquest borne,
Each fleeting triumph destined to adorn,                           260
They, that of powers and kingdoms lost and won,
Have seen the noontide and the setting sun,
Consummate still in every grace remain,
As o'er *their* heads had ages rolled in vain!
Ages, victorious in their ceaseless flight,
O'er countless monuments of earthly might!
While she, from fair Byzantium's lost domain,[22]
Who bore those treasures to her ocean-reign,
'Midst the blue deep, who reared her island-throne,
And called th' infinitude of waves her own;                        270
Venice the proud, the Regent of the sea,
Welcomes in chains the trophies of the Free!]

   And thou, whose Eagle's towering plume unfurled,
Once cast its shadow o'er a vassal world,
Eternal city! round whose Curule throne,[23]
The Lords of nations knelt in ages flown;
Thou, whose Augustan years[24] have left to time,
Immortal records of their glorious prime;
When deathless bards, thine olive-shades among,
Swelled the high raptures of heroic song;                          280
Fair, fallen Empress! raise thy languid head,
From the cold altars of th' illustrious dead,
And once again, with fond delight survey,
The proud memorials of thy noblest day.[25]

   [Lo! where thy sons, oh Rome!][26] a godlike train,
In imaged majesty return again!
Bards, chieftains, monarchs, tower with mien august,
O'er scenes that shrine their venerable dust.
Those forms, those features, luminous with soul,
Still o'er thy children seem to claim control;                     290
With awful grace arrest the pilgrim's glance,
Bind his rapt soul in elevating trance,
And bid the past, to fancy's ardent eyes,
From time's dim sepulchre in glory rise.

   Souls of the lofty! whose undying names,
Rouse the young bosom still to noblest aims;

Oh! with your images could fate restore,
Your own high spirit to your sons once more;
Patriots and Heroes! could those flames return,
That bade your hearts with freedom's ardours burn;          300
Then from the sacred ashes of the first,
Might a new Rome in phoenix-grandeur burst!
With one bright glance dispel th' horizon's gloom,
With one loud call wake Empire from the tomb;
Bind round her brows her own triumphal crown,
Lift her dread Ægis, with majestic frown,
Unchain her Eagle's wing, and guide his flight,
To bathe its plumage in the fount of Light.[27]

[Vain dream! degraded Rome! thy noon is o'er,
Once lost, thy spirit shall revive no more.          310
It sleeps with those, the sons of other days,
Who fixed on thee the world's adoring gaze;
Those, blest to live, while yet thy star was high,
More blest, ere darkness quenched its beam, to die!

Yet, tho' thy faithless tutelary powers,
Have fled thy shrines, left desolate thy towers,
Still, still to thee shall nations bend their way,
Revered in ruin, sovereign in decay!
Oh! what can realms, in fame's full zenith, boast,
To match the relics of thy splendor lost!          320
By Tiber's waves, on each illustrious hill,
Genius and Taste shall love to wander still,
For there has Art survived an Empire's doom,
And reared her throne o'er Latium's[28] trophied tomb;
She from the dust recalls the brave and free,
Peopling each scene with beings worthy thee!

Oh! ne'er again may War, with lightning-stroke,
Rend its last honours from the shatter'd oak!
Long be those works, revered by ages, thine,
To lend one triumph to thy dim decline.]          330

Bright with stern beauty, breathing wrathful fire,
In all the grandeur of celestial ire,
Once more thine own, th' immortal Archer's form,[29]
Sheds radiance round, with more than Being warm!
Oh! who could view, nor deem that perfect frame,
A living temple of ethereal flame?
[Lord of the day-star! how may words pourtray
Of thy chaste glory one reflected ray?
Whate'er the soul could dream, the hand could trace,

Of regal dignity, and heavenly grace;                           340
Each purer effluence of the fair and bright,
Whose fitful gleams have broke on mortal sight;
Each bold idea, borrowed from the sky,
To vest° th' embodied form of Deity;                    *invest, endow*
All, all in thee ennobled and refined,
Breathe and enchant, transcendently combined!
Son of Elysium![30] years and ages gone,
Have bowed, in speechless homage, at thy throne,
And days unborn, and nations yet to be,
Shall gaze, absorbed in ecstasy, on thee!                       350

    And thou, triumphant wreck,[31] e'en yet sublime,
Disputed trophy, claimed by Art and Time,
Hail to that scene again, where Genius caught
From thee its fervors of diviner thought!
Where He, th' inspired One, whose gigantic mind,
Lived in some sphere, to him alone assigned;
Who from the past, the future, and th' unseen,
Could call up forms of more than earthly mien;
Unrivalled Angelo, on thee would gaze,
Till his full soul imbibed perfection's blaze!                  360
And who but he, that Prince of Art, might dare
Thy sovereign greatness view without despair?
Emblem of Rome! from power's meridian hurled,
Yet claiming still the homage of the world.

    What hadst thou been, ere barbarous hands defaced
The work of wonder, idolized by taste?
Oh! worthy still of some divine abode,
Mould of a Conqueror! ruin of a God![32]
Still, like some broken gem, whose quenchless beam,
From each bright fragment pours its vital stream,               370
'Tis thine, by fate unconquered, to dispense
From every part, some ray of excellence!
E'en yet, informed with essence from on high,
Thine is no trace of frail mortality!
Within that frame a purer Being glows,
Thro' viewless veins a brighter current flows;
Filled with immortal life each muscle swells,
In every line supernal grandeur dwells.

    Consummate work! the noblest and the last,
Of Grecian Freedom, ere her reign was past.[33]                 380
Nurse of the mighty, she, while lingering still,
Her mantle flowed o'er many a classic hill,
Ere yet her voice its parting accents breathed,

A Hero's image to the world bequeathed;
Enshrined in thee th' imperishable ray,
Of high-souled Genius, fostered by her sway,
And bade thee teach, to ages yet unborn,
What lofty dreams were hers—who never shall return!]

And mark yon group, transfixed with many a throe,
Sealed with the image of eternal woe:                  390
With fearful truth, terrific power, exprest,
Thy pangs, Laocoon, agonize the breast,
And the stern combat picture to mankind,
Of suffering nature, and enduring mind.
Oh, mighty conflict! tho' his pains intense,
Distend each [nerve],[34] and dart thro' every sense;
Tho' fixed on him, his children's suppliant eyes,
Implore the aid avenging fate denies;
Tho' with the giant-snake in fruitless strife,
Heaves every muscle with convulsive life,                 400
And in each limb Existence writhes, enrolled
'Midst the dread circles of the venomed fold;
Yet the strong spirit lives—and not a cry,
Shall own the might of Nature's agony!
That furrowed brow unconquered soul reveals,
That patient eye to angry Heaven appeals,
That struggling bosom concentrates its breath,
Nor yields one moan to torture or to death![35]

Sublimest triumph of intrepid Art!
With speechless horror to congeal the heart,              410
To freeze each pulse, and dart thro' every vein,
Cold thrills of fear, keen sympathies of pain;
Yet teach the spirit how its lofty power,
May brave the pangs of fate's severest hour.

Turn from such conflicts, and enraptured gaze,
On scenes where Painting all her skill displays:
Landscapes, by colouring drest in richer dyes,
More mellowed sunshine, more unclouded skies;
Or dreams of bliss, to dying Martyrs given,
Descending Seraphs, robed in beams of heaven.            420

Oh! sovereign Masters of the Pencil's might,
Its depth of shadow, and its blaze of light,[36]
Ye, whose bold thought disdaining every bound,
Explored the worlds above, below, around,
Children of Italy! who stand alone,
And unapproached, 'midst regions all your own;

What scenes, what beings blest your favoured sight,
Severely grand,[37] unutterably bright!
Triumphant spirits! your exulting eye,
Could meet the noontide of eternity,                              430
And gaze untired, undaunted, uncontrolled,
On all that Fancy trembles to behold.

Bright on your view such forms their splendor shed,
As burst on Prophet-bards in ages fled:
Forms that to trace, no hand but yours might dare,
Darkly sublime, or exquisitely fair,
These o'er the walls your magic skill arrayed,[38]
Glow in rich sunshine, gleam thro' melting shade,
Float in light grace, in awful° greatness tower,            *awe-inspiring*
And breathe and move, the records of your power.            440
Inspired of Heaven! what heightened pomp ye cast,
O'er all the deathless trophies of the past!
Round many a marble fane and classic dome,
Asserting still the majesty of Rome;
Round many a work that bids the world believe,
What Grecian Art could image and achieve;
Again, creative minds, your visions throw,
Life's chastened warmth, and Beauty's mellowest glow,
And when the Morn's bright beams and mantling° dyes,        *blushing*
Pour the rich lustre of Ausonian skies,                     450
Or evening suns illume, with purple smile,
The Parian altar, and the pillared aisle,
Then, as the full, or softened radiance falls,
On Angel-groups that hover o'er the walls,
Well may those [Temples],[39] where your hand has shed
Light o'er the tomb, existence round the dead,
Seem like some world, so perfect and so fair,
That nought of earth should find admittance there,
Some sphere, where Beings, to mankind unknown,
Dwell in the brightness of their pomp, alone!               460

[Hence, ye vain fictions, fancy's erring theme,
Gods of illusion! phantoms of a dream!
Frail, powerless idols of departed time,
Fables of song, delusive, tho' sublime!
To loftier tasks has Roman Art assigned,
Her matchless pencil, and her mighty mind!
From brighter streams her vast ideas flowed,
With purer fire her ardent spirit glowed.
To her 'twas given in fancy to explore,
The land of miracles, the holiest shore;                    470

That realm where first the light of life was sent,
The loved, the punished, of th' Omnipotent!
O'er Judah's hills her thoughts inspired would stray,
Thro' Jordan's valleys trace their lonely way;
By Siloa's brook, or Almotana's deep,[40]
Chained in dead silence, and unbroken sleep;
Scenes, whose cleft rocks, and blasted deserts tell,
Where pass'd th' Eternal, where his anger fell!
Where oft his voice the words of fate revealed,
Swelled in the whirlwind, in the thunder pealed,                    480
Or heard by prophets in some palmy vale,
Breathed "still small" whispers on the midnight gale.[41]
There dwelt her spirit°—there her hand pourtrayed,          *(Roman art)*
'Midst the lone wilderness or cedar-shade,
Ethereal forms, with awful missions fraught,
Or Patriarch-seers, absorbed in sacred thought,
Bards, in high converse with the world of rest,
Saints of the earth, and spirits of the blest.
But chief to Him, the Conqueror of the grave,
Who lived to guide us, and who died to save;                    490
Him, at whose glance the powers of evil fled,
And soul returned to animate[42] the dead;
Whom the waves owned—and sunk beneath his eye,
Awed by one accent of Divinity;
To Him she gave her meditative hours,
Hallowed her thoughts, and sanctified her powers.
O'er her bright scenes sublime repose she threw,
As all around the Godhead's presence knew,
And robed the Holy One's benignant mien,
In beaming mercy, majesty serene.                    500

   Oh! mark, where Raphael's pure and perfect line
Pourtrays that form ineffably divine!
Where with transcendent skill his hand has shed
Diffusive sunbeams round the Saviour's head;[43]
Each heaven-illumined lineament imbued
With all the fulness of beatitude,
And traced the sainted group, whose mortal sight,
Sinks overpowered by that excess of light!

   Gaze on that scene, and own the might of Art,
By truth inspired, to elevate the heart!                    510
To bid the soul exultingly possess,
Of all her powers, a heightened consciousness,
And strong in hope, anticipate the day,
The last of life, the first of freedom's ray;

To realize, in some unclouded sphere,
Those pictured glories feebly imaged here!
Dim, cold reflections from her native sky,
Faint effluence of "the Day-spring from on high!"[44]]

[1] The opening of the famous *Sonetto I* of *All'Italia* (in *Poesie Toscane*; Venezia, 1708), by Count Vincenzo da Filicaja (1642–1707), senator and governor of Volterra and later of Pisa, who wrote a celebrated series of odes on the liberation of Vienna (1683). Byron translated the sonnet in *Childe Harold's Pilgrimage IV* (1818), xlii–iii, in a section praising Italy's art and lamenting its history of invasion by "robbers." FH gives her version in *Translations* (1818): "Italia! thou, by lavish Nature graced / With ill-starr'd beauty, which to thee hath been / A fatal dowry, whose effects are traced / In the deep sorrows graven on thy mien; // Oh! that more strength, or fewer charms were thine" (translating "Sorte" as "Nature" rather than "Fate").

[2] These sentences, on the first recto after the title page of *Restoration*, are quoted from Rev. John Chetwode Eustace (?1762–1815), *A Classical Tour through Italy An.* MDCCCII, 3d ed., revised and enlarged (London: J. Mawman, 1815); in *Tour*, the sentence after FH's ellipses immediately precedes the one before the ellipses (2.60). In his "Preliminary Discourse," Eustace states his "sincere and undisguised" Roman Catholic faith, his Burkean affection of English liberty and monarchy, his "abhorrence" of the French Republic and of Napoleon's "hostilities [. . .] against the liberties and the happiness of mankind," and his "horror and detestation" of "*revolutionary* France" (xiv–xvii). Germanic tribes pillaged Rome from the 3d to the 6th c. The Vatican houses vast art collections. The art collection at the Louvre (the Parisian royal palace, formerly a stable) was greatly augmented by Napoleon's loot.

[3] This first stanza takes the form of a sonnet, FH's own to Italy, in homage to Filicaja's.

[4] Etruria is ancient Tuscany; its central city, Florence, was home to Dante (1265–1321) and Petrarch (1304–74). Tivoli, east of Rome, is the site of the famous Renaissance estate, Villa d'Este, and the ruins of Emperor Hadrian's summer palace.

[5] The tomb of Virgil (1st c. B.C.) was fabled to be near Naples.

[6] Torquato Tasso (1544–95) was raised in Naples; FH includes his sonnets in *Translations*. Laurel wreaths honored military victors and later, poets; myrtle is symbolic of erotic love.

[7] Wellington (actually an Irish peer's son) led the British against Napoleon in Spain's Sierra Mountains, in the fabled Ronscesvalles pass (see *The Siege of Valencia*), and then in southern France. The next stanza celebrates his victory over Napoleon at Waterloo (June 1815). Napoleon's standard, like that of the Roman emperors, was the eagle.

[8] In medieval chivalry and romance, those who fight on behalf of another.

[9] Various fields and small farmhouses at Waterloo became shrines of the battle.

[10] Among such pilgrims, many recorded their reflections—a genre popularized most spectacularly in *Childe Harold III*, stanzas xvii ff.

[11] 117–18, 1st ed.] Where teems the soil with records of renown, / Fame's mouldering trophies, Empire's ravish'd crown,

[12] The apostrophe to Florence is another embedded sonnet. See the similar sonnet-stanzas to Rome, 351–78.

[13] 1st ed.] native radiance

[14] De' Medici rulers Lorenzo (ca.1449–92) and Cosmo (1389–1464) were patrons of the arts. FH has one of Lorenzo's sonnets in *Translations*.

[15] The famous modest nude, the Greek *Venus de' Medici* (ca. 1st c. B.C.)—of which lead copies were a vogue in 18th-c. English gardens—was plundered and removed to Paris in 1803 and returned in 1815 to the Uffizi Gallery in Florence.

[16] Cf. *Properzia Rossi* 92; the adjective means "implanted as a natural instinct" and, by extension, "impelled." Milton describes "The Chariot of the Paternal Deity" as "Itself instinct with Spirit" (*Paradise Lost* 6.751–52); by FH's day, it added the sense of "inspired, imbued or charged with, as a moving or animating force" (*OED*).

[17] Cf. Hugh Downman (1740–1809), *Poems to Thespia* (1781; 1791), XII: "Why was I born in this more polish'd clime / Amid the scenes of artificial life? / Where custom rules, long-sanctified by time, / And fashion holds with nature endless strife?" (1–4).

[18] 1st ed.] the dim scenes of life undaunted

[19] Declined from its Renaissance power, Venice remained independent until its fall in 1797 to Napoleon, who ceded it and its territories to Austria, under whose control it remained.

[20] 1st ed.] 223–26 follow 227–30. Titian (ca. 1477–1576) was famed for his mastery of color. The classical-style architecture of Andrea Palladio (1508–80), via his drawings in *Quattro libri dell'architettura* (1570) inspired English Georgian architecture in the 18th c.

[21] 227, 1st ed.] proud.

In the Crusader sack of Byzantium (Constantinople) in 1204, the Venetians looted one of four bronze horses (?2d c.; wrongly attributed to Greek sculptor Lysippus, 4th c. B.C.) and displayed it on the balcony of its richly domed San Marco cathedral in 1265; it was removed by the French in the late 1790s.

[22] The Byzantine Empire flourished after the fall of the Roman Empire (late 5th c.) and fell to the Turks in 1453.

[23] Used by the highest civic officers of ancient Rome.

[24] A literary flourishing during the reign of Augustus (27 B.C.–A.D. 14), applied by British neoclassical writers to their 18th-c. era.

[25] 1st ed.] These lines are followed by 331–36 and 389–460.

[26] 1st ed.] And lo! thy sons, O Rome!

[27] 1st ed.] Poem ends here, closing as it opened, with a sonnet stanza. The aegis is Minerva's shield, signifying her protection and patronage.

[28] The ancient name of the region in which Rome is located.

[29] The famous statue of Apollo was taken from the Vatican's Belvedere palace in 1800 for display in Paris. Antonio Canova (1757–1822), an Italian sculptor well known in Britain, superintended its return after the fall of Napoleon.

[30] See FH's *Elysium*.

[31] The Belvedere Torso, the favourite study of Michael Angelo, and of many other distinguished artists. [FH]

This marble fragment from 1st-c. B.C. Athens is in the Vatican collections.

[32] "Quoique cette Statue d'Hercule ait été maltraitée et mutilée d'une manière étrange, se trouvant sans tête, sans bras et sans jambes, elle est cependant encore un chef-d'œuvre aux yeux des Connoisseurs; et ceux qui savent percer dans les mystères de l'Art, se la représentent dans toute sa beauté. L'Artiste en voulant représenter Hercule, a formé un corps idéal au-dessus de la Nature ... Cet Hercule paroît donc ici tel qu'il dut être lorsque purifié par le feu des foiblesses de l'humanité, il obtint l'immortalité et prit place auprès des Dieux. Il est représenté sans aucun besoin de nourriture et de réparation de forces. Les veines y sont toutes invisibles." Winckelmann, *Histoire de l'Art chez les Anciens*, tom. ii. p. 248. [FH]

[Although this Statue of Hercules has been maltreated and mutilated in a strange manner, being without head, without arms and without legs, even so it is a masterpiece in the eyes of Connoisseurs; and those who know how to penetrate the mysteries of Art can represent it to themselves in all its beauty. The Artist, in wishing to represent Hercules, has formed an ideal body that surpasses Nature. [. . .] This Hercules appears here, then, as he must have been at the moment when, purified by the fire of human weaknesses, he attained immortality and took his place among the Gods. He is represented without any need for nourishment or of recuperation of his strength. The veins there are completely invisible.]

From a translation of J. J. Winckelmann (1717–68), *Geschichte der Kunst des Altertums* (History of ancient art) (Amsterdam, 1766), bk. 10, ch. 3, sec. 16 (247–48). Winckelmann celebrated the great art nourished by the political freedoms of ancient Greece.

[33] "Le Torso d'Hercule paroît un des derniers Ouvrages parfaits que l'Art ait produit en Grèce, avant la perte de sa liberté. Car après que la Grèce fut réduite en Province Romaine, l'histoire ne fait mention d'aucun Artiste célèbre de cette nation, jusqu'aux temps du Triumvirat Romain." Winckelmann, *ibid.* tom. ii. p. 250.[FH]

[The Torso of Hercules appears to be one of the last perfect Works which Art produced in Greece, before the loss of its freedom. For after Greece was reduced to a Roman Province, history makes no mention of any celebrated Artist of that nation, until the time of the Roman Triumvirate.]

*Histoire*, bk. 10, ch. 3, sec. 29 (250). The period of the Triumvirate was in the 1st c. B.C.

[34] 1st ed.] vein.

This famous 1st-c. marble sculpture, based on an episode in Virgil's *Aeneid* (2.199–231), depicts the Trojan priest Laocoön and his two sons being strangled by a serpent. It was taken to Paris in 1797 and returned to Rome in 1816.

[35] "It is not, in the same manner, in the agoniz[ing] limbs, or in the convulsed muscles of the Laocoon, that the secret grace of its composition resides; it is in the majestic air of the head, which has not *yielded* to *suffering*, and in the deep serenity of the forehead, which seems to be still *superior* to all its *afflictions*, and significant of a mind that cannot be subdued."—*Alison's Essays*, vol. ii. p. 400.

Laocoon nous offre le spectacle de la nature humaine dans la plus grande douleur dont elle soit susceptible, sous l'image d'un homme qui tâche de rassembler contre elle toute la force de l'esprit. Tandis que l'excès de la souffrance enfle les muscles, et tire violemment les nerfs, le courage se montre sur le front gonflé: la poitrine s'élève avec peine par la nécessité de la respiration, qui est également contrainte par le silence que la force de l'ame impose à la douleur qu'elle voudroit étouffer. . . . Son air est plaintif, et non criard . . . Winckelmann, *ibid.* tom. ii. 214. [FH; her italics]

[Laocoön offers us the spectacle of human nature in the greatest suffering of which it is susceptible, in the figure of a man who tries to gather against it all the strength of his soul. While the extremity of suffering expands his muscles, and violently strains his nerves, courage is displayed on his swelling brow; his breast heaves in pain from the need to breathe, which is equally constrained by the silence which the strength of his soul imposes on the suffering that it would suppress. [. . .] His expression is plaintive, not complaining.]

Archibald Alison (1757–1839), *Essays on the Nature and Principles of Taste* (Edinburgh: Constable, 1790); 2-vol. 3d ed. (1812), 2.400–401. The widely admired sermons of this Edinburgh Episcopal minister, published 1814–15, saw several editions. His wife was one of the daughters of Dr. John Gregory, famously addressed in *A Father's Legacy to His Daughters* (1774). Winckelmann, *Histoire*, bk. 10, ch. 1, sec. 16 (214–15).

[36] The contrast of light and shade (chiaroscuro); "pencil" refers to both painting and drawing.

[37] 1st ed.] gifted sight, / Profoundly grand,

[38] These aesthetic categories were given influential formulation in Edmund Burke's *A Philosophical Enquiry into the Origin of our Ideas of the Sublime and Beautiful* (1757, often reissued). "Walls" refers to painting alfresco, on fresh, undried plaster.

[39] 1st ed.] samples,

Parian is a semitransparent white marble from the Greek isle of Paros.

[40] Almotana. The name given by the Arabs to the Dead Sea. [FH]

Other names are biblical: the kingdom of, whose capital was Jerusalem; the Jordan River; the Siloa reservoir.

[41] God speaks to the prophet Elijah in a "still small voice" (1 Kings 19.12).

[42] A Latin pun: "animate" means literally "put a soul into."

[43] The Transfiguration, thought to be so perfect a specimen of art, that, in honour of Raphael, it was carried before his body to the grave. [FH]

Raphael's painting of this subject was almost complete at his death, at age 37, in 1520; it was removed to Paris in 1797.

[44] A description of Christ by John the Baptist's father (Luke 1.78).

# Modern Greece, A Poem

## (1817)

———《⁘》———

[Stung by the low sales of *The Restoration*, Hemans tested another popular subject: Greece's struggle against the Ottoman Empire. The widespread enthusiasm for the cause notwithstanding, Greece's British champions were divided about Britain's acquisition of the Elgin Marbles, sculptural fragments from the Athenian Parthenon amassed by Thomas Bruce, seventh Earl of Elgin (1766–1841), diplomatic envoy to the Ottoman Empire, 1799–1802. His removal of the Marbles, with Turkish permission and at his own expense, in 1803 and his offer to sell them to the British government in 1811 were hotly debated. Byron cried plunder (*Childe Harold's Pilgrimage* [1812] II.xi–xv) but others cheered the rescue of the Marbles from Greek neglect and Turkish abuse, as well as the preemptive snatching of the prize from Napoleonic France (Britain was the proper custodian of Greece's ancient glory, many felt, and its true successor). Their aesthetic value was derided by Richard Payne Knight and defended by Henri Fuseli, Benjamin R. Haydon, John Keats, and others. After Parliamentary hearings, in 1816 Britain paid £35,000 (less than the £50,000 Elgin said he invested), and in 1817 the British Museum displayed the Marbles. Their possession is still contested. FH's poem was advertised in Murray's *Quarterly Review* as *Modern Greece and the Elgin Marbles: A Poem*, and published in June 1817. Declining to buy the copyright, Murray agreed to split the profits. When the first edition of 500 sold out by 1821, netting over £50, Murray issued a second.

In the philhellenist spirit of the age, FH contrasts the glory that was Greece to the degraded, enslaved modern state, condemns modern tyrants (the Ottomans and Napoleon), and enters the Elgin Marbles debate with the support of forty-four scholarly notes. The anonymity of the first edition (see FH's letter to Murray, 26 February 1817) perhaps enabled her to risk in her conclusion an apocalyptic perspective, akin to that of Barbauld's harshly reviewed *Eighteen Hundred and Eleven* (1812) in which modern Britain is imagined as a future ruin, a mere tourist site rather than world power. Even so, the poem won favorable notice in the *Edinburgh Monthly* and *Blackwood's*, the latter identifying the poet as "the same lady who last year put her name to the second edition of another poem on a kindred subject, *The Restoration of the Works of Art to Italy*—namely Mrs. Hemans" (August 1817, 516). Noting the scholarship, the *Monthly Review* (September 1817) assumed a male author; the *Eclectic Review* described "a man of genuine talent and feeling" (2d ser. 10 [1817], 598), and the *New British Ladies' Magazine* guessed Byron: "We think we trace a noble and self exiled Poet here—The Poem has all his majesty and grandeur" (n.s. 1 [1817], 70). Byron was not impressed, however, sneering to Murray (letter, 4 September 1817) about the substance and the heterodox ten-line stanza (ababcdcdee), in which the quatrains and the closing couplet are patterned on a Shakespearian sonnet, with the final line's alexandrine (six iambs) evoking the similarly measured nine-line Spenserian stanza. "The measure is like the Spencerian, though different," said *Blackwood's*; "The experiment was bold, but it has not failed" (517). It quoted several stanzas. FH uses this stanza-form again in *The Last Banquet of Antony and Cleopatra*. Text: 1st ed. (1817); variants in 2d ed. are mostly accidentals.]

*O Greece! thou sapient nurse of finer arts,*
*Which to bright Science blooming Fancy bore,*
*Be this thy praise, that thou, and thou alone,*
*In these hast led the way, in these excelled,*
*Crowned with the laurel of assenting Time.*
THOMSON'S LIBERTY.[1]

I

Oh! who hath trod thy consecrated clime,
Fair land of Phidias![2] theme of lofty strains!
And traced each scene, that, midst the wrecks of time,[3]
The print of Glory's parting step retains;
Nor for awhile, in high-wrought dreams, forgot,
Musing on years gone by in brightness there,
The hopes, the fears, the sorrows of his lot,
The hues his fate hath worn, or yet may wear;
As when from mountain-heights, his ardent eye
Of sea and heaven hath track'd the blue infinity?                        10

II

Is there who views with cold unaltered mien,
His frozen heart with proud indifference fraught,
Each sacred haunt, each unforgotten scene,
Where Freedom triumph'd, or where Wisdom taught?
Souls that too deeply feel, oh, envy not
The sullen calm your fate hath never known:
Through the dull twilight of that wint'ry lot
Genius ne'er pierced, nor Fancy's sunbeam shone,
Nor those high thoughts, that, hailing Glory's trace,
Glow with the generous flames of every age and race.                    20

III

But blest the wanderer, whose enthusiast mind
Each muse of ancient days hath deep imbued
With lofty lore; and all his thoughts refined
In the calm school of silent solitude;
Pour'd on his ear, midst groves and glens retired,
The mighty strains of each illustrious clime,
All that hath lived, while empires have expired,
To float for ever on the winds of Time;
And on his soul indelibly pourtray'd
Fair visionary forms, to fill each classic shade.                        30

IV

Is not his mind, to meaner° thoughts unknown,                       *lower*
A sanctuary of beauty and of light?

There he may dwell, in regions all his own,
A world of dreams, where all is pure and bright.
For him the scenes of old renown possess
Romantic[4] charms, all veil'd from other eyes;
There every form of nature's loveliness
Wakes in his breast a thousand sympathies;
As music's voice, in some lone mountain-dell,
From rocks and caves around calls forth each echo's swell.          40

V

For him Italia's brilliant skies illume
The bard's lone haunts, the warrior's combat-plains,
And the wild-rose yet lives to breathe and bloom,
Round Doric Pæstum's solitary fanes.[5]
But most, fair Greece! on thy majestic shore,
He feels the fervors of his spirit rise;
Thou birth-place of the Muse! whose voice, of yore,
Breathed in thy groves immortal harmonies;
And lingers still around the well-known coast,
Murmuring a wild farewell to fame and freedom lost.          50

VI

By seas, that flow in brightness as they lave
Thy rocks, th' enthusiast, rapt in thought, may stray,
While roves his eye o'er that deserted wave,
Once the proud scene of battle's dread array.
—O ye blue waters! ye, of old that bore
The free, the conquering, hymn'd by choral strains,
How sleep ye now around the silent shore,
The lonely realm of ruins and of chains!
How are the mighty vanish'd in their pride!
E'en as their barks have left no traces on your tide.[6]          60

VII

Hush'd are the Pæans whose exulting tone
Swell'd o'er that tide[7]—the sons of battle[8] sleep—
The wind's wild sigh, the halcyon's voice, alone
Blend with the plaintive murmur of the deep.
Yet when those waves have caught the splendid hues
Of morn's rich firmament, serenely bright,[9]
Or setting suns the lovely shore suffuse
With all their purple mellowness of light,
Oh! who could view the scene, so calmly fair,
Nor dream that peace, and joy, and liberty, were there?          70

### VIII

Where soft the sunbeams play, the zephyrs blow,
'Tis hard to deem that misery can be nigh;
Where the clear heavens in blue transparence glow,
Life should be calm and cloudless as the sky;
—Yet o'er the low, dark dwellings of the dead,
Verdure and flowers in summer-bloom may smile,
And ivy-boughs their graceful drapery spread
In green luxuriance o'er the ruined pile;
And mantling woodbine veils the withered tree,—
And thus it is, fair land, forsaken Greece! with thee.          80

### IX

For all the loveliness, and light, and bloom,
That yet are thine, surviving many a storm,
Are but as heaven's warm radiance on the tomb,
The rose's blush that masks the canker-worm:—
And thou art desolate—thy morn hath past
So dazzling in the splendour of its way,
That the dark shades the night hath o'er thee cast
Throw tenfold gloom around thy deep decay.
Once proud in freedom, still in ruin fair,
Thy fate hath been unmatch'd—in glory and despair.          90

### X

For thee, lost land! the hero's blood hath flowed,
The high in soul have brightly lived and died;
For thee the light of soaring genius glowed
O'er the fair arts it form'd and glorified.
Thine were the minds, whose energies sublime
So distanced ages in their lightning-race,
The task they left the sons of later time
Was but to follow their illumined trace.
—Now, bow'd to earth, thy children, to be free,
Must break each link that binds their filial hearts to thee.          100

### XI

Lo! to the scenes of fiction's wildest tales,
Her own bright East, thy son, Morea! flies,[10]
To seek repose midst rich, romantic vales,
Whose incense mounts to Asia's vivid skies.
There shall he rest?—Alas! his hopes in vain
Guide to the sun-clad regions of the palm,

Peace dwells not now on oriental plain,
Though earth is fruitfulness, and air is balm;
And the sad wanderer finds but lawless foes,
Where patriarchs reign'd of old, in pastoral repose.                    110

### XII

Where Syria's mountains rise, or Yemen's groves,
Or Tigris rolls his genii-haunted wave,
Life to his eye, as wearily it roves,
Wears but two forms—the tyrant and the slave!
There the fierce Arab leads his daring horde,
Where sweeps the sand-storm o'er the burning wild,
There stern Oppression waves the wasting sword,
O'er plains that smile, as ancient Eden smiled;
And the vale's bosom, and the desert's gloom,
Yield to the injured there no shelter save the tomb.                    120

### XIII

But thou, fair world! whose fresh unsullied charms
Welcomed Columbus from the western wave,
Wilt thou receive the wanderer to thine arms,[11]
The lost descendant of the immortal brave?
Amidst the wild magnificence of shades
That o'er thy floods their twilight-grandeur cast,
In the green depth of thine untrodden glades,
Shall he not rear his bower of peace at last?
Yes! thou hast many a lone, majestic scene,
Shrined in primæval woods, where despot ne'er hath been.                130

### XIV

There, by some lake, whose blue expansive breast
Bright from afar, an inland-ocean, gleams,
Girt with vast solitudes, profusely drest
In tints like those that float o'er poet's dreams;
Or where some flood from pine-clad mountain pours
Its might of waters, glittering in their foam,
Midst the rich verdure of its wooded shores,
The exiled Greek hath fix'd his sylvan home:
So deeply lone, that round the wild retreat
Scarce have the paths been trod by Indian huntsman's feet.              140

### XV

The forests are around him in their pride,
The green savannas, and the mighty waves;

And isles of flowers, bright-floating o'er the tide,[12]
That images the fairy worlds it laves,
And stillness, and luxuriance—o'er his head
The ancient cedars wave their peopled bowers,
On high the palms their graceful foliage spread,
Cinctured with roses the magnolia towers,
And from those green arcades a thousand tones
Wake with each breeze, whose voice through Nature's temple moans.   150

XVI

And there, no traces left by brighter days,
For glory lost may wake a sigh of grief,
Some grassy mound perchance may meet his gaze,
The lone memorial of an Indian chief.
There man not yet hath marked the boundless plain
With marble records of his fame and power;
The forest is his everlasting fane,
The palm his monument, the rock his tower.
Th' eternal torrent, and the giant tree,
Remind him but that they, like him, are wildly free.                160

XVII

But doth the exile's heart serenely there
In sunshine dwell?—Ah! when was exile blest?
When did bright scenes, clear heavens, or summer-air,
Chase from his soul the fever of unrest?
—There is a heart-sick weariness of mood,
That like slow poison wastes the vital glow,
And shrines itself in mental solitude,
An uncomplaining and a nameless woe,
That coldly smiles midst pleasure's brightest ray,
As the chill glacier's peak reflects the flush of day.              170

XVIII

Such grief is theirs, who, fixed on foreign shore,
Sigh for the spirit of their native gales,°                    *breezes*
As pines the seaman, midst the ocean's roar,
For the green earth, with all its woods and vales.
Thus feels thy child, whose memory dwells with thee,
Loved Greece! all sunk and blighted as thou art:
Though thought and step in western wilds be free,
Yet thine are still the day-dreams of his heart;
The deserts spread between, the billows foam,
Thou, distant and in chains, art yet his spirit's home.             180

### XIX

In vain for him the gay liannes entwine,
Or the green fire-fly sparkles through the brakes,
Or summer-winds waft odours from the pine,
As eve's last blush is dying on the lakes.
Through thy fair vales his fancy roves the while,
Or breathes the freshness of Cithæron's height,
Or dreams how softly Athens' towers would smile,
Or Sunium's ruins, in the fading light;
On Corinth's cliff what sunset hues may sleep,
Or, at that placid hour, how calm th' Egean deep![13]     190

### XX

What scenes, what sunbeams, are to him like thine?
(The all of thine no tyrant could destroy!)
E'en to the stranger's roving eye they shine,
Soft as a vision of remembered joy.
And he who comes, the pilgrim of a day,
A passing wanderer o'er each Attic° hill,     *(of Attica)*
Sighs as his footsteps turn from thy decay,
To laughing climes, where all is splendour still;
And views with fond regret thy lessening shore,
As he would watch a star that sets to rise no more.     200

### XXI

Realm of sad beauty! thou art as a shrine
That Fancy visits with Devotion's zeal,
To catch high thoughts and impulses divine,
And all the glow of soul enthusiasts feel
Amidst the tombs of heroes—for the brave
Whose dust, so many an age, hath been thy soil,
Foremost in honour's phalanx, died to save
The land redeem'd and hallow'd by their toil;
And there is language in thy lightest gale,
That o'er the plains they won seems murmuring yet their tale.     210

### XXII

And he, whose heart is weary of the strife
Of meaner spirits, and whose mental gaze
Would shun the dull cold littleness of life,
Awhile to dwell amidst sublimer days,
Must turn to thee, whose every valley teems
With proud remembrances that cannot die.
Thy glens are peopled with inspiring dreams,

Thy winds, the voice of oracles gone by;
And midst thy laurel shades the wanderer hears
The sound of mighty names, the hymns of vanish'd years.                   220

### XXIII

Through that deep solitude be his to stray,
By Faun and Oread loved in ages past,
Where clear Peneus winds his rapid way
Through the cleft heights, in antique grandeur vast.
Romantic Tempe! thou art yet the same—
Wild, as when sung by bards of elder time:[14]
Years, that have changed thy river's classic name,[15]
Have left thee still in savage pomp sublime;
And from thine Alpine clefts, and marble caves,
In living lustre still break forth the fountain-waves.                    230

### XXIV

Beneath thy mountain battlements and towers,
Where the rich arbute's coral berries glow,[16]
Or midst th' exuberance of thy forest bowers,
Casting deep shadows o'er the current's flow,
Oft shall the pilgrim pause, in lone recess,
As rock and stream some glancing light have caught,
And gaze, till Nature's mighty forms impress
His soul with deep sublimity of thought;
And linger oft, recalling many a tale,
That breeze, and wave, and wood, seem whispering through thy dale.[17]  240

### XXV

He, thought-entranced, may wander where of old
From Delphi's chasm the mystic vapour rose,
And trembling nations heard their doom foretold,
By the dread spirit throned midst rocks and snows.
Though its rich fanes be blended with the dust,
And silence now the hallow'd haunt possess,
Still is the scene of ancient rites august,
Magnificent in mountain loneliness;
Still Inspiration hovers o'er the ground,
Where Greece her councils held,[18] her Pythian victors crown'd.         250

### XXVI

Or let his steps the rude grey cliffs explore
Of that wild pass, once dyed with Spartan blood,
When by the waves that break on Œta's shore,
The few, the fearless, the devoted,° stood!                      *faithful; doomed*

Or rove where, shadowing Mantinea's plain,
Bloom the wild laurels o'er the warlike dead,[19]
Or lone Platæa's ruins yet remain,
To mark the battle-field of ages fled;
Still o'er such scenes presides a sacred power,
Though Fiction's gods have fled from fountain, grot, and bower.          260

### XXVII

Oh! still unblamed may fancy fondly deem
That, lingering yet, benignant genii dwell,
Where mortal worth has hallow'd grove or stream,
To sway the heart with some ennobling spell;
For mightiest minds have felt their blest control,
In the wood's murmur, in the zephyr's sigh,
And these are dreams that lend a voice and soul,
And a high power, to Nature's majesty!
And who can rove o'er Grecian shores, nor feel,
Soft o'er his inmost heart, their secret magic steal?          270

### XXVIII

Yet many a sad reality is there,
That fancy's bright illusions cannot veil.
Pure laughs the light, and balmy breathes the air,
But Slavery's mien will tell its bitter tale;[20]
And there not Peace, but Desolation, throws
Delusive quiet o'er full many a scene,
Deep as the brooding torpor of repose
That follows where the earthquake's track hath been;
Or solemn calm, on Ocean's breast that lies,
When sinks the storm, and death has hush'd the seaman's cries.          280

### XXIX

Hast thou beheld some sovereign spirit, hurl'd
By Fate's rude tempest from its radiant sphere,
Doomed to resign the homage of a world,
For Pity's deepest sigh, and saddest tear?
Oh! hast thou watch'd the awful wreck of mind,
That weareth still a glory in decay?
Seen all that dazzles and delights mankind—
Thought, science, genius, to the storm a prey,
And o'er the blasted tree, the withered ground,
Despair's wild nightshade spread, and darkly flourish round?          290

### XXX

So may'st thou gaze, in sad and awe-struck thought,
On the deep fall of that yet lovely clime:
Such there the ruin Time and Fate have wrought,
So changed the bright, the splendid, the sublime!
There the proud monuments of Valour's name,
The mighty works Ambition piled on high,
The rich remains by Art bequeath'd to Fame—
Grace, beauty, grandeur, strength, and symmetry,
Blend in decay; while all that yet is fair
Seems only spared to tell how much hath perish'd there!          300

### XXXI

There, while around lie mingling in the dust,
The column's graceful shaft, with weeds o'ergrown,
The mouldering torso, the forgotten bust,
The warrior's urn,° the altar's mossy stone;          *(for funeral ashes)*
Amidst the loneliness of shattered fanes,
Still matchless monuments of other years,
O'er cypress groves, or solitary plains,
Its eastern form the minaret proudly rears;
As on some captive city's ruin'd wall
The victor's banner waves, exulting o'er its fall.          310

### XXXII

Still, where that column of the mosque aspires,
Landmark of slavery, towering o'er the waste,
There Science droops, the Muses hush their lyres,
And o'er the blooms of fancy and of taste
Spreads the chill blight—as in that orient isle,
Where the dark upas taints the gale around,[21]
Within its precincts not a flower may smile,
Nor dew nor sunshine fertilize the ground;
Nor wild birds' music float on zephyr's breath,
But all is silence round, and solitude, and death.          320

### XXXIII

Far other influence pour'd the Crescent's light,
O'er conquer'd realms, in ages past away;
Full and alone it beam'd, intensely bright,
While distant climes in midnight darkness lay.
Then rose th' Alhambra, with its founts and shades,
Fair marble halls, alcoves, and orange bowers:
Its sculptured lions,[22] richly wrought arcades,

Aërial pillars, and enchanted towers;
Light, splendid, wild, as some Arabian tale
Would picture fairy domes, that fleet before the gale.          330

### XXXIV

Then foster'd genius lent each Caliph's throne
Lustre barbaric pomp could ne'er attain;
And stars unnumber'd o'er the orient shone,
Bright as that Pleïad, sphered in Mecca's fane.[23]
From Bagdat's palaces the choral strains
Rose and re-echoed to the desert's bound,
And Science, wooed on Egypt's burning plains,
Rear'd her majestic head with glory crown'd;
And the wild Muses breathed romantic lore,
From Syria's palmy groves to Andalusia's shore.          340

### XXXV

Those years have past in radiance—they have past,
As sinks the day-star in the tropic main;
His parting beams no soft reflection cast,
They burn—are quench'd—and deepest shadows reign.
And Fame and Science have not left a trace,
In the vast regions of the Moslem's power,—
Regions, to intellect a desert space,
A wild without a fountain or a flower,
Where towers oppression midst the deepening glooms,
As dark and lone ascends the cypress midst the tombs.          350

### XXXVI

Alas for thee, fair Greece! when Asia pour'd
Her fierce fanatics to Byzantium's wall,[24]
When Europe sheathed, in apathy, her sword,
And heard unmoved the fated city's call,
No bold crusaders ranged their serried line
Of spears and banners round a falling throne;
And thou, O last and noblest Constantine![25]
Didst meet the storm unshrinking and alone.
Oh! blest to die in freedom, though in vain,
Thine empire's proud exchange the grave, and not the chain.          360

### XXXVII

Hush'd is Byzantium—'tis the dead of night—
The closing night of that imperial race![26]
And all is vigil—but the eye of light
Shall soon unfold, a wilder scene to trace:

There is a murmuring stillness on the train,
Thronging the midnight streets, at morn to die;
And to the cross, in fair Sophia's fane,
For the last time is raised Devotion's eye;
And, in his heart while faith's bright visions rise,
There kneels the high-soul'd prince, the summon'd of the skies.　　　370

### XXXVIII

Day breaks in light and glory—'tis the hour
Of conflict and of fate—the war-note calls—
Despair hath lent a stern, delirious power
To the brave few that guard the rampart walls.
Far over Marmora's waves th' artillery's peal
Proclaims an empire's doom in every note;
Tambour and trumpet swell the clash of steel,
Round spire and dome the clouds of battle float;
From camp and wave rush on the crescent's host,
And the Seven Towers[27] are scaled, and all is won and lost.　　　380

### XXXIX

Then, Greece! the tempest rose, that burst on thee,
Land of the bard, the warrior, and the sage!
Oh! where were then thy sons, the great, the free,
Whose deeds are guiding-stars from age to age?
Though firm thy battlements of crags and snows,
And bright the memory of thy days of pride,
In mountain might though Corinth's fortress rose,
On, unresisted, roll'd th' invading tide!
Oh! vain the rock, the rampart, and the tower,
If Freedom guard them not with Mind's unconquer'd power.　　　390

### XL

Where were th' avengers then, whose viewless might
Preserved inviolate their awful fane,[28]
When through the steep defiles, to Delphi's height,
In martial splendour pour'd the Persian's train?
Then did those mighty and mysterious Powers,
Arm'd with the elements, to vengeance wake,
Call the dread storms to darken round their towers,
Hurl down the rocks, and bid the thunders break;
Till far around, with deep and fearful clang,
Sounds of unearthly war through wild Parnassus rang.　　　400

### XLI

Where was the spirit of the victor-throng,
Whose tombs are glorious by Scamander's tide,
Whose names are bright in everlasting song,
The lords of war, the praised, the deified?[29]
Where he, the hero of a thousand lays,
Who from the dead at Marathon arose[30]
All-arm'd; and beaming on th' Athenians' gaze,
A battle-meteor, guided to their foes?
Or they whose forms, to Alaric's awe-struck eye,[31]
Hovering o'er Athens, blazed, in airy panoply?                          410

### XLII

Ye slept, oh heroes! chief ones of the earth![32]
High demi-gods of ancient days! ye slept.
There lived no spark of your ascendant worth,
When o'er your land the victor Moslem swept;
No patriot then the sons of freedom led,
In mountain-pass devotedly to die;
The martyr-spirit of resolve was fled,
And the high soul's unconquer'd buoyancy;
And by your graves, and on your battle-plains,
Warriors! your children knelt, to wear the stranger's chains.           420

### XLIII

Now have your trophies vanish'd, and your homes
Are moulder'd from the earth, while scarce remain
E'en the faint traces of the ancient tombs
That mark where sleep the slayers or the slain.
Your deeds are with the days of glory flown,
The lyres are hush'd that swell'd your fame afar,
The halls that echoed to their sounds are gone,
Perish'd the conquering weapons of your war;[33]
And if a mossy stone your names retain,
'Tis but to tell your sons, for them ye died in vain.                   430

### XLIV

Yet, where some lone sepulchral relic stands,
That with those names tradition hallows yet,
Oft shall the wandering son of other lands
Linger in solemn thought and hush'd regret.
And still have legends mark'd the lonely spot
Where low the dust of Agamemnon lies;
And shades of kings and leaders unforgot,

Hovering around, to fancy's vision rise.
Souls of the heroes! seek your rest again,
Nor mark how changed the realms that saw your glory's reign.     440

### XLV

Lo, where th' Albanian spreads his despot sway
O'er Thessaly's rich vales and glowing plains,[34]
Whose sons in sullen abjectness obey,
Nor lift the hand indignant at its chains:
Oh! doth the land that gave Achilles birth,
And many a chief of old illustrious line,
Yield not one spirit of unconquer'd worth,
To kindle those that now in bondage pine?
No! on its mountain-air is slavery's breath,
And terror chills the hearts whose utter'd plaints were death     450

### XLVI

Yet if thy light, fair Freedom, rested there,
How rich in charms were that romantic clime,
With streams, and woods, and pastoral valleys fair,
And walled with mountains, haughtily sublime.
Heights, that might well be deem'd the Muses' reign,
Since, claiming proud alliance with the skies,
They lose in loftier spheres their wild domain.
Meet home for those retired divinities
That love, where nought of earth may e'er intrude,
Brightly to dwell on high, in lonely sanctitude.     460

### XLVII

There, in rude grandeur, daringly ascends
Stern Pindus,[35] rearing many a pine-clad height;
He with the clouds his bleak dominion blends,
Frowning o'er vales, in woodland verdure bright.
Wild and august in consecrated pride,
There through the deep-blue heaven Olympus towers,
Girdled with mists, light-floating as to hide
The rock-built palace of immortal powers;
Where far on high the sunbeam finds repose,
Amidst th' eternal pomp of forests and of snows.[36]     470

### XLVIII

Those savage cliffs and solitudes might seem
The chosen haunts where Freedom's foot would roam;
She loves to dwell by glen and torrent-stream,
And make the rocky fastnesses her home.

And in the rushing of the mountain-flood,
In the wild eagle's solitary cry,
In sweeping winds that peal through cave and wood,
There is a voice of stern sublimity,
That swells her spirit to a loftier mood
Of solemn joy severe, of power, of fortitude.                    480

### XLIX

But from those hills the radiance of her smile
Hath vanish'd long, her step hath fled afar;
O'er Suli's frowning rocks she paused awhile,[37]
Kindling the watch-fires of the mountain-war;
And brightly glow'd her ardent spirit there,
Still brightest midst privation: o'er distress
It cast romantic splendour, and despair
But fann'd that beacon of the wilderness;[38]
And rude ravine, and precipice, and dell,
Sent their deep echoes forth, her rallying voice to swell.        490

### L

Dark children of the hills! 'twas then ye wrought
Deeds of fierce daring, rudely, sternly grand;
As midst your craggy citadels ye fought,
And woman mingled with your warrior-band.
Then on the cliff the frantic mother stood[39]
High o'er the river's darkly-rolling wave,
And hurl'd, in dread delirium, to the flood,
Her free-born infant, ne'er to be a slave.
For all was lost—all, save the power to die
The wild indignant death of savage liberty.                       500

### LI

Now is that strife a tale of vanish'd days,
With mightier things forgotten soon to lie;
Yet oft hath minstrel sung, in lofty lays,
Deeds less adventurous, energies less high.
And the dread struggle's fearful memory still
O'er each wild rock a wilder aspect throws;
Sheds darker shadows o'er the frowning hill,
More solemn quiet o'er the glen's repose;
Lends to the rustling pines a deeper moan,
And the hoarse river's voice a murmur not its own.                510

## LII

For stillness now—the stillness of the dead,
Hath wrapt that conflict's lone and awful scene,
And man's forsaken homes, in ruin spread,
Tell where the storming of the cliffs hath been.
And there, o'er wastes magnificently rude,
What race may rove, unconscious of the chain?
Those realms have now no desert unsubdued,
Where Freedom's banner may be rear'd again:
Sunk are the ancient dwellings of her fame,
The children of her sons inherit but their name.                    520

## LIII

Go, seek proud Sparta's monuments and fanes!
In scatter'd fragments o'er the vale they lie;
Of all they were not e'en enough remains
To lend their fall a mournful majesty.[40]
Birth-place of those whose names we first revered
In song and story—temple of the free!
Oh thou, the stern, the haughty, and the fear'd,
Are such thy relics, and can this be thee?
Thou shouldst have left a giant-wreck behind,
And e'en in ruin claim'd the wonder of mankind.                    530

## LIV

For thine were spirits cast in other mould
Than all beside—and proved by ruder test;
They stood alone—the proud, the firm, the bold,
With the same seal indelibly imprest.
Theirs were no bright varieties of mind,
One image stamp'd the rough, colossal race,
In rugged grandeur frowning o'er mankind,
Stern, and disdainful of each milder grace.
As to the sky some mighty rock may tower,
Whose front can brave the storm, but will not rear the flower.       540

## LV

Such were thy sons—their life a battle day!
Their youth one lesson how for thee to die!
Closed is that task, and they have past away
Like softer beings train'd to aims less high.
Yet bright on earth *their* fame who proudly fell,
True to their shields, the champions of thy cause,

Whose funeral column bade the stranger tell
How died the brave, obedient to thy laws![41]
O lofty mother of heroic worth,
How couldst thou live to bring a meaner offspring forth?          550

### LVI

Hadst thou but perish'd with the free, nor known
A second race, when Glory's noon went by,
Then had thy name in single brightness shone
A watch-word on the helm of liberty!
Thou shouldst have past with all thy light of fame,
And proudly sunk in ruins, not in chains.
But slowly set thy star midst clouds of shame,
And tyrants rose amidst thy falling fanes;
And thou, surrounded by thy warriors' graves,
Hast drain'd the bitter cup once mingled for thy slaves.          560

### LVII

Now all is o'er—for thee alike are flown
Freedom's bright noon, and Slavery's twilight cloud;
And in thy fall, as in thy pride, alone,
Deep solitude is round thee, as a shroud.
Home of Leonidas! thy halls are low,
From their cold altars have thy Lares fled,[42]
O'er thee unmark'd the sun-beams fade or glow,
And wild flowers wave, unbent by human tread;
And midst thy silence, as the grave's profound,
A voice, a step would seem as some unearthly sound.              570

### LVIII

Taygetus still lifts his awful brow,
High o'er the mouldering city of the dead,
Sternly sublime; while o'er his robe of snow
Heaven's floating tints their warm suffusions spread.
And yet his rippling wave Eurotas leads
By tombs and ruins o'er the silent plain,
While whispering there, his own wild graceful reeds
Rise as of old, when hail'd by classic strain;
There the rose laurels still in beauty wave,[43]
And a frail shrub survives to bloom o'er Sparta's grave.          580

### LIX

Oh! thus it is with man—a tree, a flower,
While nations perish, still renews its race,
And o'er the fallen records of his power

Spreads in wild pomp, or smiles in fairy grace.
The laurel shoots when those have past away
Once rivals for its crown, the brave, the free;
The rose is flourishing o'er beauty's clay,°          *mortal flesh*
The myrtle° blows when love hath ceased to be;     *(emblem of love)*
Green waves the bay° when song and bard are fled,          *laurel*
And all that round us blooms, is blooming o'er the dead.          590

### LX

And still the olive spreads its foliage round
Morea's fallen sanctuaries and towers,
Once its green boughs Minerva's votaries crown'd,
Deem'd a meet offering for celestial powers.
The suppliant's hand its holy branches bore;[44]
They waved around th' Olympic victor's head;
And, sanctified by many a rite of yore,
Its leaves the Spartan's honour'd bier o'erspread:
Those rites have vanish'd—but o'er vale and hill
Its fruitful groves arise, revered and hallow'd still.[45]          600

### LXI

Where now thy shrines, Eleusis! where thy fane
Of fearful visions, mysteries wild and high?
The pomp of rites, the sacrificial train,
The long procession's awful pageantry?
Quench'd is the torch of Ceres[46]—all around
Decay hath spread the stillness of her reign,
There never more shall choral hymns resound,
O'er the hush'd earth and solitary main;
Whose wave from Salamis deserted flows,
To bathe a silent shore of desolate repose.          610

### LXII

And oh! ye secret and terrific powers,
Dark oracles![47] in depth of groves that dwelt,
How are they sunk, the altars of your bowers,
Where superstition trembled as she knelt!
Ye, the unknown, the viewless ones! that made
The elements your voice, the wind and wave;
Spirits! whose influence darken'd many a shade,
Mysterious visitants of fount and cave!
How long your power the awe-struck nations sway'd,
How long earth dreamt of you, and shudderingly obey'd!          620

### LXIII

And say, what marvel, in those early days,
While yet the light of heaven-born truth° was not;        *Christianity*
If man around him cast a fearful gaze,
Peopling with shadowy powers each dell and grot?
Awful is nature in her savage forms,
Her solemn voice commanding in its might,
And mystery then was in the rush of storms,
The gloom of woods, the majesty of night;
And mortals heard fate's language in the blast,
And rear'd your forest-shrines, ye phantoms of the past!     630

### LXIV

Then through the foliage not a breeze might sigh
But with prophetic sound—a waving tree,
A meteor flashing o'er the summer sky,
A bird's wild flight, reveal'd the things to be.
All spoke of unseen natures, and convey'd
Their inspiration; still they hovered round,
Hallow'd the temple, whisper'd through the shade,
Pervaded loneliness, gave soul to sound;
Of them the fount, the forest, murmur'd still,
Their voice was in the stream, their footstep on the hill.     640

### LXV

Now is the train of Superstition flown,[48]
Unearthly Beings walk on earth no more;
The deep wind swells with no portentous tone,
The rustling wood breathes no fatidic° lore.        *prophetic*
Fled are the phantoms of Livadia's cave,
There dwell no shadows, but of crag and steep;
Fount of Oblivion! in thy gushing wave,[49]
That murmurs nigh, those powers of terror sleep.
Oh! that such dreams alone had fled that clime,
But Greece is changed in all that could be changed by time!     650

### LXVI

Her skies are those whence many a mighty bard
Caught inspiration, glorious as their beams;
Her hills the same that heroes died to guard,
Her vales, that foster'd art's divinest dreams!
But that bright spirit o'er the land that shone,
And all around pervading influence pour'd,
That lent the harp of Eschylus its tone,

And proudly hallow'd Lacedæmon's sword,[50]
And guided Phidias o'er the yielding stone,
With them its ardours lived—with them its light is flown.     660

### LXVII

Thebes, Corinth, Argos!—ye, renown'd of old,
Where are your chiefs of high romantic name?
How soon the tale of ages may be told!
A page, a verse, records the fall of fame,
The work of centuries—we gaze on you,
Oh cities! once the glorious and the free,
The lofty tales that charm'd our youth renew,
And wondering ask, if these their scenes could be?
Search for the classic fane, the regal tomb,
And find the mosque alone—a record of their doom!     670

### LXVIII

How oft hath war his host of spoilers pour'd,
Fair Elis! o'er thy consecrated vales?[51]
There have the sunbeams glanced on spear and sword,
And banners floated on the balmy gales.
Once didst thou smile, secure in sanctitude,
As some enchanted isle 'mid stormy seas;
On thee no hostile footstep might intrude,
And pastoral sounds alone were on thy breeze.
Forsaken home of peace! that spell is broke,
Thou too hast heard the storm, and bow'd beneath the yoke.     680

### LXIX

And through Arcadia's wild and lone retreat
Far other sounds have echoed than the strain
Of faun and dryad, from their woodland seats,
Or ancient reed of peaceful mountain-swain!
There, tho' at times Alpheus yet surveys,
On his green banks renew'd, the classic dance,
And nymph-like forms, and wild melodious lays,
Revive the sylvan scenes of old romance;
Yet brooding fear and dark suspicion dwell,
'Midst Pan's deserted haunts, by fountain, cave, and dell.     690

### LXX

But thou, fair Attica! whose rocky bound
All art and nature's richest gifts enshrined,
Thou little sphere, whose soul-illumined round
Concentrated each sunbeam of the mind;

Who, as the summit of some Alpine height
Glows earliest, latest, with the blush of day,
Didst first imbibe the splendours of the light,
And smile the longest in its lingering ray;[52]
Oh! let us gaze on thee, and fondly deem
The past awhile restored, the present but a dream.                    700

### LXXI

Let Fancy's vivid hues awhile prevail—
Wake at her call—be all thou wert once more!
Hark, hymns of triumph swell on every gale!
Lo, bright processions move along thy shore!
Again thy temples, 'midst the olive-shade,
Lovely in chaste simplicity arise;
And graceful monuments, in grove and glade,
Catch the warm tints of thy resplendent skies;
And sculptured forms, of high and heavenly mien,
In their calm beauty smile, around the sun-bright scene.              710

### LXXII

Again renew'd by thought's creative spells,
In all her pomp thy city, Theseus! towers:
Within, around, the light of glory dwells
On art's fair fabrics,° wisdom's holy bowers.                         *buildings*
There marble fanes in finish'd grace ascend,
The pencil's world° of life and beauty glows;        *(painting and drawing)*
Shrines, pillars, porticoes, in grandeur blend,
Rich with the trophies of barbaric foes;
And groves of platane wave, in verdant pride,
The sage's blest retreats, by calm Ilissus' tide.[53]                 720

### LXXIII

Bright as that fairy vision of the wave,
Raised by the magic of Morgana's wand,[54]
On summer seas, that undulating lave
Romantic Sicily's Arcadian strand;
That pictured scene of airy colonnades,
Light palaces, in shadowy glory drest,
Enchanted groves, and temples, and arcades,
Gleaming and floating on the ocean's breast;
Athens! thus fair the dream of thee appears,
As Fancy's eye pervades the veiling cloud of years.                   730

### LXXIV

Still be that cloud withdrawn—oh! mark on high,
Crowning yon hill, with temples richly graced,
That fane, august in perfect symmetry,
The purest model of Athenian taste.
Fair Parthenon! thy Doric pillars rise
In simple dignity, thy marble's hue
Unsullied shines, relieved by brilliant skies,
That round thee spread their deep ethereal blue;
And art o'er all thy light proportions throws
The harmony of grace, the beauty of repose.                740

### LXXV

And lovely o'er thee sleeps the sunny glow,
When morn and eve in tranquil splendour reign,
And on thy sculptures, as they smile, bestow
Hues that the pencil emulates in vain.
Then the fair forms by Phidias wrought, unfold
Each latent grace, developing in light,
Catch from soft clouds of purple and of gold,
Each tint that passes, tremulously bright;
And seem indeed whate'er devotion deems,
While so suffused with heaven, so mingling with its beams.        750

### LXXVI

But oh! what words the vision may pourtray
The form of sanctitude that guards thy shrine?
There stands thy goddess, robed in war's array,
Supremely glorious, awfully divine!
With spear and helm she stands, and flowing vest,
And sculptured ægis, to perfection wrought,
And on each heavenly lineament imprest,
Calmly sublime, the majesty of thought;
The pure intelligence, the chaste repose,—
All that a poet's dream around Minerva throws.              760

### LXXVII

Bright age of Pericles![55] let fancy still
Through time's deep shadows all thy splendor trace,
And in each work of art's consummate skill
Hail the free spirit of thy lofty race.
That spirit, roused by every proud reward
That hope could picture, glory could bestow,
Foster'd by all the sculptor and the bard

Could give of immortality below.
Thus were thy heroes form'd, and o'er their name
Thus did thy genius shed imperishable fame.                    770

### LXXVIII

Mark in the thronged Ceramicus, the train
Of mourners weeping o'er the martyred brave:
Proud be the tears devoted to the slain,
Holy the amaranth strew'd upon their grave![56]
And hark—unrivall'd eloquence proclaims
Their deeds, their trophies, with triumphant voice!
Hark—Pericles records their honour'd names![57]
Sons of the fallen, in their lot rejoice:
What hath life brighter than so bright a doom?
What power hath fate to soil the garlands of the tomb?         780

### LXXIX

Praise to the valiant dead! for them doth art
Exhaust her skill, their triumphs bodying forth;
Theirs are enshrined names, and every heart
Shall bear the blazon'd impress of their worth.
Bright on the dreams of youth their fame shall rise,
Their fields of fight shall epic song record,
And when the voice of battle rends the skies,
Their name shall be their country's rallying word!
While fane and column rise august to tell
How Athens honours those for her who proudly fell.             790

### LXXX

City of Theseus! bursting on the mind,
Thus dost thou rise, in all thy glory fled!
Thus guarded by the mighty of mankind,
Thus hallow'd by the memory of the dead:
Alone in beauty and renown—a scene
Whose tints are drawn from freedom's loveliest ray.
'Tis but a vision now—yet thou hast been
More than the brightest vision might pourtray;
And every stone, with but a vestige fraught
Of thee, hath latent power to wake some lofty thought.         800

### LXXXI

Fall'n are thy fabrics, that so oft have rung
To choral melodies, and tragic lore;
Now is the lyre of Sophocles unstrung,
The song that hail'd Harmodius peals no more.

Thy proud Piræus is a desart strand,
Thy stately shrines are mouldering on their hill,
Closed are the triumphs of the sculptor's hand,
The magic voice of eloquence is still;
Minerva's veil is rent[58]—her image gone,
Silent the sage's bower—the warrior's tomb o'erthrown.　　　810

### LXXXII

Yet in decay thine exquisite remains
Wondering we view, and silently revere,
As traces left on earth's forsaken plains
By vanish'd beings of a nobler sphere!
Not all the old magnificence of Rome,
All that dominion there hath left to time,
Proud Coliseum, or commanding dome,
Triumphal arch, or obelisk sublime,
Can bid such reverence o'er the spirit steal,
As aught by thee imprest with beauty's plastic° seal.　　　*pliant*　820

### LXXXIII

Though still the empress of the sun-burnt waste,
Palmyra rises, desolately grand—
Though with rich gold[59] and massy sculpture graced,
Commanding still, Persepolis may stand
In haughty solitude—though sacred Nile
The first-born temples of the world surveys,
And many an awful and stupendous pile°　　　*building*
Thebes of the hundred gates e'en yet displays;
City of Pericles! oh, who like thee
Can teach how fair the works of mortal hand may be?　　　830

### LXXXIV

Thou led'st the way to that illumined sphere
Where sovereign beauty dwells; and thence didst bear,
Oh, still triumphant in that high career!
Bright archetypes of all the grand and fair.
And still to thee th' enlightened mind hath flown,
As to her country;—thou hast been to earth
A cynosure°;—and, e'en from victory's throne,　　　*pole-star, guide*
Imperial Rome gave homage to thy worth;
And nations rising to their fame afar,
Still to thy model turn, as seamen to their star.　　　840

### LXXXV

Glory to those whose relics thus arrest
The gaze of ages! Glory to the free!
For they, they only, could have thus imprest
Their mighty image on the years to be!
Empires and cities in oblivion lie,
Grandeur may vanish, conquest be forgot:—
To leave on earth renown that cannot die,
Of high-soul'd genius is th' unrivall'd lot.
Honour to thee, O Athens! thou hast shewn
What mortals may attain, and seized the palm alone.                850

### LXXXVI

Oh! live there those who view with scornful eyes
All that attests the brightness of thy prime?
Yes; they who dwell beneath thy lovely skies,
And breathe th' inspiring ether of thy clime!
Their path is o'er the mightiest of the dead,
Their homes are midst the works of noblest arts;
Yet all around their gaze, beneath their tread,
Not one proud thrill of loftier thought imparts.
Such are the conquerors of Minerva's land,
Where Genius first reveal'd the triumphs of his hand!                860

### LXXXVII

For them in vain the glowing light may smile
O'er the pale marble, colouring's warmth to shed,
And in chaste beauty many a sculptured pile
Still o'er the dust of heroes lift its head.
No patriot feeling binds them to the soil,
Whose tombs and shrines their fathers have not rear'd,
Their glance is cold indifference, and their toil
But to destroy what ages have revered,
As if exulting sternly to erase
Whate'er might prove *that* land had nurs'd a nobler race.[60]                870

### LXXXVIII

And who may grieve that, rescued from their hands,
Spoilers of excellence and foes to art,
Thy relics, Athens! borne to other lands,
Claim homage still to thee from every heart?
Though now no more th' exploring stranger's sight,
Fix'd in deep reverence on Minerva's fane,
Shall hail, beneath their native heaven of light,

All that remain'd of forms adored in vain;
A few short years—and, vanish'd from the scene,
To blend with classic dust their proudest lot had been.          880

### LXXXIX

Fair Parthenon! yet still must fancy weep
For thee, thou work of nobler spirits flown.
Bright, as of old, the sunbeams o'er thee sleep
In all their beauty still—and thine is gone!
Empires have sunk since thou wert first revered,
And varying rites have sanctified thy shrine.[61]
The dust is round thee of the race that rear'd
Thy walls; and thou—their fate must soon be thine!
But when shall earth again exult to see
Visions divine like theirs renew'd in aught like thee?          890

### XC

Lone are thy pillars now—each passing gale
Sighs o'er them as a spirit's voice, which moan'd
That loneliness, and told the plaintive tale
Of the bright synod once above them throned.
Mourn, graceful ruin! on thy sacred hill,
Thy gods, thy rites, a kindred fate have shared:
Yet art thou honour'd in each fragment still,[62]
That wasting years and barbarous hands had spared;
Each hallow'd stone, from rapine's fury borne,
Shall wake bright dreams of thee in ages yet unborn.          900

### XCI

Yes; in those fragments, though by time defaced,
And rude insensate conquerors, yet remains
All that may charm th' enlighten'd eye of taste,
On shores where still inspiring freedom reigns.
As vital fragrance breathes from every part
Of the crush'd myrtle, or the bruised rose,
E'en thus th' essential energy of art,
There in each wreck imperishably glows![63]
The soul of Athens lives in every line,
Pervading brightly still the ruins of her shrine.          910

### XCII

Mark—on the storied frieze the graceful train,
The holy festival's triumphal throng,
In fair procession, to Minerva's fane,
With many a sacred symbol move along.

There every shade of bright existence trace,
The fire of youth, the dignity of age;
The matron's calm austerity of grace,
The ardent warrior, the benignant sage;
The nymph's light symmetry, the chief's proud mien,
Each ray of beauty caught and mingled in the scene.                    920

### XCIII

Art unobtrusive there ennobles form,[64]
Each pure chaste outline exquisitely flows;
There e'en the steed, with bold expression warm,[65]
Is clothed with majesty, with being glows.
One mighty mind hath harmonized the whole;
Those varied groups the same bright impress bear;
One beam and essence of exalting soul
Lives in the grand, the delicate, the fair;
And well that pageant of the glorious dead
Blends us with nobler days, and loftier spirits fled.                  930

### XCIV

O conquering Genius! that couldst thus detain
The subtle graces, fading as they rise,
Eternalize expression's fleeting reign,
Arrest warm life in all its energies,
And fix them on the stone—thy glorious lot
Might wake ambition's envy, and create
Powers half divine: while nations are forgot,
A thought, a dream of thine hath vanquish'd fate!
And when thy hand first gave its wonders birth,
The realms that hail them now scarce claim'd a name on earth.          940

### XCV

Wert thou some spirit of a purer sphere
But once beheld, and never to return?
No—we may hail again thy bright career,
Again on earth a kindred fire shall burn!
Though thy least relics, e'en in ruin, bear
A stamp of Heaven, that ne'er hath been renew'd—
A light inherent—let not man despair:
Still be hope ardent, patience unsubdued;
For still is nature fair, and thought divine,
And art hath won a world in models pure as thine.[66]                  950

### XCVI

Gaze on yon forms, corroded and defaced—
Yet there the germ of future glory lies!
Their virtual grandeur could not be erased,
It clothes them still, though veil'd from common eyes.
They once were gods and heroes[67]—and beheld
As the blest guardians of their native scene;
And hearts of warriors, sages, bards, have swell'd
With awe that own'd their sovereignty of mien.
—Ages have vanish'd since those hearts were cold,
And still those shattered forms retain their godlike mould.          960

### XCVII

Midst their bright kindred, from their marble throne,
They have look'd down on thousand storms of time;
Surviving power, and fame, and freedom flown,
They still remain'd, still tranquilly sublime!
Till mortal hands the heavenly conclave marr'd.
Th' Olympian groups have sunk, and are forgot;
Not e'en their dust could weeping Athens guard—
—But these were destined to a nobler lot!
And they have borne, to light another land,
The quenchless ray that soon shall gloriously expand.          970

### XCVIII

Phidias! supreme in thought! what hand but thine,
In human works thus blending earth and heaven,
O'er nature's truth hath shed that grace divine,
To mortal form immortal grandeur given?
What soul but thine, infusing all its power,
In these last monuments of matchless days,
Could, from their ruins, bid young Genius tower,
And Hope aspire to more exalted praise?
And guide deep Thought to that secluded height,
Where Excellence is throned, in purity of light.          980

### XCIX

And who can tell how pure, how bright a flame,
Caught from these models, may illume the west?
What British Angelo may rise to fame,[68]
On the free isle what beams of art may rest?
Deem not, O England! that by climes confined,
Genius and taste diffuse a partial ray;[69]

Deem not th' eternal energies of mind
Sway'd by that sun whose doom is but decay!
Shall thought be foster'd but by skies serene?
No! thou hast power to be what Athens e'er[70] hath been.        990

C

But thine are treasures oft unprized, unknown,
And cold neglect hath blighted many a mind,
O'er whose young ardors, had thy smile but shone,
Their soaring flight had left a world behind!
And many a gifted hand, that might have wrought
To Grecian excellence the breathing stone,
Or each pure grace of Raphael's pencil caught,
Leaving no record of its power, is gone!
While thou hast fondly sought, on distant coast,
Gems far less rich than those, thus precious, and thus lost.        1000

CI

Yet rise, O Land in all but Art alone,
Bid the sole wreath that is not thine be won!
Fame dwells around thee—Genius is thine own;
Call his rich blooms to life—be Thou their Sun!
So, should dark ages o'er thy glory sweep,
Should *thine* e'er be as now are Grecian plains,
Nations unborn shall track thine own blue deep,
To hail thy shore, to worship thy remains;
Thy mighty monuments with reverence trace,
And cry, "This ancient soil hath nurs'd a glorious race!"        1010

[1] James Thomson, *Liberty: A Poem* (1735–36), part 2, *Greece* 252–56, spoken in the voice of "Liberty." Across this five-part poem, Liberty narrates her history from ancient Greece, to republican Rome (compared to modern Italy), to Britain; the final part offers a "prospect," with praise for "Science, Fine Arts, and Public Works."

[2] The sculptor (5th c. B.C.) who supervised the decoration of the Acropolis.

[3] Cf. Byron's description of ruins "Swept into wrecks anon by Time's ungentle tide!" (*Childe Harold* [1812] I.xxiii).

[4] Referring to the literary genre of "romance": extravagant, imaginary, idealized.

[5] "The Pæstan rose, from its peculiar fragrancy and the singularity of blowing twice a year, is often mentioned [. . .] by the classic poets; the wild rose, which now shoots up among the ruins, is of the small single damask kind with a very high perfume; as a farmer assured me on the spot, it flowers both in spring and autumn."—Swinburne's Travels in the Two Sicilies. [FH]
Henry Swinburne (1743–1803), "Pæstum," sec. 18, *Travels in the Two Sicilies, In the Years 1777, 1778, 1779, and 1780*, 2 vols. (London: P. Elmsly, 1783), 1.131–32. Pæstum, an ancient Greek coastal colony south of Naples, is noted for its Doric architecture.

[6] Echoing "How are the mighty fallen!" (2 Samuel 1.19), which concerned the fall of Israel; cf. note to 428. At Salamis (480 B.C.), an Athenian-led Greek fleet defeated a much larger Persian one.

[7] In the naval engagements of the Greeks, "it was usual for the soldiers before the fight to sing

a *pæan*, or hymn, to Mars, and after the fight another to Apollo."—See Potter's Antiquities of Greece, vol. ii. p. 155. [FH]

John Potter (?1674–1747), Archbishop of Canterbury, *Archæologia Græca, or The Antiquities of Greece* (1697); new ed., 2 vols. (Edinburgh and London, 1813), 2.158.

[8] A frequent phrase; see *Abencerrage* 336, *Widow of Crescentius* 4, *The Last Constantine* 97, *The Voice of Scio* 16.

[9] "Serenely bright" is another habitual phrase; cf. *Dartmoor* 244, *Ivy Song* 35, *On the Death of Her Mother* 51. Pope uses it in *Autumn*, and Wordsworth in *The White Doe of Rylstone* 136.

[10] The emigration of the natives of the Morea [Peloponnesus] to different parts of Asia is thus mentioned by Chateaubriand in his "Itinéraire de Paris à Jerusalem"—"Parvenu au dernier degré du malheur, le Moraïte s'arrache de son pays, et va chercher en Asie un sort moins rigoureux. Vain espoir! [Il ne peut finir sa destinée:] il retrouve des cadis et des pachas jusques dans les sables du Jourdain et dans les déserts de Palmyre." [FH]

[At the lowest degree of misery, the Morean abandons his country, and goes to seek in Asia a lot less severe. Vain hope! [He is not able to terminate his quest:] he there finds other cadis and pachas, even in the sands of Jordan and in the deserts of Palmyra.]

From François René, Vicomte de Chateaubriand (1768–1848), *Itinéraire de Paris à Jérusalem, et de Jérusalem à Paris, en allant par la Grèce, et revenant par l'Égypte, la Barbarie et l'Espagne,* 3 vols. (Paris, 1811), 1.262. The vogue for wild Eastern tales (101–2) is marked by Byron's sensational successes in the genre (1813–16), inspiring a host of followers, including FH.

[11] In the same work, Chateaubriand also relates his having met with several Greek emigrants who had established themselves in the woods of Florida. [FH. *Itinéraire* 1.154–55]

[12] "La grace est toujours unie à la magnificence dans les scènes de la nature: et tandis que le courant du milieu entraîne vers la mer les cadavres des pins et des chênes, on voit sur les deux courant latéraux, remonter, le long des rivages des îles flottantes de Pistia & de Nénuphar, dont les roses jaunes s'élèvent comme de petits pavillons."—Description of the banks of the Mississippi, Chateaubriand's "Atala." [FH]

[Beauty is always joined to grandeur in the scenery of nature: and while the middle current hurls the cadavers of pines and oaks toward the sea, one sees on the two lateral currents, reascending, the whole length of the banks, floating isles of Duckweed & Waterlily, out of which yellow roses float like little pavillion tents / tent-flags.]

*Atala, ou les amours de deux sauvages dans le désert*, 3d ed., rev. and corrected (Paris, 1801), 7.

[13] *Cithæron*: mountain north of the city-state of Corinth. *Sunium*: a cape at the southern tip of Attica, the district containing Athens.

[14] "Looking generally at the narrowness and abruptness of this mountain-channel (Tempe), and contrasting it with the course of the Peneus through the plains of Thessaly, the imagination instantly recurs to the tradition, that these plains were once covered with water, for which some convulsion of nature had subsequently opened this narrow passage. The term *vale*, in our language, is usually employed to describe scenery, in which the predominant features are breadth, beauty, and repose. The reader has already perceived that the term is wholly inapplicable to the scenery at this spot; and that the phrase of *Vale of Tempe* is one that depends on poetic fiction. . . . The real character of Tempe, though it perhaps be less beautiful, yet possesses more of magnificence than is implied in the epithet given to it. . . . to those who have visited St. Vincent's rocks below Bristol, I cannot convey a more sufficient idea of Tempe, than by saying that its scenery resembles, though on a much larger scale, that of the former place. The Peneus, indeed, as it flows through the valley, is not greatly wider than the Avon; and the channel between the cliffs is equally contracted in its dimensions; but these cliffs themselves are much loftier and more precipitous and project their vast masses of rock with still more extraordinary abruptness over the hollow beneath."—Holland's Travels in Albania, &c. [FH; her parentheses]

Henry Holland, *Travels in the Ionian Isles, Albania, Thessaly, Macedonia, &c. during the years 1812 and 1813* (1813); 2d ed., 2 vols. (London: Longman &c, 1819), 2.12–13. Holland (1788–1873) was Byron's friend and mentor and a friend of John Murray, who at this point was publishing Byron and FH.

[15] The modern name of the Peneus is Salympria. [FH]

[16] "Towards the lower part of Tempe, these cliffs are peaked in a very singular manner, and form projecting angles on the vast perpendicular faces of rock, which they present towards the chasm. Where the surface renders it possible, the summits and ledges of the rocks are for the most part covered with small wood, chiefly oak, with the arbutus and other shrubs. On the banks of the river, wherever there is a small interval between the water and the cliffs, it is covered by the rich and widely-spreading foliage of the plane, the oak, and other forest trees, which in these situations have attained a remarkable size, and in various places extend their shade far over the channel of the stream." . . . "The rocks on each side the vale of Tempe are evidently the same; what may be called, I believe, a coarse blueish grey marble, with veins and portions of the rock, in which the marble is of finer quality."—Holland's Travels in Albania, &c. [FH; *Travels* 2.15, 2.17]

[17] Cf. the Wanderer's openness to "Nature" in Wordsworth's *Excursion* (1814), 1.150–204.

[18] The Amphictyonic council was convened in spring and autumn at Delphi or Thermopylæ, and presided at the Pythian games, which were celebrated at Delphi every fifth year. [FH]

The Pythia were the priestesses of Apollo's oracle at Delphi, who rendered his prophesies; the council was a tribal federation in primitive Greece.

[19] "This spot (the field of Mantinea) in which so many brave men were laid to rest, is now covered with laurels and rosemary."—Pouqueville's Travels in the Morea. [FH; her parentheses]

François Charles Hugues Laurent Pouqueville (1770–1838), *Travels through the Morea, Albania, and Several Other Parts of the Ottoman Empire, to Constantinople. During the Years 1798, 1799, 1800, and 1801* (Eng. trans., London, 1806), 31. The stanza names famous battle sites: at the mountain pass of Thermopylae in 480 B.C. a small Greek army held off a much larger Persian army until it was betrayed; Hercules is fabled to have died on mount Œta, the site of Thermopylæ; at Mantinea, the Spartans defeated its city-state in 418 B.C. and were defeated 362 B.C.; at Platæa, a city south of Thebes, the Greeks defeated the Persians in 479 B.C. Pouqueville, trained in medicine, was an artistic and scientific consultant in Napoleon's expedition to Egypt. Captured by pirates on his way back to France, he escaped, was seized by the Turks, and spent two years in Greece and Constantinople. *Travels* led to his appointment as consul to Ali Pasha in Albania; on returning to France, he published widely on Greece and its oppression by the Turks.

[20] Cf. stanzas XXXI and LVII. FH refers to modern Ottoman tyranny, although ancient Greek states were also slave-owning. Britain abolished the slave trade in 1807, but other European and American nations had not, and slavery itself was legal in British colonies until 1833. FH knew poet and abolitionist William Roscoe (1753–1831), author of *The Wrongs of Africa* (1787); he was one of the subscribers to her 1808 *Poems* and gave her crucial help in her career (see Letters).

[21] For the accounts of the upas or poison-tree of Java, now generally believed to be fabulous, or greatly exaggerated, see the notes to Darwin's Botanic Garden. [FH]

Erasmus Darwin, *The Botanic Garden, Part II. Containing The Loves of the Plants, A Poem. With Philosophical Notes* (Lichfield: J. Jackson, 1789), vol. 2: "Fierce in dread silence on the blasted heath / Fell UPAS sits, the HYDRA-TREE of death. / Lo! from one root, the envenom'd soil below, / A thousand vegetative serpents grow" (canto 3.237–40; notes, pp. 167–73). Darwin (1731–1802; Charles Darwin's grandfather) was a physician, medical writer, and poet. This popular poem treats botany in allegory, and is embellished with detailed scientific notes.

[22] "The court most to be admired of the Alhambra is that called the *Court of the Lions*; it is ornamented with sixty elegant columns of an architecture which bears not the least resemblance to any of the known orders, and might be called the Arabian order. . . . But its principal monument, and that from which it took its name, is an alabaster cup, six feet in diameter, supported by twelve lions, which is said to have been made in imitation of the brazen sea of Solomon's temple."—Bourgoanne's Travels in Spain. [FH]

Jean François, Baron de Bourgoing (1748–1811), *Modern State of Spain*, 4 vols. (London: Stockdale, 1808), 4.171.172; a translation of his *Nouveau voyage en Espagne* (1789). Bourgoing quotes *Essays on Spain* by M. Peyron. The Alhambra of Granada, cultural center of Muslim Spain, is famed for its gorgeous buildings. The crescent is the emblem of Islam.

[23] "Sept des plus fameux parmi les anciens poètes Arabiques, sont désignés par les écrivains orientaux sous le nom de Pleïade arabique, et leurs ouvrages étaient suspendus autour de la Caaba, ou Mosque [temple] de la Mecque."—Sismondi Littérature du Midi. [FH]

[Seven of the most famous of these ancient [Arabic] poets are denoted by oriental writers under the title of the *Arabic Pleiades*, and their works were suspended around the Caaba, or temple of Mecca.]

J. C. L. Sismondi, *De la Littérature du Midi de l'Europe* (Paris, 1813); 2d ed., 4 vols. (Paris, 1819), 1.53. *Caliph*: a Muslim religious and civil ruler, a successor (Arabic, *khalifah*) of Mohammed, founder of Islam. Andalusia is in southern Spain.

[24] Byzantium (later Constantinople), capital of the the Eastern (Christian) Roman Empire, was captured by Muslim Turks in 1453. The following stanzas refer to its famous sites: Hagia Sophia, the principal Christian church; the Sea of Marmora separating Asia from Europe; and the supposedly impregnable Seven Towers guarding the city.

[25] "The distress and fall of the last Constantine are more glorious than the long prosperity of the Byzantine Cæsars."—Gibbon's Decline and Fall, &c. vol. xii. p. 226. [FH]

Edward Gibbon (1737–94), *Decline and Fall of the Roman Empire* (1776–88), ch. 68. Constantine XI (Constantine Palæologus) was the last Byzantine emperor (see note to 357). In 1453, with a force of 8,000 Greeks, Venetians, and Genoese, for nearly two months he held off 150,000 Turkish besiegers commanded by Sultan Muhammed II; he died fighting in the fall of the city and the empire of which it was the center. Baillie's tragedy *Constantine Palæologus* (1804) inspired FH's *The Last Constantine*, in *The Siege of Valencia &c* (1823).

[26] See the description of the night previous to the taking of Constantinople by Mahomet II.—Gibbon, vol. xii. p. 225. [FH. Ch. 68]

In several features, this stanza recalls Byron's famous description of the ball before the battle of Waterloo, in *Childe Harold III* (1816), xxi ff.

[27] "This building (the Castle of the Seven Towers) is mentioned as early as the sixth century of the Christian æra, as a spot which contributed to the defence of Constantinople, and it was the principal bulwark of the town on the coast of the Propontis, in the last periods of the empire."—Pouqueville's Travels in the Morea. [FH; from 112, her parentheses]

[28] See the account from Herodotus of the supernatural defence of Delphi.—Mitford's Greece, vol. i. page 396. [FH]

William Mitford, *History of Greece* (1784–1810), ch. 8, sec. 4; 1829 ed. (London: T. Cadell), 2.55–58. Mitford undertook this vast history (up to the death of Alexander) at the suggestion of Gibbon. Infused with anti-Jacobin views, it was critical of democracy, but proved very popular. Byron read it with enthusiasm. The treasure of Delphi (on the side of Mount Parnassus), known to Persian invader Xerxes, was defended by sixty soldiers and a prophet, with the "preternatural" assistance of thunder and a landslide. The notion of divine providence guiding national affairs was strong during the Napoleonic wars. Many Britons interpreted the prolongation of the struggle as a sign of divine disfavor and Britain's eventual victory as favor restored.

[29] The Scamander flows on the Asian side of the Hellespont.

[30] "In succeeding ages, the Athenians honoured Theseus as a demi-god, induced to it as well by other reasons, as because, when they were fighting the Medes at Marathon, a considerable part of the army thought they saw the apparition of Theseus completely armed, and bearing down before them upon the barbarians."—Langhorne's Plutarch, life of Theseus. [FH]

John and William Langhorne's *Plutarch's Lives*, 6 vols. (London, 1770) was the most important translation of *Lives* after Sir Thomas North's (1579). At Marathon, northeast of Athens, a small Greek army defeated a large Persian force in 490 b.c. In legend, it was the scene of Theseus's victory over a great bull.

[31] "From Thermopylæ to Sparta, the leader of the Goths (Alaric) pursued his victorious march without encountering any mortal antagonist, but one of the advocates of expiring paganism has confidently asserted, that the walls of Athens were guarded by the goddess Minerva, with her formidable ægis, and by the angry phantom of Achilles, and that the conqueror was

dismayed by the presence of the hostile deities of Greece."—Gibbon's Decline and Fall, &c. vol. v. page 183. [FH; her parentheses, ch. 30]

Minerva's aegis (shield) bears an image of a Gorgon's head. In *The Iliad*, Achilles, a Greek general in the Trojan War, is famed for his wrathfulness.

[32] "Even all the *chief ones of the earth.*"—Isaiah, 14th chapter [FH; her italics]

When the Lord delivers Israel from bondage, Isaiah prophesies, present tyrants will confront the dead from Sheol, "even all the chief ones [i.e., Kings] of the earth" (Isaiah 14.9).

[33] "How are the mighty fallen, and the weapons of war perished!"—Samuel, 2d book, 1st chap. [FH. Verse 27; cf. stanza VI.59]

[34] Ali Pasha (1741–1822), Turkish ruler of Albania and western Greece. Byron visited him in 1809.

[35] A mountain range in northern Greece separating Thessaly from Epirus.

[36] Olympus's summit was fabled to be ever sunny; the gods lived below, amidst clouds.

[37] For several interesting particulars relative to the Suliote warfare with Ali Pasha, see Holland's Travels in Albania. [FH]

2.237. Living in independence in mountain fastholds during the Ottoman occupation of Greece, the Suliotes held off Ali Pasha from 1790 to 1802; but in 1803, having concluded a bad-faith truce with them, Ali Pasha conducted a massacre.

[38] Evoking Exodus 14.24, in which the Israelites are guided by a pillar of fire.

[39] "It is related as an authentic story, that a group of Suliote women assembled on one of the precipices adjoining the modern seraglio, and threw their infants into the chasm below, that they might not become the slaves of the enemy."—Holland's Travels, &c. [FH. 2.241]

Cf. *The Suliote Mother.*

[40] The ruins of Sparta, near the modern town of Mistra, are very inconsiderable, and only sufficient to mark the site of the ancient city. The scenery around them is described by travellers as very striking. [FH]

This ancient city-state in the Peloponnesus, renowned for its military culture, was devastated by the Goths in 395.

[41] The inscription composed by Simonides for the Spartan monument in the pass of Thermopylæ has been thus translated—"Stranger, go tell the Lacedemonians that we have obeyed their laws, and that we lie here." [FH]

Simonides (556–468 B.C.) was the first great lyric poet of Greece; he also composed elegiac epitaphs for the slain at Salamis and Marathon.

[42] Leonidas was the Spartan King and general whose army held off Persians at Thermopylae in 480 B.C. Lares are spirits of the dead who act as guardians of the living.

[43] "In the Eurotas I observed abundance of those famous reeds which were known in the earliest ages; and all the rivers and marshes of Greece are replete with rose-laurels, while the springs and rivulets are covered with [red and white striped] lilies, tuberoses, hyacinths, and *Narcissus orientalis.*"—Pouqueville's Travels in the Morea. [FH; 89]

Mount Taygetus is in the Peloponnesus, whose principal river, the Eurotas, flows past Sparta.

[44] It was usual for suppliants to carry an olive-branch bound with wool. [FH]

[45] The olive, according to Pouqueville, is still regarded with veneration by the people of the Morea. [FH]

"The Morea is perhaps the only country in the world which is covered with fine olive trees. The respect of the people for these trees is so great, that they surround and pay them a sort of worship at a time when they are loaded with fruit; and to cut off a branch would be a crime that would meet exemplary punishment" (87).

[46] It was customary at Eleusis, on the fifth day of the festival, for men and women to run about with torches in their hands, and also to dedicate torches to Ceres, and to contend who should present the largest. This was done in memory of the journey of Ceres in search of Proserpine, during which she was lighted by a torch kindled in the flames of Etna.—Potter's Antiquities of Greece, vol. i. p. 392. [FH]

2d ed. (1706), bk. 2, ch. 20; 1697 ed., 1.357–58; 1813 ed., 1.450. Northwest of Athens, this ancient city was the site of the famous Eleusian Mysteries (rites), which centered on Ceres, goddess of grain and the harvest, and her daughter Proserpine. Abducted by Dis (god of the underworld), Proserpine was sought by her grieving mother and allowed an annual return—a cycle symbolizing the seasons. Salamis (609) is one of the Greek isles, in the Gulf of Aegina.

[47] See note to stanza xxv.

[48] FH's major project of 1820–21 would be *Superstition and Error* (1821).

[49] The Fountains of Oblivion and Memory, with the Hercynian fountain, are still to be seen amongst the rocks near Livadia, though the situation of the cave of Trophonius in their vicinity cannot be exactly ascertained.—See Holland's Travels. [FH, paraphrasing 2.163–64]

In a cave in Lebadia (in Boeotia, central Greece), Trophonius presided over an oracle. *Fatidic*: prophetic.

[50] Lacedæmon is a region of Peloponnesus, often equated with Sparta.

[51] Elis was anciently a sacred territory, its inhabitants being considered as consecrated to the service of Jupiter. All armies marching through it delivered up their weapons, and received them again when they had passed its boundary. [FH]

Olympia is in Elis, in northwest Peloponnesus.

[52] "We are assured by Thucydides that Attica was the province of Greece in which population first became settled, and where the earliest progress was made toward civilization."—Mitford's Greece, vol. i. p. 35. [FH. Ch. 1, sec. 3; 1819 ed., 1.48]

[53] The Ilissus flows through Athens. Legendary hero Theseus federalized Attica under Athenian leadership. Hemans uses *barbaric* both in its Greek sense of "foreign" and in the modern one of "uncivilized." *Fabrics*: buildings. *Pencil's world*: drawing and painting.

[54] Fata Morgana. This remarkable aërial phenomenon, which is thought by the lower order of Sicilians to be the work of a fairy, is thus described by father Angelucci, whose account is quoted by Swinburne. "On the 15th August, 1643, I was surprised, as I stood at my window, with a most wonderful, spectacle: [delectable vision.] The sea that washes the Sicilian shore swelled up, and became, for ten miles in length, like a chain of dark mountains; while the waters near our Calabrian coast grew quite smooth, and in an instant appeared as one clear polished mirror. [. . .] On this glass was depicted, in *chiaro scuro*, a string of several thousands of pilasters, all equal in altitude, distance, and degrees of light and shade. In a moment they [lost half their height, and] bent into arcades, like Roman aqueducts. A long cornice was next formed at the top, and above it rose castles innumerable, all perfectly alike; these soon split into towers, which were shortly after lost in colonnades, then windows, and at last ended in pines, cypresses, and other trees."—Swinburne's Travels in the Two Sicilies. [FH]

"Journey to Reggio," *Travels* 1.366. Swinburne continues, "This is the *Fata Morgana*, which, for twenty-six years, I had thought a mere fable." *Chiaro scuro*: light and shade.

[55] Statesman and military commander, 5th c. B.C., in whose reign Athens reached the peak of its prestige and power; he commissioned the Parthenon.

[56] All sorts of purple and white flowers were supposed by the Greeks to be acceptable to the dead, and used in adorning tombs; as amaranth, with which the Thessalians decorated the tomb of Achilles.—Potter's Antiquities of Greece, vol. ii. p. 232. [FH. From bk. 4, ch. 8; 1813 ed. 2.231–32]

Amaranth was fabled to be unfading. Ceramicus: cemetery district of Athens.

[57] Pericles, on his return to Athens after the reduction of Samos, celebrated in a splendid manner the obsequies of his countrymen who fell in that war, and pronounced, himself, the funeral oration usual on such occasions. This gained him great applause; and when he came down from the rostrum, the women paid their respects to him, and presented him with crowns and chaplets, like a champion just returned victorious from the lists.—Langhorne's Plutarch, life of Pericles. [FH]

5th-c. Athenian statesman Pericles was a patron of the arts.

[58] The peplus, which is supposed to have been suspended as an awning over the statue of Minerva, in the Parthenon, was a principal ornament of the Panathenaic festival; it was

embroidered with various colours, representing the battle of the Gods and Titans, and the exploits of Athenian heroes. When the festival was celebrated, the peplus was brought from the Acropolis, and suspended as a sail to the vessel, which on that day was conducted through the Ceramicus and principal streets of Athens, till it had made the circuit of the Acropolis. The peplus was then carried to the Parthenon, and consecrated to Minerva.—See Chandler's Travels, Stuart's Athens, &c. [FH]

Richard Chandler (1738–1810), *Travels in Greece* (Oxford: Clarendon, 1776), 44–49; and James Stuart (1713–88), *The Antiquities of Athens and other Monuments of Greece* (1762); 1837 ed. (London: Charles Tilt), 38–39. Harmodius led a revolt against tyrants Hippias and Hipparchus in the late 6th c. B.C. *Piraeus*: port of Athens.

[59] The gilding amidst the ruins of Persepolis is still, according to Winckelmann, in high preservation. [FH]

J. J. Winckelmann, *Geschichte der Kunst des Altertums* (1764; trans. 1766 as *History of Ancient Art*), bk. 7, ch. 2, sec. 10 (see note below). *Palmyra*: chief city of a state northeast of Damascus. *Persepolis*: capital of the Persian empire. *Thebes*: major Egyptian city.

[60] The Turks vandalized ancient monuments, so that they would not serve as an inspiration to revolt.

[61] In the 6th c., the Parthenon became a Christian church and in the 7th c., a mosque.

[62] Detractors of the Elgin Marbles derided them as mere rough fragments.

[63] "In the most broken fragment the same great principle of life can be proved to exist as in the most perfect figure," is one of the observations of Mr. Haydon on the Elgin Marbles. [FH]

B. R. Haydon (1786–1846), *The Judgment of Connoisseurs upon Works of Art Compared with that of Professional Men; in Reference More Particularly to the Elgin Marbles* (London: Carpenter, 1816), 6–7. This polemic previously appeared in newspapers, the *Examiner* and the *Champion*. Haydon, an art critical and painter of historical subjects, admired the Marbles, and urged *Annals of the Fine Arts* to publish two sonnets by his friend John Keats praising their shadowy magnitude.

[64] "Every thing here breathes life, with a veracity, with an exquisite knowledge of art, but without the least ostentation or parade of it, which is concealed by consummate and masterly skill." —Canova's Letter to the Earl of Elgin. [FH]

10 November 1815, trans. in *Report from the Select Committee of the House of Commons on the Earl of Elgin's Collection of Sculptured Marbles; &c.* (London: John Murray, 1816), Appendix, xxiii. Italian sculptor Antonio Canova (1757–1822), founder of the Neoclassicist school, was popular in England and admired by Byron. He made several statues of Napoleon, and one of his sister reclining as Venus Victrix.

[65] Mr. West, after expressing his admiration of the horse's head in Lord Elgin's collection of Athenian sculpture, thus proceeds: "We feel the same, when we view the young equestrian Athenians; and in observing them, we are insensibly carried on with the impression, that they and their horses actually existed, as we see them, at the instant when they were converted into marble."—West's Second Letter to Lord Elgin. [FH]

20 March 1811, in *Memorandum on the Subject of the Earl of Elgin's Pursuits in Greece*, 2d. ed., corrected (London: John Murray, 1815), 54. Benjamin West (1738–1820) was an American painter (despised by Byron) who worked in England and in 1792 succeeded Sir Joshua Reynolds as president of the Royal Academy.

[66] Mr. Flaxman thinks that sculpture has very greatly improved within these last twenty years, and that his opinion is not singular, because works of such prime importance as the Elgin marbles could not remain in any country without a consequent improvement of the public taste, and the talents of the artist.—See the Evidence given in reply to interrogatories from the Committee on the Elgin Marbles. [FH]

*Report from the Select Committee* 74. John Flaxman (1755–1826), sculptor and illustrator (of works of Homer, Aeschylus, Hesiod, and Dante), was a friend of poet, engraver, and painter William Blake.

[67] The Theseus and Ilissus, which are considered by Sir T. Lawrence, Mr. Westmacott, and other distinguished artists, to be of a higher class than the Apollo Belvedere; "because there is

in them an union of [fine composition, and] very grand form, with a more true and natural expression of the effect of action upon the human frame, than there is in the Apollo, or any of the other more celebrated statues."—See the Evidence, &c. [FH; *Report* 90]

Quoting Thomas Lawrence (1769–1830), famous portrait painter, president of the Royal Academy after West. Richard Westmacott (1775–1856) was a well-known sculptor in classical style.

[68] "Let us suppose a young man at this time in London, endowed with powers such as enabled Michael Angelo to advance the arts, as he did, by the aid of one mutilated specimen of Grecian excellence in sculpture; to what an eminence might not such a genius carry art, by the opportunity of studying those sculptures in the aggregate, which adorned the Temple of Minerva at Athens?"—West's Second Letter to Lord Elgin [FH; *Memorandum* 55]

[69] In allusion to the theories of Du Bos, Winckelmann, Montesquieu, &c. with regard to the inherent obstacles in the climate of England to the progress of genius and the arts.—See Hoare's Epochs of the Arts, page 84, 5. [FH]

Prince Hoare (1755–1834), *Epochs of the Arts: Including Hints on the Use and Progress of Painting and Sculpture in Great Britain* (London: John Murray, 1813): "the ridiculous dogmas of Du Bos and Winckelmann, on the subject of atmospheric and other physical obstacles to genius have been long overthrown" (84). Hoare refers to Jean-Baptiste du Bos (1670–1742), *Réflexions critiques sur la poésie et sur la peinture* (Critical reflections on poetry and on painting, 1719) and German art historian and critic J. J. Winckelmann (1717–68), who argued in *Geschichte* (see n. 59) that the climate and political liberty of ancient Greece gave its people physical beauty, which their art imitated until the Roman conquest. The main uses of the arts, argues Hoare, is "the celebration of the essential virtue, or fundamental strength, of the individual country in which they are cultivated" (324); England's strength is the union of "pure religion" with "the wisdom of EQUAL LAWS, constituting what is denominated the *Freedom of the English Constitution*," and "the extent of our COMMERCE, maintaining and supporting our political eminence under the influence of" the Constitution (326–27). Although Hoare attacked Elgin and opposed Britain's acquisition of the Marbles, Hemans responded to the connections he made between art and political climate.

[70] Ever, but with a punning connotation of "before" (*ere*).

# Tales, and Historic Scenes, In Verse

## (1819)

—◦◦◦—

[The volume's title page reads, "By Felicia Hemans, Author of the Restoration of the Works of Art to Italy, Modern Greece, &c. &c." *Tales* was published in May 1819 in a run of 750, met favorable reviews, and sold out. Capitalizing on the success of *The Siege of Valencia* (published in June 1823), Murray published a 2d edition, also of 750, in November 1823 (dated 1824), but about 30 percent was remaindered. *Tales* is Hemans's first experiment in an orchestrated set of poems, in which recurrent tropes and concerns, such as the fate of female passion in political conflict, evolve a transhistorical, transcultural macrotext—a cumulative form with which she will achieve spectacular success in *Records of Woman* (1828). *Tales* received a detailed and admiring review in *British Critic* 12 (1819): 70–74.]

## The Widow of Crescentius

[In the late 10th c., the Holy Roman Emperor (Otto III of Germany), the Papacy, and the people contended for control of Rome. Led by Crescentius's father, the Romans seized the government, had Pope Benedict VI strangled, and elected other popes. Supported by another faction, Otto then captured the city and installed his cousin as Pope Gregory V. Self-declared patrician Johannes Crescentius Nomentanus led an uprising in 996 that installed anti-Pope John XVI. Otto returned, besieged Crescentius and his followers in the Castel Sant'Angelo on the Tiber river, formerly the tomb of Emperor Hadrian. After heroic resistance, he surrendered in April 998 on terms later broken by Otto's supporters, who had him tortured, executed, and thrown from the ramparts. Writing in the spirit of modern Romantic nationalism, historians such as Sismondi idealized figures such as Crescentius as republican patricians, inspired by "ancient glory." Adding a supplement of insurrection inspired by female domestic affection, Hemans's tale changes some potentially improper details. Sismondi (citing Latin sources) reports that the widow disguised herself as a doctor, and "sous ses habits deuil elle l'éblouit encore par ses charmes; et, comme sa maîtresse ou comme son médecin, ayant gagné sa confiance, elle lui aministra un poison qui le conduisit bientôt à une mort doloureuse" (and under her mourning clothes she still could dazzle him with her charms; and, as his mistress or as his doctor, having gained his confidence, she administered a poison to him which soon drove him to a painful death).]

> "L'orage peut briser en un moment les fleurs qui tiennent encore la tête levée."
>
> MAD[AME] DE STAEL[1]

### ADVERTISEMENT

*"In the reign of Otho III, Emperor of Germany, the Romans, excited by their Consul, Crescentius, who ardently desired to restore the ancient glory of the republic, made a bold attempt to shake off the Saxon yoke, and the authority of the Popes, whose vices rendered them objects of universal contempt. The Consul was besieged*

*by Otho in the Mole of Hadrian, which, long afterwards, continued to be called the Tower of Crescentius. Otho, after many unavailing attacks upon this fortress, at last entered into negotiations; and pledging his imperial word to respect the life of Crescentius, and the rights of the Roman citizens, the unfortunate leader was betrayed into his power, and immediately beheaded with many of his partisans. Stephania, his widow, concealing her affliction and her resentment for the insults to which she had been exposed, secretly resolved to revenge her husband and herself. On the return of Otho from a pilgrimage to Mount Gargano, which, perhaps, a feeling of remorse had induced him to undertake, she found means to be introduced to him, and to gain his confidence, and a poison administered by her was soon afterwards the cause of his painful death."—See Sismondi,* History of the Italian Republics, *vol. i.*[2]

[PART I]

Midst Tivoli's luxuriant glades,[3]
Bright-foaming falls, and olive shades,
Where dwelt, in days departed long,
The sons of battle and of song,
No tree, no shrub its foliage rears,
But o'er the wrecks of other years,
Temples and domes, which long have been
The soil of that enchanted scene.

There the wild fig-tree and the vine
O'er Hadrian's mouldering villa twine;[4]          10
The cypress, in funereal grace,
Usurps the vanish'd column's place;
O'er fallen shrine, and ruin'd frieze,
The wall-flower rustles in the breeze;
Acanthus-leaves the marble hide,
They once adorn'd, in sculptured pride,
And nature hath resumed her throne
O'er the vast works of ages flown.

Was it for this that many a pile,
Pride of Ilissus and of Nile,                      20
To Anio's banks the image lent
Of each imperial monument?[5]
Now Athens weeps her shatter'd fanes,
Thy temples, Egypt, strew thy plains;
And the proud fabrics° Hadrian rear'd,      *buildings*
From Tibur's vale have disappear'd.
We need no prescient sybil there
The doom of grandeur to declare;
Each stone, where weeds and ivy climb,
Reveals some oracle of Time;                       30

Each relic utters Fate's decree,
The future as the past shall be.

Halls of the dead! in Tibur's° vale,                    *Tivoli's*
Who now shall tell your lofty tale?
Who trace the high patrician's dome,
The bard's retreat, the hero's home?
When moss-clad wrecks alone record
There dwelt the world's departed lord!
In scenes where verdure's rich array
Still sheds young beauty o'er decay,                    40
And sunshine on each glowing hill,
Midst ruins finds a dwelling still.

Sunk is thy palace, but thy tomb,
Hadrian! hath shared a prouder doom,[6]
Though vanish'd with the days of old
Its pillars of Corinthian mould;
And the fair forms by sculpture wrought,
Each bodying some immortal thought,
Which o'er that temple of the dead,
Serene, but solemn beauty shed,                         50
Have found, like glory's self, a grave
In time's abyss, or Tiber's wave:[7]
Yet dreams more lofty, and more fair,
Than art's bold hand hath imaged e'er,
High thoughts of many a mighty mind,
Expanding when all else declined,
In twilight years, when only they
Recalled the radiance passed away,[8]
Have made that ancient pile their home,
Fortress of freedom and of Rome.                        60

There he, who strove in evil days,
Again to kindle glory's rays,[9]
Whose spirit sought a path of light,
For those dim ages far too bright,
Crescentius, long maintain'd the strife,
Which closed but with its martyr's life,
And left th' imperial tomb a name,
A heritage of holier fame.
There closed De Brescia's mission high,
From thence the patriot came to die;[10]                70
And thou, whose Roman soul the last,
Spoke with the voice of ages past,[11]
Whose thoughts so long from earth had fled,
To mingle with the glorious dead,

That midst the world's degenerate race
They vainly sought a dwelling-place,
Within that house of death didst brood
O'er visions to thy ruin woo'd.
Yet, worthy of a brighter lot,
Rienzi![12] be thy faults forgot!                          80
For thou, when all around thee lay
Chain'd in the slumbers of decay;
So sunk each heart, that mortal eye
Had scarce a *tear* for liberty;
Alone, amidst the darkness there,
Couldst gaze on Rome—yet not despair![13]

   'Tis morn, and Nature's richest dyes
Are floating o'er Italian skies;
Tints of transparent lustre shine
Along the snow-clad Apennine;                              90
The clouds have left Soracte's height,
And yellow Tiber winds in light,
Where tombs and fallen fanes have strew'd
The wide Campagna's solitude.[14]
'Tis sad amidst that scene to trace
Those relics of a vanish'd race;
Yet o'er the ravaged path of time,
Such glory sheds that brilliant clime,
Where nature still, though empires fall,
Holds her triumphant festival;                             100
E'en Desolation wears a smile,
Where skies and sunbeams laugh the while;
And Heaven's own light, Earth's richest bloom,
Array the ruin and the tomb.

   But she, who from yon convent tower
Breathes the pure freshness of the hour;
She, whose rich flow of raven hair
Streams wildly on the morning air;
Heeds not how fair the scene below,
Robed in Italia's brightest glow.                          110
Though throned midst Latium's classic plains,
Th' Eternal City's towers and fanes,
And they, the Pleiades of earth,
The seven proud hills of Empire's birth,[15]
Lie spread beneath: not now her glance
Roves o'er that vast sublime expanse;
Inspired, and bright with hope, 'tis thrown
On Adrian's° massy tomb alone;                             *Hadrian's*

There, from the storm, when Freedom fled,
His faithful few Crescentius led;                      120
While she, his anxious bride, who now
Bends o'er the scene her youthful brow,
Sought refuge in the hallow'd fane,
Which then could shelter, not in vain.
But now the lofty strife is o'er,
And Liberty shall weep no more.
At length imperial Otho's voice
Bids her devoted° sons rejoice;                *loyal, doomed*
And he, who battled to restore
The glories and the rights of yore,               130
Whose accents, like the clarion's sound,
Could burst the dead repose around,
Again his native Rome shall see,
The sceptred city of the free!
And young Stephania waits the hour
When leaves her lord his fortress-tower,
Her ardent heart with joy elate,
That seems beyond the reach of fate;
Her mien, like creature from above,
All vivified with hope and love.                   140

    Fair is her form, and in her eye
Lives all the soul of Italy!
A meaning lofty and inspired,
As by her native day-star fired;
Such wild and high expression, fraught
With glances of impassion'd thought,
As fancy sheds in visions bright,
O'er priestess of the God of Light![16]
And the dark locks that lend her face
A youthful and luxuriant grace,                150
Wave o'er a cheek, whose kindling dyes
Seem from the fire within to rise;[17]
But deepen'd by the burning heaven
To her own land of sunbeams given.
Italian art that fervid glow
Would o'er ideal beauty throw,
And with such ardent life express
Her high-wrought dreams of loveliness;—
Dreams which, surviving Empire's fall,
The shade of glory still recal.                 160

    But see,—the banner of the brave
O'er Adrian's tomb hath ceased to wave.

'Tis lower'd—and now Stephania's eye
Can well the martial train descry,
Who, issuing from that ancient dome,
Pour through the crowded streets of Rome.
Now from her watch-tower on the height,
With step as fabled wood-nymph's light,
She flies—and swift her way pursues,
Through the lone convent's avenues.                    170
Dark cypress groves,[18] and fields o'erspread
With records of the conquering dead,
And paths which track a glowing waste,
She traverses in breathless haste;
And by the tombs where dust is shrined,
Once tenanted by loftiest mind,
Still passing on, hath reach'd the gate
Of Rome, the proud, the desolate!
Throng'd are the streets, and, still renew'd,
Rush on the gathering multitude.                       180

    Is it their high-soul'd chief to greet
That thus the Roman thousands meet?
With names that bid their thoughts ascend,
Crescentius, thine in song to blend;
And of triumphal days gone by
Recall th' inspiring pageantry?
—There is an air of breathless dread,
An eager glance, a hurrying tread;
And now a fearful silence round,
And now a fitful murmuring sound,                      190
Midst the pale crowds, that almost seem
Phantoms of some tumultuous dream.
Quick is each step, and wild each mien,
Portentous of some awful scene.
Bride of Crescentius! as the throng
Bore thee with whelming force along,
How did thine anxious heart beat high,
Till rose suspense to agony!
Too brief suspense, that soon shall close,
And leave thy heart to deeper woes.                    200

    Who midst yon guarded precinct stands,
With fearless mien, but fetter'd hands?
The ministers of death are nigh,
Yet a calm grandeur lights his eye;
And in his glance there lives a mind,
Which was not form'd for chains to bind,

But cast in such heroic mould
As theirs, th' ascendant ones of old.
Crescentius! freedom's daring son,
Is this the guerdon thou has won?                                    210
O worthy to have lived and died
In the bright days of Latium's pride!
Thus must the beam of glory close
O'er the seven hills again that rose,
When at thy voice, to burst the yoke,
The soul of Rome indignant woke?
Vain dream! the sacred shields are gone,[19]
Sunk is the crowning city's throne:[20]
Th' illusions, that around her cast
Their guardian spells, have long been past.[21]               220
Thy life hath been a shot-star's° ray,                        *meteor's*
Shed o'er her midnight of decay;
Thy death at freedom's ruin'd shrine
Must rivet every chain—but thine.

    Calm is his aspect, and his eye
Now fix'd upon the deep-blue sky,
Now on those wrecks of ages fled,
Around in desolation spread;
Arch, temple, column, worn and grey,
Recording triumphs pass'd away;                                       230
Works of the mighty and the free,
Whose steps on earth no more shall be,
Though their bright course hath left a trace
Nor years nor sorrows can efface.

    Why changes now the patriot's mien,
Erewhile so loftily serene?
Thus can approaching death control
The might of that commanding soul?
No!—Heard ye not that thrilling cry
Which told of bitterest agony?                                        240
*He* heard it, and, at once subdued,
Hath sunk the hero's fortitude.
*He* heard it, and his heart too well
Whence rose that voice of woe can tell;
And midst the gazing throngs around
One well-known form his glance hath found;
One fondly loving and beloved,
In grief, in peril, faithful proved.
Yes, in the wildness of despair,
She, his devoted bride, is there.                                     250

Pale, breathless, through the crowd she flies,
The light of frenzy in her eyes:
But ere her arms can clasp the form,
Which life ere long must cease to warm;
Ere on his agonizing breast
Her heart can heave, her head can rest;
Check'd in her course by ruthless hands,
Mute, motionless, at once she stands;
With bloodless cheek and vacant glance,
Frozen and fix'd in horror's trance;                    260
Spell-bound, as every sense were fled,
And thought o'erwhelm'd, and feeling dead.[22]
And the light waving of her hair,
And veil, far floating on the air,
Alone, in that dread moment, show
She is no sculptured form of woe.

The scene of grief and death is o'er,
The patriot's heart shall throb no more:
But *hers*—so vainly form'd to prove
The pure devotedness of love,                           270
And draw from fond affection's eye
All thought sublime, all feeling high;
When consciousness again shall wake,
Hath now no refuge—but to break.
The spirit long inured to pain
May smile at fate in calm disdain;
Survive its darkest hour, and rise
In more majestic energies.
But in the glow of vernal pride,
If each warm hope *at once* hath died,                   280
Then sinks the mind, a blighted flower,
Dead to the sunbeam and the shower;
A broken gem, whose inborn light
Is scatter'd—ne'er to re-unite.

---

[1] From Staël's popular novel *Corinne, ou l'Italie* (1807), bk. 4, ch. 2. When Corinne suggests to her beloved Nelvil that he may one day see her enshrined in the Roman Pantheon, he is amazed that one so young and beautiful should imagine her death. She replies, "a storm may crush in a moment those flowers still holding their heads upright."

[2] J.C.L. Simonde de Sismondi (1773–1842), *Histoire des Républiques Italiennes du Moyen Âge*, 16 vols. (Paris, 1809–18), vol. 3. FH's translation conflates various passages from bk. 1, ch. 3. Swiss-born economist, historian, and critic Sismondi accompanied Staël on the trip to Italy that inspired *Corinne*; the liberal, republican perspective of his *Histoire* was widely influential.

[3] South of Rome, this town is the site of the Renaissance Villa d'Este, famous for its gardens and fountains, and the ruins of the vast summer villa of Roman emperor Hadrian (ruled 117–38).

[4] "J'étais allé passer quelques jours seul à Tivoli. Je parcourus les [ruines des] environs, et surtout celles de la *Villa Adriana*. Surpris par la pluie, au milieu de ma course, je me réfugiai dans les Salles des *Thermes* voisins du *Pécile* (Monumens de *la Villa*), sous un figuier qui avait renversé le pan d'un mur en s'élevant. Dans un petit salon octogone, ouvert devant moi, une vigne vierge avait percé la voûte de l'édifice, et son gros cep lisse, rouge et tortueux, montait le long du mur comme un serpent. Autour de moi, à travers les arcades des ruines, s'ouvraient des points de vue sur la campagne romaine. Des buissons de sureau remplissaient les salles désertes où venaient se refugier quelques merles solitaires. Les fragmens de maçonnerie étaient tapissés de feuilles de scolopendre, dont la verdure satinée se dessinait comme un travail en mosaïque sur la blancheur des marbres. Çà et là de hauts cyprès remplaçaient les colonnes tombées dans ces palais de la mort; l'acanthe sauvage rampait à leurs pieds, sur des débris, comme si la nature s'était plue à reproduire sur ces chefs-d'ôeuvre mutilés d'architecture, l'ornement de leur beauté passée."—*Chateaubriand, Souvenirs d'Italie*. [FH]

[I had passed some days alone at Tivoli. I traversed the [ruins of the] environs, particularly those of *Villa Adriana*. Caught by the rain, in the midst of my excursion, I took refuge in the halls of *Thermes* near *Pécile* (Monuments of the *Villa*) under a fig tree, which had overturned a section of a wall in its growth. In a small octagonal room, open before me, a young vine had pierced the vault of the building, and its big stem, red and crooked, mounted along the wall like a serpent. Around me, across the arcades of the ruins, viewpoints opened on the Roman Campagna. Thickets of elder trees filled the deserted floors, where some solitary blackbirds found refuge. Fragments of masonry were blanketed with scolopendra leaves, their satin verdure seeming like mosaic work on the whiteness of the marbles. Here and there lofty cypresses replaced the fallen columns of these palaces of death; wild acanthus crept at their feet on the wreckage, as if nature had pleased herself in reproducing, upon these mutilated masterpieces of architecture, the ornament of their past beauty.]

Vicomte François René de Chateaubriand (1768–1848), *Souvenirs d'Italie, d'Angleterre et d'Amérique, suivi de morceaux divers de morale et de littérature* (Recollections of Italy, England and America, followed by diverse pieces on morals and literature), 2 vols. (London: Colburn, 1815), 1.19–20. Acanthus leaves were often carved on column capitals, especially Corinthian.

[5] The gardens and buildings of Hadrian's villa were copies of the most celebrated scenes and edifices in his dominions; the Lycæum, the Academia, the Prytaneum of Athens, the Temple of Serapis at Alexandria, the Vale of Tempe, &c. [FH]

Aristotle taught at the Lyceum, a gymnasium near ancient Athens; the Prytaneum is a building for public hospitality; the Temple of Serapis honored Osiris, Egyptian god of the underworld; Tempe in northern Thessaly was famed for its beauty. The "Was it for this . . . ?" that launches this sonnet stanza is a classic protest-rhetoric, deployed by Virgil (*Aeneid* 2.664–67, 4.675–81), Milton (*Samson Agonistes* 361–62), Pope (*Rape of the Lock* 4.97–102), Thomson (*Autumn* 1184–88), and Helen Maria Williams (*Letters from France*, 23 January 1793), among others. FH uses it again in *Abencerrage*. The stanza names famous rivers: the Ilissus near Athens; the Nile; and the Anio of the Tivoli region, which flows into Rome's Tiber; Tibur is the Latin name of Tivoli.

[6] The mausoleum of Hadrian, now the castle of St. Angelo, was first converted into a citadel by Belisarius, in his successful defence of Rome against the Goths. "The lover of the arts," says Gibbon, "must read with a sigh that the works of Praxiteles and Lysippus were torn from their lofty pedestals, and hurled into the ditch on the heads of the besiegers." He adds, in a note, that the celebrated sleeping Faun of the Barberini palace was found, in a mutilated state, when the ditch of St. Angelo was cleansed under Urban VIII. In the middle ages, the moles Hadriani was made a permanent fortress by the Roman government, and bastions, outworks, &c. were added to the original edifice, which had been stripped of its marble covering, its Corinthian pillars, and the brazen cone which crowned its summit. [FH]

Edward Gibbon (1737–94), *The Decline and Fall of the Roman Empire* (1776, 1781, 1788), ch. 41. Byzantine general Belisarius (circa 505–65) was sent by Emperor Justinian I to recover Italy from the Goths. As the reference to fourth-century-B.C. Greek sculptors Praxiteles and Lysippus suggests, Rome too had looted conquered territories. A member of the Barberini family, Pope Urban VIII (ruled 1623–44) involved the pontificate with the Thirty Years War in Germany.

[7] "Les plus beaux monuments des arts, les plus admirables statues ont été jetées dans le Tibre, et sont cachées sous ses flots. Qui sait si, pour les chercher, on ne le détournera pas un jour de son lit? Mais quand on songe que les chefs-d'oeuvres du génie humain sont peut-être là devant nous et qu'un oeil plus perçant les verrait à travers les ondes, l'on éprouve je ne sais quelle émotion qui renaît à Rome sans cesse sous diverses formes, et fait trouver une société pour la pensée dans les objets physiques, muets par-tout ailleurs."—*Mad. de Staël.* [FH; *Corinne*, bk. 5, ch. 2, conclusion]

[The most beautiful monuments of the arts, the most admirable statues were thrown into the Tiber, and are hidden beneath its tides. Who knows if, to find them, one will not one day divert it from its bed? But when one reflects that masterpieces of human genius are perhaps there in front of us, and that a sharper eye would see them through the waves, one feels that indescribable emotion that is ceaselessly reborn in Rome, under many forms, and that brings about one society for thought among physical objects, which everywhere else are mute.]

[8] Cf. Wordsworth's *Ode: Intimations of Immortality* (1815): "... though the radiance which was once so bright / Be now for ever taken from my sight" (175–76).

[9] The couplet has two echoes: Milton, though in peril when the monarchy was restored, has the epic narrator of *Paradise Lost* claim a voice "unchang'd / ... though fall'n on evil days" (7. 24–25; cf. *Siege of Valencia* 1.98); Wordsworth laments the loss of childhood: "nothing can bring back the hour / Of splendor in the grass, of glory in the flower" ("Intimations" *Ode* 177–78).

[10] Arnold de Brescia, the undaunted and eloquent champion of Roman liberty, after unremitting efforts to restore the ancient constitution of the republic, was put to death in the year 1155 by Adrian IV. This event is thus described by Sismondi, Histoire des Républiques Italiennes, Vol. II. pages 68 and 69. "Le préfect demeuroit dans le château Saint-Ange avec son prisonnier; il le fit transporter, un matin, sur la place destinée aux exécutions, devant la porte du peuple. Arnaud de Brescia, élevé sur un bûcher, fut attaché à un poteau, en face du Corso. Il pouvoit mesurer des yeux les trois longues rues qui aboutissoient devant son échafaud; elles font presqu' une moitié de Rome. C'est là qu'habitoient les hommes qu'il avoit si souvent appelés à la liberté. Ils reposoient encore en paix, ignorant le danger de leur législateur. Le tumulte de l'exécution et la flamme du bûcher réveillèrent les Romains: ils s'armèrent, ils accoururent, mais trop tard; et les cohortes du pape repoussèrent, avec leurs lances, ceux qui, n'ayant pu sauver Arnaud, vouloient du moins recueillir ses cendres comme de précieuses reliques." [FH; *Histoire*, bk. 2, ch. 8]

[The prefect remained in the Castel Sant-Angelo with his prisoner; he had him transported, one morning, to the square designated for executions, before the Porta del Popolo. Arnaud de Brescia, raised upon the pyre, was tied to the stake, opposite the Corso. From there he could look down the three long streets that led to his scaffold; they extend through almost half of Rome. There lived the men he had so often called to freedom. They still reposed in peace, unaware of the danger to their ruler. The tumult of the execution and the flame of the pyre woke up the Romans: they took up arms and ran to the spot, but too late; and the cohorts of the pope repulsed with their lances those who, unable to save Arnaud, at least wanted to gather his ashes as precious relics.]

Italian reformer Arnaldo da Brescia (?1100–55), angered by the corrupt clergy, led a popular revolt against the Bishop of Brescia. Exiled by the Second Lateran Council, he was betrayed by Frederick I and burned at the stake in Rome.

[11] "Posterity will compare the virtues and failings of this extraordinary man; but in a long period of anarchy and servitude, the name of Rienzi has often been celebrated as the deliverer of his country, and the last of the Roman patriots."—*Gibbon's Decline and Fall, &c.* vol. xii. page 362. [FH; ch. 70]

[12] Cola (or Nicolà) di Rienzi (ca. 1313–54) aimed to restore Rome to its ancient liberties, moral probity, and power, and to unite Italy against German interference. He led a revolution against the aristocracy in 1347 but was deposed and became a pawn of the rival German and

papal powers. Having disaffected his followers, he was killed in a riot in Rome. In the sentence just prior to the one FH quotes, Gibbon reports that his body "was abandoned to the dogs, to the Jews, and to the flames." In the eighteenth and nineteenth centuries he symbolized (for better or worse) democratic revolution.

[13] "Le consul Térentius Varron avoit fui honteusement jusqu'à Vénouse: cet homme, de la plus basse naissance, n'avoit été élevé au consulat que pour mortifier la noblesse. Mais le sénat ne voulut pas jouir de ce malheureux triomphe: il vit combien il étoit nécessaire qu'il s'attirât, dans cette occasion, la confiance du peuple; il alla au devant de Varron, et le remercia de ce *qu'il n'avoit pas désespéré de la republique.*"—*Montesquieu's Grandeur et Decadence des Romains.* [FH]

[Terentius Varro the consul had fled ignominiously as far as Venusia: this man, of the lowest birth, had been raised to the consulship merely to mortify the nobles. But the Senate did not want to enjoy this unhappy triumph: they saw how necessary it was, on this occasion, for them to draw the confidence of the people; they went before Varro, and thanked him *for not having despaired of the republic.*]

Charles Louis de Secondat, Baron de la Brède et de Montesquieu (1689–1755), *Considérations sur les causes de la grandeur des Romains et de la décadence* (Reflections on the causes of the rise and fall of the Roman Empire) (1734), ch. 4, 378. *Considérations* emphasizes the vulnerability of decadent democracies to tyranny. Marcus Terentius Varro (116-?27 B.C.), a prolific man of letters, fell into disfavor during the second Triumvirate; his library was plundered and he was proscribed. He fled, but was pardoned by Augustus.

[14] *Soracte*: 2,267-foot mountain near Rome. *Campagna*: the Roman countryside.

[15] *Latium*: Latin name for the region of Rome. *Pleiades*: a group of seven stars in the constellation Taurus, likened to Rome's seven hills.

[16] Apollo's priestesses communicated their prophesies in inspired trances.

[17] Echoing Shelley's description of the veiled, visionary dream-maid of *Alastor* (1816): "the solemn mood / Of her pure mind kindled through all her frame / A permeating fire" (161–63).

[18] Cf. Byron: "Dark tree, still sad when others' grief is fled, / The only constant mourner o'er the dead!" (*The Giaour* 286–87).

[19] Of the sacred bucklers, or ancilia of Rome, which were kept in the temple of Mars, Plutarch gives the following account. "In the eighth year of Numa's reign a pestilence prevailed in Italy; Rome also felt its ravages. While the people were greatly dejected, we are told that a brazen buckler fell from heaven into the hands of Numa. Of this he gave a very wonderful account, received from Egeria and the Muses: that the buckler was sent down for the preservation of the city, and should be kept with great care; that eleven others should be made as like it as possible in size and fashion, in order, that if any person were disposed to steal it, he might not be able to distinguish that which fell from heaven from the rest. He further declared, that the place, and the meadows about it, where he frequently conversed with the Muses, should be consecrated to those divinities; and that the spring which watered the ground, should be sacred to the use of the vestal virgins, daily to sprinkle and purify their temple. The immediate cessation of the pestilence is said to have confirmed the truth of this account."—*Life of Numa.* [FH]

John and William Langhorne, translation of *Plutarch's Lives* (London, 1770). Numa Pompilius (715–672 B.C.), legendary elected king of Rome, is said to have founded many of its religious and political institutions.

[20] "Who hath taken this counsel against Tyre, the *crowning city*, whose merchants are princes, whose traffickers are the honourable of the earth?"—*Isaiah*, chap. 23. [FH]

In 23.8, Isaiah prophesies the fall of Tyre.

[21] "Un mélange bizarre de grandeur d'âme, et de foiblesse entroit dès cette époque (l'onzième siècle) dans le caractère des Romains. . . . Un mouvement généreux vers les grandes choses faisoit place tout-à-coup à l' [étoit bientôt survi par un morne] abattement; ils passoient de la liberté la plus orageuse, à la servitude la plus avilissante. On auroit dit que les ruines et les portiques déserts de la capitale du monde, entretenoient ses habitans dans le sentiment de leur impuissance: au milieu de ces monumens de leur domination passée, les citoyens éprouvoient d'une manière trop décourageante leur propre nullité. Le nom des Romains qu'ils portoient ranimoit fréquemment leur enthousiasme, comme il le ranime encore aujourd'hui; mais bientôt

la vue de Rome, du forum désert, des sept collines de nouveau rendues au pâturage des trou-peaux, des temples désolés, des monumens tombant en ruines, les ramenoit à sentir qu'ils n'étoient plus les Romains d'autrefois." —Sismondi, *Histoire des Républiques Italiennes*, vol. I. p. 172. [FH; *Histoire*, bk. 1, ch. 3, her parentheses]

[A bizarre mixture of greatness of soul and of weakness entered the Roman character from that epoch (eleventh century). A generous movement toward great things would suddenly [soon] give way to [a mournful] dejection; they went from the most tempestuous freedom to the most degrading servitude. It was as if the deserted ruins and porticoes of the world's capital city sustained in its inhabitants a sense of their own impotence: in the middle of these monu-ments to their former dominance, the citizens were too dispiritingly aware of their own worth-lessness. The name of Romans that they bore often revived their enthusiasm, as it still does today, but soon the sight of Rome, of the deserted forum, of the seven hills returned once more to pastures for the herds, of the desolated temples, of the monuments falling in ruins, brought back the feeling that they were no longer the Romans of yesteryear.]

[22] Hemans applies a gender reversal, and revision, to the maiden's vanishing from the poet's dream in *Alastor*: as she "folded his frame in her dissolving arms," "blackness veiled his dizzy eyes, and night / Involved and swallowed up the vision," leaving a "vacant brain" (187–91).

## Part II

Hast thou a scene that is not spread
With records of thy glory fled?
A monument that doth not tell
The tale of liberty's farewell?
Italia! thou art but a grave
Where flowers luxuriate o'er the brave,
And nature gives her treasures birth
O'er all that hath been great on earth.
Yet smile thy heavens as once they smiled,
When thou wert freedom's favour'd child:          10
Tho' fane and tomb alike are low,
Time hath not dimm'd thy sunbeam's glow;
And robed in that exulting ray,
Thou seem'st to triumph o'er decay;
O yet, though by thy sorrows bent,
In nature's pomp magnificent;
What marvel if, when all was lost,
Still on thy bright, enchanted coast,
Though many an omen warn'd him thence,
Linger'd the lord of eloquence?[1]          20
Still gazing on the lovely sky,
Whose radiance woo'd him—but to die:
Like him *who* would not linger there,
Where heaven, earth, ocean, all are fair?
Who midst thy glowing scenes could dwell,
Nor bid awhile his griefs farewell?
Hath not thy pure and genial air
Balm for all sadness but despair?[2]

No! there are pangs, whose deep-worn trace
Not all *thy* magic can efface!                                     30
Hearts, by unkindness wrung, may learn
The world and all its gifts to spurn;
Time may steal on with silent tread,
And dry the tear that mourns the dead;
May change fond love, subdue regret,
And teach e'en vengeance to forget:
But thou, Remorse! there is no charm,
*Thy* sting, avenger, to disarm!
Vain are bright suns and laughing skies,
To sooth thy victim's agonies:                                      40
The heart once made thy burning throne,
Still, while it beats, is thine alone.

    In vain for Otho's joyless eye
Smile the fair scenes of Italy,
As through her landscapes' rich array
Th' imperial pilgrim bends his way.
Thy form, Crescentius, on his sight
Rises when nature laughs in light,
Glides round him at the midnight hour,
Is present in his festal bower,                                     50
With awful voice and frowning mien,
By all but him unheard, unseen.
Oh! thus to shadows of the grave
Be every tyrant still a slave!

    Where through Gargano's woody dells,
O'er bending oaks the north-wind swells,[3]
A sainted hermit's lowly tomb
Is bosom'd in umbrageous gloom,
In shades that saw him live and die
Beneath their waving canopy.                                        60
'Twas his, as legends tell, to share
The converse of immortals there;
Around that dweller of the wild
There "bright appearances" have smiled,[4]
And angel-wings, at eve, have been
Gleaming the shadowy boughs between.
And oft from that secluded bower
Hath breathed, at midnight's calmer hour,
A swell of viewless harps, a sound
Of warbled anthems pealing round.                                   70
Oh, none but voices of the sky
Might wake that thrilling harmony,

Whose tones, whose very echos made
An Eden of the lonely shade!

  Years have gone by; the hermit sleeps
Amidst Gargano's woods and steeps;
Ivy and flowers have half o'ergrown,
And veil'd his low, sepulchral stone:
Yet still the spot is holy, still
Celestial footsteps haunt the hill;                    80
And oft the awe-struck mountaineer
Aërial vesper-hymns may hear,
Around those forest-precincts float,
Soft, solemn, clear,—but still remote.
Oft will Affliction breathe her plaint
To that rude shrine's departed saint,
And deem that spirits of the blest
There shed sweet influence⁵ o'er her breast.

  And thither Otho now repairs,
To sooth his soul with vows and prayers;               90
And if for him, on holy ground,
The lost-one, Peace, may yet be found,
Midst rocks and forests, by the bed,
Where calmly sleep the sainted dead,
She dwells, remote from heedless eye,
With Nature's lonely majesty.

  Vain, vain the search—his troubled breast
Nor vow nor penance lulls to rest;
The weary pilgrimage is o'er,
The hopes that cheer'd it are no more.                 100
Then sinks his soul, and day by day,
Youth's buoyant energies decay.
The light of health his eye hath flown,
The glow that tinged his cheek is gone.
Joyless as one on whom is laid
Some baleful spell that bids him fade,
Extending its mysterious power
O'er every scene, o'er every hour;
E'en thus *he* withers; and to him,
Italia's brilliant skies are dim.                      110
He withers—in that glorious clime
Where Nature laughs in scorn of Time;
And suns, that shed on all below
Their full and vivifying glow,
From him alone their power withhold,
And leave his heart in darkness cold.

Earth blooms around him, heaven is fair,
*He* only seems to perish there.

    Yet sometimes will a transient smile
Play o'er his faded cheek awhile,          120
When breathes his minstrel-boy a strain
Of power to lull all earthly pain;
So wildly sweet, its notes might seem
Th' ethereal music of a dream,
A spirit's voice from worlds unknown,
Deep thrilling power in every tone!
Sweet is that lay, and yet its flow
Hath language only given to woe;
And if at times its wakening swell
Some tale of glory seems to tell,          130
Soon the proud notes of triumph die,
Lost in a dirge's harmony:
Oh! many a pang the heart hath proved,
Hath deeply suffer'd, fondly loved,
Ere the sad strain could catch from thence
Such deep impassion'd eloquence!—
Yes! gaze on him, that minstrel boy—
He is no child of hope and joy;
Though few his years, yet have they been
Such as leave traces on the mien,          140
And o'er the roses of our prime
Breathe other blights than those of time.

    Yet, seems his spirit wild and proud,
By grief unsoften'd and unbow'd.
Oh! there are sorrows which impart
A sternness foreign to the heart,
And rushing with an earthquake's power,
That makes a desert in an hour;
Rouse the dread passions in their course,
As tempests wake the billows' force!—          150
'Tis sad, on youthful Guido's face,
The stamp of woes like these to trace.
Oh! where can ruins awe mankind,
Dark as the ruins of the mind?

    His mien is lofty, but his gaze
Too well a wandering soul betrays:
His full dark eye at times is bright
With strange and momentary light,
Whose quick uncertain flashes throw
O'er his pale cheek a hectic glow:          160

And oft his features and his air
A shade of troubled mystery wear,
A glance of hurried wildness, fraught
With some unfathomable thought.[6]
Whate'er that thought, still, unexpress'd,
Dwells the sad secret in his breast;
The pride his haughty brow reveals,
All other passion well conceals.[7]
He breathes each wounded feeling's tone,
In music's eloquence alone;                                    170
His soul's deep voice is only pour'd
Through his full song and swelling chord.

   He seeks no friend, but shuns the train
Of courtiers with a proud disdain;
And, save when Otho bids his lay
Its half unearthly power essay,
In hall or bower the heart to thrill,
His haunts are wild and lonely still.
Far distant from the heedless throng,
He roves old Tiber's banks along,                              180
Where Empire's desolate remains
Lie scatter'd o'er the silent plains:
Or, lingering midst each ruin'd shrine
That strews the desert Palatine,[8]
With mournful, yet commanding mien,
Like the sad genius° of the scene,                    *presiding spirit*
Entranced in awful thought appears
To commune with departed years.
Or at the dead of night, when Rome                             189
Seems of heroic shades° the home;               *spirits of the dead*
When Tiber's murmuring voice recalls
The mighty to their ancient halls;
When hush'd is every meaner sound,
And the deep moonlight-calm around
Leaves to the solemn scene alone
The majesty of ages flown;
A pilgrim to each hero's tomb,
He wanders through the sacred gloom;
And, midst those dwellings of decay,
At times will breathe so sad a lay,                            200
So wild a grandeur in each tone,
'Tis like a dirge for empires gone!

   Awake thy pealing harp again,
But breathe a more exulting strain,

Young Guido! for awhile forgot
Be the dark secrets of thy lot,[9]
And rouse th' inspiring soul of song
To speed the banquet's hour along!—
The feast is spread; and music's call
Is echoing through the royal hall,                    210
And banners wave, and trophies shine,
O'er stately guests in glittering line;
And Otho seeks awhile to chase
The thoughts he never can erase,
And bid the voice, whose murmurs deep
Rise like a spirit on his sleep,
The still small voice[10] of conscience die,
Lost in the din of revelry.

On his pale brow dejection lowers,°            *menaces*
But that shall yield to festal hours:                 220
A gloom is in his faded eye,
But that from music's power shall fly:
His wasted cheek is wan with care,
But mirth shall spread fresh crimson there.
Wake, Guido! wake thy numbers high,
Strike the bold chord exultingly!
And pour upon th' enraptured ear
Such strains as warriors love to hear!
Let the rich mantling goblet flow,
And banish all resembling woe;                        230
And, if a thought intrude, of power
To mar the bright convivial hour,
Still must its influence lurk unseen,
And cloud the heart—but not the mien!

Away, vain dream!—on Otho's brow,[11]
Still darker lower the shadows now;
Changed are his features, now o'erspread
With the cold paleness of the dead;
Now crimson'd with a hectic dye,
The burning flush of agony!                           240
His lip is quivering, and his breast
Heaves with convulsive pangs oppress'd;
Now his dim eye seems fix'd and glazed,
And now to heaven in anguish raised;
And as, with unavailing aid,
Around him throng his guests dismay'd,
He sinks—while scarce his struggling breath
Hath power to falter—"This is death!"

Then rush'd that haughty child of song,
Dark Guido, through the awe-struck throng;          250
Fill'd with a strange delirious light,
His kindling eye shone wildly bright,[12]
And on the sufferer's mien awhile
Gazing with stern vindictive smile,
A feverish glow of triumph dyed
His burning cheek, while thus he cried:—
"Yes! these are death-pangs—on thy brow
Is set the seal of vegeance now!
Oh! well was mix'd the deadly draught,
And long and deeply hast thou quaff'd;          260
And bitter as thy pangs may be,
They are but guerdons meet from me!
Yet, these are but a moment's throes,
Howe'er intense, they soon shall close.
Soon shalt thou yield thy fleeting breath,
*My* life hath been a lingering death;
Since one dark hour of woe and crime,
A blood-spot on the page of time!

Deem'st thou my mind of reason void?
It is not phrensied,—but destroy'd!          270
Aye! view the wreck with shuddering thought,—
That work of ruin thou hast wrought![13]

The secret of thy doom to tell,
My name alone suffices well!
Stephania!—once a hero's bride!
Otho! thou know'st the rest—*he died.*
Yes! trusting to a monarch's word,
The Roman fell, untried, unheard!
And thou, whose every pledge was vain,
How couldst *thou* trust in aught again?          280

He died, and I was changed—my soul,
A lonely wanderer, spurn'd control.
From peace, and light, and glory hurl'd,
The outcast of a purer world,
I saw each brighter hope o'erthrown,
And lived for one dread task alone.
The task is closed—fulfill'd the vow,
The hand of death is on thee now.
Betrayer! in thy turn betray'd,
The debt of blood shall soon be paid!          290
Thine hour is come—the time hath been
My heart had shrunk from such a scene;

*That* feeling long is past—my fate
Hath made me stern as desolate.

Ye that around me shuddering stand,
Ye chiefs and princes of the land!
Mourn ye a guilty monarch's doom?
—Ye wept not o'er the patriot's tomb!
*He* sleeps unhonour'd—yet be mine
To share his low, neglected shrine.                          300
His soul with freedom finds a home,
His grave is that of glory—Rome!
Are not the great of old with her,
That city of the sepulchre?
Lead me to death! and let me share
The slumbers of the mighty there!"

The day departs—that fearful day
Fades in calm loveliness away:
From purple heavens its lingering beam
Seems melting into Tiber's stream,                           310
And softly tints each Roman hill
With glowing light, as clear and still,
As if, unstain'd by crime or woe,
Its hours had pass'd in silent flow.
The day sets calmly—it hath been
Mark'd with a strange and awful scene:
One guilty bosom throbs no more,
And Otho's pangs and life are o'er.
And thou, ere yet another sun
His burning race hath brightly run,                          320
Released from anguish by thy foes,
Daughter of Rome![14] shalt find repose.—
Yes! on thy country's lovely sky
Fix yet once more thy parting eye!
A few short hours—and all shall be
The silent and the past for thee.

Oh! thus with tempests of a day
We struggle, and we pass away,[15]
Like the wild billows as they sweep,
Leaving no vestige on the deep!                              330
And o'er thy dark and lowly bed
The sons of future days shall tread,
The pangs, the conflicts, of thy lot,
By them unknown, by thee forgot.[16]

[1] "As for Cicero, he was carried to Astyra, where, finding a vessel, he immediately went on board, and coasted along to Circæum with a favourable wind. The pilots were preparing immediately to sail from thence, but whether it was that he feared the sea, or had not yet given up all his hopes in Cæsar, he disembarked, and travelled a hundred furlongs on foot, as if Rome had been the place of his destination. Repenting, however, afterwards, he left that road, and made again for the sea. He passed the night in the most perplexing and horrid thoughts; insomuch, that he was sometimes inclined to go privately into Cæsar's house and stab himself upon the altar of his domestic gods, to bring the divine vengeance upon his betrayer. But he was deterred from this by the fear of torture. Other alternatives, equally distressful, presented themselves. At last, he put himself in the hands of his servants, and ordered them to carry him by sea to Cajeta, where he had a delightful retreat in the summer, when the Etesian winds set in. There was a temple of Apollo on that coast, from which a flight of crows came with great noise towards Cicero's vessel as it was making land. They perched on both sides the sail-yard, where some sat croaking, and others pecking the ends of the ropes. All looked upon this as an ill omen; yet Cicero went on shore, and, entering his house, lay down to repose himself. In the mean time a number of the crows settled in the chamber-window, and croaked in the most doleful manner. One of them even entered it, and alighting on the bed, attempted, with its beak, to draw off the clothes with which he had covered his face. On sight of this, the servants began to reproach themselves. 'Shall we,' said they, 'remain to be spectators of our master's murder? Shall we not protect him, so innocent and so great a sufferer as he is, when the brute creatures give him marks of their care and attention?' Then partly by entreaty, partly by force, they got him into his litter, and carried him towards the sea."—*Plutarch. Life of Cicero*. [FH; from Langhorne, *Lives*]

A republican, Cicero (106–43 B.C.) feared Julius Caesar's monarchical tendencies. Though not one of Caesar's assassins, he bitterly opposed Caesar's protégé, Mark Antony. During the second triumvirate, Octavius allowed Antony to condemn Cicero to death, and he was executed.

[2]                    "Now purer air
Meets his approach, and to the heart inspires
Vernal delight and joy, able to drive
All sadness but despair."—*Milton*. [FH]

*Paradise Lost* 4.153–156, describing Satan's discovery of Eden.

[3] Mount Gargano. "This ridge of mountains forms a very large promontory advancing into the Adriatic, and separated from the Apennines on the west by the plains of Lucera and San Severo. We took a [Next morning we took a pleasant] ride into the heart of the mountains, through shady dells and noble woods, which brought to our minds the venerable groves, that in ancient times bent with the loud winds sweeping along the rugged sides of Garganus.

            'Aquilonibus
    Querceta Gargani laborant
    Et foliis viduantur orni.' —Horace.

There is still a respectable forest of evergreen and common oak, pine, horn beam, chesnut, and manna-ash. The sheltered vallies are industriously cultivated, and seem to be blest with [an excellent soil, and] luxuriant vegetation."—*Swinburne's Travels*. [FH]

Henry Swinburne (1743–1803), *Travels in the Two Sicilies, In the Years 1777, 1778, 1779, and 1780*, 2 vols. (London: P. Elmsly, 1783), "Journey to Taranto" 1.155–56. The first sentence "This ridge . . .") is not in this text; the first sentence FH quotes after the verse ("There is still . . .") precedes it. The verse is from Horace's *Carminum, Liber Secundus* IX (*non semper imbres*), translated by Samuel Johnson: "Nor Valgius, on the Armenian shores, / Do the chained waters always freeze; / Nor always furious Boreas roars, / Or bends with violent force the trees."

[4]         "In yonder nether world where shall I seek
     His bright appearances, or footstep trace?"—*Milton*. [FH]

Adam laments to the archangel Michael that he will not be able to show his children the places where God had visited him in Eden. (*Paradise Lost* 11.328–29).

⁵ A phrase from Raphael's account of God's creation of light: "the Pleiades before him danc'd / Shedding sweet influence" (*Paradise Lost* 7.374–75); cf. the description of Rome's seven hills as "the Pleiades of Earth" (1.113–14, above).

⁶ The rhymes pointedly echo those defining Stephania in part I: compare *bright / light* to 147–48, *throw / glow* to 155–56, *air / wear* to 263–64, and *fraught / thought* to 145–46. Not only is this semantic of key rhymes one Byron perfected in his tales, but readers of *The Giaour* and *Lara* would also grasp FH's allusion to a Byronic heroine in page's guise.

⁷ In Byron's portrait of the charismatic, mysterious hero of *The Corsair* (1814)—a type that is given female fashioning in Guido—this rhyme is a keynote: "And oft perforce his rising lip reveals / The haughtier thought it curbs, but scarce conceals" (1.205–6).

⁸ One of Rome's seven hills, later the site of the emperor's palace.

⁹ Cf. the rhymes at 1.79–80 and the poem's closing couplet.

¹⁰ The Lord speaks thus to the prophet Elijah (1 Kings 19.12).

¹¹ This sonnet-stanza renders a lurid parody of this traditional form for sentiment.

¹² Compare to the rhymes at 1.147–48 and 2.44.

¹³ Cf. *The Bride of the Greek Isle* 210 for an interesting recasting of this rhyme word.

¹⁴ Cf. the public history of "the sons of Rome" (1.4) and the "sons of future days" (2.332).

¹⁵ FH leaves ambiguous whether "we" is a general or gendered reference.

¹⁶ This stanza, evoking a sonnet sestet, concludes in an echo of Eloisa's lament in Pope's *Eloisa to Abelard*: "How happy is the blameless Vestal's lot! / The world forgetting by the world forgot" (197–98).

---

## The *Abencerrage*

[The last refuge of the Moors, Granada, an ornate city in southern Spain at the foot of the Sierra Nevada, was conquered in January 1492 by Ferdinand of Aragon and Isabella of Castile. FH's tale involves lovers from enemy clans, the Abencerrages and the Zegris, whose feuding made them vulnerable to conquest. As in Dryden's heroic drama *The Conquest of Granada* (1670), a love story unfolds against political conflict. Among modern influences are Byron's popular "Eastern tales," especially *The Bride of Abydos* and *The Corsair*, and a long verse tale in Thomas Moore's *Lalla Rookh* (1817), "The Fire-Worshippers," set in the time of the Gheber (Persian) resistance to the conquering Muslims, treating the doomed love of a young Gheber man and the daughter of the Arabian general sent to quell the rebellion. Following Dryden's *Conquest* and Byron's *Corsair*, FH uses heroic couplets. In the 2d edition (1824) and in *1839*, *The Abencerrage* leads *Tales*, perhaps to appeal to contemporary British interest in Spanish nationalism.]

> *Le Maure ne se venge pas parce que sa colère dure encore, mais parce que la vengeance seule peut écarter de sa tête le poids d'infamie dont il est accablé. Il se venge, parce qu'à ses yeux il n'y a qu'une âme basse qui puisse pardonner les affronts; et il nourrit sa rancune, parce que, s'il la sentoit s'éteindre, il croiroit avec elle avoir perdu une vertu.*
>
> SISMONDI¹

The events with which the following tale is interwoven, are related in the "Historia de las Guerras civiles de Granada."² They occurred in the reign of Abo Abdeli or Abdali, the last Moorish king of that city, called by the Spaniards *El Rey Chico*. The conquest of Granada, by Ferdinand and Isa-

bella, is said, by some historians, to have been greatly facilitated by the
Abencerrages, whose defection was the result of the repeated injuries they
had received from the king, at the instigation of the Zegris. One of the
most beautiful halls of the Alhambra is pointed out as the scene where so
many of the former celebrated tribe were massacred; and it still retains their
name, being called the "Sala de los Abencerrages." Many of the most interesting old Spanish ballads relate to the events of this chivalrous and romantic period.[3]

[CANTO I]

Lonely and still are now thy marble halls,
   Thou fair Alhambra! there the feast is o'er;
And with the murmur of thy fountain-falls,
   Blend the wild tones of minstrelsy no more.

Hush'd are the voices, that in years gone by,
   Have mourn'd, exulted, menaced, through thy towers;
Within thy pillar'd courts the grass waves high,
   And all uncultured bloom thy fairy bowers.

Unheeded there the flowering myrtle blows,[4]
   Through tall arcades unmark'd the sunbeam smiles,          10
And many a tint of soften'd brilliance throws
   O'er fretted walls, and shining peristyles.°          *colonnades*

And well might Fancy deem thy fabrics° lone,          *buildings*
   So vast, so silent, and so wildly fair,
Some charm'd abode of Beings all unknown,
   Powerful and viewless, children of the air.

For there no footstep treads th' enchanted ground,
   There not a sound the deep repose pervades,
Save winds and founts, diffusing freshness round,
   Through the light domes and graceful colonnades.          20

Far other tones have swell'd those courts along,
   In days romance yet fondly loves to trace;
The clash of arms, the voice of choral song,
   The revels, combats, of a vanish'd race.

And yet awhile, at Fancy's potent call,
   Shall rise that race, the chivalrous, the bold!
Peopling once more each fair, forsaken hall,
   With stately forms, the knights and chiefs of old.

   —The sun declines—upon Nevada's height,
There dwells a mellow'd flush of rosy light;          30

Each soaring pinnacle of mountain snow,
Smiles in the richness of that parting glow,
And Darro's wave° reflects each passing dye,                    *(river of Granada)*
That melts and mingles in th' empurpled sky.
Fragrance, exhaled from rose and citron bower,
Blends with the dewy freshness of the hour:
Hush'd are the winds, and Nature seems to sleep
In light and stillness; wood, and tower, and steep,
Are dyed with tints of glory, only given
To the rich evening of a southern heaven;                                        40
Tints of the sun, whose bright farewell is fraught
With all that art hath dreamt, but never caught.
—Yes, Nature sleeps; but not with her at rest
The fiery passions of the human breast.
Hark! from th' Alhambra's towers what stormy sound,
Each moment deepening, wildly swells around?
Those are no tumults of a festal throng,
Not the light zambra,⁵ nor the choral song:
The combat rages—'tis the shout of war,
'Tis the loud clash of shield and scymitar.                                      50
Within the hall of Lions,⁶ where the rays
Of eve, yet lingering, on the fountain blaze;
There, girt and guarded by his Zegri bands,
And stern in wrath, the Moorish monarch stands;
There the strife centres—swords around him wave;
There bleed the fallen, there contend the brave,
While echoing domes return the battle-cry,
"Revenge and freedom! let the tyrant die!"
And onward rushing, and prevailing still,
Court, hall, and tower, the fierce avengers fill.                                60

But first and bravest of that gallant train,
Where foes are mightiest, charging ne'er in vain;
In his red hand the sabre glancing bright,
His dark eye flashing with a fiercer light,
Ardent, untired, scarce conscious that he bleeds,
His Aben-Zurrahs⁷ there young Hamet leads;
While swells his voice that wild acclaim on high,
"Revenge and freedom! let the tyrant die!"

Yes, trace the footsteps of the warrior's wrath,
By helm and corslet shatter'd in his path;                                       70
And by the thickest harvest of the slain,
And by the marble's deepest crimson stain:
Search through the serried fight, where loudest cries
From triumph, anguish, or despair arise;

And brightest where the shivering° falchions[8] glare,                    *shattered*
And where the ground is reddest—he is there.
Yes, that young arm, amidst the Zegri host,
Hath well avenged a sire, a brother, lost.
They perish'd—not as heroes should have died,
On the red field, in victory's hour of pride,                              80
In all the glow and sunshine of their fame,
And proudly smiling as the death-pang came:
Oh! had they *thus* expired, a warrior's tear
Had flow'd, almost in triumph, o'er their bier.
For thus alone the brave should weep for those,
Who brightly pass in glory to repose.
—Not such their fate—a tyrant's stern command,
Doom'd them to fall by some ignoble hand,
As, with the flower of all their high-born race,
Summon'd, Abdallah's royal feast to grace,                                 90
Fearless in heart, no dream of danger nigh,
They sought the banquet's gilded hall—to die.
Betray'd, unarm'd, they fell—the fountain wave
Flow'd crimson with the life-blood of the brave,
Till far the fearful tidings of their fate
Through the wide city rung from gate to gate,
And of that lineage each surviving son,
Rush'd to the scene where vengeance might be won.

    For this young Hamet mingles in the strife,
Leader of battle, prodigal of life,                                        100
Urging his followers, till their foes beset
Stand faint and breathless, but undaunted yet.
Brave Aben-Zurrahs, on! one effort more,
Yours is the triumph, and the conflict o'er.

    But lo! descending o'er the darken'd hall,
The twilight-shadows fast and deeply fall,
Nor yet the strife hath ceased—though scarce they know,
Through that thick gloom, the brother from the foe;
Till the moon rises with her cloudless ray,
The peaceful moon, and gives them light to slay.                           110

    Where lurks Abdallah?—'midst his yielding train,
They seek the guilty monarch, but in vain.
He lies not number'd with the valiant dead,
His champions round him have not vainly bled;
But when the twilight spread her shadowy veil,
And his last warriors found each effort fail,
In wild despair he fled—a trusted few,
Kindred in crime, are still in danger true;

And o'er the scene of many a martial deed,
The Vega's⁹ green expanse, his flying footsteps lead.                    120
He passed th' Alhambra's calm and lovely bowers,
Where slept the glistening leaves and folded flowers
In dew and starlight—there from grot and cave,
Gush'd, in wild music, many a sparkling wave;
There, on each breeze, the breath of fragrance rose,
And all was freshness, beauty, and repose.

    But thou, dark monarch! in thy bosom reign
Storms that, once roused, shall never sleep again.
Oh! vainly bright is Nature in the course
Of him who flies from terror or remorse!                    130
A spell is round him which obscures her bloom,
And dims her skies with shadows of the tomb;
There smiles no Paradise on earth so fair,
But guilt will raise avenging phantoms there.

    Abdallah heeds not, though the light gale roves
Fraught with rich odour, stolen from orange-groves,
Hears not the sounds from wood and brook that rise,
Wild notes of Nature's vesper-melodies;
Marks not, how lovely, on the mountain's head,
Moonlight and snow their mingling lustre spread;                    140
But urges onward, till his weary band,
Worn with their toil, a moment's pause demand.
He stops, and turning, on Granada's fanes
In silence gazing, fix'd awhile remains;
In stern, deep silence—o'er his feverish brow,
And burning cheek, pure breezes freshly blow,
But waft, in fitful murmurs, from afar,
Sounds, indistinctly fearful,—as of war.
What meteor bursts, with sudden blaze, on high,
O'er the blue clearness of the starry sky?                    150
Awful it rises, like some Genie°-form,                    *demon*
Seen 'midst the redness of the desert storm,¹⁰
Magnificently dread—above, below,
Spreads the wild splendour of its deepening glow.
Lo! from th' Alhambra's towers the vivid glare
Streams through the still transparence of the air,
Avenging crowds have lit the mighty pyre,
Which feeds the waving pyramid of fire;
And dome and minaret, river, wood, and height,
From dim perspective start to ruddy light.                    160

    Oh heaven! the anguish of Abdallah's soul,
The rage, though fruitless, yet beyond control!

Yet must he cease to gaze, and raving fly,
For life—such life as makes it bliss to die!
On yon green height, the mosque, but half reveal'd
Through cypress-groves, a safe retreat may yield.
Thither his steps are bent—yet oft he turns,
Watching that fearful beacon as it burns.
But paler grow the sinking flames at last,
Flickering they fade, their crimson light is past,                        170
And spiry vapours, rising o'er the scene,
Mark where the terrors of their wrath have been.
And now his feet have reach'd that lonely pile,°                  *building*
Where grief and terror may repose awhile;
Embower'd it stands, 'midst wood and cliff on high,
Through the gray rocks a torrent sparkling nigh;
He hails the scene where every care should cease,
And all—except the heart he brings—is peace.

There is deep stillness in those halls of state,
Where the loud cries of conflict rung so late;                            180
Stillness like that, when fierce the Kamsin's blast
Hath o'er the dwellings of the desert pass'd.[11]
Fearful the calm—nor voice, nor step, nor breath,
Disturbs that scene of beauty and of death:
Those vaulted roofs re-echo not a sound,
Save the wild gush of waters—murmuring round,
In ceaseless melodies of plaintive tone,
Through chambers peopled by the dead alone.
O'er the mosaic floors, with carnage red,
Breastplate, and shield, and cloven helm are spread                       190
In mingled fragments—glittering to the light
Of yon still moon, whose rays, yet softly bright,
Their streaming lustre tremulously shed,
And smile, in placid beauty, o'er the dead:
O'er features, where the fiery spirit's trace,
E'en death itself is powerless to efface,
O'er those, who flush'd with ardent youth, awoke,
When glowing morn in bloom and radiance broke,
Nor dreamt how near the dark and frozen sleep,
Which hears not Glory call, nor Anguish weep,                             200
In the low silent house, the narrow spot,
Home of forgetfulness—and soon forgot.

But slowly fade the stars—the night is o'er—
Morn beams on those who hail her light no more;
Slumberers who ne'er shall wake on earth again,
Mourners, who call the loved, the lost, in vain.

Yet smiles the day—oh! not for mortal tear
Doth nature deviate from her calm career,
Nor is the earth less laughing or less fair,
Though breaking hearts her gladness may not share.                    210
O'er the cold urn the beam of summer glows,
O'er fields of blood the zephyr freshly blows;
Bright shines the sun, though all be dark below,
And skies arch cloudless o'er a world of woe,
And flowers renew'd in spring's green pathway bloom,
Alike to grace the banquet and the tomb.[12]

  Within Granada's walls the funeral-rite
Attends that day of loveliness and light;
And many a chief, with dirges and with tears,
Is gathered to the brave of other years:                    220
And Hamet, as beneath the cypress-shade
His martyr'd brother and his sire are laid,
Feels every deep resolve, and burning thought
Of ampler vengeance, e'en to passion wrought;
Yet is the hour afar—and he must brood
O'er those dark dreams awhile in solitude.
Tumult and rage are hush'd—another day
In still solemnity hath pass'd away,
In that deep slumber of exhausted wrath,
The calm that follows in the tempest's path.                    230

  And now Abdallah leaves yon peaceful fane,
His ravaged city traversing again.
No sound of gladness his approach precedes,
No splendid pageant the procession leads,
Where'er he moves the silent streets along,
Broods a stern quiet o'er the sullen throng;
No voice is heard—but in each alter'd eye,
Once brightly beaming when his steps were nigh,
And in each look of those, whose love hath fled
From all on earth to slumber with the dead,                    240
Those, by his guilt made desolate, and thrown
On the bleak wilderness of life alone.
In youth's quick glance of scarce-dissembled rage,
And the pale mien of calmly-mournful age,
May well be read a dark and fearful tale
Of thought that ill th' indignant heart can veil,
And passion, like the hush'd volcano's power,
That waits in stillness its appointed hour.

  No more the clarion, from Granada's walls,
Heard o'er the Vega, to the tourney calls;                    250

No more her graceful daughters, throned on high,
Bend o'er the lists° the darkly-radiant eye;          *tournament contestants*
Silence and gloom her palaces o'erspread,
And song is hush'd, and pageantry is fled.
—Weep, fated city! o'er thy heroes weep—
Low in the dust the sons of glory sleep!
Furl'd are their banners in the lonely hall,
Their trophied shields hang mouldering on the wall,
Wildly their chargers range the pastures o'er,
Their voice in battle shall be heard no more;                          260
And they, who still thy tyrant's wrath survive,
Whom he hath wrong'd too deeply to forgive,
That race, of lineage high, of worth approved,
The chivalrous, the princely, the beloved;
Thine Aben-Zurrahs—they no more shall wield
In thy proud cause the conquering lance and shield:
Condemned to bid the cherish'd scenes farewell
Where the loved ashes of their fathers dwell,
And far o'er foreign plains, as exiles roam,
Their land the desert, and the grave their home.                       270
Yet there is one shall see that race depart,
In deep, though silent, agony of heart;
One whose dark fate must be to mourn alone,
Unseen her sorrows, and their cause unknown,
And veil her heart, and teach her cheek to wear
That smile, in which the spirit hath no share;
Like the bright beams that shed their fruitless glow
O'er the cold solitude of Alpine snow.

    Soft, fresh, and silent, is the midnight hour,
And the young Zayda seeks her lonely bower;                            280
That Zegri maid, within whose gentle mind,
One name is deeply, secretly enshrined.
That name in vain stern Reason would efface,
Hamet! 'tis thine, thou foe to all her race!

    And yet not hers in bitterness to prove
The sleepless pangs of unrequited love;
Pangs, which the rose of wasted youth consume,
And make the heart of all delight the tomb,
Check the free spirit in its eagle-flight,
And the spring-morn of early genius blight;                           290
Not such her grief—though now she wakes to weep,
While tearless eyes enjoy the honey-dews of sleep.[13]

    A step treads lightly through the citron-shade,
Lightly, but by the rustling leaves betray'd—

Doth her young hero seek that well-known spot,
Scene of past hours that ne'er may be forgot?
'Tis he—but changed that eye, whose glance of fire
Could, like a sunbeam, hope and joy inspire,
As, luminous with youth, with ardor fraught,
It spoke of glory to the inmost thought;                    300
Thence the bright spirit's eloquence hath fled,
And in its wild expression may be read
Stern thoughts and fierce resolves—now veil'd in shade,
And now in characters of fire pourtray'd.
Changed e'en his voice—as thus its mournful tone
Wakes in her heart each feeling of his own.

  "Zayda, my doom is fix'd—another day,
And the wrong'd exile shall be far away;
Far from the scenes where still his heart must be,
His home of youth, and, more than all—from thee.           310
Oh! what a cloud hath gather'd o'er my lot,
Since last we met on this fair tranquil spot!
Lovely as then, the soft and silent hour,
And not a rose hath faded from thy bower;
But I—my hopes the tempest hath o'erthrown,
And changed my heart, to all but thee alone.
Farewell, high thoughts! inspiring hopes of praise,
Heroic visions of my early days!
In me the glories of my race must end,
The exile hath no country to defend!                        320
E'en in life's morn, my dreams of pride are o'er,
Youth's buoyant spirit wakes for me no more,
And one wild feeling in my alter'd breast
Broods darkly o'er the ruins of the rest.
Yet fear not thou—to thee, in good or ill,
The heart, so sternly tried, is faithful still!
But when my steps are distant, and my name
Thou hear'st no longer in the song of fame,
When Time steals on, in silence to efface
Of early love each pure and sacred trace,                   330
Causing our sorrows and our hopes to seem
But as the moonlight pictures of a dream,
Still shall thy soul be with me, in the truth
And all the fervor of affection's youth?
—If such thy love, one beam of heaven shall play
In lonely beauty, o'er thy wanderer's way."

  "Ask not, if such my love! oh! trust the mind
To grief so long, so silently resign'd!

Let the light spirit, ne'er by sorrow taught
The pure and lofty constancy of thought, 340
Its fleeting trials eager to forget,
Rise with elastic power o'er each regret!
Foster'd in tears, *our* young affection grew,
And I have learn'd to suffer and be true.
Deem not my love a frail, ephemeral flower,
Nursed by soft sunshine and the balmy shower;
No! 'tis the child of tempests, and defies,
And meets unchanged, the anger of the skies!
Too well I feel, with grief's prophetic heart,
That, ne'er to meet in happier days, we part. 350
We part! and e'en this agonizing hour,
When love first feels his own o'erwhelming power,
Shall soon to Memory's fix'd and tearful eye
Seem almost happiness—for thou wert nigh!
Yes! when this heart in solitude shall bleed,
As days to days all wearily succeed,
When doom'd to weep in loneliness, 'twill be
Almost like rapture to have wept with thee.

But thou, my Hamet, thou can'st yet bestow
All that of joy my blighted lot can know. 360
Oh! be thou still the high-soul'd and the brave,
To whom my first and fondest vows I gave,
In thy proud fame's untarnish'd beauty still
The lofty visions of my youth fulfil,
So shall it soothe me, 'midst my heart's despair,
To hold undimm'd one glorious image there!"

"Zayda, my best-beloved! my words too well,
Too soon, thy bright illusions must dispel;
Yet must my soul to thee unveil'd be shown,
And all its dreams and all its passions known. 370
Thou shalt not be deceived—for pure as heaven
Is thy young love, in faith and fervor given.
I said my heart was changed—and would thy thought
Explore the ruin by thy kindred wrought,
In fancy trace the land whose towers and fanes,
Crush'd by the earthquake, strew its ravaged plains,
And such that heart—where desolation's hand
Hath blighted all that once was fair or grand!
But Vengeance, fix'd upon her burning throne,
Sits 'midst the wreck in silence and alone, 380
And I, in stern devotion at her shrine,
Each softer feeling, but my love, resign.

—Yes! they whose spirits all my thoughts control,
Who hold dread converse with my thrilling soul;
They, the betray'd, the sacrificed, the brave,
Who fill a blood-stain'd and untimely grave,
Must be avenged! and pity and remorse,
In that stern cause, are banish'd from my course.
Zayda, thou tremblest—and thy gentle breast
Shrinks from the passions that destroy my rest;                    390
Yet shall thy form, in many a stormy hour,
Pass brightly o'er my soul with softening power,
And oft recall'd, thy voice beguile my lot,
Like some sweet lay, once heard, and ne'er forgot.

   But the night wanes—the hours too swiftly fly,
The bitter moment of farewell draws nigh,
Yet, loved one! weep not thus—in joy or pain,
Oh! trust thy Hamet, we shall meet again!
Yes, we shall meet! and haply smile at last
On all the clouds and conflicts of the past.                    400
On that fair vision teach thy thoughts to dwell,
Nor deem these mingling tears our last farewell!"

   Is the voice hush'd, whose loved, expressive tone
Thrill'd to her heart, and doth she weep alone?
Alone she weeps—that hour of parting o'er—
When shall the pang it leaves be felt no more?
The gale breathes light, and fans her bosom fair,
Showering the dewy rose-leaves o'er her hair;
But ne'er for her shall dwell reviving power,
In balmy dew, soft breeze, or fragrant flower,                    410
To wake once more that calm, serene delight,
The soul's young bloom, which passion's breath could blight;
The smiling stillness of life's morning hour,
Ere yet the day-star burns in all his power.

   Meanwhile, through groves of deep luxuriant shade,
In the rich foliage of the South array'd,
Hamet, ere dawns the earliest blush of day,
Bends to the vale of tombs his pensive way.
Fair is that scene where palm and cypress wave
On high o'er many an Aben-Zurrah's grave,                    420
Lonely and fair—its fresh and glittering leaves,
With the young myrtle there the laurel weaves,[14]
To canopy the dead—nor wanting there
Flowers to the turf, nor fragrance to the air,
Nor wood-bird's note, nor fall of plaintive stream,

Wild music, soothing to the mourner's dream.
There sleep the chiefs of old—their combats o'er,
The voice of glory thrills their hearts no more;
Unheard by them th' awakening clarion blows;
The sons of war at length in peace repose.                               430
No martial note is in the gale that sighs,
Where proud their trophied sepulchres arise,
'Mid founts, and shades, and flowers of brightest bloom,
As in his native vale some shepherd's tomb.

   There, where the trees their thickest foliage spread
Dark o'er that silent valley of the dead,
Where two fair pillars rise, embower'd and lone,
Not yet with ivy clad, with moss o'ergrown,
Young Hamet kneels—while thus his vows are pour'd,
The fearful vows that consecrate his sword.                              440
—"Spirit of him, who first within my mind
Each loftier aim, each nobler thought enshrined,
And taught my steps the line of light to trace
Left by the glorious fathers of my race,
Hear thou my voice—for thine is with me still,
In every dream its tones my bosom thrill,
In the deep calm of midnight they are near,
'Midst busy throngs they vibrate on my ear,
Still murmuring 'vengeance!'—nor in vain the call,
Few, few shall triumph in a hero's fall!                                 450
Cold as thine own to glory and to fame,
Within my heart there lives one only aim,
There, till th' oppressor for thy fate atone,
Concentring every thought, it reigns alone.
I will not weep—revenge, not grief, must be,
And blood, not tears, an offering meet for thee,
But the dark hour of stern delight will come,
And thou shalt triumph, warrior! in thy tomb.

   Thou, too, my brother! thou art pass'd away,
Without thy fame, in life's fair dawning day.                            460
Son of the brave! of thee no trace will shine
In the proud annals of thy lofty line,
Nor shall thy deeds be deathless in the lays
That hold communion with the after-days.
Yet by the wreaths thou might'st have nobly won,
Had'st thou but lived till rose thy noontide sun,
By glory lost, I swear, by hope betray'd,
Thy fate shall amply, dearly, be repaid;

War with thy foes I deem a holy strife,
And to avenge thy death, devote my life.                          470

Hear ye my vows, O spirits of the slain!
Hear, and be with me on the battle-plain;
At noon, at midnight, still around me bide,
Rise on my dreams, and tell me how ye died!"

[1] The Moor does not avenge himself because his anger still remains, but because revenge alone can relieve his head of the weight of infamy by which it is overwhelmed. He avenges himself, because in his eyes it is only a base soul that can pardon affronts, and he feeds his rancor, because if he felt it go out, he would believe with this, to have lost a virtue.
  J-C.L. Simonde de Sismondi, *Histoire des Républiques Italiennes du Moyen Âge* (Paris, 1809–18), ch. cxxvii. In this final chapter, Sismondi critiques the code of vendetta that disseminated from the Moors to Spain and then to the rest of Europe.
[2] This purported translation and adaptation by Ginés Pérez de Hita of an Arabic original (first published in the late sixteenth century) contains an account of the lovers but emphasizes clan warfare. Hemans owned "De Hita, Wars of the 'Zegrii y Abencerrages'" (Lawrence 237).
[3] *Alhambra*: a complex of ornate buildings in Granada. "Romantic" refers to the literary genre of the romance. For "ballads," see the note to *Songs of the Cid*. The opening inset song is in elegiac stanzas, so called from Thomas Gray's popular *Elegy Written in a Country Churchyard* (1751).
[4] An evergreen associated with Venus.
[5] Zambra, a Moorish dance. [FH]
  *Scimitar*: short, curved sword used by Muslim warriors.
[6] The hall of Lions was the principal one of the Alhambra, and was so called from twelve sculptured lions which supported an alabaster basin in the centre. [FH]
[7] Aben-Zurrahs; the name thus written is taken from the translation of an Arabic MS. given in the 3d volume of Bourgoanne's Travels through Spain. [FH]
  Jean François, Chevalier de Bourgoanne (1748–1811), *Nouveau voyage en Espagne*, trans. as *Travels in Spain: Containing a New, Accurate, & Comprehensive View of the Present State of that Country*, 3 vols. (London: G. G. and J. Robinson, 1789). In the Arabic MS (3.220–22), the name is "Mahomed Aben Zurrah."
[8] *Falchions*: broad swords with a convex edge.
[9] The Vega, the plain surrounding Granada, the scene of frequent actions between the Moors and Christians. [FH]
[10] An extreme redness in the sky is the presage of the Simoom.—See *Bruce's Travels*. [FH]
  James Bruce (1730–94), *Travels to Discover the Source of the Nile, in the Years 1768, 1769, 1770, 1771, 1772, and 1793*, 6 vols. (1790; Dublin, 1791) 5.321. *Simoom*: hot south wind.
[11] Of the Kamsin, a hot south wind, common in Egypt, we have the following account in Volney's Travels. "These winds are known in Egypt by the general name of winds of fifty days, because they prevail more frequently in the fifty days preceding and following the equinox. They are mentioned by travellers under the name of the poisonous winds, or hot winds of the desert: their heat is so excessive, that it is difficult to form any idea of its violence without having experienced it. When they begin to blow, the sky, at other times so clear in this climate, becomes dark and heavy; the sun loses his splendor, and appears of a violet colour; the air is not cloudy, but grey and thick, and is filled with a subtle dust, which penetrates every where: respiration becomes short and difficult, the skin parched and dry, the lungs are contracted and painful, and the body consumed with internal heat. In vain is coolness sought for; marble, iron, water, though the sun no longer appears, are hot: the streets are deserted, and a dead silence appears every where. The natives of towns and villages shut themselves up in their houses, and those of the desert in tents, or holes dug in the earth, where they wait the termination of this

heat, which generally lasts three days. Woe to the traveller whom it surprises remote from shelter: he must suffer all its dreadful effects, which are sometimes mortal." [FH]

François Chasseboeuf, Count de Volney (1757–1820), "Du Vent Chaud, ou Kamsin," *Voyage en Egypte et en Syrie* (1787; rev. 1791). FH's translation; cf. "Of the hot Wind, or Kamsin," in *Travels Through Syria and Egypt in the Years 1783, 1784, and 1785. Containing the Present Natural and Political State of Those Countries*, 2 vols. (London: G. G. and J. Robinson, 1805) 1.56–58. Traveler, economist, and historian Volney is best known for *Les Ruines; ou, Méditations sur les révolutions des empires* (Ruins, or Meditations on the revolutions of empires; 1791), inspired by his enthusiasm for the French Revolution, and revered as one of the primers of modern radical-infidel republicanism.

[12] This stanza and the next are embedded sonnets, a common Romantic-era form employed with thematic significance throughout this poem: 1.293–306; 2.253–66 and 345–58; 3.331–44, 465–78, 543–56, 557–70, 607–20 (the poem's close).

[13] "Enjoy the honey-heavy-dew of slumber."—*Shakspeare.* [FH]

Regarding his sleeping minstrel, guilt-ridden conspirator Brutus bids him "Enjoy the honey-heavy dew of slumber. / Thou hast no figures nor no fantasies / Which busy care draws in the brains of men; / Therefore thou sleep'st so sound" (*Julius Caesar* 2.1.230).

[14] Emblems, respectively, of love and military honor.


CANTO II


———*Oh! ben provvide il Cielo*
*Ch' Uom per delitti mai lieto non sia.*
ALFIERI[1]


Fair land! of chivalry the old domain,
Land of the vine and olive, lovely Spain!
Though not for thee with classic shores to vie
In charms that fix th' enthusiast's pensive eye;
Yet hast thou scenes of beauty, richly fraught
With all that wakes the glow of lofty thought;
Fountains, and vales, and rocks, whose ancient name
High deeds have raised to mingle with their fame.
Those scenes are peaceful now: the citron blows,
Wild spreads the myrtle, where the brave repose.        10
No sound of battle swells on Douro's shore,
And banners wave on Ebro's banks no more.
But who, unmoved, unawed, shall coldly tread
Thy fields that sepulchre the mighty dead?
Blest be that soil! where England's heroes share
The grave of chiefs, for ages slumbering there;[2]
Whose names are glorious in romantic lays,
The wild, sweet chronicles of elder days,
By goatherd lone, and rude serrano° sung,        *mountaineer*
Thy cypress dells, and vine-clad rocks among.        20
How oft those rocks have echo'd to the tale
Of knights who fell in Roncesvalles' vale;
Of him, renown'd in old heroic lore,

First of the brave, the gallant Campeador;
Of those, the famed in song, who proudly died,
When "Rio Verde" roll'd a crimson tide;
Or that high name, by Garcilaso's might,
On the green Vega won in single fight.[3]

Round fair Granada, deepening from afar,
O'er that green Vega rose the din of war.                           30
At morn or eve no more the sunbeams shone
O'er a calm scene, in pastoral beauty lone;
On helm and corslet tremulous they glanced,
On shield and spear in quivering lustre danced.
Far as the sight by clear Xenil° could rove,        *(river in Granada)*
Tents rose around, and banners waved above,
And steeds in gorgeous trappings, armour bright
With gold, reflecting every tint of light,
And many a floating plume, and blazon'd shield,
Diffused romantic splendor o'er the field.                         40

There swell those sounds that bid the life-blood start
Swift to the mantling cheek, and beating heart.
The clang of echoing steel, the charger's neigh,
The measured tread of hosts in war's array;
And oh! that music, whose exulting breath
Speaks but of glory on the road to death;
In whose wild voice there dwells inspiring power
To wake the stormy joy of danger's hour;
To nerve the arm, the spirit to sustain,
Rouse from despondence, and support in pain;                       50
And midst the deepening tumults of the strife,
Teach every pulse to thrill with more than life.

High o'er the camp, in many a broider'd fold,
Floats to the wind a standard rich with gold:
There, imaged on the cross, *his* form appears,
Who drank for man the bitter cup of tears.[4]
*His* form, whose word recall'd the spirit fled,
Now borne by hosts to guide them o'er the dead!
O'er yon fair walls to plant that cross on high,
Spain hath sent forth her flower of chivalry.                      60
Fired with that ardor, which, in days of yore,
To Syrian plains the bold crusaders bore;
Elate with lofty hope, with martial zeal,
They come, the gallant children of Castile;
The proud, the calmly dignified:—and there
Ebro's dark sons with haughty mien repair,

And those who guide the fiery steed of war
From yon rich province of the western star.[5]

But thou, conspicuous midst the glittering scene,
Stern grandeur stamp'd upon thy princely mien;                    70
Known by the foreign garb, the silvery vest,
The snow-white charger, and the azure crest,[6]
Young Aben-Zurrah! midst that host of foes,
Why shines *thy* helm, thy Moorish lance? Disclose!
Why rise the tents, where dwell thy kindred train,
O son of Afric, midst the sons of Spain?
Hast thou with these thy nation's fall conspired,
Apostate chief! by hope of vengeance fired?
How art thou changed! Still first in every fight,
Hamet, the Moor! Castile's devoted knight!                        80
There dwells a fiery lustre in thine eye,
But not the light that shone in days gone by;
There is wild ardor in thy look and tone,
But not the soul's expression once thine own,
Nor aught like peace within. Yet who shall say
What secret thoughts thine inmost heart may sway?
No eye but heaven's may pierce that curtain'd breast,
Whose joys and griefs alike are unexprest.

There hath been combat on the tented plain;
The Vega's turf is red with many a stain,                         90
And rent and trampled, banner, crest, and shield,
Tell of a fierce and well-contested field;
But all is peaceful now—the west is bright
With the rich splendor of departing light;
Mulhacen's peak, half lost amidst the sky,
Glows like a purple evening-cloud on high,
And tints that mock the pencil's art° o'erspread          *painting*
Th' eternal snow that crowns Veleta's head,[7]
While the warm sunset o'er the landscape throws
A solemn beauty, and a deep repose.                              100
Closed are the toils and tumults of the day,
And Hamet wanders from the camp away,
In silent musings rapt:—the slaughter'd brave
Lie thickly strewn by Darro's rippling wave.
Soft fall the dews—but other drops have dyed
The scented shrubs that fringe the river side,
Beneath whose shade, as ebbing life retired,
The wounded sought a shelter,—and expired.[8]
Lonely, and lost in thoughts of other days,
By the bright windings of the stream he strays,                  110

Till more remote from battle's ravaged scene,
All is repose, and solitude serene.
There, 'neath an olive's ancient shade reclined,
Whose rustling foliage waves in evening's wind,
The harass'd warrior, yielding to the power,
The mild sweet influence[9] of the tranquil hour,
Feels by degrees a long forgotten calm
Shed o'er his troubled soul unwonted balm;
His wrongs, his woes, his dark and dubious lot,
The past, the future, are awhile forgot;                          120
And Hope, scarce own'd, yet stealing o'er his breast,
Half dares to whisper, "Thou shalt yet be blest!"

    Such his vague musings—but a plaintive sound
Breaks on the deep and solemn stillness round;
A low, half-stifled moan, that seems to rise
From life and death's contending agonies.
He turns: Who shares with him that lonely shade?
—A youthful warrior on his death-bed laid.
All rent and stain'd his broider'd Moorish vest,
The corslet shatter'd on his bleeding breast;                     130
In his cold hand the broken falchion strain'd,
With life's last force convulsively retain'd;
His plumage soil'd with dust, with crimson dyed,
And the red lance in fragments by his side;
He lies forsaken—pillow'd on his shield,
His helmet raised, his lineaments reveal'd.
Pale is that quivering lip, and vanish'd now
The light once throned on that commanding brow;
And o'er that fading eye, still upward cast,
The shades of death are gathering dark and fast.                  140
Yet as yon rising moon her light serene
Sheds the pale olive's waving boughs between,
Too well can Hamet's conscious heart retrace,
Though changed thus fearfully, that pallid face,
Whose every feature to his soul conveys
Some bitter thought of long departed days.

    "Oh! is it thus," he cries, "we meet at last?
Friend of my soul, in years for ever past!
Hath fate but led me hither, to behold
The last dread struggle, ere that heart is cold,                  150
Receive thy latest agonizing breath,
And with vain pity soothe the pangs of death?
Yet let me bear thee hence—while life remains,

E'en though thus feebly circling through thy veins,
Some healing balm thy sense may still revive,
Hope is not lost,—and Osmyn yet may live!
And blest were he, whose timely care should save
A heart so noble, e'en from glory's grave."

Roused by those accents, from his lowly bed,
The dying warrior faintly lifts his head; 160
O'er Hamet's mien, with vague, uncertain gaze,
His doubtful glance awhile bewilder'd strays;
Till, by degrees, a smile of proud disdain
Lights up those features late convulsed with pain;
A quivering radiance flashes from his eye,
That seems too pure, too full of soul, to die;
And the mind's grandeur, in its parting hour,
Looks from that brow with more than wonted power.

"Away!" he cries, in accents of command,
And proudly waves his cold and trembling hand, 170
"Apostate, hence! my soul shall soon be free,
E'en now it soars, disdaining aid from thee:
'Tis not for thee to close the fading eyes
Of him who faithful to his country dies;
Not for *thy* hand to raise the drooping head
Of him who sinks to rest on glory's bed.
Soon shall these pangs be closed, this conflict o'er,
And worlds be mine where thou canst never soar:
Be thine existence with a blighted name,
Mine the bright death which seals a warrior's fame!" 180

The glow hath vanish'd from his cheek—his eye
Hath lost that beam of parting energy;
Frozen and fix'd it seems—his brow is chill;
One struggle more,—that noble heart is still.
Departed warrior! were thy mortal throes,
Were thy last pangs, ere Nature found repose,
More keen, more bitter, than th' envenomed dart,
Thy dying words have left in Hamet's heart?
*Thy* pangs were transient; *his* shall sleep no more
Till life's delirious dream itself is o'er; 190
But thou shalt rest in glory, and thy grave
Be the pure altar of the patriot brave.

Oh, what a change that little hour hath wrought
In the high spirit, and unbending thought!
Yet, from himself each keen regret to hide,

Still Hamet struggles with indignant pride;
While his soul rises, gathering all its force,
To meet the fearful conflict with remorse.

To thee, at length, whose artless love hath been
His own, unchanged, through many a stormy scene;       200
Zayda! to thee his heart for refuge flies;
Thou still art faithful to affection's ties.
Yes! let the world upbraid, let foes contemn,
Thy gentle breast the tide will firmly stem;
And soon thy smile, and soft consoling voice,
Shall bid his troubled soul again rejoice.

Within Granada's walls are hearts and hands,
Whose aid in secret Hamet yet commands;
Nor hard the task, at some propitious hour,
To win his silent way to Zayda's bower,       210
When night and peace are brooding o'er the world,
When mute the clarions, and the banners furl'd.
That hour is come—and o'er the arms he bears
A wandering fakir's° garb the chieftain wears:      *religious mendicant's*
Disguise that ill from piercing eye could hide
The lofty port, and glance of martial pride;
But night befriends—through paths obscure he pass'd,
And hail'd the lone and lovely scene at last;
Young Zayda's chosen haunt, the fair alcove,
The sparkling fountain, and the orange grove;      220
Calm in the moonlight smiles the still retreat,
As form'd alone for happy hearts to meet.
For happy hearts?—not such is hers, who there
Bends o'er her lute, with dark, unbraided hair;
That maid of Zegri race, whose eye, whose mien,
Tell that despair her bosom's guest hath been.
So lost in thought she seems, the warrior's feet
Unheard approach her solitary seat,
Till his known accents every sense restore—
"My own loved Zayda! do we meet once more?"      230

She starts, she turns—the lightning of surprise,
Of sudden rapture, flashes from her eyes;
But that is fleeting—it is past—and now
Far other meaning darkens o'er her brow;
Changed is her aspect, and her tone severe,
"Hence, Aben-Zurrah! death surrounds thee here!"

"Zayda! what means that glance, unlike thine own?
What mean those words, and that unwonted tone?

I will not deem thee changed—but in thy face,
It is not joy, it is not love, I trace!                                    240
It was not thus in other days we met:
Hath time, hath absence, taught thee to forget?
Oh! speak once more—these rising doubts dispel;
One smile of tenderness, and all is well!"

  "Not thus we met in other days!—oh no!
Thou wert not, warrior, then thy country's foe!
Those days are past—we ne'er shall meet again
With hearts all warmth, all confidence, as then.
But *thy* dark soul no gentler feelings sway,
Leader of hostile bands! away, away!                                      250
On in thy path of triumph and of power,
Nor pause to raise from earth a blighted flower."

  "And *thou* too changed! thine early vow forgot!
This, this alone was wanting to my lot!
Exiled and scorn'd, of every tie bereft,
Thy love, the desert's lonely fount, was left;
And thou, my soul's last hope, its lingering beam,
Thou, the good angel of each brighter dream,
Wert all the barrenness of life possest,
To wake one soft affection in my breast!                                  260
That vision ended—fate hath nought in store
Of joy or sorrow e'er to touch me more.
Go, Zegri maid! to scenes of sunshine fly,
From the stern pupil of adversity!
And now to hope, to confidence, adieu!
If thou art faithless, who shall e'er be true?"

  "Hamet! oh, wrong me not!—I too could speak
Of sorrows—trace them on my faded cheek,
In the sunk eye, and in the wasted form,
That tell the heart hath nursed a canker-worm!                           270
But words were idle—read my sufferings there,
Where grief is stamp'd on all that once was fair.

  Oh! wert thou still what once I fondly deem'd,
All that thy mien express'd, thy spirit seem'd,
My love had been devotion—till in death
Thy name had trembled on my latest breath.
But not the chief who leads a lawless band,
To crush the altars of his native land;
Th' apostate son of heroes, whose disgrace
Hath stain'd the trophies of a glorious race;                            280
Not *him* I loved—but one whose youthful name

Was pure and radiant in unsullied fame.
Hadst thou but died, ere yet dishonour's cloud
O'er that young name had gather'd as a shroud,
I then had mourn'd thee proudly—and my grief
In its own loftiness had found relief;
A noble sorrow, cherish'd to the last,
When every meaner woe had long been past.
Yes! let Affection weep—no common tear
She sheds, when bending o'er a hero's bier.          290
Let Nature mourn the dead—a grief like this,
To pangs that rend *my* bosom, had been bliss!"

   "High-minded maid! the time admits not now
To plead my cause, to vindicate my vow.
That vow, too dread, too solemn to recall,
Hath urged me onward, haply to my fall.
Yet this believe—no meaner aim inspires
My soul, no dream of poor ambition fires.
No! every hope of power, of triumph, fled,
Behold me but th' avenger of the dead!          300
One whose changed heart no tie, no kindred knows,
And in thy love alone hath sought repose.
Zayda! wilt *thou* his stern accuser be?
False to his country, he is true to thee!
Oh, hear me yet!—if Hamet e'er was dear,
By our first vows, our young affection, hear!
Soon must this fair and royal city fall,
Soon shall the cross be planted on her wall;
Then who can tell what tides of blood may flow,
While her fanes echo to the shrieks of woe?          310
Fly, fly with me, and let me bear thee far
From horrors thronging in the path of war:
Fly! and repose in safety—till the blast
Hath made a desert in its course—and past!"

   "Thou that wilt triumph when the hour is come,
Hasten'd by thee, to seal thy country's doom,
With *thee* from scenes of death shall Zayda fly
To peace and safety?—Woman too can die!
And die exulting, though unknown to fame,
In all the stainless beauty of her name!          320
Be mine unmurmuring, undismay'd, to share
The fate my kindred and my sire must bear.
And deem thou not my feeble heart shall fail,
When the clouds gather, and the blasts assail;

Thou hast but known me ere the trying hour
Call'd into life my spirit's latent power;
But I have energies that idly slept,
While withering o'er my silent woes I wept,
And now, when hope and happiness are fled,
My soul is firm—for what remains to dread?                  330
Who shall have power to suffer and to bear,
If strength and courage dwell not with Despair?

    Hamet, farewell!—retrace thy path again,
To join thy brethren on the tented plain.
There wave and wood in mingling murmurs tell,
How, in far other cause, thy fathers fell!
Yes! on that soil hath Glory's footstep been,
Names unforgotten consecrate the scene!
Dwell not the souls of heroes round thee there,
Whose voices call thee in the whispering air?               340
Unheard, in vain, they call—their fallen son
Hath stain'd the name those mighty spirits won,
And to the hatred of the brave and free
Bequeath'd his own, through ages yet to be!"

    Still as she spoke, th' enthusiast's kindling eye
Was lighted up with inborn majesty,
While her fair form and youthful features caught
All the proud grandeur of heroic thought,
Severely beauteous:[10] awe-struck and amazed,
In silent trance awhile the warrior gazed                   350
As on some lofty vision—for she seem'd
One all inspired—each look with glory beam'd,
While brightly bursting through its cloud of woes,
Her soul at once in all its light arose.
Oh! ne'er had Hamet deem'd there dwelt enshrined
In form so fragile that unconquer'd mind,
And fix'd, as by some high enchantment, there,
He stood—till wonder yielded to despair.[11]

    "The dream is vanish'd—daughter of my foes!
Reft of each hope the lonely wanderer goes.                 360
Thy words have pierced his soul—yet deem thou not
Thou could'st be once adored, and e'er forgot!
O form'd for happier love! heroic maid!
In grief sublime, in danger undismay'd,
Farewell, and be thou blest!—all words were vain
From him who ne'er may view that form again;

Him, whose sole thought, resembling bliss, must be,
He *hath* been loved, once fondly loved, by thee!"

And is the warrior gone?[12] doth Zayda hear
His parting footstep, and without a tear?                    370
Thou weep'st not, lofty maid!—yet who can tell
What secret pangs within thy heart may dwell?
*They* feel not least, the firm, the high in soul,
Who best each feeling's agony control.
Yes! we may judge the measure of the grief
Which finds in Misery's eloquence relief;
But who shall pierce those depths of silent woe,
Whence breathes no language, whence no tears may flow?
The pangs that many a noble breast hath proved,
Scorning itself that thus it *could* be moved?              380
He, He alone, the inmost heart who knows,
Views all its weakness, pities all its throes,
He who hath mercy when mankind contemn,
Beholding anguish—all unknown to them.

Fair city! thou, that 'midst thy stately fanes
And gilded minarets, towering o'er the plains,
In eastern grandeur proudly dost arise
Beneath thy canopy of deep-blue skies,
While streams that bear thee treasures in their wave,[13]
Thy citron-groves and myrtle-gardens lave;                  390
Mourn! for thy doom is fix'd—the days of fear,
Of chains, of wrath, of bitterness, are near!
Within, around thee, are the trophied graves
Of kings and chiefs—their children shall be slaves.
Fair are thy halls, thy domes majestic swell,
But there a race who rear'd them not shall dwell;
For 'midst thy councils Discord still presides,
Degenerate fear thy wavering monarch guides,
Last of a line whose regal spirit flown
Hath to their offspring but bequeath'd a throne,            400
Without one generous thought, or feeling high,
To teach his soul how kings should live and die.

A voice resounds within Granada's wall,
The hearts of warriors echo to its call.[14]
Whose are those tones with power electric fraught,
To reach the source of pure exalted thought?

See on a fortress-tower, with beckoning hand,
A form, majestic as a prophet, stand!

His mien is all impassion'd—and his eye
Fill'd with a light whose fountain is on high;                    410
Wild on the gale his silvery tresses flow,
And inspiration beams upon his brow,
While thronging round him breathless thousands gaze,
As on some mighty seer of elder days.

"Saw ye the banners of Castile display'd,
The helmets glittering and the line array'd?
Heard ye the march of steel-clad hosts?" he cries,
"Children of conquerors! in your strength arise!
O high-born tribes! O names unstain'd by fear!
Azarques, Zegris, Almoradis, hear!¹⁵                    420
Be every feud forgotten, and your hands
Dyed with no blood but that of hostile bands.¹⁶
Wake, princes of the land! the hour is come,
And the red sabre must decide your doom.
Where is that spirit which prevail'd of yore,
When Tarik's bands o'erspread the western shore?¹⁷
When the long combat raged on Xeres' plain,¹⁸
And Afric's tecbir swell'd through yielding Spain?¹⁹
Is the lance broken, is the shield decay'd,
The warrior's arm unstrung, his heart dismay'd?                    430
Shall no high spirit of ascendant worth
Arise to lead the sons of Islam forth?
To guard the regions where our fathers' blood
Hath bathed each plain, and mingled with each flood,
Where long their dust hath blended with the soil,
Won by their swords, made fertile by their toil?

O ye Sierras of eternal snow!
Ye streams that by the tombs of heroes flow,
Woods, fountains, rocks, of Spain! ye saw their might
In many a fierce and unforgotten fight!                    440
Shall ye behold their lost, degenerate race,
Dwell 'midst your scenes in fetters and disgrace?
With each memorial of the past around,
Each mighty monument of days renown'd?
May this indignant heart ere then be cold,
This frame be gather'd to its kindred mould!
And the last life-drop circling through my veins
Have tinged a soil untainted yet by chains!

And yet one struggle ere our doom is seal'd,
One mighty effort, one deciding field!                    450

If vain each hope, we still have choice to be,
In life the fetter'd, or in death the free!"

Still while he speaks, each gallant heart beats high,
And ardor flashes from each kindling eye;
Youth, manhood, age, as if inspired, have caught
The glow of lofty hope and daring thought,
And all is hush'd around—as every sense
Dwelt on the tones of that wild eloquence.

But when his voice hath ceased, th' impetuous cry
Of eager thousands bursts at once on high;    460
Rampart, and rock, and fortress, ring around,
And fair Alhambra's inmost halls resound.
"Lead us, O chieftain! lead us to the strife,
To fame in death, or liberty in life!"[20]
O zeal of noble hearts! in vain display'd!
High feeling wasted! generous hope betray'd!
Now, while the burning spirit of the brave
Is roused to energies that yet might save,
E'en now, enthusiasts! while ye rush to claim
Your glorious trial on the field of fame,    470
Your king hath yielded! Valour's dream is o'er;[21]
Power, wealth, and freedom, are your own no more;
And for your children's portion, *but* remains
That bitter heritage—the stranger's chains.

---

[1] Oh! well provides Heaven / That man may never be happy through crimes.
 Vittorio Alfieri (1749–1803), *Oreste* (1783), 1.2.27–28: Elettra's response to her mother Clitennestra's remorse for conspiring in the murder of her husband (Elettra's father). Poet and dramatist Alfieri was a champion of American and Italian independence.
 [2] Referring to those who fought in the Peninsular War against Napoleon.
 [3] Garcilaso de la Vega derived his surname from a single combat (in which he was the victor), with a Moor, on the Vega of Granada. [FH]
 FH included the verse of Garcilaso (?1503–36), celebrated lyric poet of the Spanish Golden Age, in *Translations* (1818); a soldier for Emperor Charles, he died in a reckless assault on a castle in Provence. The famed Roncesvalles pass in the Pyrenees was the site of Roland's heroic death in 778, when he was ambushed by Basque mountaineers while protecting Charlemagne's rear guard (see Ximena's ballad at the opening of *Siege of Valencia*). *Campeador* ("battlefield teacher") is national hero El Cid. *Rio Verde* (Green River), a ballad in de Hita's *Guerras* (1595), was translated as *Gentle River, Gentle River*, with a historical note, in Thomas Percy's popular *Reliques of Ancient English Poetry* (1765); cf. *Forest Sanctuary* 2.LIV. FH's version of this ballad would appear in *NMM*, January 1834.
 [4] "El Rey D[on] Fernando bolvió a la Vega, y puso su Real a la vista de Huécar, a veynte y seys días del mes de Abril, adonde fue fortificado de todo lo necesario, poniendo el Cristiano toda su gente en esquadrón, [formado] con todas sus vanderas tendidas, y su Real Estandarte, el qual llevava por divisa un Cristo crucificado."—*Historia de las guerras civiles de Granada.* [FH; Part 1]
 [King Ferdinand retreated to La Vega, and mounted the Royal standard within view of

Huecar, on the 26th day of the month of April, where he was sufficiently fortified; the Christian king arranged his men in squadrons, with their banners unfurled, and his Royal Standard, bearing the emblem of Christ crucified.]

In 1288, Ferdinand III, conqueror of Andalusia and King of Castile and León, acquiesced in the Moorish kingdom of Granada.

⁵ Andalusia signifies, in Arabic, the region of the evening of the west; in a word, the Hesperia of the Greeks.—*See Casiri. Bibliot. Arabico Hispana*, and Gibbon's *Decline and Fall, &c.* [FH]

Michaelis Casiri, "De Nomine *Andalusia*," in *Biblioteca Arabico-Hispana Escurialensis*, 2 vols. (1770), 2.327–28; cited in Edward Gibbon, *The History of the Decline & Fall of the Roman Empire* (1776–88), vol. 3, ch. 51. Casiri (1710–91), a Maronite Christian born in Syria, emigrated to Spain and became a Doctor of Theology, Regent of the Library, and Oriental linguist. *Biblioteca* is an annotated catalogue of 1,800 Arabic MSS in the library of the Escurial, a Spanish royal palace. Andalusia is a region of southern Spain; Castile, a Christian kingdom in northern Spain, led the conquest of Granada.

⁶ "Los [bravos] Abencerrages salieron con su acostumbrada librea azul y blanca, todos llenos de ricos texidos de plata, las plumas de la misma color, en sus adargas, su acostumbrada divisa; salvages que desquixalavan leones, y otros un mundo que lo deshazia un salvage con un bastón."—*Guerras civiles de Granada.* [FH]

[The brave Abencerrages sallied in their customary blue and white livery, richly embroidered with silver, their plumes of the same color; on their shields, their ancient emblems, some showing savages forcing open the jaws of lions, others a globe being shattered by a savage with a club.]

By 1492 the Moors had resided in Spain for centuries; the distinction between the "son of Afric" and the "sons of Spain" (76) is nineteenth-century racialism.

⁷ The loftiest heights of the Sierra Nevada are those called Mulhacen and Picacho de Veleta. [FH]

⁸ It is known to be a frequent circumstance in battle, that the dying and the wounded drag themselves, as it were mechanically, to the shelter which may be afforded by any bush or thicket on the field. [FH]

⁹ A phrase for starlight in *Paradise Lost* 7.325, echoed in Wordsworth's description of the Wanderer's education by Nature, *The Excursion* (1814), 1.266; cf. *Widow of Crescentius* 2.88.

¹⁰ "Severe in youthful beauty."—Milton. [FH]

Hemans admired this phrase from *Paradise Lost* 4.845, describing an archangel who has found Satan lurking in Eden (*CM* 1.90).

¹¹ This embedded sonnet both recalls the dream-maiden passage in Shelley's *Alastor* (1816), 149ff. and revises the scene in *Paradise Lost* of Satan dumbstruck by Eve's beauty (9.445–73).

¹² An echo of the Corsair's departure from his beloved in Byron's *Corsair* (1814): "'And is he gone?'—on sudden solitude / How oft that fearful question will intrude" (1.482–83).

¹³ Granada stands upon two hills separated by the Darro. The Genil runs under the walls. The Darro is said to carry with its stream small particles of gold, and the Genil, of silver. When Charles V. came to Granada with the Empress Isabella, the city presented him with a crown made of gold, which had been collected from the Darro.—*See Bourgoanne's and other Travels.* [FH]

*Travels* (1789) was republished as *Modern State of Spain*, 4 vols. (London: John Stockdale, 1808). FH cites information that Bourgoing quotes (3.84ff.) from M. Peyron, *Nouveau voyage en Espagne* (1782). Isabella was the wife of Holy Roman Emperor Charles V (1519–58), also Charles I of Spain (1516–56), successor of his grandparents, Ferdinand and Isabella.

¹⁴ "At this period, while its [Granada's] inhabitants were sunk in indolence, one of those men, whose natural and impassioned eloquence has sometimes aroused a people to deeds of heroism, raised his voice, in the midst of the city, and awakened the inhabitants from their lethargy. Twenty thousand enthusiasts, ranged under his banners, were prepared to sally forth, with the fury of desperation, to attack the besiegers, when Abo Abdeli, more afraid of his subjects than of the enemy, resolved immediately to capitulate, and made terms with the Christians, by

which it was agreed that the Moors should be allowed the free exercise of their religion and laws; should be permitted, if they thought proper, to depart, unmolested, with their effects, to Africa; and that he himself, if he remained in Spain, should retain an extensive estate, with houses and slaves, or be granted an equivalent in money, if he preferred retiring to Barbary."—*See Jacob's Travels in Spain.* [FH]

William Jacob (?1762–1851), *Travels in the South of Spain, in Letters Written A.D. 1809 and 1810* (London: J. Johnson, 1811) 270. FH corresponded with him; see "Letters." The last Moorish king of Granada, Abo Abdeli (Abu Abdalláh of Boabdil) surrendered the city in January 1492 and fled to Morocco in October 1493. He was reported to have died in battle, on behalf of his kinsman and protector, the Caliph of Fez, against a Berber invasion; other accounts say he lived in Fez, dying in abject poverty in 1538.

[15] Azarques, Zegris, Almoradis, different tribes of the Moors of Granada, all of high distinction. [FH]

[16] The conquest of Granada was greatly facilitated by the civil dissensions which, at this period, prevailed in the city. Several of the Moorish tribes, influenced by private feuds, were fully prepared for submission to the Spaniards; others had embraced the cause of Muley el Zagal, the uncle and competitor for the throne of Abdallah, (or Abo Abdeli) and all was jealousy and animosity. [FH]

Abdulla el Zagal leagued with his brother, Boabdil's father, against Boabdil.

[17] Tarik, the first leader of the Arabs and Moors into Spain.—"The Saracens landed at the pillar or point of Europe: the corrupt and familiar appellation of Gibraltar *(Gebel al Tarik)* describes the mountain of Tarik; and the intrenchments of his camp were the first outline of those fortifications, which, in the hands of our countrymen, have resisted the art and power of the house of Bourbon. The adjacent governors informed the court of Toledo of the descent and progress of the Arabs; and the defeat of his lieutenant Edeco, who had been commanded to seize and bind the presumptuous strangers, admonished Roderic of the magnitude of the danger. At the royal summons, the dukes and counts, the bishops and nobles of the Gothic monarchy, assembled at the head of their followers, and the title of king of the Romans, which is employed by an Arabic historian, may be excused by the close affinity of language, religion, and manners, between the nations of Spain."—Gibbon's *Decline and Fall, &c. Vol.* 9, p. 472, 473. [FH; Ch. 51]

In 711, Tarik, governor of Tangier, crossed the Gibraltar strait with a force of seven thousand, and with reinforcements of five thousand, defeated Visigoth king Rodrigo (or Roderick; ruled 710–11), whose regime was weakened by internal strife, tyranny, and possible collaboration of his enemies and oppressed subjects with the invading Moors. The capital, Toledo, fell without resistance, as did much of Spain soon after. England gained Gibraltar in 1704 and across the eighteenth century repelled sieges by France and Spain, both ruled by branches of Bourbon dynasty. Scott's *Don Roderick* appeared in 1811; Southey's *Roderick, Last of the Goths* in 1814.

[18] "In the neighbourhood of Cadiz, the town of Xeres has been illustrated by the encounter which determined the fate of the kingdom; the stream of the Guadalete, which falls into the bay, divided the two camps, and marked the advancing and retreating skirmishes of three successive [and bloody] days. On the fourth day, the two armies joined a more serious and decisive issue [. . .]. Notwithstanding the valour of the Saracens, they fainted under the weight of multitudes, and the plain of Xeres was overspread with sixteen thousand of their dead bodies.—'My brethren,' said Tarik to his surviving companions, 'the enemy is before you, the sea is behind; whither would ye fly? Follow your general; I am resolved either to lose my life, or to trample on the prostrate king of the Romans.' Besides the resource of despair, he confided in the secret correspondence and nocturnal interviews of Count Julian with the sons and the brother of Witiza. The two princes, and the archbishop of Toledo, occupied the most important post: their well-timed defection broke the ranks of the Christians; each warrior was prompted by fear or suspicion to consult his personal safety; and the remains of the Gothic army were scattered or destroyed in the flight and pursuit of the three following days."—*Gibbon's Decline and Fall, &c. Vol.* 9, p. 473, 474. [FH; Ch. 51]

Julian, imperial count, or governor, of Ceuta, in north Africa, attacked Spain, possibly conspiring with the sons of Witiza, Visigoth king in Spain (ruled 701–9); his daughter had been raped by Rodrigo. Walter Savage Landor (1775–1864) published his poem *Count Julian* in 1812.

[19] The *tecbir*, the shout of onset used by the Saracens in battle. [FH]

[20] Cf. Patrick Henry's famous cry for the American Revolution, "Give me liberty or give me death!"

[21] 2d ed.] The terrors occasioned by this sudden excitement of popular feeling seem even to have accelerated Abo Abdeli's capitulation. "Aterrado Abo Abdeli con el alboroto y temiendo no ser ya el Dueño de un pueblo amotinádo, se apresuró á concluir una capitulation, la menos dura que podia obtenir en tan urgentes circumstancias, y ofrecio entregor á Granada el dia seis de Enero"—*Paseos en Granada*, vol. i. p. 298. [FH]

[Abo Abdeli, terrified by the popular disturbance and fearing that he was no longer the Master of a rebellious people, hastened to conclude a surrender on the least harsh terms he could obtain in such urgent circumstances, and he offered to cede Granada on the sixth of January.]

Perhaps Cecilio García de la Leña (1726–93), *Paseos por Granada* (Walks for . . .) (Granada, 1764).

## Canto III

*Fermossi al fin il cor che balzò tanto.*
HIPPOLITO PINDEMONTE[1]

Heroes of elder days! untaught to yield,
Who bled for Spain on many an ancient field,
Ye, that around the oaken cross of yore[2]
Stood firm and fearless on Asturia's shore,
And with your spirit, ne'er to be subdued,
Hallow'd the wild Cantabrian solitude;
Rejoice amidst your dwellings of repose,
In the last chastening of your Moslem foes!
Rejoice!—for Spain, arising in her strength,
Hath burst the remnant of their yoke at length;          10
And they in turn the cup of woe must drain,
And bathe their fetters with their tears in vain.

And thou, the warrior *born in happy hour*,[3]
Valencia's lord, whose name alone was power,
Theme of a thousand songs in days gone by,
Conqueror of kings! exult, O Cid! on high.
For still 'twas thine to guard thy country's weal,
In life, in death, the watcher for Castile!

Thou, in that hour when Mauritania's bands
Rush'd from their palmy groves and burning lands,          20
E'en in the realm of spirits didst retain
A patriot's vigilance, remembering Spain![4]
Then, at deep midnight, rose the mighty sound,

By Leon heard, in shuddering awe profound,
As through her echoing streets, in dread array,
Beings, once mortal, held their viewless way;
Voices, from worlds we know not—and the tread
Of marching hosts, the armies of the dead,
Thou and thy buried chieftains—from the grave
Then did thy summons rouse a king to save,                              30
And join thy warriors with unearthly might
To aid the rescue in Tolosa's fight.
Those days are past—the crescent on thy shore,
O realm of evening! sets, to rise no more.[5]
What banner streams from high Comares' tower?[6]
The cross, bright ensign of Iberia's power!
What the glad shout of each exulting voice?
Castile and Arragon! rejoice, rejoice!
Yielding free entrance to victorious foes,
The Moorish city sees her gates unclose,                                40
And Spain's proud host, with pennon, shield, and lance,
Through her long streets in knightly garb advance.

　　Oh! ne'er in lofty dreams hath Fancy's eye
Dwelt on a scene of statelier pageantry,
At joust or tourney, theme of poet's lore,
High masque, or solemn festival of yore.
The gilded cupolas, that proudly rise
O'erarch'd by cloudless and cerulean skies,
Tall minarets, shining mosques, barbaric° towers,                     *exotic*
Fountains and palaces, and cypress bowers;                              50
And they, the splendid and triumphant throng,
With helmets glittering as they move along,
With broider'd scarf, and gem-bestudded mail,
And graceful plumage streaming on the gale;
Shields, gold-emboss'd, and pennons floating far,
And all the gorgeous blazonry of war,
All brighten'd by the rich transparent hues
That southern suns o'er heaven and earth diffuse;
Blend in one scene of glory, form'd to throw
O'er memory's page a never-fading glow.                                 60
And there too, foremost 'midst the conquering brave,
Your azure plumes, O Aben-Zurrahs! wave.
There Hamet moves; the chief whose lofty port
Seems nor reproach to shun, nor praise to court,
Calm, stern, collected—yet within his breast
Is there no pang, no struggle unconfest?

If such there be, it still must dwell unseen,
Nor cloud a triumph with a sufferer's mien.

   Hear'st thou the solemn, yet exulting sound,
Of the deep anthem floating far around?            70
The choral voices, to the skies that raise
The full majestic harmony of praise?
Lo! where, surrounded by their princely train,
They come, the sovereigns of rejoicing Spain,
Borne on their trophied car—lo! bursting thence
A blaze of chivalrous magnificence!

   Onward their slow and stately course they bend
To where th' Alhambra's ancient towers ascend,
Rear'd and adorn'd by Moorish kings of yore,
Whose lost descendants there shall dwell no more.    80

   They reach those towers—irregularly vast
And rude they seem, in mould barbaric cast:[7]
They enter—to their wondering sight is given
A Genii palace—an Arabian heaven![8]
A scene by magic raised, so strange, so fair,
Its forms and colours seem alike of air.
Here, by sweet orange-boughs, half shaded o'er,
The deep clear bath reveals its marble floor,
Its margin fringed with flowers, whose glowing hues
The calm transparence of its wave suffuse.         90
There, round the court where Moorish arches bend,
Aërial columns, richly deck'd, ascend;
Unlike the models of each classic race,
Of Doric grandeur, or Corinthian grace,
But answering well each vision that portrays
Arabian splendor to the poet's gaze:
Wild, wondrous, brilliant, all—a mingling glow
Of rainbow-tints, above, around, below;
Bright-streaming from the many-tinctured veins
Of precious marble—and the vivid stains       100
Of rich mosaics o'er the light arcade,
In gay festoons and fairy knots display'd.

   On through th' enchanted realm, that only seems
Meet for the radiant creatures of our dreams,
The royal conquerors pass—while still their sight
On some new wonder dwells with fresh delight.
Here the eye roves through slender colonnades,
O'er bowery terraces and myrtle shades,

Dark olive-woods beyond, and far on high
The vast Sierra, mingling with the sky.                              110
There, scattering far around their diamond spray,
Clear streams from founts of alabaster play,
Through pillar'd halls, where exquisitely wrought
Rich arabesques, with glittering foliage fraught,
Surmount each fretted arch, and lend the scene
A wild, romantic, oriental mien:
While many a verse, from eastern bards of old,
Borders the walls in characters of gold.[9]
Here Moslem-luxury, in her own domain,
Hath held for ages her voluptuous reign                              120
'Midst gorgeous domes, where soon shall silence brood,
And all be lone—a splendid solitude.

   Now wake their echos to a thousand songs,
From mingling voices of exulting throngs;
Tambour, and flute, and atabal, are there,[10]
And joyous clarions pealing on the air,
While every hall resounds, "Granada won!
Granada! for Castile and Arragon!"[11]

   'Tis night—from dome and tower, in dazzling maze,
The festal lamps innumerably blaze;[12]                              130
Through long arcades their quivering lustre gleams,
From every lattice tremulously streams,
'Midst orange-gardens plays on fount and rill,
And gilds the waves of Darro and Xenil;
Red flame the torches on each minaret's height,
And shines each street an avenue of light;
And midnight feasts are held, and music's voice
Through the long night still summons to rejoice.

   Yet there, while all would seem to heedless eye
One blaze of pomp, one burst of revelry,                             140
Are hearts, unsooth'd by those delusive hours,
Gall'd by the chain, though deck'd awhile with flowers;
Stern passions working in th' indignant breast,
Deep pangs untold, high feelings unexprest,
Heroic spirits, unsubmitting yet,
Vengeance, and keen remorse, and vain regret.

   From yon proud height, whose olive-shaded brow
Commands the wide, luxuriant plains below,
Who lingering gazes o'er the lovely scene,
Anguish and shame contending in his mien?                           150

He, who, of heroes and of kings the son,
Hath lived to lose whate'er his fathers won,
Whose doubts and fears his people's fate have seal'd.
Wavering alike in council and in field;
Weak, timid ruler of the wise and brave,
Still a fierce tyrant or a yielding slave.

    Far from these vine-clad hills, and azure skies,
To Afric's wilds the royal exile flies,[13]
Yet pauses on his way, to weep in vain,
O'er all he never must behold again.                          160
Fair spreads the scene around—for him *too* fair,
Each glowing charm but deepens his despair.
The Vega's meads, the city's glittering spires,
The old majestic palace of his sires,
The gay pavilions, and retired alcoves,
Bosom'd in citron and pomegranate groves;
Tower-crested rocks, and streams that wind in light,
All in one moment bursting on his sight,
Speak to his soul of glory's vanish'd years,
And wake the source of unavailing tears.                      170
—Weep'st thou, Abdallah?—Thou dost well to weep,
O feeble heart! o'er all thou couldst not keep!
Well do a woman's tears befit the eye
Of him who knew not, as a man, to die.[14]

    The gale sighs mournfully through Zayda's bower,
The hand is gone that nursed each infant flower.
No voice, no step, is in her father's halls,
Mute are the echoes of their marble walls;
No stranger enters at the chieftain's gate,
But all is hush'd, and void, and desolate.                    180

    There, through each tower and solitary shade,
In vain doth Hamet seek the Zegri maid;
Her grove is silent, her pavilion lone,
Her lute forsaken, and her doom unknown;
And through the scene she loved, unheeded flows
The stream whose music lull'd her to repose.

    But oh! to him, whose self-accusing thought
Whispers, 'twas *he* that desolation wrought;
He, who his country and his faith betray'd,
And lent Castile revengeful, powerful aid;                    190
A voice of sorrow swells in every gale,
Each wave, low rippling, tells a mournful tale;

And as the shrubs, untended, unconfined,
In wild exuberance rustle to the wind;
Each leaf hath language to his startled sense,
And seems to murmur—"Thou hast driven her hence!"
And well he feels to trace her flight were vain,
—Where hath lost love been once recall'd again?
In her pure breast, so long by anguish torn,
His name can rouse no feeling now—but scorn.          200
O bitter hour! when first the shuddering heart
Wakes to behold the void within—and start!
To feel its own abandonment, and brood
O'er the chill'd bosom's depth of solitude.
The stormy passions that in Hamet's breast
Have sway'd so long, so fiercely, are at rest;
Th' avenger's task is closed:[15]—he finds too late,
It hath not changed his feelings, but his fate.
His was a lofty spirit, turn'd aside
From its bright path by woes, and wrongs, and pride;          210
And onward in its new tumultuous course
Borne with too rapid and intense a force
To pause one moment in the dread career,
And ask—if such could be its native sphere?
Now are those days of wild delirium o'er,
Their fears and hopes excite his soul no more;
The feverish energies of passion close,
And his heart sinks in desolate repose,
Turns sickening from the world, yet shrinks not less
From its own deep and utter loneliness.          220

There is a sound of voices on the air,
A flash of armour to the sunbeam's glare,
Midst the wild Alpuxarras;[16]—there on high,
Where mountain-snows are mingling with the sky,
A few brave tribes, with spirit yet unbroke,
Have fled indignant from the Spaniard's yoke.

O ye dread scenes, where Nature dwells alone,
Severely glorious on her craggy throne;
Ye citadels of rock, gigantic forms,
Veil'd by the mists, and girdled by the storms,          230
Ravines, and glens, and deep-resounding caves,
That hold communion with the torrent-waves;
And ye, th' unstain'd and everlasting snows,
That dwell above in bright and still repose;
To you, in every clime, in every age,
Far from the tyrant's or the conqueror's rage,

Hath Freedom led her sons:—untired to keep
Her fearless vigils on the barren steep.[17]
She, like the mountain eagle, still delights
To gaze exulting from unconquer'd heights,                    240
And build her eyrie in defiance proud,
To dare the wind and mingle with the cloud.

    Now her deep voice, the soul's awakener, swells,
Wild Alpuxarras, through your inmost dells.
There, the dark glens and lonely rocks among,
As at the clarion's call, her children throng.
She with enduring strength hath nerved each frame,
And made each heart the temple of her flame,
Her own resisting spirit, which shall glow
Unquenchably, surviving all below.                            250

    There high-born maids, that moved upon the earth,
More like bright creatures of aërial birth,
Nurslings of palaces, have fled to share
The fate of brothers and of sires; to bear,
All undismay'd, privation and distress,
And smile, the roses of the wilderness.
And mothers with their infants, there to dwell
In the deep forest or the cavern cell,
And rear their offspring midst the rocks, to be,
If now no more the mighty, still the free.                    260

    And midst that band are veterans, o'er whose head
Sorrows and years their mingled snow have shed:
They saw thy glory, they have wept thy fall,
O royal city! and the wreck of all
They loved and hallow'd most:—doth aught remain
For these to prove of happiness or pain?
Life's cup is drain'd—earth fades before their eye,
Their task is closing—they have but to die.
Ask ye, why fled they hither?—that their doom
Might be, to sink unfetter'd to the tomb.                     270
And youth, in all its pride of strength, is there;
And buoyancy of spirit, form'd to dare
And suffer all things,—fall'n on evil days,[18]
Yet darting o'er the world an ardent gaze,
As on th' arena, where its powers may find
Full scope to strive for glory with mankind.

    Such are the tenants of the mountain-hold,
The high in heart, unconquer'd, uncontroll'd;

By day, the huntsmen of the wild—by night,
Unwearied guardians of the watch-fire's light.                    280
They from their bleak majestic home have caught
A sterner tone of unsubmitting thought,
While all around them bids the soul arise,
To blend with Nature's dread sublimities.
—But these are lofty dreams, and must not be
Where tyranny is near:—the bended knee,
The eye, whose glance no inborn grandeur fires,
And the tamed heart, are tributes she requires;
Nor must the dwellers of the rock look down
On regal conquerors, and defy their frown.                        290
What warrior-band is toiling to explore
The mountain-pass, with pine-wood shadow'd o'er?
Startling with martial sounds each rude recess,
Where the deep echo slept in loneliness.
These are the sons of Spain!—Your foes are near:
O, exiles of the wild Sierra! hear!
Hear! wake! arise! and from your inmost caves
Pour like the torrent in its might of waves!

   Who leads th' invaders on?—his features bear
The deep-worn traces of a calm despair;                           300
Yet his dark brow is haughty—and his eye
Speaks of a soul that asks not sympathy.
'Tis he! 'tis he again! th' apostate chief;
He comes in all the sternness of his grief.
He comes, but changed in heart, no more to wield
Falchion for proud Castile in battle-field,
Against his country's children—though he leads
Castilian bands again to hostile deeds:
His hope is but from ceaseless pangs to fly,
To rush upon the Moslem spears, and die.                          310
So shall remorse and love the heart release,
Which dares not dream of joy, but sighs for peace.
The mountain echos are awake—a sound
Of strife is ringing through the rocks around.
Within the steep defile that winds between
Cliffs piled on cliffs, a dark, terrific scene,
There Moorish exile and Castilian knight
Are wildly mingling in the serried fight.
Red flows the foaming streamlet of the glen,
Whose bright transparence ne'er was stain'd till then;            320
While swell the war-note, and the clash of spears,

To the bleak dwellings of the mountaineers,
Where thy sad daughters, lost Granada! wait,
In dread suspense, the tidings of their fate.

But he,—whose spirit, panting for its rest,
Would fain each sword concentrate in his breast—
Who, where a spear is pointed, or a lance
Aim'd at another's breast, would still advance—
Courts death in vain; each weapon glances by,
As if for him 'twere bliss too great to die.                    330
Yes, Aben-Zurrah! there are deeper woes
Reserved for thee ere Nature's last repose;
Thou know'st not yet what vengeance fate can wreak,
Nor all the heart can suffer ere it break.
Doubtful and long the strife, and bravely fell
The sons of battle in that narrow dell;
Youth in its light of beauty there hath past,
And age, the weary, found repose at last;
Till few and faint the Moslem tribes recoil,
Borne down by numbers, and o'erpower'd by toil.                 340
Dispersed, dishearten'd, through the pass they fly,
Pierce the deep wood, or mount the cliff on high;
While Hamet's band in wonder gaze, nor dare
Track o'er their dizzy path the footsteps of despair.

Yet he, to whom each danger hath become
A dark delight, and every wild a home,
Still urges onward—undismay'd to tread,
Where life's fond lovers would recoil with dread;
But fear is for the happy—*they* may shrink
From the steep precipice, or torrent's brink;                   350
They to whom earth is paradise—their doom
Lends no stern courage to approach the tomb:
Not such his lot, who, school'd by Fate severe,
Were but too blest if aught remain'd to fear.[19]
Up the rude crags, whose giant-masses throw
Eternal shadows o'er the glen below;
And by the fall, whose many tinctured spray
Half in a mist of radiance veils its way,
He holds his venturous track:—supported now
By some o'erhanging pine or ilex bough;                         360
Now by some jutting stone, that seems to dwell
Half in mid-air, as balanced by a spell:
Now hath his footstep gain'd the summit's head,

A level span, with emerald verdure spread,
A fairy circle—there the heath-flowers rise,
And the rock-rose unnoticed blooms and dies;
And brightly plays the stream, ere yet its tide
In foam and thunder cleave the mountain side;
But all is wild beyond—and Hamet's eye
Roves o'er a world of rude sublimity.                               370
That dell beneath, where e'en at noon of day
Earth's charter'd guest, the sunbeam, scarce can stray;
Around, untrodden woods; and far above,
Where mortal footstep ne'er may hope to rove,
Bare granite cliffs, whose fix'd, inherent dyes
Rival the tints that float o'er summer skies;[20]
And the pure glittering snow-realm, yet more high,
That seems a part of Heaven's eternity.

  There is no track of man where Hamet stands,
Pathless the scene as Lybia's desert sands;                         380
Yet on the calm, still air, a sound is heard
Of distant voices, and the gathering-word
Of Islam's tribes, now faint and fainter grown,
Now but the lingering echo of a tone.

  That sound, whose cadence dies upon his ear,
He follows, reckless if his bands are near.
On by the rushing stream his way he bends,
And through the mountain's forest zone ascends;
Piercing the still and solitary shades
Of ancient pine, and dark, luxuriant glades,                        390
Eternal twilight's reign:—those mazes past,
The glowing sunbeams meet his eyes at last,
And the lone wanderer now hath reach'd the source
Whence the wave gushes, foaming on its course.
But there he pauses—for the lonely scene
Towers in such dread magnificence of mien,
And, mingled oft with some wild eagle's cry,
From rock-built eyrie rushing to the sky,
So deep the solemn and majestic sound
Of forests, and of waters murmuring round,                          400
That, rapt in wondering awe, his heart forgets
Its fleeting struggles, and its vain regrets.
—What earthly feeling, unabash'd, can dwell
In Nature's mighty presence?—midst the swell
Of everlasting hills, the roar of floods,
And frown of rocks, and pomp of waving woods?

These their own grandeur on the soul impress,
And bid each passion feel its nothingness.

    Midst the vast marble cliffs, a lofty cave
Rears its broad arch beside the rushing wave;          410
Shadow'd by giant oaks, and rude, and lone,
It seems the temple of some power unknown,
Where earthly being may not dare intrude
To pierce the secrets of the solitude.

    Yet thence at intervals a voice of wail
Is rising, wild and solemn, on the gale.
Did thy heart thrill, O Hamet, at the tone?
Came it not o'er thee as a spirit's moan?
As some loved sound, that long from earth had fled,
The unforgotten accents of the dead?          420
E'en thus it rose—and springing from his trance
His eager footsteps to the sound advance.
He mounts the cliffs, he gains the cavern floor,
Its dark green moss with blood is sprinkled o'er:
He rushes on—and lo! where Zayda rends
Her locks, as o'er her slaughter'd sire she bends,
Lost in despair;—yet as a step draws nigh,
Disturbing sorrow's lonely sanctity;
She lifts her head, and all subdued by grief,
Views, with a wild, sad smile, the once loved chief;          430
While rove her thoughts, unconscious of the past,
And every woe forgetting—but the last.

    "Com'st thou to weep with me?—for I am left
Alone on earth, of every tie bereft.
Low lies the warrior on his blood-stain'd bier;
His child may call, but he no more shall hear!
He sleeps—but never shall those eyes unclose;
'Twas not my voice that lull'd him to repose,
Nor can it break his slumbers.—Dost thou mourn?
And is thy heart, like mine, with anguish torn?          440
Weep, and my soul a joy in grief shall know,
That o'er his grave my tears with Hamet's flow!"

    But scarce her voice had breathed that well-known name,
When, swiftly rushing o'er her spirit, came
Each dark remembrance; by affliction's power
Awhile effaced in that o'erwhelming hour,
To wake with tenfold strength;—'twas then her eye
Resumed its light, her mien its majesty,

And o'er her wasted cheek a burning glow
Spreads, while her lips' indignant accents flow.　　　　450

　　"Away! I dream—oh, how hath sorrow's might
Bow'd down my soul, and quench'd its native light,
That I should thus forget! and bid *thy* tear
With mine be mingled o'er a father's bier!
Did he not perish, haply by thy hand,
In the last combat with thy ruthless band?
The morn beheld that conflict of despair:—
'Twas then he fell—he fell!—and thou wert there!
Thou! who thy country's children hast pursued
To their last refuge midst these mountains rude.　　　　460
Was it for this I loved thee?—Thou hast taught
My soul all grief, all bitterness of thought!
'Twill soon be past—I bow to Heaven's decree,
Which bade each pang be minister'd by thee."

　　"I had not deem'd that aught remain'd below
For me to prove of yet untasted woe;
But thus to meet thee, Zayda! can impart
One more, one keener agony of heart.
Oh, hear me yet!—I would have died to save
My foe, but still thy father, from the grave;　　　　470
But in the fierce confusion of the strife,
In my own stern despair, and scorn of life,
Borne wildly on, I saw not, knew not aught,
Save that to perish there in vain I sought.
And let me share thy sorrows—hadst thou known
All I have felt in silence and alone,
E'en *thou* mightst then relent, and deem at last
A grief like mine might expiate all the past.

　　But oh! for thee, the loved and precious flower,
So fondly rear'd in luxury's guarded bower,　　　　480
From every danger, every storm secured,
How hast *thou* suffer'd! what hast thou endured!
Daughter of palaces! and can it be
That this bleak desert is a home for thee!
These rocks *thy* dwelling! thou, who shouldst have known
Of life the sunbeam and the smile alone!
Oh, yet forgive!—be all my guilt forgot,
Nor bid me leave thee to so rude a lot!"

　　"That lot is fix'd; 'twere fruitless to repine,
Still must a gulf divide my fate from thine.　　　　490

I may forgive—but not at will the heart
Can bid its dark remembrances depart.
No, Hamet, no!—too deeply these are traced,
Yet the hour comes when all shall be effaced!
Not long on earth, not long shall Zayda keep
Her lonely vigils o'er the grave to weep:
E'en now, prophetic of my early doom,
Speaks to my soul a presage of the tomb;
And ne'er in vain did hopeless mourner feel
That deep foreboding o'er the bosom steal!          500
Soon shall I slumber calmly by the side
Of him for whom I lived, and would have died;
Till then, one thought shall soothe my orphan lot,
In pain and peril—I forsook him not.

    And now, farewell!—behold the summer-day
Is passing, like the dreams of life, away.
Soon will the tribe of him who sleeps, draw nigh,
With the last rites his bier to sanctify.
Oh, yet in time, away!—'twere not *my* prayer
Could move their hearts a foe like thee to spare!          510
This hour they come—and dost thou scorn to fly?
Save me that one last pang—to see thee die!"

    E'en while she speaks is heard their echoing tread,
Onward they move, the kindred of the dead.
They reach the cave—they enter—slow their pace,
And calm, deep sadness marks each mourner's face,
And all is hush'd—till he who seems to wait
In silent, stern devotedness, his fate,
Hath met their glance—then grief to fury turns;
Each mien is changed, each eye indignant burns,          520
And voices rise, and swords have left their sheath:
Blood must atone for blood, and death for death!
They close around him:—lofty still his mien,
His cheek unalter'd, and his brow serene.
Unheard, or heard in vain, is Zayda's cry;
Fruitless her prayer, unmark'd her agony.
But as his foremost foes their weapons bend
Against the life he seeks not to defend,
Wildly she darts between—each feeling past,
Save strong affection, which prevails at last.          530
Oh! not in vain its daring—for the blow
Aim'd at his heart hath bade her life-blood flow;
And she hath sunk a martyr on the breast,

Where, in that hour, her head may calmly rest,
For he is saved:—behold the Zegri band,
Pale with dismay and grief, around her stand;
While, every thought of hate and vengeance o'er,
They weep for her who soon shall weep no more.
She, she alone is calm:—a fading smile,
Like sunset, passes o'er her cheek the while;                    540
And in her eye, ere yet it closes, dwell
Those last faint rays, the parting soul's farewell.

"Now is the conflict past, and I have proved
How well, how deeply thou hast been beloved!
Yes! in an hour like this 'twere vain to hide
The heart so long and so severely tried:
Still to thy name that heart hath fondly thrill'd,
But sterner duties call'd—and were fulfill'd:
And I am blest!—To every holier tie
My life was faithful,—and for thee I die!                    550
Nor shall the love so purified be vain,
Sever'd on earth, we yet shall meet again.
Farewell!—And ye, at Zayda's dying prayer,
Spare him, my kindred-tribe! forgive and spare!
Oh! be his guilt forgotten in his woes,
While I, beside my sire, in peace repose."

Now fades her cheek, her voice hath sunk, and death
Sits in her eye, and struggles in her breath.
One pang—'tis past—her task on earth is done,
And the pure spirit to its rest hath flown.                    560
But he for whom she died—Oh! who may paint
The grief, to which all other woes were faint?
There is no power in language to impart
The deeper pangs, the ordeals of the heart,
By the dread Searcher of the soul survey'd;
These have no words—nor are by words portray'd.

A dirge is rising on the mountain-air,
Whose fitful swells its plaintive murmurs bear
Far o'er the Alpuxarras;—wild its tone,
And rocks and caverns echo "Thou art gone!"[21]                    570

Daughter of heroes![22] thou art gone
    To share his tomb who gave thee birth;
Peace to the lovely spirit flown!
    It was not form'd for earth.

Thou wert a sunbeam in thy race,
Which brightly past, and left no trace.

But calmly sleep!—for thou art free,
    And hands unchain'd thy tomb shall raise.
Sleep! they are closed at length for thee,
    Life's few and evil days!                          580
Nor shalt thou watch, with tearful eye,
The lingering death of liberty.

Flower of the desert! thou thy bloom
    Didst early to the storm resign:
We bear it still—and dark *their* doom
    Who cannot weep for thine!
For us, whose every hope is fled,
The time is past to mourn the dead

The days have been, when o'er thy bier
    Far other strains than these had flow'd;            590
Now, as a home from grief and fear,
    We hail thy dark abode!
We who but linger to bequeath
Our sons the choice of chains or death.

Thou art with those, the free, the brave,
    The mighty of departed years;
And for the slumberers of the grave
    Our fate hath left no tears.
Though loved and lost, to weep were vain
For thee, who ne'er shalt weep again.                    600

Have we not seen, despoil'd by foes,
    The land our fathers won of yore?
And is there yet a pang for those
    Who gaze on *this* no more?
Oh, that like them 'twere ours to rest!
Daughter of heroes! thou art blest!

A few short years, and in the lonely cave
Where sleeps the Zegri maid, is Hamet's grave.
Sever'd in life, united in the tomb—
Such, of the hearts that loved so well, the doom!        610
Their dirge, of woods and waves th' eternal moan,
Their sepulchre, the pine-clad rocks alone.
And oft beside the midnight watch-fire's blaze,
Amidst those rocks, in long departed days,

(When Freedom fled, to hold, sequester'd there,
The stern and lofty councils of despair);
Some exiled Moor, a warrior of the wild,
Who the lone hours with mournful strains beguiled,
Hath taught his mountain-home the tale of those
Who thus have suffer'd, and who thus repose.          620

[1] Stopped at last, the heart that beat so strongly.

Ippolito Pindemonte (1753–1828), *Clizia* (1798), line 55; also an epigraph for *Arabella Stuart*. That FH's slight misquotation duplicates Staël's in *Corinne* (bk. 18, ch. 5), where Corinne speaks these words, dying of a broken heart, suggests that *Corinne* may have been her source.

[2] The oaken cross, carried by Pelagius in battle. [FH]

As the Arabs and Berbers invaded Spain, Visigoth nobles and allies retreated to the northern coastal mountains of Asturia and elected Prince Pelayo (ca. 718–37) their first king. His victory at Covadonga (ca. 720) initiated the Christian reconquest. Cf. FH's first note to *Siege of Valencia* 1.56. The Cantabrian is a mountain range.

[3] See Southey's Chronicle of the Cid, in which that warrior is frequently styled, "*he who was born in happy hour.*" [FH]

For Robert Southey's *Chronicle* (1808), see notes to *Songs of the Cid*.

[4] "Moreover when the Miramamolin brought over from Africa against King Don Alfonso, the eighth of that name, the mightiest power of the misbelievers that had ever been brought against Spain since the destruction of the Kings of the Goths, the Cid Campeador remembered his country in that great danger. For the night before the battle was fought at the Navas de Tolosa, in the dead of the night, a mighty sound was heard in the whole city of Leon, as if it were the tramp of a great army passing through. And it passed on to the Royal Monastery of St. Isidro, and there was a great knocking at the gate thereof, and they called to a priest who was keeping vigils in the Church, and told him, that the Captains of the army whom he heard were the Cid Ruydiez, and Count Ferran Gonzalez, and that they came there to call up King Don Ferrando the Great, who lay buried in that church, that he might go with them to deliver Spain. And on the morrow that great battle of the Navas de Tolosa was fought, wherein sixty thousand of the misbelievers were slain, which was one of the greatest and noblest battles ever won over the Moors."—Southey's *Chronicle of the Cid*. [FH. Bk.11.xxi (352)]

Cf. *The Cid's Rising*. Mauritania's bands are the Almoravides, Berbers, and Arabs from northwest Africa. León is a city and province in northwestern Spain.

[5] The name of Andalusia, the *region of evening or of the west*, was applied by the Arabs not only to the province so called, but to the whole peninsula. [FH]

Andalusia included the kingdom of Granada. The crescent (33) is the emblem of Islam.

[6] 2d ed.] . . . streams afar from Vela's tower?

The tower of Comares is the highest and most magnificent in the Alhambra. [FH; 2d ed. continues] "En este dia, para siempre memorable, los estandartes de la Cruz, de St Jago, y el de los Reyes de Castilla se tremoláran sobre la torre mas alta, llamada de *la Vela*; y un exercito prosternado, inundandose en lagrimas de gozo y reconocimiento, asistio al mas glorioso de los espectaculos."—*Paseos en Granada*, vol. i. p. 299.

[On this day, forever memorable, the standards of the Cross, St. James, and the Kings of Castile waved above the highest tower, called *la Vela*; and a prostrate army, awash in tears of joy and gratitude, witnessed the most glorious of spectacles.]

[7] Swinburne, after describing the noble palace built by Charles V in the precincts of the Alhambra, thus proceeds: "Adjoining (to the north) stands a huge heap of as ugly buildings as can well be seen, all huddled together, seemingly without the least intention of forming *one* habitation out of them. The walls are entirely unornamented, all gravel and pebbles, daubed over with plaster by a very coarse hand; yet this is the palace of the Moorish kings of Granada,

indisputably the most curious place within, that exists in Spain, perhaps in Europe. In many countries, you may see excellent modern as well as ancient architecture, both entire and in ruins; but nothing to be met with any where else can convey an idea of this edifice, except you take it from the decorations of an opera, or the tales of the Genii."—*Swinburne's Travels through Spain*. [FH]

Henry Swinburne (1743–1803), *Travels through Spain, in the Years 1775 and 1776* (London: P. Elmsly, 1787) 1.275–76. He refers to Rev. James Ridley (1736–64), *The Tales of the Genii* (1764), a popular collection purportedly "translated from the Persian" by "Sir Charles Morell."

[8] "Passing round the corner of the Emperor's palace, you are admitted at a plain unornamented door, in a corner. On my first visit, I confess, I was struck with amazement as I stept over the threshold, to find myself on a sudden transported into a species of fairy-land. The first place you come to is the court called the *communa*, or *del mesucar*, that is the common baths: An oblong square, with a deep bason of clear water in the middle; two flights of marble steps leading down to the bottom; on each side a parterre of flowers, and a row of orange trees. Round the court runs a peristyle paved with marble; the arches bear upon very slight pillars, in proportions and style different from all the regular orders of architecture. The ceilings and walls are incrustated with fret-work in stucco, so minute and intricate, that the most patient draughtsman would find it difficult to follow it, unless he made himself master of the general plan."—*Swinburne's Travels in Spain*. [FH; 276–77]

[9] The walls and cornices of the Alhambra are covered with inscriptions in Arabic characters. "In examining this abode of magnificence," says Bourgoanne, "the observer is every moment astonished at the new and interesting mixture of architecture and poetry. The palace of the Alhambra may be called a collection of fugitive pieces; and whatever duration these may have, time, with which every thing passes away, has too much contributed to confirm to them that title."—*See Bourgoanne's Travels in Spain*. [FH; *Modern State of Spain* 4.160]

[10] Atabal, a kind of Moorish drum. [FH]

[11] "Y ansí entraron en la ciudad y subieron al Alhambra, y encima de la Torre de Comares, tan famosa, se levantó la señal de la Santa Cruz y luego el [real] estandarte de los dos Cristianos reyes. Y al punto los reyes de armas, à grandes bozes dizieron, [Viva el rey don Fernando;] 'Granada, Granada, por su Magestad, y por la reyna su muger.' La serenísima reyna D[oña] Isabel, que vio la señal de la Santa Cruz sobre la hermosa Torre de Comares, y el su estandarte real con ella, se hincó de rodillas, y dio infinitas gracias a Dios por la victoria que le avia dado contra aquella [populosa y] gran ciudad [de Granada]. La musica real de la capilla del rey luego a canto de órgano canto *Te Deum Laudamus*. Fue tan grande el plazer, que todos lloravan. Luego del Alhambra sonaron mil instrumentos de musica de belicas trompetas. Los moros amigos del rey que querían ser Cristianos, cuya cabeza era el valeroso Muça, tomaron mil dulzaynas y añafiles, sonando grande ruydo de atambores por toda la ciudad"—*Historia de las guerras civiles de Granada*. [FH, citing de Hita]

[And thus they entered the city, and climbing up to the Alhambra, raised on that Tower of Comares, so famous, the sign of the Holy Cross and the royal standard of the two Christian monarchs. And at that moment the official marshalls of ceremonies shouted with a united voice, "Long live king Ferdinand; Granada, Granada, in the name of your Majesty, and of the queen your wife." Her most royal Queen Isabella, seeing the sign of the Cross atop the beautiful Tower of Comares, and beside it her royal standard, knelt, and gave infinite thanks to God for the victory He had given her against the populous and great city of Granada. The royal musicians of the king's chapel, accompanied by the organ, then sang the *Te Deum Laudamus*. The joy was so great that everyone wept. Then from the Alhambra sounded from a fanfare from a thousand warlike instruments. Those moorish friends of the king, who wished to become Christians, led by the valiant Musa, took up a thousand dulcimers and anafils, and raised a great clamor of drums through the whole city.] [*Te Deum* (Thee God We Praise) is part of the Mass.]

[12] "Los cavalleros moros que avemos dicho, aquella noche jugaron galanamente alcancías y cañas. [...] Andava Granada aquella noche con tanta alegría, y con tantas luminarias, que

parecía que se ardia la terra."—*Historia de las Guerras civiles de Granada.* Swinburne, in his Travels through Spain in the years 1775 and 1776, mentions, that the anniversary of the surrender of Granada to Ferdinand and Isabella was still observed in the city as a great festival and day of rejoicing; and that the populace on that occasion paid an annual visit to the Moorish palace. [FH; Swinburne, 1.312.]

[The Moorish knights of whom we spoke, that night gallantly played "alcancias y cañas"(a game of balls and canes). . . . In Granada there was so much gaiety that night, and so many lanterns, that the city itself seemed to be on fire.]

[13] "Los Gomeles todos se passaron en Africa, y el Rey Chico con ellos, que no quisò estar en España, y en Africa le mataron los Moros de aquellas partes, porque perdiò à Granada." —*Guerras civiles de Granada.* [FH]

[The Gomeles fled to Africa, and with them, el Rey Chico, who had no wish to stay in Spain, and in Africa the Moors of those regions killed him, because he lost Granada.]

El Rey Chico (the little king) is one of the names of Boabdil.

[14] Abo Abdeli, upon leaving Granada, after its conquest by Ferdinand and Isabella, stopped on the hill of Padul to take a last look of his city and palace. Overcome by the sight, he burst into tears, and was thus reproached by his mother, the Sultaness Ayxa: "Thou dost well to weep, like a woman, over the loss of that kingdom which thou knewest not how to defend and die for, like a man." [FH]

Cf. Washington Irving's account in the appendix to the revised edition of *Chronicle of the Conquest of Granada.* Ayxa is also known as Ayesha, and the hill has been called "el ultimo suspiro del Moro" (the last sigh of the Moor).

[15] "El Rey mandò, que si quedavan Zegris, que no viviessen en Granada, por la maldad que hizieron contra los Abencerrages."—*Guerras civiles de Granada.* [FH]

[The King commanded all the remaining Zegris out of Granada, for the evil they had done against the Abencerrages.]

[16] "The Alpuxarras are so lofty that the coast of Barbary and the cities of Tangier and Ceuta are discovered from their summits; they are about seventeen leagues in length from Veles Malaga to Almeria, and eleven in breadth, and abound with fruit-trees of great beauty and prodigious size. In these mountains the wretched remains of the Moors took refuge"—Bourgoanne's *Travels in Spain.* [FH. 3.171]

Barbary is on the north coast of Africa.

[17] Cf. FH's note to *Siege of Valencia* 1.156. The next stanzas refer to the revolt of Muslims living in the Alpujarras mountains against Christian Granada in 1499; in 1502 Muslims were forcibly converted to Christianity.

[18] Milton describes himself as "fall'n on evil days" (*Paradise Lost* 7.25) after the restoration of the Monarchy. Cf. 3.580 (below); *Widow of Crescentius* 1.61–68; *Siege of Valencia* 1.98.

[19] "Plût à Dieu que je craignisse!"—Andromaque. [FH]

["Please God that I may be afraid!"] Montesquieu's reference to Andromache at the end of ch. 14 of *Considérations sur les causes de la grandeur des Romains et de la décadence* (1734). Widow of prince Hector (killed in the Greek sack of Troy), Andromache is loved by her captor Phyrrus; she hates him but is willing to marry him to save the life of her son. Montesquieu may be recalling Seneca's *Troades* (vv. 632–33): "Utinam timerem. Solitus ex longo est metus: / dediscit animus sero quod didicit diu" ("I wish there was reason to fear. But fear is a habit of long custom: the mind is slow to unlearn what it has learned long since"); trans. Elaine Fantham (Princeton UP, 1982), 164–65. Fantham remarks "Andromache disclaims her fear, as a reflex from long habit (a real insight by Seneca into the psychology of mothers of little children)" (301).

[20] Mrs. Radcliffe, in her journey along the banks of the Rhine, thus describes the colours of granite rocks in the mountains of the Bergstrasse. "The nearer we approached these mountains, the more we had occasion to admire the various tints of their granites. Sometimes the precipices were of a faint pink, then of a deep red, a dull purple, or a blush approaching to lilac, and sometimes gleams of a pale yellow mingled with the low shrubs, that grew upon their sides.

The day was cloudless and bright, and we were too near these heights to be deceived by the illusions of aerial colouring; the real hues of their features were as beautiful as their magnitude was sublime." [FH]

Ann Radcliffe, "Germany," in *A Journey Made in the Summer of 1794, through Holland and the Western Frontier of Germany* 2 vols. (London: G. G. and J. Robinson, 1795), 1.466. Popular novelist Radcliffe (1764–1823) achieved sensational success in the gothic genre, including *A Sicilian Romance* (1790), *The Romance of the Forest* (1791), *The Mysteries of Udolpho* (1794), and *The Italian* (1797). *Journey* records her happy travels with her husband.

[21] A literal "echo" of 1.369, itself echoed in the next line.

[22] In *The Siege of Valencia* 1.171, Gonzalez, the governor of the Christian city, uses this term to exhort his wife to accept the martyrdom of their sons, hostages to African Moors, who demand the city's surrender.

---

## The Last Banquet of Antony and Cleopatra

[Supplementing Plutarch, Shakespeare's *Antony and Cleopatra* (1616), and Dryden's *All for Love* (1678), Hemans sets her scene on the eve of the Battle of Actium (in 31 B.C.), Antony's decisive defeat by Octavius. Egypt had a powerful resonance for Hemans's contemporaries as the site of Nelson's first major victory, his defeat of the French in the Battle of the Nile, 1798 (see *Casabianca*); like Antony, Nelson was involved in a scandalous love affair, though unlike him, he died in battle, a martyr to his country. In the stanza form reprised from *Modern Greece* (see its headnote), the final alexandrine line here effects a formalist pun on Alexandria, site of Cleopatra's palace. Both the city and the meter were named for Alexander the Great: the alexandrine was a standard French measure, derived from the twelfth-century *Roman d'Alexandre*, one of many romances woven around the legendary conqueror.]

> *"Antony, concluding that he could not die more honourably than in battle, determined to attack Cæsar at the same time both by sea and land. The night preceding the execution of this design, he ordered his servants at supper to render him their best services that evening, and fill the wine round plentifully, for the day following they might belong to another master, whilst he lay extended on the ground, no longer of consequence either to them or to himself. His friends were affected, and wept to hear him talk thus; which, when he perceived, he encouraged them by assurances that his expectations of a glorious victory were at least equal to those of an honourable death. At the dead of night, when universal silence reigned through the city, a silence that was deepened by the awful thought of the ensuing day, on a sudden was heard the sound of musical instruments, and a noise which resembled the exclamations of Bacchanals. This tumultuous procession seemed to pass through the whole city, and to go out at the gate which led to the enemy's camp. Those who reflected on this prodigy concluded that Bacchus, the god whom Antony affected to imitate, had then forsaken him."*
>
> —Langhorne's Plutarch.[1]

Thy foes had girt thee with their dread array,
    O stately Alexandria!—yet the sound
Of mirth and music, at the close of day,
    Swell'd from thy splendid fabrics,° far around          *buildings*

O'er camp and wave. Within the royal hall,
   In gay magnificence the feast was spread;
And, brightly streaming from the pictured wall,
   A thousand lamps their trembling lustre shed
O'er many a column, rich with precious dyes,
That tinge the marble's vein, 'neath Afric's burning skies.     10

And soft and clear that wavering radiance play'd
   O'er sculptured forms, that round the pillar'd scene,
Calm and majestic rose, by art array'd
   In godlike beauty, awfully serene.
Oh! how unlike the troubled guests, reclined
   Round that luxurious board!—in every face,
Some shadow from the tempest of the mind,
   Rising by fits, the searching eye might trace,
Though vainly mask'd in smiles which are not mirth,
But the proud spirit's veil thrown o'er the woes of earth.     20

Their brows are bound with wreaths, whose transient bloom
   May still survive the wearers—and the rose
Perchance may scarce be wither'd, when the tomb
   Receives the mighty to its dark repose!
The day must dawn on battle—and may set
   In death—but fill the mantling wine-cup high!
Despair is fearless, and the Fates e'en yet
   Lend her one hour for parting revelry.
They who the empire of the world possess'd,
Would taste its joys again, ere all exchanged for rest.     30

Its joys! oh! mark yon proud triumvir's mien,
   And read their annals on that brow of care!
'Midst pleasure's lotus-bowers his steps have been;[2]
   Earth's brightest pathway led him to despair.
Trust not the glance that fain would yet inspire
   The buoyant energies of days gone by;
There is delusion in its meteor-fire,
   And all within is shame, is agony!
Away! the tear in bitterness may flow,
But there are smiles which bear a stamp of deeper woe.     40

Thy cheek is sunk, and faded as thy fame,
   O lost, devoted° Roman! yet thy brow        *enrapt; doomed*
To that ascendant and undying name,
   Pleads with stern loftiness thy right e'en now.
Thy glory is departed—but hath left
   A lingering light around thee—in decay

Not less than kingly, though of all bereft,
　　Thou seem'st as empire had not pass'd away.
Supreme in ruin! teaching hearts elate,
A deep, prophetic dread of still mysterious fate!　　　　　　　　50

But thou, enchantress-queen! whose love hath made
　　His desolation—thou art by his side,
In all thy sovereignty of charms array'd,
　　To meet the storm with still unconquer'd pride.
Imperial being! e'en though many a stain
　　Of error be upon thee, there is power
In thy commanding nature, which shall reign
　　O'er the stern genius° of misfortune's hour;　　　　*presiding spirit*
And the dark beauty of thy troubled eye
E'en now is all illumed with wild sublimity.　　　　　　60

Thine aspect, all impassion'd, wears a light
　　Inspiring and inspired—thy cheek a dye,
Which rises not from joy, but yet is bright
　　With the deep glow of feverish energy.
Proud siren of the Nile! thy glance is fraught
　　With an immortal fire—in every beam
It darts, there kindles some heroic thought,
　　But wild and awful as a sybil's dream;
For thou with death hast communed, to attain
Dread knowledge of the pangs that ransom from the chain.[3]　　70

And the stern courage by such musings lent,
　　Daughter of Afric! o'er thy beauty throws
The grandeur of a regal spirit, blent
　　With all the majesty of mighty woes!
While he, so fondly, fatally adored,
　　Thy fallen Roman, gazes on thee yet,
Till scarce the soul, that once exulting soar'd,
　　Can deem the day-star of its glory set;
Scarce his charm'd heart believes that power can be
In sovereign fate, o'er him, thus fondly loved by thee.　　　80

But there is sadness in the eyes around,
　　Which mark that ruin'd leader, and survey
His changeful mien, whence oft the gloom profound,
　　Strange triumph chases haughtily away.
"Fill the bright goblet, warrior guests!" he cries,
　　"Quaff, ere we part, the generous nectar deep!
Ere sunset gild once more the western skies,
　　Your chief, in cold forgetfulness, may sleep,

While sounds of revel float o'er shore and sea,
And the red bowl again is crown'd[4]—but not for me.        90

"Yet weep not thus—the struggle is not o'er,
        O victors of Philippi![5] many a field
Hath yielded palms to us:—one effort more,
        By one stern conflict must our doom be seal'd!
Forget not, Romans! o'er a subject world
        How royally your eagle's wing hath spread,
Though from his eyrie of dominion hurl'd,[6]
        Now bursts the tempest on his crested head!
Yet sovereign still, if banish'd from the sky,
The sun's indignant bird, he must not droop—but die."        100

The feast is o'er. 'Tis night, the dead of night—
        Unbroken stillness broods o'er earth and deep;
From Egypt's heaven of soft and starry light
        The moon looks cloudless o'er a world of sleep:
For those who wait the morn's awakening beams,
        The battle signal to decide their doom,
Have sunk to feverish rest and troubled dreams;
        Rest, that shall soon be calmer in the tomb,
Dreams, dark and ominous, but *there* to cease,
When sleep the lords of war in solitude and peace.        110

Wake, slumberers, wake! Hark! heard ye not a sound
        Of gathering tumult?—Near and nearer still
Its murmur swells. Above, below, around,
        Bursts a strange chorus forth, confused and shrill.
Wake, Alexandria! through thy streets the tread
        Of steps unseen is hurrying, and the note
Of pipe, and lyre, and trumpet, wild and dread,
        Is heard upon the midnight air to float;
And voices, clamorous as in frenzied mirth,
Mingle their thousand tones, which are not of the earth.        120

These are no mortal sounds—their thrilling strain
        Hath more mysterious power, and birth more high;
And the deep horror chilling every vein
        Owns them of stern, terrific augury.
Beings of worlds unknown! ye pass away,
        O ye invisible and awful throng!
Your echoing footsteps and resounding lay
        To Cæsar's camp exulting move along.
Thy gods forsake thee, Antony! the sky
By that dread sign reveals—thy doom—"Despair and die!"[7]        130

¹ John and William Langhorne, *The Life of Antony*, in *Plutarch's Lives* (1770). *Awful*: awe-inspiring.

² In *The Odyssey* 9.82–97 (cf. Tennyson's *The Lotos-Eaters* [1832]), weary veterans of the Trojan war arrive at the land of the lotos-eaters and forget their homeward mission.

³ Cleopatra made a collection of poisonous drugs, and being desirous to know which was least painful in the operation, she tried them on the capital convicts. Such poisons as were quick in their operation, she found to be attended with violent pain and convulsions; such as were milder were slow in their effect: she therefore applied herself to the examination of venomous creatures; [. . .] and at length she found that the bite of the asp was the most eligible kind of death; for it brought on a gradual kind of lethargy.—See *Plutarch*. [FH]

*Life of Antony*. "Capital convicts" are condemned to death.

⁴ A flower-garlanded ceremonial bowl of wine ("nectar") passed around at banquets.

⁵ The site in Macedonia of the triumvirs' victory in 42 B.C. over conspirators Brutus and Cassius, who committed suicide. Antony named his sword "Philippi" in honor of this victory.

⁶ *Eyrie*: eagle's nest. The eagle was the symbol of the Roman Empire, and was adopted by Napoleon to signify his imperial destiny.

⁷       "To-morrow in the battle think on me,
      And fall thy edgeless sword; despair and die!"—*Richard III*. [FH]

In Shakespeare's play, all those whom Richard had murdered to get to the throne return to haunt him on the night before the battle in which he is fatally defeated. In these lines (5.3.135–36), the ghost of his brother speaks.

---

## *Alaric in Italy*

[Alaric (ca. 370–410) led the Visigothic troops serving Roman emperor Theodosius I, after whose death they revolted, made Alaric their king, and began a campaign of conquest. Alaric invaded Italy several times in the early 5th c., sacked Rome in 410, then set his sights on Sicily and Africa. FH's octosyllabic couplet was popular in verse narratives, recently employed by Byron in *The Giaour* and *The Bride of Abydos* (both 1813). Matthew Arnold's first published poem, *Alaric at Rome* (1840), advertises a debt to Byron, but the fact that his notes quote the same passage from Gibbon that Hemans does suggests that *Alaric in Italy* may also have been an inspiration.]

After describing the conquest of Greece and Italy by the German and Scythian hordes, united under the command of Alaric, the historian of "The Decline and Fall of the Roman Empire," thus proceeds:—"Whether fame or conquest or riches were the object of Alaric, he pursued that object with an indefatigable ardour, which could neither be quelled by adversity, nor satiated by success. No sooner had he reached the extreme land of Italy than he was attracted [attacked] by the neighbouring prospect of a fair and peaceful island. Yet even the possession of Sicily he considered only as an intermediate step to the important expedition which he already meditated against the continent of Africa. The straits of Rhegium and Messina are twelve miles in length, and in the narrowest passage about one mile and a half broad; and the fabulous monsters of the deep, the rocks of Scylla, and the whirlpool of Charybdis, could terrify none but the most timid and unskilful mariners.[1] Yet, as soon as the first division of the Goths had embarked, a sudden tempest arose, which sunk or scattered many of the transports: their courage was daunted by the terrors of a new element; and the whole design was defeated by the premature death of Alaric, which fixed, after a short illness, the fatal term of his conquests. The ferocious character of the Barbarians was displayed in the funeral of a hero, whose valour and fortune they celebrated with mournful applause. By the labour of a captive multitude they forcibly diverted the course of the Busentinus, a small river that washes the walls of Consentia. The royal sepulchre, adorned with the splendid spoils and trophies of Rome, was constructed in the vacant bed; the waters were then restored to their natural channel, and the secret spot, where the remains of Alaric had been deposited, was for ever concealed by the inhuman massacre of the prisoners who had been employed to execute the work."

—*See the Decline and Fall of the Roman Empire, Vol. 5, page* 329.[2]

Heard ye the Gothic trumpet's blast?
The march of hosts, as Alaric pass'd?
His steps have track'd that glorious clime,
The birth-place of heroic time;
But he, in northern deserts bred,
Spared not the living for the dead,[3]
Nor heard the voice, whose pleading cries
From temple and from tomb arise.
He pass'd—the light of burning fanes
Hath been his torch o'er Grecian plains;        10
And woke they not—the brave, the free,
To guard their own Thermopylæ?
And left they not their silent dwelling,
When Scythia's note of war was swelling?
No! where the bold Three Hundred slept,
Sad freedom battled not—but wept![4]
For nerveless then the Spartan's hand,
And Thebes could rouse no Sacred Band;[5]
Nor one high soul from slumber broke,
When Athens own'd the northern yoke.        20

But was there none for *thee* to dare
The conflict, scorning to despair?
O city of the seven proud hills!
Whose name e'en yet the spirit thrills,
As doth a clarion's battle-call,
Didst thou too, ancient empress, fall?
Did no Camillus from the chain
Ransom thy Capitol again?[6]

Oh! who shall tell the days to be,
No patriot rose to bleed for thee? 30

Heard ye the Gothic trumpet's blast?
The march of hosts, as Alaric pass'd?
That fearful sound, at midnight deep,[7]
Burst on th' eternal city's sleep:
How woke the mighty? She, whose will
So long had bid the world be still,
Her sword a sceptre, and her eye
Th' ascendant star of destiny!
She woke—to view the dread array
Of Scythians rushing to their prey, 40
To hear her streets resound the cries
Pour'd from a thousand agonies!
While the strange light of flames, that gave
A ruddy glow to Tyber's wave,
Bursting in that terrific hour
From fane and palace, dome and tower,
Reveal'd the throngs, for aid divine
Clinging to many a worshipp'd shrine;
Fierce fitful radiance wildly shed
O'er spear and sword, with carnage red, 50
Shone o'er the suppliant and the flying,
And kindled pyres for Romans dying.

Weep, Italy! alas! that e'er
Should tears alone thy wrongs° declare!        *sufferings*
The time hath been when *thy* distress
Had roused up empires for redress!
Now, her long race of glory run,
Without a combat Rome is won,
And from her plunder'd temples forth
Rush the fierce children of the north, 60
To share beneath more genial skies
Each joy their own rude clime denies.

Ye who on bright Campania's shore
Bade your fair villas rise of yore,
With all their graceful colonnades,
And crystal baths, and myrtle shades,
Along the blue Hesperian deep,
Whose glassy waves in sunshine sleep;[8]
Beneath your olive and your vine
Far other inmates now recline, 70

And the tall plane, whose roots ye fed
With rich libations duly shed,[9]
O'er guests, unlike your vanish'd friends,
Its bowery canopy extends:
For them the southern heaven is glowing,
The bright Falernian nectar flowing;
For them the marble halls unfold,
Where nobler beings dwelt of old,
Whose children for barbarian lords
Touch the sweet lyre's resounding chords,      80
Or wreaths of Pæstan roses twine,
To crown the sons of Elbe and Rhine.[10]

Yet though luxurious they repose
Beneath Corinthian porticoes,
While round them into being start,
The marvels of triumphant art;
Oh! not for them hath genius given
To Parian stone[11] the fire of heaven,
Enshrining in the forms he wrought
A bright eternity of thought.      90
In vain the natives of the skies
In breathing marble round them rise,
And sculptured nymphs, of fount or glade,
People the dark-green laurel shade;
Cold are the conqueror's heart and eye
To visions of divinity;
And rude his hand which dares deface
The models of immortal grace.

Arouse ye from your soft delights!
Chieftains! the war-note's call invites;      100
And other lands must yet be won,
And other deeds of havock done.
Warriors! your flowery bondage break,
Sons of the stormy north, awake!

The barks are launching from the steep,
Soon shall the Isle of Ceres weep,[12]
And Afric's burning winds afar
Waft the shrill sounds of Alaric's war.
Where shall his race of victory close?
When shall the ravaged earth repose?      110

But hark! what wildly mingling cries
From Scythia's camp tumultuous rise?

Why swells dread Alaric's name on air?
A sterner conqueror hath been there!
A conqueror—yet his paths are peace,
He comes to bring the world's release;
He of the sword that knows no sheath,
Th' avenger, the deliverer—Death!

Is then that daring spirit fled?
Doth Alaric slumber with the dead?                    120
Tamed are the warrior's pride and strength,
And he and earth are calm at length.
The land where heaven unclouded shines,
Where sleep the sunbeams on the vines;
The land by conquest made his own,
Can yield him now—a grave alone.
But his—her lord from Alp to sea—
No common sepulchre shall be!
Oh, make his tomb where mortal eye
Its buried wealth may ne'er descry!                   130
Where mortal foot may never tread
Above a victor-monarch's bed.
Let not his royal dust be hid
'Neath star-aspiring pyramid;[13]
Nor bid the gather'd mound arise,
To bear his memory to the skies.
Years roll away—oblivion claims
Her triumph o'er heroic names;
And hands profane disturb the clay
That once was fired with glory's ray;                 140
And Avarice, from their secret gloom,
Drags e'en the treasures of the tomb.[14]
But thou, O leader of the free!
That general doom awaits not thee!
Thou, where no step may e'er intrude,
Shalt rest in regal solitude,
Till, bursting on thy sleep profound,
Th' Awakener's final trumpet sound.[15]

Turn ye the waters from their course,
Bid Nature yield to human force,                      150
And hollow in the torrent's bed
A chamber for the mighty dead.
The work is done—the captive's hand
Hath well obey'd his lord's command.
Within that royal tomb are cast
The richest trophies of the past,

The wealth of many a stately dome,
And gold and gems of plunder'd Rome;
And when the midnight stars are beaming,
And ocean-waves in stillness gleaming,                    160
Stern in their grief, his warriors bear
The Chastener of the Nations there;
To rest, at length, from victory's toil,
Alone, with all an empire's spoil!

Then the freed current's rushing wave,
Rolls o'er the secret of the grave;
Then streams the martyr'd captives' blood
To crimson that sepulchral flood,
Whose conscious tide alone shall keep
The mystery in its bosom deep.                    170
Time hath past on since then—and swept
From earth the urns where heroes slept;
Temples of gods, and domes of kings,
Are mouldering with forgotten things;
Yet shall not ages e'er molest
The viewless home of Alaric's rest:
Still rolls, like them, th' unfailing river,
The guardian of his dust for ever.

---

[1] For these monsters who gave their names to these perils, see *The Odyssey* bk. 12.

[2] From ch. 31 of Edward Gibbon, *Decline and Fall*.

[3] After the taking of Athens by Sylla, "though such numbers were put to the sword, there were as many who laid violent hands upon themselves in grief for their sinking country. What reduced the best men among them to this despair of finding any mercy or moderate terms for Athens, was the well-known cruelty of Sylla; yet partly by the intercession of Midias and Calliphon, and the exiles who threw themselves at his feet, partly by the entreaties of the senators who attended him in that expedition, and being himself satiated with blood besides, he was at last prevailed upon to stop his hand, and in compliment to the ancient Athenians, he said, 'he forgave the many for the sake of the few, the *living for the dead*.'"—Plutarch. [FH, her emphasis]

John and William Langhorne, *Sylla*, in *Plutarch's Lives* (1770). Notoriously cruel Roman general and dictator Lucius Cornelius Sulla (138–78 B.C.) captured Athens in a bloody sack in 86 B.C.

[4] At the narrow pass of Thermopylae in 480 B.C., a small band of Spartans and their allies held off Xerxes' large Persian army; though eventually overwhelmed, their heroism was crucial to the Greek defense. At the same pass in 279 B.C., the Greeks held back the Gauls (who ultimately prevailed), and in 191 B.C. the Romans successfully repelled Antiochus III of Syria. Scythia (Ukraine) was home to "barbarian" tribes; see Gibbon ch. 31.

[5] The elite unit that led the resistance to Philip II of Macedon, who defeated the Thebans at the battle of Chaeronea in 338 B.C.; two years later Alexander the Great destroyed the city.

[6] The Capitoline hill is the center of Rome's political and religious life. Patrician and hero Marcus Furius Camillus (4th c. B.C.) saved Rome from the invading Gauls.

[7] "At the hour of midnight, the Salarian gate was silently opened, and the inhabitants were awakened by the tremendous sound of the Gothic trumpet. Eleven hundred and sixty-three

years after the foundation of Rome, the Imperial city, which had subdued and civilised so considerable a [part] of mankind, was delivered to the licentious fury of the tribes of Germany and Scythia."—*Decline and Fall of the Roman Empire, Vol. 5, p.* 311. [FH; Ch. 31]

⁸ Campania, in southern Italy in the area of Naples, was famed in ancient times for its wealth and luxury; the Hesperian deep is the western sea, called thus for Hesperus, the evening star.

⁹ The plane-tree was much cultivated among the Romans, upon account of its extraordinary shade, and they used to nourish it with wine instead of water, believing (as Sir W. Temple observes) "This tree loved that liquor, as well as those who used to drink under its shade."—*See the notes to Melmoth's Pliny.* [FH]

William Melmoth (1710–89) ed., *The Letters of Pliny the Consul: With Occasional Remarks* (1747), bk. 5, letter 6, to Apollonaris; cf. 9th rev. ed., 2 vols. (London: J. Dodsley, 1796), 1.266n. Nephew of Pliny the Elder (the author of *Historia Naturalis* who perished in the eruption of Vesuvius), Pliny the Younger (b. 61) was a proconsul, famed for his letters (*Epistolae*). Diplomat William Temple (1628–99) was celebrated for engineering the triple alliance against France in 1688, and in 1674, for the marriage of William and Mary. Also a man of letters and gardening enthusiast, he wrote *Upon the Gardens of Epicurus.*

¹⁰ *Falernus*: region of southern Italy famed for wine. *Paestum*: ancient city south of Naples.

¹¹ The Aegean island of Paros was famed for lustrous white marble.

¹² Sicily was anciently considered as the favoured and peculiar dominion of Ceres. [FH]

In the fair fields of Enna, Ceres' daughter Proserpine was kidnapped by Dis, god of the underworld; each spring she was allowed to return to the upper world for six months.

¹³ Napoleon's invasion of Egypt (1797–98) stimulated interest in these royal tombs.

¹⁴ In the late 18th c., ancient tombs and monuments were being looted for art collectors.

¹⁵ See Revelation 8.7–11.19; trumpet blasts announce the Apocalypse and Last Judgment.

---

## The Wife of Asdrubal

*"This [. . .] governor, who had braved death, when it was at a distance, and protested that the sun should never see him survive* Carthage, *this fierce* Asdrubal, *was so mean-spirited, as to come alone, and privately throw himself at the conqueror's feet. The general, [was well] pleased to see his proud rival humbled, [but] granted his life, and kept him to grace his triumph. The* Carthaginians *in the citadel no sooner understood that their commander had abandoned the place, than they threw open the gates, and put the proconsul in possession of* Byrsa. *The* Romans *had now no enemy to contend with but the nine hundred deserters, who, being reduced to despair, retired into the temple of* Æsculapius, *which was a second citadel within the first. There the proconsul attacked them; and those unhappy wretches, finding there was no way to escape, set fire to the temple. As the flames spread, they retreated from one part to another, till they got to the roof of the building. There* Asdrubal's *wife appeared in her best apparel, as if the day of her death had been a day of triumph [to her]; and after having uttered the most bitter imprecations against her husband, whom she saw standing below with* Æmilianus,—*Base coward! said she,* the mean things thou hast done to save thy life, shall not avail thee; thou shalt die this instant, at least, in thy two children. *Having thus spoke, she drew out a dagger, stabbed them both, and, while they were yet struggling for life, threw them from the top of the temple, and leaped down after them into the flames."*

—Ancient Universal History.¹

The sun sets brightly—but a ruddier glow
O'er Afric's heaven the flames of Carthage throw;
Her walls have sunk, and pyramids of fire
In lurid splendor from her domes aspire;
Sway'd by the wind, they wave—while glares the sky
As when the desert's red Simoom° is nigh;                    *wind*
The sculptured altar, and the pillar'd hall,
Shine out in dreadful brightness ere they fall;
Far o'er the seas the light of ruin streams,
Rock, wave, and isle, are crimson'd by its beams;          10
While captive thousands, bound in Roman chains,
Gaze in mute horror on their burning fanes;°              *temples*
And shouts of triumph, echoing far around,
Swell from the victor's tents with ivy crown'd.[2]

But mark! from yon fair temple's loftiest height
What towering form bursts wildly on the sight,
All regal in magnificent attire,
And sternly beauteous in terrific ire?
She might be deem'd a Pythia[3] in the hour
Of dread communion and delirious power;                    20
A being more than earthly, in whose eye
There dwells a strange and fierce ascendancy.
The flames are gathering round—intensely bright,
Full on her features glares their meteor-light,
But a wild courage sits triumphant there,
The stormy grandeur of a proud despair;
A daring spirit, in its woes elate,
Mightier than death, untameable by fate.
The dark profusion of her locks unbound,
Waves like a warrior's floating plumage round;            30
Flush'd is her cheek, inspired her haughty mien,
She seems th' avenging goddess of the scene.

Are those *her* infants, that with suppliant-cry
Cling round her, shrinking as the flame draws nigh,
Clasp with their feeble hands her gorgeous vest,
And fain would rush for shelter to her breast?
Is that a mother's glance, where stern disdain,
And passion awfully vindictive, reign?

Fix'd is her eye on Asdrubal, who stands,
Ignobly safe, amidst the conquering bands;               40
On him, who left her to that burning tomb,
Alone to share her children's martyrdom;

Who when his country perish'd, fled the strife,
And knelt to win the worthless boon of life.
"Live, traitor, live!" she cries, "since dear to thee,
E'en in thy fetters, can existence be!
Scorn'd and dishonour'd, live!—with blasted name,
The Roman's triumph not to grace, but shame.
O slave in spirit! bitter be thy chain
With tenfold anguish to avenge my pain!                           50
Still may the manès° of thy children rise          *avenging spirits*
To chase calm slumber from thy wearied eyes;
Still may their voices on the haunted air
In fearful whispers tell thee to despair,
Till vain remorse thy wither'd heart consume,
Scourged by relentless shadows of the tomb!
E'en now my sons shall die—and thou, their sire,
In bondage safe, shalt yet in them expire.
Think'st thou I love them not?—'Twas thine to fly—
'Tis mine with these to suffer and to die.                        60
Behold their fate!—the arms that cannot save
Have been their cradle, and shall be their grave."

Bright in her hand the lifted dagger gleams,
Swift from her children's hearts the life-blood streams;
With frantic laugh she clasps them to the breast
Whose woes and passions soon shall be at rest;
Lifts one appealing, frenzied glance on high,
Then deep midst rolling flames is lost to mortal eye.[4]

[1] *Universal History, from the Earliest Account of Time to the Present, compiled from original authors . . . ; The Ancient Part*, 7 vols. (London: J. Batley, 1736–50), 4 (1739), 778 (bk. 3, ch. 7). During the 2d and 3d centuries B.C., Carthage's sway in the western Mediterranean was challenged by Rome, which finally destroyed it in the Third Punic War (149–46 B.C.). Æmilianus is Scipio Africanus Minor, Roman general and son of Æmilius Paullus. The surviving Carthaginians were sold into slavery, and Hasdrubal lived comfortably as a state prisoner in Italy. The desperate woman's suicidal leap would become a Hemans icon, reprised (for instance) in *The Suliote Mother* and *The Last Song of Sappho*.
[2] It was a Roman custom to adorn the tents of victors with ivy. [FH]
In her commonplace book (Houghton Library MS Eng 767.89), FH credits this information to Plutarch.
[3] Medium of Apollo at the oracle of Delphi, whose entranced communications were interpreted by male priests. Cf. the image for Stephania in *The Widow of Crescentius* 1.148.
[4] An alexandrine (six-foot) meter enhances the drama.

## *Heliodorus in the Temple*

[King Seleucus IV (reigned 187–76 B.C.) sent his chief minister Heliodorus to seize treasures from the temple at Jerusalem. Drawing on Maccabees (Old Testament Apocrypha), Hemans's tale of divine protection speaks to Britain's boast, in the wake of its defeat of Napoleon, of being a modern Jerusalem, providentially protected. The verse form is the "Venus and Adonis" stanza (so named from Shakespeare's poem, and like a typical sestet in a Shakespearean sonnet.]

From Maccabees, book 2, chapter 3.—21. "Then it would have pitied a man to see the falling down of the multitude of all sorts, and the fear of the high priest, being in such an agony.—22. They then called upon the Almighty Lord to keep the things committed of trust safe and sure, for those that had committed them.—23. Nevertheless Heliodorus executed that which was decreed.—24. Now as he was there present himself with his guard about the treasury, the Lord of Spirits, and the Prince of all Power, caused a great apparition, so that all that presumed to come in with him were astonished at the power of God, and fainted, and were sore afraid.—25. For there appeared unto them an horse with a terrible rider upon him, and adorned with a very fair covering, and he ran fiercely, and smote at Heliodorus with his forefeet, and it seemed that he that sat upon the horse had complete harness[1] of gold.—26. Moreover, two other young men appeared before him, notable in strength, excellent in beauty, and comely in apparel, who stood by him on either side, and scourged him continually, and gave him many sore stripes.—27. And Heliodorus fell suddenly to the ground, and was compassed with great darkness; but they that were with him took him up, and put him into a litter.—28. Thus him that lately came with great train, and with all his guard into the said treasury, they carried out, being unable to help himself with his weapons, and manifestly they acknowledged the power of God.—29. For he by the hand of God was cast down, and lay speechless, without all hope of life."

    A sound of woe in Salem!°—mournful cries          *Jerusalem*
      Rose from her dwellings—youthful cheeks were pale,
    Tears flowing fast from dim and aged eyes,
      And voices mingling in tumultuous wail;
    Hands raised to heaven in agony of prayer,
    And powerless wrath, and terror, and despair.

    Thy daughters, Judah! weeping, laid aside
      The regal splendor of their fair array,
    With the rude sackcloth girt their beauty's pride,
      And throng'd the streets in hurrying, wild dismay;      10

While knelt thy priests before *his* awful shrine,
Who made, of old, renown and empire thine.

But on the spoiler moves—the temple's gate,
  The bright, the beautiful, his guards unfold,
And all the scene reveals its solemn state,
  Its courts and pillars, rich with sculptured gold;
And man, with eye unhallow'd, views th' abode,
The sever'd spot, the dwelling-place of God.

Where art thou, Mighty Presence! that of yore
  Wert wont between the cherubim to rest,
Veil'd in a cloud of glory, shadowing o'er
  Thy sanctuary the chosen and the blest?
Thou! that didst make fair Sion's ark[2] thy throne,
And call the oracle's recess thine own!

Angel of God! that through th' Assyrian host,
  Clothed with the darkness of the midnight-hour,[3]
To tame the proud, to hush th' invader's boast,
  Didst pass triumphant in avenging power,
Till burst the dayspring on the silent scene,
And death alone reveal'd where thou hadst been.

Wilt thou not wake, O Chastener! in thy might,
  To guard thine ancient and majestic hill,
Where oft from heaven the full Shechinah's[4] light
  Hath stream'd the house of holiness to fill?
Oh! yet once more defend thy loved domain,
Eternal one! Deliverer! rise again!

Fearless of thee, the plunderer, undismay'd,
  Hastes on, the sacred chambers to explore
Where the bright treasures of the fane are laid,
  The orphan's portion, and the widow's store;
What recks *his* heart though age unsuccour'd die,
And want consume the cheek of infancy?

Away, intruders!—hark! a mighty sound!
  Behold, a burst of light!—away, away!
A fearful glory fills the temple round,
  A vision bright in terrible array!
And lo! a steed of no terrestrial frame,
His path a whirlwind, and his breath a flame!

His neck is clothed with thunder[5]—and his mane
  Seems waving fire—the kindling of his eye

20

30

40

50

Is as a meteor—ardent with disdain
    His glance—his gesture, fierce in majesty!
Instinct with light he seems, and form'd to bear
Some dread archangel through the fields of air.

But who is he, in panoply of gold,
    Throned on that burning charger?—bright his form,
Yet in its brightness awful to behold,
    And girt with all the terrors of the storm!
Lightning is on his helmet's crest—and fear
Shrinks from the splendor of his brow severe.          60

And by his side two radiant warriors stand
    All-arm'd, and kingly in commanding grace—
Oh! more than kingly, godlike!—sternly grand
    Their port indignant, and each dazzling face
Beams with the beauty to immortals given,
Magnificent in all the wrath of heaven.

Then sinks each gazer's heart—each knee is bow'd
    In trembling awe—but, as to fields of fight,
Th' unearthly war-steed, rushing through the crowd,
    Bursts on their leader in terrific might;         70
And the stern angels of that dread abode
Pursue its plunderer with the scourge of God.

Darkness—thick darkness!—low on earth he lies,
    Rash Heliodorus—motionless and pale—
Bloodless his cheek, and o'er his shrouded eyes
    Mists, as of death, suspend their shadowy veil;
And thus th' oppressor, by his fear-struck train,
Is borne from that inviolable fane.

The light returns—the warriors of the sky
    Have pass'd, with all their dreadful pomp, away;         80
Then wakes the timbrel, swells the song on high
    Triumphant, as in Judah's elder day;
Rejoice, O city of the sacred hill!
Salem, exult! thy God is with thee still.

[1] Body armor.
[2] A sacred box in the inner chamber of the Temple at Jerusalem (Sion, Zion) that housed the tablets of the Ten Commandments.
[3] In an incident recorded in Isaiah 37 and 2 Kings 19, the prophet Isaiah counseled the Jewish king Hezekiah not to fear an invading Assyrian force; during the night God sent an angel who destroyed 185,000 of its army. Byron wrote a memorable poem on the subject, *The Destruction of Sennacherib*, in *Hebrew Melodies* (1815).
[4] Or *Shekinah* (Hebrew for "dwelling"), i.e., God's presence.

[5] "Hast thou given the horse strength? Hast thou clothed his neck with thunder?"—*Job*, chapter 39, verse 19. [FH]

The voice of God scoffing at human pretensions.

---

## Night-Scene in Genoa

[Under Roman rule, the port city of Genoa had flourished. In the 11th c., leagued with Pisa, it drove the Arabs from Corsica and Sardinia, but then contended with this ally for control of these islands. In 1284, after a long era of war, Genoa prevailed. FH's scene is set in 1169, with implied, cautionary reference to Genoa's history of factionalism. In the 15th c., in military and financial rivalry with Venice, its republic was weakened by internal strife between the Ghibellines and the Guelphs (parties supporting the emperors and popes, respectively), and their foreign influencers. France and Milan controlled the city at various times from the 14th c. to the 16th c.; in the 17th c. and 18th c., it fell under Spanish, French, and Austrian control. In 1797 Napoleon forced Genoa to join a republic, and in 1805 annexed it to France. In 1814, the Congress of Vienna (with Britain's cooperation) united this republic with the kingdom of Sardinia, a betrayal of republicanism that dismayed British liberals. Hemans's verse form is the octosyllabic couplet.]

FROM SISMONDI'S "RÉPUBLIQUES ITALIENNES"

*"En même temps que les Génois poursuivoient avec ardeur la guerre contra Pise, ils étoient déchirés eux-mêmes par une discorde civile. [. . .] Les consuls de l'année 1169, pour rétablir la paix dans leur patrie, au milieu des factions sourdes à leur voix et plus puissantes qu'eux, furent obligés d'ourdir en quelque sorte une conspiration. Ils commencèrent par s'assurer secrètement des dispositions pacifiques de plusieurs des citoyens, qui cependant étoient entraînés dans les émeutes par leur parenté avec les chefs de faction; puis, se concertant avec le vénérable vieillard Hugues, leur archevêque, ils firent, long-temps avant le lever du soleil, appeler au son des cloches les citoyens au parlement: ils se flattoient que la surprise et l'alarme de cette convocation inattendue, au milieu de l'obscurité de la nuit, rendroit l'assemblée et plus complète et plus docile. Les citoyens, en accourant au parlement général, virent, au milieu de la place publique, le vieil archevêque, entouré de son clergé en habit de cérémonies, et portant des torches allumées, tandis que les reliques de Saint Jean-Baptiste, le protecteur de Gênes, étoient exposées devant lui, et que les citoyens les plus respectables portoient à leurs mains des croix suppliantes. Dès que l'assemblée fut formée, le vieillard se leva; et de sa voix cassée il conjura les chefs de parti, au nom du Dieu de paix, au nom du salut de leurs âmes, au nom de leur patrie et de la liberté, dont leurs discordes entraîneroient la ruine, de jurer sur l'Évangile l'oubli de leurs querelles, et la paix à venir.*

*Les hérauts, dès qu'il eut fini de parler, s'avancèrent aussitôt vers Roland Avogado, le chef de l'une des factions, qui étoit présent à l'assemblée; et, secondés par les acclamations de tout le peuple, et par les prières de ses parens eux-mêmes, ils le sommèrent de se conformer au voeu des consuls et de la nation.*

*Roland, à leur approche, déchira ses habits; et, s'asseyant par terre en versant des larmes, il appela à haute voix les morts qu'il avoit juré de venger, et qui ne lui permettoient pas de pardonner leurs vieilles offenses. Comme on ne pouvoit le déterminer à s'avancer, les consuls eux-mêmes, l'archevêque et le clergé, s'approchèrent de lui; et, renouvelant leurs prières, ils l'entraînèrent enfin, et lui firent jurer sur l'Évangile l'oubli de ses inimitiés passées.*

   *Les chefs du parti contraire, Foulques de Castro et Ingo de Volta, n'étoient pas présens à l'assemblée; mais le peuple et le clergé se portèrent en foule à leurs maisons: ils les trouvèrent déjà ébranlés par ce qu'ils venoient d'apprendre; et, profitant de leur émotion, ils leur firent jurer une réconciliation sincère, et donner le baiser de paix aux chefs de la faction opposée. Alors les cloches de la ville sonnèrent en témoignage d'allégresse; et l'archevêque de retour sur la place publique, entonna un Te Deum avec tout le peuple, en honneur du Dieu de paix qui avoit sauvé leur patrie."*
              —Histoire des Républiques Italiennes, *vol. II. pages 149–50.*[1]

In Genoa, when the sunset gave
Its last warm purple to the wave,
No sound of war, no voice of fear,
Was heard, announcing danger near:
Though deadliest foes were there, whose hate
But slumber'd till its hour of fate,
Yet calmly, at the twilight's close,
Sunk the wide city to repose.

But when deep midnight reign'd around,
All sudden woke the alarm-bell's sound,            10
Full swelling, while the hollow breeze
Bore its dread summons o'er the seas.
Then, Genoa, from their slumber started
Thy sons, the free, the fearless hearted;
Then mingled with th' awakening peal
Voices, and steps, and clash of steel.
Arm, warriors, arm! for danger calls,
Arise to guard your native walls!
With breathless haste the gathering throng
Hurry the echoing streets along;             20
Through darkness rushing to the scene
Where their bold councils still convene.
—But there a blaze of torches bright
Pours its red radiance on the night,
O'er fane, and dome, and column playing,
With every fitful night-wind swaying,
Now floating o'er each tall arcade,
Around the pillar'd scene display'd,
In light relieved by depth of shade;
And now, with ruddy meteor-glare,            30
Full streaming on the silvery hair
And the bright cross of him who stands,
Rearing that sign with suppliant hands,

Girt with his consecrated train,
The hallow'd servants of the fane.

Of life's past woes, the fading trace
Hath given that aged patriarch's face
Expression holy, deep, resign'd,
The calm sublimity of mind.
Years o'er his snowy head have pass'd,                    40
And left him of his race the last;
Alone on earth—yet still his mien
Is bright with majesty serene;
And those high hopes, whose guiding-star
Shines from th' eternal worlds afar,
Have with that light illumed his eye,
Whose fount is immortality,
And o'er his features pour'd a ray
Of glory, not to pass away.
He seems a being who hath known                           50
Communion with his God alone,
On earth by nought but pity's tie
Detain'd a moment from on high!
One to sublimer worlds allied,
One, from all passion purified,
E'en now half mingled with the sky,
And all prepared—oh! not to die—
But, like the prophet, to aspire,
In heaven's triumphal car of fire.[2]

He speaks—and from the throngs around                    60
Is heard not e'en a whisper'd sound;
Awe-struck each heart, and fix'd each glance,
They stand as in a spell-bound trance:
He speaks—oh! who can hear nor own
The might of each prevailing tone?

"Chieftains and warriors! ye, so long
Aroused to strife by mutual wrong,
Whose fierce and far-transmitted hate
Hath made your country desolate;
Now by the love ye bear her name,                         70
By that pure spark of holy flame
On freedom's altar brightly burning,
But, once extinguish'd—ne'er returning;
By all your hopes of bliss to come
When burst the bondage of the tomb;

By Him, the God who bade us live
To aid each other, and forgive;
I call upon ye to resign
Your discords at your country's shrine,
Each ancient feud in peace atone,                    80
Wield your keen swords for her alone,
And swear upon the cross, to cast
Oblivion's mantle o'er the past."

No voice replies—the holy bands
Advance to where yon chieftain stands,
With folded arms and brow of gloom,
O'ershadow'd by his floating plume.
To him they lift the cross—in vain—
He turns—oh! say not with disdain,
But with a mien of haughty grief,                    90
That seeks not, e'en from heaven, relief:
He rends his robes—he sternly speaks—
Yet tears are on the warrior's cheeks.

"Father! not thus the wounds may close
Inflicted by eternal foes.
Deem'st thou *thy* mandate can efface
The dread volcano's burning trace?
Or bid the earthquake's ravaged scene
Be, smiling, as it once hath been?
No!—for the deeds the sword hath done          100
Forgiveness is not lightly won;
The words, by hatred spoke, may not
Be, as a summer breeze, forgot!
'Tis vain—we deem the war-feud's rage
A portion of our heritage.
Leaders, now slumbering with their fame,
Bequeath'd us that undying flame;
Hearts that have long been still and cold
Yet rule us from their silent mould,
And voices, heard on earth no more,              110
Speak to our spirits as of yore.
Talk not of mercy—blood alone
The stain of bloodshed may atone;
Nought else can pay that mighty debt,
The dead forbid us to forget."

He pauses—from the patriarch's brow
There beams more lofty grandeur now;

His reverend form, his aged hand,
Assume a gesture of command,
His voice is awful, and his eye                                120
Fill'd with prophetic majesty.

"The dead!—and deem'st thou *they* retain
Aught of terrestrial passion's stain?
Of guilt incurr'd in days gone by,
Aught but the fearful penalty?
And say'st thou, mortal! blood alone
For deeds of slaughter may atone?
There *hath* been blood—by HIM 'twas shed
To expiate every crime who bled;
Th' absolving God who died to save,                            130
And rose in victory from the grave!
And by that stainless offering given
Alike for all on earth to heaven;
By that inevitable hour
When death shall vanquish pride and power,
And each departing passion's force
Concentrate all in late remorse;
And by the day when doom shall be
Pass'd on earth's millions, and on thee,
The doom that shall not be repeal'd,                           140
Once utter'd, and for ever seal'd;
I summon thee, O child of clay!
To cast thy darker thoughts away,
And meet thy foes in peace and love,
As thou would'st join the blest above."

Still as he speaks, unwonted feeling
Is o'er the chieftain's bosom stealing;
Oh! not in vain the pleading cries
Of anxious thousands round him rise,
He yields—devotion's mingled sense                             150
Of faith, and fear, and penitence,
Pervading all his soul, he bows
To offer on the cross his vows,
And that best incense to the skies,
Each evil passion's sacrifice.

Then tears from warriors' eyes were flowing,
High hearts with soft emotions glowing,
Stern foes as long-loved brothers greeting,
And ardent throngs in transport meeting,

And eager footsteps forward pressing,                    160
And accents loud in joyous blessing;
And when their first wild tumults cease,
A thousand voices echo "Peace!"

Twilight's dim mist hath roll'd away,
And the rich Orient burns with day;
Then, as to greet the sunbeam's birth,
Rises the choral hymn of earth;
Th' exulting strain through Genoa swelling,
Of peace and holy rapture telling.
Far float the sounds o'er vale and steep,                170
The seaman hears them on the deep,
So mellow'd by the gale, they seem
As the wild music of a dream;
But not on mortal ear alone
Peals the triumphant anthem's tone,
For beings of a purer sphere
Bend with celestial joy, to hear.

[1] At the same time that the Genoans were hotly pursuing war against Pisa, they were being torn apart by civil discord. The consuls of the year 1169, in order to re-establish peace in their country, in the midst of factions deaf to their voice and more powerful than they, were obliged to hatch a kind of conspiracy. They began by secretly assuring themselves of the peaceful disposition of some of the citizens, who had nevertheless been drawn into the struggles by family ties with the factions' leaders; then, by agreement with the venerable old Hugues, their archbishop, long before dawn, they rang the bells, calling the citizens to parliament: they cherished the hope that the surprise and alarm in this unexpected summons, in the middle of the darkness of night, would render the assembly better attended and more docile. The citizens, hurrying to the general parliament, found, in the middle of the public square, the old archbishop surrounded by his clergy in ceremonial habits, and carrying lighted torches, while the relics of Saint John the Baptist, the protector of Genoa, were displayed before him, and the most respectable citizens of the town carried in their hands the crosses of suppliants. As soon as the assembly had gathered, the old man stood up; and in a broken voice entreated the leaders of the parties, in the name of the God of peace, in the name of the salvation of their souls, in the name of their country and of liberty, which their quarrels would bring to ruin, to swear upon the Gospel to forget the discord between them, and to bring about peace.

The heralds, as soon as he had finished speaking, advanced toward Roland Avogado, the leader of one of the factions, who was present at the assembly; and, seconded by the acclamations of all the people, and by the entreaties of his relatives themselves, charged him to conform to the wishes of the consuls and of the nation.

Roland, at their approach, rent his garments; and, sitting on the ground and weeping called loudly upon those dead he had sworn to avenge, who would not allow him to pardon their ancient offenses. As he could not be persuaded to move forward, the consuls themselves, the archbishop and the clergy approached him; and, renewing their entreaties, they at last brought him around, and made him swear on the Gospel to forget his former enmities.

The leaders of the opposing party, Foulques de Castro and Ingo de Volta, were not present at the assembly; but the people and the clergy moved en masse to their houses: they found them already shaken by what they had just learned, and, taking advantage of their emotion, they made them swear to a sincere reconciliation, and to give the kiss of peace to the leaders of the

opposing faction. Then the bells of the town rang out in joy; and the archbishop, returned to
the public square, intoning a *Te Deum* with the whole people, in honor of the God of peace who
had saved their country.

J.C.L. Sismondi, *Histoire des Républiques Italiennes du Môyen Age* (1807–17), ch. 10; 1826
Paris ed., 2.140–43. *Te Deum Laudamus* (We Praise Thee Lord) is part of the Mass.

[2] The prophet Elijah ascended to heaven in a chariot of fire (1 Kings 17ff.).

---

## The Troubadour, and Richard Cœur de Lion[1]

[Called "Lionheart" for his military exploits, especially in the Third Crusade (1190–92),
Richard I, king of England 1189–99, was celebrated by troubadour poets and featured in
Scott's *Ivanhoe* (1819). Hemans joins this tradition, eliding the less heroic aspects of Richard's career: preferring imperial conquest to home government, Richard spent only six
months of his reign in England; he sold public offices to fund his participation in the
Crusades, quarreled with his allies, and graced his victories in Palestine with atrocities,
including the massacre of 2,000 prisoners. He failed in his attempt to seize Jerusalem,
which was strongly fortified, but secured Saladin's agreement to allow Christians to visit its
holy sites. On his return home, he was captured in December 1192 by Leopold V of
Austria (a Crusader with whom he had quarreled), who pent him in a castle on the Danube. There, according to legend, his faithful minstrel Blondel de Nesle found him—the
scene that Hemans portrays. Leopold delivered him to Holy Roman Emperor Henry VI,
who in 1194 ransomed him for a huge sum (150,000 marks), raised by a heavy tax on
Richard's subjects, as well as the kingdom itself (it became a fief of the Empire). Richard
returned to England, faced more internal strife, and soon left, spending his final years in
intermittent warfare with Philip II of France, a former ally. He died of wounds, during a
siege of a castle. Hemans also elides the critique of the Crusades voiced in her own day,
even by conservatives: Hannah More put "Romantic crusades" on the same level as "the
ordeal trial, drowning of witches, the torture, and the Inquisition"—all "justly reprobated
as the foulest stain of the respective periods, in which, to the disgrace of human reason,
they existed" (*M. Dupont's Speech* [London, 1793]).

The troubadours were aristocratic poet-musicians who flourished in southern France
from the end of the 11th c. through the 13th c.; many were noblemen and Crusaders, and
some, including Richard I, were kings. In the 13th c., the Church "Crusade" in Provence
against the Albigenses (an ascetic sect deemed heretical) placed the region under suspicion,
and troubadour culture declined. Interest revived in the 18th c. with the troubadour emerging as a type of Romantic artist, a social and cultural hero; see, for example, L.E.L. (Landon), *The Troubadour* (1825) and *The Golden Violet* (1827). FH's verse is octosyllabic couplets, and the inset song is a ballad stanza.]

"Not only the place of Richard's confinement," (when thrown into prison
by the Duke of Austria) "if we believe the literary history of the times, but
even the circumstance of his captivity, was carefully concealed by his vindictive enemies: and both might have remained unknown but for the
grateful attachment of a Provençal bard, or minstrel, named Blondel, who
had shared that prince's friendship, and tasted [experienced] his bounty.
Having travelled over all the European continent to learn the destiny of his

beloved patron [who was a poet, as well as a hero], Blondel accidentally got
intelligence of a certain castle in Germany, where a prisoner of distinction
was confined, and guarded with great vigilance. Persuaded by a secret impulse that this prisoner was the King of England, the minstrel repaired to
the place. But the gates of the castle were shut against him, and he could
obtain no information relative to the name or quality of the unhappy person
[whom] it secured. In this extremity, he [thought] of an expedient for
making the desired discovery. He chaunted, with a loud voice, some verses
of a song, which had been composed partly by himself, partly by Richard;
and to his unspeakable joy, on making a pause, he heard it re-echoed and
continued by the royal captive.—(Hist. Troubadours.) To this discovery
the English monarch is said to have eventually owed his release."
—See Russell's Modern Europe, vol. 1, p. 369.[2]

The Troubadour o'er many a plain
Hath roam'd unwearied, but in vain.
O'er many a rugged mountain-scene,
And forest-wild, his track hath been;
Beneath Calabria's° glowing sky                              *(toe of Italy)*
He hath sung the songs of chivalry,
His voice hath swell'd on the Alpine breeze,
And rung through the snowy Pyrenees;
From Ebro's banks to Danube's wave,
He hath sought his prince, the loved, the brave,                 10
And yet, if still on earth thou art,
O monarch of the lion-heart!
The faithful spirit, which distress
But heightens to devotedness,
By toil and trial vanquish'd not,
Shall guide thy minstrel to the spot.

He hath reach'd a mountain hung with vine,
And woods that wave o'er the lovely Rhine;
The feudal towers that crest its height
Frown in unconquerable might;                                    20
Dark is their aspect of sullen state,
No helmet hangs o'er the massy gate[3]
To bid the wearied pilgrim rest,
At the chieftain's board a welcome guest;
Vainly rich evening's parting smile
Would chase the gloom of the haughty pile,°       *large building*
That midst bright sunshine lowers° on high,        *lours, menaces*
Like a thunder-cloud in a summer-sky.

Not these the halls where a child of song
Awhile may speed the hours along;                                30

Their echos should repeat alone
The tyrant's mandate, the prisoner's moan,
Or the wild huntsman's bugle-blast,
When his phantom-train are hurrying past.[4]

The weary minstrel paused—his eye
Roved o'er the scene despondingly:
Within the lengthening shadow, cast
By the fortress-towers and ramparts vast,
Lingering he gazed—the rocks around
Sublime in savage grandeur frown'd;                    40
Proud guardians of the regal flood,
In giant strength the mountains stood;
By torrents cleft, by tempests riven,
Yet mingling still with the calm blue heaven.
Their peaks were bright with a sunny glow,
But the Rhine all shadowy roll'd below;
In purple tints the vineyards smiled,
But the woods beyond waved dark and wild;
Nor pastoral pipe, nor convent's bell,
Was heard on the sighing breeze to swell,               50
But all was lonely, silent, rude,
A stern, yet glorious solitude.

But hark! that solemn stillness breaking,
The Troubadour's wild song is waking.
Full oft that song, in days gone by,
Hath cheer'd the sons of chivalry;
It hath swell'd o'er Judah's mountains lone,
Hermon! thy echos have learn'd its tone;
On the Great Plain[5] its notes have rung,
The leagued Crusaders['] tents among;                   60
'Twas loved by the Lion-heart, who won
The palm in the field of Ascalon;
And now afar o'er the rocks of Rhine
Peals the bold strain of Palestine.

THE TROUBADOUR'S SONG

"Thine hour is come, and the stake is set°,"          *(for impalement)*
    The Soldan° cried to the captive knight,               *Sultan*
"And the sons of the Prophet° in throngs are met       *Muhammed*
    To gaze on the fearful sight.

But be our faith by thy lips profess'd,
    The faith of Mecca's shrine,                            70

Cast down the red-cross that marks thy vest,
　　And life shall yet be thine."

"I have seen the flow of my bosom's blood,
　　And gazed with undaunted eye;
I have borne the bright cross through fire and flood,
　　And think'st thou I fear to die?

I have stood where thousands, by Salem's° towers,     *Jerusalem's*
　　Have fall'n for the name divine;
And the faith that cheer'd *their* closing hours
　　Shall be the light of mine."           80

"Thus wilt thou die in the pride of health,
　　And the glow of youth's fresh bloom?
Thou art offer'd life, and pomp, and wealth,
　　Or torture and the tomb."

"I have been where the crown of thorns was twined
　　For a dying Saviour's brow;
*He* spurn'd the treasures that lure mankind,
　　And I reject them now!"[6]

"Art thou the son of a noble line
　　In a land that is fair and blest?
And doth not thy spirit, proud captive! pine,          90
　　Again on its shores to rest?

Thine own is the choice to hail once more
　　The soil of thy fathers' birth,[7]
Or to sleep, when thy lingering pangs are o'er,
　　Forgotten in foreign earth."

"Oh! fair are the vine-clad hills that rise
　　In the country of my love;
But yet, though cloudless my native skies,
　　There's a brighter clime above!          100

The bard hath paused—for another tone
Blends with the music of his own;
And his heart beats high with hope again,
As a well-known voice prolongs the strain.

"Are there none within thy father's hall,
　　Far o'er the wide blue main,
Young Christian! left to deplore° thy fall,          *lament*
　　With sorrow deep and vain?

There are hearts that still, through all the past,
　　Unchanging have loved me well;          110

There are eyes whose tears were streaming fast
    When I bade my home farewell.

Better they wept o'er the warrior's bier
    Than th' apostate's living stain;
There's a land where those who loved, when here,
    Shall meet to love again."

'Tis he! thy prince—long sought, long lost,
The leader of the red-cross host!
'Tis he!—to none thy joy betray,
Young Troubadour! away, away!                      120
Away to the island of the brave,
The gem on the bosom of the wave,[8]
Arouse the sons of the noble soil,
To win their lion from the toil;°                          *trap*
And free the wassail-cup shall flow,
Bright in each hall the hearth shall glow;
The festal board shall be richly crown'd,
While knights and chieftains revel round,
And a thousand harps with joy shall ring,
When merry England hails her king.            130

[1] Later published in *LS* 1826, 357–62, signed "Mrs. Hemans," with full-page illustration on 356. This version shears off FH's notes (head and end) and supplies this endnote by editor Alaric Watts: "In printing Mrs. Hemans's beautiful poem 'The Troubadour and Richard Coeur de Lion,' I have deviated from the plan of the Literary Souvenir, it having already been published. I had prepared a short illustration [i.e., poem] to accompany the plate myself; but having met with this poem, I most willingly gave it the preference. Three other pieces, not less attractive of their kind, will be found in the foregoing pages, from Mrs. Hemans's pen, which were furnished by her expressly for this work" (362); these were *The Peasant Girl of the Rhone*, *The Wreck*, and *The Child and the Dove*.

[2] Paraphrased from William Russell, *The History of Modern Europe: with an Account of the Decline & Fall of the Roman Empire: and a View of the Progress of Society, from the Rise of Modern Kingdoms to the Peace of Paris in 1763; in a Series of Letters from a Nobleman to His Son. A New Edition, with a Continuation, Terminating at the Pacification of Paris, in 1815*, 7 vols. (London, 1818), 1.313n. 10, citing "Chron. T. Wykes" (Thomas Wykes [fl.1258–93], *Chronicon vulgo dictum Chronicon, 1066–1289*) and "Hist. Troubadours"—i.e., Jean Baptiste de la Curne de Sainte-Palaye, *Histoire littéraire des troubadours contenant leurs vies, les extraits de leurs pièces, & plusieurs particularités sur les moeurs, les usages & l'histoire du douzième & du treizième siècles* (Paris, 1774), trans. and abridged by Susannah Dobson (d. 1795) as *Literary History of the Troubadours* (London: Cadell, 1779; 2d ed., 1807). Like Russell, FH equates troubadour and minstrel but she knew the distinction: by the thirteenth century, *troubadour* (French, "finder" or "inventor") specified a professional with noble patronage (e.g., Blondel), originating new songs in the *langue d'oc* of Provence (rather than singing old ones, as did bards).

[3] It was a custom in feudal times to hang out a helmet on a castle, as a token that strangers were invited to enter, and partake of hospitality. So in the romance of 'Perceforest,' "ils fasoient mettre au plus hault de leur hostel ung heaume, en signe que tous les gentils hommes et gentilles femmes entrassent [trespassans leurs chemins s'embatissent] hardiement en leur hostel comme en leur propre." [FH]

They [tous gentils hommes et gentilles femmes] had placed at the top of their house a helmet, as a sign that all gentlemen and gentlewomen should enter [make their ways] boldly into their house as into their own.

*Perceforest*, part 3, vol. 2, stanza xliv, about a custom in Great Britain. The sentence continues, "car leurs biens estoient de avantaige a tous nobles hommes et nobles femmes trespassans le royaume" (for their welfare was advantageous to all noble men and noble women traversing the realm). This long fourteenth-century chivalric romance, set in mythical Britain and featuring Alexander the Great and the knight Perceforest, was first printed in Paris in 1528.

[4] Popular tradition has made several mountains in Germany the haunt of the *wild Jäger*, or supernatural huntsman—the superstitious tales relating to the Unterburg are recorded in Eustace's Classical Tour; and it is still believed in the romantic district of the Odenwald, that the knight of Rodenstein, issuing from his ruined castle, announces the approach of war by traversing the air with a noisy armament to the opposite castle of Schnellerts.—See the *"Manuel pour les Voyageurs sur le Rhin," and "Autumn on the Rhine."* [FH]

Aloys Wilhelm Schreiber (1761–1841) with Aloise Schreiber, *Manuel pour les Voyageurs sur le Rhin* (Heidelberg, J. Egelmann, 1816); Charles Edward Dodd, *An Autumn Near the Rhine; or, Sketches of Courts, Society, Scenery, &cc. in Some of the States Bordering on the Rhine* (London, 1818). *Der wilde Jäger*, a popular literary ballad by Gottfried Bürger, was translated by Scott in the 1790s. John Chetwode Eustace, *A Tour through Italy*, 3 vols. (London, 1813–19); in the 4th ed., *A Classical Tour through Italy, An. MDCCCII*, 4 vols. (London, 1817), he relates the legends of the Unterberg (1.76–77), some of which FH copied into her commonplace book, 20–22 (Houghton Library MS Eng 767).

[5] The Plain of Esdraelon, called by way of eminence the "Great Plain"; in Scripture, and elsewhere, the "field of Megiddo," the "Galilæan Plain." This plain, the most fertile part of all the land of Canaan, [. . .] has been the scene of many a memorable contest [. . .] It has been a chosen place for encampment in every contest carried on in this country, from the days of Nabuchodonosor, king of the Assyrians, [. . .] until the disastrous march of [Napoleon] Buonaparté from Egypt into Syria. [. . .] warriors out of "every nation which is under heaven," have pitched their tents upon the Plain of Esdraelon, and have beheld the various banners of their nations wet with the dews of Thabôr and of Hermon.—*Dr. Clarke's Travels*. [FH]

Paraphrasing Edward Daniel Clarke (1769–1822), "The Holy Land, From Tiberias to Napolose," in *Travels in Various Countries of Europe, Asia and Africa*, 6 vols. (London: Cadell and Davies, 1812), part. 2, sec. 1, ch. 15 (496–501). The famous Plain of Esdraelon is in northern Palestine; the term *Armageddon* is derived from the name *Megiddo*. Canaan and Judah are ancient kingdoms. From Mount Thabôr (1929 ft) in northern Israel, Barak descended with an army of 10,000 to defeat Sisera (Joshua 19.22); this mountain is believed by many Christians to be the site of Christ's Transfiguration. Mt. Hermon (9,232 ft.) is on the border of Syria and Lebanon; Ascalo is a city of Palestine; Nebuchadnezzar II of Babylonia (ruled 605–562 B.C.) besieged Jerusalem and carried the Jews into captivity in Babylon. Palestine was conquered by Alexander the Great in the 4th c. B.C., by the Romans in the 1st c. B.C., by the Persians in 7th c., by Crusaders in 1099, and fought fresh waves of Crusaders in the 12th c. and 13th c. In 1798–99 Napoleon tried to challenge Britain's hegemony in the eastern Mediterranean by seizing Egypt, Palestine, and Syria.

[6] Satan tempted Jesus with promises of wealth and power (Matthew 4.1–10).

[7] *LS*] father's birth.

The revision makes the image more domestic than dynastic.

[8] "This precious stone set in the silver sea." Shakespeare's *Richard II*. [FH]

John of Gaunt's dying lament for England's lost but perhaps redeemable grandeur (2.1.46); he also warmly praises its Crusaders, 'Renownèd for their deeds . . . far from home, / For Christian service and true chivalry" (53–54).

## The Death of Conradin

[Descendant of Holy Roman Emperors Frederick II and Conrad IV, Conradin the Younger (1252–68) was the last legitimate heir of the Hohenstauffen dynasty. Born in Bavaria, he spent his childhood in Germany while his uncle Manfred (Frederick II's illegitimate son) made himself king of Sicily. When Manfred died in 1266, Sicily went to Charles I (Count of Anjou in France), to whom Pope Urban IV had offered it and Naples in return for his support of the pro-Papal Guelph party. Conradin, allied with the anti-Papal Florentine Ghibellines, invaded Italy to pursue his own claims, finding support in several cities. But in 1268 he was defeated by Charles, captured, and executed at Naples, along with supporters and his friend Frederick of Baden. Charles himself would suffer a major defeat in the "Sicilian Vespers," a bloody rebellion in 1282, the subject of Hemans's *The Vespers of Palermo* (1823). *The Death of Conradin* glances at the fraught revival of Italian nationalism in the Napoleonic era. Napoleon invaded Italy in the late 1790s and was hailed as a liberator, but in 1806 he installed his brother Joseph as king of Naples, then in 1808 replaced him with Joachim Murat, and over all failed to unite Italy or secure its self-government. After his defeat, the Congress of Vienna (1814–15) restored the old regimes, while secret revolutionary societies such as the Carbonari continued to be active.]

FROM SISMONDI'S "RÉPUBLIQUES ITALIENNES"

"*La défaite de Conradin ne devoit mettre une terme ni à ses malheurs, ni aux vengeances du roi (Charles d'Anjou). L'amour du peuple pour l'héritier légitime du trône avoit éclaté d'une manière effrayante; il pouvoit causer de nouvelles révolutions, si Conradin demeuroit en vie; et Charles, revêtant [couvrant] sa défiance et sa cruauté des formes de la justice, résolut de faire périr sur l'échafaud le dernier rejeton de la Maison de Souabe, l'unique espérance de son parti.[. . .] Un seul juge, Provençal et sujet de Charles, dont les historiens n'ont pas voulu conserver le nom, osa voter pour la mort: d'autres se renfermèrent dans un timide et coupable silence; et Charles, sur l'autorité de ce seul juge, fit prononcer, par Robert de Bari, protonotaire du royaume, la sentence de mort contre Conradin et tous ses compagnons. Cette sentence fut communiquée à Conradin, comme il jouoit aux échecs; on lui laissa peu de temps pour se préparer à son exécution, et, le 26 d'octobre, il fut conduit, avec tous ses amis, sur la place du marché de Naples, le long du rivage de la mer: Charles étoit présent, avec toute sa cour, et une foule immense entouroit le roi vainqueur et le roi condamné.[. . .] Conradin étoit entre les mains des bourreaux: il détacha lui-même son manteau, et, s'étant mis à genoux pour prier, il se releva en s'écriant: 'Oh, ma mère! quelle profonde douleur te causera la nouvelle qu'on va te porter de moi!' Puis il tourna les yeux sur la foule qui l'entouroit: il vit les larmes, il entendit les sanglots de son peuple; alors, détachant son gant, il jeta au milieu de ses sujets ce gage d'un combat de vengeance, et tendit sa tête au bourreau. Après lui, sur le même échafaud, Charles fit trancher la tête au duc d'Autriche, aux comtes Gualférano et Bartolomméo Lancia, et aux comtes Gerard et Gavano Donoratico de Pise. Par un raffinement de cruauté, Charles voulut que le premier, fils du second, précédât son père, et mourût entre ses bras. Les cadavres, d'après ses ordres, furent exclus d'une terre sainte [de la terre consacrée des cimetières], et inhumés sans pompe sur le rivage de la mer. Charles II, cependant, fit dans la suite bâtir sur le même lieu, une église de carmélites, comme pour appaiser ces ombres irritées.*"[1]

No cloud to dim the splendor of the day
Which breaks o'er Naples and her lovely bay,
And lights that brilliant sea and magic shore
With every tint that charm'd the great of yore;
Th' imperial ones of earth—who proudly bade
Their marble domes e'en Ocean's realm invade.

That race is gone—but glorious Nature here
Maintains unchanged her own sublime career,
And bids these regions of the sun display
Bright hues, surviving empires past away.                    10

The beam of Heaven expands—its kindling smile
Reveals each charm of many a fairy isle,
Whose image floats, in softer colouring drest,
With all its rocks and vines, on Ocean's breast.
Misenum's cape hath caught the vivid ray,
On Roman streamers there no more to play;
Still as of old, unalterably bright,
Lovely it sleeps on Posilippo's height,
With all Italia's sunshine to illume
The ilex° canopy of Virgil's tomb.                    *evergreen oak*   20
Campania's plains° rejoice in light, and spread          *(near Naples)*
Their gay luxuriance o'er the mighty dead;
Fair glittering to thine own transparent skies,
Thy palaces, exulting Naples! rise;
While, far on high, Vesuvius rears his peak,
Furrow'd and dark with many a lava streak.

O ye bright shores of Circe and the Muse!
Rich with all Nature's and all fiction's hues;
Who shall explore your regions, and declare
The poet err'd to paint Elysium there?                    30
Call up his spirit, wanderer! bid him guide
Thy steps, those syren-haunted seas beside,
And all the scene a lovelier light shall wear,
And spells more potent shall pervade the air.
What though his dust be scatter'd, and his urn
Long from its sanctuary of slumber torn,[2]
Still dwell the beings of his verse around,
Hovering in beauty o'er th' enchanted ground;
His lays are murmur'd in each breeze that roves
Soft o'er the sunny waves and orange-groves.                    40
His memory's charm is spread o'er shore and sea,
The soul, the genius° of Parthenope;                    *presiding spirit*

Shedding o'er myrtle-shade and vine-clad hill
The purple radiance of Elysium still.[3]

Yet that fair soil and calm resplendent sky
Have witness'd many a dark reality.
Oft o'er those bright blue seas the gale hath borne
The sighs of exiles, never to return.[4]
There with the whisper of Campania's gale
Hath mingled oft affection's funeral-wail,                    50
Mourning for buried heroes—while to her
That glowing land was but their sepulchre.[5]
And there of old, the dread, mysterious moan
Swell'd from strange voices of no mortal tone;
And that wild trumpet, whose unearthly note
Was heard, at midnight, o'er the hills to float
Around the spot where Agrippina died,
Denouncing vengeance on the matricide.[6]

Past are those ages—yet another crime,
Another woe, must stain th' Elysian clime.                   60
There stands a scaffold on the sunny shore—
It must be crimson'd ere the day is o'er!
There is a throne in regal pomp array'd,—
A scene of death from thence must be survey'd.
Mark'd ye the rushing throngs?—each mien is pale,
Each hurried glance reveals a fearful tale;
But the deep workings of th' indignant breast,
Wrath, hatred, pity, must be all suppress'd;
The burning tear awhile must check its course,
Th' avenging thought concentrate all its force,             70
For tyranny is near—and will not brook
Aught but submission in each guarded look.

Girt with his fierce Provençals, and with mien
Austere in triumph, gazing on the scene,[7]
And in his eye a keen suspicious glance
Of jealous pride and restless vigilance,
Behold the conqueror!—vainly in his face,
Of gentler feeling hope would seek a trace;
Cold, proud, severe, the spirit which hath lent
Its haughty stamp to each dark lineament;                    80
And pleading mercy, in the sternness there,
May read at once her sentence—to despair!

But thou, fair boy! the beautiful, the brave,
Thus passing from the dungeon to the grave,[8]

While all is yet around thee which can give
A charm to earth, and make it bliss to live;
Thou on whose form hath dwelt a mother's eye,
Till the deep love that not with thee shall die
Hath grown too full for utterance—can it be?
And is this pomp of death prepared for *thee?*          90
Young, royal Conradin! who should'st have known
Of life as yet the sunny smile alone!
Oh! who can view thee, in the pride and bloom
Of youth, array'd thus richly for the tomb,
Nor feel, deep-swelling in his inmost soul,
Emotions tyranny may ne'er control?
Bright victim! to ambition's[9] altar led,
Crown'd with all flowers that heaven on earth can shed,
Who, from th' oppressor towering in his pride,
May hope for mercy—if to thee denied?          100

There is dead silence on the breathless throng,—
Dead silence all the peopled shore along,
As on the captive moves—the only sound,
To break that calm so fearfully profound,
The low, sweet murmur of the rippling wave,
Soft as it glides, the smiling shore to lave;
While on that shore, his own fair heritage,
The youthful martyr to a tyrant's rage
Is passing to his fate—the eyes are dim
Which gaze, through tears that dare not flow, on him:          110
He mounts the scaffold—doth his footstep fail?
Doth his lip quiver? doth his cheek turn pale?
Oh! it may be forgiven him, if a thought
Cling to that world, for him with beauty fraught,
To all the hopes that promised Glory's meed,
And all th' affections that with him shall bleed!
If, in his life's young day-spring, while the rose
Of boyhood on his cheek yet freshly glows,
One human fear convulse his parting breath,
And shrink from all the bitterness of death!          120
But no!—the spirit of his royal race
Sits brightly on his brow—that youthful face
Beams with heroic beauty—and his eye
Is eloquent with injured majesty.
He kneels—but not to man—his heart shall own
Such deep submission to his God alone!
And who can tell with what sustaining power
That God may visit him in fate's dread hour?

How the still voice, which answers every moan,
May speak of hope,—when hope on earth is gone? 130

That solemn pause is o'er—the youth hath given
One glance of parting love to earth and heaven;
The sun rejoices in th' unclouded sky,
Life all around him glows—and he must die!
Yet 'midst his people, undismay'd, he throws
The gage of vengeance for a thousand woes;[10]
Vengeance, that like their own volcano's fire,
May sleep suppress'd awhile—but not expire.
One softer image rises o'er his breast,
One fond regret, and all shall be at rest! 140
"Alas, for thee, my mother! who shall bear
To thy sad heart the tidings of despair,
When thy lost child is gone?"—that thought can thrill
His soul with pangs one moment more shall still.
The lifted axe is glittering in the sun—
It falls—the race of Conradin is run!
Yet from the blood which flows that shore to stain,
A voice shall cry to heaven—and not in vain!
Gaze thou, triumphant from thy gorgeous throne,
In proud supremacy of guilt alone, 150
Charles of Anjou!—but that dread voice shall be
A fearful summoner e'en yet to thee!

The scene of death is closed—the throngs depart,
A deep stern lesson graved[11] on every heart.
No pomp, no funeral rites, no streaming eyes,
High-minded boy! may grace thine obsequies.
O vainly royal and beloved! thy grave,
Unsanctified, is bath'd by ocean's wave,
Mark'd by no stone, a rude, neglected spot,
Unhonour'd, unadorn'd—but *unforgot*; 160
For thy deep wrongs° in tameless hearts shall live,          *sufferings of*
Now mutely suffering—never to forgive!                             *injustice*

The sunset fades from purple heavens away,—
A bark hath anchor'd in th' unruffled bay;
Thence on the beach descends a female form,[12]
Her mien with hope and tearful transport warm;
But life hath left sad traces on her cheek,
And her soft eyes a chasten'd heart bespeak,
Inured to woes—yet what were all the past!
*She* sunk not feebly 'neath affliction's blast, 170
While one bright hope remain'd—who now shall tell

Th' uncrown'd, the widow'd, how her loved-one fell?
To clasp her child, to ransom and to save,
The mother came—and she hath found his grave!
And by that grave, transfix'd in speechless grief,
Whose death-like trance denies a tear's relief,
Awhile she kneels—till roused at length to know,
To feel the might, the fulness of her woe,
On the still air a voice of anguish wild,
A mother's cry, is heard—"My Conradin! my child!"          180

---

[1] The defeat of Conradin was not to put an end either to his misfortunes, nor to the vengeances of the king (Charles of Anjou). The love of the people for the legitimate heir to the throne had broken out in an alarming way: it could cause new revolutions, if Conradin remained alive; and Charles, covering his mistrust and cruelty in garbs of justice, resolved to put to death on the scaffold the last heir of the House of Swabia, the sole hope of his party. One sole judge, Provençal and subject to Charles, whose name historians have not wished to preserve, ventured to vote for death: others hid in timid and guilty silence; and Charles, on the authority of this sole judge, had pronounced, by Robert de Bari, protonotary of the kingdom, the sentence of death against Conradin and all his companions. This sentence was communicated to Conradin, as he was playing chess: he was allowed little time to prepare himself for his execution, and the 26th of October, he was conducted, with all his friends, to the market square of Naples, along the seacoast: Charles was present, with all his court, and a huge crowd surrounded the victorious king and the condemned king. Conradin was in the hands of his executioners: he removed his cloak himself, and, having knelt to pray, he rose up to cry, "Oh, my mother! what deep sorrow this news of me will cause you!" Then he turned his eyes on the crowd that surrounded him: he saw the tears, he heard the sobs of his people; then, removing his glove, he threw among his subjects this pledge of a combat of vengeance, and presented his head to the executioner. After him, on the same scaffold, Charles had the executioner behead the duke of Austria, counts Gualferano and Bartolommeo Lancia, and counts Gerard and Gavano Donoratico of Pisa. With a refinement of cruelty, Charles had the former, son of the latter, precede his father, and die in his arms. The bodies, by his orders, were excluded from the consecrated ground of cemeteries, and buried without ceremony on the seashore. Charles II, however, afterward had a carmelite church built on the same spot, as if to appease the angry shades.

A conflation of passages from J.C.L. Sismondi, *Histoire* (1809), vol. 3, ch. 21 (1826 ed., 386–89); FH's parentheses.

[2] The urn, supposed to have contained the ashes of Virgil, has long since been lost. [FH]

[3] Parthenope, one of the sirens, is also an ancient name for Naples; in 1799 the French named the captured kingdom the Parthenopean Republic.

[4] Many Romans of exalted rank were formerly banished to some of the small islands in the Mediterranean, on the coast of Italy. Julia, the daughter of Augustus, was confined many years in the isle of Pandataria, and her daughter, Agrippina, the widow of Germanicus, afterwards died in exile on the same desolate spot. [FH]

Augustus (d. 14), first emperor of Rome, forced his stepson Tiberius to divorce his first wife and marry Julia (39 B.C.–A.D. 14), whom Tiberius then banished to Pandataria, on charges of adultery. When Agrippina (ca.14 B.C.–A.D. 33) accused Tiberius of having Germanicus poisoned, he exiled her to the same isle, where she starved herself to death in protest.

[5] "Quelques souvenirs du coeur, quelques noms de femmes, réclament aussi vos pleurs. C'est à Misène, dans le lieu même où nous sommes, que la veuve de Pompée, Cornélie, conserva jusqu'à la mort son noble deuil; Agrippine pleura long-temps Germanicus sur ces bords. Un jour, le même assassin qui lui ravit son époux la trouva digne de le suivre. L'île de Nisida fut

témoin des adieux de Brutus et de Porcie."—*Madame de Staël*—*Corinne* [FH; Corinne's "Improvisation," bk. 13, ch. 4]

[Some memories of the heart, some names of women, also claim your tears. It was in Miseno, in the same place where we are, that the widow of Pompey, Cornelia, kept till death her noble mourning; Agrippina long wept for Germanicus on these shores. One day, the same assassin who had robbed her of her husband found her worthy to follow him. The Isle of Nisida was witness to the farewells of Brutus and Portia.]

Cornelia (fl. 2d c. B.C.) was actually the famously devout widow of Tiberius Gracchus. In the civil war following the assassination of Julius Caesar, Brutus and other republican conspirators left for Macedonia; his wife, Portia, committed suicide in despair over his fate.

[6] The sight of that coast, and those shores, where the crime [parricide] had been perpetrated, filled [Nero] with continual horrors; besides, there were some, who imagined they heard horrid shrieks and cries [wailings] from *Agrippina*'s tomb, and a mournful sound of trumpets from the neighbouring cliffs and hills. *Nero* therefore flying from such tragical scenes [places . . .], withdrew to *Naples.—See Ancient Universal History.* [FH]

From *Universal History; The Ancient Part*, 7 vols. (London: J. Batley, 1736–40), 5 (1740), bk. 3, ch. 17 (534). FH's excerpt, from the account of matricide, sets up the inverse scene of a mother's grief for her son at the poem's end. Nero had just accomplished the assassination of his mother, on suspicion of her conspiracy against his life. The preceding sentences describe his allies' congratulations, while "*Nero* himself, by a quite opposite dissimulation, pretended to be inconsolably grieved for the death of his mother, answering those who strove to comfort him, that he hated a life, which upon such terms had been saved. However, as the face and aspect of places cannot change like the countenances of men, the sight . . ."; the last sentence of FH's excerpt reads and continues: ". . . tragical places, which incessantly reproached him with the crying greatness and enormity of his crime, withdrew to *Naples*, whence he sent letters to the senate. . . ." These letters indicted his mother's conspiracies, detailed her long history of crimes, "and concluded, that her death ought to be looked upon as a public blessing, and ascribed to the auspicious fortune of the Roman state. [. . .] No one believed the pretended conspiracy; but nevertheless the senators, with wonderful heat and competition, strove to surpass one another in decreeing new honours to Nero on this occasion" (534).

Lines 45–73 form two two embedded sonnets.

[7] "Ce Charles," dit Giovanni Villani, "fut sage et prudent dans les conseils, preux dans les armes, âpre [sévère,] et fort redouté de tous les rois du monde, magnanime et de hautes pensées qui l'égaloient aux plus grandes entreprises; inébranlable dans l'adversité, ferme et fidèle dans toutes ses promesses, parlant peu et agissant beaucoup, *ne riant presque jamais*, décent comme un religieux, zélé catholique, âpre à rendre justice, féroce dans ses regards. Sa taille étoit grande et nerveuse, sa couleur olivâtre, son nez fort grand. Il paroissoit plus fait qu'aucun autre chevalier [seigneur] pour la majesté royale. Il ne dormoit presque point. [. . .] Jamais il ne prit de plaisir aux mimes, aux troubadours, et aux gens de cour."—*Sismondi, Républiques Italiennes*, vol. 3. [FH; ch. 21; her italics]

["That Charles," said Giovanni Villani, "was wise and prudent in council, valiant in arms, harsh [severe] and feared by all the kings of the world, magnanimous and so high-minded that he was equal to the greatest enterprises; unshakeable in adversity, firm and faithful in all his promises, speaking little and doing much, *almost never laughing*, modest as a monk, a zealous catholic, eager to render justice, ferocious in his look. His figure was tall and sinewy, his complexion olive, his nose very large. He seemed more than any other knight to be made for royal majesty. He scarcely slept. He never took pleasure in mimes, or troubadours, or courtiers."]

[8] The political martyrdom of sixteen-year-old Conradin joins the fate of Asdrubal's sons and the boy-martyrs in *The Siege of Valencia* and *Casabianca*.

[9] 2d ed.] Ambition's

[10] The glove referred to above; the vengeance against Charles was the "Sicilian Vespers." The volcano is Vesuvius, long dormant (cf. line 25). In *The Vespers of Palermo*, the awaited eruption

of Etna is troped as revolutionary insurrection: "With what a deep and ominous moan, the voice / Of our great mountain swells [—] There will be soon / A fearful burst!" (1.2).

[11] *Engraved*, but also punning *buried in* (cf. *grave*, 157).

[12] "The Carmine (at Naples) calls to mind the bloody catastrophe of those royal youths, Conradine and Frederick of Austria, butchered before its door; whenever I traversed that square, my heart yearned at the idea of their premature fate, and at the deep distress of Conradine's mother, who, landing on the beach with her son's ransom, found only a lifeless trunk to redeem from the fangs of his barbarous conqueror"—*Swinburne's Travels in the Two Sicilies*. [FH]

"Naples" (1783; Dublin, 1786) 2.60 (2.63–64 in London ed. of 1783); her parentheses.

# Patriotic Effusions of the
# Italian Poets

## (1821)

—⟡⟡⟡—

[Preface to Hemans's translations of six sonnets, by Vincenzo da Filicaja, Carlo Maria
Maggi, Alessandro Marchetti, Alessandro Pegolotti, and Francesco Maria de Conti; *Edinburgh Magazine and Literary Miscellany* 8 (June 1821): 514–15. In FH's day Italian patriotism emerged from a long history of internal rivalries and foreign dominations, most recently by Napoleon. In 1798 he invaded Italy with a liberalizing agenda that won support
from those anticipating progress toward local and national independence; but by 1810 he
had incorporated Rome into the French Empire, and after his fall in 1815, Papal rule was
restored under Austrian protection. In this reactionary régime, secret revolutionary societies such as the Carbonari plotted for independence, with an abortive uprising in 1817 and
agitation into the 1820s.]

Whoever has attentively studied the works of the Italian Poets, from the days
of Dante and Petrarch to those of Foscolo and Pindemonte, must have been
struck with those allusions to the glory and the fall, the renown and the degradation of Italy, which give a melancholy interest to their pages.[1] Amidst all the
vicissitudes of that devoted country, the warning voice[2] of her bards has still been
heard to prophesy the impending storm, and to call up such deep and spirit-
stirring recollections from the glorious past, as have resounded through the land,
notwithstanding the loudest tumults of those discords which have made her

> Long, long a bloody stage,
> For petty kinglings tame,
> Their miserable game
> Of puny war to wage.[3]

There is something very affecting in these vain, though exalted aspirations
after that independence, which the Italians, as a nation, seem destined never to
regain. The strains in which their high-toned feelings on this subject are recorded, produce on our minds the same effect with the song of the imprisoned
bird, whose melody is fraught, in our imagination, with recollections of the
green woodland, the free air, and unbounded sky. We soon grow weary of the
perpetual *violets* and *zephyrs*, whose cloying sweetness pervades the sonnets and
canzoni of the minor Italian Poets, till we are ready to "die in aromatic pain";[4]
nor is our interest much more excited, even by the everlasting *laurel* which inspires the enamoured Petrarch with so ingenious a variety of *concetti*, as might
reasonably cause it to be doubted whether the beautiful Laura, of the emblematic Tree, were the real object of the bard's affection;[5] but the moment a patriotic
chord is struck, our feelings are awakened, and we find it easy to sympathize with

the emotions of a modern Roman, surrounded by the ruins of the Capitol; a Venetian, when contemplating the proud trophies won by his ancestors at Byzantium, or a Florentine amongst the tombs of the mighty dead, in the church of Santa Croce.[6] It is not, perhaps, *now*, the time to plead, with any effect, the cause of Italy; yet cannot we consider that nation as altogether degraded, whose literature, from the dawn of its majestic immortality, has been consecrated to the nurture of every generous principle and ennobling recollection; and whose "choice and master-spirits,"[7] under the most adverse circumstances, have kept alive a flame, which may well be considered as imperishable, since the "ten thousand tyrants" of the land have failed to quench its brightness.[8] We present our readers with a few of the minor effusions in which the indignant, though unavailing regrets of those, who, to use the words of Alfieri, are "Slaves, yet still *indignant* slaves,"[9] have been feelingly pourtrayed. The first of these productions must, in the original, be familiar to every reader who has any acquaintance with Italian literature.[10]

[1] Dante (1265–1321) is revered for the nationalist gesture of writing in Italian; Petrarch (1304–74) was a strong voice for Italian liberty and a supporter of Rienzi's republican movement (FH is thinking of his famous *Ode to Italy*). Venetian Ugo Foscolo (1778–1827) fought with Napoleon against Austria, hoping to restore the Venetian Republic; after Napoleon's fall and Venice's subsequent annexation to Austria, he exiled himself to London. The poetry of Ippolito Pindemonte (1753–1828) supplies epigraphs for *The Abencerrage* and *Arabella Stuart*.

[2] Alluding to the epic poet's cry at the opening of *Paradise Lost* bk. 4 (in which Satan invades the Garden of Eden in search of Adam and Eve): "O for that warning voice, which he who saw / Th' Apocalypse, hear cry in heaven aloud" (see Revelation 12.7–12). *Devoted*: doomed.

[3] Henry Hart Milman (1791–1868), *Fazio, A Tragedy* 2.1.184–87, from a song by Philario lamenting enslaved, "sad and sunken Italy! / The plunderer's common prey!"

[4] Alexander Pope's oft-quoted sarcasm about the hypersensitivity that would "Die of a rose in aromatic pain" (*An Essay on Man* [1733–34], *Epistle I*, 200). *Canzoni*: songs.

[5] *Concetti* ("conceits"): self-consciously elaborate poetic figures. Much of Petrarch's *Rime* concerns his love for Laura, whose name he puns and involves with *l'aura* (the "aura" or halo that graces her divinity); *l'oro* (the gold that is her hair, her halo); *l'ora* (the hour in which he fell in love with her); *lauro* (the laurel tree, emblem of Apollo, the god of poetry, and the source of the laurel crown for poetic fame [Petrarch became Poet Laureate of Rome]), and so forth.

[6] In 1204 Venetians and Crusaders sacked Constantinople (formerly Byzantium) and brought much of its artwork to Venice. The large Franciscan church Santa Croce is Florence's pantheon, containing frescoes by Giotto, a crucifix by Donatello, and other fine art.

[7] Shakespeare, *Julius Caesar* 3.1.161; Antony's seemingly respectful term of address to Caesar's assassins.

[8] Byron's phrase for the legion of Rome's rulers; *Childe Harold's Pilgrimage IV* (1818), cxiv.

[9] Schiavi siam, ma schiavi ognor frementi.—Alfieri. [FH]
[We are slaves, but slaves still quivering (i.e., with angry defiance)]—a famous line from *Misogallo*, sonnet 18, by poet and dramatist Vittorio Alfieri (1749–1803), an enthusiast for the American Revolution who reinvigorated the cause of Italian independence. Staël has Corinne recite this line (*Corinne*, bk. 4, ch. 3)—a bold act in 1807, given that the sonnet's anger is pointed at French invaders.

[10] Filicaja, "Italia, Italia!" which, in the original, FH used for her epigraph to *The Restoration of the Works of Art to Italy* and later rendered in *Translations*. The others appear here for the first time. FH translated eight more sonnets for "Patriotic Lays of Italy," *NMM* 40 (1834): 444–46.

# From *The Siege of Valencia; A Dramatic Poem ...*
## *With Other Poems*
### (1823)

━━◦◦◦◦━━

### *Elysium*[1]

*"In the Elysium of the ancients, we find none but heroes and persons who had either been fortunate or distinguished on earth; the children, and apparently the slaves and lower classes, that is to say, Poverty, Misfortune, and Innocence, were banished to the infernal regions."*
—*Chateaubriand*, Génie du Christianisme.[2]

    Fair wert thou, in the dreams
Of elder time, thou land of glorious flowers,
And summer-winds, and low-ton'd silvery streams,
Dim with the shadows of thy laurel-bowers![3]
    Where, as they pass'd, bright hours
Left no faint sense of parting, such as clings
To earthly love, and joy in loveliest things!

    Fair wert thou, with the light
On thy blue hills and sleepy waters cast,
From purple skies ne'er deepening into night,        10
Yet soft, as if each moment were their last
    Of glory, fading fast
Along the mountains!—but *thy* golden day
Was not as those that warn us of decay.

    And ever, through thy shades,
A swell of deep Eolian sound went by,
From fountain-voices in their secret glades,
And low reed-whispers, making sweet reply
    To summer's breezy sigh!
And young leaves trembling to the wind's light breath,     20
Which ne'er had touch'd them with a hue of death!

    And the transparent sky
Rung as a dome, all thrilling to the strain
Of harps that, midst the woods, made harmony
Solemn and sweet; yet troubling not the brain
    With dreams and yearnings vain,

And dim remembrances, that still draw birth
From the bewildering music of the earth.

    And who, with silent tread,
Mov'd o'er the plains of waving Asphodel?           30
Who, of the hosts, the night-o'erpeopling dead,[4]
Amidst the shadowy amaranth-bowers might dwell,[5]
    And listen to the swell
Of those majestic hymn-notes, and inhale
The spirit wandering in th' immortal gale?

    They of the sword, whose praise,
With the bright wine at nations' feasts, went round!
They of the lyre, whose unforgotten lays
On the morn's wing had sent their mighty sound,
    And in all regions found           40
Their echoes midst the mountains!—and become
In man's deep heart, as voices of his home!

    They of the daring thought!
Daring and powerful, yet to dust allied;
Whose flight thro' stars, and seas, and depths had sought
The soul's far birth-place—but without a guide!
    Sages and seers, who died,
And left the world their high mysterious dreams,
Born midst the olive-woods, by Grecian streams.[6]

    But they, of whose abode           50
Midst her green valleys earth retain'd no trace,
Save a flower springing from their burial-sod,
A shade of sadness on some kindred face,
    A void and silent place
In some sweet home;—thou hadst no wreaths for these,[7]
Thou sunny land! with all thy deathless trees!

    The peasant, at his door
Might sink to die, when vintage-feasts were spread,
And songs on every wind!—From *thy* bright shore
No lovelier vision floated round his head,           60
    Thou wert for nobler dead!
He heard the bounding steps which round him fell,
And sigh'd to bid the festal sun farewell!

    The slave, whose very tears
Were a forbidden luxury, and whose breast
Shut up the woes and burning thoughts of years,
As in the ashes of an urn compress'd;[8]

—*He* might not be thy guest!
No gentle breathings from thy distant sky
Came o'er *his* path, and whisper'd "Liberty!"                    70

  Calm, on its leaf-strewn bier,
Unlike a gift of nature to decay,
Too rose-like still, too beautiful, too dear,
The child at rest before its mother lay;
  E'en so to pass away,
With its bright smile!—Elysium! what wert *thou*,
To her, who wept o'er that young slumberer's brow?

  Thou hadst no home, green land!
For the fair creature from her bosom gone,
With life's first flowers just opening in her hand,                    80
And all the lovely thoughts and dreams unknown,
  Which in its clear eye shone
Like the spring's[9] wakening!—But that light was past—
—Where went the dew-drop, swept before the blast?

  Not where thy[10] soft winds play'd,
Not where thy waters lay in glassy sleep!—
Fade, with thy flowers, thou land of visions, fade!
From thee no voice came o'er the gloomy deep,
  And bade man cease to weep!
Fade, with the amaranth-plain, the myrtle-grove,                    90
Which could not yield one hope to sorrowing love![11]

  For the most lov'd are they,
Of whom Fame speaks not with her clarion-voice
In regal halls!—the shades o'erhang their way,
The vale, with its deep fountains, is their choice,
  And gentle hearts rejoice
Around their steps!—till silently they die,
As a stream shrinks from summer's burning eye.

  And the world knows not then,
Not then, nor ever, what pure thoughts are fled!                    100
Yet these are they, that on the souls of men
Come back, when night her folding veil hath spread,
  The long-remember'd dead!
But not with *thee* might aught save Glory dwell—
—Fade, fade away, thou shore of Asphodel!

---

[1] Rpt. in vol. 2 of *Forest Sanctuary &c* (Boston, 1827), and at the close of FH's last new lifetime volume, *Scenes and Hymns of Life, with other Religious Poems* (1834) 241–47, with this final endnote: "This poem, written some years ago, is re-published from a volume long out of

print; the train of thought it suggests appearing not unsuitable to the spirit of the present work"
(247). FH varies rhyme royal, making her first and fourth lines hexa- rather than deca-syllabic,
the heterometrics evoking medieval troubadour verse.

[2] François René, Vicomte de Chateaubriand (1768–1848), *Le Génie du Christianisme* (The
Genius / Spirit of Christianity) (1802), bk. 6, ch. 6 ("Conclusion of the Doctrines of Christian-
ity—State of Punishments & Rewards in a future Life—Elysium of the ancients"); FH's trans.
A major text of French Romanticism, this popular treatise was admired by Napoleon.

[3] Military victors were crowned with laurel wreaths.

[4] *Forest Sanctuary &c* (Boston ed.), 232, editor's note]: The following is an extract from a
letter of Mrs. Hemans. "There is one line in the poem of Elysium which I should wish altered;
it is the third of the fifth stanza [31], I should like it to stand thus:
        Who, call'd and sever'd from the countless dead,"
  *Asphodel*: a lily fabled to be undying.

[5] *Amaranth*: the flower of heaven or paradise.

31–32, *Scenes*] Called from the dim procession of the Dead, / Who, midst . . .

[6] *Scenes*] 92–98 inserted here, with *lov'd* italicized.

[7] 54–55, *Scenes*] A dim and vacant . . . / . . . *these*,

[8] 66–67, *Scenes*] Kept the mute woes . . . / As embers in a burial urn . . . ;
Slaves, unlike the heroes of Elysium, did not get funerary urns.

[9] *Scenes*] Like spring's first

[10] *Scenes*] thy

[11] *Scenes*] Text ends here; 92–98 are relocated (see n. 6); 99–106, deleted.
  *Myrtle*: an emblem of love.

---

# The Siege of Valencia: A Dramatic Poem

[The volume named for this poem was a respectable success, its edition of 1,000 selling out,
and earning FH and Murray each nearly £66. The subtitle announces a genre not intended
for the stage, and with a respectable lineage. "*A Dramatic Poem*" is the subtitle of Milton's
*Samson Agonistes*; so, too, in Hemans's day, James Macpherson's *Cornala* (1805), Mary
Robinson's *The Sicilian Lover* (1806), Byron's *Manfred* (1817), and George Croly's *Cataline* (1822). Favoring passions over action, the genre is akin to the poetic or "closet" drama.
Although Baillie insisted that her *Plays on the Passions* (1798–1812) were not of this genre,
they were widely admired as if they were, for "delineat[ing] the progress of the higher
passions in the human breast" ("Introductory Discourse"). FH's imaginary 13th-c. Moorish siege of Valencia, a Christian city on Spain's Mediterranean coast, involves the passions
of several intricate conflicts: Christian versus Moor, war versus peace, honor versus shame,
patriarchal versus maternal values. Her canceled subtitle, "or the Race of the Cid" (Houghton Library MS Eng. 1227 64M-40), suggests a clear national, racial, and religious bias,
but in the poem itself the sympathies are complex. On the one hand, the mother Elmina
(of Valencia's ruling family) is an impassioned critic of the human cost of patriotic-religious
warfare, while men such as stern Christian priest Hernandez and his political opponent
Abdullah (his name means "servant of God") voice inhuman, even filicidal rigor. On the
other hand, the imperatives of national honor, noble patrilineage, and patriotic self-
sacrifice—upheld by the royally named Valencian children Ximena and Alphonso, and
embodied as dynastic "honor" in the Valencian governor Gonzalez (Elmina's husband)—
are charged with anti-Napoleonic patriotism, an enthusiasm dating from Hemans's earliest
poetry (e.g., *England and Spain; or, Valour and Patriotism*) and infused with family pride:

two brothers, as well as Captain Alfred Hemans, served in the war in Spain (1808–14)—
"the events of which are so associated in my mind with the most vivid recollections of my
early youth," she wrote early in 1823, "that I could almost fancy I had passed that period
of my life in the days of Chivalry, so high and ardent were the feelings they excited" (*CM*
1.89–90).

   This girlish enthusiasm was part of a national, modern chivalric romance. Napoleon
prohibited Spain's trade with Britain, and in June 1808 replaced King Ferdinand VII with
his brother Joseph. Widespread revolts ensued, and when the French besieged Valencia, a
port central to trade, they met heroic resistance—as throughout the Peninsula. Britain
allied with Portugal and Spanish guerillas. In August Wellington's forces landed in Portugal and negotiated the controversial Convention of Cintra, securing the liberation of Lisbon by conveying the French army and its booty in British ships back to France. Then, with
Sir John Moore in command, the British invaded Spain. With various victories and defeats
(Moore's death in the retreat to Coroña made him a martyr-hero), the war concluded in
1814 with the abdication of Napoleon. British victories in Spain contributed to his down-
fall (Wellington led the victory over Napoleon at Waterloo, in 1815), revived the spirit of
chivalry at home, and raised Britain's military prestige abroad. By 1823, however, the
romance of Spanish resistance was challenged by a messier civil war. Ferdinand returned to
the throne in 1814 (the Bourbon Restoration), with the acclaim of "liberales" and patriots,
but his reactionary measures soon alienated this support and fueled an opposition that
erupted into revolution in 1820. This was put down in 1823 by the French, acting on behalf
of the Holy Alliance of monarchal powers. What had been a valiant Spanish resistance
against a foreign invader in 1808 had become, in 1823, a civil war against a reactionary king
and his French allies. The Houghton Library MS contains a wealth of substantive variants,
some of which are noted. In this draft, Ximena is more militant, Elmina gives fuller voice
to maternal claims and values, including a critique of the masculine culture of glory,
and Gonsalvo (Gonzalez) is more internally conflicted about the claims of honor over
affection.]

> Jndicio ha dado esta no vista hazaña
> Del valor que en los siglos venideros
> Tendrán los Hijos de la fuerte España,
> Hijos de tal padres herederos.
>
> Hallo solá en Numancia todo quanto
> Debe con justo titulo cantarse,
> Y lo que puede dar materia al canto.
>                    Numancia de Cervantes[1]

### ADVERTISEMENT

   The history of Spain records two instances of the severe and self-devoting
heroism, which forms the subject of the following dramatic poem. The first
of these occurred at the siege of Tarifa, which was defended in 1294 for
Sancho, King of Castile, during the rebellion of his brother, Don Juan, by
Guzman, surnamed the Good.[2] The second is related of Alonso Lopez de
Texeda, who, until his garrison had been utterly disabled by pestilence, maintained the city of Zamora for the children of Don Pedro the Cruel, against
the forces of Henrique of Trastamara.[3]

   Impressive as were the circumstances which distinguished both these
memorable sieges, it appeared to the author of the following pages that a
deeper interest, as well as a stronger colour of nationality might be imparted

to the scenes in which she has feebly attempted "to describe high passions and high actions";[4] by connecting a religious feeling with the patriotism and high-minded loyalty which had thus been proved "faithful unto death,"[5] and by surrounding her ideal dramatis personæ with recollections derived from the heroic legends of Spanish chivalry. She has, for this reason, employed the agency of imaginary characters, and fixed upon "*Valencia del Cid*" as the scene to give them

"A local habitation and a name."[6]

Dramatis Personæ

Alvar Gonzalez,[7] *Governor of Valencia*
Alphonso and Carlos, *His Sons*
Hernandez, *A Priest*
Garcias, *A Spanish Knight*
Abdullah, *A Moorish Prince, Chief of the Army
    besieging Valencia*
Elmina, *Wife to Gonzalez*
Ximena, *Her Daughter*
Theresa, *An Attendant*
*Citizens, Soldiers, Attendants, &c.*

Scene 1

*Room in a Palace of Valencia.* Ximena *singing to a Lute.*

ballad[8]

"Thou hast not been with a festal throng,
    At the pouring of the wine;
Men bear not from the Hall of Song,
    A mien so dark as thine!
        —There's blood upon thy shield,
        There's dust upon thy plume,
—Thou hast brought, from some disastrous field,
        That brow of wrath and gloom!"

"And is there blood upon my shield?
    —Maiden! it well may be!                               10
We have sent the streams from our battle-field,
    All darken'd to the sea!
        We have given the founts a stain,
        Midst their woods of ancient pine;
And the ground is wet—but not with rain,
    Deep-dyed—but not with wine!

The ground is wet—but not with rain—
    We have been in war array,

And the noblest blood of Christian Spain
  Hath bathed her soil to-day.                                   20
    I have seen the strong man die,
    And the stripling meet his fate,
Where the mountain-winds go sounding by,
    In the Roncesvalles' Strait.[9]

In the gloomy Roncesvalles' Strait
  There are helms and lances cleft;
And they that moved at morn elate
  On a bed of heath are left!
    There's many a fair young face,
    Which the war steed hath gone o'er;          30
At many a board there is kept a place
    For those that come no more!"

"Alas! for love, for woman's breast,
  If woe like this must be!
—Hast thou seen a youth with an eagle crest,
  And a white plume waving free?
    With his proud quick flashing eye,
    And his mien of knightly state?
Doth he come from where the swords flash'd high,
    In the Roncesvalles' Strait?"                 40

"In the gloomy Roncesvalles' Strait
  I saw and mark'd him well;
For nobly on his steed he sate,
  When the pride of manhood fell!
    —But it is not *youth* which turns
    From the field of spears again;
For the boy's high heart too wildly burns,
    Till it rests amidst the slain!"

"Thou canst not say that *he* lies low,
  The lovely and the brave!                          50
Oh! none could look on his joyous brow,
  And think upon the grave!
    Dark, dark perchance the day
    Hath been with valour's fate,
But *he* is on his homeward way,
    From the Roncesvalles' Strait!"

"There is dust upon his joyous brow,
  And o'er his graceful head;
And the war-horse will not wake him now,
  Tho' it bruise his greensward bed!                  60

—I have seen the stripling die,
And the strong man meet his fate,
Where the mountain-winds go sounding by,
In the Roncesvalles' Strait!"

ELMINA *enters.*

ELMINA. Your songs are not as those of other days,
Mine own Ximena!—Where is now the young
And buoyant spirit of the morn, which once
Breath'd in your spring-like melodies, and woke
Joy's echo from all hearts?

XIMENA.                             My mother, this
Is not the free air of our mountain-wilds;                    70
And these are not the halls, wherein my voice
First pour'd those gladdening strains.

ELMINA.                                   Alas! thy heart
(I see it well) doth sicken for the pure
Free-wandering breezes of the joyous hills,
Where thy young brothers, o'er the rock and heath,
Bound in glad boyhood, e'en as torrent-streams
Leap brightly from the heights. Had we not been
Within these walls thus suddenly begirt,
Thou shouldst have track'd ere now, with step as light,
Their wild wood-paths.

XIMENA.                       I would not but have shared        80
These hours of woe and peril, tho' the deep
And solemn feelings wakening at their voice,
Claim all the wrought-up spirit to themselves,
And will not blend with mirth. The storm doth hush
All floating whispery sounds, all bird-notes wild
O' th' summer-forest, filling earth and heaven
With its own awful music.—And 'tis well!
Should not a hero's child be train'd to hear
The trumpet's blast unstartled, and to look
In the fix'd face of Death without dismay?                    90

ELMINA. Woe! woe! that aught so gentle and so young
Should thus be call'd to stand i' the tempest's path,
And bear the token and the hue of death
On a bright soul so soon! I had not shrunk
From mine own lot, but thou, my child, shouldst move
As a light breeze of heaven, thro' summer-bowers,
And not o'er foaming billows. We are fall'n
On dark and evil days![10]

XIMENA.                       Aye, days, that wake[11]
All to their tasks!—Youth may not loiter now

In the green walks of spring; and womanhood                100
Is summon'd unto conflicts, heretofore
The lot of warrior-souls. But we will take
Our toils upon us nobly! Strength is born
In the deep silence of long-suffering hearts;
Not amidst joy.[12]

ELMINA.             Hast thou some secret woe
That thus thou speak'st?

XIMENA.           What sorrow should be mine,
Unknown to thee?

ELMINA.         Alas! the baleful air
Wherewith the pestilence in darkness walks
Thro' the devoted° city, like a blight               *doomed, steadfast*
Amidst the rose-tints of thy cheek hath fall'n,                110
And wrought an early withering!—Thou hast cross'd
The paths of Death, and minister'd to those
O'er whom his shadow rested, till thine eye
Hath changed its glancing sunbeam for a still,
Deep, solemn radiance, and thy brow hath caught
A wild and high expression, which at times
Fades unto desolate calmness, most unlike
What youth's bright mien should wear. My gentle child!
I look on thee in fear![13]

XIMENA.            Thou hast no cause
To fear for me. When the wild clash of steel,                120
And the deep tambour, and the heavy step
Of armed men, break on our morning dreams;
When, hour by hour, the noble and the brave
Are falling round us, and we deem it much
To give them funeral-rites, and call them blest
If the good sword, in its own stormy hour,
Hath done its work upon them, ere disease
Had chill'd their fiery blood;—it is no time
For the light mien wherewith, in happier hours,
We trod the woodland mazes, when young leaves                130
Were whispering in the gale.—My Father comes—
Oh! speak of me no more. I would not shade
His princely aspect with a thought less high
Than his proud duties claim.

                            **GONZALEZ** *enters.*

ELMINA.            My noble lord!
Welcome from this day's toil!—It is the hour
Whose shadows, as they deepen, bring repose
Unto all weary men; and wilt not thou

Free thy mail'd bosom from the corslet's weight,[14]
To rest at fall of eve?
GONZALEZ.                         There may be rest
For the tired peasant, when the vesper-bell                    140
Doth send him to his cabin, and beneath
His vine and olive, he may sit at eve,
Watching his children's sport: but unto *him*
Who keeps the watch-place on the mountain-height,
When Heaven lets loose the storms that chasten realms
—Who speaks of rest?
XIMENA.                         My father, shall I fill
The wine-cup for thy lips, or bring the lute
Whose sounds thou lovest?
GONZALEZ.                         If there be strains of power
To rouse a spirit, which in triumphant scorn
May cast off nature's feebleness, and hold               150
Its proud career unshackled, dashing down
Tears and fond thoughts to earth; give voice to those![15]
I have need of such, Ximena! we must hear
No melting music now.
XIMENA.                         I know all high
Heroic ditties of the elder time,
Sung by the mountain-Christians,[16] in the holds
Of th' everlasting hills, whose snows yet bear
The print of Freedom's step; and all wild strains
Wherein the dark serranos[17] teach the rocks
And the pine forests deeply to resound               160
The praise of later champions. Wouldst thou hear
The war-song of thine ancestor, the Cid?
GONZALEZ.  Aye, speak of him; for in that name is power,
Such as might rescue kingdoms! Speak of him!
We are his children! They that can look back
I' th' annals of their house on such a name,
How should *they* take dishonour by the hand,
And o'er the threshold of their father's halls
First lead her as a guest?[18]
ELMINA.                         Oh, why is this?
How my heart sinks!
GONZALEZ.                         It must not fail thee *yet*,               170
Daughter of heroes![19]—thine inheritance
Is strength to meet all conflicts. Thou canst number
In thy long line of glorious ancestry
Men, the bright offering of whose blood hath made
The ground it bathed e'en as an altar, whence
High thoughts shall rise for ever. Bore they not,

Midst flame and sword, their witness of the Cross,
With its victorious inspiration girt
As with a conqueror's robe, till th' infidel[20]
O'erawed, shrank back before them?—Aye, the earth          180
Doth call them martyrs, but *their* agonies
Were of a moment, tortures whose brief aim
Was to destroy, within whose powers and scope
Lay nought but dust.— And earth doth call them *martyrs!*
Why, Heaven but claim'd their blood, their lives, and not
The things which grow as tendrils round their hearts;
No, not their children![21]

ELMINA.                          Mean'st thou?—know'st thou
      aught?—
   I cannot utter it—My sons! my sons!
   Is it of them?—Oh! wouldst thou speak of them?
GONZALEZ. A mother's heart divineth but too well!          190
ELMINA. Speak, I adjure thee!—I can bear it all.—
   Where are my children?
GONZALEZ.                          In the Moorish camp
   Whose lines have girt the city.
XIMENA.                               But they live?
   —All is not lost, my mother!
ELMINA.                          Say, they live.
GONZALEZ. Elmina, still they live.
ELMINA.                          But captives!—They
   Whom my fond heart had imaged to itself
   Bounding from cliff to cliff amidst the wilds
   Where the rock-eagle seem'd not more secure
   In its rejoicing freedom!—And my boys[22]
   Are captives with the Moor!—Oh! how was this?          200
GONZALEZ. Alas! our brave Alphonso, in the pride
   Of boyish daring, left our mountain-halls,
   With his young brother, eager to behold
   The face of noble war. Thence on their way
   Were the rash wanderers captured.[23]
ELMINA                          'Tis enough.
   —And when shall they be ransom'd?
GONZALEZ.                          There is ask'd
   A ransom far too high.
ELMINA.                          What! have we wealth
   Which might redeem a monarch, and our sons
   The while wear fetters?—Take thou all for them,
   And we will cast our worthless grandeur from us,          210
   As 'twere a cumbrous robe!—Why, *thou* art one,
   To whose high nature pomp hath ever been

But as the plumage to a warrior's helm,
Worn or thrown off as lightly. And for me,
Thou knowest not how serenely I could take
The peasant's lot upon me, so my heart,
Amidst its deep affections undisturb'd,
May dwell in silence.

XIMENA.                    Father! doubt thou not
But we will bind ourselves to poverty,
With glad devotedness, if this, but this,                    220
May win them back.—Distrust us not, my father!
We can bear all things.

GONZALEZ.                    Can ye bear disgrace?

XIMENA. We were not *born* for this.

GONZALEZ.                    No, thou sayst well!
Hold to that lofty faith.—My wife, my child!
Hath earth no treasures richer than the gems
Torn from her secret caverns?—If by them
Chains may be riven, then let the captive spring
Rejoicing to the light!—But he, for whom
Freedom and life may but be worn with shame,
Hath nought to do, save fearlessly to fix                    230
His stedfast look on the majestic heavens,
And proudly die!

ELMINA.                    Gonzalez, *who* must die?

GONZALEZ (*hurriedly*). They on whose lives a fearful price is set,
But to be paid by treason!—Is't enough?
Or must I yet seek words?

ELMINA.                    That look saith more!
Thou canst not mean——

GONZALEZ.                    I do! why dwells there not
Power in a glance to speak it?—They must die!
They—must their names be told—*Our sons* must die
Unless I yield the city![24]

XIMENA.                    Oh! look up!
My mother, sink not thus!—Until the grave                    240
Shut from our sight its victims, there is hope.

ELMINA (*in a low voice*).
Whose knell was in the breeze?—No, no, not *theirs!*
Whose was the blessed voice that spoke of hope?
—And there *is* hope!—I will not be subdued—
I will not hear a whisper of despair!
For Nature is all-powerful, and her breath
Moves like a quickening spirit o'er the depths
Within a father's heart.—Thou too, Gonzalez,
Wilt tell me there is hope!

GONZALEZ (*solemnly*).　　　　Hope but in Him
　　Who bade the patriarch lay his fair young son　　　　250
　　Bound on the shrine of sacrifice, and when
　　The bright steel quiver'd in the father's hand
　　Just raised to strike, sent forth his awful voice
　　Through the still clouds, and on the breathless air,
　　Commanding to withhold!<sup>25</sup> —Earth has no hope,
　　It rests with Him.
ELMINA.　　　　　　*Thou* canst not tell me this!
　　Thou father of my sons, within whose hands
　　Doth lie thy children's fate.
GONZALEZ.　　　　　　　　If there have been
　　Men in whose bosoms Nature's voice hath made
　　Its accents as the solitary sound　　　　260
　　Of an o'erpowering torrent, silencing
　　Th' austere and yet divine remonstrances
　　Whisper'd by faith and honour, lift thy hands,
　　And, to that Heaven, which arms the brave with strength,
　　Pray, that the father of thy sons may ne'er
　　Be thus found wanting!
ELMINA.　　　　　Then their doom is seal'd!
　　Thou wilt not save thy children?
GONZALEZ.　　　　　　　　Hast thou cause,
　　Wife of my youth! to deem it lies within
　　The bounds of possible things, that I should link
　　My name to that word—*traitor?*—They that sleep　　　　270
　　On their proud battle-fields, thy sires and mine,
　　Died not for this!
ELMINA.　　　　Oh, cold and hard of heart!
　　Thou shouldst be born for empire, since thy soul
　　Thus lightly from all human bonds can free
　　Its haughty flight!—Men! men! too much is yours
　　Of vantage; ye, that with a sound, a breath,
　　A shadow, thus can fill the desolate space
　　Of rooted up affections, o'er whose void
　　Our yearning hearts must wither!—So it is,
　　Dominion must be won!—Nay, leave me not—<sup>26</sup>　　　　280
　　My heart is bursting, and I *must* be heard!
　　Heaven hath given power to mortal agony
　　As to the elements in their hour of might
　　And mastery o'er creation!—Who shall dare
　　To mock that fearful strength?—I *must* be heard!
　　Give me my sons!
GONZALEZ.　　　　That they may live to hide
　　With covering hands th' indignant flush of shame

On their young brows, when men shall speak of him
They call'd their father!—Was the oath, whereby,
On th' altar of my faith, I bound myself,[27]                    290
With an unswerving spirit to maintain
This free and christian city for my God,
And for my king, a writing traced on sand?
That passionate tears should wash it from the earth,
Or e'en the life-drops of a bleeding heart
Efface it, as a billow sweeps away
The last light vessel's wake?—Then never more
Let man's deep vows be trusted!—though enforced
By all th' appeals of high remembrances,
And silent claims o' th' sepulchres, wherein              300
His fathers with their stainless glory sleep,
On their good swords! Thinkst thou *I* feel no pangs?
He that hath given me sons, doth know the heart
Whose treasure she recalls.[28]—Of this no more.
'Tis vain. I tell thee that th' inviolate cross
Still, from our ancient temples, must look up
Through the blue heavens of Spain, though at its foot
I perish, with my race. Thou *darest* not ask
That I, the son of warriors—men who died
To fix it on that proud supremacy—                       310
Should tear the sign of our victorious faith,
From its high place of sunbeams, for the Moor
In impious joy to trample!

ELMINA.                        Scorn me not
In mine extreme of misery!—Thou art strong—
Thy heart is not as mine.—My brain grows wild;[29]
I know not what I ask!—And yet 'twere but
Anticipating fate—since it must fall,
That cross *must* fall at last! There is no power,
No hope within this city of the grave,
To keep its place on high. Her sultry air              320
Breathes heavily of death, her warriors sink
Beneath their ancient banners, ere the Moor
Hath bent his bow against them; for the shaft
Of pestilence flies more swiftly to its mark,
Than the arrow of the desert.[30] Ev'n the skies
O'erhang the desolate splendour of her domes
With an ill omen's aspect, shaping forth,
From the dull clouds, wild menacing forms and signs
Foreboding ruin. *Man* might be withstood,
But who shall cope with famine and disease,            330
When leagued with armed foes?—Where now the aid,

Where the long-promised lances of Castile?[31]
—We are forsaken, in our utmost need,
By heaven and earth forsaken!
GONZALEZ.                              If this be,
(And yet I will not deem it) we must fall
As men that in severe devotedness
Have chosen their part, and bound themselves to death,
Through high conviction that their suffering land,
By the free blood of martyrdom alone,
Shall call deliverance down.
ELMINA.                              Oh! I have stood                    340
Beside thee through the beating storms of life,
With the true heart of unrepining love,
As the poor peasant's mate doth cheerily,
In the parch'd vineyard, or the harvest-field,
Bearing her part, sustain with him the heat
And burden of the day;[32] —But now the hour,
The heavy hour is come, when human strength
Sinks down, a toil-worn pilgrim, in the dust,
Owning that woe is mightier!—Spare me yet
This bitter cup, my husband!—Let not her,                               350
The mother of the lovely, sit and mourn
In her unpeopled home, a broken stem,
O'er its fall'n roses dying!
GONZALEZ.                              Urge me not,
Thou that through all sharp conflicts hast been found
Worthy a brave man's love, oh! urge me not
To guilt, which through the midst of blinding tears,
In its own hues thou seest not!—Death may scarce
Bring aught like this!
ELMINA.                              All, all thy gentle race,
The beautiful beings that around thee grew,
Creatures of sunshine! Wilt thou doom them all?                         360
—She too, thy daughter—doth her smile unmark'd
Pass from thee, with its radiance, day by day?
Shadows are gathering round her—seest thou not?
The misty dimness of the spoiler's breath
Hangs o'er her beauty, and the face which made
The summer of our hearts, now doth but send,
With every glance, deep bodings through the soul,
Telling of early fate.
GONZALEZ.                              I see a change
Far nobler on her brow!—She is as one,
Who, at the trumpet's sudden call, hath risen                           370
From the gay banquet, and in scorn cast down

The wine-cup, and the garland, and the lute
Of festal hours, for the good spear and helm,
Beseeming sterner tasks.—Her eye hath lost
The beam which laugh'd upon th' awakening heart,
E'en as morn breaks o'er earth. But far within
Its full dark orb, a light hath sprung, whose source
Lies deeper in the soul.—And let the torch
Which but illumed the glittering pageant, fade!
The altar-flame, i' th' sanctuary's recess,                          380
Burns quenchless, being of heaven!—She hath put on
Courage, and faith, and generous constancy,
Ev'n as a breastplate.[33] —Aye, men look on her,
As she goes forth serenely to her tasks,[34]
Binding the warrior's wounds, and bearing fresh
Cool draughts to fever'd lips; they look on her,
Thus moving in her beautiful array
Of gentle fortitude, and bless the fair
Majestic vision, and unmurmuring turn
Unto their heavy toils.

ELMINA.                           And seest thou not          390
In that high faith and strong collectedness,
A fearful inspiration?—*They* have cause
To tremble, who behold th' unearthly light
Of high, and, it may be, prophetic thought,
Investing youth with grandeur!—From the grave
It rises, on whose shadowy brink thy child
Waits but a father's hand to snatch her back
Into the laughing sunshine.—Kneel with me,
Ximena, kneel beside me, and implore
That which a deeper, more prevailing voice          400
Than ours doth ask, and will not be denied;
—His children's lives!

XIMENA.                      Alas! this may not be,
Mother!—I cannot.

                                        *Exit* XIMENA.

GONZALEZ.                My heroic child!
—A terrible sacrifice thou claim'st, O God!
From creatures in whose agonizing hearts
Nature is strong as death!

ELMINA.                         Is't thus in thine?
Away!—what time is given thee to resolve
On?—what I cannot utter!—Speak! thou know'st
Too well what I would say.

GONZALEZ.                    Until—ask not!
    The time is brief.
ELMINA.                    Thou saidst—I heard not right—          410
GONZALEZ.  The time is brief.
ELMINA.                         What! must we burst all ties[35]
    Wherewith the thrilling chords of life are twined;
    And, for this task's fulfilment, can it be
    That man, in his cold heartlessness, hath dared
    To number and to mete us forth the sands
    Of hours, nay, moments?—Why, the sentenced wretch,
    He on whose soul there rests a brother's blood
    Pour'd forth in slumber, is allow'd more time
    To wean his turbulent passions from the world
    His presence doth pollute!—It is not thus!          420
    We must have Time to school us.[36]
GONZALEZ.                              We have but
    To bow the head in silence, when Heaven's voice
    Calls back the things we love.
ELMINA.  Love! love!—there are soft smiles and gentle words,
    And there are faces, skilful to put on
    The look we trust in—and 'tis mockery all!
    —A faithless mist, a desert-vapour, wearing
    The brightness of clear waters, thus to cheat
    The thirst that semblance kindled!—There is none,
    In all this cold and hollow world, no fount          430
    Of deep, strong, deathless love, save that within
    A mother's heart.—It is but pride, wherewith
    To his fair son the father's eye doth turn,
    Watching his growth. Aye, on the boy he looks,
    The bright glad creature springing in his path,
    But as the heir of his great name, the young
    And stately tree, whose rising strength ere long
    Shall bear his trophies well.—And this is love!
    This is *man's* love![37] —What marvel?—*you* ne'er made
    Your breast the pillow of his infancy,          440
    While to the fulness of your heart's glad heavings
    His fair cheek rose and fell; and his bright hair
    Waved softly to your breath!—*You* ne'er kept watch
    Beside him, till the last pale star had set,
    And morn, all dazzling, as in triumph, broke
    On your dim weary eye;[38] not *yours* the face
    Which, early faded thro' fond care for him,
    Hung o'er his sleep, and, duly as Heaven's light,
    Was there to greet his wakening! *You* ne'er smooth'd

His couch, ne'er sung him to his rosy rest,                    450
Caught his least whisper, when his voice from yours
Had learn'd soft utterance; press'd your lip to his,
When fever parch'd it; hush'd his wayward cries,
With patient, vigilant, never-wearied love!
No! these are *woman's* tasks![39] —In these her youth,
And bloom of cheek, and buoyancy of heart,
Steal from her all unmark'd!—My boys! my boys!
Hath vain affection borne with all for this?
—Why were ye given me?

GONZALEZ.                            Is there strength in man
Thus to endure?—That thou couldst read, thro' all          460
Its depths of silent agony, the heart
Thy voice of woe doth rend!

ELMINA.  Thy heart!—*thy* heart!—Away! it feels not *now!*[40]
But an hour comes to tame the mighty man
Unto the infant's weakness; nor shall Heaven
Spare you that bitter chastening!—May you live
To be alone, when loneliness doth seem
Most heavy to sustain!—For me, my voice
Of prayer and fruitless weeping shall be soon
With all forgotten sounds; my quiet place                    470
Low with my lovely ones, and we shall sleep,
Tho' kings lead armies o'er us, we shall sleep,
Wrapt in earth's covering mantle!—you the while
Shall sit within your vast, forsaken halls,
And hear the wild and melancholy winds
Moan thro' their drooping banners, never more
To wave above your race. Aye, then call up
Shadows—dim phantoms from ancestral tombs,
But all—all *glorious*—conquerors, chieftains, kings—
To people that cold void!—And when the strength            480
From your right arm hath melted, when the blast
Of the shrill clarion gives your heart no more
A fiery wakening; if at last you pine
For the glad voices, and the bounding steps,
Once thro' your home re-echoing, and the clasp
Of twining arms,[41] and all the joyous light
Of eyes that laugh'd with youth, and made your board
A place of sunshine;—When those days are come,
Then, in your utter desolation, turn
To the cold world, the smiling, faithless world,            490
Which hath swept past you long, and bid it quench
Your soul's deep thirst with *fame!* immortal *fame!*
Fame to the sick of heart!—a gorgeous robe,

A crown of victory, unto him that dies
I' th' burning waste, for water!
GONZALEZ.                              This from *thee!*
Now the last drop of bitterness is pour'd.
Elmina—I forgive thee!

*Exit* ELMINA.

Aid me, Heaven!
From whom alone is power!—Oh! thou hast set
Duties, so stern of aspect, in my path,
They almost, to my startled gaze, assume                    500
The hue of things less hallow'd! Men have sunk
Unblamed beneath such trials!—Doth not He
Who made us know the limits of our strength?
My wife! my sons!—Away! I must not pause
To give my heart one moment's mastery thus!⁴²

*Exit* GONZALEZ.

---

¹ This unprecedented deed has given an indication / Of the valor that in centuries to come / The sons of mighty Spain will possess, / Sons of such fathers the heirs. // I find in Numancia alone all / That should with just warrant be celebrated in poetry / And that which can give material for song.
    Extracted from the voice of "Fame" near the end (act 4) of Cervantes' *El Cerco de Numancia* (circa 1580–90). The last three lines supply the title-page epigraph for FH's 1823 volume. *Jndicio* (or *Indicio*), wrongly read as an erratum, was miscorrected in later editions to "Judicio." *El Cerco* treats the Numancians' mass suicide and destruction of their city, in northern Spain, after an eight-month siege (*cerco*) in 133 B.C., their action thwarting Scipio Æmilianus's honors in the Roman conquest of Spain. In its heroic repulse of attacks from the time of Cato the Elder's campaign (195 B.C.), Numancia was a rallying point for opposition to Roman imperialism. During the Napoleonic invasion (1807–9), *Numancia* was staged in Spain as an incitement to resistance.
    MS] no epigraph
² See Quintana's 'Vidas de Españoles celebres,' p. 53. [FH]
    Not in MS. Manuel José Quintana (1772–1857), *Lives of Celebrated Spaniards* (1807). This Spanish patriot and poet was famed for his odes, pamphlets, and proclamations against Napoleonic occupation. Tarifa, on the Strait of Gibraltar, was the first Roman colony in Spain. Sancho IV (?1257–95), or "Sancho the Brave," King of Castile (1284–95), regained it from the Moors in 1292. Nuño de Guzmán was a controversial Spanish conquistador (d. 1544).
³ See the Preface to Southey's "Chronicle of the Cid." [FH]
    The Preface does not show such an account. During the middle ages, control of the strategically located river city of Zamora in northwestern Spain shifted between Christians and Moors, then in civil war between the Christian kingdoms of León and Castile. Henrique II of Trastámara (?1333–79), illegitimate son of Alfonso XI of Castile (1311–50), waged several unsuccessful revolts against his half brother Don Pedro (1320–67), king of Portugal (1357–67), called "the Cruel" for harsh reprisals against his enemies. Aided by France, Henrique invaded Castile in 1366 and was crowned king, but dethroned in 1367 by English forces led by Edward, the Black Prince (Pedro's daughter was married to John of Gaunt). Then with French aid, Henrique captured and killed Pedro.
⁴ Milton's praise of classical Greek tragedians in *Paradise Regained*: "High actions, and high passions best describing" (4.266).

[5] Christ says, "be thou faithful unto death, and I will give thee a crown of life" (Revelation 2.10).

[6] Theseus's remark on poetic power in *A Midsummer Night's Dream* (5.1.17). Valencia was under Moorish rule from the 8th c. to the 18th c., except for 1094–1102. El Cid ruled from 1094 until his death in 1099, his conquest of the city the highlight of his career. His widow Ximena (namesake of FH's Ximena) endured a three-year siege before withdrawing to Castile in 1102. FH makes Gonzalez a descendant of El Cid (1.162, 4.75).

[7] MS] Gonsalvo

Gonsalvo (or Gonzalo) Fernández de Córdoba (1453–1515) was called the Great Captain, among his many engagements the conquest of Granada. Fernán González (d. 970), the first Count of Castile, established its independence from León; cf. *The Cid's Rising* 27. His exploits are recounted in a popular 13th-c. epic poem.

[8] Like the play's other songs, this ballad was a favorite in nineteenth-century anthologies. Ward's selection includes *The Ballad of Roncesvalles* (this song) and *A Dirge* (scene 9, 83ff.). Omitting the play itself, the 1914 Oxford ed. of FH offers *Lyrics from* . . . (182–85): this one (*Ballad*); *Dirge* (2.444 ff.); *Song* (5.42 ff.); *Chant* (5.311 ff.); *The Cid's Battle-Song* (6.193 ff.); *A Death-Hymn* (Ward's *Dirge*).

The MS scene is "in the citadel of Valencia," emphasizing the state of war, and there is a different ballad (not published in any collection); see Appendix 1.

[9] At Roncesvalles, a pass in the Pyrenees, Roland, the most renowned of Charlemagne's knights, was killed in 778 in an ambush of his army of 20,000 by a band of Basque mountaineers. In *Chanson de Roland* (11th c.), the Basques are represented as an attack force of 400,000 Muslims—a cultural polarization relevant to the historical situation of *The Siege*. Roncesvalles was also a famed battle site in the Napoleonic wars.

[10] An echo of Milton's description of his peril after the Restoration: "fall'n on evil days, . . . In darkness, and with dangers compassed round" (*Paradise Lost* 7.25–27); cf. *Widow of Crescentius* (1.61–68) and *Abencerrage* (3.274, 3.580). Throughout this scene, FH echoes Milton to evoke a "fall'n" paradise (cf. 110); Valencia was famed as "the garden of Spain."

93, MS] And bear deep images of Death impress'd

[11] MS] Aye, days, the sound / Of whose far-pealing thunders doth awake

[12] 103–5, MS] . . . nobly and sustain / The lofty name we bear! It is for us / To bind the breastplate on, howe'er the heart / May bleed beneath.

[13] MS] I look on thee, and tremble!—Can it be, / That thou, in all thy loveliness, art seal'd, / Unto an early doom?

[14] MS adds] And doff the helm, and lay the Falchion by,

[15] MS] . . . thoughts e'en as an Eagle shakes / The rain-drops from his pinion; sing me these!

[16] Mountain Christians, those natives of Spain, who, under their prince, Pelayo, took refuge amongst the mountains of the northern provinces, where they maintained their religion and liberty, whilst the rest of their country was overrun by the Moors. [FH]

Southey's *Chronicle* (Introduction xxiii, xv) gives an account of Pelayo, first king of Asturias in northern Spain, whose victory over the Moors at Covadonga (ca. 718–25) launched the Christian resistance; cf. FH's note to *Abencerrage* 3.3. Pelayo is Elmina's ancestor (2.156).

[17] "Serranos," mountaineers. [FH]

Torres de Serranos, fortified towers, were built in Valencia in the 14th c. on Roman foundations.

[18] 167 to the end of G.'s lines, MS] As on a Landmark, set to bound the sway / Of Ages and Oblivion, may not dare / To take Dishonour by the hand, and o'er / The Threshold of their Father's Halls / First lead her as a guest, No! rather be / That House the House of Death!

[19] Cf. the use of this phrase to open and close the elegiac lyric on the death of the heroine in *Abencerrage* (3.571–606).

[20] MS adds] By the Commanding Spirit of their Faith

[21] 187/189, MS] *their Children! / of them?*

[22] 199, MS] . . . freedom!—On my dreams they rose, / With the bright Aspect and trium-

phant step / Of boundless Liberty, as well beseem'd / Th' unconquer'd race they sprung from!—And my sons /

²³ 201–5, MS] I know not. From Abdullah's camp e'en now / A herald brought the tidings but reveal'd / Nought, save that they were prisoners.

²⁴ MS adds] —Now, be firm / My noble, my beloved!

²⁵ Abraham's near sacrifice of Isaac (Genesis 22.1–18) is typically read as a prefiguration of God's sacrifice of his Son. The patriarchal status of Abraham in Judaism, Christianity, and Islam bears directly on FH's theme of maternal resistance to the sacrifice of sons for national glory. On the martyrdom of boys, cf. *The Death of Conradin*, esp. 83–100, and *Casabianca* (1826), FH's most famous poem.

²⁶ 278–80, MS] . . . affections—Of such Mould / Those should be formed that mount the lonely steeps / Wherein Dominion sits, and trample down / Ten thousand faithful and devoted breasts, / Ere that proud height is gain'd!—Nay /

²⁷ MS] . . . faith, and midst the dust / Of noble Men, whose tombs and trophies sent / Attesting echoes back, I bound myself /

²⁸ MS] Whose treasures he recalls. *1839*] treasure he

²⁹ 315–16, MS] . . . of Misery!—from my soul / Its pressure hath effaced all images, / All feeling, save o' th' one o'erwhelming woe, / Which weighs me to the Earth!—My brain . . .

³⁰ MS inserts] Would'st thou seek / Her people, go not to the silent Mart, / Tread not the grass-grown street, their place is now / Beneath thee, not around. Her Sepulchres / Alone are crowded.

³¹ One of the Christian kingdoms reclaimed from the Moors in the 8th c. and 9th c.

³² MS inserts] . . . day!—My Soul hath still / Drawn Courage from thy glance to which it turn'd / For Hope and Inspiration, e'en as Thou / Hast turn'd to Glory! . . .

³³ MS inserts] . . . breastplate, and her aspect wears / That in its pale, inspired devotedness, / Which calls up lofty thoughts, where'er her glance / Falls brightly on sad hearts—Men look . . .

³⁴ MS inserts] (Like a lone sunbeam o'er a Battle-field) / Unblenching midst all fearful sights and sounds, /

³⁵ MS] To-morrow! was it *thus!*—What! must we tear / All feelings which the growth of Years hath made / Part of our Souls, our Being, with the hand / Of Violence from them?— Must . . .

³⁶ MS] . . . us!—Not To-morrow! / Heaven would but prove, not madden us!

³⁷ And . . . *man's* love] not in MS.

³⁸ 445–46, MS] . . . as in Mockery, broke / On the dim weary eye that would not close! / 'Twas not *your* hand that rais'd his gentle head / When Sickness bow'd it, as the heavy shower / Doth bow the wild-Bird's wing, not *yours* . . .

³⁹ Cf. Myrrha in Byron's *Sardanapalus* (1821): "The very first / Of human life must spring from woman's breast, / Your first small words are taught you from her lips, / Your first tears quench'd by her, and your last sighs / Too often breathed out in a woman's hearing, / When men have shrunk from the ignoble care / Of watching the last hour of him who led them" (1.2.509–15).

⁴⁰ MS adds] Is't not a Chief's, a Warrior's, mail'd with that, / More proof than steel, unconquerable pride?

⁴¹ Affectionate, embracing arms (cf. 4.210), rather than military "arms" (264, 2.313).

⁴² MS] . . . mastery o'er me; / There's Armour that shall press its gaspings down, / E'en if it burst!—Oh! swift and light of foot / Must be the journeyer of the dizzy path / Which winds along the Precipice!
    The perilous path is a standard image of temptation to sin.

Scene 2[1]

*The Aisle of a Gothic Church.* HERNANDEZ, GARCIAS, *and others.*

HERNANDEZ. The rites are closed. Now, valiant men, depart,
 Each to his place—I may not say, of rest;
 Your faithful vigils for your sons may win
 What must not be your own. Ye are as those
 Who sow, in peril and in care, the seed
 Of the fair tree, beneath whose stately shade
 They may not sit. But bless'd be they who toil
 For after-days!—All high and holy thoughts
 Be with you, warriors, thro' the lingering hours
 Of the night-watch!

GARCIAS.      Aye, father! we have need    10
 Of high and holy thoughts, wherewith to fence
 Our hearts against despair. Yet have I been
 From youth a son of war. The stars have look'd
 A thousand times upon my couch of heath,
 Spread midst the wild sierras, by some stream
 Whose dark-red waves look'd e'en as tho' their source
 Lay not in rocky caverns, but the veins
 Of noble hearts; while many a knightly crest
 Roll'd with them to the deep. And in the years
 Of my long exile and captivity,       20
 With the fierce Arab, I have watch'd beneath
 The still, pale shadow of some lonely palm,
 At midnight, in the desert; while the wind
 Swell'd with the lion's roar, and heavily
 The fearfulness and might of solitude
 Press'd on my weary heart.

HERNANDEZ (*thoughtfully*).    Thou little know'st
 Of what is solitude!—I tell thee, those
 For whom—in earth's remotest nook—howe'er
 Divided from their path by chain on chain
 Of mighty mountains, and the amplitude    30
 Of rolling seas—there beats one human heart,
 There breathes one being unto whom their name
 Comes with a thrilling and a gladdening sound
 Heard o'er the din of life! are not alone!
 Not on the deep, nor in the wild, alone;
 For there is that on earth with which they hold
 A brotherhood of soul!—Call *him* alone,
 Who stands shut out from this!—And let not those
 Whose homes are bright with sunshine and with love,

Put on the insolence of happiness,                                   40
Glorying in that proud lot!—A lonely hour
Is on its way to each, to all; for Death
Knows no companionship.

GARCIAS.                    I have look'd on Death
In field, and storm, and flood.[2] But never yet
Hath aught weigh'd down my spirit to a mood
Of sadness, dreaming o'er dark auguries,
Like this, our watch by midnight. Fearful things
Are gathering round us. Death upon the earth,
Omens in Heaven!—The summer-skies put forth
No clear bright stars above us, but at times,                        50
Catching some comet's fiery hue of wrath,
Marshal their clouds to armies, traversing
Heaven with the rush of meteor-steeds, the array
Of spears and banners, tossing like the pines
Of Pyrenean forests, when the storm
Doth sweep the mountains.

HERNANDEZ.                    Aye, last night I too
Kept vigil, gazing on the angry heavens;
And I beheld the meeting and the shock
Of those wild hosts i' th' air, when, as they closed,
A red and sultry mist, like that which mantles                      60
The thunder's path, fell o'er them. Then were flung
Thro' the dull glare, broad cloudy banners forth,
And chariots seem'd to whirl, and steeds to sink,
Bearing down crested warriors. But all this
Was dim and shadowy;—then swift darkness rush'd
Down on th' unearthly battle, as the deep
Swept o'er the Egyptian's armament.[3]—I look'd—
And all that fiery field of plumes and spears
Was blotted from heaven's face!—I look'd again—
And from the brooding mass of cloud leap'd forth                    70
One meteor-sword, which o'er the reddening sea
Shook with strange motion, such as earthquakes give
Unto a rocking citadel!—I beheld,
And yet my spirit sunk not.

GARCIAS.                    Neither deem
That mine hath blench'd.—But these are sights and sounds
To awe the firmest.—Know'st thou what we hear
At midnight from the walls?—Were't but the deep
Barbaric horn, or Moorish tambour's peal,
Thence might the warrior's heart catch impulses,
Quickening its fiery currents. But our ears                         80
Are pierced by other tones. We hear the knell

For brave men in their noon of strength cut down,
And the shrill wail of woman, and the dirge
Faint swelling thro' the streets. Then e'en the air
Hath strange and fitful murmurs of lament,
As if the viewless watchers of the land
Sigh'd on its hollow breezes!—To my soul,
The torrent-rush of battle, with its din
Of trampling steeds and ringing panoply,
Were, after these faint sounds of drooping woe,    90
As the free sky's glad music unto him
Who leaves a couch of sickness.

HERNANDEZ (*with solemnity*).    If to plunge
In the mid-waves of combat, as they bear
Chargers and spearmen onwards; and to make
A reckless bosom's front the buoyant mark
On that wild current, for ten thousand arrows;
If *thus* to dare were valour's noblest aim,
Lightly might fame be won!—but there are things
Which ask a spirit of more exalted pitch,
And courage temper'd with a holier fire!    100
Well mayst thou say, that these are fearful times,
Therefore be firm, be patient!—There is strength,
And a fierce instinct, e'en in common souls,
To bear up manhood with a stormy joy,
When red swords meet in lightning!—But our task
Is more, and nobler!—We have to endure,
And to keep watch, and to arouse a land,
And to defend an altar!—If we fall,
So that our blood make but the millionth part
Of Spain's great ransom, we may count it joy    110
To die upon her bosom, and beneath
The banner of her faith!—Think but on this,
And gird your hearts with silent fortitude,
Suffering, yet hoping all things—Fare ye well.

GARCIAS. Father, farewell.

       *Exeunt* GARCIAS *and his followers.*

HERNANDEZ.    These men have earthly ties
And bondage on their natures!—To the cause
Of God, and Spain's revenge, they bring but half
Their energies and hopes. But he whom Heaven
Hath call'd to be th' awakener of a land,
Should have his soul's affections all absorb'd    120
In that majestic purpose, and press on
To its fulfilment, as a mountain-born
And mighty stream, with all its vassal-rills

Sweeps proudly to the ocean, pausing not
To dally with the flowers.
                           Hark! What quick step
Comes hurrying through the gloom at this dead hour?

ELMINA enters.

ELMINA. Are not all hours as one to misery?—Why
        Should *she* take note of time, for whom the day
        And night have lost their blessed attributes
        Of sunshine and repose?
HERNANDEZ.                  I know thy griefs;                    130
        But there are trials for the noble heart
        Wherein its own deep fountains must supply
        All it can hope of comfort. Pity's voice
        Comes with vain sweetness to th' unheeding ear
        Of anguish, e'en as music heard afar
        On the green shore, by him who perishes
        Midst rocks and eddying waters.
ELMINA.                           Think thou not
        I sought thee but for pity. I am come
        For that which grief is privileged to demand
        With an imperious claim, from all whose form,            140
        Whose human form, doth seal them unto suffering!
        Father! I ask thine *aid.*
HERNANDEZ.               There is no aid
        For thee or for thy children, but with Him
        Whose presence is around us in the cloud,
        As in the shining and the glorious light.
ELMINA. There is no aid!—Art thou a man of God?
        Art thou a man of sorrow—(for the world
        Doth call thee such)—and hast thou not been taught
        By God and sorrow—mighty as they are,
        To own the claims of misery?
HERNANDEZ.                      Is there power                   150
        With me to save thy sons?—Implore of Heaven!
ELMINA. Doth not Heaven work its purposes by man?
        I tell thee, *thou* canst save them!—Art thou not
        Gonzalez' counsellor?—Unto him thy words
        Are e'en as oracles————[4]
HERNANDEZ.                   And therefore?—Speak!
        The noble daughter of Pelayo's line
        Hath nought to ask, unworthy of the name
        Which is a nation's heritage.—Dost thou shrink?
ELMINA. Have pity on me, father!—I must speak
        That, from the thought of which, but yesterday,[5]       160
        I had recoil'd in scorn!—But this is past.

Oh! we grow humble in our agonies,
And to the dust—their birth-place—bow the heads
That wore the crown of glory!—I am weak—
My chastening is far more than I can bear.

HERNANDEZ.  These are no times for weakness. On our hills
The ancient cedars, in their gather'd might,
Are battling with the tempest; and the flower
Which cannot meet its driving blast must die.
—But thou hast drawn thy nurture from a stem          170
Unwont to bend or break.—Lift thy proud head,
Daughter of Spain!—What wouldst thou with thy lord?

ELMINA.  Look not upon me thus!—I have no power
To tell thee. Take thy keen disdainful eye
Off from my soul!—What! am I sunk to this?
I, whose blood sprung from heroes!—How my sons
Will scorn the mother that would bring disgrace
On their majestic line!—My sons! my sons!
—Now is all else forgotten!—I had once
A babe that in the early spring-time lay          180
Sickening upon my bosom, till at last,
When earth's young flowers were opening to the sun,
Death sunk on his meek eyelid, and I deem'd
All sorrow light to mine!—But now the fate
Of all my children seems to brood above me
In the dark thunder-clouds![6] —Oh! I have power
And voice unfaltering now to speak my prayer
And my last lingering hope, that thou shouldst win
The father to relent, to save his sons!

HERNANDEZ.  By yielding up the city?

ELMINA.                                        Rather say          190
By meeting that which gathers close upon us
Perchance one day the sooner!—Is't not so?
Must we not yield at last?—How long shall man
Array his single breast against disease,
And famine, and the sword?

HERNANDEZ.                                  How long?—While he,
Who shadows forth his power more gloriously
In the high deeds and sufferings of the soul,
Than in the circling heavens, with all their stars,
Or the far-sounding deep, doth send abroad
A spirit, which takes affliction for its mate,          200
In the good cause, with solemn joy!—How long?
—And who art *thou*, that, in the littleness
Of thine own selfish purpose, would'st set bounds
To the free current of all noble thought

And generous action, bidding its bright waves
Be stay'd, and flow no further?—But the Power
Whose interdict is laid on seas and orbs,
To chain them in from wandering, hath assign'd
No limits unto that which man's high strength
Shall, through its aid, achieve!

ELMINA.                                        Oh! there are times,                    210
When *all* that hopeless courage can achieve
But sheds a mournful beauty o'er the fate
Of those who die in vain.

HERNANDEZ.                              *Who* dies in vain
Upon his country's war-fields, and within
The shadow of her altars?—Feeble heart!
I tell thee that the voice of noble blood,
Thus pour'd for faith and freedom, hath a tone
Which, from the night of ages, from the gulf
Of death, shall burst, and make its high appeal
Sound unto earth and heaven! Aye, let the land,                    220
Whose sons, through centuries of woe, have striven,
And perish'd by her temples, sink awhile,
Borne down in conflict!—But immortal seed
Deep, by heroic suffering, hath been sown
On all her ancient hills; and generous hope
Knows that the soil, in its good time, shall yet
Bring forth a glorious harvest! Earth receives
Not one red drop, from faithful hearts, in vain.[7]

ELMINA. Then it must be![8] —And ye will make those lives,
Those young bright lives, an offering—to retard                    230
Our doom one day!

HERNANDEZ.                        The mantle of that day
May wrap the fate of Spain!

ELMINA.                                  What led me here?
Why did I turn to *thee* in my despair?
Love hath no ties upon thee;[9] what had I
To hope from *thee*, thou lone and childless man!
Go to thy silent home!—there no young voice
Shall bid thee welcome, no light footstep spring
Forth at the sound of thine!—What knows thy heart?

HERNANDEZ. Woman! how dar'st thou taunt me with my woes?
*Thy* children too shall perish, and I say                          240
It shall be well!—Why tak'st thou thought for them?
Wearing thy heart, and wasting down thy life
Unto its dregs, and making night thy time
Of care yet more intense, and casting health,
Unpriz'd, to melt away, i' th' bitter cup

Thou minglest for thyself?—Why, what hath earth
To pay thee back for this?—Shall they not live,
(If the sword spare them now) to prove how soon
All love may be forgotten?—Years of thought,
Long faithful watchings, looks of tenderness,                    250
That changed not, though to change be this world's law?
Shall they not flush thy cheek with shame, whose blood
Marks, e'en like branding iron?—to thy sick heart
Make death a want, as sleep to weariness?
Doth not all hope end thus?—or e'en at best,
Will they not leave thee?—far from thee seek room
For th' overflowings of their fiery souls,
On life's wide ocean?—Give the bounding steed,
Or the wing'd bark to youth, that his free course
May be o'er hills and seas; and weep thou not              260
In thy forsaken home, for the bright world
Lies all before him,[10] and be sure he wastes
No thought on thee!

ELMINA.                    Not so! it is not so!
Thou dost but torture me!—*My* sons are kind,
And brave, and gentle.

HERNANDEZ.                    Others too have worn
The semblance of all good. Nay, stay thee yet;
I will be calm, and thou shalt learn how earth,
The fruitful in all agonies, hath woes
Which far outweigh thine own.

ELMINA.                                   It may not be!
*Whose* grief is like a mother's for her sons?              270

HERNANDEZ. *My* son lay stretch'd upon his battle-bier,
And there were hands wrung o'er him, which had caught
Their hue from his young blood!

ELMINA.                              What tale is this?

HERNANDEZ. Read you no records in this mien, of things
Whose traces on man's aspect are not such
As the breeze leaves on water?—Lofty birth,
War, peril, power?—Affliction's hand is strong,
If it erase the haughty characters
They grave so deep!—I have not always been
That which I am. The name I bore is not              280
Of those which perish!—I was once a chief—
A warrior!—nor as now, a lonely man!
I was a father!

ELMINA.              Then thy heart can *feel!*
Thou wilt have pity!

HERNANDEZ.                    Should I pity *thee?*
    *Thy* sons will perish gloriously—their blood—
ELMINA.  Their blood! my children's blood!—Thou speak'st
      as 'twere
    Of casting down a wine-cup, in the mirth
    And wantonness of feasting!—My fair boys!
    —Man! hast *thou* been a father?
HERNANDEZ.                              Let them die!
    Let them die *now*, thy children! so thy heart          290
    Shall wear their beautiful image all undimm'd,
    Within it, to the last! Nor shalt thou learn
    The bitter lesson, of what worthless dust
    Are framed the idols, whose false glory binds
    Earth's fetter on our souls!—Thou think'st it much
    To mourn the early dead; but there are tears
    Heavy with deeper anguish! We endow
    Those whom we love, in our fond passionate blindness,
    With power upon our souls, too absolute
    To be a mortal's trust! Within their hands          300
    We lay the flaming sword, whose stroke alone
    Can reach our hearts, and *they* are merciful,
    As they are strong, that wield it not to pierce us!
    —Aye, fear them, fear the loved!—Had I but wept
    O'er my son's grave, as o'er a babe's, where tears
    Are as spring dew-drops, glittering in the sun,
    And brightening the young verdure, *I* might still
    Have loved and trusted!
ELMINA (*disdainfully*).          But he fell in war!
    And hath not glory medicine in her cup
    For the brief pangs of nature?
HERNANDEZ.                              Glory!—Peace,          310
    And listen!—By my side the stripling grew,
    Last of my line. I rear'd him to take joy
    I' th' blaze of arms, as eagles train their young
    To look upon the day-king!—His quick blood
    Ev'n to his boyish cheek would mantle up,
    When the heavens rang with trumpets, and his eye
    Flash with the spirit of a race whose deeds—
    —But this availeth not!—Yet he *was* brave.
    I've seen him clear himself a path in fight
    As lightning through a forest, and his plume          320
    Waved like a torch, above the battle-storm,
    The soldier's guide, when princely crests had sunk,
    And banners were struck down.—Around my steps

Floated his fame, like music, and I lived
But in the lofty sound. But when my heart
In one frail ark had ventur'd all, when most
He seem'd to stand between my soul and heaven,
—Then came the thunder-stroke!

ELMINA.                                    'Tis ever thus!
And the unquiet and foreboding sense
That thus 'twill ever be, doth link itself                    330
Darkly with all deep love!—He died?

HERNANDEZ.                                    Not so!
—Death! Death!—Why, earth should be a paradise,
To make that name so fearful!—Had he died,
With his young fame about him for a shroud,
I had not learn'd the might of agony,
To bring proud natures low!—No! he fell off
—Why do I tell thee this?—What right hast *thou*
To learn how pass'd the glory from my house?
Yet listen!—He forsook me!—He, that was
As mine own soul, forsook me! trampled o'er             340
The ashes of his sires!—Aye, leagued himself
E'en with the infidel, the curse of Spain,
And, for the dark eye of a Moorish maid,
Abjured his faith, his God!—Now, talk of death![11]

ELMINA.  Oh! I can pity thee——

HERNANDEZ.                              There's more to hear.
I braced the corslet o'er my heart's deep wound,
And cast my troubled spirit on the tide
Of war and high events, whose stormy waves
Might bear it up from sinking;——

ELMINA.                                        And ye met
No more?

HERNANDEZ.  Be still!—We did!—we met *once* more.             350
God had his own high purpose to fulfil,
Or think'st thou that the sun in his bright heaven
Had look'd upon such things?—We met *once more*.
—That was an hour to leave its lightning-mark
Sear'd upon brain and bosom!—there had been
Combat on Ebro's banks, and when the day
Sank in red clouds, it faded from a field
Still held by Moorish lances. Night closed round,
A night of sultry darkness, in the shadow
Of whose broad wing, ev'n unto death I strove             360
Long with a turban'd champion; but my sword
Was heavy with God's vengeance—and prevail'd.
He fell—my heart exulted—and I stood

In gloomy triumph o'er him—Nature gave
No sign of horror, for 'twas Heaven's decree!
He strove to speak—but I had done the work
Of wrath too well—yet in his last deep moan
A dreadful something of familiar sound
Came o'er my shuddering sense.—The moon look'd forth,
And I beheld—speak not!—'twas he—my son!                          370
My boy lay dying there! He raised one glance,
And knew me—for he sought with feeble hand
To cover his glazed eyes. A darker veil
Sank o'er them soon. I will not have thy look
Fix'd on me thus!—Away!
ELMINA.                          Thou hast seen this,
    Thou hast *done* this—and yet thou liv'st?
HERNANDEZ.                                   I live!
    And know'st thou wherefore?—On my soul there fell
A horror of great darkness, which shut out
All earth, and heaven, and hope. I cast away
The spear and helm, and made the cloister's shade                 380
The home of my despair. But a deep voice
Came to me through the gloom, and sent its tones
Far through my bosom's depths. And I awoke,
Aye, as the mountain cedar doth shake off
Its weight of wintry snow, e'en so I shook
Despondence from my soul, and knew myself
Seal'd by that blood wherewith my hands were dyed,[12]
And set apart, and fearfully mark'd out
Unto a mighty task!—To rouse the soul
Of Spain, as from the dead; and to lift up                        390
The cross, her sign of victory, on the hills,
Gathering her sons to battle!—And my voice
Must be as freedom's trumpet on the winds,
From Roncesvalles to the blue sea-waves
Where Calpe[13] looks on Afric; till the land
Have fill'd her cup of vengeance!—Ask me *now*
To yield the Christian city, that its fanes
May rear the minaret in the face of Heaven!
—But death shall have a bloodier vintage-feast
Ere that day come!
ELMINA.                    I ask thee this no more,                400
    For I am hopeless now.—But yet one boon—
Hear me, by all thy woes!—Thy voice hath power
Through the wide city—here I cannot rest:—
Aid me to pass the gates!
HERNANDEZ.                      And wherefore?

ELMINA.            Thou,
 That *wert* a father, and art now—alone!
 Canst *thou* ask "wherefore?"—Ask the wretch whose sands
 Have not an hour to run, whose failing limbs
 Have but one earthly journey to perform,
 Why, on his pathway to the place of death,
 Aye, when the very axe is glistening cold     410
 Upon his dizzy sight, his pale, parch'd lip
 Implores a cup of water?—Why, the stroke
 Which trembles o'er him in itself shall bring
 Oblivion of all wants, yet who denies
 Nature's last prayer?—I tell thee that the thirst
 Which burns my spirit up is agony
 To be endured no more!—And I *must* look
 Upon my children's faces, I must hear
 Their voices, ere they perish!—But hath Heaven
 Decreed that they *must* perish?—Who shall say   420
 If in yon Moslem camp there beats no heart
 Which prayers and tears may melt?
HERNANDEZ.        There!—with the Moor!
 Let him fill up the measure of his guilt![14]
 —'Tis madness all!—How wouldst thou pass th' array
 Of armed foes?
ELMINA.    Oh! free doth sorrow pass,
 Free and unquestion'd, through a suffering world![15]
HERNANDEZ. This must not be. Enough of woe is laid
 E'en now, upon thy lord's heroic soul,
 For man to bear, unsinking. Press thou not
 Too heavily th' o'erburthen'd heart.—Away!   430
 Bow down the knee, and send thy prayers for strength
 Up to Heaven's gate.—Farewell![16]
           *Exit* HERNANDEZ.
ELMINA.        Are all men thus?
 —Why, wer't not better they should fall e'en now
 Than live to shut their hearts, in haughty scorn,
 Against the sufferer's pleadings?—But no, no!
 Who can be like *this* man, that slew his son,
 Yet wears his life still proudly, and a soul
 Untamed upon his brow?
 (*After a pause.*)   There's one, whose arms
 Have borne my children in their infancy,
 And on whose knees they sported, and whose hand  440
 Hath led them oft—a vassal of their sire's;
 And I will seek him: he may lend me aid,
 When all beside pass on.

DIRGE HEARD WITHOUT

Thou to thy rest art gone,
   High heart! and what are we,
While o'er our heads the storm sweeps on,
   That we should mourn for thee?

Free grave and peaceful bier
   To the buried son of Spain!
To those that live, the lance and spear,                450
   And well if not the chain!

Be *theirs* to weep the dead
   As they sit beneath their vines,
Whose flowery land hath borne no tread
   Of spoilers o'er its shrines!

Thou hast thrown off the load
   Which we must yet sustain,
And pour our blood where *thine* hath flow'd,
   Too blest if not in vain!

We give thee holy rite,                    460
   Slow knell, and chaunted strain!
—For those that fall to-morrow night,
   May be left no funeral-train.

Again, when trumpets wake,
   We must brace our armour on;
But a deeper note *thy* sleep must break—
   —Thou to thy rest art gone!

Happier in *this* than all,
   That, now thy race is run,
Upon thy name no stain may fall,             470
   Thy work hath well been done!

ELMINA. "Thy work hath well been done!"—so thou mayst rest!
   —There is a solemn lesson in those words—
   But now I may not pause.[17]

*Exit* ELMINA.

[1] In MS this scene is much longer, with a much more elaborate discussion of battlefield terrors and confusions, death, civic suffering, fearful omens, and impending doom.

[2] Not in MS. An echo of Othello (a Moor, a Christian and general of Venice's military forces), as he recounts his adventures "of most disastrous chances; / Of moving accidents by flood and field" (*Othello* 1.3.133–34); like Garcias, Othello had been an enemy captive.

[3] Exodus 14.23–28.

[4] MS] . . . Oracles. He turns to thee / As Men, i' th'elder Time, were wont to seek / Beneath

their shadowing Palms, the gifted seers / Upon whose lips hung Prophecy. The key / To his deep Soul is there—

[5] MS adds] With an indignant eye and burning cheek,

[6] MS inserts] Thou dar'st not scorn / Mine Anguish, for 'tis fearful!

[7] An echo of Milton's sonnet *On the Late Massacre in Piedmont*: "Their moans / The vales redoubled to the hills, and they / To Heaven. Their martyred blood and ashes sow / O'er all th' Italian fields . . . / . . . that from these may grow / A hundredfold" (8–12).

[8] 229–230, MS] . . . be!—Those young, bright Lives / Their nurture from this bosom, of whose pangs / Man knows not, recks not, must be offer'd up, / —Heaven! Heaven! is there no Mercy?—to retard

[9] not in MS; instead]

> Thou'rt like them all!—What recks the Conqueror's heart
> Although his Car, in its triumphal course,
> Crush the poor insect, which perchance had yet
> Some few brief hours to glitter in the Sun?
> Woman must love, and suffer, and be still
> In Sorrow's presence!—But for you, ye rush
> To gain some night of glory, shaking off
> Affection's hold, if on your fiery speed
> It hang too closely; and your Slave, Renown,
> Doth blazon forth your Victories, tolling nought
> Of the fond hopes that died; the gentle hearts
> That broke obscurely, when ye burst the ties
> Whereby they clung to yours!—No, we but hear
> Of Kingdoms won, not of their Vines and flowers
> Crush'd by the March of Hosts!—But what had I . . .

For "suffer, and be still," cf. *Madeline* 62.

[10] A sarcastic allusion to Adam and Eve's exit from Eden at the end of *Paradise Lost*: "The World was all before them . . ." (12.646).

[11] A lover turned infidel is the hero of *Abencerrage* (1819) and of Byron's *Siege of Corinth* (1816).

[12] This blood seal evokes both Abraham's near-sacrifice of Isaac (Genesis 22.1–13) and God's sacrifice of his Son.

[13] Part of the Gibraltar headland; for Roncesvalles, see above.

[14] MS adds] Till Earth's loud cry shall wake th'Avenger! hence!

[15] Frey geht das Unglück durch die ganze Erde.—*Schiller's Death of Wallenstein*, act iv, sc. 2. [FH]

Thekla's remark (paraphrased by Elmina) on her daring to go through enemy lines to seek the grave of her beloved, slain in battle. Cf. the epigraph for the *Records of Woman &c.*

[16] MS] . . . gate! So shalt thou rise, and gird / Thy Husband's armour on, and send him forth / With a prevailing Spirit, to fulfil / The Day's allotted Work.

[17] MS adds] Oh, happy Slumberer!—Thou art where no eye / Can wound thee with its scorn, no voice can send / The Sting of its upbraidings thro' thy Soul! / Would it were thus with me!

## Scene 3

*A Street in the City.* HERNANDEZ, GONZALEZ.

HERNANDEZ. Would they not hear?

GONZALEZ.                              They heard, as one that stands
By the cold grave which hath but newly closed
O'er his last friend doth hear some passer-by,

Bid him be comforted!—Their hearts have died
Within them!—We must perish, not as those
That fall when battle's voice doth shake the hills,
And peal through Heaven's great arch, but silently,
And with a wasting of the spirit down,
A quenching, day by day, of some bright spark,
Which lit us on our toils!—Reproach me not;          10
My soul is darken'd with a heavy cloud—
—Yet fear not I shall yield!

HERNANDEZ.                    Breathe not the word,
Save in proud scorn!—Each bitter day, o'erpass'd
By slow endurance, is a triumph won
For Spain's red cross.[1] And be of trusting heart!
A few brief hours, and those that turn'd away
In cold despondence, shrinking from your voice,
May crowd around their leader, and demand
To be array'd for battle.[2] We must watch
For the swift impulse, and await its time,          20
As the bark waits the ocean's.[3] You have chosen
To kindle up their souls, an hour, perchance,
When they were weary; they had cast aside
Their arms to slumber; or a knell, just then
With its deep hollow tone, had made the blood
Creep shuddering through their veins; or they had caught
A glimpse of some new meteor, and shaped forth
Strange omens from its blaze.

GONZALEZ.                    Alas! the cause
Lies deeper in their misery!—I have seen,
In my night's course through this beleaguer'd city          30
Things, whose remembrance doth not pass away
As vapours from the mountains.—There were some,
That sat beside their dead, with eyes, wherein
Grief had ta'en place of sight, and shut out all
But its own ghastly object. To my voice
Some answer'd with a fierce and bitter laugh,
As men whose agonies were made to pass
The bounds of sufferance, by some reckless word,
Dropt from the light of spirit.—Others lay—
—Why should I tell thee, father! how despair          40
Can bring the lofty brow of manhood down
Unto the very dust?—And yet for this,
Fear not that I embrace my doom—Oh God!
That 'twere *my* doom alone!—with less of fix'd
And solemn fortitude.—Lead on, prepare
The holiest rites of faith, that I by them

Once more may consecrate my sword, my life,
—But what are these?—Who hath not dearer lives
Twined with his own?—I shall be lonely soon—
Childless!—Heaven wills it so. Let us begone.    50
Perchance before the shrine my heart may beat
With a less troubled motion.[4]

*Exeunt* GONZALEZ *and* HERNANDEZ.

[1] The emblem of Christian Spain, but the sanguinary connotation is relevant; cf. 6.153.
    MS adds] —Doth not the struggling Land / From the protraction of our sufferings gain / The time she needed to arouse her Sons, / And gather all her might?—
    [2] MS inserts] Know you not / That then, or Men in Multitudes, are but / The Slaves of impulse?—
    [3] MS] ... the seas; and then bear on, / Making their passions as the subject waves / O'er which we ride in triumph. You ...
    [4] MS adds]

HERNANDEZ    Doubt thee not
    But we shall yet prevail. Thick clouds may heap
    Their dark embattled masses, and shut out
    The Heaven's clear azure, but the Sun, tho' veil'd,
    Is there, a Monarch still. We shall not fall!
    That Spirit is on us, whose prevailing might
    Works deeds that shall be marvels, when Mankind
    Shall call our times, the Past.
GONZALEZ    It is on *thee.*
    —But we will die in honour, tho' our fate
    Grant us not victory.
The metaphor of the veiled sun, aided by the sound of "Son," implies Christian providence.

## SCENE 4

*A Tent in the Moorish Camp.* ABDULLAH, ALPHONSO, CARLOS.

ABDULLAH.  These are bold words: but hast thou look'd on death,
    Fair stripling?—On thy cheek and sunny brow[1]
    Scarce fifteen summers of their laughing course
    Have left light traces. If thy shaft hath pierced
    The ibex of the mountains, if thy step
    Hath climb'd some eagle's nest, and thou hast made
    His nest thy spoil, 'tis much!—And fear'st thou not
    The leader of the mighty?[2]
ALPHONSO.    I have been
    Rear'd amongst fearless men, and midst the rocks
    And the wild hills, whereon my fathers fought    10
    And won their battles.[3] There are glorious tales
    Told of their deeds, and I have learn'd them all.
    How should I fear thee, Moor?
ABDULLAH.    So, thou hast seen
    Fields, where the combat's roar hath died away

Into the whispering breeze, and where wild flowers
Bloom o'er forgotten graves![4] —But know'st thou aught
Of those, where sword from crossing sword strikes fire,
And leaders are borne down, and rushing steeds
Trample the life from out the mighty hearts
That ruled the storm so late?—Speak not of death,                    20
Till thou hast look'd on such.

ALPHONSO.                         I was not born
A shepherd's son, to dwell with pipe and crook,
And peasant-men, amidst the lowly vales;
Instead of ringing clarions, and bright spears,
And crested knights!—I am of princely race,
And, if my father would have heard my suit,
I tell thee, infidel! that long ere now,
I should have seen how lances meet; and swords[5]
Do the field's work.

ABDULLAH.                         Boy! know'st thou there are sights
A thousand times more fearful?—Men may die                           30
Full proudly, when the skies and mountains ring
To battle-horn and tecbir.[6] —But not all.
So pass away in glory. There are those,
Midst the dead silence of pale multitudes,
Led forth in fetters—dost thou mark me, boy?
To take their last look of th' all gladdening sun,
And bow, perchance, the stately head of youth,
Unto the death of shame!—Hadst thou seen this—

ALPHONSO (*to* CARLOS)
Sweet brother, God is with us—fear thou not!
We have had heroes for our sires—this man                            40
Should not behold us tremble.

ABDULLAH.                         There are means
To tame the loftiest natures. Yet again,
I ask thee, wilt thou, from beneath the walls,
Sue to thy sire for life; or wouldst thou die,
With this, thy brother?

ALPHONSO.                 Moslem! on the hills,
Around my father's castle, I have heard
The mountain-peasants, as they dress'd the vines,
Or drove the goats, by rock and torrent, home,
Singing their ancient songs; and these were all
Of the Cid Campeador; and how his sword                              50
Tizona[7] clear'd its way through turban'd hosts,
And captured Afric's kings, and how he won
Valencia from the Moor.[8] ——I will not shame
The blood we draw from him!

(*A Moorish Soldier enters.*)

SOLDIER.                                  Valencia's lord
    Sends messengers, my chief.
ABDULLAH.                                 Conduct them hither.

*The Soldier goes out, and re-enters with* ELMINA, *disguised,*
*and an Attendant.*

CARLOS (*springing forward to the Attendant*).
    Oh! take me hence, Diego; take me hence
    With thee, that I may see my mother's face
    At morning, when I wake. Here dark-brow'd men
    Frown strangely, with their cruel eyes, upon us.
    Take me with thee, for thou art good and kind,                    60
    And well I know, thou lov'st me, my Diego!
ABDULLAH. Peace, boy!—What tidings, Christian, from thy lord?
    Is he grown humbler, doth he set the lives
    Of these fair nurslings at a city's worth?
ALPHONSO (*rushing forward impatiently*).
    Say not, he doth!—Yet wherefore art thou here?
    If it be so—I could weep burning tears
    For very shame!—If this *can* be, return!
    Tell him, of all his wealth, his battle-spoils,
    I will but ask a war-horse and a sword,
    And that beside him in the mountain-chase,                        70
    And in his halls and at his stately feasts,
    My place shall be no more!—but no!—I wrong,
    I wrong my father!—Moor! believe it not!
    He is a champion of the cross and Spain,
    Sprung from the Cid;—and I too, I can die
    As a warrior's high-born child!
ELMINA.                                   Alas! Alas!
    And wouldst thou die, thus early die, fair boy?
    What hath life done to thee, that thou shouldst cast
    Its flower away, in very scorn of heart,
    Ere yet the blight be come?
ALPHONSO.                                 That voice doth sound——      80
ABDULLAH. Stranger, who art thou?—this is mockery! speak!
ELMINA (*throwing off a mantle and helmet, and embracing*
    *her sons*).
    My boys! whom I have rear'd through many hours
    Of silent joys and sorrows, and deep thoughts
    Untold and unimagined; let me die
    With you, now I have held you to my heart,
    And seen once more the faces, in whose light
    My soul hath lived for years!

CARLOS.                              Sweet mother! now
    Thou shalt not leave us more.
ABDULLAH.                        Enough of this!
    Woman! what seek'st thou here?—How hast thou dared
    To front the mighty thus amidst his hosts?                90
ELMINA. Think'st thou there dwells no courage but in breasts
    That set their mail against the ringing spears,
    When helmets are struck down?[9] —Thou little know'st
    Of nature's marvels!—Chief! my heart is nerved
    To make its way through things which warrior-men,
    —Aye, they that master death by field or flood,[10]
    Would look on, ere they braved!—I have no thought,
    No sense of fear!—Thou'rt mighty! but a soul
    Wound up like mine is mightier, in the power
    Of that one feeling, pour'd through all its depths,       100
    Than monarchs with their hosts!—Am I not come
    To die with these, my children?
ABDULLAH.                             Doth thy faith
    Bid thee do this, fond Christian?—Hast thou not
    The means to save them?
ELMINA.                          I have prayers, and tears,
    And agonies!—and he—my God—the God
    Whose hand, or soon or late, doth find its hour
    To bow the crested head—hath made these things
    Most powerful in a world where all must learn
    That lone deep language, by the storm call'd forth
    From the bruised reeds of earth!—For thee, perchance,     110
    Affliction's chastening lesson hath not yet
    Been laid upon thy heart, and thou may'st love
    To see the creatures, by its might brought low,
    Humbled before thee.

                           *She throws herself at his feet.*
                  Conqueror! I can kneel!
    I, that drew birth from princes, bow myself
    E'en to thy feet! Call in thy chiefs, thy slaves,
    If this will swell thy triumph, to behold
    The blood of kings, of heroes, thus abased!
    Do this, but spare my sons!
ALPHONSO (*attempting to raise her*). Thou shouldst not kneel
    Unto this infidel!—Rise, rise, my mother!                120
    This sight doth shame our house!
ABDULLAH.                           Thou daring boy!
    They that in arms have taught thy father's land

  How chains are worn, shall school that haughty mien
  Unto another language.
ELMINA.       Peace, my son!
  Have pity on my heart!—Oh, pardon, Chief!
  He is of noble blood!—Hear, hear me yet!
  Are there no lives through which the shafts of Heaven
  May reach your soul?—He that loves aught on earth,
  Dares far too much, if he be merciless!
  Is it for those, whose frail mortality      130
  Must one day strive alone with God and death,
  To shut their souls against th' appealing voice
  Of nature, in her anguish?—Warrior! Man!
  To you too, aye, and haply with your hosts,
  By thousands and ten thousands marshall'd round,
  And your strong armour on, shall come that stroke
  Which the lance wards not!—Where shall your high heart
  Find refuge then, if in the day of might
  Woe hath lain prostrate, bleeding at your feet,
  And you have pitied not?
ABDULLAH.      These are vain words.[11]   140
ELMINA. Have you no children?—fear you not to bring
  The lightning on their heads?—In your own land
  Doth no fond mother, from the tents, beneath
  Your native palms, look o'er the deserts out,
  To greet your homeward step?—You have not yet
  Forgot so utterly her patient love—
  —For is not woman's, in all climes, the same?—
  That you should scorn *my* prayer!—Oh Heaven! his eye
  Doth wear no mercy!
ABDULLAH.     Then it mocks you not.[12]
  I have swept o'er the mountains of your land,   150
  Leaving my traces, as the visitings
  Of storms, upon them!—Shall I now be stay'd!
  Know, unto me it were as light a thing,
  In this, my course, to quench your children's lives,
  As, journeying through a forest, to break off
  The young wild branches that obstruct the way
  With their green sprays and leaves.
ELMINA.       Are there such hearts
  Amongst thy works, oh God?
ABDULLAH.     Kneel not to me.[13]
  Kneel to your lord! on his resolves doth hang
  His children's doom. He may be lightly won   160
  By a few bursts of passionate tears and words.

ELMINA (*rising indignantly*).
    Speak not of noble men!—he bears a soul
    Stronger than love or death.
ALPHONSO (*with exultation*).      He could not fail!
    I knew 'twas thus!
ELMINA.            There is no mercy, none,
    On this cold earth!—To strive with such a world,
    Hearts should be void of love!—We will go hence,
    My children! we are summon'd. Lay your heads,
    In their young radiant beauty, once again
    To rest upon this bosom. He that dwells
    Beyond the clouds which press us darkly round,        170
    Will yet have pity, and before his face
    We three will stand together! Moslem! now
    Let the stroke fall at once!
ABDULLAH.             'Tis thine own will.
    These might e'en yet be spared.
ELMINA.              *Thou* wilt not spare!
    And he beneath whose eye their childhood grew,
    And in whose paths they sported, and whose ear
    From their first lisping accents caught the sound
    Of that word—*Father*—once a name of love—
    Is——Men shall call him *stedfast*.
ABDULLAH.             Hath the blast
    Of sudden trumpets ne'er at dead of night,        180
    When the land's watchers fear'd no hostile step,
    Startled the slumberers from their dreamy world,
    In cities, whose heroic lords have been
    *Stedfast* as thine?
ELMINA.          There's meaning in thine eye,
    More than thy words.
ABDULLAH (*pointing to the city*). Look to yon towers and walls!
    Think you no hearts within their limits pine,
    Weary of hopeless warfare, and prepared
    To burst the feeble links which bind them still
    Unto endurance?
ELMINA.          Thou hast said too well.
    But what of this?
ABDULLAH.         Then there are those, to whom        190
    The Prophet's armies not as foes would pass
    Yon gates, but as deliverers. Might they not
    In some still hour, when weariness takes rest,
    Be won to welcome us?—Your children's steps
    May yet bound lightly through their father's halls!

ALPHONSO (*indignantly*). Thou treacherous Moor!
ELMINA.        Let me not thus be tried
 Beyond all strength, oh Heaven!
ABDULLAH.       Now, 'tis for *thee*,
 Thou Christian mother! on thy sons to pass
 The sentence—life or death!—the price is set
 On their young blood, and rests within thy hands.   200
ALPHONSO. Mother! thou tremblest!
ABDULLAH.      Hath thy heart resolved?
ELMINA (*covering her face with her hands*).
 My boy's proud eye is on me, and the things
 Which rush, in stormy darkness, through my soul,
 Shrink from his glance. I cannot answer *here*.
ABDULLAH. Come forth. We'll commune elsewhere.
CARLOS (*to his mother*).     Wilt thou go?
 Oh! let me follow thee!
ELMINA.     Mine own fair child!
 —Now that thine eyes have pour'd once more on mine
 The light of their young smile, and thy sweet voice
 Hath sent its gentle music through my soul,
 And I have felt the twining of thine arms—   210
 —How shall I leave thee?
ABDULLAH.     Leave him, as 'twere but
 For a brief slumber, to behold his face
 At morning, with the sun's.
ALPHONSO.     Thou hast no look
 For me, my mother!
ELMINA.    Oh! that I should live
 To say, I *dare* not look on thee!—Farewell,
 My first born, fare thee well!
ALPHONSO.     Yet, yet beware!
 It were a grief more heavy on thy soul,
 That I should blush for thee, than o'er my grave
 That thou shouldst proudly weep!
ABDULLAH. Away! we trifle here. The night wanes fast.  220
 Come forth![14]
ELMINA.   One more embrace! My sons, farewell!

    *Exeunt* ABDULLAH *with* ELMINA *and her Attendant.*

ALPHONSO. Hear me yet once, my mother!
        Art thou gone?
 But one word more!

      *He rushes out, followed by* CARLOS.

[1] MS] Fair stripling?—Has thou set thy daring breast / Against the shock of spears, or with strong hand / Borne on, thro' flashing steel and arrowy shower, / The Banner of a Host?—On thy smooth cheek /

[2] MS adds] —Fear'st thou not / The power whose stroke may crush thee?

[3] Evoking his lineage from Pelayo and, more generally, mountain-culture as the emblematic site of political independence.

[4] MS ] ... graves, and quiet flocks / Feed on the grassy Mounds which hide perchance, / The dust of Heroes!—Aye, but know'st ...

After ABDULLAH, MS] (*scornfully*)

[5] MS] ... how warriors quit themselves / When their good mail is on, and how red swords

[6] *Tecbir*, the war-cry of the Moors and Arabs. [FH]

[7] Tizona, the fire-brand. The name of the Cid's favourite sword, taken in battle from the Moorish king Bucar. [FH]

See Southey, *Chronicle*, bk. 8.VIII (259); cf. *The Cid's Funeral Procession* 82.

[8] Valencia, which has been repeatedly besieged, and taken by the armies of different nations, remained in the possession of the Moors for an hundred and seventy years after the Cid's death. It was regained from them by King Don Jayme of Aragon, surnamed the Conqueror; after whose success I have ventured to suppose it governed by a descendant of the Campeador. [FH]

After its conquest by James I in 1238, the city rose to cultural and commercial prominence.

53–53, MS] ... Moor; and in good hour / Still arm'd for Spain.—He was mine Ancestor—/ I will not shame his blood.

[9] 91–93 MS] ... no courage, but that which makes / Its breast a sheath for hostile swords?—No Strength, / Is felt thro' desolate Houses, unto which / Their Sons return no more?—Thou ...

[10] Another echo of Othello's story of his life (*Othello* 1.3.133–34).

[11] MS adds] Think'st thou to make *me* tremble at the thought / Of Death?—His power is not o'er Kingly hearts.

[12] MS inserts] Think you, if hearts were not of sterner Mould / Than to be borne away by Woman's tears, / From their high place, that Kingdoms would be won, / And nations change their Lords?—/

[13] MS inserts] My course is to Dominion, and I pass / O'er all that stands between me and the goal / Of that proud March; e'en as the Desert-winds / In mine own clime go forth, and scatter death / From their fire-wings, and pause not for the moan / Made above that they slay. Kneel not to me! /

[14] 221, MS] I will not thus be mock'd.

Elmina's completion of this metrical line (following) is not in MS.

## SCENE 5

*The Garden of a Palace in Valencia.* XIMENA, THERESA

THERESA.  Stay yet awhile. A purer air doth rove
   Here through the myrtles whispering, and the limes,
   And shaking sweetness from the orange boughs,
   Than waits you in the city.
XIMENA.        There are those
   In their last need, and on their bed of death,
   At which no hand doth minister but mine
   That wait me in the city. Let us hence.
THERESA.  You have been wont to love the music made
   By founts, and rustling foliage, and soft winds,

Breathing of citron-groves. And will you turn                    10
From these to scenes of death?
XIMENA.                                    To me the voice
Of summer, whispering through young flowers and leaves
Now speaks too deep a language! and of all
Its dreamy and mysterious melodies,
The breathing soul is sadness!—I have felt
That summons through my spirit, after which
The hues of earth are changed, and all her sounds
Seem fraught with secret warnings.—There is cause
That I should bend my footsteps to the scenes
Where Death is busy, taming warrior-hearts,            20
And pouring winter through the fiery blood,
And fettering the strong arm!—For now no sigh
In the dull air, nor floating cloud in heaven,
No, not the lightest murmur of a leaf,
But of his angel's silent coming bears
Some token to my soul.—But nought of this
Unto my mother!—These are awful hours!
And on their heavy steps, afflictions crowd
With such dark pressure, there is left no room
For one grief more.
THERESA.                            Sweet lady, talk not thus!          30
Your eye this morn doth wear a calmer light,
There's more of life in its clear tremulous ray
Than I have mark'd of late. Nay, go not yet;
Rest by this fountain, where the laurels dip
Their glossy leaves. A fresher gale doth spring
From the transparent waters, dashing round
Their silvery spray, with a sweet voice of coolness,
O'er the pale glistening marble. 'Twill call up
Faint bloom, if but a moment's, to your cheek.
Rest here, ere you go forth, and I will sing              40
The melody you love.

THERESA *sings*.[1]

Why is the Spanish maiden's grave
    So far from her own bright land?
The sunny flowers that o'er it wave
    Were sown by no kindred hand.

'Tis not the orange-bough that sends
    Its breath on the sultry air,
'Tis not the myrtle-stem that bends
    To the breeze of evening there!

But the Rose of Sharon's eastern bloom[2]                    50
    By the silent dwelling fades,
And none but strangers pass the tomb
    Which the Palm of Judah shades.

The lowly Cross, with flowers o'ergrown,
    Marks well that place of rest;
But who hath graved, on its mossy stone,
    A sword, a helm, a crest?

These are the trophies of a chief,
    A lord of the axe and spear!
—Some blossom pluck'd, some faded leaf,                    60
    Should grace a maiden's bier!

Scorn not her tomb—deny not her
    The honours of the brave!
O'er that forsaken sepulchre,
    Banner and plume might wave.

She bound the steel, in battle tried,
    Her fearless heart above,
And stood with brave men, side by side,
    In the strength and faith of love![3]

That strength prevail'd—that faith was bless'd!                    70
    True was the javelin thrown,
Yet pierced it not her warrior's breast,
    She met it with her own!

And nobly won, where heroes fell
    In arms for the holy shrine,
A death which saved what she loved so well,
    And a grave in Palestine.

Then let the Rose of Sharon spread
    Its breast to the glowing air,
And the Palm of Judah lift its head,                    80
    Green and immortal there!

And let yon grey stone, undefaced,
    With its trophy mark the scene,
Telling the pilgrim of the waste,
    Where Love and Death have been.

XIMENA. Those notes were wont to make my heart beat quick,
    As at a voice of victory; but to-day
The spirit of the song is changed, and seems

All mournful. Oh! that ere my early grave
Shuts out the sunbeam, I might hear one peal            90
Of the Castilian trumpet, ringing forth
Beneath my father's banner!—In that sound
Were life to you, sweet brothers!—But for me—
Come on—our tasks await us. They who know
Their hours are number'd out, have little time
To give the vague and slumberous languor way,
Which doth steal o'er them in the breath of flowers,
And whisper of soft winds.

                                    ELMINA *enters hurriedly.*

ELMINA. This air will calm my spirit, ere yet I meet
    *His* eye, which must be met.—Thou here, Ximena!      100

                        *She starts back on seeing* XIMENA.

XIMENA. Alas! my mother! In that hurrying step
    And troubled glance I read—
ELMINA (*wildly*).                Thou read'st it not!
    Why, who would live, if unto mortal eye
    The things lay glaring, which within our hearts
    We treasure up for God's?—Thou read'st it not!
    I say, thou canst not!—There's not one on earth
    Shall know the thoughts, which for themselves have made
    And kept dark places in the very breast
    Whereon he hath laid his slumber, till the hour
    When the graves open!
XIMENA.                     Mother! what is this?          110
    Alas! your eye is wandering, and your cheek
    Flush'd, as with fever! To your woes the night
    Hath brought no rest.
ELMINA.                    Rest!—who should rest?—not he
    That holds one earthly blessing to his heart
    Nearer than life!—No! if this world have aught
    Of bright or precious, let not him who calls
    Such things his own, take rest!—Dark spirits keep watch,
    And they to whom fair honour, chivalrous fame,
    Were as heaven's air, the vital element
    Wherein they breathed, may wake, and find their souls   120
    Made marks for human scorn!—Will they bear on
    With life struck down, and thus disrobed of all
    Its glorious drapery?—Who shall tell us this?
    —Will *he* so bear it?
XIMENA.                    Mother! let us kneel,
    And blend our hearts in prayer!—What else is left
    To mortals when the dark hour's might is on them?

  —Leave us, Theresa.—Grief like this doth find
Its balm in solitude.

                                  *Exit* THERESA.

                     My mother! peace
Is heaven's benignant answer to the cry
Of wounded spirits. Wilt thou kneel with me?         130
ELMINA.  Away! 'tis but for souls unstain'd to wear
  Heaven's tranquil image on their depths.—The stream
  Of my dark thoughts, all broken by the storm,
  Reflects but clouds and lightnings!—Didst thou speak
  Of peace?—'tis fled from earth!—but there is joy!
  Wild, troubled joy!—And who shall know, my child!
  It is not happiness?—Why, our own hearts
  Will keep the secret close!—Joy, joy! if but
  To leave this desolate city, with its dull
  Slow knells and dirges, and to breathe again      140
  Th' untainted mountain-air!—But hush! the trees,
  The flowers, the waters, must hear nought of this!
  They are full of voices, and will whisper things——
  We'll speak of it no more.
XIMENA.                   Oh! pitying heaven!
  This grief doth shake her reason!
ELMINA (*starting*).             Hark! a step!
  'Tis—'tis thy father's!—come away—not now—
  He must not see us now!
XIMENA.               Why should this be?

        GONZALEZ *enters, and detains* ELMINA.

GONZALEZ.  Elmina, dost thou shun me?—Have we not,
  E'en from the hopeful and the sunny time
  When youth was as a glory round our brows,      150
  Held on through life together?—And is this,
  When eve is gathering round us, with the gloom
  Of stormy clouds, a time to part our steps
  Upon the darkening wild?
ELMINA (*coldly*).         There needs not this.
  Why shouldst thou think I shunn'd thee?
GONZALEZ.                Should the love
  That shone o'er many years, th' unfading love,
  Whose only change hath been from gladdening smiles
  To mingling sorrows and sustaining strength,
  Thus lightly be forgotten?
ELMINA.             Speak'st *thou* thus?
  —I have knelt before thee with that very plea,     160
  When it avail'd me not!—But there are things

Whose very breathings on the soul erase
All record of past love, save the chill sense,
Th' unquiet memory of its wasted faith,
And vain devotedness!—Aye! they that fix
Affection's perfect trust on aught of earth,
Have many a dream to start from!

GONZALEZ.                          This is but
The wildness and the bitterness of grief,
Ere yet th' unsettled heart hath closed its long
Impatient conflicts with a mightier power,                    170
Which makes all conflict vain.

                          —Hark! was there not
A sound of distant trumpets, far beyond
The Moorish tents, and of another tone
Than th' Afric horn, Ximena?

XIMENA.                          Oh, my father!
I know that horn too well.—'Tis but the wind,
Which, with a sudden rising, bears its deep
And savage war-note from us, wafting it
O'er the far hills.

GONZALEZ.          Alas! this woe must be!
I do but shake my spirit from its height
So startling it with hope!—But the dread hour                 180
Shall be met bravely still. I can keep down
Yet for a little while—and Heaven will ask
No more—the passionate workings of my heart;
—And thine—Elmina?

ELMINA.                          'Tis—I am prepared.
I *have* prepared for all.

GONZALEZ.                          Oh, well I knew
Thou wouldst not fail me!—Not in vain my soul,
Upon thy faith and courage, hath built up
Unshaken trust.

ELMINA (*wildly*).      Away!—thou know'st me not!
Man dares too far, his rashness would invest
This our mortality with an attribute                          190
Too high and awful, boasting that he knows
One human heart!

GONZALEZ.                          These are wild words, but yet
I will not doubt thee!—Hast thou not been found
Noble in all things, pouring thy soul's light
Undimm'd o'er every trial?—And, as our fates,
So must our names be, undivided!—Thine,
I' th' record of a warrior's life, shall find
Its place of stainless honour.—By his side——

ELMINA.  May this be borne?—How much of agony
    Hath the heart room for?—Speak to me in wrath—        200
    I can endure it!—But no gentle words!
    No words of love! no praise!—Thy sword might slay,
    And be more merciful!
GONZALEZ.                Wherefore art thou thus?
    Elmina, my beloved!
ELMINA.             No more of love!
    —Have I not said there's that within my heart,
    Whereon it falls as living fire would fall
    Upon an unclosed wound?
GONZALEZ.             Nay, lift thine eyes
    That I may read *their* meaning!
ELMINA.              Never more
    With a free soul—What have I said?—'twas nought!
    Take thou no heed! The words of wretchedness      210
    Admit not scrutiny. Wouldst thou mark the speech
    Of troubled dreams?
GONZALEZ.           I have seen thee in the hour
    Of thy deep spirit's joy, and when the breath
    Of grief hung chilling round thee; in all change,
    Bright health and drooping sickness; hope and fear;
    Youth and decline; but never yet, Elmina,
    Ne'er hath thine eye till now shrunk back perturb'd
    With shame or dread, from mine!
ELMINA.                Thy glance doth search
    A wounded heart too deeply.
GONZALEZ.             Hast thou there
    Aught to conceal?
ELMINA.          Who hath not?
GONZALEZ.                Till this hour      220
    *Thou* never hadst!—Yet hear me!—by the free
    And unattainted fame which wraps the dust
    Of thine heroic fathers—
ELMINA.            This to me!
    —Bring your inspiring war-notes, and your sounds
    Of festal music round a dying man!
    Will his heart echo them?—But if thy words
    Were spells, to call up, with each lofty tone,
    The grave's most awful spirits, they would stand
    Powerless, before my anguish![4]
GONZALEZ.            Then, by her,
    Who there looks on thee in the purity      230
    Of her devoted youth, and o'er whose name
    No blight must fall, and whose pale cheek must ne'er

Burn with that deeper tinge, caught painfully
From the quick feeling of dishonour.—Speak!
Unfold this mystery!—By thy sons——

ELMINA.                                        My sons!
And canst *thou* name them?

GONZALEZ.                      Proudly!—Better far
They died with all the promise of their youth,
And the fair honour of their house upon them,
Than that with manhood's high and passionate soul
To fearful strength unfolded, they should live,                240
Barr'd from the lists of crested chivalry,
And pining, in the silence of a woe,
Which from the heart shuts daylight;—o'er the shame
Of those who gave them birth!—But *thou* couldst ne'er
Forget their lofty claims!

ELMINA (*wildly*).                'Twas but for them!
'Twas for them only!—Who shall dare arraign
Madness of crime?—And he who made us, knows
There are dark moments of all hearts and lives,
Which bear down reason!

GONZALEZ.                      Thou, whom I have loved
With such high trust, as o'er our nature threw                  250
A glory, scarce allow'd;—what hast thou done?
—Ximena, go thou hence!

ELMINA.                        No, no! my child!
There's pity in thy look!—All other eyes
Are full of wrath and scorn!—Oh! leave me not!

GONZALEZ. That I should live to see thee thus abased!
—Yet speak?—What hast thou done?

ELMINA.                                  Look to the gate!
Thou'rt worn with toil—but take no rest to-night!
The western gate!—Its watchers have been won—
The Christian city hath been bought and sold!
They will admit the Moor!

GONZALEZ.                      They have been won!             260
Brave men and tried so long!—Whose work was this?

ELMINA. Think'st thou all hearts like thine?[5]—Can mothers stand
To see their children perish?

GONZALEZ.                      Then the guilt
Was thine?

ELMINA.        —Shall mortal dare to call it guilt?
I tell thee, Heaven, which made all holy things,
Made nought more holy than the boundless love
Which fills a mother's heart!—I say, 'tis woe
Enough, with such an aching tenderness,

To love aught earthly!—and in vain! in vain!
—We are press'd down too sorely!
GONZALEZ (*in a low desponding voice*).  Now my life                    270
    Is struck to worthless ashes!—In my soul
    Suspicion hath ta'en root. The nobleness
    Henceforth is blotted from all human brows,
    And fearful power, a dark and troublous gift,
    Almost like prophecy, is pour'd upon me,
    To read the guilty secrets in each eye
    That once look'd bright with truth!
                      —Why then I have gain'd
    What men call wisdom!—A new sense, to which
    All tales that speak of high fidelity,
    And holy courage, and proud honour, tried,                         280
    Search'd, and found stedfast, even to martyrdom,
    Are food for mockery!—Why should I not cast
    From my thinn'd locks the wearing helm at once,
    And in the heavy sickness of my soul
    Throw the sword down for ever?—Is there aught
    In all this world of gilded hollowness,
    Now the bright hues drop off its loveliest things,
    Worth striving for again?
XIMENA.                Father! look up!
    Turn unto me, thy child!
GONZALEZ.[6]           Thy face is fair;
    And hath been unto me, in other days,                               290
    As morning to the journeyer of the deep;
    But now—'tis too like hers!
ELMINA (*falling at his feet*).      Woe, shame and woe,
    Are on me in their might!—forgive, forgive!
GONZALEZ (*starting up*).
    Doth the Moor deem that *I* have part or share,
    Or counsel in this vileness?—Stay me not!
    Let go thy hold—'tis powerless on me now—
    I linger here, while treason is at work!
                      *Exit* GONZALEZ.

ELMINA. Ximena, dost *thou* scorn me?
XIMENA.               I have found
    In mine own heart too much of feebleness,
    Hid, beneath many foldings, from all eyes                          300
    But *His* whom nought can blind;—to dare do aught
    But pity thee, dear mother!
ELMINA.             Blessings light
    On thy fair head, my gentle child, for this!

Thou kind and merciful!—My soul[7] is faint—
Worn with long strife!—Is there aught else to do,
Or suffer, ere we die?—Oh God! my sons!
—I have betray'd them!—All their innocent blood
Is on my soul!

XIMENA.                How shall I comfort thee?
—Oh! hark! what sounds come deepening on the wind,
So full of solemn hope!                                        310

*(A procession of Nuns passes across the Scene,*
*bearing relics, and chanting.)*

CHANT[8]

A sword is on the land!
He that bears down young tree and glorious flower,
Death is gone forth, he walks the wind in power!
        —Where is the warrior's hand?
Our steps are in the shadows of the grave,
Hear us, we perish! Father, hear, and save!

If, in the days of song,
The days of gladness, we have call'd on thee,
When mirthful voices rang from sea to sea,
        And joyous hearts were strong;                        320
Now, that alike the feeble and the brave
Must cry, "We perish!"—Father! hear, and save!

The days of song are fled!
The winds come loaded, wafting dirge-notes by,
But they that linger soon unmourn'd must die;
        —The dead weep not the dead!
—Wilt thou forsake us midst the stormy wave?
We sink, we perish!—Father, hear, and save!

Helmet and lance are dust!
Is not the strong man wither'd from our eye?             330
The arm struck down that held our banners high?
        —Thine is our spirit's trust!
Look through the gathering shadows of the grave!
Do we not perish?—Father, hear, and save!

HERNANDEZ *enters.*

ELMINA.  Why comest thou, man of vengeance?—What have I
        To do with thee?—Am I not bow'd enough?
        Thou art no mourner's comforter!

HERNANDEZ.                          Thy lord
        Hath sent me unto thee. Till this day's task
        Be closed, thou daughter of the feeble heart!

He bids thee seek him not, but lay thy woes                                340
Before Heaven's altar, and in penitence
Make thy soul's peace with God.

ELMINA.                                        Till this day's task
Be closed!—there is strange triumph in thine eyes—
Is it that I have fallen from that high place
Whereon I stood in fame?—But I can feel
A wild and bitter pride in thus being past
The power of thy dark glance! My spirit now
Is wound about by one sole mighty grief;
Thy scorn hath lost its sting.—Thou mayst reproach—

HERNANDEZ. I come not to reproach thee. Heaven doth work      350
By many agencies; and in its hour
There is no insect which the summer breeze
From the green leaf shakes trembling, but may serve
Its deep unsearchable purposes, as well
As the great ocean, or th' eternal fires,
Pent in earth's caves!—Thou hast but speeded that,
Which, in th' infatuate blindness of thy heart,
Thou wouldst have trampled o'er all holy ties,
But to avert one day!⁹

ELMINA.                          My senses fail—
Thou saidst—speak yet again!—I could not catch            360
The meaning of thy words.

HERNANDEZ.                        E'en now thy lord
Hath sent our foes defiance. On the walls
He stands in conference° with the boastful Moor,        *confrontation*
And awful strength is with him. Through the blood
Which this day must be pour'd in sacrifice
Shall Spain be free. On all her olive-hills
Shall men set up the battle-sign of fire,
And round its blaze, at midnight, keep the sense
Of vengeance wakeful in each other's hearts
E'en with thy children's tale!

XIMENA.                        Peace, father! peace!          370
Behold she sinks!—the storm hath done its work
Upon the broken reed. Oh! lend thine aid
To bear her hence.

                                            *They lead her away.*

---

¹ The scene of this song, in the medieval Crusades against the Arab "infidels," reflects the strife between Christian Spaniard and Muslim Moor.

² A showy flower, named for the Plain of Sharon in Palestine; the Palm of Judah (53) is named for the son of Jacob, tribal patriarch of Israel; myrtle (48) is an emblem of love.

³ The maid disguised as page or soldier, to join her beloved in wartime, is a literary convention at least as old as Sidney's *Arcadia*, romanticized in FH's day by Byron's *Lara* (1814).

[4] MS] All powerless in the stern and rigid presence / Of Grief, whose terrible reality / Gives her command o'er Phantoms!

[5] 262, MS] Why, what know'st *thou* of Nature?—If *thy* heart / Had shut its panoply against her touch, / Were all of such a mould?—Can . . .

[6] MS adds] (*in deep dejection*)

[7] MS] Oh! little, when this cold World's aspect lay / Before me in the sun, I little deem'd / Mercy so rare on Earth!—My Soul

[8] MS has a different "Chaunt"; see Appendix 1.

[9] MS] Aye, rooted up the glory of a life, / A Hero's life, to shun!

## SCENE 6

*A Street in Valencia. Several Groups of Citizens and Soldiers,*
*many of them lying on the Steps of a Church.*
*Arms scattered on the Ground around them.*

AN OLD CITIZEN. The air is sultry, as with thunder-clouds.
 I left my desolate home, that I might breathe
 More freely in heaven's face, but my heart feels
 With this hot gloom o'erburthen'd. I have now
 No sons to tend me. Which of you, kind friends,
 Will bring the old man water from the fount,
 To moisten his parch'd lip?

          *A citizen goes out.*

SECOND CITIZEN.       This wasting siege,
 Good Father Lopez, hath gone hard with you!
 'Tis sad to hear no voices through the house,
 Once peopled with fair sons!

THIRD CITIZEN.        Why, better thus,     10
 Than to be haunted with their famish'd cries,
 E'en in your very dreams![1]

OLD CITIZEN.        Heaven's will be done!
 These are dark times! I have not been alone
 In my affliction.

THIRD CITIZEN (*with bitterness*).[2] Why, we have but this thought
 Left for our gloomy comfort!—And 'tis well!
 Aye, let the balance be awhile struck even
 Between the noble's palace and the hut,
 Where the worn peasant sickens!—They that bear
 The humble dead unhonour'd to their homes,
 Pass now i' th' streets no lordly bridal train,     20
 With its exulting music; and the wretch
 Who on the marble steps of some proud hall
 Flings himself down to die, in his last need
 And agony of famine, doth behold
 No scornful guests, with their long purple robes,[3]
 To the banquet sweeping by. Why, this is just!

These are the days when pomp is made to feel
Its human mould!
FOURTH CITIZEN.          Heard you last night the sound
Of Saint Jago's bell?—How sullenly
From the great tower it peal'd!
FIFTH CITIZEN.                    Aye, and 'tis said          30
No mortal hand was near when so it seem'd
To shake the midnight streets.
OLD CITIZEN.                    Too well I know
The sound of coming fate!—'Tis ever thus
When Death is on his way to make it night
In the Cid's ancient house.[4] —Oh! there are things
In this strange world of which we have all to learn
When its dark bounds are pass'd.—Yon bell, untouch'd,
(Save by the hands we see not) still doth speak—
—When of that line some stately head is mark'd,—
With a wild hollow peal, at dead of night,          40
Rocking Valencia's towers. I have heard it oft,
Nor known its warning false.
FOURTH CITIZEN.                    And will our chief
Buy with the price of his fair children's blood
A few more days of pining wretchedness
For this forsaken city?
OLD CITIZEN.                Doubt it not!
—But with that ransom he may purchase still
Deliverance for the land!—And yet 'tis sad
To think that such a race, with all its fame,
Should pass away!—For she, his daughter too,
Moves upon earth as some bright thing whose time          50
To sojourn there is short.
FIFTH CITIZEN.                Then woe for us
When she is gone!—Her voice—the very sound
Of her soft step was comfort, as she moved
Through the still house of mourning!—Who like her
Shall give us hope again?
OLD CITIZEN.                    Be still!—she comes,
And with a mien how changed!—A hurrying step,
And a flush'd cheek!—What may this bode?—Be still!

            XIMENA *enters, with Attendants carrying a Banner.*

XIMENA. Men of Valencia! in an hour like this,
What do ye here?
CITIZEN.                We die!
XIMENA.                        Brave men die *now*
Girt for the toil, as travellers suddenly          60
By the dark night o'ertaken on their way!

These days require such death!—It is too much
Of luxury for our wild and angry times,
To fold the mantle round us, and to sink
From life, as flowers that shut up silently,
When the sun's heat doth scorch them!—Hear ye not?
A CITIZEN.  Lady! what wouldst thou with us?
XIMENA.                              Rise and arm!
E'en now the children of your chief are led
Forth by the Moor to perish!—Shall this be,
Shall the high sound of such a name be hush'd,                    70
I' th' land to which for ages it hath been
A battle-word, as 'twere some passing note
Of shepherd-music?—Must this work be done,
And ye lie pining here, as men in whom
The pulse which God hath made for noble thought
Can so be thrill'd no longer?
CITIZEN.                              'Tis even so!
Sickness, and toil, and grief, have breath'd upon us,
Our hearts beat faint and low.
XIMENA.                              Are ye so poor
Of soul, my countrymen! that ye can draw
Strength from no deeper source than that which sends            80
The red blood mantling through the joyous veins,
And gives the fleet step wings?—Why, how have age
And sensitive womanhood ere now endured,
Through pangs of searching fire, in some proud cause,
Blessing that agony?—Think ye the Power
Which bore them nobly up, as if to teach
The torturer where eternal Heaven had set
Bounds to his sway, was earthy, of this earth,
This dull mortality?—Nay, then look on me!
Death's touch hath mark'd me, and I stand amongst you,            90
As one whose place, i' th' sunshine of your world,
Shall soon be left to fill!⁵ —I say, the breath
Of th' incense, floating through yon fane, shall scarce
Pass from your path before me! But even now,
I have that within me, kindling through the dust,
Which from all time hath made high deeds its voice
And token to the nations;—Look on me!
Why hath Heaven pour'd forth courage, as a flame
Wasting the womanish heart, which must be still'd
Yet sooner for its swift consuming brightness,                   100
If not to shame your doubt, and your despair,
And your soul's torpor?—Yet, arise and arm!
It may not be too late.

A CITIZEN.            Why, what are we,
    To cope with hosts?—Thus faint, and worn, and few,
    O'ernumber'd and forsaken, is't for us
    To stand against the mighty?
XIMENA.                 And for whom
    Hath He, who shakes the mighty with a breath
    From their high places, made the fearfulness,
    And ever-wakeful presence of his power,
    To the pale startled earth most manifest,           110
    But for the weak?—Was't for the helm'd and crown'd
    That suns were stay'd at noonday?—Stormy seas
    As a rill parted?—Mail'd archangels sent
    To wither up the strength of kings with death?
    —I tell you, if these marvels have been done,
    'Twas for the wearied and th' oppress'd of men,
    They needed such!—And generous faith hath power
    By her prevailing spirit, e'en yet to work
    Deliverances, whose tale shall live with those
    Of the great elder time!—Be of good heart!        120
    *Who* is forsaken?—He that gives the thought
    A place within his breast!—'Tis not for you.
    —Know ye this banner?
CITIZENS (*murmuring to each other*). Is she not inspired?
    Doth not Heaven call us by her fervent voice?
XIMENA. Know ye this banner?
CITIZENS.               'Tis the Cid's.
XIMENA.                 The Cid's!
    Who breathes that name but in th' exulting tone
    Which the heart rings to?—Why, the very wind
    As it swells out the noble standard's fold
    Hath a triumphant sound!—The Cid's!—it moved
    Even as a sign of victory through the land,       130
    From the free skies ne'er stooping to a foe!
OLD CITIZEN. Can ye still pause, my brethren?—Oh! that youth
    Through this worn frame were kindling once again!
XIMENA. Ye linger still?—Upon this very air,
    He that was born in happy hour for Spain[6]
    Pour'd forth his conquering spirit!—'Twas the breeze
    From your own mountains which came down to wave
    This banner of his battles, as it droop'd
    Above the champion's death-bed. Nor even then
    Its tale of glory closed.—They made no moan      140
    O'er the dead hero, and no dirge was sung,[7]
    But the deep tambour and shrill horn of war
    Told when the mighty pass'd!—They wrapt him not

With the pale shroud, but braced the warrior's form
In war-array, and on his barbed[8] steed,
As for a triumph, rear'd him; marching forth
In the hush'd midnight from Valencia's walls,
Beleaguer'd then, as now. All silently
The stately funeral moved:—but who was he
That follow'd, charging on the tall white horse,                    150
And with the solemn standard, broad and pale,
Waving in sheets of snow-light?—And the cross,
The bloody cross, far-blazing from his shield,
And the fierce meteor-sword?—They fled, they fled!
The kings of Afric, with their countless hosts,
Were dust in his red path!—The scimetar°                    *scimitar*
Was shiver'd as a reed!—for in that hour
The warrior-saint that keeps the watch for Spain,
Was arm'd betimes!—And o'er that fiery field
The Cid's high banner stream'd all joyously,                    160
For still its lord was there!⁹

CITIZENS (*rising tumultuously*). Even unto death
    Again it shall be follow'd!

XIMENA.                                     Will he see
    The noble stem hewn down, the beacon-light
Which his house for ages o'er the land
Hath shone through cloud and storm, thus quench'd at once?
Will he not aid his children in the hour
Of this their uttermost peril?—Awful power
Is with the holy dead, and there are times
When the tomb hath no chain they cannot burst?
—Is it a thing forgotten, how he woke                    170
From its deep rest of old, remembering Spain
In her great danger?—At the night's mid-watch
How Leon started, when the sound was heard
That shook her dark and hollow-echoing streets,
As with the heavy tramp of steel-clad men,
By thousands marching through!¹⁰ —For he had risen!
The Campeador was on his march again,
And in his arms, and follow'd by his hosts
Of shadowy spearmen!—He had left the world
From which we are dimly parted, and gone forth,                    180
And call'd his buried warriors from their sleep,
Gathering them round him to deliver Spain;
For Afric was upon her!—Morning broke—
Day rush'd through clouds of battle;—but at eve
Our God had triumph'd, and the rescued land

Sent up a shout of victory from the field,
That rock'd her ancient mountains.
THE CITIZENS.                          Arm! to arms!
On to our chief!—We have strength within us yet
To die with our blood roused!—Now, be the word,
For the Cid's house!

*They begin to arm themselves.*

XIMENA.                     Ye know his battle-song?          190
The old rude strain wherewith his bands went forth
To strike down Paynim° swords! (*She sings*)          Pagan

### THE CID'S BATTLE SONG

The Moor is on his way!
With the tambour-peal and the tecbir-shout,
And the horn o'er the blue seas ringing out,
    He hath marshall'd his dark array!

Shout through the vine-clad land!
That her sons on all their hills may hear,
And sharpen the point of the red wolf spear,
    And the sword for the brave man's hand!          200

*(The* CITIZENS *join in the song, while they
continue arming themselves.)*

Banners are in the field!
The chief must rise from his joyous board,
And turn from the feast ere the wine be pour'd,
    And take up his father's shield!

The Moor is on his way!
Let the peasant leave his olive-ground,
And the goats roam wild through the pine-woods round!
    —There is nobler work to-day!

Send forth the trumpet's call!
Till the bridegroom cast the goblet down,          210
And the marriage-robe and the flowery crown,
    And arm in the banquet-hall!

And stay the funeral-train!
Bid the chanted mass be hush'd awhile,
And the bier laid down in the holy aile,[11]
    And the mourners girt for Spain!

*(They take up the banner, and follow* XIMENA *out.
Their voices are heard gradually dying away at a distance.)*

Ere night, must swords be red!
It is not an hour for knells and tears,
But for helmets braced, and serried spears!
To-morrow for the dead!                                    220

The Cid is in array!
His steed is barbed, his plume waves high,
His banner is up in the sunny sky,
Now, joy for the Cross to-day!

[1] MS adds] Oh God! mine ears / Ring with mine Children's yet

[2] MS] No voice direction in MS. 15–32 is much expanded in MS; see Appendix 2.

[3] Signifier of royalty. Trade in precious Tyrian purple dye, among other exotic Eastern commodities, developed in consequence of the Crusades.

[4] It was a Spanish tradition, that the great bell of the cathedral of Saragossa always tolled spontaneously before a king of Spain died. [FH]
   Named "Caesarae Augustus" for and by the Roman emperor, Saragossa was the leading city of Aragón, in northeastern Spain. The Moors took it from the Goths in the 8th c.; Charlemagne then tried unsuccessfully to reclaim it (778). El Cid fought for its Muslim Moorish ruler against the Christian count of Barcelona. It was eventually conquered by Alfonso I of Aragón in 1118, who made it his capital. FH may be conflating its two famous cathedrals, an older one (La Seo, 12th c. to 16th c.), formerly a mosque, that is contemporaneous with the setting of her drama, and a later 17th-c. one associated with St. James the Greater (Saint Jago, or Iago; line 29; cf. 9.127), because the Virgin Mary is said to have appeared to him at its site. Valencia also has a cathedral called La Seo (13th c. to 16th c.). Like Valencia, Saragossa was famous for its resistance in the Peninsular War; it repulsed the first siege in 1808 and succumbed in the second, 1808–9, only after fifty thousand of its population died.

[5] MS inserts] . . . be void!—A Being, unto whom / Each Wind bears Language from the shore unknown, / Heard by no other ear!—I say, . . .

[6] "El que en buen hora nasco"; he that was born in happy hour. An appellation given to the Cid in the ancient chronicles. [FH]

[7] For this, and the subsequent allusions to the Spanish legends, see *The Romances and Chronicle of the Cid*. [FH]

[8] This may be an erratum for *barded*, an emendation in later editions, with a footnote (perhaps FH's) defining it as "caparisoned for battle" (from Old Spanish *barda*, ornamental armor for a horse). On the other hand, FH may have meant "barbed," to evoke both aggressive armament and the barb horse, a breed related to the Arab that the Moors introduced into Spain; cf. Ximena's "Battle-Song" (222). FH rendered a playful "sheet of forgeries" from various authors showing *barb* "as applied to a steed" (*HM* 43–45).

[9] A famous legend; see *The Cid's Rising*.

[10] This strategically located city in northwestern Spain, reconquered from the Moors in the 9th c., became the center of a Christian kingdom in the 10th c., and flourished from the 11th c. through the 12th c. Cf. the legend represented in *The Cid's Rising*.

[11] Middle French for *wing* and the root for *aisle*, to which it was emended in later editions.

SCENE 7

*The Walls of the City. The Plain beneath, with the*
*Moorish Camp and Army.*
GONZALEZ, GARCIAS, HERNANDEZ.
*(A wild Sound of Moorish Music heard from below.)*

HERNANDEZ. What notes are these in their deep mournfulness
    So strangely wild?
GARCIAS.                'Tis the shrill melody
    Of the Moor's ancient death-song. Well I know
    The rude barbaric sound; but, till this hour,
    It seem'd not fearful.—Now, a shuddering chill
    Comes o'er me with its tones.—Lo! from yon tent
    They lead the noble boys!
HERNANDEZ.             The young, and pure,
    And beautiful victims!—'Tis on things like these
    We cast our hearts in wild idolatry,
    Sowing the winds with hope!—Yet this is well.         10
    Thus brightly crown'd with life's most gorgeous flowers,
    And all unblemish'd, earth should offer up
    Her treasures unto Heaven!
GARCIAS (*to* GONZALEZ).        My chief, the Moor
    Hath led your child forth.
GONZALEZ (*starting*).         Are my sons there?
    I knew they could not perish; for yon Heaven
    Would ne'er behold it!—Where is he that said
    I was no more a father?—They look changed—
    Pallid and worn, as from a prison-house!
    Or is't mine eye sees dimly?—But their steps
    Seem heavy, as with pain.—I hear the clank—        20
    Oh God! their limbs are fetter'd!
ABDULLAH (*coming forward beneath the walls*). Christian! look
    Once more upon thy children. There is yet
    One moment for the trembling of the sword;
    Their doom is still with thee.
GONZALEZ.              Why should this man
    So mock us with the semblance of our kind?
    —Moor! Moor! thou dost too daringly provoke,
    In thy bold cruelty, th' all-judging One,
    Who visits for° such things!—Hast thou no sense     *avenges*
    Of thy frail nature?—'Twill be taught thee yet,
    And darkly shall the anguish of my soul,        30
    Darkly and heavily, pour itself on thine,

When thou shalt cry for mercy from the dust,
And be denied!

ABDULLAH.          Nay, is it not thyself,
That hast no mercy and no love within thee?
These are thy sons, the nurslings of thy house;
Speak! must they live or die?

GONZALEZ (*in violent emotion*).  Is it Heaven's will
To try the dust it kindles for a day,
With infinite agony![1] —How have I drawn
This chastening on my head!—They bloom'd around me,
And my heart grew too fearless in its joy,                    40
Glorying in their bright promise!—If we fall,
Is there no pardon for our feebleness?

                    (HERNANDEZ, *without speaking,*
                         *holds up a Cross before him.*)

ABDULLAH.  Speak!

GONZALEZ (*snatching the Cross, and lifting it up*).
                    Let the earth be shaken through its depths,
But *this* must triumph!

ABDULLAH (*coldly*).          Be it as thou wilt.
—Unsheath the scimetar! (*To his Guards.*)

GARCIAS (*to* GONZALEZ).          Away, my chief!
This is your place no longer. There are things
No human heart, though battle-proof as yours,
Unmadden'd may sustain.

GONZALEZ.                    Be still! I have now
No place on earth but this!

ALPHONSO (*from beneath*).          Men! give me way,
That I may speak forth once before I die!                     50

GARCIAS.  The princely boy!—how gallantly his brow
Wears its high nature in the face of death!

ALPHONSO.  Father!

GONZALEZ.          My son! my son!—Mine eldest-born!

ALPHONSO.  Stay but upon the ramparts!—Fear thou not—[2]
There is good courage in me: oh! my father!
I will not shame thee!—only let me fall
Knowing thine eye looks proudly on thy child,
So shall my heart have strength.

GONZALEZ.                    Would, would to God,
That I might die for thee, my noble boy!
Alphonso, my fair son!

ALPHONSO.                    Could I have lived,                  60
I might have been a warrior!—Now, farewell!
But look upon me still!—I will not blench

When the keen sabre flashes—Mark me well!
Mine eyelids shall not quiver as it falls,
So thou wilt look upon me!
GARCIAS (*to* GONZALEZ).　　　　　Nay, my lord!
　We must begone!—Thou *canst* not bear it!
GONZALEZ.　　　　　　　　　　　Peace!
　—Who hath told *thee* how much man's heart can bear?[3]
　—Lend me thine arm—my brain whirls fearfully—
　How thick the shades close round!—my boy! my boy!
　Where art thou in this gloom?
GARCIAS.　　　　　　　　Let us go hence!　　　　　　70
　This is a dreadful moment!
GONZALEZ.　　　　　　　　Hush!—what saidst thou?
　Now let me look on him!—Dost *thou* see aught
　Through the dull mist which wraps us?
GARCIAS.　　　　　　　　　　I behold—
　Oh! for a thousand Spaniards to rush down—
GONZALEZ. Thou seest—My heart stands still to hear thee speak!
　—There seems a fearful hush upon the air,
　As't were the dead of night!
GARCIAS.　　　　　　　　The hosts have closed
　Around the spot in stillness. Through the spears,
　Ranged thick and motionless, I see him not;
　—But now—
GONZALEZ.　　　He bade me keep mine eye upon him,　　　80
　And all is darkness round me!—Now?
GARCIAS.　　　　　　　　　A sword,
　A sword, springs upward, like a lightning burst,
　Through the dark serried mass!—Its cold blue glare
　Is wavering to and fro—'tis vanish'd—hark!
GONZALEZ. I heard it, yes!—I heard the dull dead sound
　That heavily broke the silence!—Didst thou speak?
　—I lost thy words—come nearer!
GARCIAS.　　　　　　　　'Twas—'tis past!—
　The sword fell *then!*
HERNANDEZ (*with exultation*).[4] Flow forth thou noble blood!
　Fount of Spain's ransom and deliverance, flow
　Uncheck'd and brightly forth!—Thou kingly stream!　　90
　Blood of our heroes! blood of martyrdom!
　Which through so many warrior-hearts hast pour'd
　Thy fiery currents, and hast made our hills
　Free, by thine own free offering!—Bathe the land,
　But there thou shalt not sink!—Our very air
　Shall take thy colouring, and our loaded skies

O'er th' infidel hang dark and ominous,
With battle-hues of thee!—And thy deep voice
Rising above them to the judgment-seat
Shall call a burst of gather'd vengeance down,[5]                                    100
To sweep th' oppressor from us!—For thy wave
Hath made his guilt run o'er![6]

GONZALEZ (*endeavouring to rouse himself*). 'Tis all a dream!
    There is not one—no hand on earth could harm
    That fair boy's graceful head![7] —Why look you thus?

ABDULLAH (*pointing to* CARLOS).
    Christian! e'en yet thou hast a son!

GONZALEZ.                         E'en yet!

CARLOS. My father! take me from these fearful[8] men!
    Wilt thou not save me, father?

GONZALEZ (*attempting to unsheath his sword*). Is the strength
    From mine arm shiver'd?—Garcias, follow me!

GARCIAS. Whither, my chief?

GONZALEZ.              Why, we can die as well
    On yonder plain,—aye, a spear's thrust will do                                    110
    The little that our misery doth require,
    Sooner than e'en this anguish! Life is best
    Thrown from us in such moments.

                      *Voices heard at a distance.*

HERNANDEZ.                 Hush! what strain
    Floats on the wind?

GARCIAS.             'Tis the Cid's battle song!
    What marvel hath been wrought?

                *Voices approaching heard in chorus.*

        The Moor is on his way!
    With the tambour peal and the tecbir shout,
    And the horn o'er the blue seas ringing out,
    He hath marshall'd his dark array!

XIMENA *enters, followed by the* CITIZENS, *with the Banner.*

XIMENA. Is it too late?—My father, these are men                                    120
    Through life and death prepared to follow thee
    Beneath this banner!—Is their zeal too late?
    —Oh! there's a fearful history on thy brow!
    What hast thou seen?

GARCIAS.           It is not *all* too late.

XIMENA. My brothers!

HERNANDEZ.      All is well.
    (*To* GARCIAS)          Hush! wouldst thou chill
    That which hath sprung within them, as a flame

From th' altar-embers mounts in sudden brightness?
I say, 'tis not too late, ye men of Spain!
On to the rescue!

XIMENA.                    Bless me, oh my father!
And I will hence, to aid thee with my prayers,                    130
Sending my spirit with thee through the storm,
Lit up by flashing swords!

GONZALEZ (*falling upon her neck*).  Hath aught been spared?
Am I not all bereft?—Thou'rt left me still!
Mine own, my loveliest one, thou'rt left me still!
Farewell!—thy father's blessing, and thy God's,
Be with thee, my Ximena!

XIMENA.                    Fare thee well![9]
If, ere thy steps turn homeward from the field,
The voice is hush'd that still hath welcomed thee,
Think of me in thy victory!

HERNANDEZ.                    Peace! no more!
This is no time to melt our nature down                    140
To a soft stream of tears![10] —Be of strong heart!
Give me the banner! Swell the song again!

THE CITIZENS.

Ere night, must swords be red!
It is not an hour for knells and tears,
But for helmets braced and serried spears!
—To-morrow for the dead!

*Exeunt omnes.*

[1] Ximena's similar trope at 6.95.
[2] MS adds] That I shall bring dishonour on thy name! MS reads "Father" at 55 and through-out the scene (106, 129, 135), thus linking revered domestic Father to holy Father.
[3] MS] Why, of what sensitive dust are Men made now?
[4] MS] (*with a burst of exultation. Gonsalvo sinks back into his arms*)
[5] MS adds] As the Wind sweeps the locust-clouds away,
[6] 101–2, MS] . . . —For his guilt / Is full! Thy fount swells darkly o'er its bounds, / Rise! and awake the Heavens!
    MS] in the next stage direction, Gonzales is *raising himself* as if in exhortation.
[7] MS inserts] . . . Heaven doth not breathe / Into such glorious things the breath of Life, / That it should be so quench'd!
[8] MS] bloody
[9] MS adds stage direction] (*she returns and again embraces him*)
[10] MS revises and inserts] To a feeble stream of Womanish tears! / Bearing revolve away.

SCENE 8

*Before the Altar of a Church.* ELMINA *rises from the steps of the Altar.*

ELMINA.  The clouds are fearful that o'erhang thy ways,
        Oh, thou mysterious Heaven!—It cannot be
        That I have drawn the vials of thy wrath,
        To burst upon me through the lifting up
        Of a proud heart, elate in happiness!
        No! in my day's full noon, for me life's flowers
        But wreath'd a cup of trembling; and the love,
        The boundless love, my spirit was form'd to bear,
        Hath ever, in its place of silence, been
        A trouble and a shadow, tinging thought                           10
        With hues too deep for joy!—I never look'd
        On my fair children, in their buoyant mirth,
        Or sunny sleep, when all the gentle air
        Seem'd glowing with their quiet blessedness,
        But o'er my soul there came a shuddering sense
        Of earth, and its pale changes; even like that
        Which vaguely mingles with our glorious dreams,
        A restless and disturbing consciousness
        That the bright things must fade!—How have I shrunk
        From the dull murmur of th' unquiet voice,                        20
        With its low tokens of mortality,
        Till my heart fainted midst their smiles!—their smiles!
        —Where are those glad looks now?—Could they go down,
        With all their joyous light, that seem'd not earth's,
        To the cold grave?—My children!—Righteous Heaven!
        There floats a dark remembrance o'er my brain
        Of one who told me, with relentless eye,
        That *this* should be the hour!

                                            XIMENA *enters.*

XIMENA.                          They are gone forth
        Unto the rescue!—strong in heart and hope,
        Faithful, though few!—My mother, let thy prayers                  30
        Call on the land's good saints to lift once more
        The sword and cross that sweep the field for Spain,
        As in old battle; so thine arms e'en yet
        May clasp thy sons!—For me, my part is done!
        The flame, which dimly might have linger'd yet
        A little while, hath gather'd all its rays
        Brightly to sink at once; and it is well!
        The shadows are around me; to thy heart
        Fold me, that I may die.

ELMINA.                    My child!—What dream
   Is on thy soul?—Even now thine aspect wears                    40
   Life's brightest inspiration!
XIMENA.                         Death's!
ELMINA.                              Away!
   Thine eye hath starry clearness, and thy cheek
   Doth glow beneath it with a richer hue
   Than tinged its earliest flower!
XIMENA.                              It well may be!
   There are far deeper and far warmer hues
   Than those which draw their colouring from the founts
   Of youth, or health, or hope.
ELMINA.                              Nay, speak not thus!
   There's that about thee shining which would send
   E'en through *my* heart a sunny glow of joy,
   Wer't not for these sad words. The dim cold air                    50
   And solemn light, which wrap these tombs and shrines
   As a pale gleaming shroud, seem kindled up
   With a young spirit of ethereal hope
   Caught from thy mien!—Oh no! this is not death!
XIMENA. Why should not He, whose touch dissolves our chain,
   Put on his robes of beauty when he comes
   As a deliverer?—He hath many forms,
   They should not all be fearful!—If his call
   Be but our gathering to that distant land
   For whose sweet waters we have pined with thirst,                    60
   Why should not its prophetic sense be borne
   Into the heart's deep stillness, with a breath
   Of summer-winds, a voice of melody,
   Solemn, yet lovely?—Mother! I depart!
   —Be it thy comfort, in the after-days,
   That thou hast seen me thus!
ELMINA.                              Distract me not
   With such wild fears! Can I bear on with life
   When thou art gone?—Thy voice, thy step, thy smile,
   Pass'd from my path?—Alas! even now thine eye
   Is changed—thy cheek is fading!
XIMENA.                              Aye, the clouds                    70
   Of the dim hour are gathering o'er my sight,
   And yet I fear not, for the God of Help
   Comes in that quiet darkness!—It may soothe
   Thy woes, my mother! if I tell thee now,
   With what glad calmness I behold the veil
   Falling between me and the world, wherein
   My heart so ill hath rested.

ELMINA.                              Thine!
XIMENA.                                      Rejoice
    For her, that, when the garland of her life
    Was blighted, and the springs of hope were dried,
    Received her summons hence; and had no time,                    80
    Bearing the canker at th' impatient heart,
    To wither, sorrowing for that gift of Heaven,
    Which lent one moment of existence light,
    That dimm'd the rest for ever!
ELMINA.                              How is this?
    My child, what mean'st thou?
XIMENA.                              Mother! I have loved,
    And been beloved!—the sunbeam of an hour,
    Which gave life's hidden treasures to mine eye,
    As they lay shining in their secret founts,
    Went out, and left them colourless.—'Tis past—
    And what remains on earth?—the rainbow mist,                    90
    Through which I gazed, hath melted, and my sight
    Is clear'd to look on all things as they are!
    —But this is far too mournful!—Life's dark gift
    Hath fallen too early and too cold upon me!
    —Therefore I would go hence!
ELMINA.                              And thou hast loved
    Unknown—
XIMENA.         Oh! pardon, pardon that I veil'd
    My thoughts from thee!—But thou hadst woes enough,
    And mine came o'er me when thy soul had need
    Of more than mortal strength!—For I had scarce
    Given the deep consciousness that I was loved                  100
    A treasure's place within my secret heart,
    When earth's brief joy went from me![1]
                                         'Twas at morn
    I saw the warriors to their field go forth,
    And he—my chosen—was there amongst the rest,
    With his young, glorious brow!—I look'd again—
    The strife grew dark beneath me—but his plume
    Waved free above the lances.—Yet again—
    —It had gone down! and steeds were trampling o'er
    The spot to which mine eyes were riveted,
    Till blinded by th' intenseness of their gaze!                 110
    —And then—at last—I hurried to the gate,
    And met him there!—I met him!—on his shield,
    And with his cloven helm, and shiver'd sword,
    And dark hair steep'd in blood!—They bore him past—
    Mother!—I saw his face!—Oh! such a death

Works fearful changes on the fair of earth,
The pride of woman's eye!
ELMINA.                 Sweet daughter, peace!
Wake not the dark remembrance; for thy frame—
XIMENA. —There *will* be peace ere long. I shut my heart,
Even as a tomb, o'er that lone silent grief,          120
That I might spare it thee![2] —But now the hour
Is come when that which would have pierced thy soul
Shall be its healing balm. Oh! weep thou not,
Save with a gentle sorrow!
ELMINA.                 Must it be?
Art thou indeed to leave me?
XIMENA (*exultingly*).        Be thou glad!
I say, rejoice above thy favour'd child!
Joy, for the soldier when his field is fought,
Joy, for the peasant when his vintage-task
Is closed at eve!—But most of all for her,
Who, when her life had changed its glittering robes     130
For the dull garb of sorrow, which doth cling
So heavily around the journeyers on,
Cast down its weight—and slept!
ELMINA.                 Alas! thine eye
Is wandering—yet how brightly!—Is this death,
Or some high wondrous vision?—Speak, my child!
How is it with thee now?
XIMENA (*wildly*).         I see it still!
'Tis floating, like a glorious cloud on high,
My father's banner!—Hear'st thou not a sound?
The trumpet of Castile?—Praise, praise to Heaven!
—Now may the weary rest![3] —Be still!—Who calls     140
The night so fearful?——

                                    *She dies.*

ELMINA.             No! she is not dead!
—Ximena!—speak to me!—Oh! yet a tone
From that sweet voice, that I may gather in
One more remembrance of its lovely sound,
Ere the deep silence fall!—What! is all hush'd?
—No, no!—it cannot be!—How should we bear
The dark misgivings of our souls, if Heaven
Left not such beings with us?—But is this
Her wonted look?—too sad a quiet lies
On its dim fearful beauty!—Speak, Ximena!        150
Speak!—my heart dies within me!—She is gone,
With all her blessed smiles!—My child! my child!
Where art thou?—Where is that which answer'd me,

From thy soft-shining eyes?—Hush! doth she move?
—One light lock seem'd to tremble on her brow,
As a pulse throbb'd beneath;—'twas but the voice
Of my despair that stirr'd it!—She is gone!

     *She throws herself on the body.*
    GONZALEZ *enters, alone, and wounded.*

ELMINA (*rising as he approaches*).
  I must not *now* be scorn'd!—No, not a look,
  A whisper of reproach!—Behold my woe!
  —Thou canst not scorn me now!
GONZALEZ.        Hast thou heard *all?*   160
ELMINA. Thy daughter on my bosom laid her head,
  And pass'd away to rest.—Behold her there,
  Even such as death hath made her![4]
GONZALEZ (*bending over* XIMENA's *body*). Thou art gone
  A little while before me, oh, my child!
  Why should the traveller weep to part with those
  That scarce an hour will reach their promised land
  Ere he too cast his pilgrim staff away,
  And spread his couch beside them?
ELMINA.        Must it be
  Henceforth enough that *once* a thing so fair
  Had its bright place amongst us?—Is this all,   170
  Left for the years to come?—We will not stay![5]
  Earth's chain each hour grows weaker.
GONZALEZ (*still gazing upon* XIMENA).  And thou'rt laid
  To slumber in the shadow, blessed child!
  Of a yet stainless altar, and beside
  A sainted warrior's tomb!—Oh, fitting place
  For thee to yield thy pure heroic soul
  Back unto him that gave it!—And thy cheek
  Yet smiles in its bright paleness!
ELMINA.       Hadst thou seen
  The look with which she pass'd!
GONZALEZ (*still bending over her*).  Why, 'tis almost
  Like joy to view thy beautiful repose!   180
  The faded image of that perfect calm
  Floats, e'en as long-forgotten music, back
  Into my weary heart!—No dark wild spot
  On *thy* clear brow doth tell of bloody hands
  That quench'd young life by violence!—We have seen
  Too much of horror, in one crowded hour,
  To weep for aught, so gently gather'd hence!
  —Oh! *man* leaves other traces!

ELMINA (*suddenly starting*).          It returns
   On my bewilder'd soul!—Went ye not forth
   Unto the rescue?—And thou'rt here alone!                    190
   —Where are my sons?
GONZALEZ (*solemnly*).          We were too late!
ELMINA.                              Too late!
   Hast thou nought else to tell me?
GONZALEZ.                              I brought back
   From that last field the banner of my sires,
   And my own death-wound.
ELMINA.                    Thine!
GONZALEZ.                         Another hour
   Shall hush its throbs for ever. I go hence,
   And with me———
ELMINA.               No!—Man *could* not lift his hands—
   —Where hast thou left thy sons?
GONZALEZ.                         I *have* no sons.
ELMINA. What hast thou said?
GONZALEZ.                    That now there lives not one
   To wear the glory of mine ancient house,
   When I am gone[6] to rest.                              200
ELMINA (*throwing herself on the ground, and speaking in a low
   hurried voice*).
   In one brief hour, all gone!—and *such* a death!
   —I see their blood gush forth!—their graceful heads—
   —Take the dark vision from me, oh, my God![7]
   And such a death for *them!*—I was not there!
   They were but mine in beauty and in joy,
   Not in that mortal anguish!—All, all gone!
   —Why should I struggle more?—What *is* this Power,
   Against whose might, on all sides pressing us,
   We strive with fierce impatience, which but lays
   Our own frail spirits prostrate?
   (*After a long pause*).          Now I know                210
   Thy hand, my God!—and they are soonest crush'd
   That most withstand it!—I resist no more.
   (*She rises*).—A light, a light springs up from grief and death,
   Which with its solemn radiance doth reveal
   Why we have thus been tried!
GONZALEZ.                         Then I may still
   Fix my last look on thee, in holy love,
   Parting, but yet with hope!
ELMINA (*falling at his feet*).          Canst thou forgive?
   —Oh, I have driven the arrow to thy heart,
   That should have buried it within mine own

And borne the pang in silence!—I have cast                              220
Thy life's fair honour, in my wild despair,
As an unvalued gem upon the waves,
Whence thou hast snatch'd it back, to bear from earth,
All stainless, on thy breast.—Well hast thou done——
But I—canst thou forgive?

GONZALEZ.                            Within this hour
I have stood upon that verge whence mortals fall,
And learn'd how 'tis with one whose sight grows dim,
And whose foot trembles on the gulf's dark side.
—Death purifies all feeling—We will part
In pity and in love.

ELMINA.                        Death!—And thou too                     230
Art on thy way!—Oh, joy for thee, high heart!
Glory and joy for thee!—The day is closed,
And well and nobly hast thou borne thyself
Through its long battle-toils, though many swords
Have entered thine own soul!—But on my head
Recoil the fierce invokings of despair,
And I am left far distanced in the race,
The lonely one of earth!—Aye, this is just.
I am not worthy that upon my breast
In this, thine hour of victory, thou shouldst yield          240
Thy spirit unto God!

GONZALEZ.                        Thou art! thou art!
Oh! a life's love, a heart's long faithfulness,
Ev'n in the presence of eternal things,
Wearing their chasten'd beauty all undimm'd,
Assert their lofty claims; and these are not
For one dark hour to cancel!—We are here,
Before that altar which received the vows
Of our unbroken youth, and meet it is
For such a witness, in the sight of Heaven,
And in the face of death, whose shadowy arm               250
Comes dim between us, to record th' exchange
Of our tried hearts' forgiveness.—Who are they,
That in one path have journey'd, needing not
Forgiveness at its close?

*(A Citizen enters hastily.)*

CITIZEN.                        The Moors! the Moors!
GONZALEZ.                        How! is the city storm'd?
Oh! righteous Heaven!—for this I look'd not yet!
Hath all been done in vain?—Why then, 'tis time
For prayer, and then to rest!

CITIZEN.                              The sun shall set,
    And not a Christian voice be left for prayer,
    To-night within Valencia?—Round our walls          260
    The paynim host is gathering for th' assault,
    And we have none to guard them.
GONZALEZ.                              Then my place
    Is here no longer.—I had hoped to die
    Ev'n by the altar and the sepulchre
    Of my brave sires—but this was not to be!
    Give me my sword again, and lead me hence
    Back to the ramparts. I have yet an hour,
    And it hath still high duties.—Now, my wife!
    Thou mother of my children—of the dead—
    Whom I name unto thee in stedfast hope—          270
    Farewell!
ELMINA.          No, *not* farewell!—My soul hath risen
    To mate itself with thine; and by thy side
    Amidst the hurtling lances I will stand,
    As one on whom a brave man's love hath been
    Wasted not utterly.
GONZALEZ.                    I thank thee, Heaven!
    That I have tasted of the awful joy
    Which thou hast given to temper hours like this,
    With a deep sense of thee, and of thine ends
    In these dread visitings!
    (*To* ELMINA).          We will not part,
    But with the spirit's parting!
ELMINA.                              One farewell          280
    To her, that mantled with sad loveliness,
    Doth slumber at our feet!—My blessed child!
    Oh! in thy heart's affliction thou wert strong,
    And holy courage did pervade thy woe,
    As light the troubled waters!—Be at peace!
    Thou whose bright spirit made itself the soul
    Of all that were around thee!—And thy life
    E'en then was struck, and withering at the core![8]
    —Farewell!—thy parting look hath on me fall'n,
    E'en as a gleam of heaven, and I am now          290
    More like what thou hast been!—My soul is hush'd,
    For a still sense of purer worlds hath sunk
    And settled on its depths with that last smile
    Which from thine shone forth.—Thou hast not lived
    In vain—my child, farewell!
GONZALEZ.                              Surely for thee
    Death had no sting, Ximena![9] —We are blest,

To learn one secret of the shadowy pass,
From such an aspect's calmness. Yet once more
I kiss thy pale young cheek, my broken flower!
In token of th' undying love and hope,                                    300
Whose land is far away.

*Exeunt.*

[1] 100–102 linebreak, MS] Given to the deep and thrilling consciousness / That I was lov'd, a treasure's place within / My secret heart, when Death (oh! welcome now!) / Swept by me in my path, and left his trace / There, like a dried up torrent's!

[2] MS inserts] This is the World / For the luxurious Weeper!—Well I knew / Thou hadst a Hero's glorious toils to share / And shouldst not turn from that majestic task, / To mourn a broken reed!

[3] MS inserts and revises 140] The conqueror comes, and I go forth, array'd / In Joy to meet him, for my Work is done! / But I must slumber first—Be still! . . .

[4] "La voilà, telle que la mort nous l'a faite!"—*Bossuet, Oraisons Funèbres.* [FH]

[There she is, what death has made of her for us!]

Jacques Bénigne Bossuet (1627–1704), *Oraisons Funèbres H. d'Angl.* (1669). The French prelate was famed for these eloquent orations, which also supply FH's epigraphs for *Stanzas on the Late National Calamity: The Death of the Princess Charlotte*, in *Translations* (1818), and the title page of *The Sceptic* (1820).

[5] In MS, a version of 168–71 replaces published text 151–53, and this verse appears instead: Who will stay, / Now that each gentle spirit hath been call'd, / And all the melodies of Life are lost / In the fierce din of arms?—We need not weep, /

[6] MS] When I have sunk

[7] Stage direction, MS] *throwing herself on the body of Ximena, &* . . .

202–3 MS] . . . forth!—Oh God! to think / Of those fair features rigidly convuls'd, / Those eyes' bright laughter quench'd in Agony! /

[8] MS inserts] But thou has now thy guerdon!—Fare thee well!

[9] "O death, where is thy sting, O grave, where is thy victory?" (1 Corinthians 15.55).

SCENE 9

*The Walls of the City.* HERNANDEZ.—*A few Citizens gathered round him.*

HERNANDEZ.  Why, men have cast the treasures, which their lives
                        Had been worn down in gathering, on the pyre,
                        Aye, at their household hearths have lit the brand
                        Ev'n from that shrine of quiet love to bear
                        The flame which gave their temples and their homes,
                        In ashes, to the winds!—They have done this,
                        Making a blasted void where once the sun
                        Look'd upon lovely dwellings; and from earth
                        Razing all record that on such a spot
                        Childhood hath sprung, age faded, misery wept          10
                        And frail Humanity knelt before her God;
                        —They have done *this* in their free nobleness,
                        Rather than see the spoiler's tread pollute

Their holy places!—Praise, high praise be theirs,
Who have left man such lessons! —And these things
Made your own hills their witnesses![1]—The sky
Whose arch bends o'er you, and the seas, wherein
Your rivers pour their gold, rejoicing saw
The altar, and the birth-place, and the tomb,
And all memorials of man's heart and faith,                          20
Thus proudly honour'd!—Be ye not outdone
By the departed!—Though the godless foe
Be close upon us, we have power to snatch
The spoils of victory from him. Be but strong!
A few bright torches and brief moments yet
Shall baffle his flush'd hope, and we may die,
Laughing him unto scorn.—Rise, follow me,
And thou, Valencia! triumph in thy fate,
The ruin, not the yoke, and make thy towers
A beacon unto Spain![2]

CITIZEN.                         We'll follow thee!                   30
   —Alas! for our fair city, and the homes
Wherein we rear'd our children!—But away!
The Moor shall plant no crescent° o'er our fanes!    *emblem of Islam*
VOICE (*from a Tower on the Walls*).
   Succours!—Castile! Castile![3]
CITIZENS (*rushing to the spot*).       It is even so!
Now blessing be to Heaven, for we are saved!
Castile, Castile!
VOICE (*from the Tower*). Line after line of spears,
Lance after lance, upon the horizon's verge,
Like festal lights from cities bursting up,
Doth skirt the plain!—In faith, a noble host!
ANOTHER VOICE.
The Moor hath turn'd him from our walls, to front        40
Th' advancing might of Spain!
CITIZENS (*shouting*).             Castile! Castile!

    (GONZALEZ *enters, supported by* ELMINA *and a Citizen.*)
GONZALEZ. What shouts of joy are these?
HERNANDEZ.                         Hail, chieftain! hail!
Thus ev'n in death 'tis given thee to receive
The conqueror's crown!—Behold our God hath heard,
And arm'd himself with vengeance!—Lo! they come!
The lances of Castile![4]
GONZALEZ.              I knew, I knew
Thou wouldst not utterly, my God, forsake
Thy servant in his need!—My blood and tears

Have not sunk vainly to th' attesting earth!
Praise to thee, thanks and praise, that I have lived          50
To see this hour!

ELMINA.                    And I too bless thy name,
Though thou hast proved me unto agony!
Oh God!—Thou God of chastening!

VOICE (*from the Tower*).                    They move on!
I see the royal banner in the air,
With its emblazon'd towers!⁵

GONZALEZ.                    Go, bring ye forth
The banner of the Cid, and plant it here,
To stream above me, for an answering sign
That the good cross doth hold its lofty place
Within Valencia still!—What see ye now?

HERNANDEZ. I see a kingdom's might upon its path,          60
Moving, in terrible magnificence,
Unto revenge and victory!—With the flash
Of knightly swords, up-springing from the ranks
As meteors from a still and gloomy deep,
And with the waving of ten thousand plumes,⁶
Like a land's harvest in the autumn-wind,
And with fierce light, which is not of the sun,
But flung from sheets of steel—it comes, it comes,
The vengeance of our God!

GONZALEZ.                    I hear it now,
The heavy tread of mail-clad multitudes,          70
Like thunder-showers upon the forest-paths.

HERNANDEZ. Aye, earth knows well the omen of that sound,
And she hath echoes, like a sepulchre's,
Pent in her secret hollows, to respond
Unto the step of death!

GONZALEZ.                    Hark! how the wind
Swells proudly with the battle-march of Spain!
Now the heart feels its power!—A little while
Grant me to live, my God!—What pause is this?

HERNANDEZ. A deep and dreadful one!—the serried files
Level their spears for combat; now the hosts          80
Look on each other in their brooding wrath,
Silent, and face to face.

        VOICES HEARD WITHOUT, CHANTING.

Calm on the bosom of thy God,
    Fair spirit! rest thee now!
E'en while with ours thy footsteps trod,
    His seal was on thy brow.

    Dust, to its narrow house beneath!
      Soul, to its place on high!
    They that have seen thy look in death,
      No more may fear to die.[7]         90

ELMINA (*to* GONZALEZ).
    It is the death-hymn o'er thy daughter's bier!
    —But I am calm, and e'en like gentle winds,
    That music, through the stillness of my heart,
    Sends mournful peace.
GONZALEZ.              Oh! well those solemn tones
    Accord with such an hour, for all her life
    Breath'd of a hero's soul!
           *A sound of trumpets and shouting from the plain.*
HERNANDEZ.  Now, now they close!—Hark! what a dull dead sound
    Is in the Moorish war-shout!—I have known
    Such tones prophetic oft.—The shock is given—
    Lo! they have placed their shields before their hearts,    100
    And lower'd their lances with the streamers on,
    And on their steeds bent forward!—God for Spain!
    The first bright sparks of battle have been struck
    From spear to spear, across the gleaming field!
    —There is no sight on which the blue sky looks
    To match with this!—'Tis not the gallant crests,
    Nor banners with their glorious blazonry;
    The very nature and high soul of man
    Doth now reveal itself!
GONZALEZ.             Oh, raise me up,
    That I may look upon the noble scene!         110
    —It will not be!—That this dull mist would pass
    A moment from my sight!—Whence rose that shout,
    As in fierce triumph?
HERNANDEZ (*clasping his hands*). Must I look on this?
    The banner sinks—'tis taken!
GONZALEZ.             Whose?
HERNANDEZ.             Castile's!
GONZALEZ.  Oh, God of Battles!
ELMINA.             Calm thy noble heart!
    Thou wilt not pass away without thy meed.
    Nay, rest thee on my bosom.
HERNANDEZ.          Cheer thee yet!
    Our knights have spurr'd to rescue.—There is now
    A whirl, a mingling of all terrible things,
    Yet more appalling than the fierce distinctness    120
    Wherewith they moved before!—I see tall plumes

All wildly tossing o'er the battle's tide,
Sway'd by the wrathful motion, and the press
Of desperate men, as cedar-boughs by storms.
Many a white streamer there is dyed with blood,
Many a false corslet broken, many a shield
Pierced through!—Now, shout for Santiago,[8] shout!
Lo! javelins with a moment's brightness cleave
The thickening dust, and barbed steeds go down
With their helm'd riders!—Who, but One, can tell                    130
How spirits part amidst that fearful rush
And trampling on of furious multitudes?
GONZALEZ.
    Thou'rt silent!—See'st thou more?—My soul grows dark.
HERNANDEZ.  And dark and troubled, as an angry sea,
    Dashing some gallant armament in scorn
    Against its rocks, is all on which I gaze!
    —I can but tell thee how tall spears are cross'd,
    And lances seem to shiver, and proud helms
    To lighten with the stroke!—But round the spot,
    Where, like a storm-fell'd mast, our standard sank,              140
    The heart of battle burns.
GONZALEZ.                           Where is that spot?
HERNANDEZ.  It is beneath the lonely tuft of palms,
    That lift their green heads o'er the tumult still,
    In calm and stately grace.
GONZALEZ.                           *There*, didst thou say?
    Then God is with us, and we *must* prevail!
    For on that spot they died!—My children's blood
    Calls on th' avenger thence!
ELMINA.                             They perish'd there!
    —And the bright locks that waved so joyously
    To the free winds, lay trampled and defiled
    Ev'n on that place of death!—Oh, Merciful!                       150
    Hush the dark thought within me!
HERNANDEZ (*with sudden exultation*).    Who is he,
    On the white steed, and with the castled helm,
    And the gold-broider'd mantle, which doth float
    E'en like a sunny cloud above the fight;
    And the pale cross, which from his breast-plate gleams
    With star-like radiance?
GONZALEZ (*eagerly*).           Didst thou say the cross?
HERNANDEZ.  On his mail'd bosom shines a broad white cross,
    And his long plumage through the darkening air
    Streams like a snow-wreath.

GONZALEZ.                                That should be—
HERNANDEZ.                                                    The king!                           160
  —Was it not told us how he sent, of late,
  To the Cid's tomb, e'en for the silver cross,
  Which he who slumbers there was wont to bind
  O'er his brave heart in fight?[9]
GONZALEZ (*springing up joyfully*). My king! my king!
  Now all good saints for Spain!—My noble king!
  And thou art there!—That I might look once more
  Upon thy face!—But yet I thank thee, Heaven!
  That thou hast sent him, from my dying hands
  Thus to receive his city!

                    *He sinks back into* ELMINA'S *arms.*

HERNANDEZ.                          He hath clear'd
  A pathway midst the combat, and the light
  Follows his charge through yon close living mass,                  170
  E'en as the gleam on some proud vessel's wake
  Along the stormy waters!—'Tis redeem'd—
  The castled banner!—It is flung once more
  In joy and glory, to the sweeping winds!
  —There seems a wavering through the paynim hosts—
  Castile doth press them sore—Now, now rejoice!
GONZALEZ. What hast thou seen?
HERNANDEZ.                          Abdullah falls! He falls!
  The man of blood!—the spoiler!—he hath sunk
  In our king's path!—Well hath that royal sword
  Avenged thy cause, Gonzalez!
                   They give way,                          180
  The Crescent's van° is broken!—On the hills                  *front line*
  And the dark pine-woods may the infidel
  Call vainly, in his agony of fear,
  To cover him from vengeance!—Lo! they fly!
  They of the forest and the wilderness
  Are scatter'd, e'en as leaves upon the wind!
  Woe to the sons of Afric!—Let the plains,
  And the vine-mountains, and Hesperian seas,
  Take their dead unto them!—that blood shall wash
  Our soil from stains of bondage.
GONZALEZ (*attempting to raise himself*). Set me free!                          190
  Come with me forth, for I must greet my king,
  After his battle-field!
HERNANDEZ.                          Oh, blest in death!
  Chosen of Heaven, farewell!—Look on the Cross,
  And part from earth in peace!

GONZALEZ.                         Now charge once more!
    God is with Spain, and Santiago's sword
    Is reddening all the air!—Shout forth 'Castile!'
    The day is ours!—I go; but fear ye not!
    For Afric's lance is broken, and my sons
    Have won their first good field!

*He dies.*

ELMINA.                         Look on me yet!                         200
    Speak one farewell, my husband!—must thy voice
    Enter my soul no more!—Thine eye is fix'd—
    Now is my life uprooted,—and 'tis well.
      *(A Sound of triumphant Music is heard, and many*
        *Castilian Knights and Soldiers enter.)*

A CITIZEN. Hush your triumphal sounds, although ye come
    E'en as deliverers! But the noble dead,
    And those that mourn them, claim from human hearts
    Deep silent reverence.

ELMINA (*rising proudly*).      No, swell forth, Castile!
    Thy trumpet-music, till the seas and heavens,
    And the deep hills, give every stormy note
    Echoes to ring through Spain!—How, know ye not
    That all array'd for triumph, crown'd and robed      210
    With the strong spirit which hath saved the land,
    Ev'n now a conqueror to his rest is gone?
    —Fear not to break that sleep, but let the wind
    Swell on with victory's shout!—*He* will not hear—
    Hath earth a sound more sad?

HERNANDEZ.                         Lift ye the dead,
    And bear him with the banner of his race
    Waving above him proudly, as it waved
    O'er the Cid's battles, to the tomb, wherein
    His warrior-sires are gather'd.

*They raise the body.*

ELMINA.                         Aye, 'tis thus
    Thou shouldst be honour'd!—And I follow thee      220
    With an unfaltering and a lofty step,
    To that last home of glory. She that wears
    In her deep heart the memory of thy love
    Shall thence draw strength for all things, till the God,
    Whose hand around her hath unpeopled earth,
    Looking upon her still and chasten'd soul,
    Call it once more to thine!
    (*To the Castilians.*)          Awake, I say,

Tambour and trumpet, wake!—And let the land
Through all her mountains hear your funeral peal!
—So should a hero pass to his repose.                    230

*Exeunt omnes.*

[1] MS] Not far distant shores have so far wrought, / But your own Land hath witnessed them!—

[2] 29–30, Hernandez, MS] . . . yoke!—for thou shalt sink / Nobly, and making thy rich Palaces, / A Beacon unto Spain!
Cf. *Sardanapalus* as its title character is about to immolate himself and his palace rather than be taken by his enemies: "My fathers! whom I will rejoin, / . . . I would not leave your ancient first abode / To the defilement of usurping bondmen"; "the light of this / Most royal of funereal pyres shall be / Not a mere pillar form'd of cloud and flame, / A beacon in the horizon for a day, / And then a mount of ashes, but a light / To lesson ages" (5.423–41).

[3] *Succors!: Rescue!* Among FH's *Songs of Spain* (*NMM* 40 [1834]: 26–28) is *Old Spanish Battle Song*, the last line of which is "And shout ye, 'Castile! to the rescue of Spain!'"

[4] MS adds] —The sharp bright sword, / Which makes Earth crimson with the hues of wrath, / Leaps from its thunder-clouds!

[5] The castle towers of Castile, a city named for the many castles built in the region after the Christian nobles (among them, one surnamed González) reconquered the area from the Moors.

[6] Cf. Burke's famous lament in *Reflections on the Revolution in France* (1790) over the failure of chivalry in the arrest of Queen Marie Antoinette, a scandal "in a nation of gallant men, in a nation of men of honour and of cavaliers. I thought ten thousand swords must have leaped from their scabbards to avenge even a look that threatened her." FH's chivalric-Christian saviors evoke, by their positive presence, the related scandal of the French Republic's disestablishment of the Catholic Church.

[7] These verses were soon republished as *A Dirge* in *Lays of Many Lands* (*Forest Sanctuary &c* [1825]) and in collections thereafter, with an additional stanza: "Lone are the paths, and sad the bowers, / Whence thy meek smile is gone; / But oh!—a brighter home than ours, / In heaven, is now thine own." The first two stanzas are inscribed on a tablet above the vault beneath St. Anne's Church in Dublin, where Hemans is interred (*HM* 314).

[8] St. James, "Santiago, the tutelary Saint of Spain, the God of their battles" (Southey, *Chronicle*, Preface xxx).

[9] This circumstance is recorded of King Don Alfonso, the last of that name. He sent to the Cid's tomb for the cross which that warrior was accustomed to wear upon his breast when he went to battle, and had it made into one for himself; "because of the faith which he had, that through it he should obtain the victory."—*Southey's Chronicle of the Cid* [FH]
Bk. 11.xxx (364–65); see 365. Don Alfonso the Wise (1221–84) became king Alfonso X in 1252, the year he crushed a Muslim revolt; but his later policies produced much civil discontent.

## APPENDIX 1: MS SONGS

### Ximena's Ballad
(opening of Scene 1)

The Stars look'd down on the Battle plain,
    Where Night-winds were deeply sighing,
And with shatter'd lance, by his War-steed slain,
    Lay a youthful Chieftan dying.

He had folded round his gallant heart,
    The Banner once o'er him streaming,
For a noble shroud as he sunk to rest,
    On the couch that knows no dreaming.

Proudly he lay on his broken shield,
    By the rushing Guadalquiver,                                          10
While dark with the blood of his last red field,
    Swept on the majestic river.

There were hands which came to bind his wound,
    There were eyes o'er the Warrior weeping,
But he rais'd his head from the dewy ground,
    Where the Land's high hearts were sleeping:

And "Away!" he cried, "your aid is vain,
    My Soul may not brook recalling,
I have seen the stately flower of Spain,
    As the Autumn vine-leaves falling.                                   20

I have seen the Moorish Banners wave,
    O'er the Walls where my Youth was cherish'd!
I have drawn a sword that could not save,
    I have stood when my King hath perish'd!

Leave me to die with the free and brave,
    On the bankes of my own proud River,
Ye can give me nought but a Warrior's grave
    By the chainless Guadalquiver!"

### Nuns' Chaunt
(Scene 5.311 ff.)

A Sword is waving o'er the Land,
    Her towers are in the Spoiler's hand,
Red signs of wrath are deepening in her sky;
    The Stranger's tread is on her Vines,

The Cross torn rudely from her Shrines;
—Hear us! thou God of Armies! hear our cry!

A wail is in the Hall of State,
The Peasant's home is desolate,
The City's grass-grown streets untrodden lie!
  But in the chambers of the Tomb,      10
  The gathering Dwellers scarce find room;
—Hear us! thou God of chastening! hear our cry!

The old Man's brow is pale with thought,
The Youth's high heart with bodings fraught,
Wild fear is darkening in the Mother's eye;
  For there is that gone forth in power,
  Which bows young Tree and glorious Flower;
—Hear us! thou God of Suffering! hear our cry!

The weeper sits at Bridal-feast,
The Vintage-melodies have ceas'd,       20
The Winds come loaded, wafting dirge-notes by!
  Is our blood voiceless on the plains?
  Where sleeps th'Avenger of our Fanes?
—Hear us! thou God of Judgement! hear our cry!

Woe, for the Children of the Dead!
Woe, for the mail'd heart and crested head!
And arm struck down that held our Banners high!
  The shield is cleft, the Lance is dust!
  On Thee we pour our Spirit's trust!
—Hear us! thou God of Battles! hear our cry!    30


## APPENDIX 2

MS Scene 6 (ff. 119–22, replaced by *Siege* 14–32)

THIRD CITIZEN. Why, we have but this thought
 Left for our gloomy comfort!—There's no face
 Which, like a cloud, doth pass you silently
 Midst the dull, grass-grown street, but tells some tale
 In its unsettled eye, or hollow cheek
 Or troubled brow, of terror which hath sunk
 Pale on the Soul, or Sickness, creeping chill
 As a slow poison, thro' the restless blood;
 Or of long watchings by the bed of pain,
 Or weepings for the dead.
FOURTH CITIZEN.     We bore it well
 And manfully, while yet a hope was left;

But what avails it *now* to strive against
That which is crushing us?
OLD CITIZEN (*vehemently*)        It *doth* avail!
If but for this, that far throughout the Land,
Then, when our Sufferings shall be told, may learn
How much Man's heart and courage to endure,
And shame to yield far less!—Aye, for their cause,
Be of good cheer, my Brethren, and bear on!
FIFTH CITIZEN  I marvel oft how long our Chieftains think
We lowly Men in silence may sustain
The woes that reach not them.
OLD CITIZEN                                Shame on the thought!
Their cup is full as ours. These are not times
That blight the lowly shrub, but leave the Pine
Unscath'd upon its Hills. The Day of Wrath
Is rushing with its whirlwinds o'er the Land
And well I ween there is no Threshold mark'd
To be passed over.[1]
SIXTH CITIZEN              Aye, the hour is come
Which for awhile doth strike the balance even
[then follows *Siege*: THIRD CITIZEN, 6.17–28]
FIFTH CITIZEN [follows *Siege*: FOURTH CITIZEN 6.28–30]
[line continues]      —I could not rest
On my bed, when once that startling note
Had broken my feverish slumber!
SEVENTH CITIZEN                          Aye, tis said
No mortal hand was near, when that deep Knell
Lent forth its hollow voice, which almost seem'd
To shake the Midnight Streets.

[1] A reference to the first passover (Exodus 12.7–29).

---

## *Songs of the Cid*[1]

[Following *The Siege of Valencia* in *Siege &c*, these *Songs* are in the genre of "national songs," as are Hemans's *Greek Songs* (also in *Siege &c*), *Welsh Melodies* (1822), *Lays of Many Lands* (1825), *Songs of Spain* and *Patriotic Lays of Italy* (both in *NMM*, 1834), and *National Lyrics* (1834). *Songs of the Cid* more specifically reflects contemporary enthusiasm for early Spanish literature, especially in Britain and Germany. A chief figure in the romances (ballads) is El Cid—from the Arabic *Sidi* ("feudal lord"), also known as Campeador, from the Latin *campi doctor* ("battlefield master"): Rodrigo (or Ruy) Díaz de Vivar (or Bivar). Born ca. 1043 into an aristocratic family of northern Spain, he fought for Ferdinand I of Castile and commanded the forces of his son and successor Sancho II against his brothers, the kings of León and Galicia. After Sancho's death, El Cid served his brother and successor, Alfonso VI of Castile and León, one of the strongest rulers of the period, who in 1074 arranged El Cid's marriage to Sancho's daughter Ximena Díaz. But Alfonso, suspicious of El Cid's popularity and motives, banished him from Castile circa 1081. He turned soldier of fortune, even serving the Muslim Moorish ruler of Saragossa (the most important city of Aragón, in northeastern Spain) against the Christian count of Barcelona. When a zealous force of North African Moors, the Almoravides, invaded Spain, unseating weak Moorish rulers and threatening Christian ones, El Cid was restored to Alfonso's favor—but not for long. Accused of bungling the defense of Alfonso's territories, he resumed his independent career in 1089. His conquest of Valencia from the Moors in 1094 was a highlight, credited with halting the expansion of the Almoravid dynasty. He ruled and defended the city until his death in 1099; the Moors then besieged it, forcing Ximena's surrender in 1102. She withdrew with El Cid's remains to his lands in native Castile, where his body was interred in the monastery of San Pedro de Cardeña. The monks promoted a cult of sainthood, and even his horse Babieca, reputedly buried at the monastery, became an object of veneration.

Both the history and the legend of El Cid flourished in the literature of Christian Spain, especially after the expulsion of Moors in 1492. In ballads, narrative poems, and chronicles, he was cast as the loyal feudal and chivalric hero of Christian Castile, resisting Moorish expansion, and Ximena was celebrated as a worthy mate. Pierre Corneille adapted a Spanish play written in 1618 for *Le Cid* (1637), a European classic. By the Romantic era, El Cid had become the icon of Spanish nationalism and was an inspiration in the struggle against Napoleonic France. FDB was "quite impatient for the entire perusal" of Southey's *Chronicle of the Cid, from the Spanish* (1808), which her brother ordered for the family library (letter, 31 January 1823; *CM* 1.89–90). Southey assembled and translated several sources, including *Chronica del Famoso Cavallero Cid Ruy-Diez Campeador* (based on an inaccurate copy of a MS at Cardeña; pub. Burgos, 1593; rpt. 1604), *Poema del Cid* ("unquestionably the oldest poem in the Spanish language," reports Southey [ix]), the *Romances* (Anvers, 1566), *Romancero General* (Medina del Campo, 1602). His most important source was Juan de Escobar's *Historia del muy valeroso cavallero El Cid Ruy Diez de Bivar, en Romances, en lenguage antiguo* (Seville, 1632), partly translated in 1805 by Johann Gottfried von Herder in *Der Cid: . . . nach spanischen romanzen*, and the original was republished in 1818. FH read Escobar, *Chronica* (Lawrence 237), and Herder, admiring the "proud *clarion music*" of his "beautiful ballads of the 'Cid'": "I often think, what a dull, faded thing life,—such life as *we* lead in this later age,—would appear to one of those fiery knights of old. Only imagine 'My Cid,' spurring the good steed Bavieca through the streets of Liverpool! or coming to pass an evening with me at Wavertree!" (letter, late 1828; *CM* 1.225–56); these songs, she wrote in another letter, "carry us more completely back to the very heart of the proud olden time—the days of the lance—than any other poetry I know" (late 1828; *CM* 1.285). In 1817 Georg Bernhard Depping edited and arranged *Romancero General*, which in turn was excerpted and translated by John Gibson Lockhart in *Ancient Spanish Ballads: Historical and Romantic* (1823). FH's *Songs* resemble these translations, which she admired, but in contrast to the heroic legends, her scenes are elegiac, occupied with exile and death. In addition to *The Siege*, El Cid also figures in *The Abencerrage* (1819).]

The following ballads are not translations from the Spanish, but are founded upon some of the "wild and wonderful" traditions preserved in the romances of that language, and the ancient poem of the Cid.[2]

### THE CID'S DEPARTURE INTO EXILE

With sixty knights in his gallant train,
Went forth the Campeador of Spain;
For wild sierras and plains afar,
He left the lands of his own Bivar.[3]

To march o'er field, and to watch in tent,
From his home in good Castile he went;
To the wasting siege and the battle's van,
—For the noble Cid was a banish'd man!

Through his olive-woods the morn-breeze play'd,
And his native streams wild music made,                    10
And clear in the sunshine his vineyards lay,
When for march and combat he took his way.

With a thoughtful spirit his way he took,
And he turn'd his steed for a parting look,
For a parting look at his own fair towers;
—Oh! the Exile's heart hath weary hours!

The pennons° were spread, and the band array'd,        *banners*
But the Cid at the threshold a moment stay'd;
It *was* but a moment—the halls were lone,
And the gates of his dwelling all open thrown.              20

There was not a steed in the empty stall,
Nor a spear nor a cloak on the naked wall,
Nor a hawk on the perch, nor a seat at the door,
Nor the sound of a step on the hollow floor.[4]

Then a dim tear swell'd to the warrior's eye,
As the voice of his native groves went by;
And he said—"My foemen their wish have won—
—Now the will of God be in all things done!"

But the trumpet blew, with its note of cheer,
And the winds of the morning swept off the tear,           30
And the fields of his glory lay distant far,
—He is gone from the towers of his own Bivar!

## The Cid's Death-Bed[5]

It was an hour of grief and fear
    Within Valencia's walls,
When the blue spring-heaven lay still and clear
    Above her marble halls.

There were pale cheeks and troubled eyes,
    And steps of hurrying feet,
Where the Zambra's[6] notes were wont to rise,
    Along the sunny street.

It was an hour of fear and grief,
    On bright Valencia's shore,         10
For Death was busy with her chief,
    The noble Campeador.

The Moor-king's barks were on the deep,
    With sounds and signs of war,
For the Cid was passing to his sleep,
    In the silent Alcazar.°         *fortress*

No moan was heard through the towers of state,
    No weeper's aspect seen,
But by the couch Ximena sate,
    With pale, yet stedfast mien.[7]         20

Stillness was round the leader's[8] bed,
    Warriors stood mournful nigh,
And banners, o'er his glorious head,
    Were drooping heavily.

And feeble grew the conquering[9] hand,
    And cold the valiant breast;
—He had fought the battles of the land,
    And his hour was come to rest.

What said the Ruler[10] of the field?
    —His voice is faint and low;         30
The breeze that creeps o'er his lance and shield
    Hath louder accents now.

"Raise ye no cry, and let no moan
    Be made when I depart;
The Moor must hear no dirge's tone,
    Be ye of mighty[11] heart!

Let the cymbal-clash and the trumpet-strain
    From your walls ring far and shrill,

And fear ye not, for the saints of Spain
   Shall grant you victory still.                                    40

And gird my form with mail-array,
   And set me on my steed,
So go ye forth on your funeral-way,
   And God shall give you speed.

Go with the dead in the front of war,
   All arm'd with sword and helm,[12]
And march by the camp of King Bucar,
   For the good Castilian realm.

And let me slumber in the soil
   Which gave my fathers birth;                                    50
I have closed my day of battle-toil,
   And my course is done on earth."

—Now wave, ye glorious banners, wave![13]
   Through the lattice a wind sweeps by,
And the arms, o'er the death-bed of the brave,
   Send forth a hollow sigh.

Now wave, ye banners of many a fight!
   As the fresh wind o'er you sweeps;
The wind and the banners fall hush'd as night,
   The Campeador—he sleeps!                                    60

Sound the battle-horn on the breeze of morn,
   And swell out the trumpet's blast,
Till the notes prevail o'er the voice of wail,
   For the noble Cid hath pass'd!

### THE CID'S FUNERAL PROCESSION[14]

The Moor had beleaguer'd Valencia's towers,
And lances gleam'd up through her citron-bowers,
And the tents of the desert had girt her plain,
And camels were trampling the vines of Spain;
   For the Cid was gone to rest.

There were men from wilds where the death-wind sweeps,
There were spears from hills where the lion sleeps,
There were bows from sands where the ostrich runs,
For the shrill horn of Afric had call'd her sons
   To the battles of the West.                                    10

The midnight bell, o'er the dim seas heard,
Like the roar of waters, the air had stirr'd;

The stars were shining o'er tower and wave,
And the camp lay hush'd, as a wizard's cave;
    But the Christians woke° that night.            *stayed awake*

They rear'd the Cid on his barbed steed,
Like a warrior mail'd for the hour of need,
And they fix'd the sword in the cold right hand,
Which had fought so well for his father's land,
    And the shield from his neck hung            20

There was arming heard in Valencia's halls,
There was vigil kept on the rampart walls;
Stars had not faded, nor clouds turn'd red,
When the knights had girded the noble dead,
    And the burial-train moved out.

With a measured pace, as the pace of one,
Was the still death-march of the host begun;
With a silent step went the cuirass'd[15] bands,
Like a lion's tread on the burning sands,
    And they gave no battle-shout.            30

When the first went forth, it was midnight deep,
In heaven was the moon, in the camp was sleep.
When the last through the city's gates had gone,
O'er tent and rampart the bright day shone,
    With a sun-burst from the sea.

There were knights five hundred went arm'd before,
And Bermudez the Cid's green standard bore;[16]
To its last fair field, with the break of morn,
Was the glorious banner in silence borne,
    On the glad wind streaming free.            40

And the Campeador came stately then,
Like a leader circled with steel-clad men!
The helmet was down o'er the face of the dead,
But his steed went proud, by a warrior led,
    For he knew that the Cid was there.

He was there, the Cid, with his own good sword,
And Ximena following her noble lord;
Her eye was solemn, her step was slow,
But there rose not a sound of war or woe,
    Not a whisper on the air.            50

The halls in Valencia were still and lone,
The churches were empty, the masses done;

There was not a voice through the wide streets far,
Nor a foot-fall heard in the Alcazar,
          —So the burial-train moved out.

With a measured pace, as the pace of one,
Was the still death-march of the host begun;
With a silent step went the cuirass'd bands,
Like a lion's tread on the burning sands;
          —And they gave no battle-shout.                              60

But the deep hills peal'd with a cry ere long,
When the Christians burst on the Paynim° throng!          *Pagan*
—With a sudden flash of the lance and spear,
And a charge of the war-steed in full career,
          It was Alvar Fañez came![16]

He that was wrapt with no funeral shroud,
Had pass'd before, like a threatening cloud!
And the storm rush'd down on the tented plain,
And the Archer-Queen,[18] with her bands lay slain,
          For the Cid upheld his fame.                                 70

Then a terror fell on the King Bucar,
And the Libyan kings who had join'd his war;
And their hearts grew heavy, and died away,
And their hands could not wield an assagay,°    *slender spear, lance*
          For the dreadful things they saw!

For it seem'd where Minaya[19] his onset made,
There were seventy thousand knights array'd,
All white as the snow on Nevada's steep,
And they came like the foam of a roaring deep;
          —'Twas a sight of fear and awe!                              80

And the crested form of a warrior tall,
With a sword of fire, went before them all;[20]
With a sword of fire, and a banner pale,
And a blood-red cross on his shadowy mail,
          He rode in the battle's van!

There was fear in the path of his dim white horse,
There was death in the Giant-warrior's course!
Where his banner stream'd with its ghostly light,
Where his sword blazed out, there was hurrying flight,
          For it seem'd not the sword of man!                          90

The field and the river grew darkly red,
As the kings and leaders of Afric fled;

There was work for the men of the Cid that day!
—They were weary at eve, when they ceased to slay,
    As reapers whose task is done!

The kings and the leaders of Afric fled!
The sails of their galleys in haste were spread;
But the sea had its share of the Paynim-slain,
And the bow of the desert was broke in Spain;[21]
    —So the Cid to his grave pass'd on!            100

### THE CID'S RISING

'Twas the deep mid-watch of the silent night,
    And Leon in slumber lay,
When a sound went forth, in rushing might,
    Like an army on its way![22]
  In the stillness of the hour,
  When the dreams of sleep have power,
    And men forget the day.

Through the dark and lonely streets it went,
    Till the slumberers[23] woke in dread;—
The sound of a passing armament,            10
    With the charger's stony tread.
  There was heard no trumpet's peal,
  But the heavy tramp of steel,
    As a host's, to combat led.

Through the dark and lonely streets it pass'd,
    And the hollow pavement rang,
And the towers, as with a sweeping blast,
    Rock'd to the stormy clang!
  But the march of the viewless° train         *invisible*
  Went on to a royal fane,[24]            20
    Where a priest his night-hymn sang.

There was knocking that shook the marble floor,
    And a voice at the gate, which said—
"That the Cid Ruy Diez, the Campeador,
    Was there in his arms array'd;
  And that with him, from the tomb,
Had the Count Gonzalez come,[25]
    With a host, uprisen to aid!

And they came for the buried king that lay
    At rest in that ancient fane;            30
For he must be arm'd on the battle-day,
    With them, to deliver Spain!"

—Then the march went sounding on,
And the Moors, by noontide sun,
Were dust on Tolosa's plain.[26]

[1] Originally published in the New Monthly Magazine. [FH]
    The first song was published in *Literary Gazette*, 12 October 1822 (649), signed "H." and titled "Ballad." The next three appeared in *NMM* 7 (March and April) 1823, signed "Mrs. Hemans."
[2] In calling these songs "ballads," FH evokes the 18th-c. ballad revival. Such celebrated collections as Percy's *Reliques of Ancient English Poetry* (3 vols., 1765–94) and Scott's *Minstrelsy of the Scottish Border* (3 vols., 1802–3) were matched by European ones such as Herder's *Volkslieder* (which FH read [Lawrence 238]), and complemented by modern literary imitations, all chiming with Romantic-era nationalism. Spanish "romances" are ballads in octosyllabic lines blended with assonance instead of rhyme; English ballads are traditionally in quatrains of tetrameter (sometimes alternating with trimeter) with at least one rhyme. *Poema del* (or *Cantar de*) *mio Cid* is a 3,744-line epic fragment by an unknown Castilian bard, ca. 1140. It was incompletely copied in 1307 and published in 1779 by Tomás Antonio Sánchez as the first volume of *Coleccion de Poesias Castellanas Anteriores al Siglo XV* (1779–90).
[3] Bivar, the supposed birth-place of the Cid, was a castle, about two leagues from Burgos. [FH]
    Cf. Southey, *Chronicle*, bk. 1.ɪɪ. (2). Two leagues: about six miles.
[4] Tornaba la cabeza, e estabalos catando:        [He turned his head, and gazed upon them:
    Vio puertas abiertas, e uzos sin cañados,        He saw gates open and doors without locks,
    Alcandaras vacias, sin pielles e sin                Hooks empty without furs and without
        mantos:                                                  cloaks:
    E sin falcones, e sin adtores mudados.           And without falcons or moulted hawks.
    Sospirò mio Cid.    *Poem of the Cid.* [FH]    My Cid sighed.]
*Poema*, Canto 1, 2-6, describing Cid's departure, exiled from Castile by Alfonso; cf. Southey, *Chronicle*, bk. 3.xɪx–xx. The locks struck from the doors signal that this is no longer a safe refuge; the valuables (furs, etc.) have been confiscated; a moulted hawk is mature, and ready for hunting, hence valuable. Europe's most famous exile, Napoleon, died in 1821.
[5] Southey, *Chronicle*, bk. 11.v–vɪ (331–33) and romance 95 in de Escobar's *Romancero*.
[6] The zambra, a Moorish dance. When Valencia was taken by the Cid, many of the Moorish families chose to remain there, and reside under his government. [FH]
[7] The calm fortitude of Ximena is frequently alluded to in the romances. [FH]
[8] *NMM*] conqueror's
[9] *NMM*] mighty
[10] *NMM*] leader
[11] *NMM*] dauntless
[12] Banderas antiguas, tristes          [Banners ancient, sad
    De victorias un tiempo amadas,       Of victories at one time dear,
    Tremolando estan al viento            Were fluttering in the wind
    Y lloran aunque no hablan, &c.       And they weep but do not speak, &c.]
Herder's translation of these romances (Der Cid, nach Spanischen Romanzen besungen) are remarkable for their spirit and scrupulous fidelity. [FH]
[13] "And while they stood there they saw the Cid Ruy Diez coming up with three hundred knights; for he had not been in the battle, and they knew his *green pennon*."—*Southey's Chronicle of the Cid.* [FH, her italics. Bk. 2.xɪɪɪ (47–48)]
    *NMM*] stately banners; footnote]: See the Spanish Ballad, "*Banderas antiguas, tristes, & c.*"
[14] *NMM* footnote]: See the Legends recorded in Southey's Chronicle of the Cid. [FH]
    Bk. 11.vɪɪɪ (335–36); cf. romance 98 in Escobar's *Romancero*.
[15] *Cuirasse*: a piece of body armor originally made of leather (French, *cuir*).

[16] In *The Siege &c*, a superscript 6 marks *The Cid's Death-Bed* 53 and *The Cid's Funeral Procession* 37 (pp. 254, 258), keyed to FH's note in n.13 above. "Pero Bermudez went first with the banner of the Cid, and with him five hundred knights who guarded it" (Southey, *Chronicle* 11.VIII [336]; cf. 4.VIII, [113]).

[17] Alvar Fañez Minaya, one of the Cid's most distinguished warriors. [FH]

*NMM*] . . . bravest warriors.

Alvar was Cid's nephew and faithful companion; see Southey, *Chronicle*, bk. 11.IX (336).

[18] A Moorish Amazon, who, with a band of female warriors, accompanied King Bucar from Africa. Her arrows were so unerring, that she obtained the name of the Star of archers.

| | |
|---|---|
| Una Mora muy gallarda, | [A very gallant Mooress, |
| Gran maestra en el tirar, | Great master in archery, |
| Con Saetas del Aljava, | With Arrows from her Quiver, |
| De los arcos de Turquia | With bows from Turkey |
| Estrella era nombrada, | She was named the Star, |
| Por la destreza que avia | For the skill that she had |
| En el herir de la Xára. [FH] | In wounding with the dart.] |

From romance 98 in Escobar's *Romancero*; see Southey, *Chronicle*, bk. 11.IX (337).

[19] A title meaning "my brother," applied to Alvar Fañez in the lore of El Cid; see, for example, Southey, *Chronicle*, bk. 11.IX (336) and his excerpts from *Poema* (438, 442–43).

[20] See FH's note to *Siege of Valencia* 4.51; cf. *Chronicle*, bk. 8.VIII (259).

[21] A reference both to the archer's bow and the crescent, symbol of Islam. The terrified Moors fled into the sea, where many drowned; see Southey, *Chronicle*, bk. 11.IX (337).

[22] See Southey's Chronicle of the Cid, p. 352. [FH. Bk. 11.XXI]

León: a city in northern Spain and a medieval Christian kingdom, west of Castile. I correct the erratum in *Siege & c* ("night"); cf. *NMM*, *1839* (5.119) and Southey: "a mighty sound was heard in the whole city of Leon, as if it were the tramp of a great army passing through."

[23]*NMM*] sleepers

[24]The church of San Isidro, burial place of Fernando I of León (ruled 1035–65), who brought Castile and Galicia into his kingdom, heralding the final unification of Spain in 1492.

[25] Fernán González, military leader under Fernando I and hero of another medieval Spanish romance. See *Siege of Valencia*, scene 1, note 7.

[26] Site of the battle of Navas de Tolosa in 1212, when the forces of Alfonso VIII of Castile defeated the Almoravid Moors, thus securing the future of the Christian kingdoms in Spain.

---

## England's Dead[1]

Son of the ocean isle!
Where sleep your mighty dead?
Show me what high and stately pile
Is rear'd o'er Glory's bed.

Go, stranger! track the deep,
Free, free, the white sail spread!
Wave may not foam, nor wild wind sweep,
Where rest not England's dead.

On Egypt's burning plains,
By the pyramid o'ersway'd,                    10

With fearful power the noon-day reigns,
    And the palm-trees yield no shade.

But let the angry sun
From heaven look fiercely red,
Unfelt by those whose task is done!
    *There* slumber England's dead.[2]

The hurricane hath might
    Along the Indian shore,
And far, by Ganges' banks at night,
    Is heard the tiger's roar.                 20

But let the sound roll on!
It hath no tone of dread,
For those that from their toils are gone;
    —*There* slumber England's dead.

Loud rush the torrent-floods
    The western wilds among,
And free, in green Columbia's woods,
    The hunter's bow is strung.

But let the floods rush on!
Let the arrow's flight be sped!
Why should *they* reck whose task is done?        30
    *There* slumber England's dead!

The mountain-storms rise high
    In the snowy Pyrenees,
And toss the pine-boughs through the sky,
    Like rose-leaves on the breeze.

But let the storm rage on!
Let the forest-wreaths be shed!
For the Roncesvalles' field is won,[3]
    *There* slumber England's dead.           40

On the frozen deep's repose
    'Tis a dark and dreadful hour,
When round the ship the ice-fields close,
    To chain her with their power.

But let the ice drift on!
Let the cold-blue desert spread!
*Their* course with mast and flag is done,
    *There* slumber England's dead.

The warlike of the isles,
    The men of field and wave!             50

Are not the rocks their funeral piles,
The seas and shores their grave?

Go, stranger! track the deep,
Free, free the white sail spread!
Wave may not foam, nor wild wind sweep,[4]
Where rest not England's dead.

[1] First published in *Literary Gazette*, 19 October 1822, 664; signed "H." *The Cid's Departure into Exile* had been published the week before. *England's Dead* was immediately and widely admired; *New European Magazine* printed it in full in its review of the *The Siege &c* (3 [1823], 122–23). The *Gazette*, a popular Tory weekly (circulation circa four thousand), was founded by Henry Colburn (1782–1862), who also published *NMM*, and was edited by part-owner William Jerdan. The *Gazette* stirred great interest in the 1820s with poems by "L.E.L." (Landon), who also helped edit it.

[2] Led by Horatio Nelson, Britain's navy defeated Napoleon's in the Battle of the Nile, in 1798 (see *Casabianca*), and again at Alexandria in 1801. Subsequent stanzas refer to British campaigns in India, South America, and Spain. If, in Christopher North's famous boast, the sun never sets on the British Empire, FH's grave vision is that the sun never sets on a British cemetery, an empire of the dead. The strikingly domestic tone of "slumber" also suggests that this global graveyard is, in some ways, the largest compass of hearth and home, the site in which patriotism is learned through domestic affection (see Lootens 248).

[3] The Roncesvalles pass in the Pyrenees was a battle site in the Peninsular War against Napoleon (1808–14).

[4] *Gazette*] "Wind may not rove, nor billow sweep"

Other variants of note are the mythicizing capitals: Dead, Deep, Glory, Stranger, Pyramid, Heaven, Western, Hunter, Warlike, Men.

# From *The Forest Sanctuary;*
## *and Other Poems*

### (1825)

—⟨∿∿⟩—

## *The Forest Sanctuary*

["I am at present engaged on a poem of some length," Hemans wrote a friend in November 1824. "It relates to the sufferings of a Spanish Protestant, in the time of Philip the Second, and is supposed to be narrated by the sufferer himself." She regarded this poem, begun in that autumn and published in 1825, "as her best" (*HM* 81). Joanna Baillie, who received a copy from Hemans, told a friend that she thought it "a beautiful poem [. . .] full, perhaps too full of poetic imagery & description," with a story rendered "in an interesting, impassioned manner" (12 May 1826; *Letters* 590). Twenty-one-year-old George Eliot thought it "exquisite!" (letter; 27 October 1840), and its theme won admiration in the United States: fleeing "persecution at home to religious liberty in America," the hero "has imbibed the spirit of our own fathers," observed Andrews Norton in the *North American Review* (April 1827); "his mental struggles are described in verses, with which the descendants of the pilgrims must know how to sympathize" (rpt. in *1839* 4.76). The chief scene of part 1 is an *auto-da-fé* ("act of faith"), the torture, trial, and mass execution of heretics. By the reign of Philip II (1556–98), the notorious Spanish Inquisition—established by his grandparents Ferdinand and Isabella, with Papal approval, to root out, convert, or expel refractory Moors and Jews (long part of a pluralistic culture)—was targeting Protestants. In English gothic novels the Inquisition variously symbolized despotism, Catholic sadism, or the French Terror (1793–94). Napoleon's abolition of it was cheered even by those opposed to his presence in Spain (executions continued into the 1780s); although it was reestablished with the monarchal restoration of 1814, it was permanently abolished in the Spanish revolution of the early 1820s.

The poem also bears contemporary reference. The rebellions of the early 1820s against Spain's reactionary regime were suppressed by French forces, with approval from the Holy Alliance of European monarchies and to the dismay of many Britons (including Hemans), for whom the Spanish resistance was a "chivalric" enthusiasm. Britons meanwhile were caught up in *the* civil rights issue of their 1820s, Catholic Emancipation. Hemans recognized that her poem had "some apparent coincidence with the great subject of national debate—the Catholic question," but insisted to Rev. Samuel Butler that it was "written without the slightest view to such coincidence, (which in my opinion Poetry should always avoid,)" (5 May 1826; BL Add MS 34586, f.192).

The form is an extended monologue, in a variation of the Spenserian stanza (*ababccbdd*, instead of *ababbcbcc*). Recent orthodox uses of the stanza included Wordsworth's romance monologue *The Female Vagrant* (*Lyrical Ballads*, 1798), Tighe's epic romance *Psyche* (1805) and Byron's epic romance *Childe Harold's Pilgrimage* (1812–18). The stanza was a challenge. Although "a fine structure of verse," Wordsworth advised a female poet in 1829, it is "almost insurmountably difficult [. . .] ill adapted to conflicting passion [. . .] unfit for narrative" and difficult to rhyme. A long poem, moreover, was regarded as no venture for a "feminine" writer (so Jeffrey said of *The Forest Sanctuary* in his 1829 article on Hemans

for the *Edinburgh Review*). The "greater part of this poem was written in no more picturesque a retreat than a laundry, to which, as being detached from the house, she resorted for
undisturbed quiet and leisure" (*CM* 1.124). Its progress "was watched with great interest
in her domestic circle," reports her sister; "its touching descriptions would often extract a
tribute of tears from the fireside auditors. When completed, a family consultation was held
as to its name. Various titles were proposed and rejected, till that of *The Forest Sanctuary*
was suggested by her brother" (*HM* 81). Murray's run of 750 sold well, earning Hemans
£34 by the next year and encouraging William Blackwood to issue second and third editions (1829 and 1835, respectively). Text: 2d ed.; most 1st-ed. (1825) variants are accidentals. Chief substantive variants in the "original" MS (LL) are noted.]

*Ihr Plätze aller meiner stillen freuden,*
*Euch lass' ich hinter mir auf immerdar!*

. . . . . . . . . . . .

*So ist des geistes ruf an mich ergangen,*
*Mich treibt nicht eitles, irdisches verlangen.*
                              —Die Jungfrau von Orleans[1]

*Long time against oppression have I fought,*
*And for the native liberty of faith*
*Have bled and suffer'd bonds.*
                              —Remorse, a Tragedy[2]

The following Poem is intended to describe the mental conflicts, as well
as outward sufferings, of a Spaniard, who, flying from the religious persecu-
tions of his own country, in the sixteenth century, takes refuge, with his
child, in a North American Forest. The story is supposed to be related by
himself, amidst the wilderness which has afforded him an asylum.[3]

## PART FIRST

### I

The voices of my home!—I hear them still!
They have been with me through the dreamy night—
The blessed household voices, wont to fill
My heart's clear depths with unalloy'd delight!
I hear them still, unchang'd:—though some from earth
Are music parted,[4] and the tones of mirth—
Wild, silvery tones, that rang through days more bright!
Have died in others,—yet to me they come,
Singing of boyhood back—the voices of my home!

### II

They call me through this hush of woods, reposing            10
In the grey stillness of the summer morn,
They wander by when heavy flowers are closing,
And thoughts grow deep, and winds and stars are born;
Ev'n as a fount's remember'd gushings burst

On the parch'd traveller in his hour of thirst,
E'en thus they haunt me with sweet sounds, till worn
By quenchless longings, to my soul I say—
Oh! for the dove's swift wings, that I might flee away,—[5]

### III

And find mine ark!—yet whither?—I must bear
A yearning heart within me to the grave.                    20
I am of those o'er whom a breath of air—
Just darkening in its course the lake's bright wave,
And sighing through the feathery canes[6]—hath power
To call up shadows, in the silent hour,
From the dim past, as from a wizard's cave!—
So must it be!—These skies above me spread,
Are they my own soft skies?—Ye rest not here, my dead!

### IV

Ye far amidst the southern flowers lie sleeping,
Your graves all smiling in the sunshine clear,
Save one!—a blue, lone, distant main is sweeping          30
High o'er *one* gentle head—ye rest not here!—
'Tis not the olive, with a whisper swaying,
Not thy low ripplings, glassy water, playing
Through my own chesnut groves, which fill mine ear;
But the faint echoes in my breast that dwell,
And for their birth-place moan, as moans the ocean-shell.[7]

### V

Peace!—I will dash these fond regrets to earth,
Ev'n as an eagle shakes the cumbering rain
From his strong pinion. Thou that gav'st me birth,
And lineage, and once home,—my native Spain!             40
My own bright land—my father's land—my child's!
What hath thy son brought from thee to the wilds?
He hath brought marks of torture and the chain,
Traces of things which pass not as a breeze,
A blighted name, dark thoughts, wrath, wo,—thy gifts are these.

### VI

A blighted name!—I hear the winds of morn—
Their sounds are not of this!—I hear the shiver
Of the green reeds, and all the rustlings, borne
From the high forest, when the light leaves quiver:
Their sounds are not of this!—the cedars, waving,          50
Lend it no tone: His wide savannahs laving,

It is not murmur'd by the joyous river!
What part hath mortal name,[8] where God alone
Speaks to the mighty waste, and through its heart is known?

### VII

Is it not much that I may worship Him,
With nought my spirit's breathings to control,
And feel His presence in the vast, and dim,
And whispery woods, where dying thunders roll
From the far cataracts?—Shall I not rejoice
That I have learn'd at last to know *His* voice          60
From man's?—I will rejoice!—my soaring soul
Now hath redeem'd her birthright of the day,
And won, through clouds, to Him, her own unfetter'd way!

### VIII

And thou, my boy! that silent at my knee
Dost lift to mine thy soft, dark, earnest eyes,
Fill'd with the love of childhood, which I see
Pure through its depths, a thing without disguise;
Thou that hast breath'd in slumber on my breast,
When I have check'd its throbs to give thee rest,
Mine own! whose young thoughts fresh before me rise!          70
Is it not much that I may guide thy prayer,
And circle thy glad soul with free and healthful air?

### IX

Why should I weep on thy bright head, my boy?
Within thy fathers' halls thou wilt not dwell,
Nor lift their banner, with a warrior's joy,
Amidst the sons of mountain chiefs, who fell
For Spain of old.[9] —Yet what if rolling waves
Have borne us far from our ancestral graves?
Thou shalt not feel thy bursting heart rebel
As mine hath done; nor bear what I have borne,          80
Casting in falsehood's mould th' indignant brow of scorn.

### X

This shall not be thy lot, my blessed child!
I have not sorrow'd, struggled, liv'd in vain—
Hear me! magnificent and ancient wild;
And mighty rivers, ye that meet the main,
As deep meets deep; and forests, whose dim shade
The flood's voice, and the wind's, by swells pervade;
Hear me!—'tis well to die, and not complain,

Yet there are hours when the charg'd heart must speak,
Ev'n in the desert's ear to pour itself, or break!¹⁰                    90

### XI

I see an oak before me,¹¹ it hath been
The crown'd one of the woods; and might have flung
Its hundred arms to Heaven, still freshly green,
But a wild vine around the stem hath clung,
From branch to branch close wreaths of bondage throwing,
Till the proud tree, before no tempest bowing,
Hath shrunk and died, those serpent-folds among.
Alas! alas!—what is it that I see?
An image of man's mind, land of my sires, with thee!

### XII

Yet art thou lovely!—Song is on thy hills—                             100
Oh sweet and mournful melodies of Spain,
That lull'd my boyhood, how your memory thrills
The exile's heart with sudden-wakening pain!—
Your sounds are on the rocks—that I might hear
Once more the music of the mountaineer!—
And from the sunny vales the shepherd's strain
Floats out, and fills the solitary place
With the old tuneful names of Spain's heroic race.

### XIII

But there was silence one bright, golden day,
Through my own pine-hung mountains. Clear, yet lone,                   110
In the rich autumn light the vineyards lay,
And from the fields the peasant's voice was gone;
And the red grapes untrodden strew'd the ground,
And the free flocks untended roam'd around:
Where was the pastor?—where the pipe's wild tone?
Music and mirth were hush'd the hills among,
While to the city's gates each hamlet pour'd its throng.¹²

### XIV

Silence upon the mountains!—But within
The city's gates a rush—a press—a swell
Of multitudes their torrent way to win;                                120
And heavy boomings of a dull, deep bell,
A dead pause following each—like that which parts
The dash of billows, holding breathless hearts
Fast in the hush of fear—knell after knell;
And sounds of thickening steps, like thunder-rain,
That plashes on the roof of some vast echoing fane!

### XV

What pageant's hour approach'd?—The sullen gate
Of a strong ancient prison-house was thrown
Back to the day. And who, in mournful state,
Came forth, led slowly o'er its threshold-stone?                    130
They that had learn'd, in cells of secret gloom,
How sunshine is forgotten!—They, to whom
The very features of mankind were grown
Things that bewilder'd!—O'er their dazzled sight,
They lifted their wan hands, and cower'd before the light!¹³

### XVI

To this man brings his brother!—Some were there,
Who with their desolation had entwin'd
Fierce strength, and girt the sternness of despair
Fast round their bosoms, ev'n as warriors bind
The breast-plate on for fight: but brow and cheek                  140
Seem'd *theirs* a torturing panoply to speak!
And there were some, from whom the very mind
Had been wrung out: they smil'd—oh! startling smile
Whence man's high soul is fled!—where doth it sleep the while?¹⁴

### XVII

But onward moved the melancholy train,
For their false creeds in fiery pangs to die.
This was the solemn sacrifice of Spain—
Heaven's offering from the land of chivalry!
Thro' thousands, thousands of their race they mov'd—
Oh! how unlike all others!—the belov'd,                            150
The free, the proud, the beautiful! whose eye
Grew fix'd before them, while a people's breath
Was hush'd, and its one soul bound in the thought of death!¹⁵

### XVIII

It might be that amidst the countless throng,
There swell'd some heart with Pity's weight oppress'd,
For the wide stream of human love is strong;
And woman, on whose fond and faithful breast
Childhood is rear'd, and at whose knee the sigh
Of its first prayer is breath'd, she, too, was nigh.
—But life is dear, and the free footstep bless'd,                  160
And home a sunny place, where each may fill
Some eye with glistening smiles,—and therefore all were still—

### XIX

All still—youth, courage, strength!—a winter laid,
A chain of palsy, cast on might and mind!
Still, as at noon a southern forest's shade,
They stood, those breathless masses of mankind;
Still, as a frozen torrent!—but the wave
Soon leaps to foaming freedom—they, the brave,
Endur'd—they saw the martyr's place assign'd
In the red flames—whence is the withering spell                    170
That numbs each human pulse?—they saw, and thought it well.

### XX

And I, too, thought it well! That very morn
From a far land I came, yet round me clung
The spirit of my own. No hand had torn
With a strong grasp away the veil which hung
Between mine eyes and truth. I gaz'd, I saw,
Dimly, as through a glass.[16] In silent awe
I watch'd the fearful rites; and if there sprung
One rebel feeling from its deep founts up,
Shuddering, I flung it back, as guilt's own poison-cup.             180

### XXI

But I was waken'd as the dreamers waken
Whom the shrill trumpet and the shriek of dread
Rouse up at midnight, when their walls are taken,
And they must battle till their blood is shed
On their own threshold-floor. A path for light
Through my torn breast was shatter'd by the might
Of the swift thunder-stroke—and Freedom's tread
Came in through ruins, late, yet not in vain,
Making the blighted place all green with life again.

### XXII

Still darkly, slowly, as a sullen mass                              190
Of cloud, o'ersweeping, without wind, the sky,
Dream-like I saw the sad procession pass,
And mark'd its victims with a tearless eye.
They mov'd before me but as pictures, wrought
Each to reveal some secret of man's thought,
On the sharp edge of sad mortality,[17]
Till in his place came one—oh! could it be?
—My friend, my heart's first friend!—and did I gaze on thee?

### XXIII

On thee! with whom in boyhood I had play'd,
At the grape-gatherings, by my native streams;                           200
And to whose eye my youthful soul had laid
Bare, as to Heaven's, its glowing world of dreams;
And by whose side midst warriors I had stood,
And in whose helm was brought—oh! earn'd with blood!—
The fresh wave to my lips, when tropic beams
Smote on my fever'd brow!—Ay, years had pass'd,
Severing our paths, brave friend!—and *thus* we met at last![18]

### XXIV

I see it still—the lofty mien thou borest—
On thy pale forehead sat a sense of power!
The very look that once thou brightly worest,                            210
Cheering me onward through a fearful hour,
When we were girt by Indian bow and spear,
Midst the white Andes—ev'n as mountain deer,
Hemm'd in our camp—but thro' the javelin shower
We rent our way, a tempest of despair!—
And thou—hadst thou but died with thy true brethren there!

### XXV

I call the fond wish back—for thou hast perish'd
More nobly far, my Alvar!—making known
The might of truth;[19] and be thy memory cherish'd
With theirs, the thousands, that around her throne                       220
Have pour'd their lives out smiling, in that doom
Finding a triumph, if denied a tomb!—
Ay, with their ashes hath the wind been sown,
And with the wind their spirit shall be spread,
Filling man's heart and home with records of the dead.

### XXVI

Thou Searcher of the Soul! in whose dread sight
Not the bold guilt alone, that mocks the skies,
But the scarce-own'd, unwhisper'd thought of night,
As a thing written with the sunbeam lies;
*Thou* know'st—whose eye through shade and depth can see,                 230
That this man's crime was but to worship thee,
Like those that made their hearts thy sacrifice,
The call'd of yore; wont by the Saviour's side,
On the dim Olive-Mount to pray at eventide.[20]

XXVII

For the strong spirit will at times awake,
Piercing the mists that wrap her clay-abode;
And, born of thee, she may not always take
Earth's accents for the oracles of God;
And ev'n for this—O dust, whose mask is power!
Reed, that wouldst be a scourge thy little hour!                    240
Spark, whereon yet the mighty hath not trod,
And therefore thou destroyest!—where were flown
Our hope, if man were left to man's decree alone?

XXVIII

But this I felt not yet. I could but gaze
On him, my friend; while that swift moment threw
A sudden freshness back on vanish'd days,
Like water-drops on some dim picture's hue;
Calling the proud time up, when first I stood
Where banners floated, and my heart's quick blood
Sprang to a torrent as the clarion blew,                           250
And he—his sword was like a brother's worn,
That watches through the field his mother's youngest born.

XXIX

But a lance met me in that day's career,
Senseless I lay amidst th' o'ersweeping fight,
Wakening at last—how full, how strangely clear,
That scene on memory flash'd!—the shivery light,
Moonlight, on broken shields—the plain of slaughter,
The fountain-side—the low sweet sound of water—
And Alvar bending o'er me—from the night
Covering me with his mantle!—all the past                          260
Flow'd back—my soul's far chords all answer'd to the blast.

XXX

Till, in that rush of visions, I became
As one that by the bands of slumber wound,
Lies with a powerless, but all-thrilling frame,
Intense in consciousness of sight and sound,
Yet buried in a wildering dream which brings
Lov'd faces round him, girt with fearful things!
Troubled ev'n thus I stood, but chain'd and bound
On that familiar form mine eye to keep:—
Alas! I might not fall upon his neck and weep![21]                 270

### XXXI

He pass'd me—and what next?—I look'd on two,
Following his footsteps to the same dread place,
For the same guilt—his sisters!22—Well I knew
The beauty on those brows, though each young face
Was chang'd—so deeply chang'd!—a dungeon's air
Is hard for lov'd and lovely things to bear,
And ye, O daughters of a lofty race,
Queen-like Theresa! radiant Inez!—flowers
So cherish'd! were ye then but rear'd for those dark hours?

### XXXII

A mournful home, young sisters! had ye left,                280
With your lutes hanging hush'd upon the wall,
And silence round the aged man, bereft
Of each glad voice, once answering to his call.
Alas, that lonely father! doom'd to pine
For sounds departed in his life's decline,
And, midst the shadowing banners of his hall,
With his white hair to sit, and deem the name
A hundred chiefs had borne, cast down by you to shame!23

### XXXIII

And woe for you, midst looks and words of love,
And gentle hearts and faces, nurs'd so long!                290
How had I seen you in your beauty move,
Wearing the wreath, and listening to the song!
—Yet sat, ev'n then, what seem'd the crowd to shun,
Half veil'd upon the clear pale brow of one,
And deeper thoughts than oft to youth belong,
Thoughts, such as wake to evening's whispery sway,
Within the drooping shade of her sweet eyelids lay.

### XXXIV

And if she mingled with the festive train,
It was but as some melancholy star
Beholds the dance of shepherds on the plain,                300
In its bright stillness present, though afar.
Yet would she smile—and that, too, hath its smile—
Circled with joy which reach'd her not the while,
And bearing a lone spirit, not at war
With earthly things, but o'er their form and hue
Shedding too clear a light, too sorrowfully true.

XXXV

But the dark hours wring forth the hidden might
Which hath lain bedded in the silent soul,
A treasure all undreamt of;—as the night
Calls out the harmonies of streams that roll            310
Unheard by day. It seem'd as if her breast
Had hoarded energies, till then suppress'd
Almost with pain, and bursting from control,
And finding first that hour their pathway free:—
Could a rose brave the storm, such might her emblem be!

XXXVI

For the soft gloom whose shadow still had hung
On her fair brow, beneath its garlands worn,
Was fled; and fire, like prophecy's had sprung
Clear to her kindled eye. It might be scorn—
Pride—sense of wrong—ay, the frail heart is bound     320
By these at times, ev'n as with adamant round,
Kept so from breaking!—yet not *thus* upborne
She mov'd, though some sustaining passion's wave
Lifted her fervent soul—a sister for the brave!

XXXVII

And yet, alas! to see the strength which clings
Round woman in such hours!—a mournful sight,
Though lovely!—an o'erflowing of the springs,
The full springs of affection, deep as bright!
And she, because her life is ever twin'd
With other lives, and by no stormy wind               330
May thence be shaken, and because the light
Of tenderness is round her, and her eye
Doth weep such passionate tears—therefore she thus can die.

XXXVIII

Therefore didst *thou*, through that heart-shaking scene,
As through a triumph move; and cast aside
Thine own sweet thoughtfulness for victory's mien,
O faithful[24] sister! cheering thus the guide,
And friend, and brother of thy sainted youth,
Whose hand had led thee to the source of truth,
Where thy glad soul from earth was purified;          340
Nor wouldst thou, following him through all the past,
That he should see thy step grow tremulous at last.

### XXXIX

For thou hadst made no deeper love a guest
Midst thy young spirit's dreams,²⁵ than that which grows
Between the nurtur'd of the same fond breast,
The shelter'd of one roof; and thus it rose
Twin'd in with life.—How is it, that the hours
Of the same sport, the gathering early flowers
Round the same tree, the sharing one repose,
And mingling one first prayer in murmurs soft,                    350
From the heart's memory fade, in this world's breath, so oft?

### XL

But thee that breath had touch'd not; thee, nor him,
The true in all things found!—and thou wert blest
Ev'n then, that no remember'd change could dim
The perfect image of affection, press'd
Like armour to thy bosom!—thou hadst kept
Watch by that brother's couch of pain, and wept,
Thy sweet face covering with thy robe, when rest
Fled from the sufferer; thou hadst bound his faith
Unto thy soul—one light, one hope ye chose—one death.           360

### XLI

So didst thou pass on brightly!—but for her,
Next in that path, how may *her* doom be spoken!
—All-merciful! to think that such things were,
And *are*, and seen by men with hearts unbroken!
To think of that fair girl, whose path had been
So strew'd with rose-leaves, all one fairy scene!
And whose quick glance came ever as a token
Of hope to drooping thought, and her glad voice
As a free bird's in spring, that makes the woods rejoice!

### XLII

And she to die!—she lov'd the laughing earth                     370
With such deep joy in its fresh leaves and flowers!
—Was not her smile even as the sudden birth
Of a young rainbow, colouring vernal showers?
Yes! but to meet her fawn-like step, to hear
The gushes of wild song, so silvery clear,
Which, oft unconsciously, in happier hours
Flow'd from her lips, was to forget the sway
Of Time and Death below,—blight, shadow, dull decay!

### XLIII

Could this change be?—the hour, the scene, where last
I saw that form, came floating o'er my mind:—                    380
A golden vintage-eve;—the heats were pass'd,
And, in the freshness of the fanning wind,
Her father sat, where gleam'd the first faint star
Through the lime-boughs; and with her light guitar,
She, on the greensward at his feet reclin'd,
In his calm face laugh'd up; some shepherd-lay
Singing, as childhood sings on the lone hills at play.

### XLIV

And now—oh God!—the bitter fear of death,
The sore amaze, the faint o'ershadowing dread,
Had grasp'd her!—panting in her quick-drawn breath,                    390
And in her white lips quivering;—onward led,
She look'd up with her dim bewilder'd eyes,
And there smil'd out her own soft brilliant skies,
Far in their sultry southern azure spread,
Glowing with joy, but silent!—still they smil'd,
Yet sent down no reprieve for earth's poor trembling child.

### XLV

Alas! that earth had all too strong a hold,
Too fast, sweet Inez! on thy heart, whose bloom
Was given to early love, nor knew how cold
The hours which follow. There was one, with whom,                    400
Young as thou wert, and gentle, and untried,
Thou might'st, perchance, unshrinkingly have died;
But he was far away;—and with thy doom
Thus gathering, life grew so intensely dear,
That all thy slight frame shook with its cold mortal fear!

### XLVI

No aid!—thou too didst pass!—and all had pass'd,
The fearful—and the desperate—and the strong!
Some like the bark that rushes with the blast,
Some like the leaf swept shiveringly along,
And some as men, that have but one more field                    410
To fight, and then may slumber on their shield,—
Therefore they arm in hope. But now the throng
Roll'd on, and bore me with their living tide,
Ev'n as a bark wherein is left no power to guide.

### XLVII

Wave swept on wave. We reach'd a stately square,
Deck'd for the rites. An altar stood on high,
And gorgeous, in the midst: a place for prayer,
And praise, and offering. Could the earth supply
No fruits, no flowers for sacrifice, of all
Which on her sunny lap unheeded fall?                    420
No fair young firstling of the flock to die,
As when before their God the Patriarchs stood?—
Look down! man brings thee, Heaven! his brother's guiltless blood![26]

### XLVIII

Hear its voice, hear!—a cry goes up to thee,
From the stain'd sod; make thou thy judgment known
On him, the shedder!—let his portion° be                    *reward*
The fear that walks at midnight—give the moan
In the wind haunting him a power to say
"Where is thy brother?"—and the stars a ray
To search and shake his spirit, when alone                    430
With the dread splendor of their burning eyes!—
So shall earth own thy will—mercy, not sacrifice!

### XLIX

Sounds of triumphant praise!—the mass was sung—
Voices that die not might have pour'd such strains!
Thro' Salem's towers might that proud chant have rung,
When the Most High, on Syria's palmy plains,
Had quell'd her foes![27]—so full it swept, a sea
Of loud waves jubilant, and rolling free!
—Oft when the wind, as thro' resounding fanes,
Hath fill'd the choral forests with its power,                    440
Some deep tone brings me back the music of that hour.

### L

It died away;—the incense-cloud was driven
Before the breeze—the words of doom were said;[28]
And the sun faded mournfully from Heaven:
—He faded mournfully! and dimly red,
Parting in clouds from those that look'd their last,
And sigh'd—"Farewell, thou sun!"—Eve glow'd and pass'd—
Night—midnight and the moon—came forth and shed
Sleep, even as dew, on glen, wood, peopled spot—
Save one—a place of death—and there men slumber'd not.                    450

### LI

'Twas not within the city[29]—but in sight
Of the snow-crown'd sierras, freely sweeping,
With many an eagle's eyrie° on the height,                     *nest*
And hunter's cabin, by the torrent peeping
Far off: and vales between, and vineyards lay,
With sound and gleam of waters on their way,
And chesnut-woods, that girt the happy sleeping,
In many a peasant-home!—the midnight sky
Brought softly that rich world round those who came to die.

### LII

The darkly-glorious midnight sky of Spain,                    460
Burning with stars!—What had the torches' glare
To do beneath that Temple, and profane
Its holy radiance?—By their wavering flare,
I saw beside the pyres—I see thee *now*,
O bright Theresa! with thy lifted brow,
And thy clasp'd hands, and dark eyes fill'd with prayer!
And thee, sad Inez! bowing thy fair head,
And mantling up thy face, all colourless with dread!

### LIII

And Alvar, Alvar!—I beheld thee too,
Pale, stedfast, kingly; till thy clear glance fell            470
On that young sister; then perturb'd it grew,
And all thy labouring bosom seem'd to swell
With painful tenderness. Why came I there,
That troubled image of my friend to bear
Thence, for my after-years?—a thing to dwell
In my heart's core, and on the darkness rise,
Disquieting my dreams with its bright mournful eyes?

### LIV

Why came I? oh! the heart's deep mystery!—Why
In man's last hour doth vain affection's gaze
Fix itself down on struggling agony,                          480
To the dimm'd eye-balls freezing as they glaze?
It might be—yet the power to will seem'd o'er—
That my soul yearn'd to hear his voice once more!
But mine was fetter'd!—mute in strong amaze,
I watch'd his features as the night-wind blew,
And torch-light or the moon's pass'd o'er their marble hue.[30]

LV

The trampling of a steed!—a tall white steed,
Rending his fiery way the crowds among—
A storm's way through a forest—came at speed,
And a wild voice cried "Inez!" Swift she flung          490
The mantle from her face, and gaz'd around,
With a faint shriek at that familiar sound;
And from his seat a breathless rider sprung,
And dash'd off fiercely those who came to part,
And rush'd to that pale girl, and clasp'd her to his heart.

LVI

And for a moment all around gave way
To that full burst of passion!—on his breast,
Like a bird panting yet from fear she lay,
But blest—in misery's very lap—yet blest!—
Oh love, love, strong as death!—from such an hour          500
Pressing out joy by thine immortal power,
Holy and fervent love! had earth but rest
For thee and thine, this world were all too fair!
How could we thence be wean'd to die without despair?

LVII

But she—as falls a willow from the storm,
O'er its own river streaming—thus reclin'd
On the youth's bosom hung her fragile form,
And clasping arms, so passionately twin'd
Around his neck—with such a trusting fold,
A full deep sense of safety in their hold,          510
As if nought earthly might th' embrace unbind!
Alas! a child's fond faith, believing still
Its mother's breast beyond the lightning's reach to kill!

LVIII

Brief rest! upon the turning billow's height,
A strange sweet moment of some heavenly strain,
Floating between the savage gusts of night,
That sweep the seas to foam! Soon dark again
The hour—the scene—th' intensely present, rush'd
Back on her spirit, and her large tears gush'd
Like blood-drops from a victim; with swift rain          520
Bathing the bosom where she lean'd that hour,
As if her life would melt into th' o'erswelling shower.

### LIX

But he, whose arm sustain'd her!—oh! I knew
'Twas vain,—and yet he hop'd!—he fondly strove
Back from her faith her sinking soul to woo,
As life might yet be hers!—A dream of love
Which could not look upon so fair a thing,
Remembering how like hope, like joy, like spring,
Her smile was wont to glance, her step to move,
And deem that men indeed, in very truth,                                    530
*Could* mean the sting of death for her soft flowering youth!

### LX

He woo'd her back to life.—"Sweet Inez, live!
My blessed Inez!—visions have beguil'd
Thy heart—abjure them!—thou wert form'd to give,
And to find, joy; and hath not sunshine smil'd
Around thee ever? Leave me not, mine own!
Or earth will grow too dark!—for thee alone,
Thee have I lov'd, thou gentlest! from a child,
And borne thine image with me o'er the sea,
Thy soft voice in my soul—speak!—Oh! yet live for me!"                      540

### LXI

She look'd up wildly; these were anxious eyes
Waiting that look—sad eyes of troubled thought,
Alvar's—Theresa's!—Did her childhood rise,
With all its pure and home-affections fraught,
In the brief glance?—She clasp'd her hands—the strife
Of love, faith, fear, and that vain dream of life,
Within her woman's breast so deeply wrought,
It seem'd as if a reed so slight and weak
*Must*, in the rending storm not quiver only—break!

### LXII

And thus it was—the young cheek flush'd and faded,                          550
As the swift blood in currents came and went,
And hues of death the marble brow o'ershaded,
And the sunk eye a watery lustre sent
Thro' its white fluttering lids. Then tremblings pass'd
O'er the frail form, that shook it, as the blast
Shakes the sere leaf, until the spirit rent
Its way to peace—the fearful way unknown—
Pale in love's arms she lay—*she!*—what had lov'd was gone!

### LXIII

Joy for thee, trembler!—thou redeem'd one, joy!
Young dove set free!—earth, ashes, soulless clay,      560
Remain'd for baffled vengeance to destroy;
—*Thy* chain was riven!—nor hadst thou cast away
Thy hope in thy last hour!—though love was there
Striving to wring thy troubled soul from prayer,
And life seem'd robed in beautiful array,
Too fair to leave!—but this might be forgiven,
Thou wert so richly crown'd with precious gifts of Heaven!

### LXIV

But woe for him who felt the heart grow still,
Which, with its weight of agony, had lain
Breaking on his!—Scarce could the mortal chill      570
Of the hush'd bosom, ne'er to heave again,
And all the silence curdling round the eye,
Bring home the stern belief that she could die,
That she indeed could die!—for wild and vain
As hope might be—his soul *had* hoped—'twas o'er—
Slowly his failing arms dropp'd from the form they bore.

### LXV

They forc'd him from that spot.—It might be well,
That the fierce, reckless words by anguish wrung
From his torn breast, all aimless as they fell,
Like spray-drops from the strife of torrents flung,      580
Were mark'd as guilt.—There are, who note these things[31]
Against the smitten heart; its breaking strings
—On whose low thrills once gentle music hung—
With a rude hand of touch unholy trying,
And numbering then as crimes, the deep, strange tones replying.

### LXVI

But ye in solemn joy, O faithful pair!
Stood gazing on your parted sister's dust;
I saw your features by the torch's glare,
And they were brightening with a heavenward trust!
I saw the doubt, the anguish, the dismay,      590
Melt from my Alvar's glorious mien away;
And peace was there—the calmness of the just!
And, bending down the slumberer's brow to kiss,
"Thy rest is won," he said; "sweet sister! praise for this!"

### LXVII

I started as from sleep;—yes! he had spoken—
A breeze had troubled memory's hidden source!
At once the torpor of my soul was broken—
Thought, feeling, passion, woke in tenfold force.
—There are soft breathings in the southern wind,
That so your ice-chains, O ye streams! unbind,                    600
And free the foaming swiftness of your course!
—I burst from those that held me back, and fell
Ev'n on his neck, and cried—"Friend, brother! fare thee well!"

### LXVIII

Did *he* not say "Farewell?"—Alas! no breath
Came to mine ear. Hoarse murmurs from the throng
Told that the mysteries in the face of death
Had from their eager sight been veil'd too long.
And we were parted as the surge might part
Those that would die together, true of heart.
—*His* hour was come—but in mine anguish strong,              610
Like a fierce swimmer through the midnight sea,
Blindly I rush'd away from that which was to be.

### LXIX

Away—away I rush'd;—but swift and high
The arrowy pillars of the firelight grew,
Till the transparent darkness of the sky
Flush'd to a blood-red mantle in their hue;
And, phantom-like, the kindling city seem'd
To spread, float, wave, as on the wind they stream'd,
With their wild splendour chasing me!—I knew
The death-work was begun—I veil'd mine eyes,                   620
Yet stopp'd in spell-bound fear to catch the victims' cries.

### LXX

What heard I then?—a ringing shriek of pain,
Such as for ever haunts the tortur'd ear?
—I heard a sweet and solemn-breathing strain
Piercing the flames, untremulous and clear!
—The rich, triumphal tones!—I knew them well,
As they came floating with a breezy swell!
Man's voice was there—a clarion voice to cheer
In the mid-battle—ay, to turn the flying—
Woman's—that might have sung of Heaven beside the dying!        630

### LXXI

It was a fearful, yet a glorious thing,
To hear that hymn of martyrdom, and know
That its glad stream of melody could spring
Up from th' unsounded gulfs of human woe!
Alvar! Theresa!—what is deep? what strong?
—God's breath within the soul!—It fill'd that song
From your victorious voices!—but the glow
On the hot air and lurid skies increas'd—
Faint grew the sounds—more faint—I listen'd—they had ceas'd!

### LXXII

And thou indeed hadst perish'd, my soul's friend! 640
I might form other ties—but thou alone
Couldst with a glance the veil of dimness rend,
By other years o'er boyhood's memory thrown!
Others might aid me onward:—Thou and I
Had mingled the fresh thoughts that early die,
Once flowering—never more!—And thou wert gone!
Who could give back my youth, my spirit free,
Or be in aught again what thou hadst been to me?

### LXXIII

And yet I wept thee not, thou true and brave!
I could not weep!—there gather'd round thy name 650
Too deep a passion!—*thou* denied a grave!³²
*Thou*, with the blight flung on thy soldier's fame!
Had I not known thy heart from childhood's time?
Thy heart of hearts?—and couldst thou die for crime?
—No! had all earth decreed that death of shame,
I would have set, against all earth's decree,
Th' inalienable trust of my firm soul in thee!

### LXXIV

There are swift hours in life—strong, rushing hours,
That do the work of tempests in their might!
They shake down things that stood as rocks and towers 660
Unto th' undoubting mind;—they pour in light
Where it but startles—like a burst of day
For which th' uprooting of an oak makes way;—
They sweep the colouring mists from off our sight,
They touch with fire, thought's graven page, the roll
Stamp'd with past years—and lo! it shrivels as a scroll!³³

### LXXV

And this was of such hours!—the sudden flow
Of my soul's tide seem'd whelming me; the glare[34]
Of the red flames, yet rocking to and fro,
Scorch'd up my heart with breathless thirst for air,                     670
And solitude, and freedom. It had been
Well with me then, in some vast desert scene,
To pour my voice out, for the winds to bear
On with them, wildly questioning the sky,
Fiercely th' untroubled stars, of man's dim destiny.

### LXXVI

I would have call'd, adjuring the dark cloud;
To the most ancient Heavens I would have said
—"Speak to me! show me truth!"[35]—through night aloud
I would have cried to him, the newly dead,
"Come back! and show me truth!"—My spirit seem'd                    680
Grasping for some free burst, its darkness teem'd
With such pent storms of thought!—again I fled—
I fled, a refuge from man's face to gain,
Scarce conscious when I paus'd, entering a lonely fane.

### LXXVII

A mighty minster, dim, and proud, and vast!
Silence was round the sleepers, whom its floor
Shut in the grave;[36] a shadow of the past,
A memory of the sainted steps that wore
Erewhile its gorgeous pavement, seem'd to brood
Like mist upon the stately solitude,                                     690
A halo of sad fame to mantle o'er
Its white sepulchral forms of mail-clad men,
And all was hush'd as night in some deep Alpine glen.

### LXXVIII

More hush'd, far more!—for there the wind sweeps by,
Or the woods tremble to the streams' loud play!
Here a strange echo made my very sigh
Seem for the place too much a sound of day!
Too much my footstep broke the moonlight, fading,
Yet arch through arch in one soft flow pervading;
And I stood still:—prayer, chant, had died away,                       700
Yet past me floated a funereal breath
Of incense.—I stood still—as before God and death!

### LXXIX

For thick ye girt me round, ye long-departed![37]
Dust—imaged form—with cross, and shield, and crest;
It seem'd as if your ashes would have started,
Had a wild voice burst forth above your rest!
Yet ne'er, perchance, did worshipper of yore
Bear to your thrilling presence what *I* bore
Of wrath—doubt—anguish—battling in the breast!
   I could have pour'd out words, on that pale air,        710
To make your proud tombs ring:—no, no! I could not *there!*

### LXXX

Not midst those aisles, through which a thousand years
Mutely as clouds and reverently had swept;
Not by those shrines, which yet the trace of tears
And kneeling votaries on their marble kept!
Ye were too mighty in your pomp of gloom
And trophied age, O temple, altar, tomb!
And you, ye dead!—for in that faith ye slept,
   Whose weight had grown a mountain's on my heart,
Which could not *there* be loos'd.—I turn'd me to depart.    720

### LXXXI

I turn'd—what glimmer'd faintly on my sight,
Faintly, yet brightening, as a wreath of snow
Seen through dissolving haze?—The moon, the night,
Had waned, and dawn pour'd in;—grey, shadowy, slow,
Yet day-spring still!—a solemn hue it caught,
Piercing the storied windows, darkly fraught
With stoles and draperies of imperial glow;
   And soft, and sad, that colouring gleam was thrown,
Where, pale, a pictur'd form above the altar shone.

### LXXXII

*Thy* form, Thou Son of God!—a wrathful deep,        730
With foam, and cloud, and tempest, round Thee spread,
And such a weight of night!—a night, when sleep
From the fierce rocking of the billows fled.
A bark show'd dim beyond Thee, with its mast
Bow'd, and its rent sail shivering to the blast;
But, like a spirit in thy gliding tread,
   Thou, as o'er glass, didst walk that stormy sea
Through rushing winds, which left a silent path for Thee.[38]

### LXXXIII

So still thy white robes fell!—no breath of air
Within their long and slumberous folds had sway!          740
So still the waves of parted, shadowy hair
From thy clear brow flow'd droopingly away!
Dark were the Heavens above Thee, Saviour!—dark
The gulfs, Deliverer! round the straining bark!
But Thou!—o'er all thine aspect and array
Was pour'd one stream of pale, broad, silvery light—
Thou wert the single star of that all-shrouding night!

### LXXXIV

Aid for one sinking!—Thy lone brightness gleam'd
On his wild face, just lifted o'er the wave,
With its worn, fearful, *human* look that seem'd          750
To cry through surge and blast—"I perish—save!"
Not to the winds—not vainly!—Thou wert nigh,
Thy hand was stretch'd to fainting agony,
Even in the portals of th' unquiet grave!
O Thou that art the life! and yet didst bear
Too much of mortal woe to turn from mortal prayer!

### LXXXV

But was it not a thing to rise on death,
With its remember'd light, that face of thine,
Redeemer! dimm'd by this world's misty breath,
Yet mournfully, mysteriously divine?          760
—Oh! that calm, sorrowful, prophetic eye,
With its dark depths of grief, love, majesty!
And the pale glory of the brow!—a shrine
Where Power sat veil'd, yet shedding softly round
What told that *Thou* couldst be but for a time uncrown'd!

### LXXXVI

And more than all, the Heaven of that sad smile!
The lip of mercy, our immortal trust!
Did not that look, that very look, erewhile,
Pour its o'ershadow'd beauty on the dust?
Wert Thou not such when earth's dark cloud hung o'er Thee?          770
Surely thou wert!—my heart grew hush'd before Thee,
Sinking with all its passions, as the gust
Sank at thy voice, along its billowy way:—
—What had I there to do, but kneel, and weep, and pray?

### LXXXVII

Amidst the stillness rose my spirit's cry
Amidst the dead—"By that full cup of woe,
Press'd from the fruitage of mortality,
Saviour! for Thee—give light! that I may know
If by *thy* will, in thine all-healing name,
Men cast down human hearts to blighting shame,                          780
And early death—and say, if this be so,
Where then is mercy?—whither shall we flee,
So unallied to hope, save by our hold on Thee?

### LXXXVIII

But didst Thou not, the deep sea brightly treading,
Lift from despair that struggler with the wave?
And wert Thou not, sad tears, yet awful, shedding,
Beheld, a weeper at a mortal's grave?[39]
And is this weight of anguish, which they bind
On life, this searing to the quick of mind,
That but to God its own free path would crave,                          790
This crushing out of hope, and love, and youth,
*Thy* will indeed?—Give light! that I may know the truth!

### LXXXIX

For my sick soul is darken'd unto death,
With shadows from the suffering it hath seen
The strong foundations of mine ancient faith
Sink from beneath me—whereon shall I lean?
—Oh! if from thy pure lips was wrung the sigh
Of the dust's anguish! if like man to die,
—And earth round *him* shuts heavily—hath been
Even to *Thee* bitter, aid me!—guide me!—turn                           800
My wild and wandering thoughts back from their starless bourne!"[40]

### XC

And calm'd I rose:—but how the while had risen
Morn's orient sun, dissolving mist and shade!
—Could there indeed be wrong, or chain, or prison,
In the bright world such radiance might pervade?
It fill'd the fane, it mantled the pale form
Which rose before me through the pictured storm,
Even the grey tombs it kindled, and array'd
With life!—how hard to see thy race begun,
And think man wakes to grief, wakening to *thee*, O Sun![41]             810

### XCI

I sought my home again:—and thou, my child,
There at thy play beneath yon ancient pine,
With eyes, whose lightning laughter[42] hath beguil'd
A thousand pangs, thence flashing joy to mine;
Thou in thy mother's arms, a babe, didst meet
My coming with young smiles, which yet, though sweet,
Seem'd on my soul all mournfully to shine,
And ask a happier heritage for thee,
Than but in turn the blight of human hope to see.

### XCII

Now sport, for thou are free—the bright birds chasing,          820
Whose wings waft star-like gleams from tree to tree;
Or with the fawn, thy swift wood-playmate racing,
Sport on, my joyous child! for thou art free!
Yes, on that day I took thee to my heart,
And inly vow'd, for thee a better part
To choose; that so thy sunny bursts of glee
Should wake no more dim thoughts of far-seen woe,
But, gladdening fearless eyes, flow on—as now they flow.

### XCIII[43]

Thou hast a rich world round thee:—Mighty shades
Weaving their gorgeous tracery o'er thy head,          830
With the light melting through their high arcades,
As through a pillar'd cloister's:[44] but the dead
Sleep not beneath; nor doth the sunbeam pass
To marble shrines through rainbow-tinted glass;
Yet thou, by fount and forest-murmur led
To worship, thou art blest!—to thee is shown
Earth in her holy pomp, deck'd for her God alone.

[1] Ye places of my calm hopes, / For ever must I leave you! /. . . / Yet it is not ambition or vain glory that moves me / But the spirit's voice alone.
  Schiller, *Die Jungfrau von Orleans* (The Maid of Orleans, 1801), Prologue 4.11–12, 16–18; Joan of Arc's voice. Not in MS.
[2] Not in MS. In Coleridge's play, also set during Philip II's Inquisition, these lines (2.2.6–8) are spoken by Alvar, a Protestant returned from exile and imprisonment to confront the brother who betrayed him in order to win Alvar's beloved. Opening at Drury Lane, January 1813, *Remorse* was published the same year, and was among Coleridge's notable successes; it was produced more than forty times by the end of 1823.
[3] "Advertisement" continues in MS] . . ., and is intended more as the *record of a Mind*, than as a tale abounding with romantic and extraordinary incident.
  This intention recalls Wordsworth's disdain of the poetry of "extraordinary incident," and his effort to present poems in which "the feeling therein developed gives importance to the

action and situation, and not the action and situation to the feeling" (Preface to *Lyrical Ballads*, 1800).

[4] 6, MS] Are pass'd for ever, and . . .

[5] Cf. Psalm 55: "Oh that I had wings like a dove! for then would I fly away, and be at rest" (6), uttered by David, seeking escape from the wicked city. FH uses this line as the epigraph for *The Wings of the Dove*, in *The Forest Sanctuary &c* (2d. ed., 1829), and De Quincey voices it in his *Confessions of an English Opium-Eater* (1821), a text FH knew.

[6] The canes, in some parts of the American forests, form a thick undergrowth for many hundred miles.—See Hodgson's *Letters from North America*, vol. i. p. 242. [FH]

Adam Hodgson, Letter XIV, in *Letters from North America, Written During a Tour in the United States and Canada*, 2 vols. (London: Hurst, Robinson, 1824), 1.242 note.

19, MS] Away, and be at rest!—for I . . .

22–23, MS] A sighing breath, to which the young bright wave / And the Canes tremble by the Lake,—hath power

[7] Such a shell as Wordsworth has beautifully described.

> "I have seen
> A curious Child, who dwelt upon a tract
> Of inland ground, applying to his ear
> The convolutions of a smooth-lipped Shell;
> To which, in silence hushed, his very soul
> Listened intensely, and his countenance soon
> Brightened with joy; for murmurings from within
> Were heard,—sonorous cadences! whereby,
> To his belief, the Monitor expressed
> Mysterious union with its native Sea.
> —Even such a Shell the Universe itself
> Is to the ear of Faith."—*The Excursion*. [FH]

*The Excursion* (1814), bk. 4 ("Despondency Corrected"), 1149–57 (cf. 4.1132–42 in the 1850 text).

MS] This stanza (1.5) follows:

> Fade from my dreams, bright Land! my sunny Land,
> Far o'er the dark and many-sounding Sea!
> With all thy Vines and glistening Myrtles, fann'd
> By the soft South, let me not think of Thee!
> For then the deep and inborn Love I drew
> Ev'n from thy bosom, gushes forth anew,
> Melting away my Spirit, which to free
> From cankering bonds, I wooed the Surge and Wind
> And left my Fathers' Tombs for evermore behind!

[8] 46–53, MS]

> A blighted name! I hear the Wind—'tis bringing
> A murmur, all the Desert's!—wide around,
> Forests and Waters in their strength are springing
> With nought in sight which hath been tam'd, or bound,
> Or check'd by Man!—I hear the Cedars waving
> And the great River his Savannahs laving,
> With a rejoicing flow. What should the sound
> Of mortal name do *here*, where . . .

[9] When the Moors invaded (several centuries earlier), Christian Visigoths retreated to the mountains in the north; cf. 2.171–72.

[10] MS] This stanza (1.12) follows:

> Many there are that live and grieve alone;
> Few—some—from whose lock'd bosoms Misery's cry
> Rends not its fitful way, tho' but the moan

That passes in the wandering Wind, reply.
Yet must we speak!—and e'en in *this* the Mind
O'erwrought to Visions by its pangs, can find
That which it needs—a tone of Sympathy!
Hear me then Deserts!—answer me with Sounds!
Man's woe must find a Voice to pass your loneliest bounds.

[11] "I recollect hearing a traveller, of poetical temperament, expressing the kind of horror which he felt on beholding, on the banks of the Missouri, an oak of prodigious size, which had been, in a manner, overpowered by an enormous wild grape-vine. The vine had clasped its huge folds round the trunk, and from thence had wound about every branch and twig, until the mighty tree had withered in its embrace. It seemed like Laocoon struggling ineffectually in the hideous coils of the monster Python."—*Bracebridge Hall*. Chapter on Forest Trees. [FH]

[Washington Irving], *Bracebridge Hall or The Humourists, A Medley by "Geoffrey Crayon, Gent."* (1822). For profaning Apollo's temple, Laocoön and his sons were strangled by a serpent.

[12] 115–17, MS] And in the Hamlets every stirring tone / Of Life was hush'd: their Dwellers were away / Thronging the City's Gates that soft, bright, golden Day.

[13] 131, MS] . . . in chill and secret . . . / in lone and secret . . .
This stanza (1.18) follows:

> To this Man brings his Brother!—forth they came,
> And stillness fell on Life's wide-heaving Sea
> Around:—ev'n such as falls on Nature's frame—
> —But that is ere the Lightnings fierce and free
> Leap from their Cloud—or ere the Earthquake's Wrath
> Shakes down the Sovereign Cities in its path—
> This calm presag'd no fiery burst to be:
> Yet seems it fearful, when a Million's breath
> Is chain'd, and its One Soul bound in the thought of Death!

[14] 143, MS] Had been crush'd out
MS] This stanza (1.20) follows:

> There was a Father of that band, accused
> E'en so Men whisper'd—by his Child, his Son!
> He lifted his dim eyes, to [Day] Light unused,
> Then dropp'd their heavy lids, as if to shun
> The Sight of human faces, at whose look
> It seem'd as all that liv'd within him shook.
> —Perchance they woke some image of the one
> Which he had lov'd, and watch'd in silent joy,
> And press'd with his fond lips—as I do thine, my Boy!

[15] 146, MS] For their false creeds a fiery death to die!
152–53, MS] Grew still a moment as they pass'd, then bright / With Life's ev'n quicken'd sense, flash'd round in joyous light.

[16] "For now we see through a glass, darkly; but then face to face: now I know in part; but then shall I know even as I am known" (1 Corinthians 13.12).

[17] 194–96, MS] A sound went up at times of chaunted prayer, / A heavy Banner droop'd upon the air, / Borne on, as priest and Crucifix went by

[18] MS] This stanza (1.28) follows:

> Thou, my Soul's Brother! in the garb of shame,
> Led—and with that bright festal Sun on high!
> To the dark parting!—I, of those that came
> Forth from their quiet homes to see thee die,
> And to bear back, for their still waveless life
> An impulse from the Memory of the Strife,

> The pangs—*thy* pangs—thy fiery Agony!
> A tale to tell at purple Eve's decline,
> When they might rest beneath their Olive and their Vine!

[19] For a most interesting account of the Spanish Protestants, and the heroic devotion with which they met the spirit of persecution in the sixteenth century, see the Quarterly Review, No. 57, art. Quin's Visit to Spain. [FH]

Review of Michael Joseph Quin, *A Visit to Spain* (London, 1823), *Quarterly* 29.57 (April 1823): 246–56. The *autos-da-fě* recounted took place 1159–60.

The name of the comrade in Peru recalls Alvar Fañez, brother-companion of El Cid.

[20] Recounted in Matthew 26.30, Mark 14.26, Luke 22.34; this Soul-Searching God (226) contrasts with the unholy Inquisition; cf. *Abencerrage* 3.565.

[21] An image of fraternal love in Genesis: Esau weeps on his brother Jacob's neck (33.4), and Joseph on his brother Benjamin's (45.14).

[22] "A priest, named Gonzalez, had, among other proselytes, gained over two young females, his sisters, to the protestant faith. All three were confined in the dungeons of the Inquisition. The torture, repeatedly applied, could not draw from them the least evidence against their religious associates. Every artifice was employed to obtain a recantation from the two sisters, since the constancy and learning of Gonzalez precluded all hopes of a theological victory. Their answer, if not exactly logical, is wonderfully simple and affecting. 'We will die in the faith of our brother: he is too wise [clever] to be wrong, and too good to deceive us.' The three stakes on which they died were near each other. The priest had been gagged till the moment of lighting up the wood. The few minutes that he was allowed to speak he employed in comforting his sisters, with whom he sung the 109th Psalm, till the flames smothered their voices."—*Ibid.* [FH]

*Quarterly* 29 (255–56). David's Psalm ("Hold not thy peace, O God of my praise") calls on God for aid and vengeance. The sisters' names honor mystic and church reformer Theresa (1515–82), the most famous of Spain's female saints, and Inez de Castro (d. 1355), mistress of Prince Pedro of Portugal, murdered on orders from Pedro's father. After his accession, Pedro displayed her body and had it crowned (see *The Coronation of Inez de Castro*, in *Songs of the Affections*).

[23] The names, not only of the immediate victims of the Inquisition, were devoted to infamy, but those of all their relations were branded with the same indelible stain, which was likewise to descend as an inheritance to their latest posterity. [FH. See *Quarterly* 29 (257)]

[24] MS] noble

[25] MS] Of thy young virgin Soul

[26] Evoking Cain's murder of Abel (Genesis 4.9); cf. 429, below.

[27] An event from the late 8th c. B.C. recounted in 2 Kings 18–19: an angel destroys an Assyrian army besieging Jerusalem (Salem). Byron's famous poem on the subject, *The Destruction of Sennacherib*, was published in *Hebrew Melodies* (1815).

[28] MS] —the fearful sentence read;

[29] The piles erected for these executions were without the towns, and the final scene of an Auto da Fe was sometimes, from the length of the preceding ceremonies, delayed till midnight. [FH]

[30] MS] Variant stanza (1.59):

> Why came I there?—oh! who shall answer?—Why
> Doth he that watches by a bed of Death,
> Fix down his frozen glance on Agony,
> And take dread lessons from each struggling breath?
> —I was as one that feels a hurrying wave
> Draw his Bark on, and hath no strength to save,
> Tho' the nigh torrent shake the Gulphs beneath.
> It might be—yet the power to will seem'd o'er —
> That my Soul yearn'd to hear the Voice it lov'd once more!

Followed by this stanza (1.60):

> So near, and yet he knew not!—could I go,
> And bid him no farewell?—In our young days,
> Ev'n from our Sports we never parted so,
> And this was his last hour!—but strong amaze
> Was on me like a chain—I could not break
> Its icy rivets from my Soul, to speak.
> Silent I stood—and with a stony gaze,
> Watching his features, as the Night-wind blew,
> And torchlight, or the Morn's, pass'd o'er their marble hue.

[31] The Inquisition deployed spies to report heresy.

[32] Heretics were denied burial in consecrated ground.

[33] MS] This stanza (1.81) follows:

> Our Souls have many Wakeners. Gentle some,
> And low in tone, as whispers of the Morn,
> That bring in sounds of leaves, or wild bees' hum,
> A friend's kind Voice—a breath of flowers new-born.
> Some of the Midnight—fearful! with the dash
> Perchance of bursting waves, or sudden crash
> Of our ancestral Walls, by Time o'erworn!
> Then we start up to Darkness and the blast—
> —Stern summonings are these—mine had been like the last.

[34] 667–68, MS] Crowds were around me still—the restless flow / Of Life went sounding by—th'unquiet glare

[35] For one of the most powerful and impressive pictures perhaps ever drawn, of a young mind struggling against habit and superstition in its first aspirations after truth, see the admirable Letters from Spain by Don Leucadio Doblado. [FH]

The pseudonym of Joseph Blanco White (1775–1841), whose "delightful writings," FH told a friend, gave her "the idea of *The Forest Sanctuary*" (*CM* 1.105); he and FH frequently corresponded, especially about Spanish literature (Lawrence 310). Born in Seville, of Irish Catholic descent, White left the family business to train for the priesthood, but Enlightenment tracts led to doubts. He welcomed French intervention in Spain but soon supported the resistance, then escaped to England, where he became an anti-French propagandist for the government, though he associated with liberal political circles. He later converted to Anglicanism and became an anti-Catholic campaigner. He edited a journal, *El Español*, from 1810–14 for Whig liberal Lord Holland, who supported the Spanish constitutionalists against monarchal corruption.

[36] The wealthy and powerful secured burial beneath the church floors.

[37] "You walk from end to end over a floor of tomb-stones, inlaid in brass with the forms of the departed—mitres and crosiers, and spears, and shields, and helmets, all mingled together—all worn into glass-like smoothness by the feet and the knees of long departed worshippers. Around, on every side—each in their separate chapel—sleep undisturbed from age to age the venerable ashes of the holiest or the loftiest that of old came thither to worship—their images and their dying prayers sculptured [and painted above] the resting-places of their remains."—From a beautiful description of ancient Spanish Cathedrals, in Peter's Letters to his Kinsfolk. [FH]

John Gibson Lockhart, *Peter's Letters to his Kinsfolk*, 3d ed.; 3 vols. (Edinburgh: William Blackwood, 1819), 3.158–59. A chief contributor to *Blackwood's*, in which FH was publishing, in 1825 he became editor of the *Quarterly Review*, in which FH had been warmly reviewed.

[38] Cf. Mark 6.45–52; see FH's *Christ Stilling the Tempest*, in *The Amulet* (1827), 267.

[39] "Jesus wept" at the grave of Lazarus before raising him from the dead (John 11.35).

[40] MS] This stanza (1.97) follows:

> "Let me not fall from Thee by this despair,
> Which coils around me with its drowning hold!

Give hope! give Knowledge to my thirst and prayer,
Knowledge of Thee, as on the Earth of old
Thou wert, and art in Heaven!—Not such as Men,
Colouring their own fierce deeds to mortal ken,
Have dar'd Thine image by their own to mould!
—Art Thou not He, that taught us, when we pray'd,
Ev'n by a Father's name to ask a Father's aid?"

[41] A conventional pun on "Son" (frequent in *Paradise Lost*), as well as, in lowercase, an antic-
ipation of the speaker's return to his son.

[42] "E'l *lampeggiar* de l'angelico riso."—Petrarch. [FH]

And the lightning of her angelic smile; *Rime* 292 (6), a sonnet of longing for his dead
beloved, Laura. FH also weaves in Wordsworthian elements of "natural" childhood.

[43] Not in MS

[44] "Sometimes, their discourse was held in the deep shades of moss-grown forests, whose
gloom and interlaced boughs first suggested that Gothic architecture, beneath whose pointed
arches, where they had studied and prayed, the parti-coloured windows shed a tinged light;
scenes, which the gleams of sunshine, penetrating the deep foliage, and flickering on the varie-
gated turf below, might have recalled to their memory."—Webster's Oration on the Landing
of the Pilgrim Fathers in New England.—See Hodgson's Letters from North America, vol. ii.
p. 305 [FH; 304–5]

Daniel Webster gave his famous *Oration* on the bicentennial of the landing (1820). FH's
poem on this subject, with a similar title, is one of her most famous in the United States.
Webster is describing "the teachers and leaders" of the Plymouth Colony.

## Part Second

*Wie diese treue liebe seele*
*Von ihrem Glauben Voll,*
*Der ganz allein*
*Ihr selig machend ist, sich heilig quäle,*
*Das sie den liebsten Mann verloren halten soll!*

FAUST[1]

*I never shall smile more—but all my days*
*Walk with still footsteps and with humble eyes,*
*An everlasting hymn within my soul.*

WILSON[2]

I

Bring me the sounding of the torrent-water,
With yet a nearer swell—fresh breeze, awake![3]
And river, darkening ne'er with hues of slaughter
Thy wave's pure silvery green,—and shining lake,
Spread far before my cabin, with thy zone
Of ancient woods, ye chainless things and lone!
Send voices through the forest aisles,[4] and make
Glad music round me, that my soul may dare,
Cheer'd by such tones, to look back on a dungeon's air!

II

Oh, Indian° hunter of the desert's race!                    *New World*   10
That with the spear at times, or bended bow,
Dost cross my footsteps in thy fiery chase
Of the swift elk or blue hill's flying roe;
Thou that beside the red night-fire thou heapest,
Beneath the cedars and the star-light sleepest,
Thou know'st not, wanderer—never may'st thou know!
Of the dark holds° wherewith man cumbers earth,              *prison cells*
To shut from human eyes the dancing seasons' mirth.[5]

III

There, fetter'd down from day, to think the while
How bright in Heaven the festal sun is glowing,                       20
Making earth's loneliest places, with his smile,
Flush like the rose; and how the streams are flowing
With sudden sparkles through the shadowy grass,
And water-flowers, all trembling as they pass;
And how the rich dark summer-trees are bowing
With their full foliage;—this to know, and pine
Bound unto midnight's heart, seems a stern lot—'twas mine.

IV

Wherefore was this?—Because my soul had drawn
Light from the book whose words are grav'd in light!
There, at its well-head, had I found the dawn,                        30
And day, and noon of freedom:—but too bright
It shines on that which man to man hath given,
And call'd the truth—the very truth, from Heaven!
And therefore seeks he, in his brother's sight,
To cast the mote;[6] and therefore strives to bind
With his strong chains to earth, what is not earth's—the mind![7]

V

It is a weary and a bitter task
Back from the lip the burning word to keep,
And to shut out Heaven's air with falsehood's mask,
And in the dark urn of the soul to heap                               40
Indignant feelings—making even of thought
A buried treasure, which may but be sought
When shadows are abroad—and night—and sleep.
I might not brook it long—and thus was thrown
Into that grave-like cell, to wither there alone.[8]

### VI

And I a child of danger, whose delights
Were on dark hills and many-sounding seas—
I, that amidst the Cordillera heights°                        *Andes*
Had given Castilian° banners to the breeze,        *(Christian kingdom)*
And the full circle of the rainbow seen                        50
There, on the snows;⁹ and in my country been
A mountain wanderer, from the Pyrenees
To the Morena crags—how left I not
Life, or the soul's life, quench'd, on that sepulchral spot?

### VII

Because *Thou* didst not leave me, oh, my God!
Thou wert with those that bore the truth of old
Into the deserts from the oppressor's rod,
And made the caverns of the rock their fold;
And in the hidden chambers of the dead,
Our guiding lamp with fire immortal fed;                        60
And met when stars met, by their beams to hold
The free heart's communing with Thee,—and Thou
Wert in the midst, felt, own'd—the strengthener then as now!

### VIII

Yet once I sank. Alas! man's wavering mind!
Wherefore and whence the gusts that o'er it blow?
How they bear with them, floating uncombin'd,
The shadows of the past, that come and go,
As o'er the deep the old long-buried things,
Which a storm's working to the surface brings!
Is the reed shaken,—and must *we* be so,                        70
With every wind?¹⁰—So, Father! must we be,
Till we can fix undimm'd our stedfast eyes on Thee.

### IX

Once my soul died within me. What had thrown
That sickness o'er it?—Even a passing thought
Of a clear spring, whose side, with flowers o'ergrown,
Fondly and oft my boyish steps had sought!
Perchance the damp roof's water-drops, that fell
Just then, low tinkling through my vaulted cell,
Intensely heard amidst the stillness, caught
Some tone from memory, of the music, welling                        80
Ever with that fresh rill, from its deep rocky dwelling.

### X

But so my spirit's fever'd longings wrought,
Wakening, it might be, to the faint, sad sound,
That from the darkness of the walls they brought
A lov'd scene round me, visibly around.[11]
Yes! kindling, spreading, brightening, hue by hue,
Like stars from midnight, through the gloom it grew,
That haunt of youth, hope, manhood!—till the bound
Of my shut cavern seem'd dissolv'd, and I
Girt by the solemn hills and burning pomp of sky.[12]                    90

### XI

I look'd—and lo! the clear, broad river flowing,
Past the old Moorish ruin on the steep,[13]
The lone tower dark against a Heaven all glowing,
Like seas of glass and fire![14]—I saw the sweep
Of glorious woods far down the mountain side,
And their still shadows in the gleaming tide,
And the red evening on its waves asleep;
And midst the scene—oh! more than all—there smil'd
My child's fair face, and hers, the mother of my child!

### XII

With their soft eyes of love and gladness rais'd                        100
Up to the flushing sky, as when we stood
Last by that river, and in silence gaz'd
On the rich world of sunset:—but a flood
Of sudden tenderness my soul oppress'd,
And I rush'd forward with a yearning breast,
To clasp—alas! a vision!—Wave and wood,
And gentle faces, lifted in the light
Of day's last hectic blush, all melted from my sight.

### XIII

Then darkness!—oh! th' unutterable gloom
That seem'd as narrowing round me, making less                          110
And less my dungeon, when, with all its bloom,
That bright dream vanish'd from my loneliness!
It floated off, the beautiful!—yet left
Such deep thirst in my soul, that thus bereft,
I lay down, sick with passion's vain excess,
And pray'd to die.—How oft would sorrow weep
Her weariness to death, if he might come like sleep!

XIV

But I was rous'd—and how?—It is no tale
Even midst *thy* shades, thou wilderness, to tell!
I would not have my boy's young cheek made pale,              120
Nor haunt his sunny rest with what befel
In that drear prison-house.—His eyes must grow
More dark with thought, more earnest his fair brow,
More high his heart in youthful strength must swell;
So shall it fitly burn when all is told:—
Let childhood's radiant mist the free child yet enfold!

XV

It is enough that through such heavy hours,
As wring us by our fellowship of clay,
I liv'd, and undegraded. We have powers
To snatch th' oppressor's bitter joy away!                   130
Shall the wild Indian, for his savage fame,
Laugh and expire, and shall not Truth's high name
Bear up her martyrs with all-conquering sway?
It is enough that Torture may be vain—
I had seen Alvar die—the strife was won from Pain.

XVI[15]

And faint not, heart of man! though years wane slow!
  There have been those that from the deepest caves,
  And cells of night, and fastnesses below
  The stormy dashing of the ocean-waves,
  Down, farther down than gold lies hid, have nurs'd         140
  A quenchless hope, and watch'd their time, and burst
  On the bright day, like wakeners from the graves!
  I was of such at last!—unchain'd I trod
This green earth, taking back my freedom from my God!

XVII

That was an hour to send its fadeless trace
  Down life's far sweeping tide!—A dim, wild night,
  Like sorrow, hung upon the soft moon's face,
  Yet how my heart leap'd in her blessed light!
  The shepherd's light—the sailor's on the sea—
  The hunter's homeward from the mountains free,             150
  Where its lone smile makes tremulously bright
  The thousand streams!—I could but gaze through tears—
Oh! what a sight is Heaven, thus first beheld for years!

### XVIII

The rolling clouds!—they have the whole blue space
Above to sail in—all the dome of sky!
My soul shot with them in their breezy race
O'er star and gloom!—but I had yet to fly,
As flies the hunted wolf. A secret spot,
And strange, I knew—the sunbeam knew it not;—
Wildest of all the savage glens that lie                               160
In far sierras, hiding their deep springs,
And travers'd but by storms, or sounding eagles' wings.

### XIX

Ay, and I met the storm there!—I had gain'd
The covert's heart with swift and stealthy tread:
A moan went past me, and the dark trees rain'd
Their autumn foliage rustling on my head;
A moan—a hollow gust—and there I stood
Girt with majestic night, and ancient wood,
And foaming water.—Thither might have fled
The mountain Christian with his faith of yore,                         170
When Afric's tambour shook the ringing western shore!

### XX

But through the black ravine the storm came swelling,
—Mighty thou art amidst the hills, thou blast!
In thy lone course the kingly cedars felling,
Like plumes upon the path of battle cast!—
A rent oak thunder'd down beside my cave,
Booming it rush'd, as booms a deep sea-wave;
A falcon soar'd; a startled wild-deer pass'd;
A far-off bell toll'd faintly through the roar:—
How my glad spirit swept forth with the winds once more!               180

### XXI

And with the arrowy lightnings!—for they flash'd,
Smiting the branches in their fitful play,
And brightly shivering where the torrents dash'd
Up, even to crag and eagle's nest, their spray!
And there to stand amidst the pealing strife,
The strong pines groaning with tempestuous life,
And all the mountain-voices on their way,—
Was it not joy?—'twas joy in rushing might,
After those years that wove but one long dead of night![16]

### XXII

There came a softer hour, a lovelier moon,       190
And lit me to my home of youth again,
Through the dim chesnut shade, where oft at noon,
By the fount's flashing[17] burst, my head had lain
In gentle sleep: but now I pass'd as one
That may not pause where wood-streams whispering run,
Or light sprays tremble to a bird's wild strain,
Because th' avenger's voice is in the wind,
The foe's quick, rustling step close on the leaves behind.

### XXIII

My home of youth!—oh! if indeed to part
With the soul's lov'd ones be a mournful thing,      200
When we go forth in buoyancy of heart,
And bearing all the glories of our spring
For life to breathe on,—is it less to meet,
When these are faded?—who shall call it sweet?
—Even though love's mingling tears may haply bring
Balm as they fall, too well their heavy showers
Teach us how much is lost of all that once was ours!

### XXIV

Not by the sunshine, with its golden glow,
Nor the green earth, nor yet the laughing sky,
Nor the faint flower-scents,[18] as they come and go     210
In the soft air, like music wandering by;
—Oh! not by these, th'unfailing, are we taught
How time and sorrow on our frames have wrought,
But by the sadden'd eye, the darken'd brow
Of kindred aspects, and the long dim gaze,
Which tells us *we* are chang'd,—how chang'd from other days!

### XXV

Before my father—in my place of birth,
I stood an alien. On the very floor
Which oft had trembled to my boyish mirth,
The love that rear'd me, knew my face no more!     220
There hung the antique armour, helm and crest,
Whose every stain woke childhood in my breast,
There droop'd the banner, with the marks it bore
Of Paynim° spears; and I, the worn in frame     *Pagan, Muslim*
And heart, what there was I?—another and the same!

### XXVI

Then bounded in a boy, with clear dark eye—
How should *he* know his father?—when we parted,
From the soft cloud which mantles infancy,
His soul, just wakening into wonder, darted
Its first looks round. Him follow'd one, the bride                    230
Of my young days, the wife how lov'd and tried!
Her glance met mine—I could not speak—she started
With a bewilder'd gaze;—until there came
Tears to my burning eyes, and from my lips her name.

### XXVII

She knew me then!—I murmur'd "*Leonor!*"[19]
And her heart answer'd!—oh! the voice is known
First from all else, and swiftest to restore
Love's buried images with one low tone,
That strikes like lightning, when the cheek is faded,
And the brow heavily with thought o'ershaded,                        240
And all the brightness from the aspect gone!
—Upon my breast she sunk, when doubt was fled,
Weeping as those may weep, that meet in woe and dread.

### XXVIII

For there we might not rest. Alas! to leave
Those native towers, and know that they must fall
By slow decay, and none remain to grieve
When the weeds cluster'd on the lonely wall![20]
We were the last—my boy and I—the last
Of a long line which brightly thence had pass'd!
My father bless'd me as I left his hall—                             250
With his deep tones and sweet, tho' full of years,
He bless'd me there, and bath'd my child's young head with tears.

### XXIX

I had brought sorrow on his grey hairs down,
And cast the darkness of my branded name
(For so *he* deem'd it) on the clear renown,
My own ancestral heritage of fame.
And yet he bless'd me!—Father! if the dust
Lie on those lips benign, my spirit's trust
Is to behold thee yet, where grief and shame
Dim the bright day no more; and thou wilt know                       260
That not thro' guilt thy son thus bow'd thine age with woe!

### XXX

And thou, my Leonor! that unrepining,
If sad in soul, didst quit all else for me,
When stars—the stars that earliest rise—are shining,
How their soft glance unseals each thought of thee!
For on our flight they smil'd; their dewy rays,
Thro' the last olives, lit thy tearful gaze
Back to the home we never more might see;
So pass'd we on, like earth's first exiles, turning
Fond looks where hung the sword above their Eden burning.[21]      270

### XXXI

It was a woe to say—"Farewell, my Spain!
The sunny and the vintage land, farewell!"
—I could have died upon the battle plain
For thee, my country! but I might not dwell
In thy sweet vales, at peace.—The voice of song
Breathes, with the myrtle scent, thy hills along;
The citron's glow is caught from shade and dell;
But what are these?—upon thy flowery sod
I might not kneel, and pour my free thoughts out to God!

### XXXII

O'er the blue deep I fled, the chainless deep!—      280
Strange heart of man! that ev'n midst woe swells high,
When thro' the foam he sees his proud bark sweep,
Flinging out joyous gleams to wave and sky!
Yes! it swells high, whate'er he leaves behind;
His spirit rises with the rising wind;
For, wedded to the far futurity,
On, on, it bears him ever, and the main
Seems rushing, like his hope, some happier shore to gain.

### XXXIII

Not thus is woman. Closely *her* still heart
Doth twine itself with ev'n each lifeless thing,      290
Which, long remember'd, seem'd to bear its part
In her calm joys. For ever would she cling,
A brooding dove,[20] to that sole spot of earth
Where she hath loved, and given her children birth,
And heard their first sweet voices. There may Spring
Array no path, renew no flower, no leaf,
But hath its breath of home, its claim to farewell grief.

### XXXIV

I look'd on Leonor,—and if there seem'd
A cloud of more than pensiveness to rise
In the faint smiles that o'er her features gleam'd,                    300
And the soft darkness of her serious eyes,
Misty with tender gloom, I call'd it nought
But the fond exile's pang, a lingering thought
Of her own vale, with all its melodies
And living light of streams. Her soul would rest
Beneath your shades, I said, bowers of the gorgeous west![23]

### XXXV

Oh! could we live in visions! could we hold
Delusion faster, longer, to our breast,
When it shuts from us, with its mantle's fold,
That which we see not, and are therefore blest!                    310
But they, our lov'd and loving, they to whom
We have spread out our souls in joy and gloom,
*Their* looks and accents, unto ours address'd,
Have been a language of familiar tone
Too long to breathe, at last, dark sayings and unknown.

### XXXVI

I told my heart 'twas but the exile's woe
Which press'd on that sweet bosom;—I deceiv'd
My heart but half:—a whisper faint and low,
Haunting it ever, and at times believ'd,
Spoke of some deeper cause. How oft we seem                    320
Like those that dream, and *know* the while they dream,
Midst the soft falls of airy voices griev'd,
And troubled, while bright phantoms round them play,
By a dim sense that all will float and fade away!

### XXXVII

Yet, as if chasing joy, I woo'd the breeze
To speed me onward with the wings of morn.
—Oh! far amidst the solitary seas,
Which were not made for man, what man hath borne,
Answering their moan with his!—what *thou* didst bear,
My lost and loveliest! while that secret care                    330
Grew terror, and thy gentle spirit, worn
By its dull brooding weight, gave way at last,
Beholding me as one from hope for ever cast!

XXXVIII[24]

For unto thee, as thro' all change, reveal'd
Mine inward being lay. In other eyes
I had to bow me yet, and make a shield,
To fence my burning bosom, of disguise;
By the still hope sustain'd, ere long to win
Some sanctuary, whose green retreats within,
My thoughts unfetter'd to their source might rise,                340
Like songs and scents of morn.—But thou didst look
Thro' all my soul, and thine even unto fainting shook.

XXXIX

Fallen, fallen, I seem'd[25]—yet, oh! not less belov'd,
Tho' from thy love was pluck'd the early pride,
And harshly, by a gloomy faith reproved,
And sear'd with shame!—tho' each young flower had died,
There was the root,—strong, living, not the less
That all it yielded now was bitterness;
Yet still such love as quits not misery's side,
Nor drops from guilt its ivy-like embrace,                        350
Nor turns away from death's its pale heroic face.

XL

Yes! thou hadst follow'd me thro' fear and flight;
Thou wouldst have follow'd had my pathway led
Even to the scaffold; had the flashing light
Of the rais'd axe made strong men shrink with dread,
Thou, midst the hush of thousands, wouldst have been
With thy clasp'd hands beside me kneeling seen,
And meekly bowing to the shame thy head—
The shame!—oh! making beautiful to view
The might of human love—fair thing! so bravely true!              360

XLI

There was thine agony—to love so well
Where fear made love life's chastener.—Heretofore
Whate'er of earth's disquiet round thee fell,
Thy soul, o'erpassing its dim bounds, could soar
Away to sunshine, and thy clear eye speak
Most of the skies when grief most touch'd thy cheek.
Now, that far brightness faded! never more
Couldst thou lift heavenwards for its hope thy heart,
Since at Heaven's gate it seem'd that thou and I must part.[26]

### XLII

Alas! and life hath moments when a glance                         370
(If thought to sudden watchfulness be stirr'd),
A flush—a fading of the cheek perchance,
A word—less, less—the *cadence* of a word,
Lets in our gaze the mind's dim veil beneath,
Thence to bring haply knowledge fraught with death!
—Even thus, what never from thy lip was heard
Broke on my soul.—I knew that in thy sight
I stood—howe'er belov'd—a recreant from the light![27]

### XLIII

Thy sad sweet hymn, at eve, the seas along,—
Oh! the deep soul it breath'd![28]—the love, the woe,          380
The fervour, pour'd in that full gush of song,
As it went floating through the fiery glow
Of the rich sunset!—bringing thoughts of Spain,
With all her vesper-voices, o'er the main,
Which seem'd responsive in its murmuring flow.
—"*Ave sanctissima!*"°—how oft that lay                    *Hail, most holy*
Hath melted from my heart the martyr-strength away!

    Ave, sanctissima!
    'Tis night-fall on the sea;
      Ora pro nobis!°                              *pray for us* 390
    Our souls rise to thee!

    Watch us, while shadows lie
      O'er the dim water spread;
    Hear the heart's lonely sigh,—
      —*Thine*, too, hath bled!

    Thou that hast look'd on death,
      Aid us when death is near!
    Whisper of Heaven to faith;
      Sweet mother, hear!

      Ora pro nobis!                                      400
    The wave must rock our sleep,
      Ora, mater, ora!
    Thou star of the deep!

### XLIV

"*Ora pro nobis, mater!*"—What a spell
Was in those notes, with day's last glory dying
On the flush'd waters!—seem'd they not to swell

From the far dust, wherein my sires were lying
With crucifix and sword?—Oh! yet how clear
Comes their reproachful sweetness to mine ear!
"*Ora!*"—with all the purple waves replying,         410
  All my youth's visions rising in the strain—
And I had thought it much to bear the rack and chain!

XLV

Torture!—the sorrow of affection's eye,
Fixing its meekness on the spirit's core,
Deeper, and teaching more of agony,
May pierce than many swords!—and this I bore
With a mute pang. Since I had vainly striven
From its free springs to pour the truth of Heaven
  Into thy trembling soul, my Leonor!
Silence rose up where hearts no hope could share:—     420
Alas! for those that love, and may not blend in prayer!

XLVI

*We* could not pray together midst the deep,
Which, like a floor of sapphire, round us lay,
Through days of splendour, nights too bright for sleep,
Soft, solemn, holy!—We were on our way
Unto the mighty Cordillera-land,
With men whom tales of that world's golden strand
  Had lur'd to leave their vines.—Oh! who shall say
What thoughts rose in us, when the tropic sky
Touch'd all its molten seas with sunset's alchemy?     430

XLVII

Thoughts no more mingled!—Then came night—th'intense
Dark blue—the burning stars!—I saw *thee* shine
Once more, in thy serene magnificence,
O Southern Cross![29] as when thy radiant sign
First drew my gaze of youth.—No, not as then;
I had been stricken by the darts of men
  Since those fresh days; and now thy light divine
Look'd on mine anguish, while within me strove
The still small voice[30] against the might of suffering love.

XLVIII

But thou, the clear, the glorious! thou wert pouring     440
Brilliance and joy upon the crystal wave,
While she that met thy ray with eyes adoring,
Stood in the lengthening shadow of the grave!

—Alas! I watch'd her dark religious glance,
As it still sought thee through the Heaven's expanse,
Bright Cross!—and knew not that I watch'd what gave
But passing lustre—shrouded soon to be—
A soft light found no more—no more on earth or sea!

### XLIX

I knew not all—yet something of unrest
Sat on my heart. Wake, ocean-wind! I said;                    450
Waft us to land, in leafy freshness drest,
Where through rich clouds of foliage o'er her head,
Sweet day may steal, and rills unseen go by,
Like singing voices, and the green earth lie
Starry with flowers, beneath her graceful tread!
—But the calm bound us midst the glassy main;
Ne'er was her step to bend earth's living flowers again.

### L

Yes! as if Heaven upon the waves were sleeping,
Vexing my soul with quiet, there they lay,
All moveless through their blue transparence keeping,          460
The shadows of our sails, from day to day;
While she—oh! strongest is the strong heart's woe—
And yet I live! I feel the sunshine's glow—
And I am he that look'd, and saw decay
Steal o'er the fair of earth, th' ador'd too much!—
It is a fearful thing to love what death may touch.

### LI

A fearful thing that love and death may dwell
In the same world!—She faded on—and I—
Blind to the last, there needed death to tell
My trusting soul that she *could* fade to die!                 470
Yet, ere she parted, I had mark'd a change,—
But it breath'd hope—'twas beautiful, though strange:
Something of gladness in the melody
Of her low voice, and in her words a flight
Of airy thought—alas! too perilously bright!

### LII

And a clear sparkle in her glance, yet wild,
And quick, and eager, like the flashing gaze
Of some all wondering and awakening child,
That first the glories of the earth surveys.—

How could it thus deceive me?—she had worn      480
Around her, like the dewy mists of morn,
A pensive tenderness through happiest days,[31]
And a soft world of dreams had seem'd to lie
Still in her dark, and deep, and spiritual eye.

### LIII

And I could hope in that strange fire!—she died,
She died, with all its lustre on her mien!—
The day was melting from[32] the waters wide,
And through its long bright hours her thoughts had been,
It seem'd, with restless and unwonted yearning,
To Spain's blue skies and dark sierras turning;      490
For her fond words were all of vintage-scene,
And flowering myrtle, and sweet citron's breath—
Oh! with what vivid hues life comes back oft on death!

### LIV

And from her lips the mountain-songs of old,
In wild faint snatches, fitfully had sprung;
Songs of the orange bower, the Moorish hold,
The "*Rio verde*,"[33] on her soul that hung,
And thence flow'd forth.—But now the sun was low;
And watching by my side its last red glow,
That ever stills the heart, once more she sung      500
Her own soft "*Ora, mater!*"—and the sound
Was even like love's farewell—so mournfully profound.

### LV

The boy had dropp'd to slumber at our feet;—
"And I have lull'd him to his smiling rest
Once more!" she said:—I rais'd him—it was sweet,
Yet sad, to see the perfect calm which bless'd
His look that hour;—for now her voice grew weak;
And on the flowery crimson of his cheek,
With her white lips a long, long kiss she press'd,
Yet light, to wake him not.—Then sank her head      510
Against my bursting heart:—What did I clasp?—the dead!

### LVI

I call'd—to call what answers not our cries,
By that we lov'd to stand unseen, unheard,
With the loud passion of our tears and sighs
To see but some cold glistering ringlet stirr'd,

And in the quench'd eye's fixedness to gaze,
All vainly searching for the parted rays;
This is what waits us!—Dead!—with that chill word
To link our bosom-names!—For this we pour
Our souls upon the dust[34]—nor tremble to adore!                    520

### LVII

But the true parting came!—I look'd my last
On the sad beauty of that slumbering face;
How could I think the lovely spirit pass'd,
Which there had left so tenderly its trace?
Yet a dim awfulness was on the brow—
No! not like sleep to look upon art Thou,
Death, death!—She lay, a thing for earth's embrace,[35]
To cover with spring-wreaths. For earth's?—the wave
That gives the bier no flowers—makes moan above her grave!

### LVIII

On the mid-seas a knell!—for man was there,                          530
Anguish and love—the mourner with his dead!
A long, low-rolling knell—a voice of prayer—
Dark glassy waters, like a desert spread,—
And the pale-shining Southern Cross on high,
Its faint stars fading from a solemn sky,
Where mighty clouds before the dawn grew red:—
Were these things round me? Such o'er memory sweep
Wildly when aught brings back that burial of the deep.

### LIX

Then the broad, lonely sunrise!—and the plash
Into the sounding waves![36]—around her head                         540
They parted, with a glancing moment's flash,
Then shut—and all was still. And now thy bed
Is of their secrets, gentlest Leonor!
Once fairest of young brides!—and never more,
Lov'd as thou wert, may human tear be shed
Above thy rest!—No mark the proud seas keep,
To show where he that wept may pause again to weep.

### LX

So the depths took thee!—Oh! the sullen sense
Of desolation in that hour compress'd!
Dust going down, a speck, amidst th' immense                         550
And gloomy waters, leaving on their breast

The trace a weed might leave there!—Dust!—the thing
Which to the heart was as a living spring
Of joy, with fearfulness of love possess'd,
    Thus sinking!—Love, joy, fear, all crush'd to this—
And the wide Heaven so far—so fathomless th' abyss![37]

### LXI

Where the line sounds not, where the wrecks lie low,
What shall wake thence the dead?—Blest, blest are they
That earth to earth entrust; for they may know
And tend the dwelling whence the slumberer's clay                560
Shall rise at last, and bid the young flowers bloom,
That waft a breath of hope around the tomb;
And kneel upon the dewy turf to pray!
    But thou, what cave hath dimly chamber'd *thee?*
Vain dreams!—oh! art thou not where there is no more sea?[38]

### LXII

The wind rose free and singing:—when for ever,
O'er that sole spot of all the watery plain,
I could have bent my sight with fond endeavour
Down, where its treasure was, its glance to strain;          570
Then rose the reckless wind!—Before our prow
The white foam flash'd—ay, joyously—and thou
Wert left with all the solitary main
    Around thee—and thy beauty in my heart,
And thy meek sorrowing love—oh! where could *that* depart?

### LXIII

I will not speak of woe; I may not tell—
Friend tells not such to friend—the thoughts which rent
My fainting spirit, when its wild farewell
Across the billows to thy grave was sent,
Thou, there most lonely!—He that sits above,
In his calm glory, will forgive the love                   580
His creatures bear each other, ev'n if blent
    With a vain worship; for its close is dim
Ever with grief, which leads the wrung soul back to Him!

### LXIV

And with a milder pang if now I bear
To think of thee in thy forsaken rest,
If from my heart be lifted the despair,
The sharp remorse with healing influence press'd,

If the soft eyes that visit me in sleep
Look not reproach, though still they seem to weep;
It is that He my sacrifice hath bless'd,                    590
And fill'd my bosom, through its inmost cell,
With a deep chastening sense that all at last is well.

### LXV

Yes! thou art now—Oh! wherefore doth the thought
Of the wave dashing o'er thy long bright hair,
The sea-weed into its dark tresses wrought,
The sand thy pillow—thou that wert so fair!
Come o'er me still?—Earth, earth!—it is the hold
Earth ever keeps on that of earthly mould!
But *thou* art breathing now in purer air,
I well believe, and freed from all of error,        600
Which blighted here the root of thy sweet life with terror.

### LXVI

And if the love, which here was passing light,
Went with what died not—Oh! that *this* we knew,
But this!—that through the silence of the night,
Some voice, of all the lost ones and the true,
Would speak, and say, if in their far repose,
We are yet aught of what we were to those
We call the dead!—their passionate adieu,
Was it but breath, to perish?—Holier trust
Be mine!—thy love *is* there, but purified from dust!        610

### LXVII

A thing all heavenly!—clear'd from that which hung
As a dim cloud between us, heart and mind!
Loos'd from the fear, the grief, whose tendrils flung
A chain, so darkly with its growth entwin'd.
This is my hope!—though when the sunset fades,
When forests rock the midnight on their shades,
When tones of wail are in the rising wind,
Across my spirit some faint doubt may sigh;
For the strong hours *will* sway this frail mortality![39]

### LXVIII

We have been wanderers since those days of woe,        620
Thy boy and I!—As wild birds tend their young,
So have I tended him—my bounding roe![40]
The high Peruvian solitudes among;

And o'er the Andes' torrents borne his form,
Where our frail bridge hath quiver'd midst the storm.[41]
—But there the war-notes of my country rung,
And, smitten deep of Heaven and man, I fled
To hide in shades unpierc'd a mark'd and weary head.

### LXIX

But he went on in gladness—that fair child!
Save when at times his bright eye seem'd to dream,               630
And his young lips, which then no longer smil'd,
Ask'd of his mother!—That was but a gleam
Of Memory, fleeting fast; and then his play
Through the wide Llanos[42] cheer'd again our way,
And by the mighty Oronoco stream,
On whose lone margin we have heard at morn,
From the mysterious rocks, the sunrise-music borne.[43]

### LXX

So like a spirit's voice! a harping tone,
Lovely, yet ominous to mortal ear,
Such as might reach us from a world unknown,               640
Troubling man's heart with thrills of joy and fear!
'Twas sweet!—yet those deep southern shades oppress'd
My soul with stillness, like the calms that rest
On melancholy waves:[44] I sigh'd to hear
Once more earth's breezy sounds, her foliage fann'd,
And turn'd to seek the wilds of the red hunter's land.

### LXXI

And we have won a bower of refuge now,
In this fresh waste, the breath of whose repose
Hath cool'd, like dew, the fever of my brow,
And whose green oaks and cedars round me close,               650
As temple-walls and pillars, that exclude
Earth's haunted dreams from their free solitude;
All, save the image and the thought of those
Before us gone; our lov'd of early years,
Gone where affection's cup hath lost the taste of tears.

### LXXII

I see a star—eve's first-born!—in whose train
Past scenes, words, looks, come back. The arrowy spire
Of the lone cypress, as of wood-girt fane,
Rests dark and still amidst a heaven of fire;

The pine gives forth its odours, and the lake                    660
Gleams like one ruby, and the soft winds wake,
Till every string of nature's solemn lyre
Is touch'd to answer; its most secret tone
Drawn from each tree, for each hath whispers all its own.

### LXXIII

And hark! another murmur on the air,
Not of the hidden rills, or quivering shades!—
That is the cataract's, which the breezes bear,
Filling the leafy twilight of the glades
With hollow surge-like sounds, as from the bed
Of the blue mournful seas, that keep the dead:                   670
But *they* are far!—the low sun here pervades
Dim forest-arches, bathing with red gold
Their stems, till each is made a marvel to behold,—

### LXXIV

Gorgeous, yet full of gloom!—In such an hour,
The vesper-melody of dying bells
Wanders through Spain, from each grey convent's tower
O'er shining rivers pour'd, and olive-dells,
By every peasant heard, and muleteer,
And hamlet, round my home:—and I am here,
Living again through all my life's farewells,                    680
In these vast woods, where farewell ne'er was spoken,
And sole I lift to Heaven a sad heart—yet unbroken!

### LXXV

In such an hour are told the hermit's beads;
With the white sail the seaman's hymn floats by:
Peace be with all! whate'er their varying creeds,
With all that send up holy thoughts on high!
Come to me, boy!—by Guadalquivir's° vines,          *(river in Spain)*
By every stream of Spain, as day declines,
Man's prayers are mingled in the rosy sky.
—We, too, will pray; nor yet unheard, my child!                 690
Of Him whose voice *we* hear at eve amidst the wild.

### LXXVI

At eve?—oh! through all hours!—From dark dreams oft
Awakening, I look forth, and learn the might
Of solitude, while thou art breathing soft,
And low, my lov'd one! on the breast of night:

I look forth on the stars—the shadowy sleep
Of forests—and the lake, whose gloomy deep
Sends up red sparkles to the fire-flies' light.
A lonely world!—ev'n fearful to man's thought,
But for His presence felt, whom here my soul hath sought.[45]          700

---

[1] "This sweet soul, in loyalty, / Full of her own creed / Which alone, / She trusts, can bring salvation, lives in agony / To think her lover lost, however she may plead." Faust, speaking to Mephistopheles, of his lover, Margarete. *Goethe's Faust*, trans. Walter Kaufman (New York, 1961), part 1 (1808), 3529–33.

[2] *The Convict* (1816), by Scots writer John Wilson (1785–1854), frequent contributor to *Blackwood's*. Falsely accused of murder, the convict is about to be executed. The real murderer has just confessed and in the last scene, the convict's wife runs up to the scaffolding, redeems him from it, and utters these words (201–4); 204 continues, ". . . soul, / To the great God of Mercy."

[3] The varying sounds of waterfalls are thus alluded to in an interesting work of Mrs. Grant's. "On the opposite side the view was bounded by steep hills, covered with lofty pines, from which a waterfall descended, which not only gave animation to the sylvan scene, but was the best barometer imaginable; foretelling by its varied and intelligible sounds every approaching change, not only of the weather but of the wind."—Memoirs of an American Lady, vol. i. p. 143. [FH]

Anne Macvicar Grant (1755–1838), *Memoirs of an American Lady, with Sketches of Manners and Scenery in America as They Existed Previous to the Revolution*, 2 vols. (London, 1808). This influential and celebrated Scots poet and essayist lived in America from 1758 to 1768; the "American Lady" is her early mentor Catalina Schuyler. *Memoirs* traces the progress of an infant society "from virtuous simplicity, to the dangerous 'knowledge of good and evil' " (1.v; a reference to Genesis 2.16–17) and contrasts the virtues of native Americans to corrupt modern society. After moving to Edinburgh in 1810, Grant flourished in its literary circle, counting Scott, Hogg, Mackenzie, Campbell, Jeffrey, and Wilson among her many friends. See Jane Williams's reference to her in her essay on Hemans (below).

[4] 7, MS] Lift up your voices to the Skies

[5] MS] This stanza (2.3) follows:
> Thou hast the Wilderness o'er which to reign,
> With all its founts, Thou of the falcon-eyes!
> Thou hast the wide Savannahs, like the Main,
> Rolling their wavy verdure to the Skies.
> Nor wilt thou lay thy Warrior-Father's dust,
> Beneath his Oak, without an inborn trust
> In One above, to whom thy prayer may rise
> Untaught yet free, when by the torrent's roar
> Or the Wood's gleam thy Soul is bow'd, and doth adore.

[6] A phrase from the Sermon on the Mount: "And why beholdest thou the mote that is in thy brother's eye, but perceivest not the beam that is in thine own eye?" (Luke 6.41; Matthew 7.3).

[7] Echoing the famous opening of Byron's *Sonnet on Chillon*: "Eternal spirit of the chainless Mind!" The stanza is a critique of political and ecclesiastical tyranny.

[8] MS] This stanza (2.7) follows:
> So utterly alone!—the brooding load
> Of Silence and of Solitude, which hung
> Like Death, upon me!—thro' that dim Abode
> Oh! for a Battle-Trumpet to have rung
> Shaking its Walls!—a Trumpet wild and shrill,
> To say that human hearts were beating still!

—Sweep louder, Winds! the Forest-Aisles along,
And yet more loud!—All Earth so full of Sounds,
And not a breath to pass that Dungeon's stony bounds!

[9] The circular rainbows, occasionally seen amongst the Andes, are described by Ulloa. [FH]

George Juan and Antonio de Ulloa (1716–95), *Relacion historica del viage a la America merid-ional* (1748), bk. 6, ch. 9; trans. John Adams as *A Voyage to South America* (1758), 4th ed. (London, 1806), 442.

[10] Jesus to the multitude, concerning John the Baptist in prison, "What went ye out into the wilderness to see? A reed shaken with the wind?" (Matthew 11.7).

[11] Many striking instances of the vividness with which the mind, when strongly excited, has been known to renovate past impressions, and embody them into visible imagery, are noticed and accounted for in Dr. Hibbert's Philosophy of Apparitions. The following illustrative pas-sage is quoted in the same work, from the writings of the late Dr. Ferriar. "I remember that, about the age of fourteen, it was a source of great amusement to myself, if I had been viewing any interesting object in the course of the day, such as a romantic ruin, a fine seat, or a review of a body of troops, as soon as evening came on, if I had occasion to go into a dark room, the whole scene was brought before my eyes with a brilliancy equal to what it had possessed in daylight, and remained visible for several minutes. I have no doubt, that dismal and frightful images have been presented to young persons after scenes of domestic affliction, or public horror."

The following passage from the "Alcazar of Seville," a tale, or historical sketch, by the author of Doblado's letters, affords a further illustration of this subject. "When, descending fast into the vale of years, I strongly fix my mind's eye on those narrow, shady, silent streets, where I breathed the scented air which came rustling through the surrounding groves; where the foot-steps re-echoed from the clean watered porches of the houses, and every object spoke of quiet and contentment; . . . the objects around me begin to fade into a mere delusion, and not only the thoughts, but the external sensations, which I then experienced, revive with a reality that makes me shudder—it has so much the character of a trance or vision." [FH]

Samuel Hibbert, *Sketches of the Philosophy of Apparitions; or, An Attempt to Trace Such Illusions to Their Physical Causes* (1824), 2d ed. (Edinburgh and London, 1825), 265; quoting John Ferriar, M. D., *An Essay towards a Theory of Apparitions* (London: Cadell and Davies, 1813) 16–17. A "seat" is a country residence. FH's interest in Hibbert's work was irritated by his insistence "upon bringing those hateful engines, commonly called the 'reasoning powers,' into play against all the fabrics of imagination" (*CM* 1.199). Joseph Blanco White, *The Alcazar of Seville*, in *Forget Me Not for 1825*, 31–54; FH quotes from 32–33. The speaker is a male native of Seville, recollecting his early years as a student and contemplating the Alcazar, a palace originally built by the Arabs in the Middle Ages and rebuilt by Pedro the Cruel in the 14th c. An old man whom he met in the garden relates some of the place's history—events of murder, sexual infidelity, suspicions of female promiscuity, and state tyranny.

[12] MS] . . . the soaring Hills, and golden vesper Sky.

[13] The Moors' hold in Spain ended with the conquest of Granada in 1492 by Ferdinand and Isabella.

[14] Revelation 15.2: "And I saw as it were a sea of glass, mingled with fire."

[15] MS] This stanza (2.18) appears instead:

And drop not, Hope! and heart of Man, be strong!
Hold thine unfetter'd faith midst dungeons fast!
Thou wast endow'd to suffer well and long,
Aye, gifted to endure till all be past!
My Spirit, which a lovely dream could melt,
Stood up against the Might of Wrong, and felt
The Rock it lean'd on—and prevail'd at last!
Yes! an hour came—I rent my chain—I trod
The Earth once more and took my freedom back from God!

[16] 188, MS] . . . in fiery Might
  MS] This stanza (2.24) follows:

> This was to wake!—the tossing and the sound
> Abroad in Heaven and Earth—the Waters raving,
> And the loud Harping of the Winds around,
> What did they speak of?—and the high Cliffs, braving
> The War of blasts, yet answering every tone,
> With strange mysterious Music of their own,
> And o'er the flashing Skies the dark Woods waving,
> —What did they speak of? —Freedom!—I was free,
> And with a fearless Voice might call, my God! on Thee.

[17] MS] glittering
  190, MS] It was a softer Night, a . . .

[18] "For because the breath of flowers is farre sweeter in the aire (where it comes and goes like the warbling of musick) than in the hand, therefore nothing is more fit for that delight than to know what be the flowers and plants which doe best perfume the aire."—Lord Bacon's *Essay on Gardens*. [FH]
  Francis Bacon, *Of Gardens*, in *Essays; or, Counsels, Civill and Morall* (1625), Essay 46.

[19] MS] Leonore.
  Revised to "Leonor" perhaps to evoke "Leonor Gomez," one of the martyrs in the *auto-da-fé* recounted in *Quarterly* 29 (256), and to avoid evoking "Lenore," heroine of Gottfried Bürger's sensational ballad, whose lover's ghost returns from his grave to claim her. "Leonora" was the name of Alfonso II's sister, adored by Tasso; see FH's celebration of her in Goethe's *Tasso* ("German Studies," *NMM* 40 [January 1834], esp. 3–6).

[20] MS] . . . on its ancient wall!

[21] Adam and Eve's last view, at the end of *Paradise Lost* (12.624–49), cf. Genesis 3.24.
  266, MS] parting rays.

[22] MS] tender and true.
  FH's revision blends Milton's description of divine nurture ("Dove-like sat'st brooding" [*Paradise Lost* 1.21]) into Wordsworth's description of Margaret's fixation on her home, in book 1 of *The Excursion* (1814): "Yet still / She loved this wretched spot, nor would for worlds / Have parted thence" (953–55; cf. 910–12 in 1850 text).

[23] MS] This stanza (2.38) follows:

> Were we not on the waves?—twas but the sound
> Of their far-dashing Surge thro' day and night,
> 'Twas but the moaning Solitude around,
> Scarce broken by a snowy Sea-bird's flight
> Which weigh'd upon her Spirit, whose deep love
> Had ever its lone haunts by fount and grove,
> And of their many whispers made delight.
> —How oft I told my heart it was but this,
> And that we yet should find some forest-home of Bliss!

[24] Not in MS

[25] MS] One fall'n from Heaven

[26] MS] This stanza (2.45) follows:

> So ev'n thy pure Affections in their course
> Chang'd and perturb'd by Error, took a hue
> From inward strife, a shadow from remorse,
> A boding from Despair; until they grew
> Into destroying Angels. I had burst
> The yoke; Thou couldst not. Thy meek Nature, nurs'd
> In bondage, sank beneath it; and I knew
> What, in the bosom which I could not free,
> Fain would have pass'd unseen—but this was not to be.

[27] MS] This stanza (2.47) follows:

> Thy long, long looks on Heaven and on thy Child—
> —Oh! their deep language!—and the tearful haze,
> Whence tremulous they broke, and darkly mild,
> Yet piercing in their melancholy rays!
> —I had borne torture—I had prov'd it vain,
> Freedom and my God were mighty to sustain;
> But, by the stillness of that mournful gaze,
> My Soul was troubled—shaken—well nigh drawn
> Back to the bonds it rent, when struggling into Dawn.

[28] 378–80, MS] And thy sweet Hymn at Eve the Deep along! / —*"Ave, Sanctissima!"*—

[29] "The pleasure we felt on discovering the southern Cross was warmly shared by such of the crew as had lived in the colonies. In the solitude of the seas, we hail a star as a friend, from whom we have long been separated. Among the Portugueze and the Spaniards, peculiar motives seem to increase this feeling; a religious sentiment attaches them to a constellation, the form of which recalls the sign of the faith planted by their ancestors in the deserts of the new world. [. . .] It has been observed at what hour of the night, in different seasons, the Cross of the South is erect or inclined. It is a time-piece that advances very regularly near four minutes a day, and no other group of stars exhibits, to the naked eye, an observation of time so easily made. How often have we heard our guides exclaim in the savannahs of Venezuela, or in the desert extending from Lima to Truxillo, 'Midnight is past, the Cross begins to bend!' How often these words reminded us of that affecting scene where Paul and Virginia, seated near the source of the river of Lataniers, conversed together for the last time, and where the old man, at the sight of the southern Cross, warns them that it is time to separate!"—De Humboldt's *Travels*. [FH]

Alexander de Humboldt (1769–1854) and and Aimé Bonpland, *Voyage aux régions équinoctiales du Nouveau Continent* (1807), trans. by his friend, English poet and essayist Helen Maria Williams, as *Personal Narrative of Travels to the Equinoctial Regions of the New Continent, During the Years 1799–1804* (1814); 3d ed., 7 vols. (London: Longman &c, 1822), 2.21–22. German naturalist, travel writer, statesman, and explorer, Humboldt spent five years (1799–1804) with Bonpland on a scientific expedition through South America. In his popular novel *Paul et Virginie* (1787), Jacques Henri Bernardin de St. Pierre (1737–1814) sees nature's beauties as proof of God's existence.

[30] The Lord speaks to the prophet Elijah in a "still small voice" (1 Kings 19.12).

[31] MS] A tender sadness from her earliest days

[32] MS] The day was sinking on

[33] "Rio verde, rio verde," the popular Spanish romance, known to the English reader in Percy's translation.

> "Gentle river, gentle river,
> Lo, thy streams are stain'd with gore!
> Many a brave and noble captain
> Floats along thy willow'd shore," &c. &c. [FH]

Cf. *Abencerrage* 2.25–56 and note. *Reliques of Ancient English Poetry* (1765), by Thomas Percy (1729–1811), was an influential collection. FH gives a version (not a translation) of *The Rio Verde Song* in *Songs of Spain* (*NMM* 40 [January 1834], 26) with this note: "The name of Rio Verde (the "Gentle River" of Percy's ballad) will be familiar to every Spanish reader, as associated in song and story with the old romantic wars of the Peninsula." The Spanish ballad opens: "Rio verde, rio verde, / Quanto cuerpo en ti se baña / De Christianos y de Moros / Muertos por la dura espada!" (Green river, green river, / In you have bathed so many bodies / Of Christians and of Moors / Killed by the harsh sword!). FH's song makes the river a kind of Wordsworthian balm for the sorrowing female heart: "Flow, Rio Verde! / In melody flow; /Win her that weepeth / To slumber from woe! / Bid thy wave's music / Roll through her dreams" (1–6).

[34] Cf. the close of *Woman on the Field of Battle*.

[35] Cf. Wordsworth's *Song* ("A slumber did my spirit seal"): "she" who "seem'd a thing that could not feel / The touch of earthly years" is now "rolled round in earth's diurnal course." FH particularly liked the verses on Leonor's sea burial (*CM* 1.124–25).

[36] De Humboldt, in describing the burial of a young Asturian at sea, mentions the entreaty of the officiating priest, that the body, which had been brought upon deck during the night, might not be committed to the waves until after sunrise, in order to pay it the last rites according to the usage of the Romish church. [FH. *Voyage* (1822 ed.), 2.33–34]

[37] Cf. the fisherman's description, in Byron's *The Giaour* (a poem FH knew well), of Hassan's grieving disposal at sea of his favorite harem slave (perhaps not yet dead), who has betrayed him: "Sullen it plunged, and slowly sank, / The calm wave rippled to the bank; / I watch'd it as it sank, methought / Some motion from the current caught / Bestirr'd it more,—'twas but the beam / That checker'd o'er the living stream: / I gazed, till vanishing from view, / Like lessening pebble it withdrew; / Still less and less, a speck of white / That gemm'd the tide, then mock'd the sight; / And all its hidden secrets sleep, / Known but to Genii of the deep, / Which, trembling in their coral caves, / They dare not whisper to the waves" (374–87).

[38] "And there was no more sea."—Rev. chap. xxi. v. 1. [FH]

St. John's vision: "And I saw a new heaven and a new earth: for the first heaven and the first earth were passed away; and there was no more sea"; "earth to earth" (559) is a phrase in the Anglican funeral service.

[39] MS] This stanza (2.73) follows:

> Yet all is well;—thy meek imploring look,
> The beautiful and mournful unto Death,
> Did what the Torturer could not, when it shook
> Mine anchored heart one moment from the faith
> Which Alvar died to seal.—But oh! Belov'd!
> This might not be, and thou wert so remov'd,
> To where the flowers know not of Sorrow's breath,
> And I, from whom thy low sweet Voice had pass'd,
> Left before God to walk, unfetter'd to the last!

[40] Cf. Wordsworth's description in *Tintern Abbey* (1798) of his boyhood self: "when like a roe / I bounded o'er the mountains" (69–72).

[41] The bridges over many deep chasms amongst the Andes, are pendulous, and formed only of the fibres of equinoctial plants. Their tremulous motion has afforded a striking image to one of the stanzas in "Gertrude of Wyoming."

> "Anon some wilder portraiture he draws;
> Of Nature's savage glories he would speak,—
> The loneliness of earth, that overawes,—
> Where, resting by the tomb of old Cacique,
> The lama-driver on Peruvia's peak,
> Nor voice nor living motion marks around,
> But storks that to the boundless forest shriek;
> Or wild-cane arch, high flung o'er gulph profound,
> That fluctuates when the storms of El Dorado sound.—" [FH]

Thomas Campbell, *Gertrude of Wyoming, A Pennsylvania Tale* (1809), part 2, stanza 16. Campbell has this note: "The bridges over narrow streams in many parts of Spanish America are said to be built of cane, which, however strong to support the passenger, are yet waved in the agitation of the storm, and frequently add to the effect of a mountainous and picturesque scenery." *Gertrude* is a tale in Spenserian stanzas about European settlers who had imagined themselves in a paradisal refuge from tyranny, but were massacred in 1788 by Mohawks manipulated in British-French-American conflicts.

[42] *Llanos*, or savannas, the great plains in South America. [FH]

The *dream / gleam* rhyme that shapes this subject of fleeting memory echoes Wordsworth's lament for the world of childhood in his "Intimations" *Ode*: "Whither is fled the visionary gleam? / Where is it now, the glory and the dream?" (56–57). FH may have known that Wordsworth's mother died just before his eighth birthday.

[43] De Humboldt speaks of these rocks on the shores of the Oronoco. Travellers have heard from time to time subterraneous sounds proceed from them at sunrise, resembling those of an organ. He believes in the existence of this mysterious music, although not fortunate enough to have heard it himself; and thinks that it may be produced by currents of air issuing through the crevices. [FH. *Voyage* (1822 ed.), 4.559]

Flowing into the Caribbean, the Oronoco is the principal river of Venezuela. Versions of this and the next note are sketched in MS.

[44] The same distinguished traveller frequently alludes to the extreme stillness of the air in the equatorial regions of the new continent, and particularly on the thickly wooded shores of the Oronoco. "In this neighbourhood," he says, "no breath of wind ever agitates the foliage." [FH. *Voyage* (1822 ed.), 5.8]

643–46, MS] . . . with calmness;—not a Wind their guest, / Not a faint breeze!—their broad leaves glistening clear, / Hung as in picture, by a breath unfann'd— / —I left them for the Wilds of the Red Hunter's Land. [i.e., North America]

[45] MS] The poem concludes with this additional stanza (2.83):

> —Again that Sound, as of the rolling Wave!—
> Night-fall hath given it power,—and yet again—
> —What! shall my Spirit, that o'erswept the Grave,
> Sink if a touch press Memory into pain?
> —There is a wild Song haunts me with that moan,
> A wild low Song, and mournful!—yet a tone
> Of Hope, thro' all the sadness of the strain,
> Breathes up to Heaven:—Strange!—twas the sweet Voice fled
> Ev'n Leonor's, that sang—"Thou Sea, restore the Dead!"

Then follows, as if a continuation, *Song: The treasures of the Deep*, its last lines linking back to this stanza: "— Yet must thou hear a Voice—Restore the Dead! / Earth shall reclaim her precious things from Thee — / — Restore the Dead, Thou Sea!" FH published this *Song* in *NMM* 8 (August 1823), unsigned, and in *Forest Sanctuary &c* (1825), but not attached to the title poem.

---

# From *Lays of Many Lands*

## *The Suliote Mother*[1]

It is related, in a French Life of Ali Pacha, that several of the Suliote women, on the advance of the Turkish troops into their mountain fastnesses, assembled on a lofty summit, and, after chanting a wild song, precipitated themselves, with their children, into the chasm below, to avoid becoming the slaves of the enemy.[2]

She stood upon the loftiest peak,
    Amidst the clear blue sky,
A bitter smile was on her cheek,
    And a dark flash in her eye.

"Dost thou see them, boy?—through the dusky pines
Dost thou see where the foeman's armour shines?
Hast thou caught the gleam of the conqueror's crest?
My babe, that I cradled on my breast!
Wouldst thou spring from thy mother's arms with joy?
—That sight hath cost thee a father, boy!"        10

    For in the rocky strait beneath,
        Lay Suliote sire and son;
    They had heap'd high the piles of death
        Before the pass was won.

"They have cross'd the torrent, and on they come!
Wo for the mountain hearth and home!
There, where the hunter laid by his spear,
There, where the lyre hath been sweet to hear,
There, where I sang thee, fair babe! to sleep,
Nought but the blood-stain our trace shall keep!"        20

    And now the horn's loud blast was heard,
        And now the cymbal's clang,
    Till ev'n the upper air was stirr'd,
        As cliff and hollow rang.

"Hark! they bring music, my joyous child!
What saith the trumpet to Suli's wild!
Doth it light thine eye with so quick a fire,
As if at a glance of thine armed sire?—
Still!—be thou still!—there are brave men low—
Thou wouldst not smile couldst thou see him now!"        30

    But nearer came the clash of steel,
        And louder swell'd the horn,
    And farther yet the tambour's peal
        Through the dark pass was borne.

"Hear'st thou the sound of their savage mirth?—
Boy! thou wert free when I gave thee birth,—
Free, and how cherish'd, my warrior's son!
He too hath bless'd thee, as I have done!
Ay, and unchain'd must his lov'd ones be—
Freedom, young Suliote! for thee and me!"        40

And from the arrowy peak she sprung,
   And fast the fair child bore:—
A veil upon the wind was flung,
   A cry—and all was o'er!

[1] First published *NMM* 13 (March 1825), signed "F. H.," then in *Forest Sanctuary &c*, in the subsection, "Lays of Many Lands."

[2] *NMM* headnote] Various modern writers on Modern Greece have related the fate of those Suliote women, who threw themselves, with their infants, from the precipices of their mountainous territory, on the conquest and approach of Ali Pacha. One of those narrators adds, that a wild song was chanted by the mothers, before committing the act of desperation.

For an account, see Sir Henry Holland (1788–1833), *Travels in the Ionian Isles, Albania, etc., during the years 1812 and 1813* (London: Murray, 1819). In 1790, in part of the Russo-Turkish war, the Suliotes, an Albanian Christian tribe, held out in their mountain fasthold against Ali Pasha's troops; in 1803, when defeat seemed imminent, six men and twenty-two women leapt from a precipice; Albanian soldiers reported seeing the women throw their children down first. Cf. *Modern Greece*, stanzas 48–50, and M. J. Jewsbury, *The Women of Suli*, in *Phantasmagoria* (1825), 1.125–27. For the suicide leaps of desperate women, cf. *The Wife of Asdrubal* and *The Last Song of Sappho*.

---

# Miscellaneous Pieces

[From the Renaissance on, "Miscellany" denoted an anthology by several hands, but by the nineteenth century it could designate the work of a single author. Using such headings to gather previous publications, Hemans increased the income of her labor and widened its circulation, as well as signaled a career under way, a body of work oversupplying any particular rubric. Wordsworth put a section of "Miscellaneous Sonnets" in his collections of 1807 and 1815. Hemans thanked Jewsbury in 1826 for lending her "precious copy" of his 1820 *Miscellaneous Poems* (*CM* 1.173), a title that validated the rubric as a primary category. Seven "Miscellaneous Pieces" in the 1825 *Forest Sanctuary &c* expanded to 36 in the second edition (1829), 126 of its 324 pages. Almost half of *Records of Woman &c* is taken up by 38 "Miscellaneous Pieces." FH used Wordsworth's 1820 volume-title for subsections in *Songs of the Affections &c* and *Scenes and Hymns of Life &c*.]

## *The Treasures of the Deep*[1]

What hidest thou in thy treasure-caves and cells?
   Thou hollow-sounding and mysterious main!—
Pale glistening pearls, and rainbow-colour'd shells,
   Bright things which gleam unreck'd-of, and in vain!—
Keep, keep thy riches, melancholy sea!
   We ask not such from thee.

Yet more, the depths have more!—what wealth untold,
   Far down, and shining through their stillness lies!
Thou hast the starry gems, the burning gold,
   Won from ten thousand royal Argosies!—          10
Sweep o'er thy spoils, thou wild and wrathful main!
      Earth claims not *these* again.[2]

Yet more, the depths have more!—thy waves have roll'd
   Above the cities of a world gone by![3]
Sand hath fill'd up the palaces of old,
   Sea-weed o'ergrown the halls of revelry.—
Dash o'er them, ocean! in thy scornful play!
      Man yields them to decay.

Yet more! the billows and the depths have more!
   High hearts and brave are gather'd to thy breast!      20
They hear not now the booming waters roar,
   The battle-thunders will not break their rest.—
Keep thy red gold and gems, thou stormy grave!
      Give back the true and brave!

Give back the lost and lovely!—those for whom
   The place was kept at board and hearth so long!
The prayer went up through midnight's breathless gloom,
   And the vain yearning woke 'midst festal song!
Hold fast thy buried isles, thy towers o'erthrown—
      But all is not thine own.          30

To thee the love of woman hath gone down,
   Dark flow thy tides o'er manhood's noble head,
O'er youth's bright locks, and beauty's flowery crown,
   Yet must thou hear a voice—Restore the dead!
Earth shall reclaim her precious things from thee!—
      Restore the dead, thou sea!

[1] Drafted as "Song / The treasures of the Deep," at the end of *The Forest Sanctuary* MS; first published, unsigned, *NMM* 8 (August 1823). *NMM* variants are chiefly mythicizing capitals: Depths, Main, Ocean, Billows, Dead, Sea (the MS has still more). The verse form is a variation on the "Venus and Adonis" stanza.

[2] A theme sounded at the end of Byron's *Childe Harold's Pilgrimage* (4.179–83).

  *Argosies*: merchant fleets. The word evokes *Argonauts* but is not etymologically related.

[3] There are several myths of cities lost under the sea, Atlantis the most famous.

## Bring Flowers[1]

Bring flowers, young flowers, for the festal board,
To wreathe the cup ere the wine is pour'd;
Bring flowers! they are springing in wood and vale,
Their breath floats out on the southern gale,
And the touch of the sunbeam hath waked the rose,
To deck the hall where the bright wine flows.

Bring flowers to strew in the conqueror's path—
He hath shaken thrones with his stormy wrath!
He comes with the spoils of nations back,
The vines lie crush'd in his chariot's track,                            10
The turf looks red where he won the day—
Bring flowers to die in the conqueror's way!

Bring flowers to the captive's lonely cell,
They have tales of the joyous woods to tell;
Of the free blue streams, and the glowing sky,
And the bright world shut from his languid eye;
They will bear him a thought of the sunny hours,
And a dream of his youth—bring him flowers, wild flowers!

Bring flowers, fresh flowers, for the bride to wear!
They were born to blush in her shining hair.                             20
She is leaving the home of her childhood's mirth,
She hath bid farewell to her father's hearth,
Her place is now by another's side—
Bring flowers for the locks of the fair young bride!

Bring flowers, pale flowers, o'er the bier to shed,
A crown for the brow of the early dead!
For this through its leaves hath the white rose burst,
For this in the woods was the violet nurs'd!
Though they smile in vain for what once was ours,
They are love's last gift—bring ye flowers, pale flowers!                30

Bring flowers to the shrine where we kneel in prayer,
They are nature's offering, their place is *there!*
They speak of hope to the fainting heart,
With a voice of promise they come and part,
They sleep in dust through the wintry hours,
They break forth in glory—bring flowers, bright flowers!

[1] This poem would focus L.E.L.'s elegy (see "Reception").

# From *New Monthly Magazine*

## NOVEMBER 1826

—◦◦◦—

### *The Sound of the Sea*[1]

Thou art sounding on, thou mighty Sea!
  For ever and the same!
The ancient rocks yet ring to thee,
  Those thunders nought can tame.

Oh! many a glorious voice is gone
  From the rich bowers of earth,
And hush'd is many a lovely one
  Of mournfulness or mirth.

The Dorian flute, that sigh'd of yore
  Along thy wave, is still;                    10
The harp of Judah peals no more
  On Zion's awful° hill:[2]              *awe-inspiring*

And Memnon's lyre hath lost the chord
  That breathed the mystic tone,[3]
And the songs, at Rome's high triumphs° pour'd,   *victory parades*
  Are with her eagles flown:[4]

And mute the Moorish horn, that rang
  O'er stream and mountain free,
And the hymn the leagued Crusaders sang
  Hath died in Galilee.                20

But thou art swelling on, thou Deep!
  Through many an olden clime,
Thy billowy anthem, ne'er to sleep
  Until the close of Time.

Thou liftest up thy solemn voice
  To every wind and sky,
And all our Earth's green shores rejoice
  In that one harmony!

It fills the noontide's calm profound,
  The sunset's heaven of gold;              30
And the still midnight hears the sound
  Even as first it roll'd.

> Let there be silence, deep and strange,
> Where crowning[5] cities rose!
> *Thou* speak'st of one who doth not change—
> So may our hearts repose.

[1] Signed "F. H."; also published in *The League of the Alps &c* (1826) without the emblematic capitals of Sea (1), Deep (21), Time (24), Earth (27). The stanza, akin to a ballad's, is a standard one in medieval hymns.

[2] *Judah*: son of Jacob, eponymous ancestor of the most powerful of the twelve tribes of Israel (*Zion*).

[3] Memnon was a prince slain by Achilles in the Trojan War as he tried to protect his uncle Priam, king of Troy. A statue of him was fabled to produce music when struck by the sun.

[4] The eagle was the symbol of the Roman Empire, appropriated by Napoleon.

[5] *League* and later texts] sceptered

# From *Records of Woman:*
## *With Other Poems*

### (1828)

⟨⟨⟨ ⟩⟩⟩

[Since 1818 Hemans had been publishing poetry in *Blackwood's Edinburgh Magazine,* with favorable notice in its reviews. Edinburgh publisher William Blackwood also issued her prize-winning *Wallace's Invocation to Bruce* (1820). As Murray's interest in new volumes of poetry waned amid financial pressures, FH approached Blackwood about *Records of Woman.* He declined to purchase the copyright but agreed to front the expenses and split the profits. It was a good decision; this would be FH's most popular volume. Augmenting her income from the previous publication of most of its poems, it earned her £300 through four editions, from May 1828 to October 1830. "I have put my heart and individual feelings into it more than in any thing else I have written," she wrote to Mary Russell Mitford in March 1828. Quotation marks around attributed epigraphs in *1839* suggest that ones not thus marked are by Hemans.[1] Text: 1st ed. (1828).]

> *Mightier far*
> *Than strength of nerve or sinew, or the sway*
> *Of magic potent over sun and star,*
> *Is love, though oft to agony distrest,*
> *And though his favourite seat be feeble woman's breast.*
> WORDSWORTH[2]

> *Das ist das Los des Schönen auf der Erde!*
> SCHILLER[3]

*To*
### MRS. JOANNA BAILLIE,
*This Volume,*
*As a Slight Token of*
*Grateful Respect and Admiration,*
*is Affectionately Inscribed,*
*By*
*The Author*[4]

---

[1] My notes report the most interesting of the substantive variants from previous publications. For the full report, as well as generous quotations from and further information about sources cited by and relevant to FH, see Paula Feldman's edition (1999).

[2] *Laodamia* (first pub. 1815), 86–90; Laodamia's anguished protest to the shade of her husband Protesilaus, the first Greek soldier killed in the Trojan War (*Aeneid,* bk. 6). Pitying her grief, the gods allowed his shade to visit her for three hours. She hopes that in mercy they will restore him to life; he counsels faith and fortitude, but at his departure, "all in vain exhorted and reproved, / She perished." "Ah, judge her gently who so deeply loved! / Her, who, in reason's spite, yet without crime" (1815); the version of 1827 is more severe: "not without . . . crime."

[3] "That is the lot of the splendid in the world"; from Thekla's last monologue in Friedrich von Schiller's *Wallensteins Tod* (Act 4, scene 12), a lament for the death in battle of her beloved Max

Piccolomini and, more generally, an elegy for the fate of female affections in a world of men at war. The last of a trilogy, *Wallenstein* (1798–99) is based on the fall of Thekla's father, Count von Wallenstein, a seventeenth-century Bohemian general celebrated for his victories on behalf of Ferdinand II but subsequently tempted by dreams of personal ambition. In 1800 Coleridge rendered the second and third plays as *The Piccolomini* and *Wallenstein's Death*, translating the line FH quotes as "That is the lot of heroes upon earth!" (4.6.11, the end of Act 4). FH "could for ever find fresh beauties in *Wallenstein*, with which she was equally familiar in its eloquent original, and in Coleridge's magnificent translation" (*HM* 54); "she could never speak enough of his version of 'Wallenstein,'—no translation, but a transfusion from one language to another" (*CM* 1.79). Thekla haunted her: she frequently alludes to her sorrows in her epigraphs and notes; she translated a poem that Schiller wrote for a friend who wondered about Thekla's fate after her resolve to visit her lover's grave (*Thekla's Song; or, the Voice of Spirit,—from the German of Schiller*, *NMM* 13, January 1825; rpt. *Forest Sanctuary &c*, 2d ed.), and she shaped her own fantasy, *Thekla at Her Lover's Grave* (*Songs of the Affections*).

⁴ Baillie's *Plays on the Passions* (1798–1812) were admired by Wordsworth, Scott, and Byron. In 1823 FH praised the "gentle fortitude" and "deep, self-devoting affection" of her female characters: "so perfectly different from the pretty 'un-idea'd girls,' who seem to form the *beau idéal* of our whole sex in the works of some modern poets" (*CM* 1.196; cf. *HM* 69). When she wrote to Baillie in 1827 to ask permission for this dedication, she addressed her as one "of whom my whole sex may be proud" (*HM* 127; cf. *CM* 1.146). "I am exceedingly proud that any work of yours is indeed to be connected with my name," Baillie replied in kind; "it is an honour which every man & woman in our three Kingdoms would most highly prize" (5 May 1828; Berg Collection, New York Public Library; *Letters* 1161–62). She warmly recommended the volume to a friend as "rich in poetical beauties and well worth your perusal" (15 July 1828; Camden Local Studies and Archives Centre; *Letters* 608).

---

# Records of Woman

[Variously cast as heroic epistles, familiar epistles, soliloquies, romance narratives, lyrics, and first-person meditations, Hemans's set of 19 poems, with 7 scholarly endnotes, joins the genre of "women's lives" that emerged in the 18th c. in such prose works as *Biographium Fæmineum. The Female Worthies: or, Memoirs of the Most Illustrious Ladies of all Ages and Nations* (1766), and marked FH's era with Mary Hays's *Female Biography; or, Memoirs of Illustrious and Celebrated Women, of all Ages and Countries* (1803), Lucy Aikin's poetic *Epistles on Women, Exemplifying Their Character and Condition in Various Ages and Nations* (1810), and Mary Russell Mitford's *Narrative Poems on the Female Character* (1813). Like Aikin's and Mitford's, FH's poems treat ordinary as well as famous lives, yet all united in "Woman's lot." As in Wollstonecraft's *Vindication of the Rights of Woman* (1792), "Woman" is categorical and universal. Although less polemically analytical than Wollstonecraft, FH dramatizes the impact of the sociopolitical sphere on women's lives, their passions, and their families, especially their children. Almost all the "Records" were previously published; ten in *NMM*, 1825–27, under the main title, "Records of Woman," with a serial roman numeral, indicating an ongoing chronicle.]

## *Arabella Stuart*

[This epistle from a prisoner to a husband in exile joins a tradition descending from Ovid's *Heroides* and refreshed by Pope's *Eloisa to Abelard* (1717), one in which the uncertainty of the letter's receipt renders it a kind of a lyric monologue. Arabella Stuart (1575–1615), cousin of James I of England (James VI of Scotland) and niece of Mary Queen of Scots, was a potential claimant to the throne. Elizabeth I was sufficiently nervous about the threat, especially should Lady Arabella bear legitimate issue, that she prevented her from marrying, and placed her under house arrest when she learned of her affection for Edward Seymour. When James succeeded to the throne in 1603, he released her, but in 1610 on discovering her secret marriage to Edward's younger brother William Seymour (1588–1660) he imprisoned the newlyweds, separately. In June 1611 they eluded their jailors. Seymour arrived at their agreed-upon destination, Ostend, Belgium, but Lady Arabella was recaptured and sent to the Tower of London (the setting of this "Record"), where she died in 1615. Seymour returned in 1616 after her death; he would fight for Charles I in the Civil Wars of the 1640s and recover his family's ancestral dukedom after the Restoration.]

"The Lady Arabella," as she has been frequently entitled, was descended from Margaret, eldest daughter of Henry VII and consequently allied by birth to Elizabeth, as well as James I. This affinity to the throne proved the misfortune of her life, as the jealousies which it constantly excited in her royal relatives, who were anxious to prevent her marrying, shut her out from the enjoyment of that domestic happiness which her heart appears to have so fervently desired. By a secret, but early discovered union with William Seymour, son of Lord Beauchamp, she alarmed the cabinet of James, and the wedded lovers were immediately placed in separate confinement. From this they found means to concert a romantic plan of escape; and having won over a female attendant, by whose assistance she was disguised in male attire, Arabella, though faint from recent sickness and suffering, stole out in the night, and at last reached an appointed spot, where a boat and servants were in waiting. She embarked; and, at break of day, a French vessel, engaged to receive her, was discovered and gained. As Seymour, however, had not yet arrived, she was desirous that the vessel should lie at anchor for him; but this wish was overruled by her companions, who, contrary to her entreaties, hoisted sail, "which," says D'Israeli, "occasioned so fatal a termination to this romantic adventure. Seymour, indeed, had escaped from the Tower;—he reached the wharf, and found his confidential man waiting with a boat, and arrived at Lee.[1] The time passed; the waves were rising; Arabella was not there; but in the distance he descried a vessel. Hiring a fisherman to take him on board, he discovered, to his grief, on hailing it, that it was not the French ship charged with his Arabella; in despair and confusion he found another ship from Newcastle, which for a large sum altered its course, and landed him in Flanders."—Arabella, meantime, whilst imploring her attendants to linger, and earnestly looking out for the expected boat of her husband, was overtaken in Calais Roads[2] by a vessel in the King's service, and brought back to a captivity, under the suffering of which her mind and constitution gradually sank.—"What passed in that dreadful imprisonment, cannot perhaps be recovered for authentic history,—but enough is known; that her mind grew impaired, that she finally lost her reason, and, if the duration of her imprisonment was short, that it was only terminated by her death. Some effusions, often begun and never ended, written and erased, incoherent and rational, yet remain among her papers."—D'Israeli's *Curiosities of Literature*.[3]————The following poem, meant as some record of her fate, and the imagined fluctuations of her thoughts and feelings, is supposed to commence during the time of her first imprisonment, whilst her mind was yet buoyed up by the consciousness of Seymour's affection, and the cherished hope of eventual deliverance.

> *And is not love in vain,*
> *Torture enough without a living tomb?*
>
>                                   BYRON.[4]

> *Fermossi al fin il cor che balzò tanto.*
>
>                                   PINDEMONTE.[5]

### I

'Twas but a dream!—I saw the stag leap free,
    Under the boughs where early birds were singing,
I stood, o'ershadow'd by the greenwood tree,[6]
    And heard, it seemed a sudden bugle ringing
Far thro' a royal forest: then the fawn
Shot, like a gleam of light, from grassy lawn
To secret covert; and the smooth turf shook,
And lilies quiver'd by the glade's lone brook,
And young leaves trembled, as, in fleet career,
A princely band, with horn, and hound, and spear,          10
Like a rich masque swept forth. I saw the dance
Of their white plumes, that bore a silvery glance
Into the deep wood's heart; and all pass'd by,
Save one—I met the smile of *one* clear eye,
Flashing out joy to mine.—Yes, *thou* wert there,
Seymour! a soft wind blew the clustering hair
Back from thy gallant brow, as thou didst rein
Thy courser, turning from that gorgeous train,
And fling, methought, thy hunting-spear away,
And, lightly graceful in thy green array,                  20
Bound to my side; and we, that met and parted,
    Ever in dread of some dark watchful power,
Won back to childhood's trust, and, fearless-hearted,
    Blent the glad fulness of our thoughts that hour,
Ev'n like the mingling of sweet streams, beneath
Dim woven leaves, and midst the floating breath
Of hidden forest flowers.

II

'Tis past!—I wake,
A captive, and alone, and far from thee,
My love and friend! Yet fostering, for thy sake,
    A quenchless hope of happiness to be;　　　　　　30
And feeling still my woman's spirit strong,
In the deep faith which lifts from earthly wrong,
A heavenward glance. I know, I know our love
Shall yet call gentle angels from above,
By its undying fervour; and prevail,
Sending a breath, as of the spring's first gale,
Thro' hearts not cold; and raising its bright face,
With a free gush of sunny tears erase
The characters of anguish; in this trust,
I bear, I strive, I bow not to the dust,　　　　　　40
That I may bring thee back no faded form,
No bosom chill'd and blighted by the storm,
But all my youth's first treasures, when we meet,
Making past sorrow, by communion, sweet.

III

And thou too art in bonds!—yet droop thou not,
Oh, my belov'd!—there is *one* hopeless lot,
But one, and that not ours. Beside the dead
*There* sits the grief that mantles up its head,
Loathing the laughter and proud pomp of light,
When darkness, from the vainly-doting sight,　　　　50
Covers its beautiful![7] If thou wert gone
    To the grave's bosom, with thy radiant brow,—
If thy deep-thrilling voice, with that low tone
    Of earnest tenderness, which now, ev'n now,
Seems floating thro' my soul, were music taken
For ever from this world,—oh! thus forsaken,
Could I bear on?—thou liv'st, thou liv'st, thou'rt mine!
With this glad thought I make my heart a shrine,
And by the lamp which quenchless there shall burn,
Sit, a lone watcher for the day's return.　　　　　　60

IV

And lo! the joy that cometh with the morning,[8]
    Brightly victorious o'er the hours of care!
I have not watch'd in vain, serenely scorning
    The wild and busy whispers of despair!

Thou hast sent tidings, as of heaven.—I wait
   The hour, the sign, for blessed flight to thee.
Oh! for the skylark's wing that seeks its mate
   As a star shoots!—but on the breezy sea
We shall meet soon.—To think of such an hour!
   Will not my heart, o'erburden'd by its bliss,     70
Faint and give way within me, as a flower
   Borne down and perishing by noontide's kiss?
Yet shall I *fear* that lot?—the perfect rest,
The full deep joy of dying on thy breast,
After long-suffering won? So rich a close
Too seldom crowns with peace affection's woes.

V

Sunset!—I tell each moment—from the skies
   The last red splendour floats along my wall,
Like a king's banner!—Now it melts, it dies!
   I see one star—I hear—'twas not the call,     80
Th' expected voice; my quick heart throbb'd too soon.
I must keep vigil till yon rising moon
Shower down less golden light. Beneath her beam
Thro' my lone lattice pour'd, I sit and dream
Of summer-lands afar, where holy love,
Under the vine, or in the citron-grove,
May breathe from terror.
               Now the night grows deep,
And silent as its clouds, and full of sleep.
I hear my veins beat.—Hark! a bell's slow chime.
My heart strikes with it.—Yet again—'tis time!     90
A step!—a voice!—or but a rising breeze?
Hark!—haste!—I come, to meet thee on the seas.

*   *   *   *   *   *   *   *   *   *   *   *

VI

Now never more, oh! never, in the worth
Of its pure cause, let sorrowing love on earth
Trust fondly—never more!—the hope is crush'd
That lit my life, the voice within me hush'd
That spoke sweet oracles; and I return
To lay my youth, as in a burial-urn,
Where sunshine may not find it.—All is lost!
No tempest met our barks—no billow toss'd;     100
Yet were they sever'd, ev'n as we must be,
That so have lov'd, so striven our hearts to free

From their close-coiling fate! In vain—in vain!
The dark links meet, and clasp themselves again,
And press out life.—Upon the deck I stood,
And a white sail came gliding o'er the flood,
Like some proud bird of ocean; then mine eye
Strained out, one moment earlier to descry
The form it ached for, and the bark's career
Seem'd slow to that fond yearning: It drew near,      110
Fraught with our foes!—What boots it to recall
The strife, the tears? Once more a prison-wall
Shuts the green hills and woodlands from my sight,
And joyous glance of waters to the light,
And thee, my Seymour, thee!

               I will not sink!
  Thou, *thou* hast rent the heavy chain that bound thee;
And this shall be my strength—the joy to think
    That thou mayst wander with heaven's breath around thee,
And all the laughing sky! This thought shall yet
Shine o'er my heart, a radiant amulet,      120
Guarding it from despair. Thy bonds are broken,
And unto me, I know, thy true love's token
Shall one day be deliverance, tho' the years
Lie dim between, o'erhung with mists of tears.

VII

My friend, my friend! where art thou? Day by day,
Gliding, like some dark mournful stream, away,
My silent youth flows from me. Spring, the while,
  Comes and rains beauty on the kindling boughs
Round hall and hamlet; Summer, with her smile,
    Fills the green forest;—young hearts breathe their vows;      130
Brothers long parted meet; fair children rise
Round the glad board; Hope laughs from loving eyes:
All this is in the world!—These joys lie sown,
The dew of every path—On *one* alone
Their freshness may not fall—the stricken deer,
Dying of thirst with all the waters near.[9]

VIII

Ye are from dingle and fresh glade, ye flowers!
  By some kind hand to cheer my dungeon sent;
O'er you the oak shed down the summer showers,
    And the lark's news was where your bright cups bent,      140

Quivering to breeze and rain-drop, like the sheen
Of twilight stars. On you Heaven's eye hath been,
Thro' the leaves, pouring its dark sultry blue
Into your glowing hearts; the bee to you
Hath murmur'd, and the rill.—My soul grows faint
With passionate yearning, as its quick dreams paint
Your haunts by dell and stream,—the green, the free,
The full of all sweet sound,—the shut from me!

IX

There went a swift bird singing past my cell—
   O Love and Freedom! ye are lovely things!      150
With you the peasant on the hills may dwell,
   And by the streams; but I—the blood of kings,
A proud, unmingling river, thro' my veins
Flows in lone brightness,—and its gifts are chains!
Kings!—I had silent visions of deep bliss,
Leaving their thrones far distant, and for this
I am cast under their triumphal car,
An insect to be crush'd.—Oh! Heaven is far,—
Earth pitiless!

Dost thou forget me, Seymour? I am prov'd      160
So long, so sternly! Seymour, my belov'd!
There are such tales of holy marvels done
By strong affection, of deliverance won
Thro' its prevailing power! Are these things told
Till the young weep with rapture, and the old
Wonder, yet dare not doubt,—and thou, oh! thou,
   Dost thou forget me in my hope's decay?—
Thou canst not!—thro' the silent night, ev'n now,
   I, that need prayer so much, awake and pray
Still first for thee.—Oh! gentle, gentle friend!      170
How shall I bear this anguish to the end?

Aid!—comes there yet no aid?—the voice of blood
Passes Heaven's gate, ev'n ere the crimson flood
Sinks thro' the greensward!—is there not a cry
From the wrung heart, of power, thro' agony,
To pierce the clouds? Hear, Mercy! hear me! None
That bleed and weep beneath the smiling sun,
Have heavier cause!—yet hear!—my soul grows dark—
Who hears the last shriek from the sinking bark,
On the mid seas, and with the storm alone,      180
And bearing to th' abyss, unseen, unknown,

Its freight of human hearts?—th' o'ermastering wave!
Who shall tell how it rush'd—and none to save?

Thou hast forsaken me![10] I feel, I know,
There would be rescue if this were not so.
Thou'rt at the chase, thou'rt at the festive board,
Thou'rt where the red wine free and high is pour'd,
Thou'rt where the dancers meet!—a magic glass
Is set within my soul, and proud shapes pass,
Flushing it o'er with pomp from bower and hall;—                    190
I see one shadow, stateliest there of all,—
*Thine!*—What dost *thou* amidst the bright and fair,
Whispering light words, and mocking my despair?
It is not well of thee!—my love was more
Than fiery song may breathe, deep thought explore,
And there thou smilest, while my heart is dying,
With all its blighted hopes around it lying;
Ev'n thou, on whom they hung their last green leaf—
Yet smile, smile on! too bright art thou for grief!

Death!—what, is death a lock'd and treasur'd thing,                 200
Guarded by swords of fire?[11] A hidden spring,
A fabled fruit, that I should thus endure,
As if the world within me held no cure?
Wherefore not spread free wings—Heaven, Heaven! controul
These thoughts—they rush—I look into my soul
As down a gulph, and tremble at th' array
Of fierce forms crowding it! Give strength to pray.
So shall their dark host pass.

                  The storm is still'd.
  Father in Heaven! Thou, only thou, canst sound
The heart's great deep, with floods of anguish fill'd,               210
  For human line° too fearfully profound.                    *plumb line*
Therefore, forgive, my Father! if Thy child,
Rock'd on its heaving darkness, hath grown wild,
And sinn'd in her despair! It well may be,
That Thou shouldst lead my spirit back to Thee,
By the crush'd hope too long on this world pour'd,
The stricken love which hath perchance ador'd
A mortal in Thy place! Now let me strive
With Thy strong arm no more! Forgive, forgive!
Take me to peace!

              And peace at last is nigh.          220
  A sign is on my brow, a token sent

Th' o'erwearied dust, from home: no breeze flits by,
    But calls me with a strange sweet whisper, blent
Of many mysteries.

                    Hark! the warning tone
Deepens—its word is *Death*. Alone, alone,
And sad in youth, but chasten'd, I depart,
Bowing to heaven. Yet, yet my woman's heart
Shall wake a spirit and a power to bless,
Ev'n in this hour's o'ershadowing fearfulness,
Thee, its first love!—oh! tender still, and true!          230
Be it forgotten if mine anguish threw
Drops from its bitter fountain on thy name,
Tho' but a moment.

                Now, with fainting frame,
With soul just lingering on the flight begun,
To bind for thee its last dim thoughts in one,
I bless thee! Peace be on thy noble head,
Years of bright fame, when I am with the dead!
I bid this prayer survive me, and retain
Its might, again to bless thee, and again!
Thou hast been gather'd into my dark fate          240
Too much; too long, for my sake, desolate
Hath been thine exiled youth; but now take back,
From dying hands, thy freedom, and re-track
(After a few kind tears for her whose days
Went out in dreams of thee) the sunny ways
Of hope, and find thou happiness! Yet send,
Ev'n then, in silent hours a thought, dear friend!
Down to my voiceless chamber; for thy love
Hath been to me all gifts of earth above,
Tho' bought with burning tears! It is the sting          250
Of Death to leave that vainly-precious thing
In this cold world! What were it then, if thou,
With thy fond eyes, wert gazing on me now?
Too keen a pang!—Farewell! and yet once more,
Farewell![12]—the passion of long years I pour
Into that word: thou hear'st not,—but the wo
And fervour of its tones may one day flow
To thy heart's holy place; there let them dwell—
We shall o'ersweep the grave to meet—Farewell!

[1] A town six miles southeast of London.

[2] Natural harbors.

[3] Paraphrasing Isaac D'Israeli (1766–1848), "The Loves of 'The Lady Arabella'," *Curiosities of Literature*, second series (London: John Murray, 1823). He was a close friend of Murray and father of Benjamin Disraeli. *Curiosities* is a collection of literary and historical anecdotes.

[4] *The Prophecy of Dante* (1821) 3.147–48. Byron sets this monologue during Dante's exile, between his completion of *The Divine Comedy* and his death. In these lines, he foresees Tasso's fate with his patron Alphonso II, Duke of Ferrara, who had him confined to an asylum for several years when his behavior proved too erratic; one legend, popularized by Goethe and Byron, was that the duke was outraged by Tasso's passionate love for his sister Leonora d'Este, and released him only on condition of exile. See Byron's *Lament of Tasso* (1817), and FH's *Tasso and His Sister*.

[5] Stopped at last, the heart that had beat so strongly.

Ippolito Pindemonte (1753–1828), *Clizia* (55); in his *Poesie Varie* the line reads "Fermasi alfin quel cor. . . ." That FH's slight misquotation duplicates Staël's in *Corinne* (bk. 18, ch. 5), where Corinne quotes these words, dying of a broken heart, suggests that *Corinne* was her source; cf. the epigraph of *The Abencerrage* canto 3. *Clizia* draws on the story in Ovid's *Metamorphoses* (4.257–90) of the nymph Clytie, whose jealousy of Leucothoe, beloved of Hyperion's son, sets in motion a chain of events leading to Leucothoe's death. Clytie is devastated by his consequent scorn of her; line 55 refers to the moment when, wasting away in futile desire, she turns into a heliotrope, forever fixated on the sun godling. FH transcribed this line "in a book of manuscript extracts, belonging to a friend. [. . .] Above was written, 'Felicia Hemans' epitaph'" (*CM* 2.323). Lawrence made it the epigraph for *Recollections of Mrs. Hemans: Irregular Stanzas, Written in the Library, Wavertree Hall* (*Last Autumn* 231). FH admired Pindemonte's poetry and included his sonnet, *On the Hebe of Canova* in *Translations &c* (1818).

[6] Cf. Amiens's song celebrating the forest of Arden, a place of exile and refuge from court politics in *As You Like It* (2.5.1).

[7] "Wheresoever you are, or in what state soever you be, it sufficeth me you are mine. *Rachel wept, and would not be comforted, because her children were no more.* And that, indeed, is the remediless sorrow, and none else!"—From a letter of Arabella Stuart's to her husband.—See Curiosities of Literature." [FH]

D'Israeli prints the entire letter, sent during the couple's first imprisonment. Stuart quotes from Matthew 2.18, which describes the aftermath of Herod's Massacre of the Innocents of Bethlehem. See also Sarah Jayne Steen, ed., *The Letters of Arabella Stuart* (New York: Oxford UP, 1994) 81–97.

[8] Cf. Psalm 30: "weeping may endure for a night, but joy cometh in the morning" (5).

[9] A standard Petrarchan conceit for the desperate lover; also an echo of Cowper's famous self-description in *The Task* (1785): "I was a stricken deer that left the herd / Long since; with many an arrow deep infixt / My panting side was charged when I withdrew / To seek a tranquil death in distant shade." Cowper's victim was rescued and restored by a fellow victim (3.108 ff.).

[10] Cf. Christ on the cross: "My God, my God, why hast thou forsaken me?" (Mark 15.34).

[11] "'And if you remember of old, *I dare die.* [. . .] Consider what the world would conceive, if I should be violently enforced to do it.'—*Fragments of her Letters.*" [FH]

From two letters circa March 1611, during her second imprisonment (D'Israeli includes both). Lacking "his majesty's favour," she was fearful of all around her and was contemplating suicide. The first letter was to Thomas Erskine, the second to the Privy Council; see Steen 257–59.

[12] Lawrence uses this "Farewell!" as her title-page epigraph for the edition of *The Last Autumn* that adds her *Recollections of Mrs. Hemans.*

## The Bride of the Greek Isle[1]

["Of the Greek Isle" names not only an origin but also a spiritual fidelity to a land enslaved for centuries by the Ottoman Empire. The War for Greek Independence, sparked by a revolt in 1821 and championed by British Hellenists, including the Shelleys and Byron, would be won in 1832. As a call for renewed struggle, in 1822 Percy Shelley published *Hellas*, about ancient Greece's defeat of Xerxes' Persian grand army. In various works, especially *The Corsair* (1814) and *Don Juan IV-VI* (1821–23), Byron celebrated or exhorted the independent spirit of the Greeks against Ottoman oppression; he died in Greece in 1824 while training a regiment he had financed for the struggle. One of his best-known songs was "The Isles of Greece" (*Don Juan III* [1821]), often printed independently. Hemans's *Bride* appeals to this political context, which her literary Byronism amplifies. Byron had used octosyllabic couplets for *The Bride of Abydos* (1813), also set on a Greek isle and involving similar elements (pirates, a fatally interrupted wedding), and presenting his first "heroine." Like *Hellas* and *Sardanapalus*, Hemans's *Bride* evokes enslaved Greece in the figure of an enslaved Greek maid, but one whose imprisonment and self-annihilating resistance give an allegory of "Woman" that exceeds the specific issue of Greece.]

> *Fear!—I'm a Greek, and how should I fear death?*
> *A slave, and wherefore should I dread my freedom?*
>
> .   .   .   .   .   .   .   .   .   .   .   .   .   .   .
>
> *I will not live degraded.*
> > > > —Sardanapalus[2]

Come from the woods with the citron-flowers,
Come with your lyres for the festal hours,
Maids of bright Scio![3] They came, and the breeze
Bore their sweet songs o'er the Grecian seas;—
They came, and Eudora[4] stood rob'd and crown'd,
The bride of the morn, with her train around.
Jewels flash'd out from her braided hair,
Like starry dews midst the roses there;
Pearls on her bosom quivering shone,
Heav'd by her heart thro' its golden zone°;                    *breast-sash*
But a brow, as those gems of the ocean pale,                    11
Gleam'd from beneath her transparent veil;
Changeful and faint was her fair cheek's hue,
Tho' clear as a flower which the light looks through;
And the glance of her dark resplendent eye,
For the aspect of woman[5] at times too high,
Lay floating in mists, which the troubled stream
Of the soul sent up o'er its fervid beam.

She look'd on the vine at her father's door,
Like one that is leaving his native shore;                    20
She hung o'er the myrtle once call'd her own,
As it greenly wav'd by the threshold stone;

She turn'd—and her mother's gaze brought back
Each hue of her childhood's faded track.
Oh! hush the song, and let her tears
Flow to the dream of her early years!
Holy and pure are the drops that fall
When the young bride goes from her father's hall;
She goes unto love yet untried and new,
She parts from love which hath still been true;                     30
Mute be the song and the choral strain,
Till her heart's deep well-spring is clear again!

She wept on her mother's faithful breast,
Like a babe that sobs itself to rest;
She wept—yet laid her hand awhile
In *his* that waited her dawning smile,
Her soul's affianced, nor cherish'd less
For the gush of nature's[6] tenderness!
She lifted her graceful head at last—
The choking swell of her heart was past;                            40
And her lovely thoughts from their cells found way
In the sudden flow of a plaintive lay.[7]

### THE BRIDE'S FAREWELL

Why do I weep?—to leave the vine
  Whose clusters o'er me bend,—
The myrtle—yet, oh! call it mine!—
  The flowers I lov'd to tend.
A thousand thoughts of all things dear,
  Like shadows o'er me sweep,
I leave my sunny childhood here,
  Oh, therefore let me weep!                                   50

I leave thee, sister! we have play'd
  Thro' many a joyous hour,
Where the silvery green of the olive shade
  Hung dim o'er fount and bower.
Yes, thou and I, by stream, by shore,
  In song, in prayer, in sleep,
Have been as we may be no more—
  Kind sister, let me weep!

I leave thee, father! Eve's bright moon
  Must now light other feet,                                    60
With the gather'd grapes, and the lyre in tune,
  Thy homeward step to greet.

Thou in whose voice, to bless thy child,
 Lay tones of love so deep,
Whose eye o'er all my youth hath smiled—
 I leave thee! let me weep!

Mother! I leave thee! on thy breast,
 Pouring out joy and wo,
I have found that holy place of rest
 Still changeless,—yet I go!     70
Lips, that have lull'd me with your strain,
 Eyes, that have watch'd my sleep!
Will earth give love like *yours* again?
 Sweet mother! let me weep!

And like a slight young tree, that throws
The weight of rain from its drooping boughs,
Once more she wept. But a changeful thing
Is the human heart, as a mountain spring,
That works its way, thro' the torrent's foam,
To the bright pool near it, the lily's home!   80
It is well!—the cloud, on her soul that lay,
Hath melted in glittering drops away.
Wake again, mingle, sweet flute and lyre!
She turns to her lover, she leaves her sire.
Mother! on earth it must still be so,
Thou rearest the lovely to see them go!
They are moving onward, the bridal throng,
Ye may track their way by the swells of song;
Ye may catch thro' the foliage their white robes' gleam,
Like a swan midst the reeds of a shadowy stream.  90
Their arms bear up garlands, their gliding tread
Is over the deep-vein'd violet's bed;
They have light leaves around them, blue skies above,
An arch for the triumph of youth and love!

II

Still and sweet was the home that stood
In the flowering depths of a Grecian wood,
With the soft green light o'er its low roof spread,
As if from the glow of an emerald shed,
Pouring thro' lime-leaves that mingled on high,
Asleep in the silence of noon's clear sky.    100
Citrons amidst their dark foliage glow'd,
Making a gleam round the lone abode;
Laurels o'erhung it, whose faintest shiver
Scatter'd out rays like a glancing river;

Stars of the jasmine its pillars crown'd,
Vine-stalks its lattice and walls had bound,
And brightly before it a fountain's play
Flung showers thro' a thicket of glossy bay,
To a cypress[8] which rose in that flashing rain,
Like one tall shaft of some fallen fane.                               110

And thither Ianthis[9] had brought his bride,
And the guests were met by that fountain-side;
They lifted the veil from Eudora's face,
It smiled out softly in pensive grace,
With lips of love, and a brow serene,
Meet for the soul of the deep wood-scene.—
Bring wine, bring odours!—the board is spread—
Bring roses! a chaplet° for every head!                                *wreath*
The wine-cups foam'd, and the rose was shower'd
On the young and fair from the world embower'd,                        120
The sun look'd not on them in that sweet shade,
The winds amid scented boughs were laid;
But there came by fits, thro' some wavy[10] tree,
A sound and a gleam of the moaning sea.

    Hush! be still!—was that no more
    Than the murmur from the shore?
    Silence!—did thick rain-drops beat
    On the grass like trampling feet?—
    Fling down the goblet, and draw the sword!
    The groves are filled with a pirate-horde![11]               130
    Thro' the dim olives their sabres shine;—
    Now must the red blood stream for wine!

The youths from the banquet to battle sprang,
The woods with the shriek of the maidens rang;
Under the golden-fruited boughs
There were flashing poniards,° and darkening brows,                    *daggers*
Footsteps, o'er garland and lyre that fled;
And the dying soon on a greensward bed.

Eudora, Eudora! *thou* dost not fly!—
She saw but Ianthis before her lie,                                    140
With the blood from his breast in a gushing flow,
Like a child's large tears in its hour of wo,
And a gathering film in his lifted eye,
That sought his young bride out mournfully.—
She knelt down beside him, her arms she wound,
Like tendrils, his drooping neck around,

As if the passion of that fond grasp
Might chain in life with its ivy-clasp.

But they tore her thence in her wild despair,
The sea's fierce rovers—they left him there;                    150
They left to the fountain a dark-red vein,
And on the wet violets a pile of slain,
And a hush of fear thro' the summer-grove,—
So clos'd the triumph of youth and love!

### III

Gloomy lay the shore that night,
When the moon, with sleeping light,
Bath'd each purple Sciote° hill,—                    *(of Scio)*
Gloomy lay the shore, and still.
O'er the wave no gay guitar
Sent its floating music far;                    160
No glad sound of dancing feet
Woke, the starry hours to greet.
But a voice of mortal wo,
In its changes wild or low,
Thro' the midnight's blue repose,
From the sea-beat rocks arose,
As Eudora's mother stood
Gazing o'er th' Egean flood,
With a fix'd and straining eye—
Oh! was the spoilers' vessel nigh?                    170
Yes! there, becalm'd in silent sleep,
Dark and alone on a breathless deep,
On a sea of molten silver dark,
Brooding it frown'd that evil bark!
There its broad pennon a shadow cast,
Moveless and black from the tall still mast,
And the heavy sound of its flapping sail,
Idly and vainly wooed the gale.
Hush'd was all else—had ocean's breast
Rock'd e'en Eudora that hour to rest?                    180

To rest?—the waves tremble!—what piercing cry
Bursts from the heart of the ship on high?
What light through the heavens, in a sudden spire,
Shoots from the deck up? Fire! 'tis fire!
There are wild forms hurrying to and fro,
Seen darkly clear on that lurid glow;[12]
There are shout, and signal-gun, and call,
And the dashing of water,—but fruitless all!

Man[13] may not fetter, nor ocean tame
The might and wrath of the rushing flame!                                  190
It hath twined the mast like a glittering snake,
That coils up a tree from a dusky brake;
It hath touch'd the sails, and their canvass rolls
Away from its breath into shrivell'd scrolls;
It hath taken the flag's high place in air,
And redden'd the stars with its wavy glare,
And sent out bright arrows, and soar'd in glee,
To a burning mount midst the moonlight sea.
The swimmers are plunging from stern and prow—
Eudora, Eudora! where, where art thou?                                      200
The slave and his master alike are gone.—
Mother! who stands on the deck alone?
The child of thy bosom!—and lo! a brand
Blazing up high in her lifted hand![14]
And her veil flung back, and her free dark hair
Sway'd by the flames as they rock and flare,[15]
And her fragile form to its loftiest height
Dilated, as if by the spirit's might,
And her eye with an eagle-gladness fraught,—
Oh! could this work be of woman wrought?[16]                                210
Yes! 'twas her deed!—by that haughty smile
It was her's!—She hath kindled her funeral pile!
Never might shame on that bright head be,
Her blood was the Greek's, and hath made her free.

Proudly she stands, like an Indian bride
On the pyre with the holy dead beside;[17]
But a shriek from her mother hath caught her ear,
As the flames to her marriage-robe draw near,
And starting, she spreads her pale arms in vain
To the form they must never infold again.                                   220
One moment more, and her hands are clasp'd,
Fallen is the torch they had wildly grasp'd,
Her sinking knee unto Heaven is bow'd,
And her last look rais'd thro' the smoke's dim shroud,
And her lips as in prayer for her pardon move—
Now the night gathers o'er youth and love![18]

[1] Founded on a circumstance related in the Second Series of the Curiosities of Literature, and forming part of a picture in the "Painted Biography" there described. [FH]

D'Israeli, "Of a Biography Painted," in *Curiosities* (1823). The *NMM* note names D'Israeli and adds: "The scene of the catastrophe is [. . .] transferred from Cyprus to the Greek Isles." This eighteen-page biography, writes D'Israeli, gives "the travels and adventures of Charles Magius, a noble Venetian" in "a series of highly-finished miniature paintings on vellum, some executed by the hand of Paul Veronese." Magius himself had been captured and enslaved by the Turks. One of the paintings shows "two ships on fire; a young lady of Cyprus preferring death to the loss of her honour and the miseries of slavery, determined to set fire to the vessel in which she was carried; she succeeded, and the flames communicated to another."

First published *NMM* 14 (October 1825), 370–74, *Records of Woman, No. III*, signed "F.H."

[2] Not in *NMM*. *Sardanapalus* is set during the last days of this Assyrian king and his lover, his Greek slave Myrrha. FH's first epigraph (1.2.479–80) is her heroic pledge to die with him if he is defeated by his enemies; the second (1.2.629) is his determination—part self-indulgence, part narcissism, part self-pity, part heroism—to commit suicide rather than be taken captive, exiled, or worse, enslaved. They die together in a self-ignited immolation as the palace is attacked.

[3] Scio (Chois) is the reputed birthplace of Homer. FH's opening lines have several echoes of the opening stanzas of Byron's *Bride of Abydos*. In 1822 the Ottomans attacked this isle, massacring 20,000 and enslaving 45,000. Delacroix's lurid and provocative painting, *Scenes from the Chios Massacre* (1824) galvanized public outrage, and FH treats the subject, in aftermath, in *Greek Song: The Voice of Scio* (unsigned, *NMM* 7 [April, 1823]) and *The Sisters of Scio* (*LS* 1830, 181–82, with a full-page engraved illustration, signed "Mrs. Hemans"; rpt. *Songs of the Affections &c*).

[4] Her name means "good gift"; it also evokes "Medora," the loyal, loving, fatally devoted wife of Byron's pirate-hero in *The Corsair*.

[5] *NMM*] Woman; also in line 210.

[6] *NMM*] Nature's

[7] A Greek Bride, on leaving her father's house, takes leave of her friends and relatives frequently in extemporaneous verse.—See Fauriel's Chants Populaires de la Grèce Moderne. [FH]

*NMM*] A Greek bride, before she quits her father's house, "fait de tendres adieux à son père, à sa mère, à ses proches, à ses amies, à tout son voisinage, et aux lieux où se sont passés les jours de son enfance.[. . .] en certains endroits, la douleur de la fiancée s'exprime par une formule d'usage." [FH]

["bids tender farewells to her father, to her mother, to her kindred, to her friends, to all her neighbors, and to all those places where the days of her childhood were passed.[. . .] in certain points, the bride's sorrow is expressed by a customary formula."]

Claude Charles Fauriel (1772–1844), *Chants Populaires de la Grèce Moderne*, 2 vols. (Paris: Didot, 1824), 1.xxxv. Protégé of Staël, Fauriel meant this translated and annotated collection both to bring the songs to French attention and to fuel the cause of Greek independence. *Chants* opened "a world of new ideas and feelings" to FH, and suggested "some of her sweetest lyrics" (*HM* 166 n). Charles B. Sheridan's English translation of Fauriel was published in London in 1824.

[8] A symbol of mourning; cf. Byron's *Bride*: after the bride and her beloved die, "dark above" their palace the "sad but living cypress glooms, / And withers not, though branch and leaf / Are stamp'd with an eternal grief" (2.665–68).

[9] This wedding stanza is a (tetrameter) sonnet, the last lines with the drama of a Shakespearean couplet. Perhaps inspired by sonnet stanzas in Byron's *Giaour* (374–87; 674–88), *Bride of Abydos* (2.VII, 2.X), and *Corsair* (1.III, 3.194–207, XII, 567–80), FH used such forms thematically in *Tales, and Historic Scenes*; see *Widow of Crescentius* and *Abencerrage*. "Ianthus" derives from a word meaning "violet" (cf. 92, 152), a perennial often used to symbolize rebirth and hope (ironic here). The female name, Ianthe, has notable lineage: she is the heroine of William D'Avenant's play, *The Siege of Rhodes* (1656), who saves her husband and the defenders of this Greek isle against Sulayman the Magnificent (whose Ottoman forces succeeded in 1523); the dedicatee of Byron's *Childe Harold's Pilgrimage I–II* (1812); Shelley's daughter by his first wife, lost in a highly publicized custody case (1817), in which figured prominently his controversial poem *Queen Mab* (1813), with a character named Ianthe.

[10] *NMM*] whispery

[11] Piracy was widespread in the Mediterranean in the 18th c. and early 19th c., operating with a political independence and commercial disruption that threatened Ottoman control of the eastern region. FH conflates piracy with Ottoman oppression, even as she uses the pirate raid as the creative emergency of romance tradition.

[12] The hellish atmosphere and Satanic-Byronic energy of the scene is amplified by its recollection of Milton's depiction of hell as a fiery "darkness visible" (*Paradise Lost* 1.63ff.).

[13] In the political structure of the poem, this word seems gender-specific, with "fetter" (whether by pirate enslavement or patriarchal marriage) playing against the "free" state Eudora claims for herself (205, 214) just before her death.

[14] *Brand / hand* is a signature rhyme in Byron's "Eastern tales." FH aligns Eudora's act with their heroes' violent heroics (e.g., *The Corsair* 1.131–32, 1.163–64, 2.483–84). The blazing brand also evokes the spiritual rigor of the "flaming Brand" with which Archangel Michael's Seraphim raze fallen Eden (*Paradise Lost* 12.643).

[15] Unbound female hair traditionally signifies release from inhibitions and proprieties and an emergence into political and erotic liberation; cf. Stephania (*Widow of Crescentius* 1.107–8) and Maimuna in *The Indian City*. See also the visionary dream-maiden in Shelley's *Alastor*, "Her dark locks floating in the breath of night" (178) and Byron's heroines: Gulnare who, after killing the Pacha, "threw back her dark far-floating hair" (*The Corsair* 3.410); Myrrha, turned warrior to defend Sardanapalus: "her kindled cheek; / Her large black eyes that flash'd through her long hair / As it stream'd o'er her; her blue veins that rose / Along her most transparent brow; her nostril / Dilated from its symmetry; her lips / Apart" (3.1.387–92).

[16] A reworking of the rhyme from *The Widow of Crescentius* where vengeful Stephania-Guido indicts Otho with the effects of his treachery on her: "Aye! view the wreck with shuddering thought,— / The work of ruin thou hast wrought!" (2.271–72).

[17] The suttee (from the Sanskrit for "faithful wife"), a suicide rite culturally compelled and sometimes violently enforced, was still prevalent in 1828 (it would be abolished by the British Raj in 1829). Jewsbury's *Song of the Hindoo Women, While Accompanying a Widow to the Funeral Pile of Her Husband* (*Phantasmagoria* [1825]), which FH knew, is prefaced by an idealized description from James Forbes's *Oriental Memoirs* (London, 1813). In the trappings of a second marriage, the widow immolates herself on her husband's funeral pyre, ostensibly to join him beyond the grave. In temporal terms, such suicide reflects a consensus about the worthlessness of widows, and within the severe patriarchal culture it was security against a miserable or ambitious wife conspiring to murder her husband. In *Sardanapalus*, Myrrha declares her superiority to the suttee when she willingly joins the king in a suicide conflagration.

[18] "Originally published, as well as several other of these Records, in the *New Monthly Magazine*." [FH]

---

# The Switzer's Wife[1]

Werner Stauffacher, one of the three confederates of the field of Grutli, had been alarmed by the envy with which the Austrian Bailiff, Landenberg, had noticed the appearance of wealth and comfort which distinguished his dwelling. It was not, however, until roused by the entreaties of his wife, a woman who seems to have been of an heroic spirit, that he was induced to deliberate with his friends upon the measures by which Switzerland was finally delivered.[2]

*Nor look nor tone revealeth aught*
*Save woman's quietness of thought;*
*And yet around her is a light*
*Of inward majesty and might.*

M.J.J.[3]

*Wer solch ein Herz an seinen Busen drückt,*
*Der kann für Herd und Hof mit Freuden fechten.*

WILHELM TELL[4]

It was the time when children bound to meet
    Their father's homeward step from field or hill,
And when the herd's returning bells are sweet
    In the Swiss valleys, and the lakes grow still,
And the last note of that wild horn swells by,
Which haunts the exile's heart with melody.[5]

And lovely smil'd full many an Alpine home,
    Touch'd with the crimson of the dying hour,
Which lit its low roof by the torrent's foam,
    And pierced its lattice thro' the vine-hung bower;      10
But one, the loveliest o'er the land that rose,
Then first look'd mournful in its green repose.

For Werner sat beneath the linden-tree,
    That sent its lulling whispers through his door,
Ev'n as man sits whose heart alone would be
    With some deep care, and thus can find no more
Th' accustom'd joy in all which evening brings,
Gathering a household with her quiet wings.

His wife stood hush'd before him,—sad, yet mild
    In her beseeching mien;—he mark'd it not.      20
The silvery laughter of his bright-hair'd child
    Rang from the greensward round the shelter'd spot,
But seem'd unheard; until at last the boy
Rais'd from his heap'd up flowers a glance of joy,

And met his father's face: but then a change
    Pass'd swiftly o'er the brow of infant glee,
And a quick sense of something dimly strange
    Brought him from play to stand beside the knee
So often climb'd, and lift his loving eyes
That shone through clouds of sorrowful surprise.      30

Then the proud bosom of the strong man shook;
    But tenderly his babe's fair mother laid
Her hand on his, and with a pleading look,
    Thro' tears half quivering, o'er him bent, and said,

"What grief, dear friend, hath made thy heart its prey,[6]
That thou shouldst turn thee from our love away?

It is too sad to see thee thus, my friend!
   Mark'st thou the wonder on thy boy's fair brow,
Missing the smile from thine? Oh! cheer thee! bend
   To his soft arms, unseal thy thoughts e'en now!     40
Thou dost not kindly to withhold the share
Of tried affection in thy secret care."

He looked up into that sweet earnest face,
   But sternly, mournfully: not yet the band
Was loosen'd from his soul; its inmost place
   Not yet unveil'd by love's o'ermastering hand.
"Speak low!" he cried, and pointed where on high
The white Alps glitter'd thro' the solemn sky:

"We must speak low amidst our ancient hills
   And their free torrents; for the days are come     50
When tyranny lies couch'd by forest-rills,
   And meets the shepherd in his mountain-home.
Go, pour the wine of our own grapes in fear,
Keep silence by the hearth! its foes are near.

The envy of th' oppressor's eye hath been
   Upon my heritage. I sit to-night
Under my household tree, if not serene,
   Yet with the faces best-belov'd in sight:
To-morrow eve may find me chain'd, and thee—
How can I bear the boy's young smiles to see?"     60

The bright blood left that youthful mother's cheek;
   Back on the linden-stem she lean'd her form,
And her lip trembled, as it strove to speak,
   Like a frail[7] harp-string, shaken by the storm.
'Twas but a moment, and the faintness pass'd,
And the free Alpine spirit woke at last.

And she, that ever thro' her home had mov'd
   With the meek thoughtfulness and quiet smile
Of woman, calmly loving and belov'd,
   And timid in her happiness the while,     70
Stood brightly forth, and stedfastly, that hour,
Her clear glance kindling into sudden power.

Ay, pale she stood, but with an eye of light,
   And took her fair child to her holy breast,
And lifted her soft voice, that gather'd might
   As it found language:—"Are we thus oppress'd?

Then must we rise upon our mountain-sod,
And man must arm, and woman call on God!

I know what thou wouldst do,—and be it done!
　　Thy soul is darken'd with its fears for me.　　　　　　80
Trust me to Heaven, my husband!—this, thy son,
　　The babe whom I have born thee, must be free!
And the sweet memory of our pleasant hearth
May well give strength—if aught be strong on earth.

Thou hast been brooding o'er the silent dread
　　Of my desponding tears; now lift once more,
My hunter of the hills! thy stately head,
　　And let thine eagle glance my joy restore!
I can bear all, but seeing *thee* subdued,—
Take to thee back thine own undaunted mood.　　　　　　90

Go forth beside the waters, and along
　　The chamois-paths, and thro' the forests go;
And tell,[8] in burning words, thy tale of wrong
　　To the brave hearts that midst the hamlets glow.
God shall be with thee, my belov'd!—Away!
Bless but thy child, and leave me,—I can pray!"

He sprang up like a warrior-youth awaking
　　To clarion-sounds upon the ringing air;
He caught her to his breast, while proud tears breaking
　　From his dark eyes, fell o'er her braided hair,—　　　　100
And "Worthy art thou," was his joyous cry,
"That man for thee should gird himself to die.

My bride, my wife, the mother of my child!
　　Now shall thy name be armour to my heart;
And this our land, by chains no more defiled,
　　Be taught of thee to choose the better part!
I go—thy spirit on my words shall dwell,
Thy gentle voice shall stir the Alps—Farewell!"

And thus they parted, by the quiet lake,
　　In the clear starlight: he, the strength to rouse　　　　110
Of the free[9] hills; she, thoughtful for his sake,
　　To rock her child beneath the whispering boughs
Singing its blue, half-curtain'd eyes to sleep,
With a low hymn, amidst the stillness deep.

[1] First published in *NMM* 16 (January 1826): 23–25, as *Records of Woman—No. V*; signed "F. H."

[2] In *NMM* this was a footnote to the title. In the 14th c., on the Rütli (Grütli) meadows on the shores of Lake Lucerne, canton Uri, met representatives of Uri, Schywz, and Unterwald to swear the Rütli Oath, the foundation of Swiss freedom in defiance of Austrian rule, especially the tyranny of the local bailiffs. FH had treated this event, featuring legendary hero William Tell, in *The League of the Alps* (1826). The home of Werner Stauffacher and his wife, historically based characters in Schiller's *Wilhelm Tell* (1804; English trans. 1825), is at Steinen, in Schwyz, the scene of the dialogue (1.2) that inspires FH (this wife is even more forceful than FH's). For the connections between "the Swiss woman's release of her husband to protect a family home and a British woman's sacrifice in sending her husband off to defend an empire," see Lootens 244.

[3] Jewsbury, *Arria* (*Phantasmagoria* [1825]), 5–8; the poem's title is in *NMM*. Arria is the wife of Paetus, a Roman couple imprisoned by their enemies. Paetus expires in prison, and Arria commits noble suicide.

[4] Not in *NMM*. "Whoever clasps such a Heart to his Bosom, / Can fight for Hearth and Home with joy," says Werner to his wife in *Wilhelm Tell* near the end of 1.2, just after she has vowed suicide if the Austrians prevail.

[5] The verse form is the "Venus and Adonis" stanza, so named from Shakespeare's poem. The most popular sextain, it was widely used in the Renaissance, and a typical sestet in a Shakespearean sonnet; Wordsworth used it for seven poems, including *Laodamia* (which supplies an epigraph for the *Records* volume).

[6] See the beautiful scene between Stauffacher and his wife in Schiller's Wilhelm Tell—"So ernst, mein freund? Ich kenne dich nicht mehr," &c. [FH]
["So serious my dear? I scarcely know you"]—the wife's first words in 1.2.

[7] *NMM*] wild

[8] A light pun on (William) Tell. A chamois is a mountain-antelope.

[9] *NMM*] deep

---

## Properzia Rossi

[Bolognese sculptor, painter, and poet Properzia de'Rossi (?1491–1530) is discussed in Giorgio Vasari's *Le Vite de' piu eccellenti Pittori, Scultori et Architettori*, 2d. ed. (Florence, 1568), which reports that although she had some professional success, she had difficulties with her commissions, got into scrapes with the law, and died young, poor, and friendless. Drawing on the fable of her involvement with a young nobleman (who married into his own class after her death), Hemans casts her poem in the form of a lover's epistle that, even more radically than Arabella Stuart's, devolves into an isolated monologue. "No emotion is more truly, or more often pictured in her song," said L.E.L., "than that craving for affection which answers not unto the call" ("On the Character of Mrs. Hemans's Writings" 428). The lovelorn female artist unfulfilled by her fame is a recurring figure in FH's poetry of the 1820s and 1830s, one whose type is Staël's Corinne. When Chorley reviewed Barrett Browning's *Aurora Leigh* (1855), he connected the "admission of failure" in its conclusion to *Properzia Rossi*: "The moral is the insufficiency of Fame and Ambition, be either ever so generous, to make up for the absence of Love:—a class-vindication wound up by an appeal against class-separation. Thus, as in all the works of its kind, which women have so freely poured out from their full hearts during late years, we see the agony more clearly than the remedy" (*Athenæum*, 22 November 1856).]

Properzia Rossi, a celebrated female sculptor of Bologna, possessed also of talents for poetry and music, died in consequence of an unrequited attachment.—A painting by Ducis, represents her showing her last work, a basso-relievo of Ariadne, to a Roman Knight, the object of her affection, who regards it with indifference.[1]

> ————*Tell me no more, no more*
> *Of my soul's lofty gifts! Are they not vain*
> *To quench its haunting thirst for happiness?*
> *Have I not lov'd, and striven, and fail'd to bind*
> *One true heart unto me, whereon my own*
> *Might find a resting-place, a home for all*
> *Its burden of affections? I depart,*
> *Unknown, tho' Fame goes with me; I must leave*
> *The earth unknown. Yet it may be that death*
> *Shall give my name a power to win such tears*
> *As would have made life precious.*[2]

# I

One dream of passion and of beauty more!
And in its bright fulfilment let me pour
My soul away! Let earth retain a trace
Of that which lit my being, tho' its race
Might have been loftier far.—Yet one more dream!
From my deep spirit one victorious gleam
Ere I depart! For thee alone, for thee!
May this last work, this farewell triumph be,
Thou, lov'd so vainly! I would leave enshrined
Something immortal of my heart and mind,                    10
That yet may speak to thee when I am gone,
Shaking thine inmost bosom with a tone
Of lost affection;—something that may prove
What she hath been, whose melancholy love
On thee was lavish'd; silent pang and tear,
And fervent song, that gush'd when none were near,
And dream by night, and weary thought by day,
Stealing the brightness from her life away,—
While thou——Awake! not yet within me die,
Under the burden and the agony                               20
Of this vain tenderness,—my spirit, wake!
Ev'n for thy sorrowful affection's sake,
Live! in thy work breathe out!—that he may yet,
Feeling sad mastery there, perchance regret
Thine unrequited gift.

## II

It comes,—the power
Within me born, flows back; my fruitless dower
That could not win me love. Yet once again
I greet it proudly, with its rushing train
Of glorious images:—they throng—they press—
A sudden joy lights up my loneliness,—      30
I shall not perish all!
         The bright work grows
Beneath my hand, unfolding, as a rose,
Leaf after leaf, to beauty; line by line,
I fix my thought, heart, soul, to burn, to shine,
Thro' the pale marble's veins. It grows—and now
I give my own life's history to thy brow,
Forsaken Ariadne! thou shalt wear
My form, my lineaments; but oh! more fair,
Touch'd into lovelier being by the glow
   Which in me dwells, as by the summer-light      40
All things are glorified. From thee my wo
   Shall yet look beautiful to meet his sight,
When I am pass'd away. Thou art the mould
Wherein I pour the fervent thoughts, th' untold,
The self-consuming! Speak to him of me,
Thou, the deserted by the lonely sea,
With the soft sadness of thine earnest eye,
Speak to him, lorn one! deeply, mournfully,
Of all my love and grief! Oh! could I throw
Into thy frame a voice, a sweet, and low,      50
And thrilling voice of song! when he came nigh,
To send the passion of its melody
Thro' his pierc'd bosom—on its tones to bear
My life's deep feeling, as the southern air
Wafts the faint myrtle's breath,—to rise, to swell,
To sink away in accents of farewell,
Winning but one, *one* gush of tears, whose flow
Surely my parted spirit yet might know,
If love be strong as death!

## III

         Now fair thou art,
Thou form, whose life is of my burning heart!      60

Yet all the vision that within me wrought,
    I cannot make thee! Oh! I might have given
Birth to creations of far nobler thought,
    I might have kindled, with the fire of heaven,
Things not of such as die! But I have been
Too much alone;[3] a heart whereon to lean,
With all these deep affections, that o'erflow
My aching soul, and find no shore below;
An eye to be my star, a voice to bring
Hope o'er my path, like sounds that breathe of spring,     70
These are denied me—dreamt of still in vain,—
Therefore my brief aspirings from the chain,
Are ever but as some wild fitful song,
Rising triumphantly, to die ere long
In dirge-like echoes.

IV

           Yet the world will see
Little of this, my parting work, in thee,
    Thou shalt have fame! Oh, mockery! give the reed
From storms a shelter,—give the drooping vine
Something round which its tendrils may entwine,—
    Give the parch'd flower a rain-drop, and the meed     80
Of love's kind words to woman! Worthless fame!
That in *his* bosom wins not for my name
Th' abiding-place it ask'd! Yet how my heart,
In its own fairy world of song and art,
Once beat for praise!—Are those high longings o'er?
That which I have been can I be no more?—
Never, oh! never more; tho' still thy sky
Be blue as then, my glorious Italy!
And tho' the music, whose rich breathings fill
Thine air with soul, be wandering past me still,     90
And tho' the mantle of thy sunlight streams,
Unchang'd on forms, instinct[4] with poet-dreams;
Never, oh! never more! Where'er I move,
The shadow of this broken-hearted love
Is on me and around! Too well *they* know,
    Whose life is all within, too soon and well,
When there the blight hath settled;—but I go
    Under the silent wings of peace to dwell;
From the slow wasting, from the lonely pain,
The inward burning of those words—"*in vain,*"     100

Sear'd on the heart—I go. 'Twill soon be past.
Sunshine, and song, and bright Italian heaven,
    And thou, oh! thou, on whom my spirit cast
Unvalued wealth,—who know'st not what was given
In that devotedness,—the sad, and deep,
And unrepaid—farewell! If I could weep
Once, only once, belov'd one! on thy breast,
Pouring my heart forth ere I sink to rest!
But that were happiness, and unto me
Earth's gift is *fame*. Yet I was form'd to be                    110
So richly blest! With thee to watch the sky,
Speaking not, feeling but that thou wert nigh;
With thee to listen, while the tones of song
Swept ev'n as part of our sweet air along,
To listen silently;—with thee to gaze
On forms, the deified of olden days,
This had been joy enough;—and hour by hour,
From its glad well-springs drinking life and power,
How had my spirit soar'd, and made its fame
    A glory for thy brow!—Dreams, dreams!—the fire                120
Burns faint within me. Yet I leave my name—
    As a deep thrill may linger on the lyre
When its full chords are hush'd—awhile to live,
And one day haply in thy heart revive
Sad thoughts of me:—I leave it, with a sound,
A spell o'er memory, mournfully profound,
I leave it, on my country's air to dwell,—
Say proudly yet— " *'Twas her's who lov'd me well!*"

---

[1] French painter of historical subjects, Louis Ducis (1775–1847) displayed the piece to which
FH refers as part of a commissioned series at the Paris Salon (1812–14), *Arts Under the Empire
of Love*, which celebrated chivalry "in a mythical era of love, poetry and reverie, when Woman
was seen as the protectress of the arts and the instigator of noble actions by men." In the
allegories "de la *Poésie*, de la *Musique*, de la *Peinture* et de la *Sculpture*," *Properzia de'Rossi and
her Last Bas-relief* represented sculpture. Ducis painted other subjects of interest to FH: *Tasso
and His Sister; Tasso and Léonore d'Este; Corinne and Oswald at Naples*. Ariadne was the daughter of King Minos of Crete, who imprisoned the Greek prince Theseus in his labyrinth, there
to be devoured by the Minotaur. In love with Theseus, Ariadne told him how to slay the
monster and escape the labyrinth. He married her, but after they left Crete, he abandoned her
on the Greek isle of Naxos, where she pined away for him. He married her sister Phaedra.
[2] By FH (Lawrence 298–99; FH to William Blackwood, 8 April 1828 [BA MS 4021, f.
263]). The blank verse evokes a Shakespearean soliloquy. "How exquisitely is the doom of a
woman, in whose being pride, genius, and tenderness contend for mastery, shadowed in the
lines that succeed! The pride bows to the very dust; [. . .] and the tenderness turns away with
a crushed heart to perish in neglect" (L.E.L., "On the Character" 428). The poem proper is
chiefly in romance couplets (iambic pentameter marked by enjambment and feminine rhyme),
with Rossi's outpouring deftly troped in the pouring of syntax over line breaks, often with
formalist punning at the endword (e.g., *pour, grow, throw, flow*).

³ Echoing Byron's *Mazeppa*, with a difference: "she would not delay / Her due return:—while she was gone, / Methought I felt too much alone. // She came . . ." (837–40).
⁴ "Implanted as a natural instinct" and, by extension, "impelled"; cf. *Restoration of the Works of Art to Italy* 198.

---

### Gertrude, or Fidelity till Death[1]

The Baron Von Der Wart, accused, though it is believed unjustly, as an accomplice in the assassination of the Emperor Albert, was bound alive on the wheel, and attended by his wife Gertrude, throughout his last agonizing hours, with the most heroic devotedness.[2] Her own sufferings, with those of her unfortunate husband, are most affectingly described in a letter which she afterwards addressed to a female friend, and which was published some years ago, at Haarlem, in a book entitled Gertrude Von Der Wart, or Fidelity unto Death.[3]

> *Dark lowers our fate,*
> *And terrible the storm that gathers o'er us;*
> *But nothing, till that latest agony*
> *Which severs thee from nature, shall unloose*
> *This fix'd and sacred hold. In thy dark prison-house,*
> *In the terrific face of armed law,*
> *Yea, on the scaffold, if it needs must be,*
> *I never will forsake thee.*
>
>                                        JOANNA BAILLIE[4]

Her hands were clasp'd, her dark eyes rais'd,
    The breeze threw back her hair;
Up to the fearful wheel she gaz'd—
    All that she lov'd was there.
The night was round her clear and cold.
    The holy heaven above,
Its pale stars watching to behold
    The might of earthly love.

"And bid me not depart," she cried,
    "My Rudolph, say not so!                                        10
This is no time to quit thy side,
    Peace, peace! I cannot go.
Hath the world aught for *me* to fear,
    When death is on thy brow?
The world! what means it?—*mine* is *here*—
    I will not leave thee now.

I have been with thee in thine hour
    Of glory and of bliss;

Doubt not its memory's living power
   To strengthen me thro' *this!*                    20
And thou, mine honour'd love and true,
   Bear on, bear nobly on!
We have the blessed heaven in view,
   Whose rest shall soon be won."

And were not these high words to flow
   From woman's breaking heart?
Thro' all that night of bitterest wo
   She bore her lofty part;
But oh! with such a glazing eye,
   With such a curdling cheek—                    30
Love, love! of mortal agony,
   Thou, only *thou* shouldst speak!

The wind rose high,—but with it rose
   Her voice, that he might hear:
Perchance that dark hour brought repose
   To happy bosoms near;
While she sat striving with despair
   Beside his tortured form,
And pouring her deep soul in prayer
   Forth on the rushing storm.                    40

She wiped the death-damps from his brow,
   With her pale hands and soft,
Whose touch upon the lute-chords low,
   Had still'd his heart so oft.
She spread her mantle o'er his breast,
   She bath'd his lips with dew,
And on his cheek such kisses press'd
   As hope and joy ne'er knew.

Oh! lovely are ye, Love and Faith,
   Enduring to the last!                    50
She had her meed—one smile in death—
   And his worn spirit pass'd.
While ev'n as o'er a martyr's grave
   She knelt on that sad spot,
And, weeping, bless'd the God who gave
   Strength to forsake it not!

---

[1] First published in *NMM* 16 (May 1826): 469–70, as *Records of Woman.—No. VII. Gertrude*, signed "F. H.," with a footnote to the title: "The author was not aware, at the time this little poem was written, that the courage and affection of Gertrude Von der Wart had previously been celebrated by another writer in a yet unpublished poem."

This writer is unknown. FH's octave stanza assimilates two balladlike quatrains. Words-worth used a similar rhyme pattern in *Goody Blake, and Harry Gill; Simon Lee;* and *To a Sexton* (all in *Lyrical Ballads* (1798–1805), and in *Yarrow Unvisited* (1807), *Yarrow Visited, September 1814* (1815), the last two cited in FH's letter to Jewsbury, 1826 (*CM* 1.174–75, and below).

[2] *NMM*] heroic fidelity

[3] Albert I (?1250–1308), king of Germany and Holy Roman Emperor, had a contentious reign, involving challenges from the Rhenish Electors, Pope Boniface VIII, and Wenceslaus II. His imperial ambitions antagonized factions in Swabia and Switzerland, and he was assassi-nated on 1 May 1308 by a band of four that included his nephew. Baron Rudolph von Wart was the only one arrested. FH's source is Johann Conrad Appenzeller, *Gertrude de Wart; or, Fidelity unto Death* (London, 1826), a translation of *Gertraud von Wart: oder Treue bis in den Tod* (Zurich, 1813). FH depicts Albert's death in *A Monarch's Death-Bed* (first published as the lead piece in *Friendship's Offering* for 1826, and collected in the Miscellaneous Poems of *Records*).

[4] From Baillie's best-known play, *De Monfort* (revised version, 5.4.66–73). Jane de Monfort (played by Sarah Siddons in 1800) is speaking to her beloved brother, just before he is arrested for murdering her betrothed. Baillie's revisions were prompted by Byron, who in 1815 wanted the play for Drury Lane with Edmund Kean starring, and by Kean himself, who acted it for five nights in November 1821. Byron urged her to "alter the ending" for a better "stage effect," she told Scott in 1815; she made it "more dramatic by killing De Mon[t] on the stage [. . .] I really think it is a great improvement" (NLS MS 3886, ff. 162–65, 266–68; *Letters* 1.338, 343). Kean, who "was anxious to die upon the stage, [. . .] did not like the death which I had formerly provided for him," she told William Sotheby in 1821; "so after [. . .] hearing him explain his notions on the subject, I have written a new last scene, where he is made to die of a broken spirit after having the chains put on his limbs. [. . .] I am informed that he is now quite satisfied" (Royal College of Surgeons, Hunter-Baillie papers, MS HB ix-56; *Letters* 1.206).

The epigraph is not in *NMM*. Other variants of note are "freezing eye" (29) and symbolizing capitals: Woman (26), Death (51).

---

## *Imelda*[1]

————*Sometimes*
*The young forgot the lessons they had learnt,*
*And lov'd when they should hate,—like thee, Imelda!*[2]
—Italy, a Poem.

*Passa la bella Donna, e par che dorma.*
TASSO[3]

We have the myrtle's breath around us here,
    Amidst the fallen pillars;—this hath been
Some Naiad's fane of old. How brightly clear,
    Flinging a vein of silver o'er the scene,
Up thro' the shadowy grass, the fountain wells,
    And music with it, gushing from beneath
The ivied altar!—that sweet murmur tells
    The rich wild flowers no tale of wo or death;
Yet once the wave was darken'd, and a stain

Lay deep, and heavy drops—but not of rain— 10
On the dim violets by its marble bed,
And the pale shining water-lily's head.

Sad is that legend's truth.—A fair girl met
   One whom she lov'd, by this lone temple's spring,
Just as the sun behind the pine-grove set,
   And eve's low voice in whispers woke, to bring
All wanderers home. They stood, that gentle pair,
   With the blue heaven of Italy above,
And citron-odours dying[4] on the air,
   And light leaves trembling round, and early love 20
Deep in each breast.—What reck'd *their* souls of strife
Between their fathers? Unto them young life
Spread out the treasures of its vernal years;
And if they wept, they wept far other tears
Than the cold world wrings forth. They stood, that hour,
Speaking of hope, while tree, and fount, and flower,
And star, just gleaming thro' the cypress boughs,[5]
Seem'd holy things, as records of their vows.

But change came o'er the scene. A hurrying tread
   Broke on the whispery shades. Imelda knew 30
The footstep of her brother's wrath, and fled
   Up where the cedars make yon avenue
Dim with green twilight: pausing there, she caught—
Was it the clash of swords?—a swift dark thought
   Struck down her lips' rich crimson as it pass'd,
And from her eye the sunny sparkle took
One moment with its fearfulness, and shook
Her slight frame fiercely, as a stormy blast
Might rock the rose. Once more, and yet once more,[6]
She still'd her heart to listen,—all was o'er;
Sweet summer winds alone were heard to sigh, 40
Bearing the nightingale's deep spirit by.[7]
That night Imelda's voice was in the song,
Lovely it floated thro' the festive throng,
Peopling her father's halls. That fatal night
Her eye look'd starry in its dazzling light,
And her cheek glow'd with beauty's flushing dyes,
Like a rich cloud of eve in southern skies,
A burning, ruby cloud. There were, whose gaze
Follow'd her form beneath the clear lamp's blaze, 50
And marvell'd at its radiance. But a few
Beheld the brightness of that feverish hue,

With something of dim fear; and in that glance
    Found strange and sudden tokens of unrest,
Startling to meet amidst the mazy dance,
    Where thought, if present, an unbidden guest,
Comes not unmask'd. Howe'er this were, the time
Sped as it speeds with joy, and grief, and crime
Alike: and when the banquet's hall was left
Unto its garlands of their bloom bereft,                   60
When trembling stars look'd silvery in their wane,
And heavy flowers yet slumber'd, once again
There stole a footstep, fleet, and light, and lone,
Thro' the dim cedar shade; the step of one
That started at a leaf, of one that fled,
Of one that panted with some secret dread:—
What did Imelda there? She sought the scene
Where love so late with youth and hope had been;[8]
Bodings were on her soul—a shuddering thrill
Ran thro' each vein, when first the Naiad's rill         70
Met her with melody—sweet sounds and low;
*We* hear them yet, they live along its flow—
*Her* voice is music lost! The fountain-side
She gain'd—the wave flash'd forth—'twas darkly dyed
Ev'n as from warrior-hearts; and on its edge,
    Amidst the fern, and flowers, and moss-tufts deep,
There lay, as lull'd by stream and rustling sedge,
    A youth, a graceful youth. "Oh! dost thou sleep?
"Azzo!" she cried, "my Azzo! is this rest?"
But then her low tones falter'd:—"On thy breast        80
Is the stain,—yes 'tis blood!—and that cold cheek—
That moveless lip!—thou dost not slumber?—speak,
Speak, Azzo, my belov'd!—no sound—no breath—
What hath come thus between our spirits?—Death!
Death?—I but dream—I dream!"—and there she stood,
A faint, frail trembler, gazing first on blood,
With her fair arm around yon cypress thrown,
Her form sustain'd by that dark stem alone,
And fading fast, like spell-struck maid of old,
Into white waves dissolving, clear and cold;        90
When from the grass her dimm'd eye caught a gleam—
'Twas where a sword lay shiver'd° by the stream—     *shattered*
Her brother's sword!—she knew it; and she knew
'Twas with a venom'd point that weapon slew!
Wo for young love! but love is strong. There came
Strength upon woman's fragile heart and frame.

There came swift courage! On the dewy ground
She knelt, with all her dark hair floating round,
Like a long silken stole; she knelt, and press'd
Her lips of glowing life to Azzo's breast,                                    100
Drawing the poison forth. A strange, sad sight!
Pale death, and fearless love, and solemn night!—
So the moon saw them last.
       The morn came singing
 Thro' the green forests of the Appenines,
With all her joyous birds their free flight winging,
 And steps and voices out amongst the vines.
What found that day-spring *here?* Two fair forms laid
Like sculptured sleepers; from the myrtle shade
Casting a gleam of beauty o'er the wave,
Still, mournful, sweet. Were such things for the grave?            110
Could it be so indeed? That radiant girl,
Deck'd as for bridal hours!—long braids of pearl
Amidst her shadowy locks were faintly shining,
 As tears might shine, with melancholy light;
And there was gold her slender waist entwining;
 And her pale graceful arms—how sadly bright!
And fiery gems upon her breast were lying,
And round her marble brow red roses dying.—
But she died first!—the violet's hue had spread
 O'er her sweet eyelids with repose oppress'd,                     120
She had bow'd heavily her gentle head,
 And, on the youth's hush'd bosom, sunk to rest.
So slept they well!—the poison's work was done;
Love with true heart had striven—but Death had won.

[1] First published in *NMM* 13 (May 1825): 467–69, as *Records of Woman.—No. I*, signed "F.H."

[2] The tale of Imelda is related in Sismondi's Histoire des Republiques Italienne. Vol. iii, p. 443. [FH. Ch. 22 (3.425–29)]

*Italy, a Poem* (1822 and 1828) was an immensely popular set of tales by Samuel Rogers (1763–1855). "The Campagna of Florence" briefly refers to Imelda (230–45); FH's epigraph is 228–30, the "lessons" being the "Law" of vengeance. In *Histoire des Républiques Italiennes du Moyen Âge* (Paris, 1826) J.C.L. Sismondi, who is sharply critical of *vendetti* (wars of vengeance), relates the story of these lovers from bitterly rival families in the civil strife of 13th-c. Italy. Imelda's family, the Lambertazzis, are Ghibellines, the imperial and aristicratic faction; Boniface's family, the Giéréméi, are Guelphs, the Papal faction. The murder of Boniface led to forty days of continuous violence and six years of intermittent warfare.

[3] The beautiful Lady dies and seems to sleep.

Tasso, *Gerusalemme Liberata* (1575) 12.69. The reference is to Clorinda, accidentally slain in battle by her beloved, Tancred, who bends over her as she dies forgiving him. This is one of Corinne's favorite texts in Staël's *Corinne* (bk. 8, ch. 4). The epigraph is not in *NMM*.

[4] *NMM*] fainting

<sup>5</sup> Emblem of grief and mourning.
 <sup>6</sup> An echo of the opening line of Milton's *Lycidas*— "Yet once more, O ye Laurels, and once more . . ."—and so a signal of death and impending mourning.
 <sup>7</sup> In literary tradition, the nightingale's song is melancholy, associated with the myth of Philomel, or more generally, with a heart pierced by a thorn. Recent treatments in FH's age include poems by Charlotte Smith, Coleridge, Wordsworth, and Keats.
 <sup>8</sup> *NMM*] Love / Youth / Hope

---

### Edith, a Tale of the Woods[1]

*Du Heilige! rufe dein Kind zurück!*
*Ich habe genossen das irdische Glück,*
*Ich habe gelebt und geliebet.*
WALLENSTEIN[2]

The woods—oh! solemn are the boundless[3] woods
　　Of the great Western World, when day declines,
And louder sounds the roll of distant floods,
　　More deep the rustling of the ancient pines;
When dimness gathers on the stilly air,
　　And mystery seems o'er every leaf to brood,
Awful it is for human heart to bear
　　The might[4] and burden of the solitude!
Yet, in that hour, midst those green wastes, there sate
One young and fair; and oh! how desolate!　　　　　　10
But undismay'd; while sank the crimson light,
And the high cedars darken'd with the night.
Alone she sate: tho' many lay around,
They, pale and silent on the bloody[5] ground,
Were sever'd from her need and from her wo,
　　Far as Death severs Life. O'er that wild spot
Combat had rag'd, and brought the valiant low,
　　And left them, with the history of their lot,
Unto the forest oaks. A fearful scene
For her whose home of other days had been　　　　　20
Midst the fair halls of England! but the love
　　Which fill'd her soul was strong to cast out fear,
And by its might upborne all else above,
　　She shrank not—mark'd not that the dead were near.
Of him alone she thought, whose languid head
　　Faintly upon her wedded bosom fell;
Memory of aught but him on earth was fled,
　　While heavily she felt his life-blood well

Fast o'er her garments forth, and vainly bound
With her torn robe and hair the streaming wound,          30
Yet hoped, still hoped!—Oh! from such hope how long
    Affection wooes the whispers that deceive,
Ev'n when the pressure of dismay grows strong,
    And we, that weep, watch, tremble, ne'er believe
The blow indeed can fall! So bow'd she there,
Over the dying, while unconscious prayer
Fill'd all her soul. Now pour'd the moonlight down,
Veining the pine-stems thro' the foliage brown,
And fire-flies, kindling up the leafy place,
Cast fitful radiance o'er the warrior's face,          40
Whereby she caught its changes: to her eye,
    The eye that faded look'd through gathering haze,
Whence love, o'ermastering mortal agony,
    Lifted a long deep melancholy gaze,
When voice was not: that fond sad meaning pass'd—
She knew the fulness of her wo at last!
One shriek the forests heard,—and mute she lay,
And cold; yet clasping still the precious clay
To her scarce-heaving breast. O Love and Death!
Ye have sad meetings on this changeful earth,          50
Many and sad! but airs of heavenly breath
Shall melt the links which bind you, for your birth
Is far apart.

        Now light, of richer hue
Than the moon sheds, came flushing mist and dew;
The pines grew red with morning; fresh winds play'd,
Bright-colour'd birds with splendour cross'd the shade,
Flitting on flower-like wings; glad murmurs broke
    From reed, and spray, and leaf, the living strings
Of earth's Eolian lyre,[6] whose music woke
    Into young life and joy all happy things.          60
And she too woke from that long dreamless trance,
The widow'd Edith: fearfully her glance
Fell, as in doubt, on faces dark and strange,
And dusky forms. A sudden sense of change
Flash'd o'er her spirit, ev'n ere memory swept
The tide of anguish back with thoughts that slept;
Yet half instinctively she rose, and spread
Her arms, as 'twere for something lost or fled,
Then faintly sank again. The forest-bough,
With all its whispers, wav'd not o'er her now,—          70

Where was she? Midst the people of the wild,
   By the red hunter's fire: an aged chief,
Whose home look'd sad—for therein play'd no child—
   Had borne her, in the stillness of her grief,
To that lone cabin of the woods; and there,
Won by a form so desolately fair,
Or touch'd with thoughts from some past sorrow sprung,
O'er her low couch an Indian matron hung,
While in grave silence, yet with earnest eye,
The ancient warrior of the waste stood by,        80
Bending in watchfulness his proud grey head,
   And leaning on his bow.
                        And life return'd,
Life, but with all its memories of the dead,
   To Edith's heart; and well the sufferer learn'd
Her task of meek endurance, well she wore
The chasten'd grief that humbly can adore,
Midst blinding tears. But unto that old pair,
Ev'n as a breath of spring's awakening air,
Her presence was; or as a sweet wild tune
Bringing back tender thoughts, which all too soon    90
Depart with childhood. Sadly they had seen
   A daughter to the land of spirits go,
And ever from that time her fading mien,
   And voice, like winds of summer, soft and low,
Had haunted their dim years; but Edith's face
Now look'd in holy sweetness from her place,
And they again seem'd parents. Oh! the joy,
The rich, deep blessedness—tho' earth's alloy,
Fear, that still bodes, be there—of pouring forth
The heart's whole power of love, its wealth and worth   100
Of strong affection, in one healthful flow,
On something all its own!—that kindly glow,
Which to shut inward is consuming pain,
Gives the glad soul its flowering time again,
When, like the sunshine, freed.—And gentle cares
Th' adopted Edith meekly gave for theirs
Who lov'd her thus:—her spirit dwelt, the while,
With the departed, and her patient smile
Spoke of farewells to earth;—yet still she pray'd,
Ev'n o'er her soldier's lowly grave, for aid       110
*One* purpose to fulfil, to leave one trace
Brightly recording that her dwelling-place
Had been among the wilds; for well she knew
The secret whisper of her bosom true,

Which warn'd her hence.
            And now, by many a word
Link'd unto moments when the heart was stirr'd,
By the sweet mournfulness of many a hymn,
Sung when the woods at eve grew hush'd and dim,
By the persuasion of her fervent eye,
All eloquent with child-like piety,                   120
By the still beauty of her life, she strove
To win for heaven, and heaven-born truth, the love
Pour'd out on her so freely.—Nor in vain
Was that soft-breathing influence to enchain
The soul in gentle bonds: by slow degrees
Light follow'd on, as when a summer breeze
Parts the deep masses of the forest shade
And lets the sunbeam through:—her voice was made
Ev'n such a breeze; and she, a lowly guide,
By faith and sorrow rais'd and purified,            130
So to the Cross her Indian fosterers led,
Until their prayers were one. When morning spread
O'er the blue lake, and when the sunset's glow
Touch'd into golden bronze the cypress-bough,
And when the quiet of the Sabbath time
Sank on her heart, tho' no melodious chime
Waken'd the wilderness, their prayers were one.
—Now might she pass in hope, her work was done.
And she *was* passing from the woods away;
The broken flower of England might not stay        140
Amidst those alien shades; her eye was bright
Ev'n yet with something of a starry light,
But her form wasted, and her fair young cheek
Wore oft and patiently a fatal streak,
A rose whose root was death. The parting sigh
Of autumn thro' the forests had gone by,
And the rich maple o'er her wanderings lone
Its crimson leaves in many a shower had strown,
Flushing the air; and winter's blast had been
Amidst the pines; and now a softer green        150
Fring'd their dark boughs; for spring again had come,
The sunny spring! but Edith to her home
Was journeying fast. Alas! we think it sad
To part with life, when all the earth looks glad
In her young lovely things, when voices break
Into sweet sounds, and leaves and blossoms wake:
Is it not brighter then, in that far clime
Where graves are not, nor blights of changeful time,

If *here* such glory dwell with passing blooms,
Such golden sunshine rest around the tombs?          160
So thought the dying one. 'Twas early day,
And sounds and odours with the breezes' play,
Whispering of spring-time, thro' the cabin-door,
Unto her couch life's farewell sweetness bore;
Then with a look where all her hope awoke,
"My father!"—to the grey-hair'd chief she spoke—
"Know'st thou that I depart?"[7]—"I know, I know,"
He answer'd mournfully, "that thou must go
To thy belov'd, my daughter!"—"Sorrow not
    For me, kind mother!" with meek smiles once more     170
She murmur'd in low tones;[8] "one happy lot
    Awaits, us, friends! upon the better shore;
For we have pray'd together in one trust,
And lifted our frail spirits from the dust,
To God, who gave them. Lay me by mine own,
Under the cedar-shade: where he is gone
Thither I go. There will my sisters be,
And the dead parents, lisping at whose knee
My childhood's prayer was learn'd,—the Saviour's prayer
Which now *ye* know,—and I shall meet you there,     180
Father, and gentle mother!—ye have bound
The bruised reed, and mercy shall be found
By Mercy's children."—From the matron's eye
Dropp'd tears, her sole and passionate reply;
But Edith felt them not; for now a sleep,
Solemnly beautiful, a stillness deep,
Fell on her settled face. Then, sad and slow,
And mantling up his stately head in wo,
"Thou'rt passing hence," he sang, that warrior old,
In sounds like those by plaintive waters roll'd.     190

✧   ✧   ✧

    "Thou'rt passing from the lake's green side,
        And the hunter's hearth away;
    From the time of flowers, for the summer's pride,
        Daughter! thou canst not stay.

    Thou'rt journeying to thy spirit's home,
        Where the skies are ever clear;
    The corn-month's golden hours will come,
        But they shall not find thee here.

    And we shall miss thy voice, my bird!
        Under our whispering[9] pine;     200

Music shall midst the leaves be heard,
      But not a song like thine.

A breeze that roves o'er stream and hill,
      Telling of winter gone,
Hath such sweet falls—yet caught we still
      A farewell in its tone.

But thou, my bright one! thou shalt be
      Where farewell sounds are o'er;
Thou, in the eyes thou lov'st, shalt see
      No fear of parting more.                                        210

The mossy grave thy tears have wet,
      And the wind's wild moanings by,
Thou with thy kindred shalt forget,
      Midst flowers—not such as die.

The shadow from thy brow shall melt,
      The sorrow from thy strain,
But where thine earthly smile hath dwelt,
      Our heart shall thirst in vain.

Dim will our cabin be, and lone,
      When thou, its light, art fled;                                220
Yet hath thy step the pathway shown
      Unto the happy dead.

And we will follow thee, our guide!
      And join that shining band;
Thou'rt passing from the lake's green side—
      Go to the better land!"

                  ❖      ❖      ❖

The song had ceas'd—the listeners caught no breath,
That lovely sleep had melted into death.

[1] Founded on incidents related in an American work, "Sketches of Connecticut." [FH]
    First published *NMM* 20 (July 1827): 33–37, as *Records of Woman.—No. IX. Edith*, signed
"F. H." In *NMM*, this first note, with slightly different wording, is appended to the poem's last
line. FH cites Lydia Howard Huntley (Lydia Sigourney), *Sketches of Connecticut, Forty Years
Since* (Hartford, 1824). In its review of this work the *United States Literary Gazette* (vol. 1,
no. 8 [1 August 1824], 120–21) excerpts the death scene of Oriana, a young English bride
adopted by a Mohegan couple after her husband is killed in battle in 1781. FH's poem recon-
ceives the genre of the American frontier "captivity" narrative (see *The American Forest Girl*),
substituting for its violence a tale of domestic affections and Christian conversion. Sigourney
(1791–1865) later published poetry, some influenced by FH, and was called "The American
Hemans"; she wrote the introduction for the American edition of Hughes's *Memoir*.
[2] Thou Holy One, call thy child home. I have enjoyed the happiness of this world, I have lived
and have loved (Coleridge's prose translation of Schiller in a footnote in *The Piccolomini*).

Schiller, *Die Piccolomini* 1764–66. Thekla's song, just after her beloved Max has torn himself away from her (the end of 2.6). Coleridge translates the lines just before: "the heart is dead, the world is empty." FH had an "almost actual, relation-like love" for Max and Thekla (*HM* 54).

*NMM*] no epigraph.

[3] *NMM*] mighty

[4] *NMM*] gloom

[5] *NMM]* dewy

[6] An instrument of tuned strings, issuing music made by the wind. Coleridge's poem titled *The Eolian Harp* was published in 1817.

[7] In the passage from *Sketches* quoted by the *Gazette* (121): "'Knowest thou, Father, that I am about to leave thee?' Fixing his keen glance upon her for a moment, and kneeling at her side, he answered—'I know it, my daughter. Thy blue eye hath already the light of that sky to which thou art ascending. Thy brow hath the smile of the angels who wait for thee.'"

[8] *NMM*] murmur'd, but with pain

[9] *NMM*] lonely. Other significant variants are emblematic capitals, among them: Him (25; the deifying effect may account for the lowercase in *Records*); Hunter / Chief (72), Warrior (80), Land of Spirits (92), Earth's (98), Heaven (122), Hope (139), Mother / Daughter (169–70, 182). Mercy (181) was lowercase.

---

## The Indian City[1]

> *What deep wounds ever clos'd without a scar?*
> *The heart's bleed longest, and but heal to wear*
> *That which disfigures it.*
> —Childe Harold[2]

### I

Royal in splendour went down the day
On the plain where an Indian city lay,
With its crown of domes o'er the forest high,
Red as if fused in the burning sky,
And its deep groves pierced by the rays which made
A bright stream's way thro' each long arcade,
Till the pillar'd vaults of the Banian° stood,          *Asian mulberry*
Like torch-lit aisles midst the solemn wood,
And the plantain glitter'd with leaves of gold,
As a tree midst the genii-gardens old,          10
And the cypress lifted a blazing spire,
And the stems of the cocoas were shafts of fire.
Many a white pagoda's gleam
Slept lovely round upon lake and stream,
Broken alone by the lotus-flowers,
As they caught the glow of the sun's last hours,
Like rosy wine in their cups, and shed
Its glory forth on their crystal bed.
Many a graceful Hindoo maid,

With the water-vase from the palmy shade,                    20
Came gliding light as the desert's roe,
Down marble steps to the tanks below;
And a cool sweet plashing was ever heard,
As the molten glass of the wave was stirr'd;
And a murmur, thrilling the scented air,
Told where the Bramin³ bow'd in prayer.

There wandered a noble Moslem boy
Thro' the scene of beauty in breathless joy;
He gazed where the stately city rose
Like a pageant of clouds in its red repose;                  30
He turn'd where birds thro' the gorgeous gloom
Of the woods went glancing on starry plume
He track'd the brink of the shining lake,
By the tall canes feathered in tuft and brake,
Till the path he chose, in its mazes wound
To the very heart of the holy ground.

And there lay the water, as if enshrin'd
In a rocky urn from the sun and wind,
Bearing the hues of the grove on high,
Far down thro' its dark still purity.                        40
The flood beyond, to the fiery west
Spread out like a metal-mirror's breast,
But that lone bay in its dimness deep,
Seem'd made for the swimmer's joyous leap,
For the stag athirst from the noontide chase,
For all free things of the wild-wood's race.

Like a falcon's glance on the wide blue sky,
Was the kindling flash of the boy's glad eye,
Like a sea-bird's flight to the foaming wave,
From the shadowy bank was the bound he gave;                 50
Dashing the spray-drops, cold and white,
O'er the glossy leaves in his young delight,
And blowing his locks to the waters clear—
Alas! he dreamt not that fate was near.

His mother look'd from her tent the while,
O'er heaven and earth with a quiet smile:
She, on her way unto Mecca's fane,⁴
Had stay'd the march of her pilgrim-train,
Calmly to linger a few brief hours,
In the Bramin city's glorious bowers;                        60
For the pomp of the forest, the wave's bright fall,
The red gold of sunset—she lov'd them all.

II

The moon rose clear in the splendour given
To the deep-blue night of an Indian heaven;
The boy from the high-arch'd woods came back—
Oh! what had he met in his lonely track?
The serpent's glance, thro' the long reeds bright?
The arrowy spring of the tiger's might?
No!—yet as one by a conflict worn,
With his graceful hair all soil'd and torn,            70
And a gloom on the lids of his darken'd eye,
And a gash on his bosom—he came to die!
He look'd for the face to his young heart sweet,
And found it, and sank at his mother's feet.

"Speak to me!—whence doth the swift blood run?
What hath befall'n thee, my child, my son?"
The mist of death on his brow lay pale,
But his voice just linger'd to breathe the tale,
Murmuring faintly of wrongs and scorn,
And wounds from the children of Brahma born:        80
This was the doom for a Moslem found
With foot profane on their holy ground,
This was for sullying the pure waves free
Unto them alone—'twas their God's decree.

A change came o'er his wandering look—
The mother shriek'd not then, nor shook:
Breathless she knelt in her son's young blood,
Rending her mantle to staunch its flood;
But it rush'd like a river which none may stay,
Bearing a flower to the deep away.             90
That which our love to the earth would chain,
Fearfully striving with Heaven in vain,
That which fades from us, while yet we hold,
Clasp'd to our bosoms, its mortal mould,
Was fleeting before her, afar and fast;
One moment—the soul from the face had pass'd!

Are there no words for that common wo?
—Ask of the thousands, its depths that know!
The boy had breathed, in his dreaming rest,
Like a low-voiced dove, on her gentle breast;      100
He had stood, when she sorrow'd, beside her knee,
Painfully stilling his quick heart's glee;
He had kiss'd from her cheek the widow's tears,

With the loving lip of his infant years;
He had smil'd o'er her path like a bright spring-day—
Now in his blood on the earth he lay!
*Murder'd!*—Alas! and we love so well
In a world where anguish like this can dwell!

She bow'd down mutely o'er her dead—
They that stood round her watch'd in dread;                    110
They watch'd—she knew not they were by—
Her soul sat veil'd in its agony.
On the silent lip she press'd no kiss,
Too stern was the grasp of her pangs for this;
She shed no tear as her face bent low,
O'er the shining hair of the lifeless brow;
She look'd but into the half-shut eye,
With a gaze that found there no reply,
And shrieking, mantled her head from sight,
And fell, struck down by her sorrow's⁵ might!                    120

And what deep change, what work of power,
Was wrought on her secret soul that hour?
How rose the lonely one?—She rose
Like a prophetess from dark repose!
And proudly flung from her face the veil,
And shook the hair from her forehead pale,
And 'midst her wondering handmaids stood,
With the sudden glance of a dauntless mood.
Ay, lifting up to the midnight sky⁶
A brow in its regal passion high,                    130
With a close and rigid grasp she press'd
The blood-stain'd robe to her heaving breast,
And said—"Not yet—not yet I weep,
Not yet my spirit shall sink or sleep,
Not till yon city, in ruins rent,
Be piled for its victim's monument.
—Cover his dust! bear it on before!
It shall visit those temple-gates once more."

And away in the train of the dead she turn'd,
The strength of her step was the heart that burn'd;                    140
And the Bramin groves in the starlight⁷ smil'd,
As the mother pass'd with her slaughter'd child.

### III

Hark! a wild sound of the desert's horn
Thro' the woods round the Indian city borne,

A peal of the cymbal and tambour afar—
War! 'tis the gathering of Moslem war!
The Bramin look'd from the leaguer'd towers—
He saw the wild archer amidst his bowers;
And the lake that flash'd through the plantain shade,
As the light of the lances along it play'd;　　　　150
And the canes that shook as if winds were high,
When the fiery steed of the waste swept by;
And the camp as it lay, like a billowy sea,
Wide round the sheltering Banian tree.

There stood one tent from the rest apart—
That was the place of a wounded heart.
—Oh! deep is a wounded heart, and strong
A voice that cries against mighty wrong;
And full of death, as a hot wind's blight,
Doth the ire of a crush'd affection light.　　　　160

Maimuna from realm to realm had pass'd,
And her tale had rung like a trumpet's blast.
There had been words from her pale lips pour'd,
Each one a spell to unsheath the sword.
The Tartar had sprung from his steed to hear,
And the dark chief of Araby grasp'd his spear,
Till a chain of long lances begirt the wall,
And a vow was recorded that doom'd its fall.

Back with the dust of her son she came,
When her voice had kindled that lightning flame;　　　　170
She came in the might of a queenly foe,
Banner, and javelin, and bended bow;
But a deeper power on her forehead sate—
*There* sought the warrior his star of fate;
Her eye's wild flash through the tented line
Was hail'd as a spirit and a sign,
And the faintest tone from her lip was caught,
As a Sybil's breath of prophetic thought.

Vain, bitter glory!—the gift of grief,
That lights up vengeance to find relief,　　　　180
Transient and faithless!—it cannot fill
So the deep voice of the heart, nor still
The yearning left by a broken tie,
That haunted fever of which we die!

Sickening she turn'd from her sad renown,
As a king in death might reject his crown;

Slowly the strength of the walls gave way—
*She* wither'd faster, from day to day.
All the proud sounds of that banner'd plain,
To stay the flight of her soul were vain;                    190
Like an eagle caged, it had striven, and worn
The frail dust ne'er for such conflicts born,
Till the bars were rent, and the hour was come
For its fearful rushing thro' darkness home.

The bright sun set in his pomp and pride,
As on that eve when the fair boy died;
She gazed from her couch, and a softness fell
O'er her weary heart with the day's farewell;
She spoke, and her voice in its dying tone
Had an echo of feelings that long seem'd flown.                    200
She murmur'd a low sweet cradle song,
Strange midst the din of a warrior throng,
A song of the time when her boy's young cheek
Had glow'd on her breast in its slumber meek;
But something which breathed from that mournful strain
Sent a fitful gust o'er her soul again,
And starting as if from a dream, she cried—
"Give him proud burial at my side!
There, by yon lake, where the palm-boughs wave,
When the temples are fallen, make there our grave."                    210

And the temples fell, tho' the spirit pass'd,
That stay'd not for victory's voice at last;
When the day was won for the martyr-dead,
For the broken heart, and the bright blood shed.

Thro' the gates of the vanquish'd the Tartar steed
Bore in the avenger with foaming speed;
Free swept the flame thro' the idol-fanes,
And the streams glow'd red, as from warrior-veins,
And the sword of the Moslem, let loose to slay,
Like the panther leapt on its flying prey.                    220
Till a city of ruin begirt[8] the shade,
Where the boy and his mother at rest were laid.

Palace and tower on that plain were left,
Like fallen trees by the lightning cleft;
The wild vine mantled the stately square,
The Rajah's throne was the serpent's lair,[9]
And the jungle grass o'er the altar sprung—
This was the work of one deep heart wrung!

[1] From a tale in Forbes's Oriental Memoirs. [FH]

First published in *NMM* 14 (December 1925): 574–78, as *Records of Woman.—No. IV*, signed "F. H."

*NMM* footnote to the title] See Forbes's Oriental Memoirs, vol. ii, p. 337, in which this story is related of Dhuboy, a city in Guzerat.

James Forbes (1749–1819), *Oriental Memoirs, Selected and Abridged from a Series of Familiar Letters Written During Seventeen Years Residence in India*, 4 vols. (London: White, Cochrane, 1813), 2.337–38: "Dhuboy for a long time was inhabited only by Hindoos, no Mussulman being permitted [. . .] but a young Mahomedan stranger [. . .] on a pilgrimage with his mother [. . .] rashly ventured to bathe in the sacred lake: the brahmins, deeming the water polluted, prevailed on the rajah to punish the delinquent by cutting off his hands, to deter others from following his example; [. . .] weak with the loss of blood, he could but just reach his mother at the caravansary, and there expired." The mother, a member of an influential family, "laid aside her pilgrimage, and vowed revenge." She was able to engage "a large army" to march on Dhuboy and lay siege to the city for several years, during which the she died, and the besieged citizens starved. The siegers ultimately prevailed with "dreadful slaughter."

FH's verse form is octosyllabic couplets, used by Byron for some of his "Eastern Tales."

[2] Byron, *Childe Harold's Pilgrimage* 3.84 (the antecedent of "heart's" is "wounds"), where the verse continues, "and they who war / With their own hopes, and have been vanquished, bear / Silence, but not submission."

*NMM*] no epigraph

[3] A Hindu of the priestly class; Hindus and Muslims were often at war in India.

[4] *NMM*] This pilgrimage was undertaken from the interior parts of Hindostan. [FH]

Faithful Muslims are expected to make a pilgrimage to the holy city of Mecca, Mohammed's birthplace.

[5] *NMM*] misery's

[6] *NMM*] morn's clear sky

[7] *NMM*] to the Orient

[8] *NMM*] City of Death spread round

222, footnote *NMM*] Their tombs are still remaining, according to Forbes, in a grove near the city. [FH]

The mother "was revered as a saint, and buried in a grove near the gate of diamonds, where her tomb still remains" (Forbes, 2.338).

[9] The Muslim-Hindu warfare, which disrupted the business of the East India Company, was one justification used by the British for their takeover of India.

---

## *The Peasant Girl of the Rhone*[1]

*There is but one place in the world.*
*Thither where he lies buried!*

*. . . . . . . . .*

*There, there is all that still remains of him,*
*That single spot is the whole earth to me.*
                    —*Coleridge's* Wallenstein.[2]

*Alas! our young affections run to waste,*
*Or water but the desert.*
                    —Childe Harold.[3]

There went a warrior's funeral thro' the night,
A waving of tall plumes, a ruddy light
Of torches, fitfully and wildly thrown
From the high woods, along the sweeping Rhone,
Far down the waters. Heavily and dead,
Under the moaning trees the horse-hoof's tread
In muffled sounds upon the greensward fell,
As chieftains pass'd; and solemnly the swell
Of the deep requiem, o'er the gleaming river
Borne with the gale, and with the leaves low shiver,　　　　10
Floated and died. Proud mourners there, yet pale,
　　Wore man's mute anguish sternly;—but of *one*
Oh! who shall speak? What words *his* brow unveil?
　　A father following to the grave his son!
That is no grief to picture! Sad and slow,
　　Thro' the wood-shadows moved the knightly train,
With youth's fair form upon the bier laid low,
　　Fair even when found, amidst the bloody slain,
Stretch'd by its broken lance. They reached the lone
　　Baronial chapel, where the forest gloom　　　　20
Fell heaviest, for the massy boughs had grown
　　Into thick archways, as to vault the tomb.
Stately they trod the hollow ringing aisle,
A strange deep echo shuddered thro' the pile,
Till crested heads at last, in silence bent
Round the De Coucis' antique monument,
When dust to dust was given:—and Aymer slept
　　Beneath the drooping banners of his line,
Whose broider'd folds the Syrian wind had swept
　　Proudly and oft o'er fields of Palestine:[4]　　　　30
So the sad rite was clos'd.—The sculptor gave
Trophies, ere long, to deck that lordly grave,
And the pale image of a youth, arrayed
As warriors are for fight, but calmly laid
　　In slumber on his shield.—Then all was done,
All still, around the dead.—His name was heard
Perchance when wine-cups flow'd, and hearts were stirr'd
　　By some old song, or tale of battle won,
Told round the hearth: but in his father's breast
Manhood's high passions woke again, and press'd　　　　40
On to their mark; and in his friend's clear eye
There dwelt no shadow of a dream gone by;
And with the brethren of his fields, the feast
Was gay as when the voice whose sounds had ceas'd

Mingled with theirs.—Ev'n thus life's rushing tide
Bears back affection from the grave's dark side:
Alas! to think of this!—the heart's void place
 Filled up so soon!—so like a summer-cloud,
All that we lov'd to pass and leave no trace!—
 He lay forgotten in his early shroud.     50
Forgotten?—not of all!—the sunny smile
Glancing in play o'er that proud lip erewhile,
And the dark locks whose breezy waving threw
A gladness round, whene'er their shade withdrew
From the bright brow; and all the sweetness lying
 Within that eagle-eye's jet radiance deep,
And all the music with that young voice dying,
 Whose joyous echoes made the quick heart leap
As at a hunter's bugle—these things lived
Still in one breast, whose silent love survived   60
The pomps of kindred sorrow.—Day by day,
On Aymer's tomb fresh flowers in garlands lay,
Thro' the dim fane soft summer-odours breathing,
And all the pale sepulchral trophies wreathing,
And with a flush of deeper brilliance glowing
In the rich light, like molten rubies flowing
Thro' storied windows down. The violet there
Might speak of love—a secret love and lowly,
And the rose image all things fleet and fair,
And the faint passion-flower, the sad and holy,   70
Tell of diviner hopes. But whose light hand,
As for an altar, wove the radiant band?
Whose gentle nurture brought, from hidden dells,
That gem-like wealth of blossoms and sweet bells,
To blush thro' every season?—Blight and chill
Might touch the changing woods, but duly still,
For years, those gorgeous coronals renewed,
 And brightly clasping marble spear and helm,
Even thro' mid-winter, filled the solitude
 With a strange smile, a glow of summer's realm.  80
Surely some fond and fervent heart was pouring
Its youth's vain worship on the dust, adoring
In lone devotedness![5]
       One spring-morn rose,
 And found, within that tomb's proud shadow laid—
Oh! not as midst the vineyards, to repose
 From the fierce noon—a dark-hair'd peasant maid:

Who could reveal her story?—That still face
  Had once been fair; for on the clear arch'd brow,
And the curv'd lip, there lingered yet such grace
  As sculpture gives its dreams; and long and low          90
The deep black lashes, o'er the half-shut eye—
For death[6] was on its lids—fell mournfully.
But the cold cheek was sunk, the raven hair
Dimm'd, the slight form all wasted, as by care.
Whence came that early blight?—*Her* kindred's place
Was not amidst the high De Couci race;
Yet there her shrine had been!—She grasp'd a wreath—
The tomb's last garland!—This was love in death!

[1] First published in *LS* 1826, 81–84, as *Aymer's Tomb*, signed "Mrs. Hemans." FH had three more poems thus signed in this volume (*The Wreck, The Child and the Dove*, and *The Troubadour and Richard Cœur de Lion*), amidst contributions from "Miss L. E. Landon" (not yet "L.E.L."), Bernard Barton, W. L. Bowles, M.J.J. (Jewsbury), James Hogg, John Clare, Thomas Campbell, "Robert Southey, Esq. the Poet Laureate," and Coleridge. FH's verse form is the "romance" couplet. The two epigraphs were not in *LS*.

[2] *The Death of Wallenstein* 4.5.5–6 and 8–9. Wallenstein's daughter, Thekla, asks to be taken to the coffin of her beloved Max Piccolomini, slain in battle. FH used lines 6 and 9 as the epigraph for *Thekla at Her Lover's Grave*.

[3] Byron, *Childe Harold's Pilgrimage IV*.cxx.

[4] The renowned de Coucy family of medieval France married into the family of Edward III of England and participated in the Crusades. Feldman (*Records* 177–78) suggests that Aymer may be Aymer de Valence, who was buried at Westminster Abbey in 1324 and whose father, William of Valence (d. 1296), fought in Palestine.

[5] *LS*] With a sad constancy!—

[6] *LS*] For night

---

## Indian Woman's Death-Song

*An Indian woman, driven to despair by her husband's desertion of her for another wife, entered a canoe with her children, and rowed it down the Mississippi towards a cataract. Her voice was heard from the shore singing a mournful death-song, until overpowered by the sound of the waters in which she perished. The tale is related in Long's "Expedition to the Source of St. Peter's River."[1]*

*Non, je ne puis vivre avec un coeur brisé. Il faut que je retrouve la joie, et que je m'unisse avec les esprits libres de l'air.*
              —Bride of Messina, *Translated by Madame De Staël*[2]

*Let not my child be a girl, for very sad is the life of a woman.*
              —The Prairie[3]

Down a broad river of the western wilds,
Piercing thick forest glooms, a light canoe
Swept with the current: fearful was the speed
Of the frail bark, as by a tempest's wing
Borne leaf-like on to where the mist of spray
Rose with the cataract's thunder.⁴—Yet within,
Proudly, and dauntlessly, and all alone,
Save that a babe lay sleeping at her breast,
A woman stood: upon her Indian brow
Sat a strange gladness, and her dark hair wav'd          10
As if triumphantly. She press'd her child,
In its bright slumber, to her beating heart,
And lifted her sweet voice, that rose awhile
Above the sound of waters, high and clear,
Wafting a wild proud strain, her song of death.

Roll swiftly to the Spirit's land, thou mighty stream and free!
Father of ancient waters,⁵ roll! and bear our lives with thee!
The weary bird that storms have toss'd, would seek the sunshine's calm,
And the deer that hath the arrow's hurt, flies to the woods of balm.

Roll on!—my warrior's eye hath look'd upon another's face,          20
And mine hath faded from his soul, as fades a moonbeam's trace;
My shadow comes not o'er his path, my whisper to his dream,
He flings away the broken reed—roll swifter yet, thou stream!

The voice that spoke of other days is hush'd within *his* breast,
But *mine* its lonely music haunts, and will not let me rest;
It sings a low and mournful song of gladness that is gone,
I cannot live without that light—Father of waves! roll on!

Will he not miss the bounding step that met him from the chase?
The heart of love that made his home an ever sunny place?
The hand that spread the hunter's board, and deck'd his couch of yore?—     30
He will not!—roll, dark foaming stream, on to the better shore!

Some blessed fount amidst the woods of that bright land must flow,
Whose waters from my soul may lave the memory of this wo;
Some gentle wind must whisper there, whose breath may waft away
The burden of the heavy night, the sadness of the day.

And thou, my babe! tho' born, like me, for woman's weary lot,
Smile!—to that wasting of the heart, my own! I leave thee not;
Too bright a thing art *thou* to pine in aching love away,
Thy mother bears thee far, young Fawn! from sorrow and decay.

She bears thee to the glorious bowers where none are heard to weep,          40
And where th' unkind one hath no power again to trouble sleep;

And where the soul shall find its youth, as wakening from a dream,—
One moment, and that realm is ours—On, on, dark rolling stream!

[1] William Hypolitus Keating (1799–1840), *Narrative of an Expedition to the Source of St. Peter's River*, 2 vols. (1824; London, 1825), based on notes by Major Stephen Harriman Long (1784–1865), the expedition's commander. His account of the American plains includes a story told by a Dakota of an Indian woman who, in despair over her husband's second marriage, "launched her light canoe, entered into it with her children, and paddled down the stream singing her death song. [. . .] her voice was drowned in the sound of the cataract" (1.299–301; FH reduces "children" to one infant daughter). Keating includes accounts of other such suicides (1.284 and 1.394). There is also an account of maternal infanticide among "the red Indians" in Lucy Aikin's *Epistles on Women* (1810), *Epistle II*, 67–102, inspired by a passage in William Robertson's widely read *History of America*, 3 vols. (Dublin, 1777), 2.105: "Die, little wretch; die once and be at peace! / Why shouldst thou live, in toil, and pain, and strife, / To curse the names of mother and of wife?" (76–78); "'tis love, dear babe, that stops thy breath; / Tis mercy lulls thee to the sleep of death: / Ah! would for me, by like indulgent doom, / A mother's hand had raised the early tomb!" (91–94).

[2] No, I cannot live with a broken heart. I need to recover joy, and unite myself with the free spirits of the air.

Schiller, *Die Braut von Messina* (1803); tr. Staël, *De l'Allemagne* (Paris, 1810; 2d ed. 1813), 242, in a summary of *La Fiancée de Messine* at the end of ch. 19. Don Cesar explains to his mother and sister/bride (the Sophoclean/Gothic plot involves a family curse, unwitting romance, fraternal rivalry), why he must kill himself for having killed his brother. *De l'Allemagne* was instrumental in bringing Schiller and other German writers to international attention.

[3] James Fenimore Cooper (1759–1851), *The Prairie* (1827), ch. 26. A Sioux chief has proposed a fourth marriage to Inez, a "white" Mexican captured by his tribe, promising her the status of favorite. His heartbroken third wife and late favorite begs him, for the sake of their infant son, to remember his love for her. Accepting her doom, she strips herself of her ornaments and offers them, with the son, to Inez. "A strange tongue will tell my boy the manner to become a man. He will [. . .] forget the voice of his mother. It is the will of the Wahcondah, and a Sioux girl should not complain. [. . .] Let him not be a girl, for very sad is the life of a woman. Teach him to keep his eyes on the men. Show him how to strike them that do him wrong, and let him never forget to return blow for blow. When he goes to hunt, the flower of the palefaces" (her husband's epithet for Inez) "will whisper softly in his ears that the skin of his mother was red and that she was once the Fawn of the Dakotas." Inez eventually escapes, but the third wife never fully recovers from her husband's betrayal and her sense of inferiority to the white woman.

[4] The imagery evokes the Poet's visionary quest in Shelley's *Alastor* (republished 1824), as he commits his little boat to the winds and waves: "rapidly / Along the dark and ruffled waters fled / The straining boat.—A whirlwind swept it on, / With fierce gusts and precipitating force, [. . .] Down the steep cataract of a wintry river" (318–21, 346).

[5] "Father of waters," the Indian name for the Mississippi. [FH]

The gendered trope is sharpened by the context of male betrayal and female martyrdom. The song is patently Byronic; cf. "Roll on, thou deep and dark blue Ocean—roll!" (*Childe Harold's Pilgrimage IV*.clxxix ff.), a passage FH enjoyed reading aloud (*HM* 128). The dramatic shift from unrhymed, irregular verse into fourteener (heptameter) couplets (the verse form of Chapman's *Iliad*) adds an epic aura to the tone of ritual incantation. FH uses such couplets for *Juana* and for the inset song of *The Sicilian Captive*.

## *Joan of Arc, in Rheims*[1]

[Claiming counsel from holy voices, Jeanne d'Arc (?1412–31) encouraged the Dauphin to resist English incursions on to France. In May 1429 she raised the siege of Orléans, and in July escorted the Dauphin to Rheims cathedral, where she was honored and he was crowned Charles VII. Joan continued to lead the war against the English but suffered defeats. She was captured in 1430 and, with Charles's acquiescence, turned over to the French Inquisition in 1431. Provoked by her claims of holy inspiration and fearing her popularity and power, it tried her for witchcraft, blasphemy, and dressing in male armor. Then, uneasy about prosecuting a popular heroine, it handed her over to the English, who convicted her of treason and burned her at the stake. Lines spoken by Joan from Schiller's play *Die Jungfrau von Orleans* (The Maid of Orléans) (1801) supply the first epigraph for *The Forest Sanctuary*, their theme echoed in this Record. In post-Revolutionary representation, Joan was a contested symbol: sometimes a righteous opponent of tyranny and hence the embodiment of French nationalism, especially against English challenges; sometimes a martyr of conscience to royal treachery and political corruption.]

> *Jeanne d'Arc avait eu la joie de voir à Chàlons quelques amis de son enfance. Une joie plus ineffable encore l'attendoit à Rheims, au sein de son triomphe. [La respectable] Jacques d'Arc, son père, [. . .] y se trouva, aussitôt que de troupes de Charles VII y furent entrées; et comme les deux frères de notre héroïne l'avoient accompagnée, elle se vit, pour un instant, au milieu de sa famille, dans les bras d'un père vertueux.*
>
> —Vie de Jeanne d'Arc.[2]

> *Thou hast a charmed cup, O Fame!*
> *A draught that mantles high,*
> *And seems to lift this earth-born frame*
> *Above mortality:*
> *Away! to me—a woman—bring*
> *Sweet waters from affection's spring.*[3]

That was a joyous day in Rheims of old,
When peal on peal of mighty music roll'd
Forth from her throng'd cathedral; while around,
A multitude, whose billows made no sound,
Chain'd to a hush of wonder, tho' elate
With victory, listen'd at their temple's gate.
And what was done within?—within, the light
 Thro' the rich gloom of pictured windows flowing,
Tinged with soft awfulness a stately sight,
 The chivalry of France, their proud heads bowing     10
In martial vassalage!—while midst that ring,
And shadow'd by ancestral tombs, a king
Receiv'd his birthright's crown. For this, the hymn
 Swell'd out like rushing waters, and the day
With the sweet censer's misty breath grew dim,
 As thro' long aisles it floated o'er th' array

Of arms and sweeping stoles. But who, alone
And unapproach'd, beside the altar-stone,
With the white banner, forth like sunshine streaming,
And the gold helm, thro' clouds of fragrance gleaming,          20
Silent and radiant stood?—the helm was rais'd,
And the fair face reveal'd, that upward gaz'd,
 Intensely worshipping:—a still, clear face,
Youthful, but brightly solemn!—Woman's cheek
And brow were there, in deep devotion meek,
 Yet glorified with inspiration's trace
On its pure paleness; while, enthron'd above,
The pictur'd virgin, with her smile of love,
Seem'd bending o'er her votaress.—That slight form!
Was that the leader thro' the battle storm?          30
Had the soft light in that adoring eye,
Guided the warrior where the swords flash'd high?
'Twas so, even so!—and thou, the shepherd's child,
Joanne,[4] the lowly dreamer of the wild!
Never before, and never since that hour,
Hath woman, mantled with victorious power,
Stood forth as *thou* beside the shrine didst stand,
Holy amidst the knighthood of the land;
And beautiful with joy and with renown,
Lift thy white banner o'er the olden crown,          40
Ransom'd for France by thee!

       The rites are done.
Now let the dome with trumpet-notes be shaken,
And bid the echoes of the tombs awaken,
 And come thou forth, that Heaven's rejoicing sun
May give thee welcome from thine own blue skies,
 Daughter of victory!—A triumphant strain,
A proud rich stream of warlike melodies,
 Gush'd thro' the portals of the antique fane,
And forth she came.—Then rose a nation's sound[5]—
Oh! what a power to bid the quick heart bound,          50
The wind bears onward with the stormy cheer
Man gives to glory on her high career!
Is there indeed such power?—far deeper dwells
In one kind household voice, to reach the cells
Whence happiness flows forth!—The shouts that fill'd
The hollow heaven tempestuously, were still'd
One moment; and in that brief pause, the tone,
As of a breeze that o'er her home had blown,

Sank on the bright maid's heart.—"Joanne!"—Who spoke
   Like those whose childhood with *her* childhood grew      60
Under one roof?—"Joanne!"—*that* murmur broke
   With sounds of weeping forth!—She turn'd—she knew
Beside her, mark'd from all the thousands there,
In the calm beauty of his silver hair,
The stately shepherd; and the youth, whose joy
From his dark eye flash'd proudly; and the boy,
The youngest-born, that ever lov'd her best:
"Father! and ye, my brothers!"—On the breast
Of that grey sire she sank—and swiftly back,
Ev'n in an instant, to their native track      70
Her free thoughts flowed.—She saw the pomp no more—
The plumes, the banners:—to her cabin-door,
And to the Fairy's fountain in the glade,[6]
Where her young sisters by her side had play'd,
And to her hamlet's chapel, where it rose
Hallowing the forest unto deep repose,
Her spirit turn'd.—The very wood-note, sung
   In early spring-time by the bird, which dwelt
Where o'er her father's roof the beech-leaves hung,
   Was in her heart; a music heard and felt,      80
Winning her back to nature.[7]—She unbound
   The helm of many battles from her head,
And, with her bright locks bow'd to sweep the ground,
   Lifting her voice up, wept for joy, and said,—
"Bless me, my father, bless me! and with thee,
To the still cabin and the beechen-tree,
Let me return!"[8]
               Oh! never did thine eye
Thro' the green haunts of happy infancy
Wander again, Joanne!—too much of fame
Had shed its radiance on thy peasant-name;      90
And bought alone by gifts beyond all price,[9]
The trusting heart's repose, the paradise
Of home with all its loves, doth fate allow
The crown of glory unto woman's brow.[10]

[1] First published *NMM* 17 (October 1826): 314–16, as *Records of Woman.—No. VIII*, unsigned.

[2] Joan of Arc had the pleasure of seeing some childhood friends at Chalons. A still more inexpressible pleasure awaited her at Rheims, in the heart of her triumph: Jacques d'Arc, her father, [. . .] arrived just as Charles VII's troops made their entry; and as the two brothers of our heroine had accompanied him, she found herself, for an instant, in the midst of her family, in the arms of a good father.

*Jeanne d'Arc ou La Pucelle d'Orleans*, in *Almanach de Gotha pour l'Année 1822* (Gotha: Justus Perthes), 2d pagination, 102 (*Pucelle*: Virgin). FH elides "le bon Durand Laxart, son oncle" and adapts "se trouvèrent" accordingly. *Almanach 1822*'s frontispiece features a brawny, armored, Minerva-like Joan. This genealogical, statistical and diplomatic annual had been published since 1763.

*NMM*] The epigraph is a footnote to line 68, citing *Almanach* and continuing, "auquel cette vertueuse fille se plut à renvoyer ces hommages d'estime, [. . .] dont elle étoit entourée" (to whom this virtuous daughter was pleased to transfer these homages of esteem by which she was surrounded). FH elides "de respect et d'amour" (respect and love).

³ Not in *NMM*. Stanza 1 of *Woman and Fame* (not yet published in 1828). Implying that this is Joan's interior voice, FH means to recuperate the stereotype of a woman who "wanders [. . .] far beyond the limits prescribed to her sex" (the words of conduct-advisor Hannah More, linking Joan with Thalestris, Queen of the Amazons ("On Religion" [1777]).

⁴ FH's hybrid of French Jeanne and English Joan.

⁵ This anachronism (France was not a "nation" but a dynastic territory) is the language of emergent Romantic nationalism.

⁶ A beautiful fountain near Domremi, believed to be haunted by fairies, and a favourite resort of Jeanne d'Arc in her childhood. [FH]

*NMM*] A tree and fountain near Domremi, the native village of Joanne d'Arc, was believed to be haunted by fairies, and were much frequented by the young girls of the neighbouring hamlets, who often suspended wreaths from the branches of the tree, which was a beech of remarkable size and beauty.

⁷ Not just the world of nature but also her deepest female "nature."
*NMM*] Nature. Other such symbolizing capitals: Cathedral (2), Virgin (28), Glory (52), Paradise (92), Fate (93).

⁸ Cf. Jesus' parable of the prodigal son (Luke 15.11–32) and *The Spells of Home*. The unbinding of the hair from the helmet evokes Spenser's knight Britomart, revealing her female heart (*Faerie Queene*, bk. 4, canto 1, stanzas 12–15).

⁹ Echoing 2 Peter on salvation through Christ: "Through [His] might and splendour he has given us promises, great beyond all price, and through Him you may escape the corruption" of "the world" (1.4, New English Bible).

¹⁰ "Thou never from that hour in Paradise / Found'st either sweet repast, or sound repose," Milton writes of Eve as she leaves Adam's side (*Paradise Lost* 9.406–7).

---

## *Pauline*¹

> To die for what we love!—Oh! there is power
> In the true heart, and pride, and joy, for this;
> It is to live without the vanish'd light
> That strength is needed.²

> Così trapassa al trapassar d'un Giorno
> Della vita mortal il fiore e'l verde.
> TASSO³

Along the star-lit Seine went music swelling,
   Till the air thrill'd with its exulting mirth;
Proudly it floated, even as if no dwelling
   For cares or stricken hearts were found on earth;

And a glad sound the measure lightly beat,
A happy chime of many dancing feet.

For in a palace of the land that night,
    Lamps, and fresh roses, and green leaves were hung,
And from the painted walls a stream of light
    On flying forms beneath soft splendour flung:        10
But loveliest far amidst the revel's pride
Was one, the lady from the Danube-side.[4]

Pauline, the meekly bright!—tho' now no more
    Her clear eye flash'd with youth's all tameless glee,
Yet something holier than its dayspring wore,
    There in soft rest lay beautiful to see;
A charm with graver, tenderer, sweetness fraught—
The blending of deep love and matron thought.

Thro' the gay throng she moved, serenely fair,
    And such calm joy as fills a moonlight sky,        20
Sate on her brow beneath its graceful hair,
    As her young daughter in the dance went by,
With the fleet step of one that yet hath known
Smiles and kind voices in this world alone.

Lurk'd there no secret boding in her breast?
    Did no faint whisper warn of evil nigh?
Such oft awake when most the heart seems blest
    Midst the light laughter of festivity:
Whence come those tones!—Alas! enough we know,
To mingle fear with all triumphal show!        30

Who spoke of evil, when young feet were flying
    In fairy rings around the echoing hall?
Soft airs thro' braided locks in perfume sighing,
    Glad pulses beating unto music's call?
Silence!—the minstrels pause—and hark! a sound,
A strange quick rustling which their notes had drown'd!

And lo! a light upon the dancers breaking—
    Not such their clear and silvery lamps had shed!
From the gay dream of revelry awaking,
    One moment holds them still in breathless dread:        40
The wild fierce lustre grows—then bursts a cry—
Fire! thro' the hall and round it gathering—fly!

And forth they rush—as chased by sword and spear—
    To the green coverts of the garden-bowers;
A gorgeous masque of pageantry and fear,
    Startling the birds and trampling down the flowers:

While from the dome behind, red sparkles driven
Pierce the dark stillness of the midnight heaven.

And where is she, Pauline?—the hurrying throng
    Have swept her onward, as a stormy blast          50
Might sweep some faint o'erwearied bird along—
    Till now the threshold of that death is past,
And free she stands beneath the starry skies,
Calling her child—but no sweet voice replies.

"Bertha! where art thou?—Speak, oh! speak, my own!"
    Alas! unconscious of her pangs the while,
The gentle girl, in fear's cold grasp alone,
    Powerless hath sunk within the blazing pile;
A young bright form, deck'd gloriously for death,[5]
With flowers all shrinking from the flame's fierce breath!    60

But oh! thy strength, deep love!—there is no power
    To stay the mother from that rolling grave,
Tho' fast on high the fiery volumes tower,
    And forth, like banners, from each lattice wave
Back, back she rushes thro' a host combined—
Mighty is anguish, with affection twined!

And what bold step may follow, midst the roar
    Of the red billows, o'er their prey that rise?
None!—Courage there stood still—and never more
    Did those fair forms emerge on human eyes!    70
Was one brief meeting theirs, one wild farewell?
And died they heart to heart?—Oh! who can tell?

Freshly and cloudlessly the morning broke
    On that sad palace, midst its pleasure-shades;
Its painted roofs had sunk—yet black with smoke
    And lonely stood its marble colonnades:
But yester-eve their shafts with wreaths were bound—
Now lay the scene one shrivell'd scroll around!

And bore the ruins no recording trace
    Of all that woman's heart had dared and done?    80
Yes! there were gems to mark its mortal place,
    That forth from dust and ashes dimly shone!
Those had the mother on her gentle breast,
Worn round her child's fair image, there at rest.[6]

And they were all!—the tender and the true
    Left this alone her sacrifice to prove,
Hallowing the spot where mirth once lightly flew,
    To deep, lone, chasten'd thoughts of grief and love.

Oh! we have need of patient faith below,
To clear away the mysteries of such wo! 90

[1] First published *NMM* 19 (February 1827): 155–57, as *Records of Woman.—No. X*, signed
"F. H." Other than the epigraphs, significant variants are capitals: Evil (31), Heaven (48),
Death (52, 59), Love (61), Faith (89).
  [2] In *NMM*, there is only this epigraph:

> One adequate support
> For the calamities of mortal life
> Exists, one only;—an assured belief
> That the procession of our fate, howe'er
> Sad or disturb'd, is order'd by a Being
> Of infinite benevolence and power,
> Whose everlasting purposes embrace
> All accidents, converting them to Good.
>
> WORDSWORTH

From *The Excursion* (1814), the Wanderer's reproof of the indulgence of excess compassion for
human sufferers (4.10–17).
  [3] Thus passes in the passing of a Day / The flower and the leaf of mortal life.
  *Gerusalemme Liberata* 16.15.1–2. The context is a *carpe diem* song ("O gather then the rose
while you have time") caroled by a bird in the garden of the enchantress Armida's palace, where
Rinaldo, a lapsed Crusader, is imprisoned. Staël quotes these lines in her epigraph for her
passionate recounting of the story of "La princesse Pauline de Schwartzenberg" (see next note).
  [4] The Princess Pauline Schwartzenberg. The story of her fate is beautifully related in L'Allemagne. Vol. iii. p. 336. [FH]
  *Germany; by the Baroness Staël-Holstein* (London: John Murray 1813), 3.338–39. In *NMM*
with slightly different wording the note is attached to the title. Napoleon, who had first exiled
Staël in 1803, confiscated and destroyed *De l'Allemagne* when it was printed in 1810, and again
exiled her. She managed to preserve three copies, and it was published in 1813, in Paris. In
London, Murray brought it out both in English (*Germany*) and in French (*De l'Allemagne, par
Mme La baronne de Stael Holstein*). The story of Pauline appears on 549–50, at the beginning
of part 4, ch. 6, "De la douleur." When a fire erupted at a Parisian ballroom in 1810, Austrian
princess Pauline de Schwartzenberg rushed in to save her daughter. She succeeded at the cost
of her life, her corpse identifiable only by a gemmed choker: "her hand seized that of her
daughter, her hand saved her daughter; and although the fatal blow then struck her, her last act
was maternal; her last act preserved the object of her affection; it was at this sublime instant that
she appeared before God; and it was impossible to recognise what remained of her upon earth
except by the impression on a medal, given by her children, which also marked the place where
this angel perished. [. . .] This generous Paulina will hereafter be the saint of mothers" (*Germany* 3.338–39). FH has the daughter die, too. Paulina's son, Prince Felix of Schwartzenberg
(1800–52), later became Austrian premier, and her choker remained a cherished family heir-
loom until it was seized by Hitler.
  [5] Evoking the suttee, the ritual suicide of an Indian widow on her husband's funeral pyre; see
*The Bride of the Greek Isle* 216ff. and note.
  [6] *NMM*] "L'on n'a pu reconnaître ce qui restait d'elle sur la terre qu'au chiffre de ses enfants,
qui marquait encore la place où cet ange avait péri." MADAME DE STAEL. [FH]
  *De l'Allemagne* (1813), 550; cf. *Germany* 338 (note 4: "it was impossible to recognise . . .").

## *Juana*[1]

Juana, mother of the Emperor Charles V, upon the death of her husband, Philip the Handsome of Austria, who had treated her with uniform neglect, had his body laid upon a bed of state in a magnificent dress, and being possessed with the idea that it would revive, watched it for a length of time incessantly, waiting for the moment of returning life.[2]

> *It is but dust thou look'st upon. This love,*
> *This wild and passionate idolatry,*
> *What doth it in the shadow of the grave?*
> *Gather it back within thy lonely heart,*
> *So must it ever end: too much we give*
> *Unto the things that perish.*

The night-wind shook the tapestry round an ancient palace-room,
And torches, as it rose and fell, waved thro' the gorgeous gloom,
And o'er a shadowy regal couch threw fitful gleams and red,
Where a woman with long raven hair sat watching by the dead.

Pale shone the features of the dead, yet glorious still to see,
Like a hunter or a chief struck down while his heart and step were free;
No shroud he wore, no robe of death, but there majestic lay,
Proudly and sadly glittering in royalty's array.

But she that with the dark hair watch'd by the cold slumberer's side,
On *her* wan cheek no beauty dwelt, and in her garb no pride;                    10
Only her full impassion'd eyes as o'er that clay she bent,
A wildness and a tenderness in strange resplendence blent.

And as the swift thoughts cross'd her soul, like shadows of a cloud,
Amidst the silent room of death, the dreamer spoke aloud;
She spoke to him who could not hear, and cried, "Thou yet wilt wake,
And learn my watchings and my tears, belov'd one! for thy sake.

They told me this was death, but well I knew it could not be;
Fairest and stateliest of the earth! who spoke of death for *thee?*
They would have wrapt the funeral shroud thy gallant form around,
But I forbade—and there thou art, a monarch, rob'd and crown'd!                  20

With all thy bright locks gleaming still, their coronal beneath,
And thy brow so proudly beautiful—who said that this was death?
Silence hath been upon thy lips, and stillness round thee long,
But the hopeful spirit in my breast is all undimm'd and strong.

I know thou hast not lov'd me yet; I am not fair like thee,
The very glance of whose clear eye threw round a light of glee!

A frail and dropping form is mine—a cold unsmiling cheek,
Oh! I have but a woman's heart, wherewith *thy* heart to seek.

But when thou wak'st, my prince, my lord! and hear'st how I have kept
A lonely vigil by thy side, and o'er thee pray'd and wept;                    30
How in one long deep dream of thee my nights and days have past,
Surely that humble, patient love *must* win back love at last!

And thou wilt smile—my own, my own, shall be the sunny smile,
Which brightly fell, and joyously, on all *but* me erewhile!
No more in vain affection's thirst my weary soul shall pine—
Oh! years of hope deferr'd were paid by one fond glance of thine!

Thou'lt meet me with that radiant look when thou comest from the chase,
For me, for me, in festal halls it shall kindle o'er thy face!
Thou'lt reck no more tho' beauty's gift mine aspect may not bless;
In thy kind eyes this deep, deep love, shall give me loveliness.              40

But wake! my heart within me burns, yet once more to rejoice
In the sound to which it ever leap'd, the music of thy voice:
Awake! I sit in solitude, that thy first look and tone,
And the gladness of thine opening eyes may all be mine alone."

In the still chambers of the dust, thus pour'd forth day by day,
The passion of that loving dream from a troubled soul found way,
Until the shadows of the grave had swept o'er every grace,
Left midst the awfulness of death on the princely form and face.

And slowly broke the fearful truth upon the watcher's breast,
And they bore away the royal dead with requiems to his rest,                  50
With banners and with knightly plumes all waving in the wind—
But a woman's broken heart was left in its lone despair behind.

---

[1] First published as *Joanna*, *NMM* 20 (October 1827), 358–59. The fourteener couplet is also used for the inset songs of the "Indian Woman" and the "Sicilian Captive"—a formal link between these various songs of "woman's broken heart" in "its lone despair."

[2] Upon the death of her mother, Isabella I, in 1504, Juana, "Joanna the Mad" (1479–1555) became Queen of Castile under the regency of her father, Ferdinand II. To strengthen his hand against France, he arranged her marriage in 1496 to ambitious and famously handsome Phillip, Archduke of Austria (1478–1506). Phillip contested Ferdinand's regency, and in 1506 became joint ruler with Juana. He was publicly unfaithful to and neglectful of her, and his death of fever the same year aggravated her mental instability. Her father continued as regent and "Juana la Loca" remained a virtual prisoner for the rest of her life. Her son Charles V (1500–1558) ruled as Holy Roman Emperor from 1519–56.

## The American Forest-Girl[1]

[More so than *Edith*, this is a "captivity narrative," a primary genre in the literature of New World encounters, initiated by Captain John Smith's account of his captivity in *Generall Historie of Virginia, New-England, and the Summer Isles* (1624, often reprinted). His rescue by Pocohantas is FH's figurative background. Blending Puritan spiritual autobiography into the genre, *The Soveraignty and Goodness of God, together with the Faithfulness of His Promises Displayed; Being a Narrative of the Captivity and Restauration of Mrs. Mary Row-landson* (1682, also often reprinted) influenced FH's "conversion" tales, such as *Edith*. John Dunn Hunter's popular and controversial *Memoirs of a Captivity among the Indians of North America, from Childhood to the Age of Nineteen* (1823) inspired FH's *The Child of the Forests* (*NMM*, March 1824; see *HM* 95). FH also read Catherine Maria Sedgwick's *Hope Leslie* (*CM* 1.228), a novel published in 1827 about the Pequod War in 17th-c. New England.]

> *A fearful gift upon thy heart is laid,*
> *Woman!—a power to suffer and to love,*
> *Therefore thou so canst pity.*

Wildly and mournfully the Indian drum
   On the deep hush of moonlight forests broke;—
"Sing us a death-song, for thine hour is come,"—
   So the red warriors to their captive spoke.
Still, and amidst those dusky forms alone,
   A youth, a fair-hair'd youth of England stood,
Like a king's son; tho' from his cheek had flown
   The mantling crimson of the island-blood,
And his press'd lips look'd marble.—Fiercely bright,
And high around him, blaz'd the fires of night,                    10
Rocking beneath the cedars to and fro,
As the wind pass'd, and with a fitful glow
Lighting the victim's face:—But who could tell
Of what within his secret heart befel,
Known but to heaven that hour?—Perchance a thought
Of his far home then so intensely wrought,
That its full image, pictured to his eye
On the dark ground of mortal agony,
Rose clear as day!—and he might *see* the band,
Of his young sisters wandering hand in hand,                       20
Where the laburnums droop'd; or haply binding
The jasmine, up the door's low pillars winding;
Or, as day clos'd upon their gentle mirth,
Gathering with braided hair, around the hearth
Where sat their mother;—and that mother's face
Its grave sweet smile yet wearing in the place

Where so it ever smiled!—Perchance the prayer
Learn'd at her knee came back on his despair;
The blessing from her voice, the very tone
Of her "*Good-night*" might breathe from boyhood gone!—          30
He started and look'd up:—thick cypress boughs
   Full of strange sound, wav'd o'er him, darkly red
In the broad stormy firelight;—savage brows,
   With tall plumes crested and wild hues o'erspread,
Girt him like feverish phantoms; and pale stars
Look'd thro' the branches as thro' dungeon bars,
Shedding no hope.—He knew, he felt his doom—
Oh! what a tale to shadow with its gloom
That happy hall in England!—Idle fear!
Would the winds tell it?—Who might dream or hear          40
The secret of the forests?—To the stake
   They bound him; and that proud young soldier strove
His father's spirit in his breast to wake,
   Trusting to die in silence! He, the love
Of many hearts!—the fondly rear'd,—the fair,
Gladdening all eyes to see!—And fetter'd there
He stood beside his death-pyre, and the brand
Flamed up to light it, in the chieftain's hand.
He thought upon his God.—Hush! hark!—a cry
Breaks on the stern and dread solemnity,—          50
A step hath pierc'd the ring!—Who dares intrude
On the dark hunters in their vengeful mood?—
A girl—a young slight girl—a fawn-like child
Of green Savannas and the leafy wild,
Springing unmark'd till then, as some lone flower,
Happy because the sunshine is its dower;
Yet one that knew how early tears are shed,—
For *hers* had mourn'd a playmate brother dead.

She had sat gazing on the victim long,
Until the pity of her soul grew strong;          60
And, by its passion's deepening fervour sway'd,
Ev'n to the stake she rush'd, and gently laid
His bright head on her bosom, and around
His form her slender arms to shield it wound
Like close Liannes°; then rais'd her glittering eye          *climbing vines*
And clear-toned voice that said, "He shall not die!"

"He shall not die!"—the gloomy forest thrill'd
   To that sweet sound. A sudden wonder fell
On the fierce throng; and heart and hand were still'd,
   Struck down, as by the whisper of a spell.          70

They gaz'd,—their dark souls bow'd before the maid,
She of the dancing step in wood and glade!
And, as her cheek flush'd thro' its olive hue,
As her black tresses to the night-wind flew,
Something o'ermaster'd them from that young mien—
Something of heaven, in silence felt and seen;
And seeming, to their child-like faith, a token
That the Great Spirit by her voice had spoken.

They loos'd the bonds that held their captive's breath;
From his pale lips they took the cup of death;                    80
They quench'd the brand beneath the cypress tree;
"Away," they cried, "young stranger, thou art free!"

¹ First published in *NMM* 16 (April 1826): 407–8, as *Records of Woman.—No. VI*, signed
"F. H.," without the epigraph.

-------------------

## Costanza¹

> *Art thou then desolate?*
> *Of friends, of hopes forsaken?—Come to me!*
> *I am thine own.—Have trusted hearts prov'd false?*
> *Flatterers deceiv'd thee? Wanderer, come to me!*
> *Why didst thou ever leave me? Know'st thou all*
> *I would have borne, and call'd it joy to bear,*
> *For thy sake? Know'st thou that thy voice had power*
> *To shake me with a thrill of happiness*
> *By one kind tone?—to fill mine eyes with tears*
> *Of yearning love? And thou—oh! thou didst throw*
> *That crush'd affection back upon my heart;—*
> *Yet come to me!—it died not.*²

She knelt in prayer. A stream of sunset fell
Thro' the stain'd window of her lonely cell,
And with its rich, deep, melancholy glow
Flushing her cheek and pale Madonna-brow,³
While o'er her long hair's flowing jet it threw
Bright waves of gold—the autumn forest's hue—
Seem'd all a vision's mist of glory, spread
By painting's touch around some holy head,
Virgin's or fairest martyr's. In her eye,
Which glanced as dark clear water to the sky,                     10
What solemn fervour lived! And yet what wo,
Lay like some buried thing, still seen below

The glassy tide! Oh! he that could reveal
What life had taught that chasten'd heart to feel,
Might speak indeed of woman's blighted years,
And wasted love, and vainly bitter tears!
But she had told her griefs to heaven alone,
And of the gentle saint no more was known,
Than that she fled the world's cold breath, and made
A temple of the pine and chestnut shade,                    20
Filling its depths with soul, whene'er her hymn
Rose thro' each murmur of the green, and dim,
And ancient solitude; where hidden streams
Went moaning thro' the grass, like sounds in dreams,
Music for weary hearts! Midst leaves and flowers
She dwelt, and knew all secrets of their powers,
All nature's balms, wherewith her gliding tread
To the sick peasant on his lowly bed,
Came, and brought hope; while scarce of mortal birth
He deem'd the pale fair form, that held on earth           30
Communion but with grief.

                              Ere long a cell,
     A rock-hewn chapel rose, a cross of stone
Gleam'd thro' the dark trees o'er a sparkling well,
     And a sweet voice, of rich, yet mournful tone,
Told the Calabrian wilds,[4] that duly there
Costanza lifted her sad heart[5] in prayer.
And now 'twas prayer's own hour. That voice again
Thro' the dim foliage sent its heavenly strain,
That made the cypress quiver where it stood
In day's last crimson soaring from the wood                40
Like spiry flame. But as the bright sun set,
Other and wilder sounds in tumult met
The floating song. Strange sounds!—the trumpet's peal,
Made hollow by the rocks; the clash of steel,
The rallying war-cry.—In the mountain-pass,
There had been combat; blood was on the grass,
Banners had strewn the waters; chiefs lay dying,
And the pine-branches crash'd before the flying.

And all was chang'd within the still retreat,
Costanza's home:—there enter'd hurrying feet,             50
Dark looks of shame and sorrow; mail-clad men,
Stern fugitives from that wild battle-glen,
Scaring the ringdoves from the porch-roof, bore
A wounded warrior in: the rocky floor

Gave back deep echoes to his clanging sword,
As there they laid their leader, and implor'd
The sweet saint's prayers to heal him; then for flight,
Thro' the wide forest and the mantling night,
Sped breathlessly again.—They pass'd—but he,
The stateliest of a host—alas! to see                    60
What mothers' eyes have watch'd in rosy sleep
Till joy, for very fulness, turn'd to weep,
Thus changed!—a fearful thing! His golden crest
Was shiver'd,° and the bright scarf on his breast—        *shattered*
Some costly love-gift—rent:—but what of these?
There were the clustering raven-locks—the breeze
As it came in thro' lime and myrtle flowers,
Might scarcely lift them—steep'd in bloody showers
So heavily upon the pallid clay
Of the damp cheek they hung! the eyes' dark ray—          70
Where was it?—and the lips!—they gasp'd apart,
With their light curve, as from the chisel's art,
Still proudly beautiful! but that white hue—
Was it not death's?—that stillness—that cold dew
On the scarr'd forehead? No! his spirit broke
From its deep trance ere long, yet but awoke
To wander in wild dreams; and there he lay,
By the fierce fever as a green reed shaken,
The haughty chief of thousands—the forsaken
Of all save one!—*She* fled not. Day by day—             80
Such hours are woman's birthright—she, unknown,
Kept watch beside him, fearless and alone;
Binding his wounds, and oft in silence laving
His brow with tears that mourn'd the strong man's raving.
He felt them not, nor mark'd the light veil'd form
Still hovering nigh; yet sometimes, when that storm
Of frenzy sank, her voice, in tones as low
As a young mother's by the cradle singing,
Would sooth him with sweet *aves*,° gently bringing    *Ave-Maria prayers*
Moments of slumber, when the fiery glow                   90
Ebb'd from his hollow cheek.

     At last faint gleams
Of memory dawn'd upon the cloud of dreams,
And feebly lifting, as a child, his head,
And gazing round him from his leafy bed,
He murmur'd forth, "Where am I? What soft strain
Pass'd, like a breeze, across my burning brain?

Back from my youth it floated, with a tone
Of life's first music, and a thought of one—
Where is she now? and where the gauds of pride
Whose hollow splendour lured me from her side?          100
All lost!—and this is death!—I *cannot* die
Without forgiveness from that mournful eye!
Away! the earth hath lost her. Was *she* born
To brook abandonment, to strive with scorn?
My first, my holiest love!—her broken heart
Lies low, and I—unpardon'd I depart."

But then Costanza rais'd the shadowy[6] veil
From her dark locks and features brightly pale,
And stood before him with a smile—oh! ne'er
Did aught that *smiled* so much of sadness wear—          110
And said, "Cesario! look on me; I live
To say my heart hath bled, and can forgive.
I loved thee with such worship, such deep trust
As should be Heaven's alone—and Heaven is just!
I bless thee—be at peace!"

            But o'er his frame
Too fast the strong tide rush'd—the sudden shame,
The joy, th' amaze!—he bow'd his head—it fell
On the wrong'd bosom which had lov'd so well;
And love still perfect, gave him refuge there,—
His last faint breath just wav'd her floating hair.          120

---

[1] First published *NMM* 14 (August 1825) 110–12, *Records of Woman, No. II.*, signed "F.H."
"Costanza" is a feminine Italian noun meaning "constancy, steadiness, loyalty." The verse is in
romance couplets and, as in *Properzia Rossi*, enjambments reinforce sense, with such terminal
words as *fell*, *threw*, and *spread* carrying the syntax across the lines—here muting but not
silencing some of the rhymes.

[2] *NMM*] no epigraph

[3] *NMM*] Flushing the marble beauty of her brow

[4] District of ancient Italy in the boot-heel of the peninsula.

[5] *NMM*] soul

[6] *NMM*] shadowing

## *Madeline, a Domestic Tale*[1]

*Who should it be?—Where shouldst thou look for kindness?*
*When we are sick where can we turn for succour,*
*When we are wretched where can we complain;*
*And when the world looks cold and surly on us,*
*Where can we go to meet a warmer eye*
*With such sure confidence as to a mother?*
                                          JOANNA BAILLIE[2]

"My child, my child, thou leav'st me!—I shall hear
The gentle voice no more that blest mine ear
With its first utterance; I shall miss the sound
Of thy light step amidst the flowers around,
And thy soft-breathing hymn at twilight's close,
And thy "Good-night" at parting for repose.
Under the vine-leaves I shall sit alone,
And the low breeze will have a mournful tone
Amidst their tendrils, while I think of thee,
My child! and thou, along the moonlight sea,                    10
With a soft sadness haply in thy glance,
Shalt watch thine own, thy pleasant land of France,
Fading to air.—Yet blessings with thee go!
Love guard thee, gentlest! and the exile's wo
From thy young heart be far!—And sorrow not
For me, sweet daughter! in my lonely lot,
God shall[3] be with me.—Now farewell, farewell!
Thou that hast been what words may never tell
Unto thy mother's bosom, since the days
When thou wert pillow'd there, and wont to raise                20
In sudden laughter thence thy loving eye
That still sought mine:—those moments are gone by,
Thou too must go, my flower!—Yet with thee dwell
The peace of God!—One, one more gaze—farewell!"

This was a mother's parting with her child,
A young meek Bride on whom fair fortune smil'd,
And wooed her with a voice of love away
From childhood's home; yet there, with fond delay[4]
She linger'd on the threshold, heard the note
Of her caged bird thro' trellis'd rose-leaves float,            30
And fell upon her mother's neck, and wept,
Whilst old remembrances, that long had slept,

Gush'd[5] o'er her soul, and many a vanish'd day,
As in one picture traced, before her lay.

But the farewell was said; and on the deep,
When its breast heav'd in sunset's golden sleep,
With a calm'd heart, young Madeline ere long
Pour'd forth her own sweet solemn vesper-song,
Breathing of home:[6] thro' stillness heard afar,
And duly rising with the first pale star,                                40
That voice was on the waters; till at last
The sounding ocean-solitudes were pass'd,
And the bright land was reach'd, the youthful world
That glows along the West: the sails were furl'd
In its clear sunshine, and the gentle bride
Look'd on the home that promis'd hearts untried
A bower of bliss to come.[7]—Alas! we trace
The map of our own paths, and long ere years
With their dull steps the brilliant lines efface,
On sweeps the storm, and blots them out with tears.                     50
That home was darken'd soon: the summer breeze
Welcom'd with death the wanderers from the seas,
Death unto one, and anguish how forlorn!
To her, that widow'd in her marriage-morn,
Sat in her voiceless[8] dwelling, whence with him,
    Her bosom's first belov'd, her friend and guide,
Joy had gone forth, and left the green earth dim,
    As from the sun shut out on every side,
By the close veil of misery!—Oh! but ill,
    When with rich hopes o'erfraught, the young high heart             60
    Bears its first blow!—it knows not yet the part
Which life will teach—to suffer and be still,[9]
And with submissive love to count the flowers
Which yet are spared, and thro' the future hours
To send no busy dream!—*She* had not learn'd
Of sorrow till that hour,[10] and therefore turn'd,
In weariness from life: then came th' unrest,
The heart-sick[11] yearning of the exile's breast,
The haunting sounds of voices far away,
And household steps; until at last she lay                              70
On her lone couch of sickness, lost in dreams
Of the gay vineyards and blue-rushing streams
In her own sunny land, and murmuring oft
Familiar names, in accents wild, yet soft,
To strangers round that bed, who knew not aught
Of the deep spells wherewith each word was fraught.

To strangers?—Oh! could strangers raise the head
Gently as *hers* was rais'd?—did strangers shed
The kindly tears which bath'd that feverish brow
And wasted cheek[12] with half unconscious flow?               80
Something was there, that thro' the lingering[13] night
Outwatches patiently the taper's light,
Something that faints not thro' the day's distress,
That fears not toil, that knows not weariness;[14]
Love, true and perfect love!—Whence came that power,
Uprearing thro' the storm the drooping flower?[15]
Whence?—who can ask?—the wild[16] delirium pass'd,
And from her eyes the spirit look'd at last
Into her *mother's* face, and wakening knew
The brow's calm grace, the hair's dear silvery hue,            90
The kind sweet smile of old!—and had *she* come,
Thus in life's evening, from her distant home,
To save her child?—Ev'n so—nor yet in vain:
In that young heart a light sprung up again,
And lovely still, with so much love to give,
Seem'd this fair world, tho' faded; still to live
Was not to pine forsaken. On the breast
That rock'd her childhood, sinking in soft rest,
"Sweet mother, gentlest mother! can it be?"
The lorn one cried, "and do I look[17] on thee?                100
Take back thy wanderer from this fatal shore,[18]
Peace shall be ours beneath[19] our vines once more."

---

[1] Originally published in the Literary Souvenir for 1828. [FH]

*LS* (22–25): titled *Madeline*, no epigraph, signed "Mrs. Hemans." *LS* 1828 also included FH's *The Wings of the Dove, The Voice of Home, Ancient Song of Victory*, and *The Memory of the Dead*, and pieces by M.J.J. (Jewsbury), L.E.L. (Landon), Mitford, Coleridge, W. L. Bowles, Caroline Bowles, Clare, Hood, Southey, Alan Cunningham, and Barry Cornwall. The romance couplets link *Madeline* formally and thematically with *Costanza*. The genre of "Domestic Tale," featuring sympathies tuned to moral understanding, arose in the 18th-c. culture of sensibility, among the most popular works, *The Young Lady's Tale: The Two Emilys* (1798) by Sophia Lee, and *Madeline Mowbray, or the Mother and Daughter, A Tale* (1804), *Simple Tales* (1806), and *Madeline* (1822), all by Amelia Alderson Opie. Associated with women writers, the genre attracted Wordsworth, too: see *The Brothers* and *Michael* (*Lyrical Ballads* [1800]), and several tales in *The Excursion* (1814).

[2] *Rayner: A Tragedy*, in *Miscellaneous Plays* (1804) 4.2.15–20; spoken by the countess as she unmasks herself to her ailing son, both of them in disguise.

[3] *LS*] will

[4] 26–28, *LS*] Fortune / Love / Childhood

[5] *LS*] Streamed

[6] *LS*] low solemn vesper-song / To chiming waves.

[7] The youthful world to the West suggests the Americas, but the "bower of bliss" is a fallen world in Spenser's *Faerie Queene* (bk. 2, canto 12, stanza 69).

[8] *LS*] lonely

[9] *LS*] still!
Cf. *Siege of Valencia* MS (note 50). A prescription widely sounded (perhaps first here) in the nineteenth century. See Sarah Stickney Ellis, *The Daughters of England* (London, 1845), 73.
[10] *LS*] blight
[11] *LS*] vague sad
[12] *LS*] pale young brow, / And feverish cheek
[13] *LS*] heavy
[14] *LS*] bows not to . . . / That knows not change, that fears . . .
[15] *LS*] Upbearing through the storm the fragile flower?
A reworking of the line from Staël's *Corinne* that supplies the epigraph for *The Widow of Crescentius*.
[16] *LS*] long
[17] *LS*] gaze
[18] Laodamia recalls the "matchless courage" that "propelled" her husband Protesilaus to Troy's "fatal shore" (*Laodamia* 52). The first Greek to alight, he was killed by Hector.
[19] *LS*] amidst

## *The Queen of Prussia's Tomb*[1]

"*This tomb is in the garden of Charlottenburgh, near Berlin. [. . .] It was not without surprise that I came suddenly, among trees, upon a fair white Doric temple. I might, and should, have deemed it a mere adornment of the grounds, [. . .] but the cypress and the willow declare it a habitation of the dead. [. . .] Upon a sarcophagus of white marble lay a sheet; and the outline of the human form was plainly visible beneath its folds. [. . .] The person with me reverently turned it back, and displayed the statue of his queen. It is a portrait-statue recumbent, said to be a perfect resemblance,—not as in death, but when she lived to bless and be blessed. Nothing can be more calm and kind than the expression of her features. The hands are folded on the bosom; the limbs are sufficiently crossed to show the repose of life.[. . .] Here the King [. . .] brings her children annually, to offer garlands at her grave. These hang in withered mournfulness above this living image of their departed mother.*"
—*Sherer's Notes and Reflections during a Ramble in Germany.*[2]

*In sweet pride upon that insult keen*
*She smiled; then drooping mute and broken-hearted,*
*To the cold comfort of the grave departed.*
MILMAN[3]

It stands where northern willows weep,
 A temple fair and lone;
Soft shadows o'er its marble sweep,
 From cypress-branches thrown;
While silently around it spread,
Thou feel'st the presence of the dead.[4]

And what within is richly shrined?
 A sculptur'd woman's form,

Lovely in perfect rest reclined,
  As one beyond the storm:                         10
Yet not of death, but slumber, lies
The solemn sweetness on those eyes.[5]

The folded hands, the calm pure face,
  The mantle's quiet flow,
The gentle, yet majestic grace,
  Throned on the matron brow;
These, in that scene of tender gloom,
With a still glory robe the tomb.

There stands an eagle, at the feet
  Of the fair image wrought;                       20
A kingly emblem—nor unmeet
  To wake yet deeper thought:
She whose high heart finds rest below,
Was royal in her birth and wo.

There are pale garlands hung above,
  Of dying scent and hue;—
She was a mother—in her love
  How sorrowfully true!
Oh! hallow'd long be every leaf,
The record of her children's grief!                30

She saw their birthright's warrior-crown
  Of olden glory spoil'd,
The standard of their sires borne down,
  The shield's bright blazon soiled:
She met the tempest meekly brave,
Then turn'd, o'erwearied, to the grave.[6]

She slumber'd; but it came—it came,
  Her land's redeeming hour,
With the glad shout, and signal-flame,
  Sent on from tower to tower!                     40
Fast thro' the realm[7] a spirit moved—
'Twas hers, the lofty and the loved.

Then was her name a note[8] that rung
  To rouse bold hearts from sleep,
Her memory, as a banner flung
  Forth by the Baltic deep;
Her grief, a bitter vial pour'd
To sanctify th'avenger's sword.

And the crown'd eagle[9] spread again
   His pinion to the sun;                                              50
And the strong land shook off its chain—
   So was the triumph won!
But wo for earth, where sorrow's tone
Still blends with victory's!—*She* was gone!

[1] Originally published in the Monthly Magazine. [FH]

*MM*, n.s. 2 (December 1826), 627–28, signed "F. H." This version has capitals for Avenger's, Sorrow's, and Victory's (48–54), and a lowercased, unitalicized "she" (54). In *Records &c* FH's note is a footnote at the end of the poem.

[2] Moyle Sherer (1789–1869), *Notes and Reflections During a Ramble in Germany* (London: Longman &c, 1826), 392–94. Sherer, a travel writer, was a "friend and correspondent" of FH (Lawrence 309). FH also read a "Memoir of the Queen of Prussia" in 1822 (*CM* 1.85). Queen Louise of Mecklenburg-Strelitz (1776–1810), who bore ten children, was widely admired for her patriotism during the Napoleonic wars, when Germany allied with Britain against France. She is buried with her husband, Frederick William III of Prussia (1770–1840), in the mausoleum in the palace park of Charlottenburg, a much-visited shrine.

[3] Henry Hart Milman (1791–1868), *Judicium Regale, An Ode*, 74–76. The Queen has been insulted by a horseman of a conquering Baron: "the beautiful, the delicate, / The Queenly, but too gentle for a Queen— / But in sweet pride . . ." (then follow the lines of FH's epigraph). Milman, professor of poetry at Oxford (1821–31), dramatist, and ecclesiastical historian, encouraged FH's efforts at drama. *Judicium* is a dream vision in which Napoleon, Queen Louise, and others are brought to judgment. Sherer, in the paragraph just previous to FH's quotation, writes that the queen was revered "by an entire people, who respected her pure example, as a wife and a mother, and adored her patriot spirit as their queen. The subject of indignities, which never have been, and never will be, forgiven to the iron Napoleon; and the witness of public calamities, which, although they could not subdue her generous and royal mind, corroded the inward principle of life, stole the bloom from her youthful cheek, the light from her fair eyes, bowed down her beautiful form, broke her young heart, and laid her in the tomb" (392). In *MM*, the sole epigraph is:

>    Courage was cast about her like a dress
>       Of solemn comeliness;
>    A gathered mind and an untroubled face
>       Did give her dangers grace.

William Cartwright (1611–43), *On the Queens Return from the Low Countries* (1643), 7–10. FH later used these lines as an epigraph for *The Lady of Provence*, in *Songs of the Affections* (1830), attributing them to Donne, an error that persisted in nineteenth-century editions.

[4] Cypress and willow are funereal emblems. The verse form is a balladlike variation of the "Venus and Adonis" stanza.

[5] *MM*] The character of this monumental statue is that of the deepest serenity; the repose, however, of sleep—not the grave.—See the description in Russell's "Germany." [FH]

John Russell, *A Tour in Germany, and some of the Southern Provinces of the Austrian Empire in the Years 1820, 1821, and 1822* (London and Edinburgh: Constable, 1824), 263–64; this work includes a description of the character of the queen and her reign (265–68).

[6] Louise accompanied her husband on the Jena campaign, October 1806, in which a Prussian-Russian alliance unsuccessfully resisted Napoleon, who entered Berlin on the 25th. Louise, who exhausted herself in trying to maintain the alliance with Russia, died 18 July 1810.

[7] *MM*] land.

Prussia resumed its fight against Napoleon in 1813, now in alliance with Austria and Britain as well as Russia.

[8] *MM*] word

<sup>9</sup> *MM*] proud
    The crowned eagle is a symbol of Prussia, in contrast to the uncrowned eagle that was the symbol of Napoleonic France.

----

### The Memorial Pillar[1]

*On the road-side between Penrith and Appleby, stands a small pillar, with this inscription:—"This pillar was erected in the year 1656, by Ann, Countess Dowager of Pembroke, for a memorial of her last parting, in this place, with her good and pious mother, Margaret, Countess Dowager of Cumberland, on the 2d April, 1616."—See Notes to the "Pleasures of Memory."[2]*

> *Hast thou, thro' Eden's wild-wood vales pursued*
> *Each mountain-scene, magnificently rude,*
> *[. . .]*
> *Nor with attention's lifted eye, revered*
> *That modest stone, by pious Pembroke rear'd,*
> *Which still records, beyond the pencil's power,*
> *The silent sorrows of a parting hour?*
>                                         ROGERS[3]

Mother and child! whose blending tears
    Have sanctified the place,
Where, to the love of many years,
    Was given one last embrace;
Oh! ye have shrin'd a spell of power,
Deep in your record of that hour!

A spell to waken solemn thought,
    A still, small under-tone,[4]
That calls back days of childhood, fraught
    With many a treasure gone;                                    10
And smites, perchance, the hidden source,
Tho' long untroubled—of remorse.

For who, that gazes on the stone
    Which marks your parting spot,
Who but a mother's love hath known
    The *one* love changing not?
Alas! and haply learn'd its worth
First with the sound of "Earth to earth?"[5]

But thou, high-hearted daughter! thou,[6]
    O'er whose bright, honour'd head,                             20
Blessings and tears of holiest flow,
    Ev'n here were fondly shed,

Thou from the passion of thy grief,
In its full burst, couldst draw relief.

For oh! tho' painful be th' excess,
    The might wherewith it swells,
In nature's fount no bitterness
    Of nature's mingling, dwells;
And thou hadst not, by wrong or pride,
Poison'd the free and healthful tide.          30

But didst thou meet the face no more,
    Which thy young heart first knew?
And all—was all in this world o'er,
    With ties thus close and true?
It was!—On earth no other eye
Could give thee back thine infancy.

No other voice could pierce the maze
    Where deep within thy breast,
The sounds and dreams of other days,
    With memory lay at rest;          40
No other smile to thee could bring
A gladd'ning, like the breath of spring.

Yet, while thy place of weeping still
    Its lone memorial keeps,
While on thy name, midst wood and hill,
    The quiet sunshine sleeps,
And touches, in each graven line,
Of reverential thought a sign;

Can I, while yet these tokens wear
    The impress of the dead,          50
Think of the love embodied there,
    As of a vision fled?
A perish'd thing, the joy and flower
And glory of one earthly hour?[7]

Not so!—I will not bow me so,
    To thoughts that breathe despair!
A loftier faith we need below,
    Life's farewell words to bear.
Mother and child!—Your tears are past—
Surely your hearts have met at last!          60

¹ First published in *NMM* 19 (June 1827): 522–23, signed "F. H." This poem reflects FH's grief for her mother, who died in January 1827. The verse form repeats that of *Queen of Prussia*.

² *NMM*] Headnote is a footnote to the title, the last sentence continuing, "in memory whereof she hath left an annuity of 4*l*. [pounds] to be distributed to the poor of the parish of Brougham, every 2d day of April for ever, upon the stone table placed hard by. Laus Deo!" [Praise God!] Samuel Rogers (1763–1855) made his name with *The Pleasures of Memory* (1792), which reached fifteen editions by 1806. Lady Anne Clifford (1590–1676), Countess of Pembroke, was a friend of George Herbert; her mother, Margaret Russell Clifford (1560–1616), Countess of Cumberland, was admired for her talent and beauty and served as a pall-bearer at Elizabeth I's funeral, which Lady Anne attended. Lady Anne's diary records her "grevious & heavy Parting" from her mother on 2 April 1616, and on the 29th, "the heavy news of my Mother's death, which I held as the greatest & most lamentable Cross that could have befallen me."

³ Part 2.173–74, 177–80. FH elides 175–76: "To note the sweet simplicity of life, / Far from the din of Folly's idle strife." She also alters 177: "Nor there awhile with lifted eyes . . ."; Rogers extends the question: "Still to the musing pilgrim points the place / Her sainted spirit most delights to trace?" (179–80).

⁴ An echo of 1 Kings 19.12: the Lord speaks to the prophet Elijah in a "still small voice."

⁵ See Genesis 3.19 and Ecclesiastes 3.20–21.

⁶ *NMM*] true-hearted Daughter.

Other significant variants are emblematic capitals: Nature (27–28), Memory (40), Spring (42), Dead (50), Child (59).

⁷ The pillar is located in Wordsworth country (near Brougham Castle, in the area of Penrith, Cumberland), a connection Hemans acknowledges with echoes of Wordsworth's famous lament for the lost world of childhood in his "Immortality" *Ode*: "Whither is fled the visionary gleam? / Where is it now, the glory and the dream?" (56–57); "nothing can bring back the hour / Of splendour in the grass, of glory in the flower" (177–78).

---

## The Grave of a Poetess¹

*"Ne me plaignez pas—si vous saviez*
*Combien de peines ce tombeau m'a épargnées!"²*

I stood beside thy lowly grave;—
  Spring-odours breath'd around,
And music, in the river-wave,
  Pass'd with a lulling sound.

All happy things that love the sun
  In the bright air glanc'd by,
And a glad murmur seem'd to run
  Thro' the soft azure sky.³

Fresh leaves were on the ivy-bough
  That fring'd the ruins near;
Young voices were abroad—but thou
  Their sweetness couldst not hear.

10

And mournful grew my heart for thee,
    Thou in whose woman's mind
The ray that brightens earth and sea,
    The light of song was shrined.

Mournful, that thou wert slumbering low,
    With a dread curtain drawn
Between thee and the golden glow
    Of this world's vernal dawn.                                    20

Parted from all the song and bloom
    Thou wouldst have lov'd so well,
To thee the sunshine round thy tomb
    Was but a broken spell.

The bird, the insect on the wing,
    In their bright reckless play,
Might feel the flush and life of spring,—
    And thou wert pass'd away!

But then, ev'n then, a nobler thought
    O'er my vain sadness came;                                      30
Th' immortal spirit woke, and wrought
    Within my thrilling frame.

Surely on lovelier things, I said,
    Thou must have look'd ere now,
Than all that round our pathway shed
    Odours and hues below.

The shadows of the tomb are here,
    Yet beautiful is earth!
What seest thou then where no dim fear,
    No haunting dream hath birth?                                  40

Here a vain love to passing flowers
    Thou gav'st—but where thou art,
The sway is not with changeful hours,
    *There* love and death must part.

Thou hast left sorrow in thy song,
    A voice not loud, but deep!
The glorious bowers of earth among,
    How often didst thou weep!

Where couldst thou fix on mortal ground
    Thy tender thoughts and high?—                                 50
Now peace the woman's heart hath found,
    And joy the poet's eye.[4]

[1] "Extrinsic interest has lately attached to the fine scenery of Woodstock, near Kilkenny, on account of its having been the last residence of the author of Psyche. Her grave is one of many in the church-yard of the village. The river runs smoothly by. The ruins of an ancient abbey that have been partially converted into a church, reverently throw their mantle of tender shadow over it."—*Tales by the O'Hara Family*. [FH]

First published in *NMM* 20 (July 1827): 69–70, signed "F. H." *Tales* is a collection of stories of Irish peasant life (London: Simpkin, 1825) by the "O'Hara" brothers, John Banim (1798–1842) and Michael Banim (1796–1874). In *NMM*, the note continues: "It is the very spot for the grave of a poetess." The author of *Psyche, or The Legend of Love* is Mary Tighe (1772–1810), unhappily married and dead of tuberculosis before her fortieth birthday. *Psyche* was printed privately in 1805, and with other poems in 1811. After reading some of her early poems in manuscript, FH wrote a sonnet, *On Records of Immature Genius* ("Oh! judge in thoughtful tenderness") (*HM* 239; *CM* 2.219); see *CM* 208–21 for FH's interest in her. For FH's visit to her grave, see her letters of 1831 (some in *HM* 237–39) and *Written after Visiting a Tomb, Near Woodstock, in the County of Kilkenney* ("I stood where the lip of song lay low") (1831).

[2] Do not pity me—if you knew / How many pains this tomb has spared me!

Staël, *Corinne*, bk. 18, end of ch. 3, "Le séjour à Florence" (the inscription is prose, as it is in *NMM*). Wandering through a graveyard in Florence, Corinne is fixated by this epitaph, on the tombstone of a man, dead in youth: "Quel détachment de la vie des paroles inspirent, dit Corinne, en versant des pleurs!" (What detachment from life those words inspire, said Corinne, turning to tears!)

[3] Echoing stanza 2 of Wordsworth's *Resolution and Independence*: "All things that love the sun are out of doors; / The sky rejoices in the morning's birth." FH's verse form is also Wordsworthian, used in several of the *Lyrical Ballads*: *We Are Seven, The Tables Turned, The Two April Mornings, The Fountain*, and most of the "Lucy" songs.

[4] 51–52, *NMM*] Woman / Poet

This is the only one of "Records" that treats a historically contemporary Englishwoman. Lawrence used the last two stanzas as the title-page epigraph for *Recollections of Mrs. Hemans*.

# Miscellaneous Pieces

## The Homes of England

[Leading the Miscellaneous Pieces (following "Records of Woman," with all their ravaged homes), this anthology favorite has provoked debate. Does its blend of domestic affection and patriotism echo, in traditional ballad meters, the conservative themes of Edmund Burke's *Reflections on the Revolution in France* (1790), mystifying class differences in a vision of an organically united England? Victorian anthologizer Frederic Rowton thought so: in these "beautiful lines [. . .] every class is made to participate in domestic pleasures" (387). Yet "is made" suggests why others see the patently conventional iconography as conceding an artificial, sentimental ideal.]

> *Where's the coward that would not dare*
> *To fight for such a land?*
> —Marmion[1]

The stately Homes of England,
   How beautiful they stand!
Amidst their tall ancestral trees,
   O'er all the pleasant land.
The deer across their greensward bound
   Thro' shade and sunny gleam,
And the swan glides past them with the sound
   Of some rejoicing stream.

The merry Homes of England!
   Around their hearths by night,           10
What gladsome looks of household love
   Meet, in the ruddy light!
There woman's voice flows forth in song,
   Or childhood's tale is told,
Or lips move tunefully along
   Some glorious page of old.

The blessed Homes of England!
   How softly on their bowers
Is laid the holy quietness
   That breathes from Sabbath-hours!      20
Solemn, yet sweet, the church-bell's chime
   Floats through their woods at morn;
All other sounds, in that still time,
   Of breeze and leaf are born.

The Cottage Homes of England!
   By thousands on her plains,
They are smiling o'er the silvery brooks,
   And round the hamlet-fanes.
Thro' glowing orchards forth they peep,
   Each from its nook of leaves,          30
And fearless there the[2] lowly sleep,
   As the bird beneath their eaves.

The free, fair Homes of England!
   Long, long, in hut and hall,
May hearts of native proof be rear'd
   To guard each hallowed wall!
And green for ever be the groves,
   And bright the flowery sod,
Where first the child's glad spirit loves
   Its country and its God![3]          40

<sup>1</sup> *Marmion, A Tale of Flodden Field* (1808), Scott's six-canto poem, situated in 1513; the epigraph is from 4 ("The Camp"), stanza xxx—an exclamation by Fitz-Eustace, as he and Marmion witness the massing of the Scots army across the beautiful landscape of Scotland, prior to the battle of Flodden Field, in Northumberland, just across the border from Scotland. First published in *Blackwood's* 21 (April 1827): 92, signed "F. H.," with this epigraph:

> A land of peace,
> Where yellow fields unspoil'd, and pastures green,
> Mottled with herds and flocks, who crop secure
> Their native herbage, nor have ever known
> A stranger's stall, smile gladly.
> See through its tufted alleys to Heaven's roof
> The curling smoke of quiet dwellings rise.
>
> JOANNA BAILLIE

*Ethwald: A Tragedy* (1802), part 2, 1.2.76–82, preceded by these lines: "O see before thee / Thy native land, freed from ills of war, / And hard oppressive power, a land of peace ..."

<sup>2</sup> *Blackwood's*] they

<sup>3</sup> Originally published in Blackwood's Magazine. [FH]

---

## The Sicilian Captive[1]

> *I have dreamt thou wert*
> *A captive in thy hopelessness; afar*
> *From the sweet home of thy young infancy,*
> *Whose image unto thee is as a dream*
> *Of fire and slaughter; I can see thee wasting,*
> *Sick for thy native air.*
>
> L.E.L.[2]

The champions had come from their fields of war,
Over the crests of the billows far,
They had brought back the spoils of a hundred shores,
Where the deep had foam'd to their flashing oars.

They sat at their feast round the Norse-king's board,
By the glare of the torch-light the mead was pour'd,
The hearth was heap'd with the pine-boughs high,
And it flung a red radiance on shields thrown by.

The Scalds had chaunted in Runic rhyme,
Their songs of the sword and the olden time,                    10
And a solemn thrill, as the harp-chords rung,
Had breath'd from the walls where the bright spears hung.

But the swell was gone from the quivering string,
They had summon'd a softer voice to sing,
And a captive girl, at the warriors' call,
Stood forth in the midst of that frowning hall.

Lonely she stood:—in her mournful eyes
Lay the clear midnight of southern skies,
And the drooping fringe of their lashes low,
Half veil'd a depth of unfathom'd wo.[3]                    20

Stately she stood—tho' her fragile frame
Seem'd struck with the blight of some inward flame,
And her proud pale brow had a shade of scorn,
Under the waves of her dark hair worn.

And a deep flush pass'd, like a crimson haze,
O'er her marble cheek by the pine-fire's blaze;
No soft hue caught from the south-wind's breath,
But a token of fever, at strife with death.

She had been torn from her home away,
With her long locks crown'd for her bridal day,                    30
And brought to die of the burning dreams
That haunt the exile by foreign streams.

They bade her sing of her distant land—
She held its lyre with a trembling hand,
Till the spirit its blue skies had given her, woke,
And the stream of her voice into music broke.

Faint was the strain, in its first wild flow,
Troubled its murmur, and sad, and low;
But it swell'd into deeper power ere long,
As the breeze that swept over her soul grew strong.                    40

✧      ✧      ✧

"They bid me sing of thee, mine own, my sunny land! of thee![4]
Am I not parted from thy shores by the mournful-sounding sea?
Doth not thy shadow wrap my soul?—in silence let me die,
In a voiceless dream of thy silvery founts, and thy pure deep sapphire sky;
How should thy lyre give *here* its wealth of buried sweetness forth?
Its tones, of summer's breathings born, to the wild winds of the north?

Yet thus it shall be once, once more!—my spirit shall awake,
And thro' the mists of death shine out, my country! for thy sake!
That I may make *thee* known, with all the beauty and the light,
And the glory never more to bless thy daughter's yearning sight!                    50
Thy woods shall whisper in my song, thy bright streams warble by,
Thy soul flow o'er my lips again—yet once, my Sicily!

There are blue heavens—far hence, far hence! but oh! their glorious blue!
Its very night is beautiful, with the hyacinth's deep hue!
It is above my own fair land, and round my laughing home,
And arching o'er my vintage-hills, they hang their cloudless dome,

And making all the waves as gems, that melt along the shore,
And steeping happy hearts in joy—that now is mine no more.

And there are haunts in that green land—oh! who may dream or tell,
Of all the shaded loveliness it hides in grot and dell!                       60
By fountains flinging rainbow-spray on dark and glossy leaves,
And bowers wherein the forest-dove her nest untroubled weaves;
The myrtle dwells there, sending round the richness of its breath,
And the violets gleam like amethysts, from the dewy moss beneath.

And there are floating sounds that fill the skies thro' night and day,
Sweet sounds! the soul to hear them faints in dreams of heaven away!
They wander thro' the olive-woods, and o'er the shining seas,
They mingle with the orange-scents that load the sleepy breeze;
Lute, voice, and bird, are blending there;—it were a bliss to die,
As dies a leaf, thy groves among, my flowery Sicily!                          70

*I* may not thus depart[5]—farewell! yet no, my country! no!
Is not love stronger than the grave? I feel it must be so!
My fleeting spirit shall o'ersweep the mountains and the main,
And in thy tender starlight rove, and thro' thy woods again.
Its passion deepens—it prevails!—I break my chain—I come
To dwell a viewless thing, yet blest—in thy sweet air, my home!"

                    ❖      ❖      ❖

    And her pale arms dropp'd the ringing[6] lyre,
    There came a mist o'er her eye's wild fire,
    And her dark rich tresses, in many a fold,
    Loos'd from their braids, down her bosom roll'd.                          80

    For her head sank back on the rugged wall,—
    A silence fell o'er the warrior's hall;
    She had pour'd out her soul with her song's last tone;
    The lyre was broken, the minstrel gone!

[1] Originally published in *NMM* 14 (August 1825): 122–23, signed "F. H." The frame is in the verse form Shelley used for *The Sensitive Plant* (*Prometheus Unbound &c* [1820]).
[2] Letitia Elizabeth Landon (L.E.L.), *Unknown Female Head* (14–19), first published in *Literary Gazette* 316 (8 February 1823): 91. Not in *NMM*.
[3] 19–20, *NMM*] And their drooping lids—oh! the world of woe, / The cloud of dreams, that sweet veil below!
[4] This inset song is in fourteeners, best known from Chapman's *Iliad* (1616). The fourteen-syllable, four-line ballad-stanza is a common adaptation. FH uses fourteeners for the inset poems of *Indian Woman's Death Song* and *Juana*—thus linking the exiled Sicilian to their misery.
[5] *NMM*] perish thus
[6] *NMM*] singing

## The Lady of the Castle[1]

*From the "Portrait Gallery," an unfinished Poem.*

> *If there be but one spot upon thy name,*
> *One eye thou fear'st to meet, one human voice*
> *Whose tones thou shrink'st from—Woman! veil thy face,*
> *And bow thy head—and die!*[2]

Thou seest her pictured with her shining hair,
  (Famed were those tresses in Provençal song,)
Half braided, half o'er cheek and bosom fair
  Let loose, and pouring sunny waves along
Her gorgeous vest. A child's[3] light hand is roving
Midst the rich curls, and oh! how meekly loving
Its earnest looks are lifted to the face,
Which bends to meet its lip in laughing grace!
Yet that bright lady's eye methinks hath less
Of deep, and still, and pensive tenderness,          10
Than might beseem a mother's;—on her brow
  Something too much there sits of native scorn,
And her smile kindles with a conscious glow,
  As from the thought of sovereign beauty born.
—These may be dreams—but how shall woman tell
Of woman's shame, and not with tears?—She fell!
That mother left that child!—went hurrying by
Its cradle—haply, not without a sigh,
Haply one moment o'er its rest serene
She hung—but no! it could not thus have been,          20
For *she went on*—forsook her home, her hearth,
All pure affection, all sweet household mirth,
To live a gaudy and dishonour'd thing,
Sharing in guilt the splendours of a king.

Her lord, in very weariness of life,
Girt on his sword for scenes of distant strife;
He reck'd no more of glory—grief and shame
Crush'd out his fiery nature, and his name
Died silently. A shadow o'er his halls
Crept year by year; the minstrel pass'd their walls;          30
The warder's horn hung mute;—meantime the child,
On whose first flowering thoughts no parent smiled,
A gentle girl, and yet deep-hearted, grew
Into sad youth; for well, too well, she knew
Her mother's tale! Its memory made the sky
Seem all too joyous for her shrinking eye;

Check'd on her lip the flow of song, which fain
Would there have linger'd; flush'd her cheek to pain,
If met by sudden glance; and gave a tone
Of sorrow, as for something lovely gone, 40
Ev'n to the spring's glad voice. Her own was low,
And plaintive—oh!⁴ there lie such depths of wo
In a *young* blighted spirit! Manhood rears
A haughty brow, and age has done with tears;
But youth bows down to misery, in amaze
At the dark cloud o'ermantling its fresh days,—
And thus it was with her. A mournful sight
  In one so fair—for she indeed was fair—
Not with her mother's dazzling eyes of light,
   *Hers* were more shadowy, full of thought and prayer, 50
And with long lashes o'er a white-rose cheek,
Drooping in gloom, yet tender still and meek,
Still that fond child's—and oh! the brow above,
So pale and pure! so form'd for holy love
To gaze upon in silence!—but she felt
That love was not for her, tho' hearts would melt
Where'er she mov'd, and reverence mutely given
Went with her; and low prayers, that call'd on Heaven
To bless the young Isaure.

              One sunny⁵ morn,
  With alms before her castle gate she stood, 60
Midst peasant-groups; when breathless and o'erworn,
  And shrouded in long weeds of widowhood,
A stranger thro' them broke:—the orphan maid
With her sweet voice, and proffer'd hand of aid,
Turn'd to give welcome; but a wild sad look
Met hers; a gaze that all her spirit shook;
And that pale woman, suddenly subdued
By some strong passion in its gushing mood,
Knelt at her feet, and bath'd them with such tears
As rain the hoarded agonies of years 70
From the heart's urn; and with her white lips press'd
The ground they trod; then, burying in her vest
Her brow's deep flush, sobb'd out—"Oh! undefiled!
I am thy mother—spurn me not, my child!"

Isaure had pray'd for that lost mother; wept
O'er her stain'd memory, while the happy slept
In the hush'd midnight; stood with mournful gaze
Before yon picture's smile of other days,

But never breath'd in human ear the name
Which weigh'd her being to the earth with shame.                    80
What marvel if the anguish, the surprise,
The dark remembrances, the alter'd guise,
Awhile o'erpower'd her?—from the weeper's touch
She shrank—'twas but a moment—yet too much
For that all humbled one; its mortal stroke
Came down like lightning, and her full heart broke
At once in silence. Heavily and prone
She sank, while, o'er her castle's threshold-stone,
Those long fair tresses—*they* still brightly wore
Their early pride, tho' bound with pearls no more—                  90
Bursting their fillet, in sad beauty roll'd,
And swept the dust with coils of wavy gold.

Her child bent o'er her—call'd her—'twas too late—
Dead lay the wanderer at her own proud gate!
The joy of Courts, the star of knight and bard,—
How didst thou fall, O bright-hair'd Ermengarde!

---

[1] First published in *NMM* 14 (September 1825): 207–8, signed "F. H.," then in *League &c* (1826). FH sketched plans for a *Portrait Gallery* in a notebook (*HM* 113–16), but this poem was "the only one ever completed." She imagined "a connected series of poems," in this frame: "A young bride leads her husband through the castle of her ancestors, an ancient chateau in Provence, or Languedoc. Her favourite haunt is the Picture Gallery, where she passes hours with him every day, relating to him stories of the sons and daughters of the house" (113). Cf. *CM* 1.131.
[2] Not in *NMM*.
[3] *NMM*] Child's
  Other emblematic capitals: Lady (9), Mother's (11), Mother / Child (17), etc.
[4] *NMM*] As drooping bird's—
[5] *NMM*] laughing

---

## *Tasso and his Sister*[1]

*"Devant vous est Sorrente; là demeurait la soeur du Tasse, quand il vint en pèlerin demander à cette obscure amie, un asile contre l'injustice des princes: ses longues douleurs avaient presque égaré sa raison; il ne lui restait plus que du génie."*
                                                        —Corinne[2]

She sat, where on each wind that sigh'd,
    The citron's breath went by,
While the red gold of eventide
    Burn'd in th' Italian sky.

Her bower was one where daylight's close
　　Full oft sweet laughter found,
As thence the voice of childhood rose
　　To the high vineyards round.

But still and thoughtful, at her knee,
　　Her children stood that hour,           10
Their bursts of song and dancing glee,
　　Hush'd as by words of power.
With bright, fix'd, wondering eyes, that gaz'd
　　Up to their mother's face,
With brows thro' parted ringlets rais'd,
　　They stood in silent grace.

While she—yet something o'er her look
　　Of mournfulness was spread—
Forth from a poet's magic book,
　　The glorious numbers° read;        *metrical verse*
The proud undying lay, which pour'd       21
　　Its light on evil years;
*His* of the gifted pen and sword,³
　　The triumph—and the tears.

She read of fair Erminia's flight,
　　Which Venice once might hear
Sung on her glittering seas at night,
　　By many a Gondolier;
Of him she read, who broke the charm
　　That wrapt the myrtle grove;       30
Of Godfrey's deeds, of Tancred's arm,
　　That slew his Paynim love.⁴

Young cheeks around that bright page glow'd,
　　Young holy hearts were stirr'd;
And the meek tears of woman flow'd
　　Fast o'er each burning word.
And sounds of breeze, and fount, and leaf,
　　Came sweet, each pause between;
When a strange voice of sudden grief
　　Burst on the gentle scene.       40

The mother turn'd—a way-worn man,
　　In pilgrim-garb stood nigh,
Of stately mien, yet wild and wan,
　　Of proud yet mournful⁵ eye.

But drops which would not stay for pride,
    From that dark eye gush'd free,
As pressing his pale brow, he cried,
    "Forgotten! ev'n by thee!

Am I so changed?—and yet we two
    Oft hand in hand have play'd;—         50
This brow hath been all bath'd in dew,
    From wreaths which thou hast made;
We have knelt down and said one prayer,
    And sung one vesper-strain;
My soul is[6] dim with clouds of care—
    Tell me those words again!

Life hath been heavy on my head,
    I come a stricken deer,[7]
Bearing the heart, midst crowds that bled,
    To bleed in stillness here."—         60
She gaz'd—till thoughts that long had slept,
    Shook all her thrilling frame—
She fell upon his neck and wept,
    Murmuring her brother's name.

Her *brother's* name!—and who was he,
    The weary one, th'unknown,
That came, the bitter world to flee,
    A stranger to his own?—
He was the bard of gifts divine
    To sway the souls[8] of men;         70
He of the song for Salem's shrine,[9]
    He of the sword and pen!

---

[1] Previously published, without the epigraph, in *League &c* (1826). FH's octave stanza is formed of two balladlike stanzas, *ababcdcd*, alternating tetrameter and trimeter.

[2] Before you is Sorrento; there lived Tasso's sister, when he came as a pilgrim to seek from this humble friend asylum from the injustice of princes: his long sufferings had almost deranged his sanity; nothing was left to him but his genius.
Staël, *Corinne*, "Improvisation de Corinne dans le Campagne de Naples," bk. 13, ch. 4. Tasso (1544–95), a brilliantly precocious poet, had a tragic life, marked by strife with Church authorities, a traumatic attack by a court attaché, delusions, profound depression, and imprisonment. He escaped his confinement at the convent of St. Francis in Ferrara and arrived in Sorrento disguised as a shepherd, greeting his sister Cornelia with the news of his death. Only when he was assured of her fidelity did he reveal himself. "There is much in the story of his sufferings which intensely interests me, and perhaps, deepens my reverence for his poetry," FH wrote to a close friend, 10 April 1831 (*CM* 2.198). Byron's *Lament of Tasso* (1817) supplies an epigraph for *Arabella Stuart*. See also FH's *The Release of Tasso* (*NMM* 8 [November 1823]: 464–66, signed "F. H."), and her essay on Goethe's *Tasso*, *NMM* 40 (January 1834): 1–8.

[3] "It is scarcely necessary to recall the well-known Italian saying, that Tasso with his sword and pen was superior to all men." [FH]

[4] Characters, some historically based, in *Gerusalemme Liberata*, Tasso's late-16th-c. epic about the First Crusade in the late 11th c. Goffredo is the Christian general. Erminia is a Syrian princess whose life is spared at the battle of Antioch by the Christian knight Tancredi, with whom she falls in love. Tancredi unknowingly delivers a fatal wound to Clorinda, a Muslim warrior maid from Persia who met and fell in love with him at this same battle. After the fall of Jerusalem in 1099, Godfrey of Boulogne ordered the massacre of Muslims, and Tancrèd de Hauteville claimed fame as "Prince of Galilee." Like Tasso, FH treats both Crusaders as heroes.

[5] *League*] restless

[6] *League*] thoughts are

[7] FH has Tasso knowingly use a standard Petrarchan image of the heartsick lover, a trope her readers would also sift through Cowper's famous reprisal of it, in a more general tenor, in *The Task* 3.108–16. 14th-c. Italian poet Petrarch was tormented and inspired by love.

[8] *League*] hearts

[9] The tomb of Christ; the "song" is *Gerusalemme Liberata*.

---

## To Wordsworth[1]

Thine is a strain to read among the hills,
    The old and full of voices;—by the source
Of some free stream, whose gladdening presence fills
    The solitude with sound; for in its course
Even such is thy deep song, that seems a part
Of those high scenes, a fountain from their heart.

Or its calm spirit fitly may be taken
    To the still breast, in sunny garden-bowers,
Where vernal winds each tree's low tones awaken,
    And bud and bell with changes mark the hours.         10
There let thy thoughts be with me, while the day
Sinks with a golden and serene decay.

Or by some hearth where happy faces meet,
    When night hath hush'd the woods, with all their birds,
There, from some gentle voice, that lay were sweet
    As antique music, link'd with household words.
While, in pleased murmurs, woman's lip might move,
And the rais'd eye of childhood shine in love.

Or where the shadows of dark solemn yews
    Brood silently o'er some lone burial-ground,         20
Thy verse hath power that brightly might diffuse
    A breath, a kindling, as of spring, around;
From its own glow of hope and courage high,
And steadfast faith's victorious constancy.

True bard, and holy!—thou art ev'n as one
  Who, by some secret gift of soul or eye,
In every spot beneath the smiling sun,
  Sees where the springs of living waters lie:
Unseen awhile they sleep—till,[2] touch'd by thee,
Bright healthful waves flow forth to each glad wanderer free.        30

---

[1] Published in the *Literary Magnet*, n.s. 1 (April 1826): 169–70, as *To the Author of the Excursion and the Lyrical Ballads*, and in *League &c* (1826) as *To the Poet Wordsworth*. The *Magnet* was edited by Alaric Watts, who also edited *Literary Souvenir*. Sometime between 1826 and early 1828, FH sent this poem to Jewsbury with a letter about Wordsworth's poetry (see "Letters"). The verse form is the "Venus and Adonis" stanza used in Wordsworth's *Laodamia*, and there are several homages to his phrasings and subjects. This is one of FH's rare unmelancholy poems. She would dedicate *Scenes and Hymns of Life* (1834) to Wordsworth.
[2] *League*] Thou mov'st through nature's realm, and

---

## The Landing of the Pilgrim Fathers in New England[1]

*Look now abroad—another race has fill'd*
  *Those populous borders—wide the wood recedes,*
*And towns shoot up, and fertile realms are till'd;*
  *The land is full of harvests and green meads.*
                                            BRYANT[2]

The breaking waves dash'd high
  On a stern and rock-bound coast,
And the woods against a stormy sky
  Their giant branches toss'd;

And the heavy night hung dark,
  The hills and water o'er,
When a band of exiles moor'd their bark
  On the wild New-England shore.

Not as the conqueror comes,
  They, the true-hearted came;                                10
Not with the roll of the stirring drums,
  And the trumpet that sings of fame:

Not as the flying come,
  In silence and in fear;—
They shook the depths of the desert gloom
  With their hymns of lofty cheer.

Amidst the storm they sang,
  And the stars heard and the sea!

And the sounding[3] aisles of the dim woods rang
   To the anthem of the free.          20

The ocean-eagle soar'd
   From his nest by the white wave's foam,
And the rocking pines of the forest roar'd—
   This was their welcome home!

There were men with hoary hair,
   Amidst that pilgrim band;—
Why had *they* come to wither there,
   Away from their childhood's land?

There was woman's fearless eye,
   Lit by her deep love's truth;          30
There was manhood's brow serenely high,
   And the fiery heart of youth.

What sought they thus afar?
   Bright jewels of the mine?
The wealth of seas, the spoils of war?—
   They sought a faith's pure shrine!

Ay, call it holy ground,
   The soil where first they trod!
They have left unstain'd[4] what there they found—
   Freedom to worship God.[5]          40

[1] First published in *NMM* 14 (November 1825): 402, signed "F. H.," then in *League &c* (Boston, 1826), the first of its "Miscellaneous Poems." The verse is a standard hymn form. FH knew Daniel Webster's celebrated bicentenary oration, *The Landing of the Pilgrim Fathers in New England* (1820), published in Adam Hodgson's *Letters from North America, Written During a Tour in the United States and Canada* (London, 1824), to which she refers in her notes to *The Forest Sanctuary*. One of her most famous poems, this was often printed as a gift-book; one such, *The Breaking Waves Dashed High (The Pilgrim Fathers)*, "With Designs by Miss L. B. Humphrey, Engraved by Andrew" (Boston: Lee and Shepard), went through several editions in the 1880s. For some of the illustrations, see Feldman's edition of *Records* 16, 40, 76, 134.

[2] American poet William Cullen Bryant (1794–1878), *The Ages* (1821), 280–84 (stanza 32); the arrival of Europeans in a world marked by "savage" "Indian" warfare. *The Ages*, a poem of 35 Spenserian stanzas, recounts the rise of civilization, from primitive times through ancient civilizations, eighteenth-century revolutions, New World colonialism and triumphal American expansion.

epigraph, *NMM*] "Their dauntless hearts no meteor led / In terror o'er the ocean; / From fortune and from fame they fled / To Heaven and its devotion."— An American Poet. [FH]

Robert Treat Paine (1731–1814), *Ode* ("Wide o'er the wilderness of waves"), written "for and sung at the anniversary of American Independence, July 4, 1806," published 1812. FH owes several details of her poem to this ode about the voyage of the pilgrim fathers.

*League*] No epigraph.

[3] *League*] surrounding

[4] *NMM*] undimm'd

<sup>5</sup> *League*] These glorious verses will find an echo in the breast of every true descendant of the Pilgrims; and give the name of their authoress a place in many hearts. She has laid our community under a common obligation of gratitude. Every one must feel the sublimity and poetical truth, with which she has conceived the scene presented, and the inspiration of that deep and holy strain of sentiment, which sounds forth like the pealing of an organ. Ed. [Andrews Norton]

---

## The Palm-Tree[1]

It wav'd not thro' an Eastern sky,
Beside a fount of Araby;
It was not fann'd by southern breeze
In some green isle of Indian seas,
Nor did its graceful shadow sleep
O'er stream of Afric, lone and deep.

But fair the exil'd Palm-tree grew
Midst foliage of no kindred hue;
Thro' the laburnum's dropping gold
Rose the light shaft of orient mould,                          10
And Europe's violets, faintly sweet,
Purpled the moss-beds at its feet.

Strange look'd it there!—the willow stream'd
Where silvery waters near it gleam'd;
The lime-bough° lured the honey-bee          *(linden, not citrus)*
To murmur by the Desert's Tree,
And showers of snowy roses made
A lustre in its fan-like shade.

There came an eve of festal hours—
Rich music fill'd that garden's bowers:                        20
Lamps, that from flowering branches hung,
On sparks of dew soft colours flung,
And bright forms glanc'd—a fairy show—
Under the blossoms to and fro.

But one, a lone one, midst the throng,
Seem'd reckless all of dance or song:
He was a youth of dusky mien,
Whereon the Indian sun had been,
Of crested brow, and long black hair—
A stranger, like the Palm-tree there.                          30

And slowly, sadly, mov'd his plumes,
Glittering athwart the leafy glooms:

He pass'd the pale green olives by,
Nor won the chestnut-flowers his eye;
But when to that sole Palm he came,
Then shot a rapture through his frame!

To him, to him, its rustling spoke,
The silence of his soul it broke!
It whisper'd of his own bright isle,
That lit the ocean with a smile;                    40
Aye, to his ear that native tone
Had something of the sea-wave's moan!

His mother's cabin home, that lay
Where feathery cocoas fring'd the bay;
The dashing of his brethren's oar,
The conch-note heard along the shore;—
All thro' his wakening bosom swept:
He clasp'd his country's Tree and wept!

Oh! scorn him not!—the strength, whereby
The patriot girds himself to die,                   50
Th' unconquerable power, which fills
The freeman battling on his hills,
These have one fountain deep and clear—
The same whence gush'd that child-like tear!

---

[1] This incident is, I think, recorded by De Lille, in his poem of "Les Jardins." [FH]

Jacques J. Montanier Abbé de Lille (1738–1813), *Les Jardins, ou l'Art d'embellir le paysage* (1782), translated as *The Garden; or, The Art of Laying Out Grounds* (1789). See the close of bk. 2: "Haply the stranger views those shades again, / He once had lov'd upon another plain / Awhile the welcome sight beguiles his woe, / At once the tears of joy and sorrow flow / . . . / The artless mourner mark'd with wild surprise / A plant familiar to his infant eyes; / The sudden sight inspires his heavy heart, / He runs, he flies, and all untaught in art, / With tears he clasps it to his beating breast, / And ev'ry sense with joy awhile is blest. / Again his home, his happy home he sees . . ." (431ff.).

Francis Jeffrey lavished praise on the way FH's "fine descriptions [. . .] tell upon the heart, with a deep moral and pathetic impression" (*Edinburgh Review* 50 [1829], 37).

---

## The Illuminated City[1]

The hills all glow'd with a festive light,
For the royal city rejoic'd by night:
There were lamps hung forth upon tower and tree,
Banners were lifted and streaming free;
Every tall pillar was wreath'd with fire,
Like a shooting meteor was every spire;

And the outline of many a dome on high
Was traced, as in stars, on the clear dark sky.

I pass'd thro' the streets; there were throngs on throngs—
Like sounds of the deep were their mingled songs;                    10
There was music forth from each palace borne—
A peal of the cymbal, the harp, and horn;
The forests heard it, the mountains rang,
The hamlets woke to its haughty clang;
Rich and victorious was every tone,
Telling the land of her foes o'erthrown.

Didst thou meet not a mourner for all the slain?
Thousands lie dead on their battle-plain!
Gallant and true were the hearts that fell—
Grief in the homes they have left must dwell;                        20
Grief o'er the aspect of childhood spread,
And bowing the beauty of woman's head:
Didst thou hear, midst the songs, not one tender moan,
For the many brave to their slumbers gone?

I saw not the face of a weeper there—
Too strong, perchance, was the bright lamp's glare!
I heard not a wail midst the joyous crowd—
The music of victory was all too loud!
Mighty it roll'd on the winds afar,
Shaking the streets like a conqueror's car;                          30
Thro' torches and streamers its flood swept by—
How could I listen for moan or sigh?

Turn then away from life's pageants, turn,
If its deep story thy heart would learn!
Ever too bright is that outward show,
Dazzling the eyes till they see not wo.
But lift the proud mantle which hides from thy view
The things thou shouldst gaze on, the sad and true;
Nor fear to survey what its folds conceal—
So must thy spirit be taught to feel!                                40

---

[1] First published in *MM*, n.s. 2 (November 1826): 515, signed "F. H." To celebrate Napoleon's defeat and exile to Elba, in the summer of 1814 all of London's newly installed gas lamps were lit. This battle-haunted speaker epitomizes the double consciousness of FH's patriotic poetics.

---

### The Spells of Home[1]

*There blend the ties that strengthen*
*Our hearts in hours of grief,*
*The silver links that lengthen*
*Joy's visits when most brief*
                              BERNARD BARTON[2]

By the soft green light in the woody glade,
On the banks of moss where thy childhood play'd;
By the household[3] tree thro' which thine eye
First look'd in love to the summer-sky;
By the dewy gleam, by the very breath
Of the primrose tufts in the grass beneath,
Upon thy heart there is laid a spell,
Holy and precious—oh! guard it well!

By the sleepy ripple of the stream,
Which hath lull'd thee into many a dream;                    10
By the shiver of the ivy-leaves
To the wind of morn at thy casement-eaves,
By the bees' deep murmur in the limes,
By the music of the Sabbath-chimes,
By every sound of thy native shade,
Stronger and dearer the spell is made.

By the gathering round the winter hearth,
When twilight call'd unto household mirth;
By the fairy tale or the legend old
In that ring of happy faces told,                           20
By the quiet hour when hearts unite
In the parting prayer and the kind "Good night";
By the smiling eye and the loving tone,
Over thy life has the spell been thrown.

And bless that gift!—it hath gentle might,
A guardian power and a guiding light.
It hath led the freeman forth to stand
In the mountain-battles of his land;
It hath brought the wanderer o'er the seas
To die on the hills of his own fresh breeze;                30
And back to the gates of his father's hall,
It hath led[4] the weeping prodigal.

Yes! when thy heart in its pride would stray
From the pure first loves of its youth away;
When the sullying breath of the world would come
O'er the flowers it brought from its childhood's home;

Think thou again of the woody glade,
And the sound by the rustling ivy made,
Think of the tree at thy father's[5] door,
And the kindly spell shall have power once more!          40

[1] First published in *MM*, n.s. 3 (February 1827): 141.
[2] *Home* (13–16), in *Poetic Vigils* (London, 1824). For Barton, see *Evening Prayer at a Girls' School*.
   *MM* epigraph includes 17–20] Then dost thou sigh for pleasure! / O! do not widely roam, / But seek the hidden treasure / At home, dear home!
[3] *MM*] waving
[4] *MM*] won
   The Prodigal Son (Luke 15.11–32), also evoked at the end of *Joan of Arc*.
[5] *MM*] parent's

---

## The Graves of a Household[1]

They grew in beauty, side by side,
   They filled one home with glee;—
Their graves are sever'd, far and wide,
   By mount, and stream, and sea.[2]

The same fond mother bent at night
   O'er each fair sleeping brow;
She had each folded flower in sight,—
   Where are those dreamers now?

One, midst the forest of the west,
   By a dark stream is laid—          10
The Indian knows his place of rest,
   Far in the cedar shade.

The sea, the blue lone sea, hath one,
   He lies where pearls lie deep;
*He* was the lov'd of all, yet none
   O'er his low bed may weep.

One sleeps where southern vines are drest
   Above the noble slain:
He wrapt his colours round his breast,
   On a blood-red field of Spain.          20

And one—o'er *her* the myrtle showers
   Its leaves, by soft winds fann'd;
She faded midst Italian flowers,—
   The last of that bright band.

And parted thus they[3] rest, who play'd
    Beneath the same green tree;
Whose voices mingled as they pray'd
    Around one parent knee!

They that with smiles lit up the hall,
    And cheer'd with song the hearth,—
Alas, for love! if *thou* wert all,
    And naught beyond, oh, earth!       30

---

[1] First published in *NMM* 14 (December 1825): 534, signed "F. H.," then in *League &c* (1826). Francis Jeffrey admired "how well the graphic and pathetic [. . .] set off each other" (*Edinburgh Review* 50 [1829], 38). The "exceptional ease" with which this poem can be translated "into Latin elegiacs," remarks Kingsley Amis, "encourages a second look at that superficially superficial piece" (*The Faber Popular Reciter* [London: Faber, 1978], 15). A second look also yields a double exposure: "the homes of England" as a global cemetery (the *Reciter* also included *The Homes of England*).

[2] According to Hughes (*HM* 8n), this stanza refers to their brother, Claude Scott Browne (one year younger than FH), who died in Kingston (Ontario) in 1821. Both the geographic dispersal of siblings and the ballad stanza recall Wordsworth's *We are Seven* (1798).

[3] *NMM*] they

---

## The Image in Lava[1]

Thou thing of years departed!
    What ages have gone by,
Since here the mournful seal was set
    By love and agony!

Temple and tower have moulder'd,
    Empires from earth have pass'd,—
And woman's heart hath left a trace
    Those glories to outlast!

And childhood's fragile image
    Thus fearfully enshrin'd,       10
Survives the proud memorials rear'd
    By conquerors of mankind.

Babe! wert thou brightly[2] slumbering
    Upon thy mother's breast,
When suddenly the fiery tomb
    Shut round each gentle guest?

A strange dark fate o'ertook you,
　　Fair babe and loving heart!
One moment of a thousand pangs—
　　Yet better than to part!　　　　　　　　　　　20

Haply of that fond bosom,
　　On ashes here impress'd,
Thou wert the only treasure, child!
　　Whereon a hope might rest.

Perchance all vainly lavish'd,
　　Its other love had been,
And where it trusted, nought remain'd
　　But thorns on which to lean.

Far better then to perish,
　　Thy form within its clasp,　　　　　　　　　　30
Than live and lose thee, precious one!
　　From that impassion'd grasp.

Oh! I could pass all relics
　　Left by the pomps of old,
To gaze on this rude monument,
　　Cast in affection's mould.

Love, human love! what art thou?
　　Thy print upon the dust
Outlives the cities of renown
　　Wherein the mighty trust!　　　　　　　　　　40

Immortal, oh! immortal
　　Thou art, whose earthly glow
Hath given these ashes holiness—
　　It must, it *must* be so!

---

[1] The impression of a woman's form, with an infant clasped to the bosom, found at the uncovering of Herculaneum. [FH]

First published in *NMM* 20 (September 1827): 255–56, unsigned. The stanza form is the same as that of *The Landing of the Pilgrim Fathers*.

headnote *NMM*] . . . of Pompeii.

In a sudden catastrophic eruption in A.D. 79, lava and ash from Mount Vesuvius buried both coastal towns, along with many inhabitants. Herculaneum was discovered in 1709 and Pompeii in 1748, with major excavations from 1763 to 1820. Plaster casts were made of some of the impressions left by the bodies caught in the lava, and are still on display at Pompeii.

[2] *NMM*] calmly

# A Parting Song[1]

*"Oh! mes Amis, rappelez-vous quelquefois mes vers; mon âme y est empreinte."*
CORINNE[2]

When will ye think of me, my friends?
    When will ye think of me?—
When the last red light, the farewell of day,
From the rock and the river is passing away,
When the air with a deep'ning hush is fraught,
And the heart grows burden'd with tender thought—
    Then let it be!

When will ye think of me, kind friends?
    When will ye think of me?—
When the rose of the rich midsummer time           10
Is fill'd with the hues of its glorious prime;
When ye gather its bloom, as in bright hours fled,
From the walks where my footsteps no more may tread;
    Then let it be!

When will ye think of me, sweet friends?
    When will ye think of me?
When the sudden tears o'erflow your eye
At the sound of some olden melody;
When ye hear the voice of a mountain stream,
When ye feel the charm of a poet's dream;          20
    Then let it be!

Thus let my memory be with you, friends!
    Thus ever think of me!
Kindly and gently, but as of one
For whom 'tis well to be fled and gone;
As of a bird from a chain unbound,[3]
As of a wanderer whose home is found;—
    So let it be.

[1] The closing poem of the volume.

[2] Oh! my Friends, remember my verse sometimes; my soul is imprinted there.
   Staël, *Corinne*, "Dernier Chant de Corinne" (Corinne's Last Song), the conclusion (bk. 20, ch. 5). FH adds "Oh! mes Amis!" She was particularly impressed by this song (Chorley, *Athenæum* 402 [11 July 1835], 529; *CM* 1.228, 304). "If the soul, without the form, be enough to constitute poetry, then [*Dernier Chant*] surely is poetry of the very highest order" (FH; *HM* 160). The *Chant* continues, "mais des muses fatales, l'amour et le malheur, ont inspiré mes derniers chants" (but fatal muses, love and unhappiness, have inspired my last songs). As the *Chant* concludes, the hall murmurs its applause for the dying poet, and Corinne's beloved Lord Nelvil, who has fatally broken her heart, sobs and faints.

[3] Cf. *The Broken Chain*.

# From *The Forest Sanctuary:*
## *With Other Poems*

(2d ed., 1829)

—⟋⟋⟍—

## Miscellaneous Pieces

### *The Traveller at the Source of the Nile*[1]

In sunset's light, o'er Afric thrown,
  A wanderer proudly stood
Beside the well-spring, deep and lone,
  Of Egypt's awful flood;
The cradle of that mighty birth,
So long a hidden thing to earth!

He heard its life's first murmuring sound,
  A low mysterious tone;
A music sought, but never found,
  By kings and warriors gone;             10
He listened—and his heart beat high—
That was the song of victory!

The rapture of a conqueror's mood
  Rush'd burning through his frame,—
The depths of that green solitude
  Its torrents could not tame;
Though stillness lay, with eve's last smile—
Round those far fountains of the Nile.

Night came with stars:—across his soul
  There swept a sudden change,             20
E'en at the pilgrim's glorious goal
  A shadow dark and strange
Breathed from the thought, so swift to fall
O'er triumph's hour—*and is this all?*[2]

No more than this!—what seem'd it *now*
  First by that spring to stand?
A thousand streams of lovelier flow
  Bathed his own mountain land!

Whence far o'er waste and ocean track,
Their wild, sweet voices called him back.                                30

They called him back to many a glade,
   His childhood's haunt of play,
Where brightly through the beechen shade
   Their waters glanced away;
They called him, with their sounding waves,
Back to his fathers' hills and graves.

But darkly mingling with the thought
   Of each familiar scene,
Rose up a fearful vision, fraught
   With all that lay between;                                      40
The Arab's lance, the desert's gloom,
The whirling sands, the red simoom!°          *desert wind*

Where was the glory of power and pride?
   The spirit born to roam?
His altered[3] heart within him died
   With yearnings for his home!
All vainly struggling to repress
That gush of painful tenderness.

He wept—the stars of Afric's heaven
   Behold his bursting tears,                                      50
E'en on that spot where fate had given
   The meed of toiling years!—
Oh, happiness! how far we flee
Thine own sweet paths in search of thee!

---

[1] First published in *MM*, n.s. 2 (July 1826): 11–12, and *League &c* (1826). The stanza is a balladlike version of the "Venus and Adonis" stanza.

[2] A remarkable description of feelings thus fluctuating from triumph to despondency, is given in Bruce's Abyssinian Travels. The buoyant exultation of his spirits on arriving at the source of the Nile, was almost immediately succeeded by a gloom, which he thus pourtrays: "I was, at that very moment, in possession of what had, for many years, been the principal object of my ambition and wishes: indifference, which from the usual infirmity of human nature, follows, at least for a time, complete enjoyment, had taken place of it. The marsh, and the fountains {of the Nile}, upon comparison with the rise of many of our rivers, became now a trifling object in my sight. I remembered that magnificent scene in my own native country, where the Tweed, Clyde, and Annan, rise in one hill. [. . .] I began, in my sorrow, to treat the inquiry about the source of the Nile as a violent effort of a distempered fancy." [FH]

A famous passage from James Bruce (1730–94), *Travels to Discover the Source of the Nile, in the Years 1768, 1769, 1770, 1771, 1772, and 1773* (1790), 6 vols. (Dublin, 1791), 4.328–29. FH elides these sentences: "three rivers, as I now thought, not inferior to the Nile in beauty, preferable to it in the cultivation of those countries through which they flow; superior, vastly superior to it in the virtues and qualities of the inhabitants, and in the beauty of its flocks; crowding its pastures in peace, without fear of violence from man or beast. I had seen the rise of the Rhine and the Rhone, and the more magnificent sources of the Saone." Just after, he quotes Hamlet's amazement at an actor's passion, "What's Hecuba to him, or he to Hecuba, / That he should weep for her?" (2.2.569–70), then reports, "Grief or despondency now rolling upon me like a torrent."

*League*, footnote to the poem's last line] The arrival of Bruce at what he considered to be the source of the Nile, was followed almost immediately by feelings thus suddenly fluctuating from triumph to despondence. See his *Travels in Abyssinia*.

³ *League*] weary

---

## Casabianca¹

[In Nelson's stunningly sweeping victory over the French fleet in the Battle of the Nile, 1 August 1798, young Giacomo Jocante Casabianca was one of a thousand-plus souls on board its admiral ship *L'Orient*, the name signifying Napoleon's imperial ambitions, commanded by fellow Corsican Louis de Casabianca. Robert Southey's *Life of Horatio, Lord Nelson* (1813, much reissued) is FH's likely source, but with revisions. He reports that "Casa-Bianca, and his son, a brave boy, only ten years old [...] were seen floating on a shattered mast when the ship blew up." Setting her poem in this signal British victory, FH heroizes the French boy, joining him to her gallery of child martyrs, including the boy-hostages of *The Siege of Valencia*. *Casabianca* became an anthology standard, its ballad form making it easy to memorize for public recitals (and attracting numerous, often scurrilous parodies). Walter Savage Landor's encomium to the poetry of "female hands" ("I have seen princes," *Examiner*, June 1847) eulogizes FH as "she / Who shrouded *Casa-Bianca*"—a confirmation of the poem's fame.

To write about French heroics in a battle with England's premier military martyr-hero was a daring gambit, even in post-Napoleonic England. In 1798, British magazines were flooded with poems of triumph or gloating over the Nile victory (e.g., *Nelson's Victory*, in *Monthly Magazine* 6, and *Ode on the Late Glorious Victory*, in *The Lady's Magazine* 29). Nelson would die in the Battle of Trafalgar (1805), his even more celebrated triumph over the restored French fleet, and FDB's early poems sang his praises: Nelson, wielding "destruction's flame, / Clos'd in its dreadful blaze a life of fame" (*War and Peace* 177–78); "Nelson fell; with fame immortal crown'd" (*England and Spain; or Valour and Patriotism* 110). Just after the Nile victory, one of Nelson's captains presented him with a coffin made from *L'Orient*'s mainmast (to which the Casabiancas had clung), so that he might be buried in this trophy. It did convey Nelson's corpse home from Trafalgar. But it did not serve his burial; instead, it was "cut in pieces, which were distributed as relics," reports Southey.]

> The boy stood on the burning deck
>     Whence all but he had fled;
> The flame that lit the battle's wreck,
>     Shone round him o'er the dead.
>
> Yet beautiful and bright he stood,
>     As born to rule the storm;
> A creature of heroic blood,
>     A proud, though child-like form.

The flames rolled on—he would not go,
    Without his Father's word;                   10
That Father, faint in death below,
    His voice no longer heard.

He called aloud:—"Say, Father, say
    If yet my task is done?"
He knew not that the chieftain lay
    Unconscious of his son.

"Speak, Father!" once again he cried,
    "If I may yet be gone!
And"[2]—but the booming shots replied,
    And fast the flames rolled on.              20

Upon his brow he felt their breath,
    And in his waving hair,
And looked from that lone post of death,
    In still, yet brave despair;

And shouted but once more aloud,
    "My Father! must I stay?"
While o'er him fast, through sail and shroud,
    The wreathing fires made way.

They wrapt the ship in splendour wild,
    They caught the flag on high,             30
And streamed above the gallant child,
    Like banners in the sky.

There came a burst of thunder-sound—
    The boy—oh! where was he?
Ask of the winds that far around
    With fragments strewed the sea!—[3]

With mast, and helm, and pennon fair,
    That well had borne their part—
But the noblest thing which perished there
    Was that young faithful heart![4]       40

[1] Young Casabianca, a boy about thirteen years old, son to the Admiral of the Orient, remained at his post (in the Battle of the Nile) after the ship had taken fire, and all the guns had been abandoned; and perished in the explosion of the vessel, when the flames had reached the powder. [FH]

First published in the *MM*, n.s. 2 (August, 1826): 164, signed "F. H.," and in *League &c* (1826); republished in *Poetical Album* (1830). FH makes the boy three years older than Southey reports.

[2] *League*] gone!" / —And but . . .

Revising the punctuation, American editor Andrews Norton compromises the drama of FH's ruptured sentence; he also lowercases all her capitalizations of "Father," by which FH simultaneously allies patriotic duty with religious faith and piety and ironizes such fidelity in the figure of a dead, nonresponding father.

³ "The tremendous explosion was followed by a silence not less awful: the firing immediately ceased on both sides; and the first sound which broke the silence was the dash of her shattered masts and yards, falling into the water from the vast height to which they been exploded. [. . .] no incident in war [. . .] has ever equalled the sublimity of this co-instantaneous pause, and all its circumstances. About seventy of the *Orient*'s crew were saved by English boats" (Southey).

⁴ An exception to the legion of parodies is Elizabeth Bishop's *Casabianca* (1942), which takes seriously FH's blending of filial affection and patriotic martyrdom. This is the first stanza:

> Love's the boy stood on the burning deck
> trying to recite "The boy stood on
> the burning deck." Love's the son
>         stood stammering elocution
>         while the poor ship in flames went down.

(Elizabeth Bishop, *The Complete Poems 1929–1979* [Farrar, Straus and Giroux / North Point Press, 1979]).

---

## Our Daily Paths¹

[Dugald Stewart (1753–1828), professor of moral philosophy at Edinburgh University (1785–1810), inspired this poem. "The admiration he always expressed for Mrs Hemans's poetry was mingled with regret that she so generally made choice of melancholy subjects"; he asked her to "employ her fine talents in giving more consolatory views of the ways of Providence, thus infusing comfort and cheer into the bosoms of her readers, in a spirit of Christian philosophy," rather "than dwelling on what was painful and depressing, however beautifully and touchingly such subjects might be treated of." Attributing her melancholy to a sense "that a cloud hung over her head which she could not always rise above," FH sent this poem in reply. Stewart was "in the highest degree charmed and gratified with the result of his suggestions; and some of the lines which pleased him more particularly were often repeated to him during the few remaining weeks of his life" (*Poems of Felicia Hemans* [Blackwood, 1873], 370 n). Yet the poem keeps a double focus that recalls the conflicting rhetoric of such early and iconic poems as *The Domestic Affections*. Its verse form, significantly, is the fourteener couplet used in *Juana* and in the mournful inset songs of *The Sicilian Captive* and *The Indian Woman's Death Song*.]

> *Nought shall prevail against us, or disturb*
> *Our cheerful faith, that all which we behold*
> *Is full of blessings.*
>                         WORDSWORTH²

There's beauty all around our paths, if but our watchful eyes
Can trace it 'midst familiar things, and through their lowly guise;
We may find it where a hedge-row showers its blossoms o'er our way,
Or a cottage window sparkles forth in the last red light of day.

We may find it where a spring shines clear, beneath an aged tree,
With the foxglove o'er the water's glass borne downwards by the bee;

Or where a swift and sunny gleam on the birchen stems is thrown,
As a soft wind playing parts the leaves, in copses green and lone.

We may find it in the winter boughs, as they cross the cold, blue sky,
While soft on icy pool and stream their pencilled shadows lie,      10
When we look upon their tracery, by the fairy frost-work bound,
Whence the flitting redbreast shakes a shower of crystals to the ground.

Yes! beauty dwells in all our paths—but sorrow too is there;
How oft some cloud within us dims the bright, still summer air!
When we carry our sick hearts abroad amidst the joyous things,
That through the leafy places glance on many-coloured wings!

With shadows from the past we fill the happy woodland shades,
And a mournful memory of the dead is with us in the glades;
And our dream-like fancies lend the wind an echo's plaintive tone
Of voices, and of melodies, and of silvery laughter gone.      20

But are we free to do ev'n thus—to wander as we will—
Bearing sad visions through the grove, and o'er the breezy hill?
No! in our daily paths lie cares, that ofttimes bind us fast,
While from their narrow round we see the golden day fleet past.

They hold us from the woodlark's haunts, and violet dingles, back,
And from all the lovely sounds and gleams in the shining river's track;
They bar us from our heritage of spring-time, hope, and mirth,
And weigh our burdened spirits down with the cumbering dust of earth.

Yet should this be?—Too much, too soon, despondingly we yield!
A better lesson we are taught by the lilies of the field!      30
A sweeter by the birds of heaven—which tell us, in their flight,
Of One that through the desert air for ever guides them right.[3]

Shall not this knowledge calm our hearts, and bid vain conflicts cease?
Ay, when they commune with themselves in holy hours of peace;
And feel that by the lights and clouds through which our pathway lies,
By the beauty and the grief alike, we are training for the skies!

[1] First published in *MM*, n.s. 4 (October 1827): 352, signed "F. H." The chief variants are capitals: Beauty (1, 13, 36), Sorrow (13), Grief (36).
[2] Adapting *Tintern Abbey* 132–34. These lines are preceded by a hymn to "Nature," that involves no little melancholy: Nature "can so inform / The mind that is within us, so impress / With quietness and beauty, and so feed / With lofty thoughts, that neither evil tongues, / Rash judgments, nor the sneers of selfish men, / Nor greetings where no kindness is, nor all / The dreary intercourse of daily life, / Shall e'er prevail . . ." (126–32).
[3] An allusion to the Sermon on the Mount: "Behold the fowls of the air: for they sow not, neither do they reap. [. . .] Yet your heavenly Father feedeth them [. . .] Consider the lilies of the field, how they grow; they toil not, neither do they spin" (Matthew 6.26ff.).

## The Lost Pleiad[1]

*"Like the lost Pleiad seen no more below."*
BYRON[2]

And is there glory from the heavens departed?—
  Oh! void unmark'd!—thy sisters of the sky
    Still hold their place on high,
Though from its rank thine orb so long hath started,
  Thou, that no more art seen of mortal eye!

Hath the night lost a gem, the regal night?
  She wears her crown of old magnificence,
    Though thou art exil'd thence—
No desert seems to part those urns of light,
  'Midst the far depths of purple gloom intense.                    10

They rise in joy, the starry myriads burning—
  The shepherd greets them on his mountains free;
    And from the silvery sea
To them the sailor's wakeful eye is turning—
  Unchang'd they rise, they have not mourn'd for thee.

Couldst thou be shaken from thy radiant place,
  E'en as a dew-drop from the myrtle spray,
    Swept by the wind away?
Wert thou not peopled by some glorious race?
  And was there power to smite them with decay?                    20

Why, who shall talk of thrones, of sceptres riven?—
  Bow'd be our hearts to think on what *we* are,[3]
    When from its height afar
A world sinks thus—and yon majestic heaven
  Shines not the less for that one vanish'd star!

[1] First published *NMM* 8 (December 1823): 526, signed "F. H." In 1829, L.E.L. published a poem of nearly five hundred lines by the same title. Six of the Pleiad stars are visible to the naked eye. Named for the daughters of the nymph Pleione and the god Atlas, these "Seven Sisters" were changed into stars to escape the rapacious pursuit of the hunter Orion. The "lost" Pleiad is either Electra or Merope. Electra, mother of Zeus of Dardanus (founder of Troy), disappeared in grief at the fall of the city. There are two legends of Merope: in one, she hid in shame for having married a mortal, Sisyphus, king of Corinth; in another, she is raped by Orion, in a rage over her father's disapproval of his love for her. FH's quintain (a rare stanza in English after the Renaissance) adapts one of the rhyme schemes of the octosyllabic Spanish quintilla stanza (*abbab*) to pentameter (her third line a trimeter). Wordsworth used a more balladlike quintain for *The Idiot Boy* (1798) and *Peter Bell* (1819).

[2] *Beppo* (1818), stanza 14: the narrator's rapture over all the anonymous, lost women a man has loved in youth, "Whose course and home we knew not, nor shall know, / Like the lost Pleiad seen no more below." In tune with this satire, FH's poem is more playful than her usual

treatments of unmourned loss. It may be a comment on the fading of Byron's Regency celebrity in England (Jerome McGann, *Poetics of Sensibility* 159–64).

³ *NMM*] It is too sad to think . . .

---

## The Dying Improvisatore[1]

*My heart shall be pour'd over thee—and break.*
—Prophecy of Dante[2]

> The spirit of my land!
> It visits me once more!—though I must die
> Far from the myrtles which thy breeze hath fann'd,
>     My own bright Italy!
>
> It is, it is thy breath,
> Which stirs my soul e'en yet, as wavering flame
> Is shaken by the wind;—in life and death
>     Still trembling, yet the same!
>
> Oh! that love's quenchless power
> Might waft my voice to fill thy summer sky,                    10
> And through thy groves its dying music shower,
>     Italy! Italy!
>
> The nightingale is there,
> The sunbeam's glow, the citron-glower's perfume,
> The south-wind's whisper in the scented air—
>     It will not pierce the tomb!
>
> Never, oh! never more,
> On thy Rome's purple heaven mine eye shall dwell,
> Or watch the bright waves melt along thy shore—
>     My Italy, farewell!                                        20
>
> Alas!—thy hills among,
> Had I but left a memory of my name,
> Of love and grief one deep, true, fervent song,
>     Unto immortal fame!
>
> But like a lute's brief tone,
> Like a rose-odour on the breezes cast,
> Like a swift flush of dayspring, seen and gone,
>     So hath my spirit pass'd!

Pouring itself away,
As a wild bird amidst the foliage turns                              30
That which within him triumphs, beats, or burns,
Into a fleeting lay;[3]

That swells, and floats, and dies,
Leaving no echo to the summer woods
Of the rich breathings and impassion'd sighs,
Which thrill'd their solitudes.

Yet, yet remember me!
Friends! that upon its murmurs oft have hung,
When from my bosom, joyously and free,
The fiery fountain sprung.                                          40

Under the dark rich blue
Of midnight heavens, and on the star-lit sea,
And when woods kindle into spring's first hue,
Sweet friends! remember me!

And in the marble halls,
Where life's full glow the dreams of beauty wear,
And poet-thoughts embodied light the walls,
Let me be with you there!

Fain would I bind for you
My memory with all glorious things to dwell;                        50
Fain bid all lovely sounds my name renew—
Sweet friends, bright land, farewell!

[1] Sestini, the Roman Improvisatore, when on his death-bed at Paris, is said to have poured forth a Farewell to Italy, in his most impassioned poetry. [FH]
    First published in *NMM* 22 (May 1828): 403–4. Chief variants are mythicizing capitals: Love's (9), South (15), Heaven (18), Love and Grief (23), Fame (24), Spring's (43), Friends (44), Life's (46), Poet (47), Friends / Land (52). A long tradition in Italy, improvisation is spontaneously inspired oral performance and, more to the point, unpublished. Staël's Corinne is such an artist, and L.E.L. imaged herself thus, even in print: the title of her collection of 1824 features *The Improvisatrice*, the impassioned outpourings of a female Italian artist.
    [2] Byron's four-canto poem (1821), a terza-rima monologue, in Dante's voice from his exile in Ravenna. He laments his vision into the future of his beloved Italy: "A spirit forces me to see and speak, / And for my guerdon grants *not* to survive; / My heart shall be pour'd over thee and break" (3.32–34).
    [3] In a despairing letter of 1835, FH quotes these lines in self-reference. The Improvisatore (and later, FH) ruefully puns on "foliage," a printed volume (e.g., Leigh Hunt's *Foliage, or Poems Original and Translated* [1818]).

# From THE ANNUALS

## (1826–30)

———◦◦◦———

[These immensely popular volumes, flourishing in the 1820s and 1830s, were a French and German fad imported to England by German-born London printer Rudolph Ackermann (1764–1834), also credited with establishing lithography in England. In 1822 he issued *Forget Me Not*, initiating a series "expressly designed to serve as tokens of remembrance, friendship, or affection," the volumes including ornate presentation plates. The annuals were published at the end of the year, so that the holiday gift-giving could be served (thus, the first *Forget Me Not* is dated 1823, but appeared at the end of 1822). In 1824, M. J. Jewsbury's friend Alaric Watts ("Father of the Annuals") brought out *The Literary Souvenir, or Cabinet of Poetry and Romance*, which he edited from 1825 to 1835. It debuted in octavo, bound in pastel boards, its pages gilt-edged and featuring steel engravings of the works of great painters. Strategically priced at 12 shillings, it sold 6,000 copies in its first two weeks; the 1826 *Souvenir* sold 10,000. The preface to the 1827 *Souvenir* bruited "embellishments" such as "the most splendid series of prints ever introduced in any work of the same class, including an engraving of 'The Last Portrait Painted of Byron'" (by W. E. West). The same year welcomed Samuel Carter Hall's editing of the *Amulet* and Smith & Elder's publication of *Friendship's Offering*. In the preface *The Keepsake* for 1829, editor Fredric Mansel Reynolds boasted in italics that "*eleven thousand guineas*" had been spent on the production.

Cherished for display as well as for contents, the annuals were aimed chiefly at women eager for a small luxury that signified taste and literacy. The titles—*Affection's Gift, Book of Beauty, Gem, Cabinet of Literary Gems, Emerald, Pearl, Cabinet, Jewel, Amulet, Keepsake, Friendship's Offering, Love's Offering, Forget Me Not, Literary Souvenir, Talisman, Wreath, Cameo*—cued their status as ornaments and gifts. Women writers profited from this culture, gaining a supportive professional community as well as income. Not only Hemans but also Howitt, L.E.L, Mitford, Opie, and Shelley found a hospitable and lucrative market for their work, and the handsome compensation lured many men of note, including Coleridge, Wordsworth, Lamb, Moore, Hood, Clare, Scott, and Tennyson, who all managed to overcome the taint of female culture and commercialism. Southey blamed the slow sales of his books on the annual competition, but not able to lick it, joined up, always seeing to it that he was listed as "The Poet Laureate." "The world [. . .] seems mad about 'Forget me Nots' and Christmas boxes," Scott exclaimed in 1828 when Charles Heath offered him £800 a year to edit *The Keepsake*. He declined, but sold Heath a tale for £500, enough to support a middle-class family for five years. Even as Wordsworth sneered at these "ornamented [. . .] greedy receptacles of trash, those bladders upon which the Boys of Poetry try to swim," he, too, took the guineas.

From 1825 to 1835 Hemans published about 100 poems in the annuals: *Literary Souvenir* (22, including *Aymer's Tomb, The Troubadour and Richard Cœur de Lion, The Better Land, Corinna at the Capitol, Madeline, The Sisters of Scio*, and *The Mirror in the Deserted Hall*); *Forget Me Not* (14, including *Evening Prayer at a Girls' School* and *The Cliffs of Dover*); *Winter's Wreath* (24), *Amulet* (17, including *Woman and Fame*), and dozens more in *Friendship's Offering, Pledge of Friendship, Bijou, Cameo, Keepsake, Juvenile Keepsake, Juvenile Forget-me-not, New Year's Gift, Remembrance*, and *Christmas Box*. For a census, see

Andrew Boyle, *Index to the Annuals* (Worcester: Andrew Boyle, 1967), 1.120–22; Frederick W. Faxon, *Literary Annuals and Gift Books: A Bibliography, 1823–1903* (Boston, 1912; rpt. with supplementary essays, Middlesex, U.K.: Private Library Association, 1973). For the culture of the annuals, see Ian Jack, *English Literature 1815–1832* (Oxford: Clarendon P, 1963); Bradford Booth, *A Cabinet of Gems* (Berkeley: U of California P, 1938); Margaret Reynolds's introduction to *Victorian Women Poets* (Oxford: Blackwell, 1995), and Peter J. Manning, "Wordsworth in the *Keepsake*," in *Literature in the Marketplace*, ed. J. Jordan and R. Patten (Cambridge: Cambridge UP, 1995).]

# Forget Me Not

## Evening Prayer at a Girls' School[1]

> *Now in thy youth, beseech of Him*
> *Who giveth, upbraiding not,*
> *That his light in thy heart become not dim,*
> *And his love be unforgot;*
> *And thy God, in the darkest of days, will be*
> *Greenness, and beauty, and strength, to thee.*
> BERNARD BARTON[2]

Hush! 'tis a holy hour!—the quiet room
   Seems like a temple, while yon soft lamp sheds
A faint and starry radiance, through the gloom
   And the sweet stillness, down on bright[3] young heads,
With all their clustering locks, untouch'd by care,
And bow'd—as flowers are bowed with[4] night—in prayer.

Gaze on, 'tis lovely!—childhood's[5] lip and cheek,
   Mantling° beneath its earnest brow of thought!         *blushing*
Gaze, yet what seest thou in those fair and meek
   And fragile things, as but for sunshine wrought?         10
—Thou seest what grief must nurture for the sky,
What death must fashion for eternity!

O joyous creatures! that will sink to rest
   Lightly, when those pure orisons are done,
As birds with slumber's honey-dew oppress'd,
   Midst the dim folded leaves, at set of sun;
Lift up your hearts! tho' yet no sorrow lies
Dark in the summer-heaven of those clear eyes.

Though fresh within your breasts th' untroubled springs
   Of hope make melody where'er ye tread,         20
And o'er your sleep bright shadows, from the wings
   Of spirits visiting but youth, be spread;

Yet in those flute-like voices, mingling low,
Is woman's tenderness—how soon her woe!

Her lot is on you!—silent tears to weep,
    And patient smiles to wear through suffering's hour,
And sumless riches, from affection's deep,
    To pour on broken reeds—a wasted shower![6]
And to make idols, and to find them clay,
And to bewail that worship—therefore pray!                    30

Her lot is on you!—to be found untir'd,
    Watching the stars out by the bed of pain,
With a pale cheek, and yet a brow inspir'd,
    And a true heart of hope, though hope be vain!
Meekly to bear with wrong, to cheer decay,
And, oh! to love through all things—therefore pray!

And take the thought of this calm vesper-time,
    With its low murmuring sounds and silvery light,
On through the dark days fading from their prime,
    As a sweet dew to keep your souls from blight!              40
Earth will forsake—Oh! happy to have given
Th' unbroken heart's first fragrance unto Heaven.

[1] *Forget Me Not; A Christmas and New Year's Present for 1826* (London: R. Ackermann) 156–58, with an engraving of the girls at prayer, facing 156. This anthology favorite also appeared in *League &c* (1826) and *Forest Sanctuary &c* (1829). FH genders a common theme, an adult's knowledge of childhood's doomed innocence; famous precedents include Gray's *Ode on a Distant Prospect of Eton College* (1747) and sonnet 27 of Charlotte Smith's *Elegiac Sonnets* ("Sighing I see yon little troop at play") (1800).

[2] The last stanza of *The Ivy, Addressed to a Young Friend* (43–48), in *Poems* (1825). FH's friend Bernard Barton (1784–1849), "the Quaker poet" (he was initially sponsored by his Quaker sect), published frequently in *Forget Me Not* and other annuals. After he dedicated *Household Verses* (1845) to Queen Victoria, he secured a government pension. FH's verse is the "Venus and Adonis" stanza.

[3] *Forest*] fair

[4] *Forest* ] in

[5] *Forest*] Childhood's
    also capitalized: Death, Eternity (12), Hope (20).

[6] Standard tropes: "suffering's hour" is any affliction, but particularly childbirth; "broken reeds" are children who die young.

## The Cliffs of Dover[1]

Rocks of my country! let the cloud
    Your crested heights array;
And rise ye like a fortress proud,
    Above the surge and spray!

My spirit greets you as ye stand,
    Breasting the billow's foam;
Oh, thus for ever guard the land,
    The sever'd land of home![2]

I have left sunny[3] skies behind,
    Lighting up classic shrines,                   10
And music in the southern wind,
    And sunshine on the vines.

The breathings of the myrtle flowers
    Have floated o'er my way,
The pilgrim's voice at vesper hours
    Hath sooth'd me with its lay.

The isles of Greece, the hills of Spain,
    The purple heavens of Rome,—[4]
Yes, all are glorious;—yet again
    I bless thee, land of home!                  20

For thine the Sabbath peace, my land;
    And thine the guarded hearth;
And thine the dead, the noble band
    That make thee holy earth.

Their voices meet me in thy breeze;
    Their steps are on thy plains;
Their names, by old majestic trees,
    Are whisper'd round thy fanes:

Their blood hath mingled with the tide
    Of thine exulting sea;—                  30
Oh, be it still a joy, a pride,
    To live and die for thee!

---

[1] *Forget Me Not: A Christmas and New Year's Present for* MDCCCXVII 69–70, signed "Mrs. Hemans," with an engraving of the cliffs and ships at sea facing 69. Rpt. in *Forest Sanctuary &c* (1829), with this epigraph: "The inviolate Island of the sage and free. BYRON" (from the poet's farewell to England; *Childe Harold's Pilgrimage IV*, viii). The stanzas are in ballad form.

[2] *Forest*] Land of Home (also at 20)

[3] *Forest*] rich blue

<sup>4</sup> *Forest*] Isles / Hills / Heavens
  "The Isles of Greece," a song in Byron's *Don Juan III* (following lxxxviii), was so popular that it was often anthologized as an independent piece.

———————

## *Night-Blowing Flowers*[1]

Call back your odours, lonely[2] flowers,
    From the night-wind call them back,
And fold your leaves till the laughing hours
    Come forth on the sunbeam's track!

The lark lies couch'd in his grassy nest,
    And the honey-bee is gone,
And all bright things are away to rest—
    Why watch ye thus alone?

Is not your world a mournful one,
    When your sisters close their eyes,                    10
And your soft breath meets not a lingering tone
    Of song in the starry skies?

Take ye no joy in the dayspring's birth,
    When it kindles the sparks of dew?
And the thousand strains of a forest's mirth,
    Shall they gladden all but you?

Shut your sweet bells till the fawn comes out
    On the sunny turf to play,
And the woodland child, with a fairy shout,
    Goes dancing on his way.                    20

Nay, let our shadowy beauty bloom;[3]
    When the stars give quiet light;
And let us offer our faint perfume
    On the silent shrine of night.

Call it not wasted, the scent we lend
    To the breeze when no step is nigh;
Oh! thus for ever the earth should send
    Her grateful breath on high!

And love us as emblems, night's dewy flowers,
    Of hopes unto sorrow given,                    30
That spring through the gloom of the darkest hours,
    Looking alone to Heaven!

[1] *Forget Me Not: A Christmas and New Year's Present for* MDCCCXVII 237–38, signed "Mrs. Hemans." The title in *1839* is *The Wanderer and the Night Flowers*, and the poem just before it ("Children of night!") is titled *Night-Blowing Flowers* (7.15–17); both are in a subsection called *Songs of a Guardian Spirit*, which includes *The Last Song of Sappho*. The stanzas are ballad form.

[2] *1839*] lovely

[3] *1839*] 21–32 are in quotation marks.

---

# *The Keepsake* for MDCCCXXIX

[FH earned £45 for this piece. The volume also boasted stories by Scott (£50 for 11 pages), tales from M. Shelley, three poetic *Fragments* by P. B. Shelley and the first publication of his essay *On Love*, three poems by Wordsworth, several *Epigrams* by Coleridge as well as *The Garden of Boccaccio* and *To a Critic*, two poems by L.E.L., a *Distich* by Lord Holland, and an *Extempore* from Thomas Moore. When William Harrison Ainsworth (1805–82), briefly editor of *The Keepsake*, invited FH to write for *The Christmas Box*, she replied warmly, "I thought the 'Keepsake' extremely beautiful, and regret that it is to be discontinued; I sent a copy to some friends in New England, as a specimen of the perfection to which such works had arrived in England" (22 May 1828; Princeton University Parrish Collection, AM 17976). She sent him *The Name of England* for the next volume.]

## *The Broken Chain*[1]

*Lift not the festal mask!*

SCOTT[2]

I am free!—I have burst through my heavy chain,
The life of young eagles is mine again!
I may cleave with my bark the glad sounding sea,
I may rove where the wind roves—my path is free!

The streams dash in joy down the tameless hill,
The birds pierce the depths of the skies at will;
The arrow goes forth with the singing breeze—
And is not my spirit as one of these?

Oh! the glad earth, with its wealth of flowers,
And the voices that ring through its forest-bowers,                    10
And the laughing glance of the founts that shine,
Lighting the valleys—all, all are mine!

I may urge through the desert my foaming steed,
The wings of the morning shall lend him speed[3]
I may meet the storm in its rushing glee,
Its blasts and its lightnings are not more free!

Captive! and hast thou then riven thy chain?
Art thou free in the wilderness, free on the main?
Yes! *these* thy spirit may proudly soar,
But must thou not mingle with crowds once more?                    20

The bird, when he pineth, may cease his song,
Till the hour when his heart shall again be strong;
But thou—wilt thou turn in thy woe aside,
And weep midst thy brethren?[4]—no, not for pride!

May the fiery word from thy lip find way,
When the thought burning in thee would rush to day?—
May the love or the grief of thy haunted breast,
Look forth from thy features, the banquet's guest?—

No! with the shaft in thy bosom borne,
Thou must hide the wound from the eye of scorn;                    30
Thou must fold the mantle that none may see,
And mask thee with laughter, and say thou art free.

Free!—thou art bound, till thy race is run,
By the might of all in the soul of one;
On thy heart, on thy lip, must the fetter be—
Dreamer, fond dreamer! oh! who is free?

[1] *Keepsake* (1829) 262–63, signed "Mrs. Hemans." For the key image, cf. the last stanza of *A Parting Song*. Variants are from the MS in Charles Scribner's Sons Collection, Princeton University (AM 21300).
[2] Source unidentified.
[3] MS] lines 13 and 14 end in exclamation points.
[4] MS] Bitterness

## *The Amulet, or Christian and Literary Remembrancer*

### *Woman and Fame*[1]

[Early in 1827 FH wrote in her notebook: "What is fame to a heart yearning for affection, and finding it not? Is it not as a triumphal crown to the brow of one parched with fever, and asking for one fresh healthful draught—the 'cup of cold water'?" (*HM* 111), echoing Jesus in Matthew 10.42: "whoever shall give to drink unto one of the little ones a cup of cold water only in the name of a disciple, verily I say unto you, he shall in no wise lose his reward." She was haunted by the miseries of fame for women: cf. *Joan of Arc, in Rheims*; *Properzia Rossi*; *Corinne at the Capitol*.]

*Happy—happier far than thou,*
*With the laurel on thy brow;*
*She that makes the humblest hearth,*
*Lovely but to one on earth.*[2]

Thou hast a charmed cup, O Fame!
   A draught that mantles° high,          *bubbles*
And seems to lift this earthly frame
   Above mortality.
Away! to me—a woman—bring
Sweet waters from affection's spring.[3]

Thou hast green laurel-leaves that twine
   Into so proud a wreath;
For that resplendent gift of thine,
   Heroes have smiled in death.          10
Give *me* from some kind hand a flower,
The record of one happy hour!

Thou hast a voice, whose thrilling tone
   Can bid each life-pulse beat,
As when a trumpet's note hath blown,
   Calling the brave to meet:
But mine, let mine—a woman's breast,
By words of home-born love be bless'd.

A hollow sound is in thy song,
   A mockery in thine eye,          20
To the sick heart that doth but long
   For aid, for sympathy;
For kindly looks to cheer it on,
For tender accents that are gone.

Fame, Fame! thou canst not be the stay
   Unto the drooping reed,
The cool fresh fountain, in the day
   Of the soul's feverish need;
Where must the lone one turn or flee?—
Not unto thee, oh! not to thee!          30

[1] *Amulet* (1829) 89–90, signed "Mrs. Hemans." First collected, posthumously, in *Poetical Works* (Philadelphia, 1836). The verse form is a balladlike adaptation of the "Venus and Adonis" stanza. The 1829 *Amulet* opens with FH's *The Angels' Call* and its title page features lines from "Mrs. Hemans." It includes John Clare's sonnet *Fame* (266), a kind of Byronic meditation on the hollowness of fame.

[2] *Corinna at the Capitol* (*LS* 1827) and *Corinne at the Capitol* (1830), 45–48.

[3] The epigraph of *Joan of Arc, in Rheims,* in *Records of Woman* (1828).

## *The Literary Souvenir*

### *The Mirror in the Deserted Hall*[1]

O dim, forsaken Mirror!
How many a stately throng
Hath o'er thee gleamed, in vanished hours
Of the wine-cup and the song!

The song hath left no echo,
The bright wine hath been quaffed,
And hushed is every silvery voice
That lightly here hath laughed.

O Mirror, lonely Mirror,
Thou of the silent Hall!      10
Thou hast been flush'd with beauty's bloom—
Is this too vanished all?

It is, with the scattered garlands
Of triumphs long ago,
With the melodies of buried lyres,
With the faded rainbow's glow.

And for all the gorgeous pageants,
For the glance of gem and plume,
For lamp, and harp, and rosy wreath,
And vase of rich perfume;      20

Now, dim, forsaken Mirror,
Thou giv'st but faintly back
The quiet stars and the sailing moon,
On her solitary track.

And thus with man's proud spirit
Thou tellest me 't will be,
When the forms and hues of this world fade
From his memory, as from thee:

And his heart's long-troubled waters
At last in stillness lie,      30
Reflecting but the images
Of the solemn world on high.

---

[1] *LS* (1830), 356–70, signed "Mrs. Hemans"; each stanza was roman-numbered. Rpt. as the closing poem of *Songs of the Affections &c.* Compare *The Deserted House.*

---

# From *Songs of the Affections,*
## *with Other Poems*
### (1830)

—⟨ɷɷɷ⟩—

[Following the solid sales of *Records of Woman &c* (the book had earned £300 by late 1830), and the 2d and 3d editions of *The Forest Sanctuary &c* (£100 by the end of 1828), FH earned £200 for two editions of *Songs of the Affections* (1830 and 1835). "There are some exquisite things amongst them in her own peculiar strain of melancholy tenderness," Baillie remarked; "woman becomes a most-noble & generous being, painted by her hand!" (19 July ?1830 [Camden Local Studies and Archives Centre; *Letters* 709]). For the collected pieces in the volume, FH changes her former subsection title, "Miscellaneous Pieces" (*Forest Sanctuary* and *Records of Woman*), to "Miscellaneous Poems." Wordsworth felt sufficiently established by 1820 to offer a volume of *Miscellaneous Poems*, the interest of which was necessarily the poet. By using this exact title, even for a subsection, FH is declaring her similar view of her own career at this point. The 31 miscellaneous poems that follow the thirty *Songs of the Affections* comprise almost half of the volume's 259 pages. In her next volume, which she dedicated to Wordsworth, *Scenes and Hymns of Life, With Other Religious Poems* (1834), the 45 "Miscellaneous Poems" that follow 23 *Scenes and Hymns* account for nearly a third of the 247 pages.

The title plate of *Songs of the Affections* bears these verses (by Hemans):

> They tell but dreams—a lonely spirit's dreams—
> Yet ever through their fleeting imagery
> Wanders a vein of melancholy love,
> An aimless thought of home:—as in the song
> Of the caged skylark ye may deem there dwells
> A passionate memory of blue skies and flowers,
> And living streams—far off!¹

¹ Gerard Manley Hopkins's sonnet *The Caged Skylark* may owe its title to these lines.]

---

# Songs

## *A Spirit's Return*

[The subject of this poem, "as peculiar as it was almost dangerously fascinating, was suggested by a fire-side conversation. It had long been a favourite amusement to wind up our evenings by telling ghost stories. One night, however, the store of thrilling narratives was exhausted, and we began to talk of the feelings with which the presence and the speech of a visitant from another world (if, indeed, a spirit *could* return,) would be most likely to impress the person so visited. After having exhausted all the common varieties of fear and terror in our speculations, Mrs. Hemans said that she thought the predominant sensations at the time must at once partake of awe and rapture, and resemble the feelings of those who listen to a revelation, and at the same moment know themselves to be favoured above all men, and humbled before a being no longer sharing their own cares or passions; but that the person so visited must thenceforward and for ever be inevitably separated from this world and its concerns: for the souls which had once enjoyed such a strange and spiritual communion, which had been permitted to look, though but for a moment, beyond the mysterious gates of death, *must* be raised, by its experience, too high for common grief again to perplex, or common joy to enliven. She spoke long and eloquently upon this subject, and I have reason to believe that this conversation settled her wandering fancy, and gave rise to the principal poem in her next volume" (*CM* 2.70–72). It was the lead piece in *Songs of the Affections*. "I prefer that poem to anything else I have written," Hemans said, "but [. . .] it almost made me tremble as I sounded 'the deep places' of my soul" (2.157). Chorley thought it "perhaps, her finest" ("Mrs Hemans" 392); "Still it was far from satisfy- ing her," reports her sister; "and she was worn and excited during its composition, by what she was wont to call 'that weary striving after ideal beauty which one never can grasp,' and yet more by those awful contemplations of the visionary world, on which it led her to dwell with an interest too intense, a curiosity too disquieting" (*HM* 203; cf. Lawrence 310–13). Communion with a ghost-beloved is treated in Bürger's ballad *Lenore*, Byron's gothic dramatic poem *Manfred* (1817), Wordsworth's *Laodamia*, and Keats's *Isabella*. *Laodamia* "completely seized her mind—she could not dispossess herself of it," Lawrence reported (313). FH was also rapt by *Lenore*: "She was never tired of hearing [it], for the sake of its wonderful rhythm and energy," recalled her close friend Lodge; "I remember how on one very stormy dark evening, I was bid to repeat it from the beginning to the end" (*CM* 1.289). A related theme is the abandonment of mortal ties for eroticized spiritual communion— the theme of Shelley's *Alastor* (1816) and *Epipsychidion* (1821) and of Keats's *Endymion* (1818). Like Keats, FH writes in romance couplets, and often deploys Shelleyan diction and imagery.]

> *This to be a mortal,*
> *And seek the things beyond mortality!*
> —Manfred[1]

Thy voice prevails; dear Friend, my gentle Friend!
This long-shut heart for thee shall be unseal'd,
And though thy soft eye mournfully will bend
Over the troubled stream, yet once reveal'd
Shall its freed waters flow; then rocks must close
For evermore, above their dark repose.

Come while the gorgeous mysteries of the sky
Fused in the crimson sea of sunset lie;
Come to the woods, where all strange wandering sound
Is mingled into harmony profound;                                    10
Where the leaves thrill with spirit while the wind
Fills with a viewless being, unconfined,

The trembling reeds and fountains;—Our own dell,
With its green dimness and Æolian breath,
Shall suit th'unveiling of dark records well—
Hear me in tenderness and silent faith!

Thou knew'st me not in life's fresh vernal noon—
I would thou hast!—for then my heart on thine
Had pour'd a worthier love; now, all o'erworn
By its deep thirst for something too divine,          20
It hath but fitful music to bestow,
Echoes of harp-strings, broken long ago.

Yet even in youth companionless I stood,
As a lone forest-bird midst ocean's foam;
For me the silver cords of brotherhood
Were early loosed;—the voices from my home
Pass'd one by one, and Melody and Mirth
Left me a dreamer by a silent hearth.

But, with the fulness of a heart that burn'd
For the deep sympathies of mind, I turn'd          30
From that unanswering spot, and fondly sought
In all wild scenes with thrilling murmurs fraught,
In every still small voice² and sound of power,
And flute-note of the wind through cave and bower,
A perilous delight!—for then first woke
My life's lone passion, the mysterious quest
Of secret knowledge; and each tone that broke
From the wood-arches or the fountain's breast,
Making my quick soul vibrate as a lyre,³
But minister'd to that strange inborn fire.          40

Midst the bright silence of the mountain-dells,
In noontide-hours or golden summer-eves,
My thoughts have burst forth as a gale that swells
Into a rushing blast, and from the leaves
Shakes out response;—O thou rich world unseen!
Thou curtain'd realm of spirits!—thus my cry
Hath troubled air and silence—dost thou lie
Spread all around, yet by some filmy screen
Shut from us ever?—The resounding woods,
Do their depths teem with marvels?—and the floods,          50
And the pure fountains, leading secret veins
Of quenchless melody through rock and hill,
Have they bright dwellers?—are their lone domains
Peopled with beauty, which may never still

*Our* weary thirst of soul?—Cold, weak and cold,
Is Earth's vain language, piercing not one fold
Of our deep being!—Oh, for gifts more high!
For a seer's glance to rend mortality!
For a charm'd rod, to call from each dark shrine,
The oracles divine!                                                    60

I woke from those high fantasies, to know
My kindred with the Earth—I woke to love:—
O, gentle Friend! to love in doubt and woe,
Shutting the heart the worshipp'd name above,
Is to love deeply—and *my* spirit's dower
Was a sad gift, a melancholy power
Of so adoring;—with a buried care,
And with the o'erflowing of a voiceless prayer,
And with a deepening dream, that day by day,
In the still shadow of its lonely sway,                                70
Folded me closer;—till the world held nought
Save the *one* Being to my centred thought.
There was no music but his voice to hear,
No joy but such as with *his* step drew near;
Light was but where he look'd—life where he moved—
Silently, fervently, thus, thus I loved.
Oh! but such love is fearful!—and I knew
Its gathering doom:—the soul's prophetic sight
Even then unfolded in my breast, and threw
O'er all things round a full, strong, vivid light.                     80
Too sorrowfully clear!—an under-tone
Was given to Nature's harp, for me alone
Whispering of grief.—Of grief?—be strong, awake!

Hath not thy love been victory, O, my soul?
Hath not its conflict won a voice to shake
Death's fastnesses?—a magic to control
Worlds far removed?—from o'er the grave to thee
Love hath made answer; and *thy* tale should be
Sung like a lay of triumph!—Now return,
And take thy treasure from its bosom'd urn,°           *(for funeral ashes)*
And lift it once to light!

         In fear, in pain,                                91
I said I loved—but yet a heavenly strain
Of sweetness floated down the tearful stream,
A joy flash'd through the trouble of my dream!
I knew myself beloved!—we breathed no vow,
No mingling visions might our fate allow,

As unto happy hearts; but still and deep,
Like a rich jewel gleaming in a grave,
Like golden sand in some dark river's wave,
So did my soul that costly knowledge keep                    100
So jealously!—a thing o'er which to shed,
When stars alone behind the drooping head,
Lone tears! yet ofttimes burden'd with the excess
Of our strange nature's quivering happiness.

But, oh! sweet Friend! we dream not of love's might
Till Death has robed with soft and solemn light
The image we enshrine!—Before *that* hour,
We have but glimpses of the o'ermastering power
Within us laid!—*then* doth the spirit-flame
With sword-like lightning rend its mortal frame;            110
The wings of that which pants to follow fast
Shake their clay-bars, as with a prison'd blast,—
The sea is in our souls![4]

       He died, *he* died,
On whom my lone devotedness was cast!
I might not keep one vigil by his side,
*I*, whose wrung heart watch'd with him to the last!
I might not once his fainting head sustain,
Nor bathe his parch'd lips in the hour of pain,
Nor say to him, "Farewell!"—He pass'd away—
Oh! had *my* love been there, its conquering sway           120
Had won him back from death!—-but thus removed,
Borne o'er the abyss no sounding line hath proved,
Join'd with the unknown, the viewless,—he became
Unto my thoughts another, yet the same—
Changed—hallow'd—glorified!—and his low grave
Seem'd a bright mournful altar—mine, all mine:—
Brother and Friend soon left me *that* sole shrine,
The birthright of the Faithful!—*their* world's wave
Soon swept them from its brink.—Oh! deem thou not
That on the sad and consecrated spot                        130
My soul grew weak!—I tell thee that a power
There kindled heart and lip;—a fiery shower
My words were made;—a might was given to prayer,
And a strong grasp to passionate despair,
And a dread triumph!—Know'st thou what I sought?
For what high boon my struggling spirit wrought?
—Communion with the dead!—I sent a cry,
Through the veil'd empires of eternity,

A voice to cleave them! By the mournful truth,
By the lost promise of my blighted youth, 140
By the strong chain a mighty love can bind
On the beloved, the spell of mind o'er mind;
By words, which in themselves are magic high,
Arm'd, and inspired, and wing'd with agony;
By tears, which comfort not, but burn, and seem
To bear the heart's blood in their passion-stream;
I summon'd, I adjured!—with quicken'd sense,
With the keen vigil of a life intense,
I watch'd, an answer from the winds to wring,
I listen'd, if perchance the stream might bring 150
Token from worlds afar: I taught *one* sound
Unto a thousand echoes; one profound
Imploring ascent to the tomb, the sky;
One prayer to night,— "Awake, appear, reply!"

Hast thou been told that from the viewless bourne,
The dark way never hath allow'd return?[5]
That all, which tears can move, with life is fled,
That earthly love is powerless on the dead?
Believe it not!—there is a large lone star,[6]
Now burning o'er yon western hill afar, 160
And under its clear light there lies a spot,
Which well might utter forth—Believe it not!

I sat beneath that planet,—I had wept
My woe to stillness; every night-wind slept;
A hush was on the hills; the very streams
Went by like clouds, or noiseless founts in dreams,
And the dark tree o'ershadowing me that hour,
Stood motionless, even as the grey church-tower
Whereon I gazed unconsciously:—there came
A low sound, like the tremor of a flame, 170
Or like the light quick shiver of a wing,
Flitting through twilight woods, across the air;
And I look'd up!—Oh! for strong words to bring
Conviction o'er thy thought!—Before me there,
He, the Departed, stood!—Aye, face to face—
So near, and yet how far!—his form, his mien,
Gave to remembrance back each burning trace
Within:—Yet something awfully serene,
Pure,—sculpture-like,—on the pale brow, that wore
Of the one beating heart no token more;[7] 180
And stillness on the lip—and o'er the hair
A gleam, that trembled through the breathless air;

And an unfathom'd calm, that seem'd to lie
In the grave sweetness of the illumined eye;
Told of the gulfs between our being set,
And, as that unsheathed spirit-glance I met,
Made my soul faint:—with *fear?*—Oh! *not* with fear!
With the sick feeling that in *his* far sphere
*My* love could be as nothing!—But he spoke—
How shall I tell thee of the startling thrill                        190
In that low voice, whose breezy tones could fill
My bosom's infinite?—O Friend, I woke
*Then* first to heavenly life!—Soft, solemn, clear,
Breathed the mysterious accents on mine ear,
Yet strangely seem'd as if the while they rose
From depths of distance, o'er the wide repose
Of slumbering waters wafted, or the dells
Of mountains, hollow with sweet echo-cells;
But, as they murmur'd on, the mortal chill
Pass'd from me, like a mist before the morn,                         200
And, to that glorious intercourse upborne,
By slow degrees, a calm, divinely still,
Possess'd my frame:—I sought that lighted eye,—
From its intense and searching purity
I drank in *soul!*—I question'd of the dead—
Of the hush'd, starry shores their footsteps tread—
And I was answer'd:—if remembrance there,
With dreamy whispers fill the immortal air;
If Thought, here piled from many a jewel-heap,
Be treasure in that pensive land to keep;                            210
If Love, o'ersweeping change, and blight, and blast,
Find *there* the music of his home at last;
I ask'd, and I was answer'd:—Full and high
Was that communion with eternity,
Too rich for aught so fleeting!—Like a knell
Swept o'er my sense its closing words,—"Farewell,
On earth we meet no more!"—and all was gone—
The pale bright settled brow—the thrilling tone—
The still and shining eye!—and never more
May twilight gloom or midnight hush restore                          220
That radiant guest!—One full-fraught hour of Heaven,
To earthly passion's wild implorings given,
Was made my own—the ethereal fire hath shiver'd
The fragile censer in whose mould it quiver'd,
Brightly, consumingly!—What now is left?—
A faded world, of glory's hues bereft,

A void, a chain!—I dwell, 'midst throngs, apart,
In the cold silence of the stranger's heart;
A fix'd, immortal shadow stands between
My spirit and life's fast-receding scene;
A gift hath sever'd me from human ties,                    230
A power is gone from all earth's melodies,
Which never may return:—their chords are broken—
The music of another land hath spoken,—
No after-sound is sweet!—this weary thirst!—
And I have heard celestial fountains burst!—
What *here* shall quench it?
                              Dost thou not rejoice,
When the spring sends forth an awakening voice
Through the young woods?—Thou dost!—And in that birth
Of early leaves, and flowers, and songs of mirth,          240
Thousands, like thee, find gladness!—Couldst thou know
How every breeze then summons *me* to go!
How all the light of love and beauty shed
By those rich hours, but woos me to the Dead!
The *only* beautiful that change no more,
The only loved!—the dwellers on the shore
Of spring fulfill'd!—The Dead!—*whom* call we so?
They that breathe purer air, that feel, that know
Things wrapt from us!—Away!—within me pent,
That which is barr'd from its own element                  250
Still droops or struggles!—But the day *will* come—
Over the deep the free bird finds its home,
And the stream lingers midst the rocks, yet greets
The sea at last; and the wing'd flower-seed meets
A soil to rest in:—shall not *I*, too, be,
My spirit-love! upborne to dwell with thee?
Yes! by the power whose conquering anguish stirr'd
The tomb, whose cry beyond the stars was heard,
Whose agony of triumph won thee back
Through the dim pass no mortal step may track,             260
Yet shall we meet!—that glimpse of joy divine,
Proved thee for ever and for ever mine!

---

[1] The voice of a spirit after the phantom of Manfred's beloved Astarte vanishes, the event leaving him "convulsed" (2.4.159–60).

[2] The Lord speaks to the prophet Elijah in a "still small voice" (1 Kings 19.12); FH frequently echoes this phrase.

[3] Cf. *Alastor* (1816, repub. 1824, in *Posthumous Poems*), where the frame poet-narrator invokes the "Mother of this unfathomable world" (18): "Enough from incommunicable dream, / And twilight phantasms, and deep noonday thought, / Has shone within me, that serenely now /

And moveless, as a long-forgotten lyre / Suspended in the solitary dome / Of some mysterious and deserted fane, / I wait thy breath" (39–45).

[4] Cf. the end of *Epipsychidion*, as the poet realizes he can never unite with his visionary beloved: "Woe is me! / The winged words on which my soul would pierce / Into the height of love's rare Universe, / Are chains of lead around its flight of fire" (587–90).

[5] Cf. Hamlet's apprehension about the afterlife: "the undiscovered country, from whose bourn / No traveler returns" (3.1.79–80).

[6] The lone burning star is a frequent symbol in Shelley's poetry for the ideal beyond this world: in *Adonais*, it is the soul of Adonais; in *To a Sky-Lark*, it is Venus; and in *Epipsychidion*, it is "love's folding star."

[7] "Sometimes I think that I have sacrificed too much in the apparition scene, to the idea that sweetness and beauty might be combined with supernatural effect; the character of the Greek sculpture, which has so singular a hold upon my imagination, was much in my thoughts at the time," FH wrote to an unnamed man (*CM* 2.82–83). Also in this fantasy reunion may have been its negative: her husband's rejection of her offer to join him in Italy after her mother's death.

---

## The Two Homes[1]

*Oh! If the soul immortal be,*
*Is not its love Immortal too?*[2]

Seest thou my home?—'tis where yon woods are waving,
In their dark richness, to the summer air;
Where yon blue stream, a thousand flower-banks laving,
Leads down the hills a vein of light,—tis there!

'Midst those green wilds how many a fount lies gleaming,
Fringed with the violet, colour'd with the skies!
My boyhood's haunt, through days of summer dreaming,
Under young leaves that shook with melodies.

My home! the spirit of its love is breathing
In every wind that plays across my track;                        10
From its white walls the very tendrils wreathing,
Seem with soft links to draw the wanderer back.

There am I loved—there pray'd for—there my mother
Sits by the hearth with meekly thoughtful eye;
There my young sisters watch to greet their brother
—Soon their glad footsteps down the path will fly.

There, in sweet strains of kindred music blending,
All the home-voices meet at day's decline;
One are those tones, as from one heart ascending,—
There laughs *my* home—sad stranger! where is thine?            20

Ask'st thou of mine?—In solemn peace 'tis lying,
Far o'er the deserts and the tombs away;
'Tis where *I*, too, am loved with love undying,
And fond hearts wait my step—But where are they?

Ask where the earth's departed have their dwelling;
Ask of the clouds, the stars, the trackless air!
I know it not, yet trust the whisper, telling
My lonely heart, that love unchanged is there.

And what is home, and where, but with the loving?
Happy *thou* art, that so canst gaze on thine                    30
My spirit feels but, in its weary roving,
That with the dead, where'er they be, is mine.

Go to thy home, rejoicing son and brother!
Bear in fresh gladness to the household scene!
For me, too, watch the sister and the mother,
I well believe—but dark seas roll between.

[1] FH's "elegiac" stanza (*abab* iambic pentameter) signals a genre and a poetic lineage: named
from Gray's popular *Elegy Written in a Country Churchyard* (1751), the stanza is Wordsworth's
allusion in his own *Elegiac Stanzas Suggested by a Picture of Peele Castle* (1807).
[2] Amelia Opie (1769–1853), *Song* ("Fond dream of love by love repaid"), in *Poems* (1811).
Opie provides a note: "Florian" [Jean-Pierre Claris de Florian (1755–94)]: "si l'âme est im-
mortelle / L'amour ne l'est-il pas?" [If the soul is immortal, / Is not love?]

## The Land of Dreams[1]

> *And dreams, in their development, have breath,*
> *And tears, and tortures, and the touch of joy;*
> *They leave a weight upon our waking thoughts,*
> *[. . .]*
> *They make us what we were not—what they will,*
> *And shake us with the vision that's gone by.*
>                                                            BYRON

O Spirit-Land! thou land of dreams!
A world thou art of mysterious gleams,
Of startling voices, and sounds at strife,—
A world of the dead in the hues of life.

Like a wizard's magic glass thou art,
When the wavy shadows float by, and part:
Visions of aspects, now loved, now strange,
Glimmering and mingling in ceaseless change.

Thou art like a city of the past,
With its gorgeous halls into fragments cast,                    10
Amidst whose ruins there glide and play
Familiar forms of the world's to-day.

Thou art like the depths where the seas have birth,
Rich with the wealth that is lost from earth,—
All the sere flowers of our days gone by,
And the buried gems in thy bosom lie.

Yes! thou art like those dim sea-caves,
A realm of treasures, a realm of graves!
And the shapes through thy mysteries that come and go,
Are of beauty and terror, of power and woe.                    20

But for *me*, O thou picture-land of sleep!
Thou art all one world of affections deep,—
And wrung from my heart is each flushing dye,
That sweeps o'er thy chambers of imagery.

And thy bowers are fair—even as Eden fair;
All the beloved of my soul are there!
The forms my spirit most pines to see,
The eyes, whose love hath been life to me:

They are there, and each blessed voice I hear,
Kindly, and joyous, and silvery clear;                    30
But under-tones are in each, that say,—
"It is but a dream; it will melt away!"

I walk with sweet friends in the sunset's glow;
I listen to music of long ago;
But one thought, like an omen, breathes faint through the lay,—
"It is but a dream; it will melt away!"

I sit by the hearth of my early days;
All the home-faces are met by the blaze,—
And the eyes of the mother shine soft, yet say,—
"It is but a dream; it will melt away!"                    40

And away, like a flower's passing breath, 'tis gone,
And I wake more sadly, more deeply lone!
Oh! a haunted heart is a weight to bear,—
Bright faces, kind voices! where are ye, where?

Shadow not forth, O thou land of dreams,
The past, as it fled by my own blue streams!
Make not my spirit within me burn
For the scenes and the hours that may ne'er return!

Call out from the *future* thy visions bright,
From the world o'er the grave, take thy solemn light,     50
And oh! with the loved, whom no more I see,
Show me my home, as it yet may be!

As it yet may be in some purer sphere,
No cloud, no parting, no sleepless fear;
So my soul may bear on through the long, long day,
Till I go where the beautiful melts not away!

[1] First published in *Blackwood's Edinburgh Magazine* 24 (December 1828): 783–84, signed."F. H." Shelley used this *aabb* tetrameter quatrain in *The Sensitive Plant* (1820); the formal continuity and visionary yearning for renewal after catastrophe make FH's poem seem a sequel to his, as well as a conversation with the poem by Byron quoted in the epigraph, *The Dream* (1816) 5–7; 15–16.

---

## *Woman on the Field of Battle*[1]

> *Where hath not woman stood,*
> *Strong in affections' might? a reed, upborne*
> *By an o'ermastering current!*[2]

Gentle and lovely form,
   What didst thou here,
When the fierce battle-storm
   Bore down the spear?

Banner and shivered crest,
   Beside thee strown,
Tell, that amidst the best,
   Thy work was done!

Yet strangely, sadly fair,
   O'er the wild scene,     10
Gleams, through its golden hair,
   That brow serene.

Low lies the stately head,—
   Earth-bound the free;
How gave those haughty dead
   A place to thee?

Slumberer! *thine* early bier
   Friends should have crown'd,
Many a flower and tear
   Shedding around.     20

Soft voices, clear and young,
    Mingling their swell,
Should o'er thy dust have sung
    Earth's last farewell.

Sisters, above the grave
    Of thy repose,
Should have bid violets wave
    With the white rose.

Now must the trumpet's note,
    Savage and shrill,             30
For requiem o'er thee float,
    Thou fair and still!

And the swift charger sweep,
    In full career,
Trampling thy place of sleep,—
    Why camest thou here?

Why?—ask the true heart why
    Woman hath been
Ever, where brave men die,
    Unshrinking seen?           40

Unto this harvest ground
    Proud reapers came,—
Some, for that stirring sound,
    A warrior's name;

Some, for the stormy play
    And joy of strife;
And some, to fling away
    A weary life;—

But thou, pale sleeper, thou,
    With the slight frame,           50
And the rich locks, whose glow
    Death cannot tame;

Only one thought, one power,
    *Thee* could have led,
So, through the tempest's hour,
    To lift thy head!

Only the true, the strong,
    The love, whose trust
Woman's deep soul too long
    Pours on the dust!          60

SUPPLEMENT

TO THE MEMORY OF LORD CHARLES MURRAY
*Who died in the Cause, and lamented by the People of Greece*[3]

*Time cannot teach Forgetfulness*
*When Grief's full heart is fed by Fame.*[4]

Thou shouldst have slept beneath the stately pines,
And with th' ancestral trophies of thy race;
Thou that hast found, where alien tombs and shrines
Speak of the past, a lonely dwelling-place!
Far from thy brethren hath thy couch been spread,
Thou young bright Stranger midst the mighty Dead!

Yet to thy name a noble rite was given!
Banner and dirge met proudly o'er thy grave,
Under that old and glorious Grecian heaven,
Which unto death so oft hath led the brave;                    10
And thy dust blends with mould heroic there,
With all that sanctifies th' inspiring air.

Vain voice of Fame! Sad sound for those that weep!
For her, the mother, in whose bosom lone
Thy childhood dwells! Whose thoughts a record keep
Of smiles departed and sweet accents gone;
Of all thine early grace and gentle worth—
A vernal promise, faded now from earth!

But a bright memory claims a proud regret;
A lofty sorrow finds its own deep springs                      20
Of healing balm; and *She* hath treasures yet,
Whose soul can number with Love's holy things
A name like thine!—Now past all cloud or spot,
A gem is hers, laid up where change is not.

---

[1] "A few days ago I had the pleasure of receiving your very elegant pieces 'To the Memory of Lord C. Murray' and 'Woman on the field of Battle,'" Blackwood wrote to FH on 27 September 1827; "Unfortunately this Nº was all at press before they came to hand but they will appear in the next one. [. . .] I would be most happy if you found it agreeable to write pieces of greater length whether in prose or verse" (BA MS 30310, ff. 282–83). Both poems first appeared in sequence in *Blackwood's* 22 (November 1827): 585–88, signed "F. H." The starkly alternating dimeter and trimeter lines of *Woman* mime the drumbeat of a funeral dirge. In a far more lurid *The Field of Battle*, a young maid discovers her beloved horribly wounded and dying (*Gentleman's and London Magazine*, May 1794; *Courier*, 11 January 1800; rpt. Bennett's anthology 112–13), author unknown.

[2] FH's epigraph; cf. a "reed shaken with the wind" (Matthew 11.7).

[3] The "Cause" is the Greek War for Independence, an enthusiasm for many English, including Byron, who also died in Greece in April 1824. In Blackwood's 1873 edition, the title adds

"Son of the Duke of Atholl" after "Charles Murray," signaling his status as an aristocrat, like Lord Byron. The verse form is the "Venus and Adonis" stanza.

⁴ Byron, *On the Death of Sir Peter Parker, Bart.* (*Morning Chronicle*, 7 October 1814, 31–32); rpt. *Hebrew Melodies* (1815) and *Childe Harold's Pilgrimage* (1815 ed.). Parker, Byron's first cousin and brother of his boyhood love Margaret Parker, was killed in 1814 in the British assault on Baltimore; "he was a very gallant & popular officer—young & not long married," Byron remarked.

---

## *The Deserted House*[1]

Gloom is upon thy lonely hearth,
O silent house! once fill'd with mirth;[2]
Sorrow is in the breezy sound
Of thy tall poplars whispering round.

The shadow of departed hours
Hangs dim upon thine early flowers;
Even in thy sunshine seems to brood
Something more deep than solitude.

Fair art thou, fair to a stranger's gaze,
Mine own sweet home of other days!                    10
My children's birth-place! yet for me,
It is too much to look on thee.

Too much! for all about thee spread,
I feel the memory of the dead,
And almost linger for the feet
That never more my step shall meet.

The looks, the smiles, all vanish'd now,
Follow me where thy roses blow;
The echoes of kind household-words
Are with me 'midst thy singing birds.                 20

Till my heart dies, it dies away
In yearnings for what might not stay;
For love which ne'er deceived my trust,
For all which went with "dust to dust!"[3]

What now is left me, but to raise
From thee, lorn spot! my spirit's gaze,
To lift, through tears, my straining eye
Up to my Father's house on high?

Oh! many are the mansions there,[4]
But not in one hath grief a share!                    30

No haunting shade from things gone by,
May there o'ersweep the unchanging sky.

And *they* are there, whose long-loved mien
In earthly home no more is seen;
Whose places, where they smiling sate,
Are left unto us desolate.

We miss them when the board is spread;
We miss them when the prayer is said;
Upon our dreams their dying eyes
In still and mournful fondness rise.                                    40

But they are where these longings vain
Trouble no more the heart and brain;
The sadness of this aching love
Dims not our Father's house above,

Ye are at rest, and I in tears,[5]
Ye dwellers of immortal spheres!
Under the poplar boughs I stand,
And mourn the broken household band.

But, by your life of lowly faith,
And by your joyful hope in death,                                       50
Guide me, till on some brighter shore,
The sever'd wreath is bound once more!

Holy ye were, and good, and true!
No change can cloud my thoughts of you;
Guide me, like you to live and die,
And reach my Father's house on high!

[1] First published *NMM* 20 (March 1827): 238–39, signed "F. H." The stanza is the same as that of *The Land of Dreams*, not only linking the two poems but also joining them to Shelley's *The Sensitive Plant*. FH wrote this poem just after the death of her mother, in January. In 1824, the family had moved from Bronwylfa, their home of many years.

[2] Cf. Ecclesiastes: "The heart of the wise is in the house of mourning, but the heart of fools is in the house of mirth" (7.4).

[3] Genesis 3.19; cf. the final line of *Woman on the Field of Battle*.

[4] In my Father's house there are many mansions. JOHN, chap. xiv. [FH]

[5] From an ancient Hebrew dirge: / "Mourn for the mourner, and not for the dead; / For he is at rest, and we in tears!" [FH]

From *The Talmud of Babylonia* (25, column B); cf. trans. Jacob Neusner (Atlanta, Ga.: Scholars Press, 1992) 105. FH's translation is closer to the Hebrew than his.

*NMM*] and *I* in tears [the italic enhancing the metrical stress]. "They" (33) was not italicized. Other variants of note are symbolic capitals: Home (10), House (2, 28, 44, 56).

# Miscellaneous Poems

## *Corinne at the Capitol*

[In the 1827 *Literary Souvenir* (189–91), the title was *Corinna at the Capitol*, an allusion to Corinna (fl. 5th c. B.C.), the most renowned Boeotian poet of Greek antiquity after Pindar, reportedly winning five victories over him for the lyric (singing) prize. FH changes her poem's title here to match the English title of book 2 of Staël's popular novel *Corinne, ou l'Italie* (1807). Germaine de Staël (1766–1817) herself was famous for her intellect and social charm, her essays and frank conversation (including blunt criticism of Napoleon); her salons were attended by political and literary celebrities, and she often styled herself after her famous heroine. Quickly translated into English, *Corinne* deeply impressed many women, not only Hemans but also Jane Austen, Mary Godwin (Shelley), Elizabeth Barrett, George Eliot, and Harriet Beecher (see Ellen Moers, *Literary Women*). It was the definitive story of female "genius"—at once an inspiration and a cautionary fable about the cost in domestic happiness of fame and creative fulfillment. Half English and half Italian, Corinne is a famous improvisatrice (performing poet) living in Italy, where she meets English Lord Nelvil. It is from his point of view that we see her for the first time, at the Roman Capitol, where she is celebrated in all her glorious genius. Staël elaborates her triumph, even giving the text of "Corinne's Improvisation at the Capitol," and concluding in a female apotheosis: "No longer a fearful woman, she was an inspired priestess, joyously devoting herself to the cult of genius." Corinne and Nelvil fall in love, but she declines his proposal of marriage, fearing the constraints of life as an English wife. He returns to England and marries her half-sister, a proper English maid, and when Corinne learns of this, she dies of a broken heart.

   FH wrote "C'est moi" next to this passage at the end of bk. 4 of her copy of *Corinne*: "de toutes mes facultés la plus puissante, c'est la faculté de souffrir. Je suis née pour le bonheur, mon caractère est confiant, mon imagination est animée; mais la peine excite en moi je ne sais quelle impétuosité qui peut troubler ma raison ou me donner de la mort. Je vous le répète encore, ménagez-moi; la gaieté, la mobilité ne me servent qu'en apparence: mais il y a dans mon ame des abîmes de tristesse dont je ne pouvais me défendre qu'en me préservant de l'amour" (*CM* 1.304); "Of all my faculties, the most powerful is the faculty of suffering. I was born for happiness, my character is confident, my imagination is inspired; but pain excites in me I know not what impetuosity that can disturb my reason, or kill me. I repeat to you again, be caring of me; gaiety, mobilité [resilience] serve me only in appearance: but there are in my soul abysses of sadness against which I cannot protect myself except by keeping myself away from love."]

> *"Les femmes doivent penser [. . .] qu'il est dans cette carrière bien peu de sorts qui puissent valoir la plus obscure vie d'une femme aimée et d'une mère heureuse."*
>                                                    MADAME DE STAËL[1]

Daughter of th' Italian heaven!
Thou, to whom its fires are given,
Joyously thy car hath roll'd
Where the conqueror's pass'd of old;

And the festal sun that shone,
O'er three² hundred triumphs gone,
Makes thy day of glory bright,
With a shower of golden light.

Now thou tread'st th' ascending road,
Freedom's foot so proudly trode;                    10
While, from tombs of heroes borne,
From the dust of empire shorn,
Flowers upon thy graceful head,
Chaplets of all hues, are shed,
In a soft and rosy rain,
Touch'd with many a gemlike stain.

Thou hast gain'd the summit now!
Music hails thee from below;—
Music, whose rich notes might stir
Ashes of the sepulchre;                             20
Shaking with victorious notes
All the bright air as it floats.
Well may woman's³ heart beat high
Unto that proud harmony!

Now afar it rolls—it dies—
And thy voice is heard to rise
With a low and lovely tone
In its thrilling power alone;
And thy lyre's deep silvery string,
Touch'd as by a breeze's wing,                      30
Murmurs tremblingly at first,
Ere the tide of rapture burst.

All the spirit of thy sky
Now hath lit thy large dark eye,
And thy cheek a flush hath caught
From the joy of kindled thought;
And the burning words of song
From thy lip flow fast and strong,
With a rushing stream's delight
In the freedom of its might.                        40

Radiant daughter of the sun!
Now thy living wreath is won.
Crown'd of Rome!—Oh! art thou not
Happy in that glorious lot?—

Happier, happier far than thou,
With the laurel on thy brow,[4]
She that makes the humblest hearth
Lovely but to one on earth!

[1] Women must realize that there is in this career very little of the conditions that are equal in worth to the most obscure life of a beloved wife and a happy mother.

*De l'influence des Passions sur le Bonheur des Individus et des Nations* (Lausanne, Switzerland, 1796; Paris, Treuttel et Würtz, 1820), ch. 3, "De la Vanité" 103–4 (*femme* means both "woman" and "wife"). FH was reading this passage: En étudiant le petit nombre de femmes qui ont de vrais titres à la gloire, on verra que cet effort de leur nature fut toujours aux dépens de leur bonheur. Après avoir chanté les plus douces leçons de la morale et de la philosophie, Sapho [sic] se précipita du haut du rocher de Leucade; Élisabeth, après avoir dompté les ennemis de l'Angleterre, périt victime de sa passion pour le comte d'Essex. Enfin, avant d'entrer dans cette carrière de gloire, soit que trône des Césars, ou les couronnes du génie littéraire en soient le but, les femmes doivent penser que, pour la gloire même, il faut renoncer au bonheur et au repos de la destinée de leur sexe: et qu'il est dans cette carrière bien peu de sorts qui puissent valoir la plus obscure vie d'une femme aimée et d'une mère heureuse. (In studying the small number of women who have true titles to glory, one will see that this effort of their nature was always at the expense of their happiness. After having sung the sweetest lessons of morality and philosophy, Sappho threw herself from the top of the rock of Leucade; Elizabeth, after having conquered the enemies of England, perished victim of her passion for the earl of Essex. Finally, before entering on this career of glory, whether the goal be the throne of the Caesars or the crowns of literary genius, women must realize that, for glory itself, it is necessary to renounce the happiness and the peaceful destiny of their sex: and that in this career . . .).

[2] The trebly hundred triumphs.—Byron. [FH]

*Childe Harold's Pilgrimage IV*, lxxxii (731), a lament on the number of triumphs (victory parades) that were the glory of ancient Rome.

[3] *LS*] Woman's

[4] Poets were honored with wreaths of laurel, the badge of Apollo, god of the sun and poetry.

---

## *The Diver*[1]

*"They learn in suffering what they teach in song."*
SHELLEY[2]

Thou hast been where the rocks of coral grow,
    Thou hast fought with eddying waves;—
Thy cheek is pale, and thy heart beats low,
    Thou searcher of ocean's caves!

Thou hast looked on the gleaming wealth of old,
    And wrecks where the brave have striven;
The deep is a strong and a fearful hold,
    But thou its bar hast riven!

A wild and weary life is thine;
  A wasting task[3] and lone,                                10
Though treasure-grots for thee may shine,
  To all besides unknown!

A weary life! but a swift decay
  Soon, soon shall set thee free;
Thou'rt passing fast from thy toils[4] away,
  Thou wrestler with the sea!

In thy dim eye, on thy hollow cheek,
  Well are the death-signs read—
Go! for the pearl in its cavern seek,
  Ere hope and power be fled!                               20

And bright in beauty's coronal
  That glistening gem shall be;
A star to all in the festive hall—
  But who will think on *thee?*

None!—as it gleams from the queen-like head,
  Not one 'midst throngs will say,
"A life hath been like a rain-drop shed,
  For that pale quivering ray."

Woe for the wealth thus dearly bought!—
  —And are not those like thee                              30
Who win for earth the gems of thought?
  O wrestler with the sea!

Down to the gulfs of the soul they go,
  Where the passion-fountains burn,
Gathering the jewels far below
  From many a buried urn:

Wringing from lava-veins the fire,
  That o'er bright words is pour'd!
Learning deep sounds, to make the lyre
  A spirit in each chord.                                   40

But, oh! the price of bitter tears,
  Paid for the lonely power
That throws at last, o'er desert years,
  A darkly-glorious dower!

Like flower-seeds, by the wild wind spread,
  So radiant thoughts are strewed;
—The soul whence those high gifts are shed,
  May faint in solitude!

And who will think, when the strain is sung,
  Till a thousand hearts are stirr'd,                                    50
What life-drops, from the minstrel wrung,
  Have gush'd with every word?

None, none!—his treasures live like thine,
  *He* strives and dies like thee;
—Thou, that hast been to the pearl's dark shrine,
  O wrestler with the sea!

---

[1] First published in *NMM* 28 (January 1830): 62–63, signed "Felicia Hemans." Jane Williams (see below) uses lines 41–52 as her epigraph for her chapter on FH. The stanza is a ballad form.
   [2] From Shelley's *Julian and Maddalo* (1824), spoken by the benevolent but disillusioned Maddalo (clearly Byron), about a lovelorn maniac: "Most wretched men / Are cradled into poetry by wrong, / They learn in suffering what they teach in song" (544–46). *NMM* epigraph begins at "wretched" and Shelley is unnamed. For FH's uneasiness about citing Shelley, see her letter of 14 February ?1828. For FH's "passionate admiration" of his poetry, especially *Marianne's Dream*, *Ode to the West Wind*, and *Prometheus Unbound*, see *CM* 1.296 and Lawrence 341. Shelley had drowned at sea in 1822, and was known to be suicidal.
   [3] *NMM*] toil
   [4] *NMM*] the strife

# Late Poems

## (1831–34)

———⟨∾⟩———

## *The Last Song of Sappho*[1]

[The poetry of Sappho of the isle of Lesbos (fl. 610 B.C.) survives only in fragments. In FH's day, her story was hetero- rather than homosexual: a suicide in love-despair over boatman Phaon. See Pope's translation of Ovid's fifteenth epistle, *Sappho to Phaon* (1707): "If not from Phaon I must hope for ease, / Ah let me seek it from the raging seas: / To raging seas unpited I'll remove, / And either cease to live or cease to love!" (256–59). FH loved Grillparzer's German verse tragedy *Sappho* (1818) (*CM* 1.272, 290), and she knew Staël's verse tragedy *Sappho, drame en cinq actes* (1821). Mary Robinson established her poetic fame with her sonnet sequence *Sappho and Phaon* (1796) and signed her work thereafter "Sappho." In L.E.L.'s *The Improvisatrice* (1824), the heroine's first inset poem is her version of the farewell, *Sappho's Song*. FH's numerous echoes of these precedents define a melancholy Sapphic sorority. For the tradition, see Margaret Reynolds, Lawrence Lipking, Yopie Prins.]

> *What is Poesy, but to create*
>    *From overfeeling, good or ill, and aim*
> *At an external life beyond our fate,*
> *[. . .]*
>    *Bestowing fire from Heaven, and then, too late,*
> *Finding the pleasure given repaid with pain!*
>    *And vultures to the heart of the bestower,*
> *Who, having lavish'd his high gift in vain,*
>    *Lies chain'd to his lone rock by the sea shore?*
>                       —Byron's Prophecy of Dante[2]

Sound on, thou dark, unslumbering sea!
   My dirge is in thy moan;
My spirit finds response in thee,
To its own ceaseless cry—"Alone, alone!"

Yet send me back one other word,
   Ye tones that never cease!
Oh! let your secret caves be stirr'd,
And say, deep waters! can ye give me peace?[3]

Away!—my weary soul hath sought
   In vain one echoing sigh,                                    10
One answer to consuming thought
In human hearts—and will the *wave* reply?

Sound on, thou dark, unslumbering sea!
   Sound in thy scorn and pride!
I ask not, alien world! from *thee*,
What my own kindred earth hath still denied!

And yet I loved that earth so well,
   With all its lovely things!
Was it for *this* the death-wind fell
On my rich lyre, and quench'd its living strings?         20

Let them lie silent at my feet!
   Since, broken even as they,
The heart, whose music made them sweet,
Hath pour'd on desert sands its wealth away.

Yet glory's light hath touch'd my name,
   The laurel-wreath is mine—
With a worn[4] heart, a weary frame,
O restless Deep! I come to make them thine!

Give to that crown, that burning crown,
   Place in thy darkest hold!                  30
Bury my anguish, my renown,
With hidden wrecks, lost gems, and wasted gold!

Thou sea-bird on the billow's crest!
   Thou hast thy love, thy home!
They wait thee in the quiet nest—
And I—unsought, unwatch'd-for—I too come!

I, with this winged nature fraught,
   These visions, brightly[5] free,
This boundless love, this fiery thought—
*Alone* I come—O! give me peace, dark Sea!        40

[1] Text: *Blackwood's Edinburgh Magazine* 29 (January 1831): 129, signed "Mrs. Hemans." Rpt.
*National Lyrics and Songs for Music* (1834).

[2] Published 1821. Cf. 4.11–19, but eliding 14: "And be the new Prometheus of new men."
Prometheus was punished for stealing fire from heaven and giving it to man. In 4.1–10 (which
may have reflected FH's melancholy about her fame), Byron's Dante contemplates the happiness of those poets who "compress'd / The god within them, and rejoin'd the stars / Unlaurell'd
upon earth, but far more blest / Than those who are degraded by the jars / Of passion, and their
frailties link'd to fame, / Conquerors of high renown, but full of scars" (4–9).

   epigraph in *Lyrics*] Suggested by a beautiful sketch, the design of the younger Westmacott.
It represents Sappho sitting on a rock above the sea, with her lyre cast at her feet. There is a
desolate grace about the whole figure, which seems penetrated with the feeling of utter
abandonment.

   In addition to the picture by Richard Westmacott (1799–1872), FH was deeply impressed
by the "statue of Sappho, representing her at the moment she receives the tidings of Phaon's

desertion," by Westmacott's associate John Gibson (1790–1866). See her letter of 1831 on Sappho, *CM* 2.172–73, and Lawrence 343–44.

  [3] *Lyrics*] dark waters! will ye give me *peace?*
  [4] *Lyrics*] lone
  [5] *Lyrics*] wildly

## To My Own Portrait

[Alaric Watts, editor of the *Literary Souvenir,* commissioned William Edward West (famed for having "painted the last likeness ever taken of Lord Byron" and of his mistress Teresa Guiccioli in 1822) to do a portrait of Hemans for his gallery of "the living authors of Great Britain." He did three in autumn 1827 at her home, Rhyllon, presenting the last to her sister, an engraving of which appears as the frontispiece of her *Memoir.* Another was exhibited the following May in London at the Royal Academy, Somerset House, where Baillie hoped to see it, telling FH (whom she had never met) that she expected none to be "more sought for and observed" (5 May 1828; *Letters* 1162); she had seen it by 4 June (HL, ALS). See also FH to Mitford, 23 March 1828, *HM* 129, and Lawrence 348. In the summer of 1830, FH reacts to another celebrity icon: "Imagine my dismay on visiting Mr. [Angus] Fletcher's sculpture-room, on beholding at least *six Mrs. Hemans,* placed as if to greet me in every direction. There is something absolutely frightful in this multiplication of one's self to *infinity*" (*CM* 2.150). Lawrence liked this marble bust (which was commissioned by Sir Robert Liston and later exhibited in London, Liverpool, and elsewhere): "excellent [. . .] very like her, and very pleasing" (347). Text: *Poetical Remains.* In his review of this volume for *Athenæum* 437 (12 March 1836), Chorley quotes the poem entire.]

How is it that before mine eyes,
  While gazing on thy mien,
All my past years of life arise,
  As in a mirror seen?
What spell within thee hath been shrined,
To image back my own deep mind?

Even as a song of other times,
  Can trouble memory's springs;
Even as a sound of vesper-chimes,
  Can wake departed things;          10
Even as a scent of vernal flowers
Hath records fraught with vanished hours;

Such power is thine!—they come, the dead,
  From the grave's bondage free,
And smiling back the changed are led,
  To look in love on thee;
And voices that are music flown
Speak to me in the heart's full tone.

This portrait of Felicia Hemans, at once wistful, modest, and fetching, was painted by William E. West. It inspired her poem *To My Own Portrait*, and her sister reports that the family considered it "the best ever taken of her." Edward Scriven's engraving, with Hemans's signature underneath, served as the frontispiece for volume 1 of Blackwood's *Works of Mrs. Hemans* (Edinburgh, 1839), which contains the *Memoir*

Till crowding thoughts my soul oppress,
   The thoughts of happier years,                           20
And a vain gush of tenderness
   O'erflows in child-like tears;
A passion which I may not stay,
A sudden fount that must have way.

But thou, the while—oh! almost strange,
   Mine imaged self! it seems
That on *thy* brow of peace no change
   Reflects my own swift dreams;
Almost I marvel not to trace
Those lights and shadows in *thy* face.                        30

To see *thee* calm, while powers thus deep—
   Affection—Memory—Grief—
Pass o'er my soul as winds that sweep
   O'er a frail aspen leaf!
Oh, that the quiet of thine eye
Might sink there when the storm goes by!

Yet look thou still serenely on,
   And if sweet friends there be
That when my song and soul are gone
   Shall seek my form in thee,                            40
Tell them of One for whom 'twas best
To flee away and be at rest!

---

## The Lyre and Flower[1]

A lyre its plaintive sweetness pour'd
   Forth on the wild wind's track;
The stormy wanderer jarr'd the chord,
   But gave no music back.
     Oh! child of song,
   Bear hence to heaven thy fire!
What hop'st thou from the reckless throng?
    Be not like that lost lyre—
     Not like that lyre!

A flower its leaves and odour cast                              10
   On a swift-rolling wave;
Th' unheeding torrent darkly pass'd,
   And back no treasure gave.

Oh! heart of love,
Waste not thy precious dower!
Turn to thine only home above!
Be not like that lost flower—
Not like that flower!

[1] One of a group of seven *Words for Melodies*, in *NMM* 39 (December 1832), 412, signed "Mrs. Hemans." With melodies by Chorley and J. Z. Hermann, these songs were also published by Power (see Jewsbury's *Athenæum* essay).

---

## From *Records of the Autumn of 1834:*
### *Design and Performance*

[Some of FH's first poems were sonnets, and in 1818 she published her translations of sonnets, sixteen by 16th-c. Portuguese poet Luis de Camoens, and others by 16th- and 17th-c. European poets, some well known (Filicaja, Quevedo, Tasso, Petrarch, and Pindemonte) and some less so (Pastorini, Della Casa, Bentivoglio, Juan de Tarsis, Francesco Lorenzini, Francisco Manuel, Bernardo Tasso). In the 1830s she returned to sonnets in earnest. The "Miscellaneous Poems" in *Scenes, and Hymns of Life* (1834) includes two sonnet sequences (many first published in *Blackwood's*, 1833–34): 15 grouped as *Female Characters of Scripture* and seventeen as *Sonnets, Devotional and Memorial*—a sequence she planned to extend with 22 more sonnets, in *Records of the Spring 1834* (about half published in *NMM* in 1834). Her last composition was a set of eight sonnets, *Thoughts During Sickness*, intended as a sequel to a ten-sonnet sequence, *Records of the Autumn of 1834*. Seven *Thoughts* sonnets were published in *NMM* in March 1835; the last, *Sabbath Sonnet*, she dictated to her brother just weeks before her death in mid-May; it appeared in *Blackwood's* in July. *Design and Performance* is the seventh sonnet of *Records of the Autumn*; it was first published in *Poetical Remains* (1836). Chorley quoted it in *CM* up to "I sink" (10) (giving the title as "Desire and Performance") and remarked that FH suffered "severely [...] from feeling the impossibility of doing justice to her own conceptions, of giving adequate utterance to the thoughts which arose within her, all the more brightly and fervently as she approached the close of her career" (2.298).]

They float before my soul, the fair designs
Which I would body forth to Life and Power,
Like clouds, that with their wavering hues and lines
Pourtray majestic buildings:—Dome and tower,
Bright spire, that through the rainbow and the shower
Points to th' unchanging stars; and high arcade
Far-sweeping to some glorious altar, made
For holiest rites:—meanwhile the waning hour
Melts from me, and by fervent dreams o'erwrought,
I sink:—O friend! O link'd with each high thought

Aid me, of those rich visions to detain
All I may grasp; until thou see'st fulfill'd,
While time and strength allow, my hope to build
For lowly hearts devout, but *one* enduring fane!

*October* 18.

---

# From *Blackwood's Edinburgh Magazine,* July 1835:
## *Sabbath Sonnet*

*Composed by Mrs Hemans a few days before her death,
and dedicated to her brother*

How many blessed groups this hour are bending
Through England's primrose meadow paths their way,
Towards spire and tower, 'midst shadowy elms ascending,
Whence the sweet chimes proclaim the hallowed day.[1]
The Halls from old heroic ages grey
Pour their fair children forth; and hamlets low
With those thick orchard-blooms the soft winds play,
Send out their inmates in a happy flow,
Like a freed vernal stream. I may not tread[2]
With them those pathways,—to the feverish bed          10
Of sickness bound;—yet, oh my God! I bless
Thy mercy, that with Sabbath peace hath filled
My chastened heart, and all its throbbings stilled
To one deep calm of lowliest thankfulness.

[1] HM 311] day!
[2] HM 311] *I* may not tread

# LETTERS

—❧—

**To her aunt** in Liverpool, 19 December 1808.[1] "The noble Spaniards!"

You have, I know, perused the papers (as I have done,) with <u>anxiety</u>, though, perhaps, without the <u>tremors</u> which I continually experience. The noble Spaniards! surely, surely, they will be crowned with success: I have never given up the cause, notwithstanding the late disastrous intelligence; but I think their prospects begin to wear a brighter appearance, and we may hope that the star of freedom, though long obscured by clouds, will again shine with transcendent radiance. You will smile, my dear aunt, but you know not what an <u>enthusiast</u> I am in the cause of Castile[2] and liberty: my whole heart and soul are interested for the gallant patriots, and though females are forbidden to interfere in politics, yet as I have a dear, dear brother, at present on the scene of action, I may be allowed to feel some ardour on the occasion. [. . .] You see I am writing on the anniversary of George's birthday;[3] and I know you will pray that every year may see his progress in virtue and true heroism. I am proud that he is at present on the theatre of glory; and I hope he will have an opportunity of signalizing his courage, and of proving an honour to his family and an ornament to his profession. I am this very moment wishing that I possessed a small portion of that patience with which my mother is so eminently gifted, for the paper is not yet arrived, and you may imagine the petulance of your "<u>little obstreperous niece</u>." I have been reading a most delightful French romance, by Madame de Genlis, "Le Siege de la Rochelle"; you would be in raptures with it. [. . .] I think it excels "Corinne," which is certainly bestowing a very high eulogium upon any work.[4] Lady Kirkwall paid us a long and highly agreeable visit a few days ago, and brought me these volumes, which I have perused with such enthusiasm: she bestowed great commendation upon "Valour and Patriotism," and I hope it will justify her encomiums.[5] [. . .] Glorious, glorious Castilians! may victory crown your noble efforts. Excuse me for dwelling so much on this subject; for Spain is the subject of my thoughts and words--"my dream by night, my vision of the day."[6] Can you be surprised at my enthusiasm? My head is half turned, but still steady enough to assure you that I remain ever, my dearest aunt,

Your attached and affectionate<br>"Felicia"

[1] *CM* 1.30–33. The two sisters of FH's mother (the Misses Wagner) lived in Liverpool.

[2] A medieval Christian kingdom, later a powerful dynasty. Napoleon invaded Spain in 1807, put his brother on the throne and forbade trade with Britain. Britain immediately allied with

Portugal and Spanish resisters; Captain Hemans and FDB's brothers Thomas and George served in the Peninsular War, George under the hero-martyr Sir John Moore.

[3] Her brother, in Spain. He would return from war disillusioned with a military career.

[4] Germaine de Staël's popular novel (1807). Stéphanie Félicité de Crest de Saint-Aubin, Comtesse de Genlis, later Marchionesse de Sillery Brulart (1746–1830), was famous for her romances and didactic children's literature. A liberal aristocrat, she initially supported the French Revolution (Helen Maria Williams gives an account of her in *Letters from France*) but, like many aristocrats, fled during the Terror. *Le Siège de la Rochelle* concerns the devastation of this French Atlantic coast city about halfway between Nantes and Bordeaux, a Protestant-Huguenot stronghold in the sixteenth century. During the reign of Louis XIII (1601–43), La Rochelle sided with the English. As part of a campaign of suppression Chief Minister Cardinal Richelieu ordered it besieged in 1627 and had constructed a vast sea wall to prevent aid from English ally Charles I. It fell in 1628 after fourteen months, three-quarters of its population having starved. Byron's friend R. C. Dallas published a translation, *The Siege of La Rochelle, or the Christian Heroine*, in 1813.

[5] *England and Spain; or Valour and Patriotism* (1808), later translated into Spanish. For encouraging her efforts, FDB thanked Viscountess Kirkwall with stanzas in *Poems* (1808).

[6] Perhaps remembering Pope's *Sappho to Phaon* (1736): "'Tis thou art all my care and my delight / My daily longing, and my dream by night" (143–44); or more recently, Robert Southey's Proem to *Carmen Nuptial: The Lay of the Laureate*: "How then to build the imperishable lay / Was then my daily care, my dream by night" (7–8).

---

**To Matthew Nicholson,** Richmond Row, Liverpool. Bronwylfa, 17 July 1811.[1] Reynolds's discourses; "reading a *Romance*"; learning Spanish

[...] Harriett and myself are going to Conway[2] next Friday & I shall take advantage of the picturesque scenery by which we shall be surrounded, to improve myself in drawing; as I am convinced that the practice of taking views from nature, is the principal way of acquiring that spirit and correctness, which alone constitute superior excellence. I have been reading lately the memoirs of Sir Joshua Reynolds, with his discourses to the Royal Academy, & I am so enthusiastic an admirer of the beauties of painting, that I derived both pleasure and instruction from the perusal. Will you assume a very good grave, <u>mentorial</u> face, & give me a long lecture, when I tell you I have also <u>been guilty</u> of reading a <u>Romance</u>? It is "The Scottish Chiefs," by Miss Porter,[3] & though I am by no means an Advocate for <u>Historical</u> Novels as they bewilder our ideas, by confounding truth with fiction, yet this animated Authoress has painted her Hero, the Patriot William Wallace, in such glowing colours, that you cannot avoid catching a spark of her own enthusiasm, as you follow him through the incidents of the Narrative—I am teaching myself Spanish, and find it much easier than I expected, but I envy all Latin Scholars, for the great facility with which <u>they</u> must acquire every new language, in consequence of an advantage from which so many are debarred. [...]

[1] LL MS 920 NIC 29/96; cf. Francis Nicholson, "Correspondence" 32–33. This article also supplies the following information. Matthew Nicholson (1746–1819) was educated at the Warrington Academy, a dissenting institution. Among his teachers were Joseph Priestley and the headmaster, John Aikin, whose brilliant daughter Anna (later Barbauld) was also a student

at the time. Nicholson became a cotton merchant in Manchester and was sufficiently successful that he was able to retire at age forty-three to a home outside Liverpool (Richmond Row) and devote himself to various avocations, among them literature. He subscribed to four copies of FDB's 1808 *Poems*, fell in love with her when he met her, and told his sister that were he twenty years younger he would have proposed marriage. He organized the publication of *The Domestic Affections &c* from various poems he collected from FDB and her mother. Bronwylfa, the Browne family's home, is variously spelled; I follow that inscribed on FH's sketch in *1839*, volume 2 title page.

² To stay with their mother's friends, in this coastal town about ten miles away.

³ Jane Porter (1776–1850), *The Scottish Chiefs* (1810). In the vogue for historical novels sparked by Edgeworth and climaxing in Scott, this "biographical romance" about Scots nationalist Wallace (?1272–1305) was a stunning success, admired by Thomas Campbell, Mary Russell Mitford, Joanna Baillie. Reynolds (1723–92) was the first president of the Royal Academy. His fifteen famous *Discourses* (London: Edwin Malone, 1797; often republished) had been delivered as lectures from 1769 to 1790 .

---

**Felicity Browne (mother) to Matthew Nicholson,** Richmond Row, Liverpool. Bronwylfa, 7 February 1812.¹ Publishing *The Domestic Affections &c*; FDB's marriage and literary projects

[. . .] with regard to the offer of Messrs. Cadell & Davies, I am such a novice on the subject, as to be quite incompetent to judge of its liberality; but I would much rather depend upon your judgment, & that of Mr. Roscoe,² than upon my own; & whatever you think most advisable, will certainly appear to me the most so—if you act as you would for yourself, you will most oblige Felicia & me & you have unlimited discretionary powers on the occasion—I will, however, remark, that as Messrs. C. D have had the publication of the two first works,³ it appears to me most <u>respectable</u> that <u>any</u> future productions should come out through the same channel; even though more liberal terms might be obtained from others & I am sure C. & D. have it fully as much in their power to promote the sale of a work & thereby make it popular, as any Book-sellers in London, if they would think it worth their while to exert themselves a little in the cause; but they have certainly been hitherto very supine, & I have no reason to speak of their liberality, <u>excepting</u> that they have not called upon me for the expences of printing "England & Spain"—What a number of copies of that work they must have on hand, which a very little exertion might have enabled them to dispose of—If it is thought advisable that Mr. Millar⁴ should be spoken to, my friend & relation Mrs. Hurt, would write any letter for me to him, I am sure—she has a library worth some thousands of pounds, & he is her bookseller in London, so that it could not go through a more respectable channel; but I am decidedly of opinion that it would be better <u>eventually</u>, to remain with Messrs. C. D. & perhaps to accept the present offer—though again I repeat, that I would rather rely on your judgment than decide myself—

I must now, my dear Sir, expatiate with you upon a subject very near my heart, & which all your words & actions prove you to have a most sincere interest in—I need not say that this relates to the future hopes & fears for my beloved Felicia, whose youth & peculiar frame of mind, make her naturally an object of my most anxious maternal solicitations, on the present momentous occasion of her life— You will perhaps be surprised to hear that, young as she is, her present attachment has been the cause of much anxiety to herself & the object of it, for four years past; & perhaps I may say it has, in a great degree, alienated her mind from all delight in what the <u>world</u> generally calls <u>pleasure</u> & from every wish but that of domestic happiness—though she is a child in years, yet her mind is so mature, that I think her quite competent to decide for herself, on a subject wherein she alone, is most deeply concerned; & as splendor & riches were never objects of any consideration with her (nor with me for her) I trust she has as much prospect of happiness with the man of her choice, & I hope, a competence, as can reasonably be expected in this state of probation——He is a man whose morals & manners are unexceptionable & in whom I feel an affectionate interest, very little, (if at all,) less, than in my own sons—this will, I know, have great weight with you in the judgment you will form on this occasion—& I trust the progress of Felicia's Genius towards perfection will not be impeded by the additional motive she will have to cultivate it & that the "Domestic Affections," beautiful as some of its ideas are, is but a humble pledge of what we are to receive from her future pen—She has been wishing to write to you herself, for some time past, but thought she could not do it without mentioning this subject & it was too delicate for her to touch upon—now that you have spoken upon it, you will hear from her soon—I saw in the paper some time ago, that two thousand pounds would be given for the best translation of Lucian Bonaparte's poem of Charlemagne—Could you enquire where information respecting this could be had?—it is a work for which Felicia's perfect knowledge of the French tongue & poetical genius make her quite competent[5]—I read in the paper, of the fall of Ciudad Rodrigo & I see four men of the 23d. wounded at the siege,[6] but thank GOD the names of my sons are not in the fatal list & I hope soon to have George's account of the operations of the army—my last news from his brother & him were as favorable as I could possibly wish—Accept, my dear Sir, the best wishes & grateful expressions of the girls & myself, for all your goodness, & present our compliments & thanks to Mr. Roscoe—

believe me your obliged friend

F. D. Browne

[1] LL MS 920 NIC 29/104. Cf. Nicholson 34–35.

[2] Thomas Cadell Jr. (1773–1836) assumed his father's publishing firm, with William Davies as principal partner, until the latter's death. FH's mother was very dissatisfied with their neglect of *Poems* and *England and Spain*. William Stanley Roscoe (1782–1843), leading figure in Liverpool and a partner in his father's bank, wrote the Advertisement (preface) to and managed the subscription of FDB's 1808 *Poems*; Nicholson was among his many acquaintances. His father, William Roscoe (1753–1831), attorney, Whig M.P. (1806–7), rare book and print collector, poet, scholar, botanist, philanthropist, abolitionist, supporter of the French Revolution and Catholic rights, was a widely liked figure at the center of Liverpool's cultural life and Whig politics.

[3] *Poems* and *England and Spain* (both 1808).

⁴ William Miller (1769–1844), a leading publisher, was succeeded on his retirement in 1812 by John Murray, publisher of most of FH's volumes from 1816 to 1825.

⁵ Lucien Bonaparte (1775–1840), differing politically with his older brother Napoleon, embarked for the United States, but was interned by the British government at Ludlow, Shropshire; there he wrote *Charlemagne; ou, l'Eglise Délivrée* (London, 1814; Paris, 1815), a twenty-two-canto poem of 15,400 lines, dedicated to Pope Pius VIII. A notice in *Examiner* 196 (29 September 1811) announced the sale of the poem, "now in the press," and the poet's ambition for an English translation, for which "he has, though the bookseller, made an overture to [Thomas] Campbell [. . .] to undertake it for a remuneration of [£]2000" (626).

⁶ A fortified town in central Spain.

---

**To Matthew Nicholson,** Richmond Row, Liverpool. Bronwylfa, 12 March 1812.¹ Prospective marriage; literary projects

[. . .] be assured no change of prospect or situation will ever lessen the pleasure and improvement I shall always derive from your letters—You seem to think, my dear Sir, in your last letter, that my having "concentrated my affections" will interfere with the pursuit of my favorite studies; on the contrary, as the object of those affections, (to whom they have been long devoted, with all the enthusiasm of a first attachment & an ardent mind;) will have delight in encouraging my progress, & will know how to appreciate excellence—if I should ever attain it, I shall have in his approbation, an additional stimulus to exert. Were you fully acquainted with him, (which I w[ish] you were,) you would feel satisfied, that the happiness of your young friend could not rest on a more secure basis than his worth & attachment; on which I rely with the most deserved confidence, for all that is to cheer & illumine my future life.

—I have a particular desire to attempt a new style of writing, & think I should succeed in translation —could you, or would Mr. Roscoe, recommend any poem in French, Italian, or Spanish, which you think would be desirable? I have so few books in any of those languages, that though I have acquired the two latter without any assistance, I am not sufficiently acquainted with their literature to know if they possess any work of merit which has not yet had an English dress—
[. . .]

Your obliged and affectionate
Felicia Browne

¹ LL MS 920 NIC 29/105. Cf. Nicholson 35–36. By 2 March 1811, FDB was addressing Nicholson as "my dear, provoking Mentor" (Nicholson 27).

---

**To W[illiam] Stanley Roscoe.** Daventry, 22 October 1813.¹ Getting published

Dear Sir,

I avail myself of your kind offer to undertake the disposal of my manuscripts for me, persuaded as I am that they cannot be in the hands of one who will make more disinterested exertions for a perfect stranger—I leave it entirely to you to offer them either to Messrs. Longman &c, or to Mr. Johnstone,[2] but I do not wish my name to appear on the occasion—if they should be inclined to purchase the copy-right, you will perhaps have the goodness to fix what you would consider as an adequate compensation—I know not what apology to make for thus troubling you, but that I am so little conversant with subjects of this nature, & that I have no literary friends to interest themselves in bringing me forward— — I shall be extremely happy if this little work should obtain your approbation, in translating the <u>sonnets</u> of Camoens, &c which compose the greater part of the volume,[3] I have not attempted any adherence to the rules of that species of composition, the difficulties of which deterred me from endeavouring to overcome them in any continued series of translations—I should not have attempted to translate any of Camoens's sonnets, as Lord Strangford had published so numerous a collection, if I had not compared his works with the originals without being able to discover any pretensions to fidelity.[4] I shall be much indebted if you will inform me that you have received these manuscripts safely, & remain

Dear Sir<br>your obliged &c<br>Felicia Hemans

[1] LL 920 ROS 1991.

[2] The Edinburgh printing and engraving firm of Johnstone (brothers John and James) was employed by Blackwood and Cadell. The firm sometimes published, too. Thomas Norton Longman III (1771–1842), head of the firm founded by his father, published many Romantic-era writers, including Baillie, Coleridge, Southey, Scott, Wordsworth, and Thomas Moore.

[3] FH sent this MS to Murray November 1817; he published *Translations from Camoens &c* in 1818. The translations comprised 55 of 95 pages; "original poetry" included several dirges and elegies, the most famous, its closing piece, *Stanzas on the Late National Calamity, the Death of the Princess Charlotte* (first published as FH's debut in *Blackwood's Edinburgh Magazine*, April 1818). Murray's run of 200 earned modest profits but did not sell out.

[4] Percy Clinton Sydney Smythe, 6th Viscount Strangford (1780–1850), a diplomat, was posted to Lisbon in 1802; his *Poems from the Portuguese of Camoens* (1803) was ridiculed in Byron's *English Bards and Scotch Reviewers* (1809, lines 295–308). Strangford had a distinguished diplomatic career and a wide circle of literary friends, including John Wilson Croker (one of the subscribers to FDB's 1808 *Poems*), Thomas Moore, and Samuel Rogers, and was a frequent contributor to the *Gentleman's Magazine*.

---

**To John Murray.** Bronwylfa, 26 February 1817.[1] Sales and promotion

Dear Sir,

I send the M.S. by the Mail of to-day, and shall be extremely happy if it meets with your approbation—Had I been more fully aware of the very limited taste for the Arts which you inform me is displayed by the Public, I should certainly have applied myself to some other subject; but from having seen so many works advertised on Sculpture, Painting, &c. I was naturally led to imagine the contrary—I am much concerned to hear of your loss by the "Restoration" &c[2] and have reason to think that part of the second edition would have sold very well at

Oxford, as I have been told by friends that <u>many</u> of their acquaintance there, had enquired for it, and would have purchased it immediately had it been on the spot—I should have mentioned this circumstance to you at the time the 2d. Edition made its appearance, but imagined you must have been aware of it—As I have several friends at both Universities, and one in particular of great interest and high literary reputation at Cambridge, I cannot but think that the present work, if published, would be well received there and at Oxford,—and I could easily procure their exertions, even were it to appear without my name— Perhaps it would be more advantageous that it should not be known to proceed from a female pen, but this point I leave entirely to your decision—Should you, however, decide against its publication at all, I shall be much favored by your suggesting to me any subject, or style of writing, likely to be more popular, and also beg to be informed when Campbell's Lectures on English Poetry are to make their appearance[3]—I shall be happy to hear from you as soon as you have leisure, and remain, Dear Sir

your obliged servant
Felicia Hemans—

[1] MA. John Murray (1778–1843), son of the founder of the publishing firm and later its head, published Byron, Campbell, Austen, and many others, including a host of travel writers; he founded the influential *Quarterly Review* in 1809.

[2] *The Restoration of the Works of Art to Italy*. Although it received critical praise and went into a second edition (1816), it did not make much money for Murray. With this letter, FH enclosed *Modern Greece* for his approval. He published it in June.

[3] Campbell, already famous for *The Pleasures of Hope*, *Gertrude of Wyoming*, and several shorter poems, published *Specimens of the British Poets* with Murray in 1819 (Thomas Carlyle— uncharacteristically—gave it high praise, finding it "good" in both its "criticisms and pieces"). In the 1820s Campbell edited *NMM*, to which FH frequently contributed.

---

**To John Murray.** Bronwylfa, November 1817.[1] Seeking advice

[. . .] Accept my best thanks for the privilege you have kindly offered me of consulting you whenever I shall have fixed upon a subject likely to excite a more general interest than my former publications could claim—It is, I assure you, a privilege which I shall value highly, and of which I hope soon to avail myself [. . . .] I have now seen how little any work of mere sentiment or description is likely to obtain popularity, and have had warning enough to give up that style of writing altogether[. . . .] The sum you have given [for Byron's poems] really seems immense—I observe you have his Lordship upon your seal, I really think he ought to wear <u>you</u> on his.[2] [. . .]

[1] MA, Ledger B, f. 132.

[2] The stamp used on sealing-wax. In 1816, Murray paid £2,000 for *Childe Harold's Pilgrimage III* and *The Prisoner of Chillon*, improving on the £600 for *Childe Harold I–II*. He had probably mentioned to FH Byron's asking price for *Childe Harold IV*, "two thousand five hundred guineas" (£2,625). This was stated in a letter to Murray, 4 September 1817 (the same in which he

ridiculed *Modern Greece*), noting that Murray had offered Campbell 3,000 guineas for *Speci-mens*, that Moore received this same sum from Longman for *Lalla Rookh*, and that John Chetwode Eustace had been promised 2,000 for a long poem on education.

---

**To James Simpson, Esq.** Bronwylfa, 22 October 1819.[1]
Promoting a religious poem; reading societies; her signature; a subvention; Mary Brunton

My dear Sir,

The enclosed note will show that I have not been unmindful of your wishes with regard to the Monthly Edinburgh Review,[2] and you will, I trust, pardon the liberty I took in showing your last letter to me, as I thought it would recommend that work so much more powerfully than any thing I could say—the note is from the Dean of St. Asaph,[3] who is a man of distinguished literary taste and father-in-law to M$^r$ Reginald Heber, the author of "Palestine"; no one could so well contribute to make the work known in this country, his approbation being considered here as quite a sort of imprimatur—I shall now have the pleasure of reading the Review myself, as the Dean kindly allows me access to his library—There is a reading society at Denbeigh into which, though I am not a member, I think I can have it introduced, and my Mother has mentioned it to several of her correspondents who are subscribers to the public Libraries—My last letter to you must, I think have been rather an incoherent composition, as I was extremely unwell at the time I wrote; I forgot to mention in it what I fear it is now too late to suggest, that I wish to appear as Mrs. Hemans in the title page of the prize poem;[4] as that infelix Felicia is the subject of so many animadversions and allusions to Rosa Matilda, Laura Maria, and all the Della Cruscan tribe, that I am determined wholly to bid it good-bye[5]—I wish all parents would take warning from my fate, and give their Daughters such names as may be fit for the common purposes of life, such as Anne, Jane, or any other convenient monosyllable, as it is very tormenting to carry about with one a constant target for all the arrows of satire, which it is impossible ever to get quit of—Mr Blackwood's very liberal offer with regard to selling the prize-poem, I heard of through M$^{rs}$ Tucker [?], and beg you will offer my best thanks for his kindness[6]—Indeed, my dear sir, I have hardly any thing to do when I write to you, but to acknowledge some fresh instance of a disinterested liberality; I begin to feel almost the attachment of a native to your "own romantic town," and "had I the wings of a dove," should certainly fly thither to visit my unknown friends[7]—I have been much interested in the perusal of a work sent me some time since by Mr. Murray, the memoirs of the late M$^{rs}$ Brunton, and her beautiful though unfinished tale of "Emme-line."[8] I was delighted with the delicacy of feeling and principle displayed throughout the work, as well as the simple elegance of the style; it is altogether an affecting memorial of a character, whose virtue and talents seem to have been beautifully harmonized by the soft green of the the soul, on which the eye loves to repose.

Mrs. Simpson and your little family are, I trust, quite well; my Mother begs to write in every good wish to them and yourself, with, my dear Sir, your

most truly obliged

F. Hemans

[1] BL Add MS 33964, ff. 256–57. Simpson, a friend of Scott, was best known for *A Visit to Flanders in July 1815, chiefly being an account of the field of Waterloo* (Edinburgh: William Blackwood, 1815); based on his visit immediately after the celebrated British victory, it quickly went through nine editions. He would later publish *Letters to Sir Walter Scott, Bart. on the moral and political character and Effects of the Visit to Scotland in August 1822 of His Majesty King George IV* in *Blackwood's Edinburgh Magazine* 7.58 (1822)—a visit Scott arranged and managed.

[2] Perhaps *Edinburgh Monthly Review*, which would praise FH's works the next year; more likely, *Edinburgh Monthly Magazine*, edited by Rev. Robert Morehead, to which FH was an occasional contributor (*HM* 41).

[3] This is Dr. Shipley. Heber (1783–1826), Cathedral prebendary of St. Asaph, would be appointed Bishop of Calcutta in 1823. His Oxford prize-poem *Palestine* was published in 1807, and he had subscribed to FDB's 1808 *Poems*. FDB admired and memorized his *Europe* (1809), a poem of 424 lines in heroic couplets on the war in Spain. A famous hymn-writer and frequent contributor to the *Quarterly* and the *Christian Observer*, Heber counted Scott and Baillie among his friends. FH was looking for a publisher for *The Sceptic*; after Murray published it in 1820, Heber encouraged her to begin another defense of Christianity, which she provisionally titled *Superstition and Revelation* (*HM* 40), and he remained a valuable literary advisor (*HM* 39). Among the "Miscellaneous Pieces" of *Records &c* is *To the Memory of Heber*.

[4] *The Meeting of Wallace and Bruce on the Banks of the Carron* had been published in *Blackwood's*, September 1819. When Blackwood issued a separate volume, *Wallace's Invocation to Bruce, A Poem*, the title page read "By Mrs Hemans, Author of 'The Restoration of the Works of Art to Italy,' 'Modern Greece,' 'Tales and Historic Scenes,' and other poems."

[5] Founded in 1784 by self-styled ladies' poet Robert Merry, the self-dramatizing Society della Crusca volleyed coterie poetry back and forth, using quasi-literary, Italianate pseudonyms—"Della Crusca" (Merry), "Anna Matilda" (playwright Hannah Cowley), "Laura Maria" (Mary Darby Robinson, onetime mistress of the Prince Regent), "Rosa Matilda" (Gothic novelist Charlotte Dacre). Their extravagant artifice, literary allusiveness, theatricality, wit and eroticism, earned fame and infamy. The Society was brutally satirized by Tory William Gifford in *The Baviad* (1794) and *The Maeviad* (1795). In 1819 FH was seeking advice about her poetry from Gifford (now editing the *Quarterly*) and developing a cordial friendship with him.

[6] Mrs. Tucker may be the patron who underwrote Blackwood's publication of 500 copies in April 1820, priced at 3.5 shillings, with the proceeds going to FH; see *Edinburgh Magazine and Literary Miscellany* 84 (November 1819), 448, and Feldman, *KSJ* 156.

[7] The "romantic town" is Edinburgh; in Psalms 55, David yearns for the wings of a dove.

[8] FH loved the memoir of novelist Mary Brunton (b. 1778); in one letter she transcribes a lengthy passage from its conclusion, on Christian consolation (*HM* 36–38). Brunton died 19 December 1818 in Edinburgh, from a fever following the birth of a stillborn son, leaving unfinished her third novel, *Emmeline*, a cautionary tale of a couple who divorce their spouses in order to marry one another; it was published by Murray in 1819, with a memoir by her husband Dr. Alexander Brunton, professor at Edinburgh University and a preacher. Her first two novels were *Self-Control* (1811) and *Discipline* (1814), the latter supplying FH's epigraph for *Message from the Dead* (*Blackwood's* 24 [September 1828]: 353).

**To B. P. Wagner.** Bronwylfa, November 1819.[1] Favorable reviews of *Tales, and Historic Scenes*; "popular style"; brother George and his wife

My dear Uncle,

Encouraged by your very gratifying encomiums on my former publication, I venture to offer you a copy of the last, and need not say how highly I shall value your approbation, if you think the performance worthy of it—I have had the satisfaction of seeing it reviewed most favourably, in more than one popular work, and it has been honoured with the commendations of many who rank high in the literary world, but my pecuniary gains from it are all yet to come,[2] and I fear I must not expect much from a production the style of which is little suited to the present fashionable taste —Our first poets, such as Lord Byron, Walter Scott, and Moore have all set the example of writing what I call Novels in Verse, and those who hope for popularity and profit, must follow in the path these Leaders of the public taste, have marked out for them—I shall certainly ere long, make an attempt to write something in this popular style, though I must own it will be much against my inclination—Before you receive this you will I hope, have seen George and his Wife, & we shall be anxious to know your opinion of the latter—Though she possesses none of those brilliant qualities calculated to strike a superficial Observer she is amply endowed with all the less dazzling, but far more valuable ones of temper and heart which win and secure the affections, and her amiable disposition has endeared her to us all. [. . .][3]

[your] affectionate niece
Felicia Hemans

[1] HL MS 2137.

[2] The reviews were favorable. By the end of 1819, Murray split profits of £23.15.1 with FH, and by March 1821, split further profits of £94.19.1 (Feldman, *KSJ* 155).

[3] By this time, FH had separated from her husband, who reportedly complained that "it was the curse of having a literary wife that he could never get a pair of stockings mended" (*A Short Sketch of the Life of Mrs. Hemans* [1835], 32).

---

**To Harriett Browne (sister).** Wavertree Lodge, October 1820.[1]
The excitement of Liverpool, Kean's acting

I cannot tell you how much I have enjoyed the novelty of all the objects around me. The pastoral seclusion and tranquillity of the life I have led for the last seven or eight years, had left my mind in that state of blissful ignorance particularly calculated to render every new impression an agreeable one; and accordingly, gas-lights, steam-boats, Mr. Kean, casts from the Elgin marbles, and tropical plants in the Botanic Garden, have all in turn, been the objects of my wondering admiration. I saw Kean in two characters, Richard the Third, and Othello, and can truly say, I felt as if I had never understood Shakspeare till then. I shall never forget the sort of electric light which seemed to flash across my mind from the bursts of power he displayed in several of my favourite passages.[2]

<sup>1</sup> *HM* 42. Jane Williams's specifying of the addressee (418) may apply to some of the other letters in *HM* with unstated addressees. FH was visiting the family of Henry Park, Esq. His son John (1778–1847) was a member of the Royal College of Surgeons, the Linnean society, and was also a visionary theologian. His writings ranged from *Pathology of Fever* (1822) to tracts on the coming apocalypse. He was Baillie's neighbor in Hampstead in 1830.

<sup>2</sup> The passionate acting of Edmund Kean (1787–1833), at the height of his fame during the Regency, revolutionized the Shakespearean stage; among his celebrated roles were Richard III and Othello. "To his splendid *meteoric* talent [FH] did full justice; she said that 'seeing him act was like reading Shakspeare by flashes of lightning'" (*CM* 1.80). Coleridge is usually cited for the famous remark that "to see [Kean] act, is like reading Shakspeare by flashes of lightning" (27 April 1823; *Table Talk*, 2d ed., 1836), but editor Carl Woodring's admission that there is no manuscript, only hearsay, for this credit (*Table Talk* [1990] 1.xcii) makes it possible that FH's striking simile was reported to Coleridge, and (characteristically) he claimed it as his own. Cf. Hazlitt's disapproval, in *A View of the English Stage* (1818), of Kean's acting of Iago as "an excellent good fellow": "the light which illumines the character, should rather resemble the flashes of lightning in the murky sky, which make the darkness more terrible."

---

**To William Jerdan.** Bronwylfa, St. Asaph, 11 June 1821.<sup>1</sup>
Royal Society of Literature poetry prize competition

Mrs. Hemans presents her best compliments to the Editor of the 'Literary Gazette,' with many acknowledgments for his very polite attention in sending her the number of his Journal which has announced her success to the public in so gratifying a manner. She has also to express her sense of his kindness in procuring the insertion of the paragraph containing this intelligence in the principal newspapers—an attention which cannot fail to be serviceable to her publications.

With regard to the remarks on Mrs. Hemans' works, which have occasionally appeared in the 'Literary Gazette,' she begs to assure the Editor of that highly respectable Journal, that she can never feel otherwise than satisfied by any expression of fair and impartial criticism, and trusts she may always have sufficient candour to derive advantage from all observations dictated by such a spirit.<sup>2</sup>

Mrs. Hemans waits to be decided by the opinion of her literary friends on the subject of publishing the poem which has been so highly honoured by the Royal Society of Literature. Should those friends not recommend its separate publication, it will give her much pleasure to avail herself of the privilege offered by the Editor of the 'Literary Gazette.' If, in the mean time, the accompanying unpublished little pieces, to which her name may be affixed, should be considered worthy of insertion in that Journal, Mrs. H. begs the Editor will do her the favour of accepting them.<sup>3</sup>

Mrs. Hemans cannot conclude without a renewal of her sincere thanks for that gentleman's liberal assurances of his disposition to serve her, and kind congratulations on her present very unexpected success.

<sup>1</sup> *The Autobiography of William Jerdan* (London: Arthur Hall, 1853) 3.321. On 9 June the widely-read *Literary Gazette* announced that the Royal Society of Literature prize for "the best poem on Dartmoor" been given to "a lady, of celebrity in the Literary world—Mrs. HEMANS;

who has, we understand, produced a beautiful poem [. . .] likely to add to her fame" (362). FH
received 50 guineas (£52.5) on 21 June 1821 for *Dartmoor* (334 lines in heroic couplets), one
of seven submissions; it was printed the same year "by order of the society" in a limited edition
for its members. Jerdan (1782–1869), the *Gazette's* editor since 1817, offered to publish another edition.

    Just below prize announcement in the "Literary Intelligence" column was news that "The
publisher of Shelley's Queen Mab has been indited by the Society for the Suppression of Vice";
adding that it "is dreadful to think that for the chance of miserable pecuniary profit, any man
would become the active agent to disseminate principles so subversive of the happiness of
Society," the *Gazette* ruefully noted that a pirated edition would appear within two months.
    [2] The *Gazette* had reviewed *Tales, and Historic Scenes* (18 September 1819) and *The Sceptic*
(22 January 1820); for Jerdan's criticisms of FH, see *Autobiography* 3.57. Beginning in 1820,
poems by Landon (L.E.L.) in the *Gazette* had been creating a sensation, and it was to her
memory that Jerdan dedicated his *Autobiography*.
    [3] *England's Dead* and *The Cid's Departure into Exile* appeared in the *Gazette* in October 1822.

---

## To ?, Bronwylfa, 1822.[1] No peace at home

    I entreat you to pity me—I am actually in the melancholy situation of Lord
Byron's "scorpion girt by fire"—"Her circle narrowing as she goes,"[2] for I have
been pursued by the household troops through every room successively, and
begin to think of establishing my <u>métier</u> in the cellar; though I dare say, if I were
to fix myself as comfortably in a hogshead, as Diogenes himself, it would immediately be discovered that some of the hoops or staves wanted repair.[3]

    When you talk of tranquillity and a quiet home, I stare about in wonder,
having almost lost the recollection of such things, and the hope that they may
probably be regained some time or other. I believe I told you that I had been
obliged to vacate my own room, and submit to the complete dislodgement of my
books, together with the dust, cobwebs, and other appurtenances thereunto belonging. "If there be any love of mercy"[4] in you, I hope you will feel a proper
degree of commiseration towards me in my extremity.

    [*a few weeks later*] We continue in the same state of tumult and confusion,
wherein we have existed, as it appears to my recollection, time immemorial.
There is a war of old grates with new grates, and plaister and paint with dust and
cobwebs, carrying on in this once tranquil abode, with a vigour and animosity
productive of little less din than that occasioned by "lance to lance, and horse to
horse."[5] I assure you, when I make my escape about "fall of eve" to some of the
green, quiet hay-fields by which we are surrounded, and look back at the house,
which, from a little distance, seems almost, like Shakspeare's moonlight, to
"sleep upon the bank," I can hardly conceive how so gentle-looking a dwelling
can contrive to send forth such an incessant clatter of obstreperous sound
through its honeysuckle-fringed window.[6] It really reminds me of a pretty
shrew, whose amiable smiles would hardly allow a casual observer to suspect the
possibility of so fair a surface being occasionally ruined by storms.

[1] *HM* 59–60.

[2] FH's wry, female-domestic parody of the tormented, alienated Byronic hero (whose mind is still gendered feminine); see *The Giaour* (1813): "The Mind, that broods o'er guilty woes, / Is like the Scorpion girt by fire, / In circle narrowing as it glows, / The flames around their captive close, / Till inly search'd by thousand throes, / And maddening in her ire . . ." (422–27).

[3] This Greek philosopher (ca. 412–323 B.C.), a proponent of simplicity, lived in a tub.

[4] Perhaps echoing S. Wesley the younger's *The Prisons Open'd* (1728): "and learn the love of mercy from my song."

[5] Thomas Gray, *The Bard* (1757): "Heard ye the din of battle bray, / Lance to lance and horse to horse" (83–84); the pattern of 84 is standard in heroic poetry, dating from classical literature, parodied by Croker in his mock-epic *The Amazoniad* (1806) (5.343), and frequently used by Byron in his "Eastern tales."

[6] The phrase "fall of eve" appears in Baillie's plays *De Monfort*, *Ethwald*, and *Rayner*, and FH will soon use it in *The Siege of Valencia* (1.139). "How sweet the moonlight sleeps upon this bank!" Lorenzo exclaims to Jessica in *The Merchant of Venice* (5.1.54).

---

## To Fanny Luxmoore, The Palace. Bronwylfa, mid-July 1822.[1]
The second Royal Society of Literature poetry prize competition

My dear Miss Fanny

I have been much surprized this morning by the appearance of the enclosed advertisement in the Morning Post, in consequence of which I really think the best thing I can do will be to publish "Constantinople"[2] either immediately, or at the beginning of the winter—One strong inducement to adopt this plan is that I can no longer hope for an <u>unbiased</u> decision should I leave the poem to await it another year, as my name is doubtless known by this time to all the council. It certainly seems a very unfair proceeding on the part of the Society, and I should imagine their object in leaving the competition open so long, must be to obtain names of greater distinction for the purpose of giving weight to the Institution. I consider my name being known, so serious a disadvantage as hardly leaves me a <u>chance</u> of gaining the prize next March; and I have many reasons for wishing to publish something as early as possible, therefore be so kind to take the matter into consideration, and if the Bishop[3] will favour me with his advice, I shall feel much indebted. Were I to resolve upon the publication, I should add Dartmoor, and several other minor poems, which would make a volume of respectable size. I must confess I should greatly regret losing the poem on Constantinople entirely as I never bestowed greater pains on any thing; and you know if I leave it still in the hands of the Society, and it should not succeed, I never can publish it as a rejected poem. If you will send me word about what time you are likely to be disengaged this morning, I will walk down to the Palace.

Ever yours truly
F.H.

Let me have the advertisement again when you have done with it.

<sup>1</sup> Princeton University AM19365. John Luxmoore (1756–1830), Bishop of St. Asaph, was "a firm and fatherly friend" who showed "paternal kindness" to FH and her sons; at his home, in spring 1820, she met Reginald Heber (*HM* 30–31; Howitt, *Homes and Haunts* 109).

<sup>2</sup> For "the best Poem on the Fall of Constantinople, in the Fifteenth Century," the prize announced was the same as for "Dartmoor," 50 guineas (£52.5). Submissions again were anonymous, marked with a code-motto. After reviewing ten, including FH's *The Last Constantine* (in 105 Spenserian stanzas), the Society posted a notice in various periodicals, the *Literary Gazette* (13 July 1822, 445), and *NMM* 6 (1 August 1822, 351) announcing that a decision would be "postponed until 23d of March 1823" and that authors wanting to "withdraw their Compositions for the purpose of any alterations they may think proper" could have them "at Messrs. Hatchard & Son's, Booksellers, Piccadilly." Ultimately no prize was awarded; in later contests, the prize would be a gold medal rather than cash. For details of the contests, see Jerdan, *Autobiography* 3, ch. 11, and David Gardner Williams, *The Royal Society of Literature and the Patronage of George IV* (Cambridge: Harvard U, 1947; New York: Garland, 1987), chs. 4–6.

<sup>3</sup> Luxmoore was a member of the Royal Society of Literature; he resided at "the Palace."

---

**To William Jacob, Esq.** Bronwylfa, 1 May 1823.<sup>1</sup> *The Vespers of Palermo*; his daughter's health

My dear Sir

Since I had the pleasure of receiving your very obliging letter, Mr. Milman has favoured me with a full explanation of the circumstances alluded to in your postscript. They are such as have convinced me that the permanent interest of my tragedy will be best provided for, by the delay of its representation until another season. I have accordingly consented to leave it in Mr. Kemble's hands, and am fully satisfied that he has every intention to do it ample justice.<sup>2</sup> Indeed, however I may regret the long protracted suspense which this change of plan must occasion me, I should ill deserve the consideration and liberality with which M<sup>r.</sup> Kemble has treated me throughout the whole of the transaction, if I did not assure my friends that whatever may be my disappointment, it does not involve with it the slightest cause of complaint. Allow me very sincerely to thank you for your kind offers of service, of which I hope to avail myself at some future opportunity. May I now trouble you to acquaint Mr Murray with the alteration of my intentions, and at the same time to convey him my acknowledgments for the promptitude with which his assistance was promised me? As I have no reason to expect that I shall be obliged to "keep the piece nine years," I trust no very long time will elapse before it is brought forward under his auspices.<sup>3</sup>

I rejoice to hear that your anxiety on your Daughter's account is so much alleviated, and trust that the approach of summer will still further establish her health. If the weather in town at all resembles what we have been visited with amongst the Hills, it must be particularly trying to Invalids. We see few other signs of Spring, than the ribbands of the May-dancers, who, according to our old Welsh custom, have been scouring the country the whole day. I beg my kindest remembrances to Miss Jacob, to whose letter nothing but want of leisure should have prevented my replying long ere now. I hope soon to make amends for the delay. My Brother and the rest of my family desire me to present you their best regards and allow me, dear Sir, to assure you of the respect with which I am very truly your obliged F. Hemans

[1] BL Add MS 33964, ff. 258–59. William Jacob (?1762–1851) was a traveler and well-known writer. His *Travels in the South of Spain, in a letter written A.D. 1809 and 1810* (London: J. Johnson and W. Miller, 1811) is cited by FH in *The Abencerrage*. He and his daughter visited FH at Bronwylfa in the autumn of 1822, and he remained a lifelong friend (*HM* 64).
[2] Poet, playwright, hymnist, and historian Henry Hart Milman (1791–1868), with whom FH had been corresponding, warmly recommended *The Vespers of Palermo*, though not written for the stage, for production at Covent Garden. With Charles Kemble in the role of the tormented hero, and featuring Charles Young, the play opened on 12 December and closed immediately, the poor reviews attributed to Fanny Kelley's inept acting. With support from Baillie, Sarah Siddons, and Scott, it had better success the following year in Scotland.
[3] Murray paid FH £220 for the copyright (among her biggest single earnings) and published the play in November, hoping to promote and then capitalize on its impending production.

---

**To William Jerdan.** Bronwylfa, St. Asaph, 8 May 1823.[1]
Withdrawing from the poetry prize competition

Dear Sir,

As I am ignorant of the proper medium of communication with the Royal Society of Literature, and am aware that you are one of its members, may I request you would do me the favour of making known to that society, in whatever manner you consider most expedient, that it is my intention to publish, without delay, a poem of mine, now in their hands, and originally written for the prize offered by them in 1821. The present season of the year being considered the most favourable for publication, I have been advised, on that account, no longer to wait the adjudgment of the prize. As I think it right that the society should be made acquainted with this without delay, it will be a satisfaction to me if you will have the kindness to inform me that it has been done. My poem [FH identifies the code-motto] will be in the hands of Mr. Murray by the time you receive this.[2]

Should you be induced to visit this country in the course of the ensuing summer, I trust you will not pass St. Asaph without giving me an opportunity of assuring you that       I am,

Dear sir, very truly,
Your obliged, &c.,
F. Hemans.

[1] Jerdan, *Autobiography* 3.154–55.
[2] *The Last Constantine* would be the opening piece of *The Siege of Valencia &c.*

---

**To Miss ?** Bronwylfa, 15 May 1823.[1] Baillie's tragedies

My Dear Miss———,

[. . .] Have you seen a collection of poems by living authors, edited by Joanna Baillie, for the benefit of a friend? She was kind enough to send me a copy, as I was one of her contributors: I mention it to you, principally to call your attention, should you meet with the book, to a very fine translation by Sotheby, of Schiller's magnificent "Lied von der Glöcke," a piece so very difficult to translate with effect, that I should have hardly thought it possible to give it so much spirit and grace in another language. The other poems in the volume are, I think, inferior to what might be expected from the high names of the authors: I was best pleased with Sir Walter Scott's and Mr. Milman's.[2] I never, until very lately, met with a tragedy of Miss Baillie's, which is, I believe, less generally known than her other works; "The Family Legend." I was much pleased with it, particularly her delineation of the heroine. Indeed, nothing in all her writings delights me so much as her general idea of what is beautiful in the female character. There is so much gentle fortitude, and deep self-devoting affection in the women whom she portrays, and they are so perfectly different from the pretty "un-idea'd girls," who seem to form the beau ideal of our whole sex in the works of some modern poets.[3] The latter remind me of a foolish saying, I think of Diderot's, that in order to describe a woman, you should write with a pen made of a peacock's feather, and dry the writing with the dust from butterflies' wings.[4] Have you seen the lately published Memoirs of Lady Griseld Baillie? She was an ancestress, I believe, of Joanna's, and her delightful character seems to have been the model her descendant has copied in some of the dramas she introduces.[5] I believe I never told you how fully I agreed with you in your opinion of the "Trials of Margaret Lyndsay."[6] The book is certainly full of deep feeling and beautiful language, but there are many passages which, I think, would have been better omitted; and although I can bear as much fictitious woe as most people, I really began to feel it an infliction at last.

> With much regard,
> Believe me very truly yours,
> Felicia Hemans

[1] *CM* 1.95–97.

[2] In Schiller's *Lied von der Glöcke* (Song of the clock), the casting of a clock bell becomes an allegorical fable. William Sotheby (1757–1853), poet, playwright, translator, was the butt of Byron's jests in *Beppo* (1819), and FH's letter of January 1830 to Murray indicates that she knew the ridicule. Baillie's *Collection of Poems, Chiefly Manuscript and from Living Authors* (London: Longman &c, 1823), a volume organized to help an ailing friend, also included FH's *Belshazzar's Feast* (rpt. *Siege &c*), Scott's *Mac Duff's Cross*, Milman's *The Loss of Royal George*, and pieces by Wordsworth, Barbauld, Southey, Campbell, Rogers, Crabbe, Anne Grant, Anna Maria Porter, and many other luminaries. With such a roster, Baillie had a subscription (advance sale) of £2,000.

[3] *The Family Legend: a tragedy*, a highland play Baillie wrote to assist a needy family, had strong support from Scott, who wrote a prologue. It had a tremendous success on the Edinburgh stage early in 1810 and was published in Edinburgh, by Ballantyne, the same year, both independently and bound with her *Miscellaneous Plays*.

⁴ Denis Diderot remarked in "Sur les femmes" (1772, review of Antoine-Leonard Thomas's *Dissertation sur les femmes*), "Quand on ecrit sur les femmes, il faut tremper sa plume dans l'arc-en-ciel et jeter sur sa ligne la poussière des ailes du papillon" (When one writes of women, one must dip one's pen into the rainbow and sprinkle over the line the dust of butterfly wings).

⁵ *Memoirs of Lady Griseld Baillie* was published by her daughter Lady Murray in 1822. The youthful adventures of poet Griseld Baillie (1665–1746) became the stuff of legend: she sheltered her family (aristocratic Scottish covenanters) from government prosecution and acted as a go-between for imprisoned Jacobites. Joanna Baillie's poems about her in *Metrical Legends of Exalted Characters* (1821) was singled out for admiration by the *Monthly Review*.

⁶ *The Trials of Margaret Lindsay* (1823), a psychological novel by John Wilson (1785–1854); Wilson wrote as "Christopher North" of *Blackwood's*, whose staff he joined in 1817.

---

**To William Jerdan.** Bronwylfa, St. Asaph, 19 May 1823.[1]

Dear Sir,

I feel particularly obliged by the kindness and consideration with which you have fulfilled the wishes I took the liberty of communicating to you, on the subject of my poem. It appears to me, however, that it would be taking an advantage hardly fair, of the permission to publish granted by the R. S. L., to leave the piece amongst those of the candidates for the offered prize, after laying it before the public. I had indeed imagined that the very request which the society have done me the favour to grant, amounted to a withdrawal of my claim as a candidate. [. . .]

I have requested Mr. Murray to transmit you a copy of the little volume immediately on its publication. You will, I hope, receive, and favour me by accepting it, in the course of a few days. I have have called it the 'Last Constantine,' having seen a poem advertised some time ago, by the title of the 'Fall of Constantinople.'[2] [. . .] With much esteem, believe me,

Dear Sir,<br>
Your obliged servant,<br>
F. Hemans.

[1] Jerdan, *Autobiography* 3.155–56.
[2] Probably David Douglas, *The Fall of Constantinople; a Poem*, reviewed in the *Literary Chronicle*, 24 May 1823. With ample quotation, the *Gazette* featured FH's poem in a front-page review, 21 June 1823. She also won high praise from *Constable's Magazine* (September 1823) and some warm, though equivocal praise from the *British Review*, August 1823.

---

**To Maria Jane Jewsbury,** mid-1826.[1] Wordsworth's poetry

The inclosed lines, an effusion of deep and sincere admiration, will give you some idea of the enjoyment, and, I hope I may say, advantage, which you have been the means of imparting, by so kindly entrusting me with your precious copy of Wordsworth's Miscellaneous Poems. It has opened to me such a treasure of thought and feeling, that I shall always associate your name with some of my pleasantest recollections, as having introduced me to the knowledge of what I

can only regret should have been so long a "Yarrow unvisited."[2] I would not write
to you sooner, because I wished to tell you that I had really <u>studied</u> these poems,
and they have been the daily food of my mind ever since I borrowed them. There
is hardly any scene of a happy, though serious, domestic life, or any mood of a
reflective mind, with the spirit of which some one or other of them does not
beautifully harmonize. This author is the true <u>Poet of Home</u>, and of all the lofty
feelings which have their root in the soil of home affections. His fine sonnets to
Liberty, and indeed, all his pieces which have any reference to political interest,
remind me of the spirit in which Schiller has conceived the character of William
Tell, a calm, single-hearted herdsman of the hills, breaking forth into fiery and
indignant eloquence, when the sanctity of his hearth is invaded.[3] Then, what
power Wordsworth condenses into single lines, like Lord Byron's "curdling a
long life into one hour."

> "The still sad music of humanity."—
>
> "The river glideth at his own sweet will"—
>
> "Over his own sweet voice the stock-dove broods."—[4]

And a thousand others, which we must some time, (and I hope not a very distant
one,) talk over together. Many of these lines quite haunt me, and I have a strange
feeling, as if I must have known them in my childhood, they come over me so
like old melodies. I can hardly speak of <u>favourites</u> among so many things that
delight me, but I think "The Narrow Glen," the lines on "Corra Linn," the
"Song for the Feast of Brougham Castle," "Yarrow visited," and "The Cuckoo,"
are among those which take hold of imagination the soonest, and recur most
frequently to memory. . . . I know not how I can have so long omitted to mention the "Ecclesiastical Sketches," which I have read, and do constantly read
with deep interest.[5] Their beauty grows upon you and develops as you study it,
like that of the old pictures by the Italian masters. My sister [. . .] desires I will
not fail to ask if you can throw any light for us on the piece of "The Danish Boy."
Its poetry is beautiful, but the subject requires explanation; does it refer to any
wild mountain legend of the "Land of Lakes?"[6] I had many more things to say
respecting all that I have thought and felt during the perusal of these works, but
my interruptions, consisting of morning visits from the Bishop down to the
tailor of the diocese (which latter guest, to the mother of five boys, is by no
means an unimportant one), have been incessant, to say nothing of the boys
themselves. My mother being unwell, and my sister engaged, all the duties of
politeness have devolved upon me for the day. I must, in a future letter, name to
you, according to your wish, a few books, the perusal of which may be advantageous to you, though I can sincerely say that I should be far from discovering the
deficiencies which you imagine in yourself, from any thing I have seen in your
writings. I cannot help, however, mentioning, as works from which I have derived much clear and general information, those of Sismondi; in particular his
"Littérature du Midi," and "Républiques Italiennes," but you are probably acquainted with both.[7] I regret that I should have been obliged to answer your

interesting letter in so hurried, and, I fear, incoherent a manner, and hope it will not prevent your writing to me again; and believe me, with unfeigned esteem, my dear Miss Jewsbury,

Your sincere friend,

F. Hemans.

[1] *CM* 1.173–77. Chorley and Hughes date the inception of FH's correspondence with Jewsbury, originating in their mutual admiration of Wordsworth, "considerably prior" to their first meeting in 1828. With this letter, FH enclosed *To the Poet Wordsworth*, first published in April 1826 in the *Literary Magnet* (with a different title); in the same annual Jewsbury had published *The Poet's Home*, about Wordsworth's residence at Rydal Mount. Jewsbury (1800–33), fiction writer, sparkling essayist, satirist, journalist, and poet, became a close friend, and dedicated *Lays of Leisure Hours* (1829) to FH.

[2] *Miscellaneous Poems* (four volumes, 1820) included new and republished pieces, including *Yarrow Unvisited* (1807) and *Yarrow Visited, September 1814*.

[3] In Schiller's *Wilhelm Tell* (1804), the hero finally rises to revolt against foreign tyranny (act 3) after his son is arrested. *Sonnets Dedicated to Liberty* (*Miscellaneous Poems*) included three celebrating the Spanish resistance to the French, and *Höfer*, in which the Swiss martyr is imagined as "Tell's great Spirit, from the dead / Returned, to animate an age forlorn."

[4] Byron, *The Dream* (1816), 26; Wordsworth, *Tintern Abbey* 91, *Composed upon Westminster Bridge* 12, *Resolution and Independence* 5—all republished in *Miscellaneous Poems*.

[5] *Glen-Almain; Composed at Cora Linn, in the Sight of Wallace's Tower; Song at the Feast of Brougham Castle; Yarrow Visited, September 1814*, and *To the Cuckoo* are all in *Miscellaneous Poems*. *Ecclesiastical Sketches* was published in 1822.

[6] The Lake District of Cumbria, Wordsworth's home for most his life. The poem was one of the "Poems of the Fancy" in his 1815 *Poems*; when Wordsworth republished it in 1827 it had a headnote referring to "the story of a Danish Prince who had fled from battle, and, for the sake of the valuables about him, was murdered by the inhabitant of a cottage in which he had taken refuge. The house fell under a curse, and the Spirit of the Youth, it was believed, haunted the valley where the crime had been committed."

[7] J-C. L. Simonde de Sismondi's *De la Littérature du Midi de L'Europe* (1813) and *Histoire des Républiques Italiennes du Moyen Âge* (1809–18) were widely admired and influential. FH cites both often in her notes to her poems.

---

**To "an old and much valued friend," January 1827.**[1] Death of her mother

I cannot suffer you to remain in anxiety about me, which I know is painful. My soul is indeed "exceeding sorrowful,"[2] dear friend; but, thank God! I can tell you that composure is returning to me, and that I am enabled to resume those duties which so imperiously call me back to life. What I have lost, none better knows than yourself. I have lost the faithful, watchful, patient love, which for years had been devoted to me and mine; and I feel that the void it has left behind, must cause me to bear "a yearning heart within me to the grave";[3] but I have her example before me, and I must not allow myself to sink.

You have, I know, been told of the wonderful collectedness she displayed to the last. Sickness and suffering, and sorrowful affection we have witnessed; but no despondence, no perplexity, nothing which can in any way connect horror with the awfulness of death. I was almost in a stupor for a few days after, but it is past, and I do not think my health will suffer, though I now feel wearied and worn, and longing, as she did, for rest. That rest was almost, indeed, perfect in her last hours, so deep and still was the slumber into which she had sunk, and which our selfish hearts almost longed to hear broken even by the renewed sickness of the preceding night; for the utter separation from us implied by such a state of solemn tranquillity, seemed almost "greater than we could bear." Oh! this earthly weakness, when we should praise God for one "departed this life in His faith and fear."[4]

[1] *HM* 100–101.
[2] "My soul is exceeding sorrowful, even unto death," Jesus tells his disciples in the Garden of Gesthemane (Matthew 26.38).
[3] A self-quotation, *The Forest Sanctuary* 3.19–20.
[4] Cf. Christopher Smart, Psalm 149, 2d version (*Translation of the Psalms* [1765]) about "glorious saints" who from earth are "severed in His faith and fear."

---

**To William Blackwood,** Bookseller, Edinburgh. Rhyllon, St. Asaph, 13 June 1827.[1] Fee for contributions to *Blackwood's Edinburgh Magazine*

Sir,

I beg to thank you for your obliging letter and valuable present of books, from the perusal of which I have derived great pleasure. The little work called "Solitary hours"[2] interested me particularly; some of the pieces it contains had before struck me in your Magazine, and I think it altogether full of talent and good feeling.—I am extremely happy that the little poem which I meant as a trifling acknowledgement of the kindness with which my name had been treated in your work, proved so acceptable.

With regard to the subject of your letter, I really shall have pleasure in becoming an occasional contributor to a work possessing so many writers of talent, provided you should not object to the mode of remuneration to which I am accustomed, and which, in order to prevent any future mistake, it would perhaps be better that I should mention at once.—I receive from other Publishers for whom I write, 24 guineas a sheet for poetry,[3] with the liberty of drawing upon them for the value of the contributions, at my own convenience—The remote situation in which I live, renders this latter arrangement a particular convenience to me, and if it be not otherwise to you, I shall be happy sometimes to join the band of your writers.—I can at any time hear from you under cover to the Bishop of St. Asaph,[4] whose present address is 78 Gloucester Place, Portman Square, London.

I enclose a little piece for the Magazine[5] and beg you to believe me, Sir,

Your obliged and obedient s.

F. Hemans

[1] BA MS 4019, f. 183. William Blackwood (1776–1834) founded *Blackwood's* in 1817, where FH would publish frequently; his firm published *Records of Woman &c* and the second edition of *Forest Sanctuary &c.*

[2] Caroline Bowles (1786–1854), *Solitary Hours*, a collection of prose and verse, published by Blackwood in 1826; in 1839 she married Robert Southey, whom she had met in 1820.

[3] A sheet is folded into pages. *Blackwood's* was printed in octavo (eight pages on each side of a sheet, for a total of sixteen pages); a guinea is £1 and one shilling. FH is asking for £1, 11½ s. per page, and will later up this to two guineas—a rate, Feldman reports, exceeding that commanded by Thomas Hood, Caroline Bowles, Scott, and Hartley Coleridge.

[4] The recipient had to pay for mail; as a bishop, Luxmoore had the "frank" ("free" postage).

[5] *Song of Emigration* (fifty lines), *Blackwood's* 22 (July 1827): 32, signed "F. H."

----

**To William Blackwood.** Rhyllon, St. Asaph, 3 November 1827.[1]
Literary signature; *Records of Woman*

Sir

I had the pleasure of receiving your obliging letter, and I enclose another little poem for the Magazine. I fear I cannot allow more than my initials to be affixed to it, because having refused the same request to the Editors of other periodical Works, I might make myself enemies by granting it in the present instance.[2]—I wish to consult you respecting the publication of a little Volume which I have now nearly completed. It is a series of poetic tales entitled Records of Woman, and illustrative of the female character, affections and fate. [List of titles.] I should like to have the volume published by you, provided we can come to an agreement respecting the terms.[3] —It is to be dedicated to Mrs. Joanna Baillie.

Believe me to remain, Sir,
Very truly yours
F. Hemans

[1] BA MS 4719, f. 101.

[2] Blackwood had closed his letter of 27 September 1827, "Would you have any objections to my affixing your name in full at your contributions?" (BA MS 30310, f. 283); writing back on 22 November, he agreed to initials: "I am satisfied with your reasons for only giving your initials which indeed designate you about as well as your name at full length" (30310, ff. 319–21). When another writer began publishing as "F. H.," she asked that her full name be printed (see below).

[3] For the consequence of this proposal, see note 2 to FH's letter to Blackwood of 1 March 1828.

----

**To William Blackwood.** Rhyllon, St. Asaph, 14 February 1828.[1] Shelley

Dear Sir
Some of my friends, who saw the little poem I had the pleasure of sending you a few days since, objected much to my having taken a motto from Shelley. I had really thought no more about it, than that the lines happened to be particularly

appropriate to my poem; will you however be kind enough to have his <u>name</u> omitted, though I should wish the motto to remain.[2]—I hope soon to hear from you respecting the "Records," and beg you to believe me, Sir,

Your faithful servant<br>
F. Hemans

[1] BA MS 4719, f. 89.

[2] The epigraph for *The Broken Lute* is *When the lamp is shatter'd* 1–12 (in Shelley's *Posthumous Poems*, 1824). "Your Poem was printed off before I read your note," Blackwood replied at the end of his letter, 22 February 1828; it appeared in the March *Blackwood's*, 291–93; signed "F. H.," with Shelley's name in small capitals. Blackwood assured FH that Shelley's name "does not signify" perilously, for "with all his follies and impieties, [he] was a true poet" (BA 30310, f. 419). Shelley had champions in the 1820s, but his rehabilitation from atheist revolutionary to true poet—pressed by Mary Shelley's preface to *Posthumous Poems* (FH admired her "earnest eloquence" [*CM* 2.194])—would not take firm hold until the 1840s.

---

## To Reverend Samuel Butler, 19 February 1828.[1] Loneliness

[. . .] Still I can but too well imagine the mingled feelings with which you and M[rs] Butler must look forward to the event, for I am about to lose in a similar manner, my only sister, and I may almost say, my only <u>Companion</u>; since we have for years been linked together in a community of thoughts and pursuits, which I must never hope to have renewed. Unfortunately for me, interchange of thought is an habitual <u>want</u> of my mind, and I pine without it, as the Swiss Exile does for his native Air, so that I look with a feeling almost of alarm, to the loneliness (not literal, but <u>mental</u> loneliness,) which seems awaiting me.— [. . .] I <u>did</u> take to rearing Gera[niums] some time since, by way of a less exciting amusement than my usual ones; but I am almost ashamed to tell the result; in Summer I forgot to water them, and in Winter I forgot to shelter them, so the last frost, these my ill-used adopted Children all withered away. It would be too cruel to try similar experiments upon <u>live things</u> (though my conscience was sorely smitten upon reading the other day a gravely maintained opinion that plants can <u>feel</u>). So I fear I must not think of the Bees and Chickens.—

I do not know whether you are at all a Lover of German Literature, but there is a poem in that Language, a beautiful nuptial benediction pronounced by a Father over his child at the moment of his leaving him, which some parts of your letter recalled to my mind. I have copied Madame de Stael's translation of it, and take the liberty of including it for you.[2]—

[1] BL Add MS 34587, f. 8. Butler (1774–1839), headmaster of Shrewsbury School since 1798, made it one of the leading boys' schools in England; he would leave in 1836 on becoming bishop of St. Asaph and Coventry. The "event" is his daughter's impending marriage.

[2] Johann Heinrich Voss (1751–1826), "Ma fille, lui dit-il avec une voix émue, que la bénédiction de Dieu soit avec toi," in Staël's *De l'Allemagne* (Paris, 1813), ch. 12 (161–62).

---

**To William Blackwood.** Rhyllon, St. Asaph, 1 March 1828.[1]
Publishing *Records of Woman*

Dear Sir

I feel, I assure you, very sensibly, all the kindness of your letter, and it has only increased my wish to place the work in your hands, from a conviction that you will give it every advantage in your power. I agree to the terms you propose, being aware that what you say respecting the demand for poetry at present, is perfectly correct;[2] but I have other reasons, besides the hope of profit, for wishing to publish this volume, in parts of which I have expressed more of my own personal feelings, than in any thing I have ever before written.—I should think it had better be printed of the same size with my former publications, (which I believe is about the one you suggest) as I now often hear of their being ordered in sets, to be bound together, and I believe 1000 copies to be the number generally printed of them. I had better receive the proof-sheets to correct myself, particularly as they contain so much German, and it will not cause much delay, as I shall always be able to send them back by return of post. The remaining part of the M.S.S. I will transmit in a few days; I suppose I may take the liberty of sending them to Sir Francis Freeling,[3] mentioning that they belong to those which were forwarded to you some time since.

> Believe me, dear Sir,
> Very truly yours
> Felicia Hemans.

[1] BA MS 4719, ff. 91–92.

[2] On 22 November 1827 Blackwood responded warmly but cautiously to FH's initial feeler: "I am very much flattered by your applying to me with regard to your intended publication of 'Records of Woman' and if I find I can meet your terms I shall be happy to be your publisher. I would beg the favour of you therefore to write me what [?] you expect for the volume, and as I never engage on any publication until perusing the MS. I hope you will have no objection to send it to me" (BA MS 30310, f. 319). Hearing her proposal, he replied: "I would not wish on any account to publish the Work unless I could do it as advantageously for you as what your London publisher has been accustomed to do with regard to your works. I shall of course be most happy to publish the volume, but I regret to say in the present state of sales for poetry I could not venture to offer a sum for it, I could only take on myself the expenses of paper & printing, and divide profits with you in the normal way after the expenses were paid from sales, but I need hardly say that I would use my utmost exertion to promote its sale but [. . .] I know this plan could not be so satisfying to you as receiving a sum at once for the volume. I hope therefore that you will feel that [?you may put] the publication into other hands if you find you can make a better arrangement" (30310, ff. 417–19). He published 1,000 copies of *Records* in May 1828, on a profit-sharing plan. Scott, a writer and publisher who kept track of every pound, remarked in his Preface to *The Lay of the Last Minstrel* that "the usual terms" are "division of profits between the author and publisher."

[3] Blackwood received mail through Freeling (1764–1836), a book collector and postal reformer.

**To Mary Russell Mitford.** St. Asaph, 23 March 1828.[1] Mothers, fame,
*Records of Woman*

My dear Miss Mitford,

I ought long since to have thanked you for your very kind letter, although it brought disappointment with it, in the conviction that I must not hope to see you here. You are happy in having such reasons to assign, for the difficulty of your leaving home; every day impresses more forcibly on my mind the truth and the full meaning of Gray's remark, "We can have but one mother";[2] it is now about a year since I have been deprived of mine, and will you think me weak when I tell you that I shed tears over your letter, from the idea of the pleasure it would have given her? I am sure that you will agree with me, that fame can only afford reflected delight to a woman. Do you know that I often think of you, and the happiness you must feel in being able to run to your father and mother, with all the praises you receive. For me that joy is past;[3] but I will not write in sadness to her whose writings have often thrown sunshine over my own variable spirits. How are all my old friends of "Our Village?" Lizzy and Lucy and May, and the pleasant people at the "Vicarage," and the merry men of the cricket-ground? do tell me something of them all. I became acquainted with your delightful bird-catcher last month, and have only to hope that you were not the worse for that fog in which you encountered him, and the very description of which almost took my hair out of curl whilst reading it.[4] Your autograph, which I transmitted to my American friends,[5] was very gratefully received,—and is enshrined in a book amidst I know not how many other "bright names";[6] for aught I know, Washington himself may be there, side by side with you; and not improbably is, for they are going to send me an original letter of his, which I shall prize much. If you are likely soon to pay one of your flying visits to London, I should very much like you to see my portrait, for which I sat a few months since;[7] I am sure you will understand why I wish you to see it; it would be giving me something of a personal introduction to one whom I esteem so highly. The picture is at the rooms of the artist, Mr. West, 63, Margaret Street, Cavendish Square: it is considered a very striking likeness. I am about to publish a little volume, called "Records of Woman," of which I shall beg your acceptance: I have put my heart and individual feelings into it more than any thing else I have written; but, whether it will interest my friends more for this reason, remains to be seen. May I offer my kindest respects to your father and mother, and beg you to believe me,

Dear Miss Mitford,
Very faithfully yours,
Felicia Hemans

---

[1] *CM* 1.158–161. Mitford (1787–1855) was a popular sketch writer, novelist, poet, dramatist, and critic.

[2] Thomas Gray, whose mother died in 1753, wrote to Norton Nicholls, 26 August 1766, "I had discovered a thing very little known, which is, that in one's whole life one never can have more than a single mother"; FH's epigraph for *The Voice of the Wind* in *Blackwood's* (November

1828, 639) credits "Gray's Letters." On the death of his mother, Byron wrote to Dr. Pigot, "I now feel the truth of Mr. Gray's observation, 'That we can only have *one* mother'" (2 August 1811; Moore, *Life of Byron* 1.272–73).

[3] Of his childhood, Wordsworth wrote, "That time is past, / And all its aching joys are now no more" (*Tintern Abbey* 83–84).

[4] Published serially in the *Lady's Magazine*, Mitford's *Our Village: Sketches of Rural Character and Scenery*, 5 vols. (1824–32), was quite popular. The references are to *Lucy*, *A Visit to Lucy*, *The Country Cricket-Match*, and *The Bird-Catcher* (which begins with a tour de force comparing London fogs to country fogs). "Lizzy" is the three-year-old daughter of the cabinetmaker, and "May" ("Mayflower") is the narrator's white greyhound, both accompanying her on various "Walks." Mitford kills off Lucy by the third series.

[5] Principally, Harvard Divinity Professor Andrews Norton, editor of and broker for the publication of FH's work in Boston.

[6] Cf. Byron, "bright names will hallow song" (*Childe Harold's Pilgrimage III*, xxix); also a self-quotation: in *Farewell to Abbotsford*, FH wishes that Scott's home will always be honored by "bright names worthy" of his (20); and in *A Fragment* ("Rest on your battlefield"), she laments, "We on changeful days are cast, / When bright names from their place fall fast" (13–14). See also her friend and publisher Alaric Watts's *Posthumous Fame* (1828), converting Byron's military heroism to poetic fame: there are few "bright names, / Who, when the roll of glory is unfurled, / Upon posterity can show such claims / As Milton, Shakspeare, Spenser" (26–29).

[7] See *To My Own Portrait*.

---

**To William Henry Atherton,** Rodney Street, Liverpool. Rhyllon, St. Asaph, 9 May 1828.[1] Panic at going to Liverpool

Dear Mr. Atherton,

I cannot tell you how much I feel obliged by your kind promise of meeting me at the Liverpool Pier. Miss Parke indeed tells me it is possible you may come as far as Bagillt,[2] and I need not say how welcome an apparition you would be, but I know your health is not strong, and therefore beg you will not on my account, expose yourself to unsuitable hours, or unnecessary fatigue, however glad I should be to see you there, provided you could come without inconvenience. I shall be very grateful for your protection through that <u>Pandemonium</u>, the Liverpool landing-place, where the whirl of all unfamiliar and discordant sights and sounds absolutely bewilders me. I believe if I were left to myself there, I should do what I have heard of Travellers doing from a similar feeling though excited by very opposite causes, amidst the mighty Solitude of an American forest—sit down in a sort of stupid despondence and utter inability either to advance or retreat.—Ought I not to be ashamed of so much helplessness—partly natural and partly acquired? It is indeed time that I should throw it from me, but you know what a caged Bird I have been, and how I have been watched and guarded with a tenderness which now, alas! I must expect no more.

Well, we shall meet very soon, and as a Syrian proverb says, "the <u>Daughter of the Voice</u> is better than the <u>Son of ink</u>" [. . .] believe me till then, and afterwards too, dear Mr. Atherton

Very faithfully yours
Felicia Hemans

¹ HL MS 1826. Atherton may be a scion of the old Liverpool family, which has a mid-eighteenth-century member named William Atherton.

² A "Miss Parke" was on the subscription list for FDB's 1808 *Poems*. Eliza Park, the "warm-hearted and accomplished daughter" of Henry Park (Lawrence 302), at whose home FH would be staying, did meet her at Bagillt, a village on the northern coast of Wales (near Flint Castle) from which the packet for Liverpool departed. The sail was enjoyable, but the entry into the Liverpool harbor was "difficult and disagreeable" (*HM* 152; Williams 441, 444). With her family dispersed from Rhyllon, FH was moving with her three younger boys to Wavertree, where resided the Parks, Rose Lawrence, John Lodge and the Chorley family.

---

**To William Blackwood.** Rhyllon, St. Asaph, 29 July 1828.¹
Success of *Records of Woman*, 2d ed. of *The Forest Sanctuary*

Dear Sir

I beg to acknowledge with many thanks, your kind letter of yesterday, with its liberal enclosure. I hear with very great pleasure of the success of the Records, and am quite sensible how much I am indebted to your zeal and exertion in favour of the Work. I shall attentively look over the book; there [are] no errors in it, I never had anything more correctly printed, but I should wish to make some additions, and will send you by degrees the pieces to be inserted.—Do you think it would answer to publish with it, of an uniform size my last previous work, the Forest Sanctuary with Lays of Many Lands?—It is now out of print, and is, I have heard, a good deal inquired for, and I have not disposed of the copy-right.—I am afraid I must give up, for the present at least, my plan of residing in Edinburgh; my health has suffered so much of late that I have scarcely been able to quit the sofa for the last two months; it is now beginning to improve, and I hope will at last allow me to *visit* the Queen of the North on some future occasion, and to make acquaintance with all the bright stars that shine in her crown.—In a few days I hope to have the pleasure of sending something for Maga;² "Christopher North in Edinburgh and London" in one of the late Nᵒˢ was delightful. [. . . ]

Believe me, Dear Sir,
Very sincerely yr obligd
Felicia Hemans

Just before receiving your last letter, I had drawn upon you for my contributions to the Magazine.—

¹ BA MS 4719, ff. 98–99. Replying to Blackwood's letter, 22 July 1828, in which he reported, "The Records of woman had met with a very favourable acceptance"; he paid FH £75 for her "share in the profits" and was planning a 2d edition for "early next Winter" (BA MS 30311, ff. 24–26); it came out sooner, in October. *Records* had a 4th edition by 1833.

² Nickname of *Blackwood's Edinburgh Magazine*. *The Two Voices* appeared in October (497), signed "F. H."

**To Mary Russell Mitford.** Wavertree, 10 November 1828.[1]
Mitford's success; her sadness

My dear Miss Mitford,

Accept my late, though sincere and cordial congratulations on the brilliant success of "Rienzi," of which I have read with unfeigned gratification.[2] I thought of your father and Mother, and could not help imagining, that your feelings must be like those of the Greek General who declared that his greatest delight in Victory arose from the thought of his parents—I have no doubt that your enjoyment of <u>your</u> triumph has been of a similar Nature—I ought to have acknowledged long, long since, your kind present of the little Volume of plays valued both for your sake and <u>theirs</u>, for they are indeed full of Beauty, but I have been a drooping creature for months, ill and suffering much from the dispersion of a little Band of Brothers and Sisters,[3] amongst whom I had lived, and who are now all scattered—and, strange as it may seem to say, I am now for the first time in my life holding <u>the reins of government</u>—independent—managing a Household myself—and I never liked any thing less than "ce triste empire de Soi-même."[4] It really suits me as ill as the <u>Southron</u> climate did your wild Orkney school-girls whom perhaps, <u>you</u>, the creator of so many fair forms and images, may have forgotten but I have not. I have changed my residence since I last wrote to you, and my address is now at Wavertree, near Liverpool, where I shall, as the Welsh country-people say, "Take it very kind" if you write to me; and I really cannot help venturing to hope that you <u>will</u>.—I have yet only read of Rienzi a few noble passages given by the Newspapers and Magazines, but in a few days I hope to be acquainted with the whole—every Woman ought to be proud of your triumph—in this Age too, when dramatic triumph seems of all others the most difficult.—How are May and Mossy, and Lucy and Jack Hatch[5]—no, Jack Hatch actually <u>died</u>, to the astonishment of myself and my Boys, who thought I believe he had been "painted for Eternity"—and Mrs. Allen, and the rest of the dear villagers?—And your Parents? I trust they are well.—your mother, I believe, is always an Invalid, but I hope she is able fully to enjoy the success of her Daughter, as only a Mother <u>can</u> enjoy it. How hollow sounds the Voice of fame to an Orphan!—Farewell, my dear Miss Mitford— long may you have the delight of gladdening a Father and Mother!—Believe me, ever faithfully yours

Felicia Hemans

[1] LL MS 920 / HEM 10/1. Cf. *CM* 1.231–235. FH has taken up residence in this village, about three miles from Liverpool, seeking better education for her sons and society for herself.

[2] *Rienzi* (1828), one of Mitford's most successful dramas, is based on the dynamic career of Cola di Rienzi (twelfth century).

[3] A rueful echo of Henry V's famous address to his allies before battle: "We few, we happy few, we band of brothers" (Shakespeare, *Henry V* 4.3.60).

[4] this sorrowful empire of oneself (source unidentified)

[5] Characters in Mitford's *Our Village* (1824–32); see letter to Mitford, 23 March 1828.

**To a close friend** in Wales, early 1829.[1] Weariness with fame, nostalgia for childhood

"Safe in the grave,"[2]—what deep meaning there is in those words, and how often does the feeling they convey come over me amidst the varied excitements of my strange, unconnected life! How I look back upon the comparative peace and repose of Bronwylfa and Rhyllon—a walk in the hay-field—the children playing round me—my dear mother coming to call me in from the dew—and you, perhaps, making your appearance just in the "gloaming," with a great bunch of flowers in your kind hand! How have these things passed away from me, and how much more was I formed for their quiet happiness, than for the weary part of femme célèbre, which I am now enacting! But my heart is with those home enjoyments, and there, however tried, excited, and wrung, it will ever remain.

¹ *HM* 176; addressee specified by Williams (449).

² Cf. Matthew Prior (1664–1721), *Solomon on the Vanity of the World*: "Tired in the Field of life, I hope Retreat / In the still Shades of Death: for Dread and Pain, / And Grief will find their Shafts elanc'd in vain, / And their Points broke, retorted from the head, / Safe in the Grave, and free among the Dead" (3.513–17); and Mary Wortley Montagu (1689–1762), *An Elegy on Mrs. Thompson* (*Poetical Works*, 1768): "How far more blest than those yet left behind! / Safe in the grave, thy griefs with thee remain; / And life's tempestuous billows break in vain" (6–8).

---

**To William Blackwood.** Wavertree, ca. January 1830.[1] Her signature; Lady Morgan

Dear Sir,

I should like to have my pieces in Maga announced, for some time to come, with my name at full length in the table of contents, and without any signature. Some One, for whose perpetrations I am not at all desirous to be answerable, has adopted the signature of F.H., and I am rather perplexed as to the best means of proving my own Identity.—Even if I lay aside the use of the initials altogether, I fear I should not quite free myself from the imputations of Mʳ. F. H's poetry, which really is "so middling, bad were better."[2] Perhaps you can give me some advice on the subject. I enclose two more of the Songs.[3] It is my still unsettled health which prevents me from yet making any more continuous effort, but I live in constant hope that the obstacle will ere long be removed. Many thanks for the Magazine; I have now received them all, and deeply interesting they are.—May I trouble you to order that a copy of the Records shall be sent to Colburn, for Lady Morgan.—Her Ladyship (entre nous) addressed me a very patronizing letter some time since, and I have a particular reason for wishing her to see the volume.—[4]

¹ BA MS 4027, ff. 174–75. Feldman speculatively dates this letter some time in 1830; if so, it was probably before FH read of and read Moore's *Life of Byron*, which dismayed her.

² Byron, *Beppo* (1818), from the couplet that crowns stanza 74, a string of sneers at the hack

author (and his bluestocking devotees), "Translating tongues he knows not even by letter, / And sweating plays so middling, bad were better."

[3] Hereafter her poems in *Blackwood's* would be signed with her full name; "Songs" is probably *Songs of the Affections*.

[4] The 2d edition of *Records* (1828) had sold out; a 3d was planned. Publisher Henry Colburn specialized in novels and inexpensive best-sellers; in 1814 he founded *NMM*, to which FH frequently contributed. Sydney Owenson, later Lady Morgan (1777–1859), was a prolific, best-selling writer. An Irish nationalist and Protestant advocate for Catholic rights, she drew nasty Tory reviews (especially from Gifford and Croker, who admired FH's poems). Among her most popular works were her novels, *The Wild Irish Girl* (1806), for which she receive an advance of £300) and *The O'Briens and the O'Flahertes* (1827); *The Lay of an Irish Harp; or Metrical Fragments* (1807); and a travelogue that Byron admired, *Italy* (1821), for which Colburn advanced £2,000. Tighe and Staël were among her friends.

---

## To? Rydal Mount, 22 June 1830.[1] Meeting Wordsworth

[. . .] my nervous fear at the idea of presenting myself to Mr. Wordsworth, grew upon me so rapidly, that it was more than seven before I took courage to leave the inn.[2] I had indeed little cause for such trepidation. I was driven to a lovely cottage-like building, almost hidden by a profusion of roses and ivy; and a most benignant-looking old man greeted me in the porch:[3] this was Mr. Wordsworth himself; and when I tell you that, having rather a large party of visitors in the house, he led me to a room apart from them, and brought in his family by degrees, I am sure that little trait will give you an idea of considerate kindness which you will both like and appreciate. In half an hour I felt myself as much at ease with him as I had been with Sir Walter Scott in half a day. I laughed to find myself saying, on the occasion of some little domestic occurrence, "Mr. Wordsworth, how <u>could</u> you be so giddy?" He has, undeniably, a lurking love of mischief. [. . .] There is an almost patriarchal simplicity, an absence of all pretension about him. [. . .] all is free, unstudied—"the river winding at its own sweet will"[4]—in his manner and conversation there is more of impulse about them than I had expected, but in other respects I see much that I should have looked for in the poet of meditative life: frequently his head droops, his eyes half close, and he seems buried in quiet depths of thought. I have passed a delightful morning to-day in walking with him about his own richly-shaded grounds, and hearing him speak of the old English writers, particularly Spenser, whom he loves, as he himself expresses it, for his "earnestness and devotedness." [. . .] I must not forget to tell you that he not only admired our exploit in crossing the Ulverston sands, as a deed of "derring do," but as a decided proof of taste; the Lake scenery, he says, is never seen to such advantage as after the passage of what he calls its majestic barrier.[5]

[1] *CM* 2.111–13

[2] In Ambleside, the village near Wordsworth's home at Rydal Mount.

[3] "She writes enthusiastically of Wordsworth and appreciates him becomingly," H. C. Robinson commented as he read *CM* (7 October 1836), "but it is his moral and religious character

that seems to have chiefly attracted her. She writes with equal warmth in admiration of the man. But I do not like her calling him always *the old man*" (*On Books and Their Writers*, ed. Edith J. Morley [London: Dent, 1938], 505).

[4] Wordsworth's *Composed on Westminster Bridge*: "The river glideth at its own sweet will" (12); FH may be punning on the poet's first name in this quotation.

[5] In his "Directions and Information for Tourists" at the front of *Guide to the Lakes* (1835), Wordsworth advertised the trek across Ulverstone Sands, a seven-mile tidal plain: "They who wish to see the celebrated ruins of Furness Abbey, and are not afraid of crossing the Sands, may go from Lancaster to Ulverston"; in an appendix, he advised, "the Stranger from the moment he sets his foot upon the Sands seems to leave the turmoil & the traffic of the world behind him, & crossing the majestic Plain from which the Sea has retired & which in a few hours the Waters will cover again" may gain a remarkable view of the mountains and valleys.

---

**To John Lodge.** Rydal Mount, 24 June 1830.[1] The Lakes, Wordsworth, Byron   My dear Mr. L——,

[. . .] You can scarcely conceive a more beautiful little spot than Rydal Mount; my window is completely embowered in ivy and roses, and Winandermere lies gleaming among the hills before it:—what a contrast to the culinary regions about Liverpool! I am charmed with Mr. Wordsworth himself; his manners are distinguished by that frank simplicity which I believe to be ever the characteristic of real genius; his conversation perfectly free and unaffected, yet remarkable for power of expression and vivid imagery; when the subject calls forth any thing like enthusiasm, the poet breaks out frequently and delightfully, and his gentle and affectionate playfulness in the intercourse with all the members of his family, would of itself sufficiently refute Moore's theory in the Life of Byron, with regard to the unfitness of genius for domestic happiness.[2] I have much of his society, as he walks by me while I ride to explore the mountain glens and waterfalls, and he occasionally repeats passages of his own poems in a deep and thinking tone, which harmonizes well with the spirit of these scenes. [. . .]

[1] *CM* 2.114–15. "Mr. L——" is FH's and Chorley's friend, John Lodge (later, John Lodge Ellerton), Esq. (1801–73) of Liverpool, a well-known amateur musician. FH wrote several songs for his melodies (*1839* 7.1 n; cf. 19 n, 87 n); many of her songs, in turn, "were beautifully set" by Lodge, "with whom she long corresponded on the subject" (Lawrence 339–40). His "powers of amateurship were never more happily displayed than in the spirited and pathetic music to which he has united many of Mrs. Hemans' songs, some written purposely for him" (*CM* 1.253). FH also composed "a great many airs to lyric pieces of [her] own"; she showed these to Lodge, who "was so much pleased, that he has kindly arranged them with symphonies and accompaniments" (2.185). Chorley acknowledges "his kind assistance" with *Memorials*.

[2] Referring to Thomas Moore's *Life of Byron* (1830), "year 1814": "The truth is, I fear, that rarely, if ever, have men of the higher order of genius shown themselves fitted for the calm affections and comforts that form the cement of domestic life," a sentence that initiates a long essay (1832 ed., 3.125–36) elaborating the subject of Byron's spectacularly failed marriage and coming to his defense. FH would also have read Byron's unkind remarks about her in letters to their then mutual publisher Murray, which Moore printed (see below).

**To Rose Lawrence.** Rydal Mount, ca. 24 June, 1830.[1] Wordsworth at home

I have been making you a little drawing of Mr Wordsworth's house, which, though it has no other merit than that of fidelity, will, I know, find favour in your sight. The steps up the front lead to a little grassy mound, commanding a view always so rich, and sometimes so brightly solemn, that one can well imagine its influence traceable in many of the poet's writings. On this mount he frequently sits all evening, and sometimes seems borne away in thought.

[1] Lawrence 330–31. Cf. *HM* 208; my dating is derived from its placement among dated letters. FH was a capable landscape-sketcher; engravings of her drawings appear on the title pages of the volumes of *1839*. Lawrence, a friend of FH in Wavertree, was also a poet.

---

**To ?H. F. Chorley.** Rydal Mount, 24 June 1830.[1] Charmed with Wordsworth

[. . .] I seem to be writing to you almost from the spirit-land; all is here so brightly still, so remote from every-day cares and tumults, that sometimes I can scarcely[2] persuade myself I am not dreaming. It scarcely seems to be "the light of common day,"[3] that is clothing the woody mountains before me; there is something almost visionary in its soft gleams and ever-changing shadows. I am charmed with Mr. Wordsworth, whose kindness to me has quite a soothing influence over my spirits. Oh! what relief, what blessing there is in the feeling of admiration, when it can be freely poured forth! "There is a daily beauty in his life,"[4] which is in such lovely harmony with his poetry, that I am thankful to have witnessed and felt it. He gives me a good deal of his society, reads to me, walks with me, leads my poney when I ride, and I begin to talk with him as with a sort of paternal friend. The whole of this morning, he kindly passed in reading to me a great deal from Spenser, and afterwards his own "Laodamia," my favourite "Tintern Abbey," and many of those noble sonnets which you, like myself, enjoy so much. His reading is very peculiar, but, to my ear, delightful; slow, solemn, earnest in expression more than any I have ever heard: when he reads or recites in the open air, his deep, rich tones seem to proceed from a spirit-voice, and belong[5] to the religion of the place; they harmonize so fitly with the thrilling tones of woods and waterfalls. His expressions are often strikingly poetical; such as—"I would not give up the mists that spiritualize our mountains, for all the blue skies of Italy." Yesterday evening he walked beside me as I rode on a long and lovely mountain-path high above Grasmere Lake: I was much interested by his showing me, carved deep into the rock, as we passed, the initials of his wife's name, inscribed there many years ago by himself; and the dear old man, like "Old Mortality," renews them from time to time.[6] I could scarcely help exclaiming "Esto perpetua!"[7]

[1] *CM* 2.116–18; previously published in the *Athenæum*, 27 June 1835, 494. Lawrence notes that the letters Chorley published in the *Athenæum* were ones "addressed to his family" (334 n), and it seems likely that this one was addressed to Chorley himself.

[2] *HM* 208] hardly

[3] A turn on Wordsworth's phrase for the loss of childhood's "celestial light," which the adult sees "fade into the light of common day" (*Ode: Intimations of Immortality* 76).

[4] A peculiar echo of Iago's envy of Michael Cassio: "He hath a daily beauty in his life / That makes me ugly" (*Othello* 5.1.19–20).

[5] *Athenæum*] belong

[6] *Old Mortality* (1816), the first of Scott's novels in the series *Tales of My Landlord* and the nickname of its storyteller, who wandered about Scotland in the 18th c., repairing the tombs of the Cameronians, a militant sect of strict Covenanters during the reign of James II.

[7] May this last forever! (Spanish motto)

**To a male friend** from Coniston. Rydal Mount, 25 June 1830.[1]
Wordsworth's opinions

My dear Sir,

[. . .] You will be pleased to hear that the more I see of Mr. Wordsworth, the more I admire, and I may almost say, love him. It is delightful to see a life in such perfect harmony with all that his writings express—"true to the kindred points of heaven and home!"[2] You may remember how much I disliked, and I think you agreed with me in reprobating that shallow theory of Mr. Moore's with regard to the unfitness of genius for domestic happiness. I was speaking of it yesterday to Mr. Wordsworth, and was pleased by his remark, "It is not because they possess genius that they make unhappy homes, but because they do not possess genius <u>enough</u>; a higher order of mind would enable them to see and feel all the beauty of domestic ties." He has himself been singularly fortunate in long years of almost untroubled domestic peace and union. . . .[3]

How much I was amused yesterday, by a sudden burst of indignation in Mr. Wordsworth which would have enchanted————. We were sitting on a bank overlooking Rydal Lake, and speaking of Burns. I said, "Mr. Wordsworth, do you not think his war ode 'Scots who hae wi' Wallace bled,' has been a good deal over-rated? especially by Mr. Carlyle, who calls it the noblest lyric in the language?"[4] "I am delighted to hear you ask the question," was his reply, "over-rated!—trash!—stuff!—miserable inanity! without a thought—without an image!" &c. &c. &c.—then he recited the piece in a tone of unutterable scorn; and concluded with a <u>Da Capo</u> of "wretched stuff!" I rode past De Quincy's cottage the other evening.[5] . . .

I hope you will write <u>very</u> soon. I really long for a "voice from home."[6]

[1] *CM* 2.119–20.

[2] Wordsworth, *To a Sky-lark* (1825), 12.

[3] *HM* (210) omits this last sentence and fills in the ellipses] His mind, indeed, may well inhabit an untroubled atmosphere, for, as he himself declares, no wounded affections, no embittered feelings, have ever been his lot; the current of his domestic life has flowed on, bright, and pure, and unbroken. Hence, I think, much of the high, sculpture-like repose which invests both his character and writings with so tranquil a dignity.

[4] In an unsigned, influential review of Lockhart's *Life of Burns* (1828), Carlyle writes, "Why should we speak of *Scots wha hae wi' Wallace bled*; since all know of it, from the king to the

meanest of his subjects? [. . .] So long as there is warm blood in the heart of Scotchman or man, it will move in fierce thrills under this war-ode; the best, we believe, that was ever written by any pen" (*Edinburgh Review* 48.96 [1828]). Burns's most famous patriotic song, subtitled "Robert Bruce's Address to his Army, before the Battle of Bannockburn" (1794), is a rally for the battle in 1314 in which a Scots army of 30,000 under Bruce (who reigned 1306–29) defeated Edward II's English army, which outnumbered them more than threefold. Bruce invokes the memory of Scots patriot-martyr Sir William Wallace (ca. 1270–1305), who was betrayed to the English, hanged, drawn, and quartered.

⁵ Between Grasmere and Rydal. FH admired Thomas De Quincey's *Confessions of an English Opium Eater* (1821), from which she took her epigraph for *The Dreamer* (*Forest Sanctuary*, 2d ed.).

⁶ "Wilt thou not pine to hear / Voices from home?" ("Song" from *The Sisters, A Ballad*).

---

**To "Mr.——." Rydal Mount, 2 July 1830.¹ Dove Nest**

Will you not like to think of me at that lovely little Dove's Nest which we both of us admired so much from the lake, my dear Mr.——? I was agreeably surprised to find it a lodging-house, and have taken apartments there for a fortnight;² probably I may remain longer, but I almost fear that its <u>deep</u> though beautiful seclusion, would, for any length of time, be too much for one upon whom solitude bears back so many subjects of melancholy thought. If you were but near enough to come and pass the evenings with me! How I should enjoy making your coffee at the window, which looks forth to that glorious lake with all its glancing sails and woody islets! But I am sure your thoughts will sometimes be with me, when you can free them from the turmoil of your busy life, and the <u>resounding</u> streets, and I hope you will write to me very often. You may be quite sure that I always write to you from impulse, and the strong wish of communion rendered even stronger to <u>my</u> nature by beautiful scenery and new impressions. [. . .] As you have so particularly requested me to tell you about my health, I must own that I am not quite so well as I was at the beginning of my sojourn here. [. . .] Yesterday I rode round Grasmere and Rydal Lake; it was a glorious evening, and the imaged heaven in the waters more completely <u>filled</u> my mind, even to overflowing, than I think any object in nature ever did before. I quite longed for you: we should have stood³ in silence before the magnificent vision for an hour, as it flushed and faded, and darkened at last into the deep sky of a summer night. I thought of the scriptural expression, "A sea of glass mingled with fire";⁴ no other words are fervid enough to convey the least impression of what lay burning before me.

¹ *CM* 2.121–23.

² FH and her sons (Henry, Charles, and Claude) stayed several weeks, leaving for Scotland in August. Dove Nest is a lodging house "near Ambleside" (*CM* 2.123).

³ *HM* (211) truncates the beginning of this sentence and emends to "I could have stood."

⁴ Revelation 15.2: "And I saw, as it were, a sea of glass, mingled with fire."

**To Thomas Cadell.** Rydal Mount, 5 July ?1830.[1] Request not to republish
*The Domestic Affections*

Sir

In reply to your obliging letter, I am under the necessity of informing you, that both my friends and myself would consider the re-appearance of the Volume to which you allude, and which was written at the Age of fourteen, so injurious to my present literary reputation, that I have earnestly to request no steps may be taken to re-produce it.—Its accidental coincidence of title with the Volume just published by Mr. Blackwood[2] would make it interfere very disadvantageously with the sale of the latter, and many reasons would render it unpleasant to me and my friends that my present name should appear on its title page; I should indeed think such a measure seriously detrimental to the interests of my late Works as well as their Publisher.

I am, Sir,
Your obedient Ser[t]
F. Hemans

[1] HL RB 137748, a letter bound in copy of FDB, *Poems* (1808).
[2] *Songs of the Affections &c* (1830); Cadell & Davies published *The Domestic Affections &c* (1812) and *Poems* (1808). Blackwood's posthumous editions of FH place some of the poems from both volumes in an appendix of "Juvenalia."

---

**To ?Harriett Hughes.** Dove Nest, Ambleside, early July 1830.[1]
Wordsworth and the Paradise of the Lakes

Mr. Wordsworth's kindness has inspired me with a feeling of confidence which it is delightful to associate with those of admiration and respect, before excited by his writings;—and he has treated me with so much consideration, and gentleness, and care!—they have been like balm to my spirit after all the <u>fades</u> flatteries with which I am <u>blasée</u>. I wish I had time to tell you of mornings which he has passed in reading to me, and of evenings when he has walked beside me, whilst I rode through the lovely vales of Grasmere and Rydal; and of his beautiful, sometimes half-unconscious recitation, in a voice so deep and solemn, that it has often brought tears into my eyes. One little incident I <u>must</u> describe. We had been listening, during one of these evening rides, to various sounds and notes of birds, which broke upon the stillness, and at last I said—"Perhaps there may be a deeper and richer music pervading all Nature, than we are permitted, in this state, to hear." He answered by reciting those glorious lines of Milton's,

> Millions of spiritual creatures walk the earth,
> Unseen, both when we wake and when we sleep, &c.[2]

and this in tones that seemed rising from such depths of veneration! I cannot describe the thrill with which I listened; it was like the feeling which Lord Byron has embodied in one of his best and purest moments, when he so beautifully says,—

> And not a breath crept through the rosy air,
> And yet the forest leaves seemed stirred with prayer.[3]

Mr. Wordsworth's daily life in the bosom of his family, is delightful—so affectionate and confiding. I cannot but mournfully feel, in the midst of their happiness, "Still, still, I am a stranger here!"—But where am I not a stranger <u>now</u>?

[1] *HM* 210–11. Cf. *CM* 2.127, FH's letter of 6 July 1830.
[2] Adam's assurance to Eve in prelapsarian Eden (*Paradise Lost* 4.677–78).
[3] A description of twilight in *Don Juan III*, cii.

---

**To ?H. F. Chorley's sister.** Dove Nest, Ambleside, mid-July 1830.[1]
Kitchen scales

My dear ———,

I must frankly own that it is my necessities which impel me so soon to address you again. From the various dilapidations which my wardrobe has endured since I came into this country, I am daily assuming more and more the appearance of "a decayed gentlewoman";[2] and if you could only behold me in a certain black gown, which came with me here in all the freshness of youth, your tender heart would be melted into tearful compassion. The ebony bloom of the said dress is departed for ever: the waters of Winandermere, (thrown up by oars in unskilful hands,) have splashed and dashed over it, the rains of Rydal have soaked it, the winds from Helm-crag have wrinkled it, and it is altogether somewhat in the state of

> "Violets plucked, which sweetest showers,
> May ne'er make grow again."[3]

Three yards of black silk, however, will, I believe, restore me to respectability of appearance, . . . if ——— will add a supply of chocolate, without which there is no getting through the fatigue of existence for me—and if ——— or your brother will also send me a volume or two of Schiller—not the plays, but the poems—to read with Mr. Wordsworth, I shall then have a complete brown-paper full of happiness.[4] Imagine, my dear ———, a bridal present made by Mr. Wordsworth, to a young lady in whom he is much interested—a poet's daughter, too! You will be thinking of a broach in the shape of a lyre, or a butterfly-shaped aigrette, or a forget-me-not ring, or some such "small gear"—nothing of the sort, but a good, handsome, substantial, useful-looking pair of scales, to hang up in her store-room! "For you must be aware, my dear Mrs. Hemans," said he to me very gravely, "how necessary it is occasionally for every lady to see things weighed herself." "<u>Poveretta me!</u>"[5] I looked as <u>good as I could</u>, and, happily for me, the poetic eyes are not very clear-sighted, so that I believe no suspicion derogatory to my notability of character, has yet flashed upon the mighty master's mind:[6] indeed I told him that I looked upon scales as particularly graceful things, and had great thoughts of having my picture taken with a pair in my hand.[7]

[1] *CM* 2.140–42. First published in the *Athenæum*, 27 June 1835, 495, where the addressee is named as "a correspondent of her own sex" (494), presumably in Chorley's household; the "brother" mentioned is probably he. Chorley feels the need to say that the tone of the anecdote about the bridal gift ought not "be misunderstood" as anything other than affectionate.

[2] Describing characters in Charlotte Lennox's *Harriot Stuart* (1751) and in Henry Brooke's *The Fool of Quality* (1765–70). See also Eaton Stannard Barrett, *All the Talents* (1807), Dialogue the Second, praising British freedoms, but commenting that in Ireland, "Catholic Emancipation now goes begging from door to door like a decayed gentlewoman" (31 n).

[3] *The Friar of Orders Gray*, collected in Thomas Percy's *Reliques of Ancient English Poetry* (1765): "Weep no more, lady, weep no more, / Thy sorrowe is in vaine: / For violets pluckt the sweetest showers / Will ne'er make grow againe" (45–48).

[4] In a later letter, FH indicates that Wordsworth, impressed with (or unable to resist) her strong enthusiasm, agreed to read Schiller with her. She planned to offer "him some of my own *first loves* in Schiller—'The Song of the Bell,' 'Cassandra,' or 'Thekla's Spirit-voice,' with none of which he is acquainted" (*CM* 2.145).

After the verse inset, *Athenæum*] Will you, therefore, be so kind as to send me as soon as possible, the *material* for this *rifacciamento*? [*rifacciamento*: Italian for "remaking"]

[5] Italian: Poor little me!

[6] A light reference to Wordsworth's "I wandered lonely as a cloud": in memory, images "flash upon [the] inward eye." For Wordsworth's chagrin at FH's amusement with his effort at instruction (and probably at Chorley's publication of the anecdote), see his headnote to *Extempore Effusion*, below. A "notable" woman is famed for household management.

[7] A notable woman's version of the icon of justice, blindfolded with a sword—not only aestheticizing the instrument of instruction but using it in playful judgment of his didacticism.

---

**To John Lodge.** Dove Nest, Ambleside, 20 July 1830.[1]
Deepest retirement, fans

My dear Mr. L——,
[. . .] I am anxious to know whether you received my little volume [. . . .] very little of its contents would be new to you, though the arrangement of the whole might, I hope, afford you some pleasure.[2] [. . .] I remained at Mr. Wordsworth's rather more than a fortnight, and then came to my present residence, a lonely, but beautifully situated cottage on the banks of Winandermere. I am so much delighted with the spot, that I scarcely know how I shall leave it. The situation is one of the deepest retirement; but the bright lake before me, with all its fairy barks and sails, glancing like "things of life"[3] over its blue water, prevents the solitude from being overshadowed by any thing like sadness. I contrive to see Mr. Wordsworth frequently, but am little disturbed by other visitors: only the other evening, just as I was about to go forth upon the lake, a card was brought to me.——— Think of my being found out by American tourists in Dove's Nest! [. . .] but however, they brought credentials I could not but acknowledge. The young ladies, as I feared, brought an Album concealed in their shawls, and it was levelled at me like a pocket-pistol before all was over.[4] [. . .]

[1] *CM* 2.142–44.

[2] *Songs of the Affections &c*, published in June.

[3] See George Croly, *Cataline: A Dramatic Poem* (1822): "The Spirit of your fiery land of spells / Is colouring the common things of life / Into mysterious splendour" (2.1); Barbauld, *To Mr. S. T. Coleridge* (1825): "Athwart the mists, / Far into vacant space, huge shadows stretch / And seem realities; while things of life, / Obvious to sight and touch, all glowing round, / Fade to the hue of shadows" (9–13); Mark Lemon, *Arnold of Winkelried* (1825): "yonder fleecy clouds / Will sometimes shape themselves to things of life / And still are vapour" (4.3).

[4] The credentials may have been a letter of introduction from Andrews Norton. An album is a sort of commonplace book in which one also gathered celebrity autographs and inscriptions; one of the more famous was that of Dora Wordsworth (the poet's daughter), with poems inscribed by FH, Jewsbury, Scott, Charles Lamb, Coleridge, and Dorothy Wordsworth.

**To Rose Lawrence.** Dove Nest, Ambleside, late July, 1830.[1] Albums

Here I have left behind me all the dust of celebrity: I have been only asked to write in two Albums since I came into this country. Mr. W[ordsworth] tells me that when he was more troubled with those importunities than he is at present, he found it convenient to administer the same line to all patients. The one he selected for the purpose, and adhered to a considerable time, was

"The proper study of mankind, is <u>man</u>."[2]

Think of this in the midst of the butterfly-winged cupids and roses of a young lady's Album!

[1] Lawrence 332–33.
[2] Pope's *Essay on Man: Epistle II* (1733), 2; emphasis added.

**To a new friend** in Dublin, Fall 1830.[1] Menai Bridge; Northern Lights

[. . .] that bold mountain-chain rose upon me, in all its grandeur, with the crowning Snowdon [. . . .] And the Menai bridge, which I thought I should scarcely have noticed in the presence of those glorious heights, really seems, from its magnificence, a native feature of the scene, and nobly asserts the pre-eminence of <u>mind</u> above all other things. I could scarcely have conceived such an union of strength and grace; and its chain-work is so airy in appearance, that to drive along it seems almost like passing thought the trellis of a bower: it is quite startling to look down from any thing which appears so fragile, to the immense depth below.[2] . . . . My journey lay along the sea-shore rather late at night, and I was surprised by quite a splendid vision of the northern lights, on the very spot where I had once, and once only, before seen them in early childhood. They shot up like slender pillars of white light, with a sort of arrowy motion, from a dark cloud above the sea; their colour varied in ascending, from that of silver to a faint orange, and then a very delicate green: and sometimes the motion was changed,

and they chased each other <u>along</u> the edge of the cloud, with a dazzling brightness and rapidity. I was almost startled by seeing them <u>there</u> again; and after so
long an interval of thoughts and years, it was like the effect produced by a sudden
burst of familiar and yet long forgotten music.

[1] *CM* 2.155–56. Cf. *HM* 222–23.
[2] Thomas Telford's famous 1,265-foot suspension bridge, begun in 1819 and completed in
1826, extended the carriage road from Bangor, North Wales, across the Menai Strait to the
island of Anglesey (on to Holyhead, port of departure to Ireland). Depending on tides and
season, the bridge hung at least one hundred feet above the water. Mount Snowdon rises about
3,650 feet.

---

**To a new friend** in Dublin, early 1831.[1] Sappho, fame, Hamlet, Byron

Since I wrote last, I have been quite confined to the house; but before I caught
my last very judicious cold, I went to see an exquisite piece of sculpture, which
has been lately sent to this neighbourhood from Rome by Gibson, with whose
name as an artist you are most likely familiar. It is a statue of Sappho, representing her at the moment she receives the tidings of Phaon's desertion. I think I
prefer it to almost any thing I ever saw of Canova's, as it possesses all his delicacy
and beauty of form, but is imbued with a far deeper sentiment.[2] There is a sort
of willowy drooping in the figure, which seems to express a weight of unutterable sadness, and one sinking arm holds the lyre so carelessly, that you almost
fancy it will drop while you gaze. Altogether, it seems to speak piercingly and
sorrowfully of the nothingness of Fame, at least to woman. There was a good
collection of pictures in the same house, but they were almost unaccountably
vulgarized in my sight by the presence of the lonely and graceful statue. [. . .] I
wish I could be with you to see Young's performance of Hamlet,[3] of all
Shakspeare's characters the one which interests me most; I suppose from the
never-ending conjectures in which it involves one's mind. Did I ever mention to
you Goëthe's beautiful remark upon it? He says, that Hamlet's naturally gentle
and tender spirit, overwhelmed with its mighty tasks and solemn responsibilities, is like a China vase, fit only for the reception of delicate flowers, but in
which an oak tree has been planted; the roots of the strong tree expand, and the
fair vase is shivered.[4] [. . .] Some <u>Quarterly Reviews</u> have lately been sent to me,
one of which contains an article on Byron, by which I have been deeply and
sorrowfully impressed. His character, as there portrayed, reminded me of some
of those old Eastern cities, where travellers constantly find a squalid mud hovel
built against the ruins of a gorgeous temple; for alas! the best part of that fearfully mingled character is but ruin—the wreck of what might have been.[5]

[1] *HM* 226–27. Cf. *CM* 2.172–73, 176–78.
[2] See *The Last Song of Sappho* (1831); English sculptor John Gibson (1790–1866), living in
Rome, and Italian sculptor Antonio Canova (1757–1822) were both neoclassicists.
[3] Charles Mayne Young (1777–1856) made his debut as Hamlet in 1807 and after 1811
became the lead actor at Covent Garden as well as the premier actor in London until the

emergence of Kean and Macready; Hamlet was one of his best parts. In 1823 he had a featured role in FH's *Vespers of Palermo* at Covent Garden.

[4] In a famous passage on Hamlet in *Wilhelm Meister* (1795), Goëthe writes, "Shakespeare meant [. . .] to represent the effects of a great action laid upon a soul unfit for the performance of it. [. . .] there is an oak-tree planted in a costly jar, which should have borne only pleasant flowers in its bosom; the roots expand, the jar is shivered."

[5] Lockhart's review of Moore's *Byron* in the *Quarterly* (January 1831) was more mixed than negative, praising the poet's genius but attacking his political opinions, especially of George III, and voicing disgust at his debauchery, especially in Venice. Stung by Byron's nasty remarks about him that had already appeared in various memoirs, Murray was not averse to publishing detractions of Byron's character in the *Quarterly*. A scathing essay on Moore's *Byron* appeared in the April *British Critic*.

---

**To ?,** after 12 February 1831.[1] "Felicia Hemans" in the *Athenæum*

I send you a number of the Athenæum, (which seems almost the best literary journal of the day,) for the sake of an account it contains of the Necker family and Madame de Staël, which I think particularly interesting. From the style, I imagine it to be written by a friend of mine, Miss Jewsbury.[2] . . . I send another number, in which I think you will read with interest a paper, by the sudden appearance of which, with the portentous title "Felicia Hemans," I was somewhat startled yesterday morning. Some parts of it are, however, beautifully written, though I hope you will quite enter into my feelings when I utterly disclaim all wish for the post of "Speaker to the Feminine Literary House of Commons."

[1] *CM* 2.173–74. FH seems not to know that Jewsbury is the author of "Literary Sketches No. 1: Felicia Hemans," which appeared unsigned in *Athenæum* 172 (12 February 1831): 104–5.

[2] *Athenæum* 171 (5 February 1831): 86–88.

---

**To John Lodge.** The Hermitage, Kilkenny, Ireland, July 1831.[1]
Visit to Mary Tighe's grave

I wish to give you an account of an interesting day I lately passed, before its images become faint in my recollection. We went to Woodstock, the place where the late Mrs. Tighe, whose poetry has always been very touching to my feelings, passed the latest years of her life, and near which she is buried.[2] The scenery of the place is magnificent, of a style which I think I prefer to every other; wild profound glens, rich with every hue and form of foliage, and a rapid river sweeping through them, now lost, and now lighting up the deep woods with <u>sudden</u> flashes of its waves. Altogether it reminded me more of Hawthornden, than any thing I have seen since—though it wants the solemn rock pinnacles of that romantic place. I wish I could have been alone with Nature and my thoughts; but, to my surprise, I found myself the object of quite a <u>reception</u>. The chief Justice and many other persons had been invited to meet me, and I was to be made completely the lady of the day. There was no help for it, though I never felt so much as if I wanted a <u>large leaf</u> to wrap me up and shelter me from all curiosity and attention. Still one cannot but feel grateful for kindness, and much was shown me. I should have told you that Woodstock is now the seat of Mr and Lady Louisa Tighe. . . . Amongst other persons of the party was Mr Henry Tighe, the widower of the poetess. He had just been exercising, I found, one of his accomplishments in the translation into Latin of a little poem of mine; and I am told that his version is very elegant.[3] We went to the tomb, "the grave of a poetess," where there is a monument by Flaxman: it consists of a recumbent female figure, with much of the repose, the mysterious sweetness of happy death, which is to me so affecting in monumental sculpture. There is, however, a very small <u>Titania</u>-looking sort of figure with wings, sitting at the head of the sleeper, and intended to represent Psyche, which I thought interfered wofully with the singleness of effect which the tomb would have produced: unfortunately, too, the monument is carved in very rough stone, which allows no delicacy of touch.[4] That place of rest made me very thoughtful; I could not but reflect on the many changes which had brought me to the spot I had commemorated three years since, without the slightest idea of ever visiting it; and though surrounded by attention and the appearance of interest, my heart was envying the repose of her who slept there. [. . .]

[1] *CM* 208–11. Cf. *HM* 237–39. FH's brother George Browne resided at The Hermitage.
[2] See *The Grave of a Poetess*, in *Records of Woman*.
[3] *The Graves of a Household* (*HM* 239); cf. Kingsley Amis's remark (423 above).
[4] John Flaxman (1755–1826), English sculptor and friend of Blake, best known for his neoclassical memorial sculptures. Titania is the Fairy Queen in *A Midsummer Night's Dream*.

**To Clara Graves.** The Hermitage, Kilkenny, July 1831.[1]
Mary Tighe, her widower

[. . .] Woodstock is a place with really superb scenery; old stately woods, and deep glens, with a fine River sweeping through, and lighting them up by occasional gleams of its waters. I visited of course, the tomb of the late Mrs. Tighe, which is in a beautiful grass Church-Yard, close to the ruins of an old Abbey.— It has a monument by Flaxman, a sleeping female figure, with much grace and softness, but unfortunately carved in a very rough stone, which has allowed no delicacy of touch. I was sorry to find that I must give up my beau idéal of Mrs. Tighe's Character; at least in a great measure; much of her domestic sorrow I learned, was caused by her excessive passion for shining in Society, which quite carried her away from all Home-enjoyments, until her Health gave way, and she was compelled to relinquish this career of dissipation.—How one is obliged to resign one's fair visions of excellence, my dear Clara, when the strong <u>daylight</u> of truth is thrown upon them; and how painful is the feeling with which we see them melt away!—I thought several times of Lord Byron's 'Implora pace,'[2] whilst listening to these details, which were given me <u>at the tomb itself</u>.—Mr.

Henry Tighe, the widower of the Poetess, was amongst our party; he had just
been translating a poem of mine into Latin, which I am told is very elegant. He
is very intelligent & gentlemanly, nevertheless, "I did not like this Dr. Fell."[3]
[...]

[1] HL MS 4253. The education of FH's son Charles was superintended by Clara's brother,
Robert Perceval Graves (1810–93), then a student at Trinity College (*HM* 243–44). With
FH's overtures and Wordsworth's help, Robert later secured a curacy in the Lake District. FH's
doctor in Dublin was Clara and Robert's father, eminent physician and professor of divinity at
Dublin University, Robert Graves (1796–1853) (Lawrence 374).

[2] (Beg for peace.) FH refers to letters that Byron wrote in June 1819 (Moore's *Byron* [1830;
cf. 1832 ed. 4.159, 162]) about epitaphs at Ferrara that read simply "Implora pace": "Can any
thing be more full of pathos? Those few words say all that can be said or sought; the dead had
had enough of life; all they wanted was rest, and this they *implore!*" (162). Byron told Murray
that this is what he wanted for his epitaph. FH made "*Implora pace!*" her epigraph for *The
Fountain of Oblivion*, the last of the *Songs of the Affections* (1830), and cited Byron's letters in a
footnote (p. 135). "She frequently referred to that touching epitaph, '*Implore pace,*' mentioned
in one of Lord Byron's letters, as the words she would wish to be inscribed on her own monument" (*CM* 2.323).

[3] Dr. John Fell (1625–86), Dean of Christ Church, Oxford, promised to cancel a sentence of
expulsion on Thomas Brown (1663–1704) if he could translate extempore Martial's twenty-
third epigram: "Non amo te, Sabidi, nec possum dicere quare; / Hoc tantum possum non amo
te" (I do not love you, Sabidi, nor can I say why; / This much I can say—I do not love you).
Brown's quatrain became famous: "I do not love thee Dr. Fell, / The reason why I cannot
tell; / But this I know, and know full well, / I do not love thee Dr. Fell."

---

**To William Blackwood,** Edinburgh. Dublin, 18 September 1831.[1]
Remuneration

Dear Sir
[...] Mr. Colburn has lately raised the terms on which I sometimes wrote for
him, to two guineas a page—if I should not hear from you to the contrary, I shall
conclude that you will not be less liberal.[2] [...]

**William Blackwood,** replying to FH, Edinburgh, 26 September 1831.[3]

My dear Madam
I had the pleasure of seeing your two beautiful Poems fortunately just in time to
put them into this n° of Maga [...] Though 2 guineas a page is so much higher
than what I pay even to my most gifted friend, I will not grudge it to you, as I
look forward to your bringing out another volume in which these can be inserted.[4] I hope therefore you have some long Poem in view, as now that you are
in Ireland, you must be meeting with some sterling tales which would make a
splendid story.[5]

[1] BA MS 4029, f. 243.
[2] Henry Colburn, publisher of *NMM*, had set this rate as the maximum on 14 October 1824
(BL Add MS 38108, f. 331).
[3] BA MS 30312, f. 234.

<sup>4</sup> The two poems are *The Freed Bird* and *Marguerite of France*. The gifted friend is John Wilson ("Christopher North"), major contributor since 1817. While FH earned more per page, his total earnings, based on volume, were considerably higher.

<sup>5</sup> He continued to urge her: "I hope you are proposing some prose articles for me, and that you are likewise going on with a poem of some length—an interesting Irish tale would be very popular, and be much more effective, for beautiful as your little pieces are, people look for something different from you" (24 October 1831; BA MS 30312, f. 244).

---

### To ?Harriett Hughes. Dublin, May 1832.<sup>1</sup> Cholera

I cannot describe to you the strange thrill that came over me, when, on accidentally going to the window yesterday, I saw one of the black covered litters, which convey the cholera patients to the hospital, passing by, followed by policemen with sabres in their hands. This last precaution is necessary to guard the litters from the infatuated populace, who imagine that the physicians are carrying on some nefarious work (<u>smothering</u> is, I believe, their favourite theory) within the vehicle. But the sight I have described to you was so like the actual presence of some dark power sweeping past, that I was for the moment, completely overcome;—and oh! the strange contrasts of life! there were May-dancers in the street scarcely a moment afterwards! Notwithstanding the sick sensation of which I have spoken, my spirits are perfectly composed, and I have not the least intention of taking flight, which many families are now doing. To me there is something extremely solemnizing, something which at once awes and calms the spirit, instead of agitating it, in the presence of this viewless danger, between which and ourselves, we cannot but feel that the only barrier is the mercy of God. I never felt so penetrated by the sense of an entire dependence upon Him; and though I adopt some necessary precautions on account of Charles, my mind is in a state of entire serenity.

<sup>1</sup> *HM* 256–57. The cholera epidemic was international by the 1830s, raging from India (taking the life of Jewsbury), Europe, and the United States; it hit particularly hard in the cities. Charles is FH's son.

---

### To ?H. F. Chorley. Ireland, August 1832.<sup>1</sup> Being a *Poetess*

The society of the neighbourhood seems as <u>borné</u> as usual in most country places. I appear to be regarded as rather a "curious thing"; the gentlemen treat me as I suppose they would the muse Calliope, were she to descend amongst them;<sup>2</sup> that is, with much <u>solemn</u> reverence, and constant allusions to poetry; the ladies, every time I happen to speak, look as if they expected sparks of fire, or some other marvellous thing, would proceed from my lips, as from those of the Sea-Princess in Arabian fiction. If I were in higher spirits, I should be strongly tempted to do something <u>very</u> strange amongst them, in order to fulfil the ideas I imagine they entertain of that altogether foreign monster, a <u>Poetess</u>, but I feel too much subdued for such <u>cappricci</u><sup>3</sup> at present.

[1] *CM* 2.279–80. According to H. G. Hewlett, several of the letters FH sent to Chorley from Dublin were used in *CM* (*Henry Fothergill Chorley: Autobiography, Memoir, and Letters*, 2 vols. [London: Richard Bentley, 1873], 1.128); this seems to be one such.

[2] *borné* (French): bound, limited, confined; Calliope is muse of epic poetry.

[3] Italian: caprices.

---

**To Rev. Samuel Butler.** Dublin, 7 November 1833.[1] Son Henry's education

[. . .] I will no longer, my dear Dr. Butler, disdain accepting the kindness you so frankly offer, to assist in carrying through my Boy's education. I may say to you in confidence, though you must be partly aware of it, that I have to struggle against much domestic Wrong, of a kind the most crushing to a Woman's health and Mind, and I do not think it the pride of a generous Nature to refuse the generosity offered cordially by another. [. . .]

[1] BL Add MS 34588, f. 396.

---

**To Wordsworth,** before April 1834.[1] Dedication of *Scenes and Hymns of Life*

My dear Sir,

I earnestly wish that the little volume here inscribed to you, in token of affectionate veneration, were pervaded by more numerous traces of those strengthening and elevating influences which breathe from all your poetry "a power to virtue friendly." I wish, too, that such a token could more adequately convey my deep sense of gratitude for moral and intellectual benefit long derived from the study of that poetry—for the perpetual fountains of "serious faith and inward glee" which I have never failed to discover amidst its pure and lofty regions—for the fresh green places of refuge which it has offered me in many an hour when

——— "The fretful stir
Unprofitable, and the fever of the world
Have hung upon the beatings of my heart";

and when I have found in your thoughts and images such relief as the vision of your "Sylvan Wye," may, at similar times, have afforded to yourself.[2]

May I be permitted, on the present occasion, to record my unfading recollections of enjoyment from your society—of delight in having heard from your own lips, and amidst your own lovely mountain-land, many of those compositions, the remembrance of which will ever spread over its hills and waters a softer colouring of spiritual beauty? Let me also express to you, as to a dear and most honoured friend, my fervent wishes for your long enjoyment of a widely-extended influence, which cannot but be blessed—of a domestic life, encircling you with yet nearer and deeper sources of happiness; and of those eternal hopes, on whose foundation you have built, as a Christian poet, the noble structure of your works.

I rely upon your kindness, my dear Sir, for an indulgent reception of my offering, however lowly, since you will feel assured of the sincerity with which it is presented by

Your ever grateful and affectionate<br>Felicia Hemans

<sup>1</sup> *HM* 270–72. First published in *HM*, together with the "*Intended Dedication of the 'Scenes and Hymns of Life,' to William Wordsworth, Esq.*" For Wordsworth's response, see his letters, ca. 30 April 1834 and September 1834 (below). The published dedication read: "To William Wordsworth, Esq., in token of deep respect for his character, and fervent gratitude for moral and intellectual benefit derived from reverential communion with the spirit of his poetry, this Volume is affectionately inscribed by Felicia Hemans."

<sup>2</sup> Quoting Wordsworth's Wanderer: "there is often found / In mournful thoughts, and always might be found, / A power to virtue friendly" (*The Excursion* 1.632–34); the poet of *O Nightingale!*, who prefers the stock-dove's song "Of serious faith, and inward glee" (19) to the nightingale's passion; and *Tintern Abbey* 52–54, 56.

----

### To? Dublin, 28 June 1834.<sup>1</sup> Jewsbury's death

I was, indeed, deeply and permanently affected by the untimely fate of one so gifted, and so affectionately loving me, as our poor lost friend. It hung the more heavily upon my spirits as the subject of death and the mighty future had so many many times been that of our most confidential communion. How much deeper power seemed to lie <u>coiled up</u>, as it were, in the recesses of her mind, than was ever manifested to the world in her writings! Strange and sad does it seem, that only the broken music of such a spirit have been given to the earth—the full and finished harmony never drawn forth! Yet I would rather, a thousand times, that she should have perished thus, in the path of her chosen duties, than have seen her become the merely brilliant creature of London literary life, living upon those poor <u>succès de société</u>, which I think utterly ruinous to all that is lofty, and holy, and delicate in the nature of a highly-endowed woman.<sup>2</sup>

### To a friend. Dublin, ?28 June 1834.<sup>3</sup> Jewsbury's death

I was ill in bed all yesterday from having walked too much and got a little wet, but am now a good deal better, though my spirits have been depressed ever since the tidings of my poor friend's death arrived. I never expected to meet her again in this life, but there was a strong chain of interest between us, that spell of <u>mind on mind</u>, which, once formed, can never be broken. I felt, too, that my whole nature was understood and appreciated by her, and this is a sort of happiness which I consider the most rare in all earthly affection. Those who feel and think deeply, whatever playfulness of manner may brighten the <u>surface</u> of their character, are fully <u>unsealed</u> to very few indeed. You must not be surprised to see me wearing a slight mourning when we meet; I know she would have put it on for me. Dearest————, I could say much more to you on her character, and my own feelings with regard to her loss—they have been the more solemn from this cause—that the subject of death and the mighty future had been many times that of our deepest conversation. With all my regret, I had rather, a thousand times, that she had perished thus in the path of her duties and the brightness of her <u>improving</u> mind, than become, what I once feared was likely, the merely brilliant creature of London life: <u>that</u> is, indeed, a worthless lot for a nobly-gifted woman's nature! I send you the second volume of "Phantasmagoria," since you liked the first, but it was the production of quite an immature mind, in a youth which had many disadvantages.[4]

**To a friend.** Dublin, early July 1834.[5] Jewsbury's death

Will you tell Mr. Wordsworth this anecdote of poor Mrs. Fletcher? I am sure it will interest him. During the time that the famine in the Deccan was raging, she heard that a poor Hindoo woman had been found lying dead in one of the temples at the foot of an idol, and with a female child, still living, in her arms. She and her husband immediately repaired to the spot, took the poor little orphan away with them, and conveyed it to their own home. She tended it assiduously, and one of her last cares was to have it placed at a female missionary school, to be brought up as a Christian. My sister informs me that her terror of death seemed quite subsided at the last, and that she sank away quite calmly, in utter exhaustion. [. . .]

[1] *CM* 2.312–13; cf. *HM* 276–77. Just after Jewsbury's marriage to Rev. William Kew Fletcher in August 1832, they left for India, where he was posted as chaplain for the East India Company. "I am very sorry to say that she is soon going to India," FH wrote to Lodge; "One can indeed ill afford to lose a friend in this cold harsh world, more especially a *gifted* friend. How few have the least influence over one's feelings or imagination" (December 1831; *CM* 2.249–50). Jewsbury continued to write for the *Athenæum* as a foreign correspondent; she died at Poona, 4 October 1833, in the cholera epidemic. The news was slow to reach England; FH is reacting to the *Athenæum*'s obituary, "Mrs. Fletcher," 21 June 1834.

[2] Alluding, in part, to Jewsbury's *History of an Enthusiast* (from *The Three Histories* [1830]). *HM* text] adds: "I put on mourning for her with a deep feeling of sadness,—"; continues with sentences duplicating the next letter's, from "I never expected" to "very few indeed."

[3] *CM* 2.313–15.

[4] *Phantasmagoria; or Sketches of Life and Literature* (1825); at least three poems therein—*The Women of Suli, Joan of Arc, Woman's Love*—treat subjects that animate FH's own poetry, and lines from a fourth, *Arria*, supply FH's epigraph for *The Switzer's Wife*.

[5] *CM* 2.315–16. *HM* (227) presents this as an additional paragraph to the letter of "28 June" in *CM*. The Wordsworths, particularly the poet and daughter Dora, adored Jewsbury.

**To Archdeacon Samuel Butler.** Dublin, 26 July 1834.[1] *National Lyrics* and *Scenes and Hymns of Life*

[. . .] I am anxious that my friends should see in it some traces of that which I am ever earnestly and fervently seeking—<u>improvement.</u>—I look upon it also as but the opening of a plan which I hope to mature, if God grants me amended health. I would fain achieve some thing of <u>permanent</u> usefulness; of true, however lowly worth; but I have too much cause to feel in my troubled life what some old Sacred Poet has affectingly said—

> "Our peaceful flame that <u>would point up to Heaven,</u>
>     Is still disturb'd, and turn'd aside;
>         And every blast of air
>     Commits such <u>Waste</u> in Man, as Man cannot repair." [unidentified]

[. . .] the frequent fluctuations of my health all interfere materially with my correspondence [. . . .] I have some thoughts of passing a few weeks this summer in Westmoreland where I shall see my friend Mr. Wordsworth [. . .]

Believe me always
my dear Sir
very gratefully yours
Felicia Hemans

¹ BL Add MS 34589, ff. 95–96.

---

**To Robert Peel.** Dublin, 10 February 1835.¹ A grant in aid for her; a living for her son Henry

Sir,

I beg to acknowledge with the deepest gratitude the very liberal pecuniary assistance which I have just had the honour of receiving from you; and which, acceptable as my circumstance renders it, is made yet more so, by the expressions of esteem and approbation which accompany it.—

It is indeed too true that my health is in a most precarious state, and that it has given way under a long and unaided struggle with many difficulties; I cannot but feel however, as if the hope which your letter afforded me, would do much toward its revival.—

I accept, Sir, most gratefully, your welcome offer of a Clerkship in one of the Public Offices for my son; it is indeed what I have long and vainly been trying to procure for him, and its attainment will relieve me from the pressure of a heavy anxiety.—He is a youth of high principle and good ability, and will, I have every reason to hope, prove not unworthy of your kindness.—He will be ready to attend your summons, whenever given.—With my sincerest acknowledgments for your most [?]—for liberality, and a deep sense of the value of that approbation which you express for my writings, I have the honour to be

Sir
your most grateful servant
Felicia Hemans

¹ BL Add MS 40414, f. 14. Peel was briefly Prime Minister from November 1834 to April 1835; see his letter to FH in "Reception." Lawrence dedicated *Recollections of Mrs. Hemans* to Peel, "whose noble and generous kindness soothed and comforted her last hours." Henry, Charles, and FH's sister Harriett, would be the chief organizers of *1839*.

**To Rose Lawrence,** 13 February 1835.[1] Writing for money vs.
"noble" work

[. . .] It has ever been one of my regrets that the constant necessity of providing
sums of money to meet the exigencies of the boys' education, has obliged me to
waste my mind in what I consider mere desultory effusions:

> ——Pouring myself away,
> As a wild bird, amidst the foliage, turns
> That which within him thrills, and beats and burns,
> Into a fleeting lay.[2]

My wish ever was to concentrate all my mental energy in the production of
some more noble and complete work; something of pure and holy excellence (if
there be not too much presumption in the thought), which might <u>permanently</u>
take its place as the work of an English poetess—I have always, hitherto, written
as if in the breathing times of Autumn storms and billows—perhaps it may not
even yet be too late to accomplish what I wish, though I sometimes feel my
health so deeply prostrated, that I cannot imagine how I am ever to be raised up
again. But a greater freedom from those cares, of which I have been obliged to
bear up under the whole responsibility, may do much to restore me; and though
my spirits are greatly subdued by long sickness, I feel the powers of my mind in
full maturity. [. . .] I am very, very weary of writing so long; yet still feel as if I
had a thousand things to say to you. [. . .]

Your most affectionate
Felicia Hemans

[1] MS, private collection, with words missing from damage supplied from *HM* (296–97) and
Lawrence; Lawrence misdates the letter 10 February, exclaiming "The *last!*" FH died in May.
Chorley gives an excerpt (*CM* 2.256–67), and in a footnote protests Lawrence's charge of
"treachery" in his publishing FH's personal letters.

[2] A self-quotation, from *The Dying Improvisatore* (28–34), with "itself" (the poet's spirit) now
"myself."

# RECEPTION

# Lifetime

[The publication of FDB's "prodigy" volume, *Poems* (1808), enabled by subscription and subvention, received unenthusiastic reviews, focused on the immaturity of "the genuine productions of a young lady, written between the ages of 8 and 13 years" (so read the volume advertisement). An unsigned notice in the *Monthly Review* (by Anna Barbauld) resisted the call for "an indulgent reception [. . .] when a little girl publishes a large quarto": a few pieces could be praised for their "poetic strain," "good thoughts and forcible images," but the whole was "extremely jejune," with "some erroneous and some pitiable lines." It advised the "youthful author [. . .] to content herself for some years with reading instead of writing." The *Annual Review* admired the poet's "excellent ear," but seconded the critique. The *Poetical Register* was gentlest, finding the verses "pretty, and not devoid of poetical ideas," and it urged "the fair authoress to form her taste upon the best models, and to beware of being too easily satisfied with her own compositions."[1] It was not until *The Restoration of the Works of Art to Italy* (1816) that FH achieved a modest critical and commercial success, the accomplishment of reading and study, refined skill, and careful attention to mainstream culture and popular subjects. Other volumes, prize poems, translations, and magazine pieces followed, and by the early 1820s, the press on "Mrs. Hemans" was broadcasting two related themes: she is to be admired for what she *is*—the epitome of British "feminine" excellence and womanly propriety—and praised for want she is *not*—an "unfeminine" woman of intellectual force and political opinion. Within this formation, any contrary strains in the poetry—the tones of bitterness, the recurrent melancholy—were generally elided, or if recognized, then contained as a hyper-"feminine" passion, rather than sounded for subversive implications, emergent opposition, protest, or critique.[2] The public reception of "Mrs. Hemans" seemed determined to develop a cultural text in which her work is made to represent prior interests, especially on questions of gender. Private reactions and transactions tended to more variety, sometimes reflecting and participating in the public discourse, sometimes responding to FH's difference from "Mrs. Hemans."]

[1] *Annual Review* 7 (1808): 525–26; *Monthly Review* 60 (1809): 323; *Poetical Register* 7 (1808): 550. Duncan Wu identifies Barbauld as the *Monthly*'s reviewer (*Romantic Women Poets* 489).

[2] For my fuller discussion of this dynamic, especially on the reception of *The Siege of Valencia*, see my essay in *The Doors of Reception.*

## Percy Bysshe Shelley, 1808–11

*A report from Thomas Medwin*[1]

[Thomas Medwin (1788–1869) met Felicia Browne on a visit to Wales in 1807 or 1808, and was so impressed that he brought *Poems* to his cousin Percy Bysshe Shelley (1792–1822). Shelley was completing his education at Eton, the last two years of which (1808–10) were marked by a romantic correspondence with another cousin, Harriet Grove.]

In the beginning of [1808] I showed Shelley some poems to which I had sub-scribed by Felicia Browne, whom I had met in North Wales, where she had been on a visit at the house of a connection of mine. She was then sixteen,[2] and it was impossible not to be struck with the beauty (for beautiful she was), the grace, and charming simplicity and *naiveté* of this interesting girl—and on my return from Denbighshire, I made her and her works the frequent subject of conversation with Shelley. Her juvenile productions, remarkable certainly for her age—and some of those which the volume contained were written when she was a mere child—made a powerful impression on Shelley, ever enthusiastic in his admira-tion of talent; and with a prophetic spirit he foresaw the coming greatness of that genius, which under the name of Hemans afterwards electrified the world. He desired to become acquainted with the young authoress, and using my name, wrote to her, as he was in the habit of doing to all those who in any way excited his sympathies. This letter produced an answer, and a correspondence of some length passed between them, which of course I never saw, but it is to be sup-posed that it turned on other subjects besides poetry. I mean, that it was scepti-cal.[3] [. . .] One may indeed suppose this to have been the case, from the circum-stance of her mother writing to my father, and begging him to use his influence with Shelley to cease from any further communication with her daughter,—in fact, prohibiting their further correspondence.

*Percy Bysshe Shelley to Felicia Browne, 13 March 1811*[4]

[Shelley matriculated at Oxford University in 1810. Early the next year he met Harriet Westbrook, a sixteen-year-old friend of his sisters and daughter of a prosperous London merchant, and collaborated with classmate T. J. Hogg on *The Necessity of Atheism*, a pam-phlet that by mid-March they distributed to university officials and every Anglican bishop in the Kingdom. Both were promptly expelled from Oxford. Impressed by the 1808 *Poems* and Medwin's reports, Shelley initiated a correspondence, which Mrs. Browne terminated on perceiving his heterodox opinions. In July he was still singing the poet's praises, writing to Hogg that "Miss F. D. Browne (certainly a tigress) [. . .] surpasses my sister in poetical talents—this every dispassionate criticism <u>must</u> allow."[5] By August, he would elope with Harriet Westbrook, and a little more than a year later he would meet Mary Godwin, with whom he would elope to the Continent, abandoning Harriet and their infant daughter Ianthe.]

My Father and Mother have both written to M[rs]. Browne, and I confess I am not a little hurt that she has not even condescended to answer their letters—I must doubtless appear very impertinent for again addressing you, perhaps you will hear before you condemn me.—Your reasons for refusing to correspond with me are that you do not know me, that my religious sentiments are widely different, that not only my opinions but those of my father & mother are in direct contradiction to those of the rest of the world.—Even supposing that I am as vile as many have supposed me, I do not see how it would injure my dear Felicia to indulge me in a correspondence—The sun shines on many a dunghill, but its rays are so pure, so celestial that they never were contaminated by it.— May I be permitted to consider what injury you might derive from my correspondence—If I am in the wrong, you might restore me to the path of virtue, if your opinions should be incorrect which is possible I might succeed in persuading you to adopt others which are less deficient.—surely it is no advantage to be in error, it is no virtue to be mistaken, if Felicia <u>can</u> mistake. . We ought not to oppose truth, in whatever form it is offered, provided it <u>is</u> truth.. Pray endeavour to persuade M<sup>rs</sup>. Browne to permit me to correspond with you—if she is inexorable, must I also be hopeless? I confess I once thought that continued passive obedience was the duty of a daughter to her Parents. . but my Mother with some difficulty succeeded in almost convincing me that we ought to judge for ourselves.—If we blindly obey the dictates of another how can we be either virtuous or vicious, how can reason, free will exist.—If we be either virtuous or vicious, how can reason, free will exist.—If [yo] we do not judge for ourselves, if we do not exert our own powers, how shall we be able to support ourselves, when those upon whom we lean are removed—I weep to think that sooner or later this must be the case. We shall have no originality of character, our virtues will at best be imitations, we shall be at best servile copies of our parents, to an original genius, I need not express my contempt for Copy—but supposing the worst, that you will not write to me, you surely would not pass such a cruel sentence upon me, upon my Mother, who has incessantly regretted my dissapointment, for she attributes it entirely to what she calls her faults.— Without some substantial reason, which I cannot conceive, the refusal would give me pain, how much that would be augmented by the idea of which I could not then divest myself, that Felicia was irrational.—Supposing the worst you will write once to tell me why you can only write once. If your reasons are solid, I will cheerfully acquiesce in them, for, believe me, however great the pleasure might be to my Mother & myself, we would by no means wish to purchase it by any, the slightest transgression of the commands of reason on your part. much as we may desire our own happiness, we should consider it, at best as contemptible, when weighed against the perfection of one whom we value. Supposing that you refuse even this, yet do not think <u>ill</u>, <u>very</u> ill of me. this would give me pain—let me enumerate my offences—My Mother valued the happiness of my father, more than the opinion of mankind. I need not say how frivolous that is. how often it is opposite to truth. . for they abused your Poems, they still abuse my Mother. I examined the grounds upon which Theism is founded, they appeared to me weak, <u>thro' deficiency of proof</u> I became an Atheist. I read, I repeated your Poems I admired them, it gave me much regret, to find among so many beauties one fault, one glaring fault, I wrote to you, I informed you of it your letter entirely removed the only cause of complaint, a fear that you approved of fatal sanguinary wars[6]—Your last letter, the plaintive verses it contained induced me, nay compelled me to solicit your correspondence—I take the liberty of persisting in that request, I desire to reform my errors, to instruct my mind by your lessons, but principally to remove my dear Mother's regret this is a correct statement of my faults. if you refuse any other request, grant this one, this final wish, let not the amiable Felicia think very very ill of her affectionate Philippe Sidney[7]

PS. M^rs^. Browne in her letter seemed to intimate that I attempted to flatter you. this accusation has afflicted me much—I venture to think for myself regardless of the abuse so liberally poured on me. —I do this thro' a love of truth., has my conduct been that of a flatterer, my past motive for adressing you, the subject of my first letter was to tell you of a fault, in this I have studiously avoided the most remote appearance of it. I have told you my opinions sincerely, altho' they were such as woud at first be rather hostile to my wishes. is this the conduct of a flatterer?—Can you indeed be so cruel as to accuse me of that odious vice— Adieu—

[1] Medwin's memoirs of Shelley were published in *The Athenæum* in the early 1830s and as *The Life of Percy Bysshe Shelley* in 1847. His continued to develop this *Life*, but it was left unpublished at his death. "A New Edition" edited by H. Buxton Forman (London: Humphrey Milford, 1913) is the source of these remarks (58–59), which did not appear in the *Athenæum* memoirs.

[2] She was fourteen.

[3] Expressing doubts about Christianity.

[4] Shelley's letter to "Miss F D Browne / Bronwhilfa / St Asaph / FlintS———" is written from 49 Lincoln's Inn Fields. My text is Bodleian Library MS Don. c. 180, ff. 13–16, a stylus copy to Hogg interpreted by Dr. Bruce C. Barker-Benfield (BCBB 30 January 1991) and Duncan Wu. For unclear script they have normalized spelling if the word itself not in question. Shelley's deletions are indicated by [-].

[5] Letter to Hogg, 28 July 1811, in Thomas Jefferson Hogg, *The Life of Shelley*, ed. Humbert Wolfe, *The Life of Percy Bysshe Shelley*, 2 vols. (London: J. M. Dent), 1.228.

[6] Among the 1808 *Poems* are *The Spartan Mother and Her Son, To Patriotism, To My Younger Brother, on His Entering the Army*. Shelley's misgivings were justified. FDB wrote to Matthew Nicholson (18 April 1809) about her brother Thomas in Spain: "Deeply as I feel for the sufferings my dearest Brother must have endured, still I can hardly regret that he has received a wound in so glorious a cause, and as a trophy of so brilliant a victory; it will ever be his pride that he has bled in the service of his country" (Nicholson 13–14).

[7] "Percy Shelley" shares initials with the 16th-c. poet, scholar, and courtier, often regarded as the perfect gentleman. The signature may be a code, or a light jest. While "Philippe" was an acceptable Renaissance spelling of the man's name, Bruce Barker-Benfield has suggested (in a letter to me) that Shelley may have been writing under the cover of a feminine-sounding pseudonym.

*The British Critic*, n.s. 7 (September 1816): 311–13, on *The Restoration of the Works of Art to Italy*, 2d ed.

[Famous for hostile reviews of Godwin, Hunt, and Shelley, this Tory, High-Church monthly was founded to oppose the dissenting, reformist slant of other monthly reviews, such as the *Analytic*, the *Critical*, and the *Monthly*.]

This is a poem of no ordinary merit. The authoress is possessed of a powerful imagination and of a commanding mind. Her taste appears to have been cast in the mould of ancient days. Her periods are long, and generally well sustained; occasionally however they taper off towards the conclusion, which considerably diminishes the effect of the preceding beauties. [quotes the opening stanza; . . .] We were much pleased with with Apostrophe to Florence [quotes 131–44; . . .] the spirited invocation of the Medici [quotes 165–86] [and] the strain of piety in which the poem is concluded. This is the first time that we have met with any composition of our authoress. She has certainly great power and a mind truly classical. Her fault is that [. . .] [s]he rises too often into the turgid. [. . .] if the bubble bursts, the *bathos* most assuredly yawns below to receive the unfortunate victim.[1]

[1] In the wake of the *British*, the review of *The Restoration* in the *Monthly* (82 [March 1817]: 326–26) made a point of forgiving occasional faults of style ("verbiage"), and lavished praise: "We have much pleasure in hailing the classical and elegant production of a female writer," it began, and quoted for admiration 295–309, on Rome's ancient glory, and 331–50, on the Apollo Belvedere.

*The Monthly Review*, 2d ser. 90 (December 1819): 408–12; on *Tales, and Historic Scenes*

[Founded in 1749, the *Monthly Review* was known for even temper and fair-mindedness, but the brash new reviews were making it seem a bit tame.]

When we consider the cultivation of the female mind in the present day, and the great taste and relish which exist among the ladies of our country for the finest and highest department of literature, it is certainly strange that we find so few poetesses of celebrity. The beautiful story of Psyche, indeed, raised the name of Tighe to an enviable and well-merited height in the public estimation: but, although since the publication of that poem we have had several fair candidates for public favour whose merits have been very considerable, we think that none can offer such strong claims to it as the writer of these "Tales and Historic Scenes." [. . .] Her first publication of poems, written when she was very young, gave a promise of increasing excellence, which her subsequent productions [. . .] have honourably fulfilled. Her "Modern Greece" was an elegant and spirited poem, and some portions of it would almost bear a comparison with the works of the first poets of our day.[1]

Mrs. Hemans's talents, however, are not of the highest order. Her poetry is graceful, and in many parts rises into the finer and more impassioned soundings of the lyre: but her verses do not possess that uniform deep colour of poetic feeling, by which the touch of a master-poet is so easily distinguished: they contain little of the "breathing and burning," or of that powerful strength of expression which stamps itself on our imagination. [. . .] with the exception of this great qualification, we think that Mrs. Hemans has all the requisites which make a poet. She displays a strain of high and pure feeling, a great power of poetical expression, a correct taste, and a fund of good sense: which last is perhaps as essential to the poet as any of the former qualities, in order to prevent him from running into that affectation and mannerism which so many writers of the present day conceive to be the distinguishing mark of true genius. To these excellences may also be added a flowing and correct versification, and a careful propriety of style and arrangement. [. . .]

The Abencerrage is the longest, and in our opinion the best:—the others being rather poetical pictures than tales, and presenting to the reader a single scene of action rather than a chain of continued events. In the design and execution of this tale, as well as in some of the sentiments, we perceive a resemblance to the Fire-Worshippers of Moore.[2] Of the other tales, "The Widow of Crescentius" is perhaps the best. [. . .] Mrs. Hemans is rather too fond of description: but her delineation of the scenes which are enriched by classical association is masterly[3] and touching. Of this power, the commencement of "Alaric in Italy" may be mentioned as an example. When Liberty strings her lyre, she frequently rises into a more elevated and impressive strain of poetry, of which we could give many proofs from the present volume.

We shall always greet with gladness the appearance of this lady before the public; feeling assured that we shall never receive any production from her pen which is not consonant to pure feelings and correct taste.

[1] "This is certainly an elegant production; bearing the stamp of scholarship, and inspired by very considerable poetical genius," opened the review of this poem (*Monthly Review* 84 [September 1817]: 30–34).

[2] An inset verse tale in Thomas Moore's *Lalla Rookh* (1817).

[3] May we use this word with application to a female? [reviewer]

---

*The Edinburgh Monthly Review* 3 (April 1820): 373–83, on *The Sceptic*

[This short-lived Tory periodical (1819–21) was published by William Blackwood. Following FH's title page, the review headline advertises "Mrs. Hemans" as "author of 'The Restoration of Works of Art to Italy'; 'Modern Greece'; 'Tales and Historic Scenes'; 'Wallace's Invocation to Bruce.'"]

We have, on more than one occasion, expressed the very high opinion which we entertain of the talents of this lady: and it is gratifying to find, that she gives us no reason to retract or modify in any degree the applause already bestowed, and that every fresh exhibition of her powers enhances and confirms her claims upon our admiration. Mrs. Hemans is indeed but in the infancy of her poetical career, but it is an infancy of unrivalled beauty and of very high promise. [. . .We] think at once of the merit and the modesty of Mrs. Hemans, for whose gentle hands the auxiliary club of political warfare, and the sharp lash of personal satire are equally unsuited.

The verses of Mrs. Hemans appear the spontaneous offspring of intense and noble feeling, governed by a clear understanding, and fashioned into elegance by an exquisite delicacy and precision of taste. With more than the force of many of her masculine competitors, she never ceases to be strictly *feminine* in the whole current of her thought and feeling, nor approaches by any chance, the verge of that free and intrepid course of speculation, of which the boldness is more conspicuous than the wisdom, but into which some of the most remarkable among the female literati of our times have freely and fearlessly plunged. She has, in the poem before us, made choice of a subject of which it would have been very difficult to have reconciled the treatment, in the hands of *some* female authors, to the delicacy which belongs to the sex, and the tenderness and enthusiasm which form its finest characteristic. A coarse and chilling cento of the exploded fancies of modern scepticism, done into rhyme by the hand of a woman, would have been doubly disgusting by the revival of absurdities long consigned to oblivion, and by the revolting exhibition of a female mind, shorn of all its attractions, and wrapt in darkness and defiance. But Mrs. Hemans has chosen the better and the nobler cause, and while she has left in the poem before us every trace of vigorous intellect of which the subject admitted, and has far transcended in energy of thought the prosing pioneers of unbelief, she has sustained throughout a tone of warm and confiding piety. [. . .]

Nothing surely can be more beautiful and attractive than such a character as this,—richly endowed with every gift which is calculated to win regard or to command esteem, yet despising all false brilliancy, and keeping every talent in sweet and modest subordination to the dignity of womanhood,—emulating the other sex in the graceful vigour of genius, but scrupulously abstaining from all that may betray unfeminine temerity or coarseness in its exhibitions,—touching the dark regions of metaphysical debate, and striking upon them as with a sunbeam from her own pure and spotless spirit, and thus reinforcing the sterner champions of her country's faith with the charm of gentle but glowing sentiment, and the resistless appeal of the most impressive eloquence. It is here that we recognize the graceful and appropriate direction of the female intellect, and not in that sneering scepticism which in man is offensive—in woman, monstrous and revolting. [. . .] the author before us is not only free from every stain, but breathes all moral beauty and loveliness; and it will be a memorable coincidence, if the era of a woman's sway in literature shall become coeval with the return of its moral purity and elevation.

*The British Review and London Critical Journal* 15 (June 1820): 299–310,
on *The Restoration of the Works of Art to Italy* and *The Sceptic*

[In 1819 Byron ridiculed "the *British*" as "my grandmother's review" (*Don Juan* 1.209).
Aimed at political conservatives, this quarterly advocated moral reform under the leadership of the clergy and the ruling classes.]

We know not whether the Authoress of these Poems will consider it a compliment, or otherwise, when we state that in examining her "Modern Greece" [. . .]
we conceived it to be the work of an academical, and certainly not a female,
pen. It is not to disparage either sex to say that as they usually live in different
worlds, so they must naturally write in different styles. Mrs. Hemans's productions, however, possess much of that chaste correctness and classical spirit which
characterize Pope's Messiah, or Heber's Palestine, poems which have furnished
a sort of accredited model for our university prize compositions.[1] From being
early and deeply imbued with the elegant literature of Greece and Rome, the
poetry of men of education, even when it does not rise much above mediocrity
in other respects, often evinces an elaborate finish which does not usually fall to
the lot of female writers. [. . .] In most respects the education of women is
unfavourable to the cultivation of the higher branches of poetry. The standards
with which they are most conversant are usually defective; and they do not learn
early in life that mental discipline which true poetry requires even when it seems
most unconstrained. We might perhaps add to this that the mind of women is
not usually favourable to that deep-toned emotion which constitutes the very
essence of the higher kinds of poetry. Tenderness, which is a very necessary
quality of poetry, will not of course be denied to that sex, one of whose characteristic epithets, in common parlance, is that of "tender"; but poetry is in truth
a thing of study; strong feeling is indeed necessary to its perfection; but it is the
feeling of a *spectator* rather than of a *sufferer*. Those who feel most acutely, are
least able to analyse their sensations; nor are the ladies usually in the habit of
examining so closely into the springs of human emotion as to touch them at
their pleasure. [. . .] Perhaps in all instances of this kind we might make a useful
distinction between what might be called *sentimental* emotion and *passionate*
emotion. [. . .]

[1] Reginald Heber (1783–1826) won a student poetry competition at Oxford in 1803 with
*Palestine* (pub. 1807). Pope's *Messiah* was published in 1712.

---

**Hannah More,** Letter to a Friend, ca. 1820, on *Modern Greece* and *The Sceptic*

[Hannah More (1745–1833) began her career as a dramatist and poet in the bluestocking
culture of the mid-eighteenth century, her subjects including this culture, "sensibility," and
the evils of slavery. She rose to prominence in the 1790s with her widely circulated Cheap
Repository Tracts, aimed at the poor and working classes, exhorting them to sobriety, hard
work, and cautioning against political discontent. Other best-sellers were *Strictures on the*

*Modern System of Female Education* (1799), which saw 13 editions and was in demand for decades, selling 19,000 copies, and her didactic "conduct" novel of 1809, *Coelebs in Search of a Wife* (eight editions in its first two months). Both were still widely read in 1820. An evangelical Christian, More was an opponent of democracy, the rights of woman, and any remedy for social ills that did not insist primarily on individual moral probity and salvation in the afterlife. Text: *HM* 33–34 n.]

I cannot refuse myself the gratification of saying, that I entertain a very high opinion of Mrs Hemans's superior genius and refined taste. I rank her, as a poet, very high, and I have seen no work on the subject of her *Modern Greece*, which evinces more just views, or more delicate perceptions of the fine and the beautiful. I am glad she has employed her powerful pen, in this new instance [*The Sceptic*], on a subject so worthy of it; and anticipating the future by the past, I promise myself no small pleasure in the perusal, and trust it will not only confer pleasure, but benefit.

*The Quarterly Review* 24 (October 1820): 130–39; omnibus review of
*The Restoration of the Works of Art to Italy; Tales, and Historic Scenes; Translations from Camoens &c; The Sceptic; and Stanzas to the Memory of the Late King*

[Blackwood's 1873 edition of FH attributes this review to William Gifford (190). In the 1790s Gifford (1756–1826) was a major contributor to the reactionary *Anti-Jacobin*, and became its editor in 1797. In 1809 he became the first editor of the Tory *Quarterly*, one of the most powerful, influential reviews of the day. The *Quarterly* upheld Church and King against opposition; among its steady contributors were Scott, Southey, and John Wilson Croker, on whose ridicule of Keats's *Endymion* (1818) Shelley would blame the poet's demise. Gifford was famously acerbic and widely despised, especially by political liberals and radicals such as Shelley, Leigh Hunt, and William Hazlitt. Hemans got off easy, perhaps because all the publications discussed were issued by John Murray, also the *Quarterly*'s publisher.]

This certainly is not the age in which those who speak slightingly of female talent should expect to be listened to with much attention. In almost every department of literature, and in many of art and science, some one or other of our own contemporaries and countrywomen will be found, in spite of all the disadvantages of an imperfect education, occupying a respectable, at least, if not a prominent situation. And this remark, if true anywhere, is undoubtedly so when applied to poetry: no judicious critic will speak without respect of the tragedies of Miss Baillie, or the Psyche of Mrs. Tighe; and, unless we deceive ourselves greatly, the author of the poems before us requires only to be more generally known and read to have her place assigned at no great distance from that of the two distinguished individuals just mentioned. Mrs. Hemans indeed, if we may judge from her writings, is not merely a clever woman, but a woman of very general reading, and of a mind improved by reflection and study. [. . .] Mrs. Hemans is a woman in whom talent and learning have not produced the

ill effects so often attributed to them; her faculties seem to sit meekly on her, at
least we can trace no ill humour or affectation, no misanthropic gloom, no quer-
ulous discontent; she is always pure in thought and expression, cheerful, affectionate, and pious. It is something at least to know, that whether the emotions
she excites be always those of powerful delight or not, they will be at least
harmless, and leave no sting behind: if our fancies are not always transported,
our hearts at least will never be corrupted: we have not found a line which a
delicate woman might blush to have written. When speaking of an English lady
this ought to be no more than common praise, for delicacy of feeling has long
been, and long may it be, the fair and valued boast of our countrywomen; but we
have had too frequent reason of late to lament, both in female readers and
writers, the display of qualities very opposite in their nature. Their tastes, at
least, have not escaped the infection of that pretended liberality, but real licen-
tiousness of thought, the plague and the fearful sign of the times. Under its
influence they lose their relish for what is simple and sober, gentle or dignified,
and require the stimulus of excessive or bitter passion, or sedition, or audacious
profaneness. Certain we are, that the most dangerous writer of the present day[1]
finds his most numerous and most enthusiastic admirers among the fair sex; and
we have many times seen very eloquent eyes kindle in vehement praise of the
poems, which no woman should have read, and which it would have been far
better for the world if the author had never written. The earliest on the list is a
Poem on the Restoration of the Works of Art to Italy, [. . .] decidedly inferior
to all that follow it. [. . .]

   The next volume, the "Tales and Historic Scenes," is a collection, as the title
imports, of Narrative Poems. Perhaps it was not upon consideration that Mrs.
Hemans passed from a poem of picture-drawing and reflection to the writing of
tales; but if we were to prescribe to a young poet his *course* of practice, this would
certainly be our advice. [. . .] The principal poem in this volume is the Abencerrage. [. . .] [H]er last two publications are works of a higher stamp—works,
indeed, of which no living poet need to be ashamed. The first of them is entitled,
the Sceptic, and is devoted, as our readers will easily anticipate, to advocating the
cause of religion. Undoubtedly the poem must have owed its being to the circumstances of the times, to a laudable indignation at the course which literature
in many departments seemed lately to be taking in this country, and at the
doctrines disseminated with industry, principally (but by no means exclusively,
as has been falsely supposed), among the lower orders. Mrs. Hemans, however,
does not attempt to reason learnedly or laboriously in verse.[. . .] But the argument of the Sceptic is one of irresistible force to confirm a wavering mind; it is
simply resting the truth of religion on the necessity of it, on the utter misery and
helplessness of man without it. [. . .]

   The last poem is to the memory of his late Majesty: unlike courtly themes in
general, this is one of the deepest, and most lasting interest. Buried as the King
had long been in mental and visual darkness, and dead to the common joys of
the world, his death, perhaps, did not occasion the shock, or the piercing sorrow
which we have felt on some other public losses; but the heart must be cold

indeed, that could, on reflection, regard the whole fortune and fate of that venerable, gallant, tender-hearted and pious man, without a more than common sympathy.[2] There was something in his character so truly national; his very errors were of so amiable a kind, his excellencies bore so high a stamp, his nature was so genuine and unsophisticated, he stood in his splendid court amidst his large and fine family, so true a husband, so good a father, so safe an example; [. . .] [H]er poem is beyond all comparison with any which we have seen on the subject; it is full of fine and pathetic passages, and it leads us up through all the dismal colourings of the fore-ground to that bright and consoling prospect, which should close every Christian's reflections on such a matter. [. . .]

[W]ho or what Mrs. Hemans is, we know not; we have been told that, like a poet of antiquity,

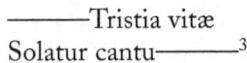

————Tristia vitæ
Solatur cantu————[3]

if it be so (and the most sensible breasts are not uncommonly nor unnaturally the most bitterly wounded), she seems from the tenor of her writings to bear about her a higher and a surer balsam than the praises of men, or even the "sacred muse" herself can impart. Still there is a pleasure, an innocent and an honest pleasure, even to a wounded spirit, in fame fairly earned; and such fame as may wait upon our decision, we freely and conscientiously bestow:—in our opinion all her poems are elegant and pure in thought and language; her later poems are of higher promise, they are vigorous, picturesque, and pathetic.

[1] Byron. John Murray also published Byron's poetry; but as Gifford makes clear, not every *Quarterly* reviewer admired Byron.
[2] George III (who died in 1820) suffered a history of mental illness that reached a crisis in November 1810; in January 1811 the Prince of Wales (later George IV) was appointed Regent.
[3] "The sorrows of life / She lightens through song" (source unidentified).

## George Gordon, Lord Byron

[The fame of Byron (1788–1824) flourished during the years he wrote these letters to his and FH's publisher John Murray. *Childe Harold's Pilgrimage* was an overnight sensation in 1812, followed by a series of spectacularly successful "Eastern tales," further cantos of *Childe Harold*, and the first two cantos of *Don Juan*. Except for the letter of 12 August 1820 (from Leslie Marchand's edition), texts are from *The Works of Lord Byron* (London: John Murray, 1832); FH read excerpts of the 1830 edition in the reviews of 1830–31.]

*On* The Restoration of the Works of Art to Italy, *30 September 1816*[1]

At present I must lay by a little, having pretty well exhausted myself in what I have sent you. Italy or Dalmatia and another summer may, or may not, set me off again. I have no plans, and am nearly as indifferent what may come as where I go. I shall take Felicia Hemans's Restoration, & c. with me; it is a good poem—very.

### On Modern Greece, 4 September 1817[2]

Why do you send me such trash—worse than trash, the Sublime of Mediocrity? Thanks for Lalla, however, which is good [. . .] Paris in 1815, & c.—good.[3] Modern Greece—good for nothing; written by some one who has never been there, and not being able to manage the Spenser stanza has invented a thing of his own, consisting of two elegiac stanzas, an heroic line, and an Alexandrine, twisted on a string.[4] Besides, why "modern?" You may say modern Greeks, but surely Greece itself is rather more ancient than ever it was.

### On The Sceptic, 7 June 1820[5]

Mrs. Hemans is a poet [. . .], but too stiltified and apostrophic,—and quite wrong. Men died calmly before the Christian era, and since, without Christianity: witness the Romans, and, lately, Thistlewood, Sandt, and Lo[u]vel—men who ought to have been weighed down with their crimes, even had they believed.[6] A deathbed is a matter of nerves and constitution, and not of religion. Voltaire was frightened, Frederick of Prussia not: Christians the same, according to their strength rather than their creed.

### On Hemans and Wordsworth; 12 August 1820[7]

"no more modern poesy—I pray—neither Mrs. Hewoman's—nor any female or male Tadpole of Poet Turdsworth's—nor any of his ragamuffins."

### On Hemans's learning and poetic style; 28 September 1820

"I do not despise [Mrs. Heman[8]]—but if [she] knit blue stockings instead of wearing them it would be better. You are taken in by that false stilted trashy style, which is a mixture of all the styles of the day, which are all bombastic (I don't except my own—no one has done more through negligence to corrupt the language); but it is neither English nor poetry. Time will show.

---

[1] *Works* 3.254–55; cf. Marchand 5.108. Blackwood's 1873 edition of FH prints this remark as an endnote to *Restoration* (27).

[2] *Works* 4.59; cf. Marchand 5.262–63.

[3] Thomas Moore's *Lalla Rookh* (1817), a series of Eastern tales set in a prose frame, would prove a sensational success. Rev. George Croly's *Paris in 1815* (1817) is a poem in the style of *Childe Harold*.

[4] Byron seems not to have identified the anonymous poet as FH. The reading in Marchand is "it's own" rather than "his own." For the stanza, see the headnote to the poem. In an issue of *Blackwood's* that Byron eventually read (August 1817), both the stanza and the poem were praised: "With the exception of Lord Byron, who has made the theme peculiarly his own, no one has more feelingly contrasted ancient with modern Greece" (57).

[5] *Works* 4.321; cf. Marchand 7.113.

[6] Arthur Thistlewood, a Painite revolutionary sentenced to death for his role in the Cato Street Conspiracy (1820), remained theatrically defiant in the face of execution. Charles Sandt, a student who despised the reactionary propaganda of German dramatist, politician, and czarist agent August von Kotzbue, assassinated him in 1819; Louvel was the assassin of the duc de Berri.

[7] Marchand 7.158.

[8] Moore tactfully substitutes asterisks for the name (*Works* 4.343), filled in by Marchand (7.182). Byron's punning distorts pronunciation; according to Rose Lawrence, "when it is sounded rightly," "Hemans" "seems as if there were two *m*'s in it" (349n); Wordsworth often spelled her name as "Hemmans" in his correspondence.

---

*The British Critic*, n.s. 20 (July 1823): 50–61

[This Tory, High-Church monthly reflects not only FH's warm reception in such quarters but also her discursive value in the abuse of other women writers. The occasion was a review of *The Siege of Valencia*.]

We heartily abjure Blue Stockings.[1] We make no compromise with any variation of the colour, from sky-blue to Prussian blue, blue stockings are an outrage upon the eternal fitness of things. It is a principle with us to regard an Academicienne of this Society, with the same charity that a cat regards a vagabond mouse. We are inexorable to special justifications. We would fain make a fire in Charing-Cross, of all the bas blus in the kingdom, and albums, and common-place books, as accessaries before or after the fact should perish in the conflagration.

Our forefathers never heard of such a thing as a Blue Stocking, except upon their sons' legs; the writers of Natural History make no mention of the name; it is not to be accounted for by the all-sufficient sensation and reflection of Mr. Locke; it has no place even amongst the phantasms of Bishop Berkeley.[2] Shakspeare, who painted all sorts and degrees of persons and things, who compounded or created thousands, which, perhaps, never existed, except in his own prolific mind, even he, in the wildest excursion of his fancy never dreamed of such an extraordinary combination as a Blue Stocking! No! it is a creature of modern growth, and capable of existing only in such times as the present.

Formerly there were two styles of female education, and consequently two styles of women; the really learned, and the really simple; the first, nurtured in classic lore, and disciplined in scholastic exercises; the second taught to sow neatly, and read the English Bible distinctly; the one skilful in drawing conclusions, the other in drawing pancakes. You had your Lady Jane Grey with Plato on her breakfast table, or a living Sophia Western with orange marmalade of her own making, and a dozen national tunes on the harpsichord of your own choosing.[3] Both of these were well; they proposed several ends, and adopted several means towards the attaining of them; there was a fitness, and a moral perfection in each. In such times, and under such institution, the anomaly in question *could* not have existed; the ingredients of its composition, and the sphere of its action, were equally wanting.

A Blue Stocking is the natural product of an age in which knowledge is lost in accomplishments.[4] It is the vapoury offspring of ignorance, impregnated by conceit. It is the epicene *tertium aliquid* between a fool and a coquette. It is the infallible consequence of the Loves of the Angels fastened upon Conversations on Chemistry, and swallowed according to the prescription of the Mathematical Professor in the University of Lagado.[5] It is the plague and the punishment of a time and nation, in which, as a system, female education is no more understood, than Mr. Payne Knight's Theory of the Iliad, or Mr. Burges's Play on the Troades.[6]

Without being positively criminal, a Blue Stocking is the most odious character in society; nature, sense, and hilarity fly at her approach; affectation, absurdity, and peevishness, follow in her train; she sinks, wherever she is placed, like the yolk of an egg, to the bottom, and carries the filth and the lees with her.

In a drawing-room she is detestable enough, no doubt, but the creature bears a feminine exterior, and we are obliged to refrain ourselves. But when, not contented with infesting private society, she proceeds to outrage public decorum; when satiated with *talking* of books, she advances to the *printing* from books, she leaves the position which ensured to her impunity, and deserts the asylum within the precincts of which alone she could hope to escape the vengeance of insulted literature. Many such fugitives, from sanctuary are rambling about the town and country; their example is evidently contagious;

> "For they write not, who never wrote before,
> And those who always wrote, now write the more!"

We thought it becoming the sound principles, and manly character, of our Review, to declare ourselves thus openly upon this subject; and we hereby give notice to all whom it may concern, that it is our intention henceforth, to visit enormities of this description, with the severity they so justly deserve.

We now turn to Mrs. Hemans, and we do so with pleasure and confidence. She will feel convinced, that whatever we may say, will be sincere, and though we do not pretend to fix the value of our advice, yet at all events after the foregoing denunciations, the praises we bestow, may reasonably be entitled to some consideration at her hands. Mrs. Hemans is a woman of that undoubted genius, that it is her legitimate vocation to attend at the altars of the Muses. She has regularly advanced in intellectual power, from her earliest work, which was simply blameless, to the present, which contains instances of a vigour of conception, luxuriance of feeling, and splendor of language, which may be compared without disadvantage, to the best efforts of Mrs. Joanna Baillie. Indeed in point of richness, and fertility of description, Mrs. Hemans is much superior. She is especially excellent in painting the strength, and the weaknesses of her own lovely sex, and there is a womanly nature throughout all her thoughts and her aspirations, which is new and inexpressibly touching. A mother *only* could have poured forth the deep and passionate strain of eloquence which follows. We hardly remember any thing more exquisitely beautiful. It is conceived in the truest spirit of essential poetry. The speakers are husband and wife.

[Quotation from *Siege of Valencia* 1.421–59]

When a woman can write like this, she *ought* to write. Her mind is national property. In the grand scheme of a popular literature, there are many departments which can alone be filled by the emanations of female genius. There is a fineness of apprehension, and a subtlety of feeling, peculiar to the weaker sex, and perhaps the result of that very weakness, which enables them to set some subjects in such lights, and to paint them in such colours, as the more robust intellect of men could never have imagined. A woman is so much more a creature of passion than man; her virtues and her failings flow so much more directly and visibly from the impulse of affection; her talent and her genius, her thoughts and her wishes, her natural qualities, and her acquired accomplishments are so interchangeably blended, and all but identified with each other, that there results a *wholeness* of conception, and a vividness and reality of colouring in her mental efforts, which advantageously distinguishes them from the most powerful productions of men on the same subjects. Let the golden fragments of Sappho bear testimony to the truth of this remark; let those two mutilated bursts of female passion, be compared with the most happy and finished parts of Ovid or Tibullus, and we may have good reason to wish that envious time had spared to us but a hundred more lines of the Lesbian Lady's, even at the price of one thousand hexameters and pentameters from the pens of the gentlemen of the Augustan age.[7] There have been indeed such things as female translators of Newton, and female interpreters of Kant;[8] but although these, and such like these, have, without doubt, displayed wonderful efforts of intellect, yet there is nothing in them peculiar to the sex; the same things are done as well, and for the most part better, by men; we admire them more for their novelty and strangeness, than for their intrinsic worth; we are surprised, rather than pleased.

[Then follows a chastising inventory of faults, ones often imputed to writers lacking formal education, i.e., women and commoners: Mrs. Hemans appears not to have sufficiently "*studied* the great masters of the English language; [. . .] her style is not characteristic, her grammar not accurate, and her diction splendid rather than rich"; she seems to be "trading before she has amassed a substantial capital" of "acquaintance with foreign literature"; "barbarous" diction, such as *hymn-notes* ("a delicate monster of hers") accompanies other "sins against technical grammar," "vulgarism," and "innumerable" "sins against logical grammar." Yet "these are [. . .] blemishes only; they obscure and weaken, but do by no means eclipse the light."]

[1] By the 1820s, this was a derisive term for learned women, having evolved from a more neutral descriptive in the second half of the eighteenth century.

[2] Idealist philosopher Bishop Berkeley (1685–1753) disputed the materialist philosophy of John Locke (1632–1704).

[3] Lady Jane Grey (1537–54) was queen of England for nine days before she was executed for treason; Sophia Western is loved by the hero of Fielding's *Tom Jones* (1749).

[4] The skills acquired for female "finishing": dancing, drawing, needlework, singing, sketching, piano playing, conversational Italian and French.

[5] *Tertium aliquid*: a third thing, usually illogical or unnatural. *The Loves of the Angels* (1823), Thomas Moore's poem about three fallen angels enamored of mortal women, was widely translated and very popular. *Conversations on Chemistry, intended especially for the Female Sex*, by Jane Marcet (1769–1858), was published in 1806, and often reprinted. In Swift's *Gulliver's Travels* (1726), scholars at the Grand Academy of Projectors at Lagado pursue a variety of fantastic experiments; one master of mathematics writes his lessons on a thin wafer with ink

composed of a cephalic tincture and asks his students to swallow it, on the theory that the tincture will rise to the brain as the wafer is digested.

⁶ Richard Payne Knight (1747–1829), an ardent Hellenist, published *An Inquiry into the Symbolic Language of Ancient Art and Mythology* in 1818. Seneca (1st-c. Rome) has a play titled *Troades*.

⁷ The poetry of Sappho (resident of Lesbos) survives only in fragments. Ovid wrote elegant elegiac meters (dactylic hexameter and pentameter); his Augustan contemporary Albius Tibullus was an elegiac poet.

⁸ Isaac Newton (1642–1727) wrote his treatises in Latin; philosopher Immanuel Kant (1724–1804) wrote in in German but was widely translated.

---

*The British Review and London Critical Journal* 21 (August 1823): 196–202; on *The Siege of Valencia &c*

[. . .] Elmina principally appears in the character of a distressed mother, overwhelmed with grief, and losing, in the prevalence of maternal affection, all sight and sense of rectitude and propriety. But we also see in her a peculiar spirit of pride and loftiness, even after the death of her sons, after her own reconciliation with her husband, and his death [. . .] [T]here is too much vehemence, too much effort in our authoress, especially when she enters on scenes that require the exhibition of tender or ardent feeling; but it is in the latter that she puts forth her energy most conspicuously. [. . .] [S]he has a strong predilection for warlike affairs, for bold, fervid, and daring characters. We must, however, remark, that the military spirit that breathes and glows in many of her pages, does not add to their real excellence. We do not like Bellona as a Muse.¹ [. . .] To be full, clear, and equal, as well as dignified and splendid, ought to be the aim of the poet: nor, if wise, will he try to astonish his readers by singular thought, by dazzling imagery, by forced expressions, or by unusual metres. Mrs. Hemans cannot claim entire exemption from the censure, implied in these remarks. [. . .] [W]e must express our regret, that the volume before us does not contain more in it, that has an immediate reference to the highest interests of man, especially, as in the principal poem one character [Hernandez], and one not the least conspicuous, is a minister of our holy religion, whose appearance in the faithful discharge of his peculiar duties, amidst the calamities of his fellow-citizens, would, by adding a moral dignity to the poem, and by infusing into it the softness and sweetness of religious consolation, have materially aided its effect. [. . .]

¹ Roman goddess of war

*The Monthly Review,* 2d ser., 102 (October 1823) 177–81; on
*The Siege of Valencia &c*

[. . .] [T]he present work [. . .] exhibits a more strict and intimate acquaintance with poetic feelings than the fair writer has hitherto displayed, and a happier and easier use of poetic diction. [. . .] [S]he has now ventured on a dramatic attempt, and has added some lyrical specimens, which are exceedingly creditable to her pen.

By the selection of subjects for her muse, Mrs. Hemans has in this volume displayed considerable tact and knowledge of her own powers of verse. A chivalrous and even a martial strain flows freely from her lyre, which never sends forth nobler sounds than when it celebrates the battles of freedom or the achievements of romance. With such dispositions, the fame of the Cid naturally attracted her regards. Indeed, the history of that hero possesses a singular charm, celebrated as he has been in the rude but fascinating ballads of his country; and we know not any writer by whom the high romantic character of that old poetry has been more successfully caught than by Mrs. Hemans, who has transferred it into her elegant and polished verse with great fidelity and happiness. We would instance the lyrical songs with which the "Siege of Valencia" is interspersed, as specimens of this kind of composition in which she has been most successful; and which have an air of romantic magnificence and grandeur thrown around them, that is admirably suited to the subject. [. . .]

When we contemplate the achievements of this illustrious hero, whether it be in the rude but splendid ballads of his native land or in the fine imitations of them which Mrs. Hemans has produced, we cannot refrain from expressing a sentiment of degradation and shame at the fate with which Spain is at this moment visited.[1] Is there not, among her nobility or her captains, one unyielding arm or one faithful heart to emulate the heroic virtues of "the Campeador"? Apathy seems to have unnerved the hands of her soldiers, and treason to have corrupted the hearts of her commanders. [. . .]

In conclusion, we can only exhort this fair votary of the muses to persevere in the course which she has hitherto pursued with so much success. When we review the progress which she has made, and more especially when we turn to this last production of her pen, we feel assured that she cannot be under better guidance than that of her own taste and judgment. Let her continue to study, with the same devotion and fervour as heretofore, the works of our great poets:—let her cherish that high moral sense which pervades all her writings;— and we do not doubt that we shall see her assume her merited station among the leading poets of her age.

[1] Despite British protests, the French invaded Spain in April 1823, at the request of the reactionary Spanish king Ferdinand VII, to suppress the insurrection led by "liberales" demanding a constitutional monarchy.

## Joanna Baillie, 1824–27

[Widely admired poet and dramatist Baillie took an interest in FH's work, publishing one of her poems, praising her work to her friends, and helping to get *The Vespers of Palermo* a successful staging in Edinburgh after it failed in London. FH dedicated *Records of Woman &c* to her.]

*To William Sotheby. Hampstead, 24 June 1823.*[1] The Last Constantine,
The Siege of Valencia &c

My dear Sir,

I received on Sunday from the Author M$^{rs}$ Heman's [*sic*] new volume which is rich in high-toned beautiful poetry, and of the longer pieces I particularly admire that which she stiles "the last of the Constantines.["] Had it been a dramatic form, she would as you said, have run me very hard and perhaps more than that. But fortunately for me she has shaped it into a poem in the Spencerian measure, and now it belongs to Lord Byron to be jealous of her and not me. Her Dramatic poem, The Siege of Valencia, is finely written and the songs or old Spanish (supposed to be) ballads &c are excellent. But there is a short thing at the end of all called the voice of Spring which is my great favorite and is quite exquisite.[2] I think there can be no doubt that this publication will be of great advantage to her worldly affairs as well as her reputation, high as that was already.— [. . .]

every truly yours
J Baillie

*To Sir Walter Scott. Hampstead, 1 July 1823.*[3] Siege &c

My dear Sir Walter,

[. . .] The admiration [*Belshazzar's Feast*] has received will now, I hope, be of use to her, and make her volume of Poems, just come out, be more eagerly sought for at first, tho' its own merit afterwards could not have failed to procure it a very honourable reception. She is a woman of high genius and respectable in every way, and the Public I hope will do themselves honour by supporting her as she deserves. There are many striking passages of the highest toned poetry in her Constantine, and there is a short poem at the end of the book called "The voice of the Spring" which is to my fancy quite exquisite. There is a great deal of character too in her Spanish Songs & ballads and M$^r$ Lockhart I think will be pleased with them.[4] — [. . .]

always most truly
J Baillie

*To Walter Scott. Hampstead, 6 February 1824.*[5] The Vespers of Palermo

My dear Sir Walter,

[. . .] I suppose you received about a week ago my letter concerning M$^{rs}$ Heman's [*sic*] Tragedy, and I hope you are according to the nature of your kind, friendly heart, inclined to smooth its way to the Edin$^r$ boards, where the beauty of the writing will be more attended to, and the Actors, perhaps more suited to their characters than at Covent Garden. [...]

yours my dear Sir Walter

truly & kindly

J. Baillie

*To Walter Scott, Bart., Edinburgh. Hampstead, 10 May 1824.*[6]

*The success of* Vespers

My dear Sir Walter,

[...] I ought long ere this to have thanked you a second time for your friendly exertions in favour of M$^{rs}$ Heman's [*sic*] Tragedy, now that they have happily led to complete success [....] The only account I received of its reception, for some time, was from the Edin$^r$ news paper which some friend or other sent me by post, and it seems to have been quite triumphant—every thing in short that her friends could desire; graced also with a prologue from the pen of a celebrated Baronet, so that both she & I have good cause to make you our grateful courtesies to the very ground. [...] I thank you again with all my heart. [...]

your grateful & affectionate

J Baillie

*To Margaret Holford Hodson. Hampstead 12 May 1826.*[7]

*A fantasy about Captain Hemans; Baillie has received a gift copy of*

The Forest Sanctuary *from FH*

[...] She is a woman of great genius, and unfortunately circumstanced. Her letter [...] was sealed with black and her husband has long been in bad health—perhaps he is dead, and then she will be relieved from a continued cause of embarrassment & anxiety; for he has been, I understand, a great clogg upon her. She supports (I am told) herself & four children on the produce of her pen, and is a woman of excellent character; if she could but get rid of her husband there would be no fear of her doing well. To marry a stupid Dandy at fifteen is a perverse fate for a woman of such endowments; for her acquirements, they say, are as great as her natural talents. [...]

*To Felicia Hemans, Rhyllon. London, 11 May 1827.*[8]

*Mothers and daughters*

In truth you are very <u>very</u> good to me, my dear M$^{rs}$ Hemans, and I thank you most heartily for it. Yesterday your American volume from the Author was put into my hands, and in dipping into it here & there without cutting the leaves,[9] I see that it is full of Poetic beauty of the highest value, and that I have a rich feast abiding me [...] What a proud thing it is for you to be taken into the arms as it were of another nation and one fresh & flourishing in a progressive state. I honour them for it, and sympathize in the feelings it must naturally awaken in your breast. [...] Had I not received your book, I still meant to have written to you to thank for what is more gratifying to me than any gift, the friendly communication of your own feelings as a Daughter cherishing the memory of a kind and good Mother. It is the first time that any allusion has been made by you to your own particular state, and I feel as if I had made one step nearer to your heart, a progress which I should dearly prize. Ay, you say well; no friend can sympathize & rejoice in the honour we receive like a Parent. But you have children to be proud of <u>you</u>, and to be stimulated & guided by that pride in a course of honourable virtue & exertion; and a fair field for hope lying before you, that which is behind softens & recedes, though it never fades away.[10] [. . .]

Many thanks again; and believe me always

Sincerely & gratefully yours

J Baillie

[1] Royal College of Surgeons of England, Hunter-Baillie papers, H-B ix 31; *Letters* 1.227. Poet, playwright, and translator William Sotheby (1757–1833) introduced Baillie to Scott in 1806. Among his many acquaintances in the literary world were Wordsworth, Coleridge, Byron, Rogers, Edgeworth, and Southey. In 1799 he published a victory ode, *The Battle of the Nile*, on the event that is the scene of FH's *Casabianca*. His eldest son was killed in battle at Waterloo.

[2] The opening poem in *Siege &c* (1823), named in the volume's full title, is *The Last Constantine*, its scene set in the fall of Constantinople to the Ottomans. Baillie's similarly situated play, *Constantine Paleologus*, in *Miscellaneous Plays* (Longman, 1804), was staged in London in 1817 and Edinburgh in 1820. Byron's epic romance *Childe Harold's Pilgrimage* (1812–18) brought new popularity to the Spenserian stanza. *Siege &c* included *The Voice of Spring*, previously published in *NMM* 7 (April 1823): 439–40, signed "F. H."

[3] NLS MS 3897, ff. 3–4; cf. *Letters* 1.420–21. Baillie published FH's *Belshazzar's Feast* (also in Spenserian stanzas) in *A Collection of Poems, Chiefly Manuscript, and from Living Authors* (Longman, 1823), in which she also included Scott, and many other literary lights.

[4] John Gibson Lockhart, Scott's son-in-law, published *Ancient Spanish Ballads: Historical and Romantic, Translated* in 1823.

[5] NLS MS 3898, ff. 56–57; cf. *Letters* 1.423–24. FH's stirring tragedy of political and domestic conflicts, set against the "Sicilian Vespers" uprising against French rule in 1282, failed at Covent Garden (London) in December 1823, the weak acting in the female lead blamed. The play still had strong support from its initial champions Charles Kemble, Reginald Heber and Henry Hart Milman. See FH's letter to William Jacob, May 1823; *CM* 1.64–79, 91–93, 99; *HM* 50–51, 69–76. Baillie persuaded Scott to approach Charles Kemble's sister, the renowned tragic actress Sarah Siddons (1755–1831), retired since 1812, about a staging at the Edinburgh Theatre, which was managed by her eldest son Henry and his wife Harriet Murray Siddons. *Vespers* was staged in April 1824 with Harriet Siddons in the female lead, and a new prologue written by Scott and recited by Sarah Siddons; it earned favorable reviews.

[6] NLS MS 3898, ff. 163–66; cf. *Letters* 1.426–28.

[7] Camden Local Studies and Archives Centre; *Letters* 2.590. Hodson (1778–1852) was a poet.

[8] ALS, Harry Ransom Humanities Research Center, University of Texas; cf. *Letters* 2.1174. The dating is my determination (Slagle says "1838?," but FH was near death by 11 May 1836): the "American volume" Baillie mentions is the combined 1826 and 1827 volumes; FH's mother died January 1827; the contents of the letter make it clear that Baillie is replying to FH's letter from Rhyllon, St. Asaph, 8 April 1827 (*CM* 1.140–42).

[9] This volume was a quarto, formed by printing four pages on each side of a sheet, folding it twice, and stitching a binding along one fold. The other fold was left uncut, for the purchaser to cut or not. Without cutting, only one side of the sheet's pages would be easily readable.

[10] Baillie was childless. For FH's reply to this letter, 31 May 1827, see *CM* 1.143–51.

## Walter Scott, 1823–29

[Prolific novelist, poet, and antiquarian, Scott (1771–1832) was a regular contributor to the *Quarterly Review*, and father-in-law of one of *Blackwood's* chief contributors, John Gibson Lockhart, who become the *Quarterly's* editor in 1825. FH visited Scott in 1829.]

*To Joanna Baillie, 11 July 1823.*[1] *Felicia Hemans's poetry*

[. . .] Mrs. Hemans is somewhat too poetical for my taste—too many flowers I mean, and too little fruit—but that may be the cynical criticism of an elderly gentleman; for it is certain that when I was young, I read verses of every kind with infinitely more indulgence. [. . .]

*To Joanna Baillie, Hampstead. Edinburgh, 9 February 1824.*[2]
The Vespers of Palermo

My Dear Miss Baillie,
To hear is to obey, and the enclosed line will show that the Siddonses are agreeable to act Mrs. Hemans's drama. When you tell the tale say nothing about me, for on no earthly consideration would I like it to be known that I interfered in theatrical matters;—it brings such a torrent of applications which it is impossible to grant, and often very painful to refuse. Everybody thinks they can write blank verse—and a word of yours to Mrs. Siddons, etc. etc. [. . .] I have great pleasure, however, in serving Mrs. Hemans, both on account of her own merit, and because of your patronage. I trust the piece will succeed; but there is no promising, for Saunders is meanly jealous of being thought less critical than John Bull,[3] and may, perhaps, despise to be pleased with what was less fortunate in London. I wish Mrs. H. had been on the spot to make any alterations, etc. which the players are always demanding. I will read the drama over more carefully than I have yet done, and tell you if anything occurs. [. . .] I am afraid that I cannot flatter myself with much interest that can avail her. I go do little out [. . .] but anything within my power shall not be left undone. I hope you will make my apology to Mrs. Hemans for the delay which has taken place; if anything should occur essential to be known to the authoress, I will write immediately.—Always yours, my dear friend,

Walter Scott

*To Joanna Baillie, 12 February 1824.*[4] Vespers of Palermo

My Dearest Friend,
[. . .] I wrote with Mrs. Siddons's consent to give Mrs. Hemans's tragedy a trial. I hope that her expectations are not very high, for I do not think our ordinary theatrical audience is either more judicious or less fastidious than those of England. They care little about poetry on the stage—it is situation, passion, and rapidity of action which seem to be the principal requisites for ensuring the success of a modern drama; but I trust, by dint of a special jury, the piece may have a decent success—certainly I should not hope for much more. I must see

they bring it out before 12th March, if possible, as we go to the country that day. I have not seen Mrs. Siddons and her brother William Murray since their obliging answer. [. . .] Always yours, with sincere respect and affection,

Walter Scott

Journal entries, July 1829.[5] Hemans's visit

[14 July] went to Chiefswood[6] and had the pleasure of a long walk with a lady well known in the world of poetry, Mrs. Hemans. She is young and pretty though the mother of five children she tells me. There is taste and spirit in her conversation. My daughters are critical and call her <u>blue</u> but I think they are hypercritical.

[18 July] She is a very clever person and has been pretty. I had a long walk with her tete-a-tete.

[1] Lockhart, *Life of Sir Walter Scott* (Edinburgh, 1837–39); cf. 1902 ed. (Edinburgh: Constable), 158. A reply to hers of 1 July, in which she praised *The Voice of Spring*, a flower-laden poem.

[2] Lockhart, *Life* 211–13. A reply to hers of 6 February, in which she refers to a letter she had written to him in January on the subject. Scott had been distracted by illness and family crises.

[3] Slang, respectively, for a typical Scotsman and a typical Englishman.

[4] Lockhart, *Life* 216–17.

[5] *The Journal of Walter Scott*, ed. W.E.K. Anderson (Oxford: Clarendon P, 1972), 5861.

[6] A countryhouse formerly owned by Lockhart, now by FH's host, Captain John Hamilton.

---

**William Blackwood,** Letters to Felicia Hemans on the success of *Records of Woman*[1]

22 July 1828 (f. 24)

Dear Madam,

Shortly after my return from London I wrote you a few lines enclosed with a No of my Magazine which was sent in my London parcel to the Bishop of St. Asaph's home.[2] Not having had the pleasure of hearing from you since, I fear the packet has not reached you.

I mentioned in my letter that The Records of Woman had met with a very favourable acceptance and I am happy to say that the sale has continued to go on so that I expect very soon to be able to put another edition to press. I have great pleasure therefore in enclosing you a draft on the Bank of England for £75—as your share of the Profits of this edition, which I hope will be agreeable to you.[3]

As I fully expect to be able to publish a new edition early next winter, you had better look over the whole in case any errors should have escaped, so that I may put to press whenever I may find it necessary. [. . .] Two or three months ago one of our Edin Papers had a paragraph stating that you were intending to take up your residence here. I shall be happy to hear that this is correct.

20 August 1828 *(ff. 46–48)*

[. . .] I am happy to inform you that The Records of Woman are now very nearly all sold off and therefore the sooner you send me any corrections so much the better, as I will instantly put the book into the hands of the Printer. It will also give me great pleasure to bring out a new edition of The Forest Sanctuary, and Lays of Many Lands, for I am quite confident of its success. The one will help the other.[4] Be so good therefore as send both Books corrected with your earliest convenience. [. . .] Your beautiful verses "The Message to the Dead" are in this No of Maga.[5] [. . .] Next month I intend to bring out two Nᵒˢ at once, and if you can send me any thing about the 11th or 12th it will be a great favour. Besides your delightful poetry, I still think [you] could send me some charming prose articles.

I had almost forgot to say that I think it would be better to insert any additional pieces in the new edition of "The Forest Sanctuary" rather than in The Records of Woman, because the latter being so recently published, the purchasers of the first edition might complain, while the former being longer out many might be tempted to purchase the new edition of it as being uniform with the Records and a much better size.

I hope to have the pleasure of hearing from you very soon [. . .]

4 September 1828 *(ff. 55–56)*

[. . .] I intend to put the new edition to press without delay [. . .] therefore send me any corrections with your earliest convenience. Since I wrote you I have had accounts from Mr. Cadell[6] saying he had not a copy left, and as I have now none to send him, I write you now to request you will be so good as write me by return of post saying if you have corrections or alterations in the first three or four sheets, for if you could specify these [. . .] it would enable the Printer to go and you could either send off in a day or two by Coach the corrected copy, or mention by letter such corrections as you wished to have made. I hope you will be able to send The Forest Sanctuary soon.

Your Poem and Miss Jewsbury's will appear in next No.[7]

I am glad to hear you are meditating another volume, which though it may in fact be and will appear to be a second volume of the Records of Woman, yet I would not call it a second volume. It is quite easy for you to give it a distinct title, which is always much better, for many will buy a single volume which appears complete in itself, who would not look at a 2nd volume.

23 October 1828 *(ff. 79–80)*

[. . .] I have published the second edition of The Records of Woman, and I shall enclose in a parcel to Liverpool tomorrow or next day, half a dozen of copies for your friends. I think Mr. Johns had done even more justice to this edition than to the former one.[8] I shall also enclose the sheet which we printed off of The Forest Sanctuary. I find that with all its additional Poems that volume will not extend to more than 240 or 250 pages. And I think it wd be advisable to add 40 or 50 pages more, which you could easily do from what has appeared in my Magazine, the Annuals or what you may have lying [?about] you. Besides making the volume more uniform with The Records it will also give those added more [?publicity.][9]

I would be most obliged to you when you write if you would send me a chronological list of your writings. I expect to have a splendid article soon upon your poetic works, and I would wish to give my friend an exact list of the whole, whatever he may notice.[10]

24 December 1829, crediting her account with £43.60 *(ff. 476–77)*

[. . .] I was glad to see Mr. Jeffrey's article in the last Edin Review. The second edition of the Records of Woman is I am happy to say nearly sold off, and I hope the Forest Sanctuary will go off by & bye

29 January 1830 *(ff. 509–10)*

[. . .] I was very happy to receive your beautiful poem The Lady of Provence just in time for our second No. It will I am sure be a great favourite.

I am glad you are preparing another volume, and the sooner we can go on with it the better. I intend to put another edition of the Records of Woman to press immediately as Cadell has sold all his copies, and I have only a few left here. Should you have any corrections be so good as write me by return of post [. . .]

[1] All letters (NLS BA MS 30311) are addressed from Edinburgh to FH in St. Asaph. Folio numbers are given in parentheses after the date.

[2] FH had franking (the free receipt of mail) through John Luxmoore, Bishop of St. Asaph.

[3] By 18 December 1828, Blackwood would pay her £150 for the 2d editions of *Records* and *Forest Sanctuary* and expected to pay another £25 for the latter (ff. 149–50).

[4] *Lays of Many Lands* followed *The Forest Sanctuary* in the 1825 volume. The 2d edition, with over two dozen new "Miscellaneous Pieces" (adding to the original seven), was published by Blackwood in 1829; *Records* had a 2d edition in October 1828. Blackwood is responding to FH's suggestion in her letter of 29 July 1828.

[5] *Blackwood's Edinburgh Magazine*, September.

[6] Thomas Cadell, London bookseller and Blackwood's London agent.

[7] FH's *The Two Voices* appeared in *Blackwood's* 24 (October 1828): 437; *Tasso's Coronation* and *The Voice of the Wind* in November (614, 639); all signed "F. H."

[8] John Johnstone, 18 St. James Square, Edinburgh, printed both editions of *Records* and the second edition of *The Forest Sanctuary*.

[9] The 2d edition of *The Forest Sanctuary* had 324 pages; *Records* had 320.

[10] Francis Jeffrey was preparing his essay for the *Edinburgh Review* (October 1829).

---

From *Noctes Ambrosianae No. XXXIX, Blackwood's Edinburgh Magazine*, November 1828, 674

[This popular series of conversations between "Shepherd" and "North," pseudonyms of James Hogg ("the Ettrick Shepherd") (1770–1835) and John Wilson (1785–1854), covered everything from politics to literature. At the end of this installment, they dwell on the prodigious success of the gift-book annuals.]

SHEPHERD

Does that dear, delightfu' cretur, Mrs Hemans, continue to contribute to ilka annual, ane or twa o' her maist beautifu' poems?

NORTH

She does so.

SHEPHERD

It's no in that woman's power, sir, to write ill; for, when a feeling heart and a fine genius forgather in the bosom o' a young matron, every line o' poetry is like a sad or cheerful smile frae her een, and every poem, whatever be the subject, in ae sense a picture o' hersell—sae that a' she writes has an affectin' and an endearin' mainnerism and moralism about it, that inspires the thochtfu' reader to say in to himsell—that's Mrs. Hemans.

NORTH

From very infancy, Felicia Dorothea was beloved by the Muses. I remember patting her fair head when she was a child of nine year—and versified even then with a touching sweetness about sylphs and fairies.

---

**Francis Jeffrey,** *Edinburgh Review* 50 (October 1829) 32–47, on the second editions of *Records of Woman* (1828) and *The Forest Sanctuary* (1829)

[Jeffrey (1773–1850) cofounded the influential quarterly *Edinburgh Review* in 1802 and was editor and chief literary reviewer until 1829, the year of its demise. Among his nearly 200 essays on literature and public issues, his relentless attacks on the Lake poets were infamous. His unsigned but recognizable authorship of this essay on FH was a credit to her popularity, and the essay subsequently proved a force in her reception, generously excerpted in editions of her works. One such, "Annotations on 'Records of Woman' &c." in *1839* (5.317–26), bore this headnote: "We feel certain that every admirer of the genius of Mrs Hemans will be obliged to us for here reprinting, almost at length, the admirable Critique on her writings which appeared in [. . .] the *Edinburgh Review*. The acumen, the clear-sightedness, the taste, and elegance of Lord Jeffrey, are evident throughout" (317). Jeffrey's "Critique" is also notable for its opening comments about women writers, its designations of "masculine" and "feminine" skills and strengths, and its summary guess about which (male) poets seemed destined for posterity.]

Women, we fear, cannot do every thing; nor even every thing they attempt. But what they can do, they do, for the most part, excellently—and much more frequently with an absolute and perfect success, than the aspirants of our rougher and more ambitious sex. They cannot, we think, represent naturally the fierce and sullen passions of men—nor their coarser vices—nor even scenes of actual business or contention—and the mixed motives, and strong and faulty characters, by which affairs of moment are usually conducted on the great theatre of the world. For much of this they are disqualified by the delicacy of their training and habits, and the still more disabling delicacy which pervades their conceptions and feelings; and from much they are excluded by their actual inexperience of the

realities they might wish to describe—by their substantial and incurable ignorance of business—of the way in which serious affairs are actually managed—
and the true nature of the agents and impulses that give movement and direction
to the stronger currents of ordinary life. Perhaps they are also incapable of long
moral or political investigations, where many complex and indeterminate elements are to be taken into account, and a variety of opposite probabilities to be
weighed before coming to a conclusion. They are generally too impatient to get
at the ultimate results, to go well through with such discussions; and either stop
short at some imperfect view of the truth, or turn aside to repose in the shadow
of some plausible error. This, however, we are persuaded, arises entirely from
their being seldom set on such tedious tasks. Their proper and natural business
is the practical regulation of private life, in all its bearings, affections, and concerns; and the questions with which they have to deal in that most important
department, though often of the utmost difficulty and nicety, involve, for the
most part, but few elements; and may generally be better described as delicate
than intricate;—requiring for their solution rather a quick tact and fine perception than a patient or laborious examination. For the same reason, they rarely
succeed in long works, even on subjects the best suited to their genius; their
natural training rendering them equally averse to long doubt and long labour.

For all other intellectual efforts, however, either of the understanding or the
fancy, and requiring a thorough knowledge either of man's strength or his
weakness, we apprehend them to be, in all respects, as well qualified as their
brethren of the stronger sex; while, in their perceptions of grace, propriety, ridicule—their power of detecting artifice, hypocrisy, and affectation—the force and
promptitude of their sympathy, and their capacity of noble and devoted attachment, and of the efforts and sacrifices it may require, they are, beyond all doubt,
our superiors.

Their business being, as we have said, with actual or social life, and the colours
it receives from the conduct and disposition of individuals, they unconsciously
acquire, at a very early age, the finest perception of character and manners, and
are almost as soon instinctively schooled in the deep and dangerous learning of
feeling and emotion; while the very minuteness with which they make and med-
itate on these interesting observations, and the finer shades and variations of
sentiment which are thus treasured and recorded, trains their whole faculties to
a nicety and precision of operation, which often discloses itself to advantage in
their application to studies of a very different character. When women, accordingly, have turned their minds—as they have done but too seldom—to the expo-
sition or arrangement of any branch of knowledge, they have commonly exhibited, we think, a more beautiful accuracy, and a more uniform and complete
justness of thinking, than their less discriminating brethren. There is a finish
and completeness about every thing they put out of their hands, which indicates
not only an inherent taste for elegance and neatness, but a habit of nice observation, and singular exactness of judgment.

It has been so little the fashion, at any time, to encourage women to write for
publication, that it is more difficult than it should be, to prove these truths by

examples. Yet there are enough, within the reach of a very careless and superficial glance over the open field of literature, to enable us to explain, at least, and illustrate, if not entirely to verify, our assertions. No *man*, we will venture to say, could have written the Letters of Madame de Sevigné, or the Novels of Miss Austin [*sic*] or the Hymns and Early Lessons of Mrs Barbauld, or the Conversations of Mrs Marcet.[1] These performances, too, are not only essentially and intensely feminine, but they are, in our judgment, decidedly more perfect than any masculine productions with which they can be brought into comparison. They accomplish more completely all the ends at which they aim, and are worked out with a gracefulness and felicity of execution which excludes all idea of failure, and entirely satisfies the expectations they may have raised. We might easily have added to these instances. There are many parts of Miss Edgeworth's earlier stories, and of Miss Mitford's sketches and descriptions, and not a little of Mrs Opie's, that exhibit the same fine and penetrating spirit of observation, the same softness and delicacy of hand, and unerring truth of delineation, to which we have alluded as characterising the purer specimens of female art.[2] The same distinguishing traits of a woman's spirit are visible through the grief and the piety of Lady Russel [*sic*], and the gaiety, the spite, and the venturesomeness of Lady Mary Wortley. We have not as yet much female poetry; but there is a truly feminine tenderness, purity, and elegance, in the Psyche of Mrs Tighe, and in some of the smaller pieces of Lady Craven.[3] On some of the works of Madame de Staël—her Corinne especially—there is a still deeper stamp of the genius of her sex. Her pictures of its boundless devotedness—its depth and capacity of suffering—its high aspirations—its painful irritability, and inextinguishable thirst for emotion, are powerful specimens of that morbid anatomy of the heart, which no hand but that of a woman's was fine enough to have laid open, or skilful enough to have recommended to our sympathy and love.[4] There is the same exquisite and inimitable delicacy, if not the same power, in many of the happier passages of Madame de Souza and Madame Cottin—to say nothing of the more lively and yet melancholy records of Madame de Staal, during her long penance in the court of the Duchesse de Maine.[5]

But we are preluding too largely; and must come at once to the point, to which the very heading of this article has already admonished the most careless of our readers that we are tending. We think the poetry of Mrs Hemans a fine exemplification of Female Poetry—and we think it has much of the perfection which we have ventured to ascribe to the happier productions of female genius.

It may not be the best imaginable poetry, and may not indicate the very highest or most commanding genius; but it embraces a great deal of that which gives the very best poetry its chief power of pleasing; and would strike us, perhaps, as more impassioned and exalted, if it were not regulated and harmonized by the most beautiful taste. It is infinitely sweet, elegant, and tender—touching, perhaps, and contemplative, rather than vehement and overpowering; and not only finished throughout with an exquisite delicacy, and even serenity of execution, but informed with a purity and loftiness of feeling, and a certain sober and humble tone of indulgence and piety, which must satisfy all judgments, and allay the apprehensions of those who are most afraid of the passionate exaggerations of poetry. The diction is always beautiful, harmonious, and free—and the themes, though of infinite variety, uniformly treated with a grace, originality and judgment, which mark the same master hand. These themes she has borrowed, with the peculiar interest and imagery that belong to them, from the legends of different nations, and the most opposite states of society; and has contrived to retain much of what is interesting and peculiar in each of them, without adopting, along with it, any of the revolting or extravagant excesses which may characterise the taste or manners of the people or the age from which it has been derived. She has thus transfused into her German or Scandinavian legends the imaginative and daring tone of the originals, without the mystical exaggerations of the one, or the painful fierceness and coarseness of the other—she has preserved the clearness and elegance of the French, without their coldness or affectation—and the tenderness and simplicity of the early Italians, without their diffuseness or languor. Though occasionally expatiating, somewhat fondly and at large, amongst the sweets of her own planting, there is, on the whole, a great condensation and brevity in most of her pieces, and, almost without exception, a most judicious and vigorous conclusion. The great merit, however, of her poetry, is undoubtedly in its tenderness and its beautiful imagery. The first requires no explanation; but we must be allowed to add a word as to the peculiar charm and character of the latter.

It has always been our opinion, that the very essence of poetry, apart from the pathos, the wit, or the brilliant description which may be embodied in it, but may exist equally in prose, consists in the fine perception and vivid expression of that subtle and mysterious analogy which exists between the physical and the moral world—which makes outward things and qualities the natural types and emblems of inward gifts and emotions, and leads us to ascribe life and sentiment to every thing that interests us in the aspects of external nature. [. . .][6] [Poetry] has substantially two functions, and operates in two directions. In the *first* place, it strikes vividly out, and flashes at once on our minds, the conception of an inward feeling or emotion, which it might otherwise have been difficult to convey, by the presentment of some bodily form or quality, which is instantly felt to be its true representative, and enables us to fix and comprehend it with a force and clearness not otherwise attainable; and, in the *second* place, it vivifies dead and inanimate matter with the attributes of living and sentient mind, and fills the whole visible universe around us with objects of interest and sympathy, by tinging them with the hues of life, and associating them with our own passions and affections.[7] This magical operation the poet too performs, for the most part, in one of two ways—either by the direct agency of similes and metaphors, more or less condensed or developed, or by the mere graceful presentment of such visible objects on the scene of his passionate dialogues or adventures, as partake of the character of the emotion he wishes to excite, and thus form an appropriate accompaniment or preparation for its direct indulgence or display. The former of those methods has perhaps been most frequently employed, and certainly has most attracted attention. But the latter, though less obtrusive, and perhaps less frequently resorted to of set purpose, is, we are inclined to think, the most natural and efficacious of the two; and is often adopted, we believe, unconsciously by poets of the highest order;—the predominant emotion of their minds overflowing spontaneously[8] on all the objects which present themselves to their fancy, and calling out from them, and colouring with its own hues, those that are naturally emblematic of its character, and in accordance with its general expression. It would be easy to show how habitually this is done by Shakspeare, and Milton especially, and how much many of their finest passages are indebted both for force and richness of effect to this general and diffusive harmony of the external character of their scenes with the passions of their living agents—this harmonizing and appropriate glow with which they kindle the whole surrounding atmosphere, and bring all that strikes the sense into unison with all that touches the heart.

But it is more to our present purpose to say, that we think the fair writer before us is eminently a mistress of this poetical secret; and, in truth, it was solely for the purpose of illustrating this great charm and excellence in her imagery, that we have ventured upon this little dissertation. Almost all her poems are rich with fine descriptions, and studded over with images of visible beauty. But these are never idle ornaments: All her pomps have a meaning; and her flowers and her gems are arranged, as they are said to be among Eastern lovers, so as to speak the language of truth and of passion. This is peculiarly remarkable in some little pieces, which seem at first sight to be purely descriptive—but are soon found to tell upon the heart, with a deep moral and pathetic impression. But it is a truth nearly as conspicuous in the greater part of her productions; where we scarcely meet with any striking sentiment that is not ushered in by some such symphony of external nature—and scarcely a lovely picture that does not serve as a foreground to some deep or lofty emotion. We may illustrate this proposition, we think, by opening either of these little volumes at random, and taking what they first present to us.—The following exquisite lines, for example, on a Palm-tree in an English garden. [Prints *The Palm-Tree* . . .] 'Graves of a Household,' has rather less of external scenery, but serves, like the others, to show how well the graphic and pathetic may be made to set off each other: [prints the poem.]

We have taken these pieces chiefly on account of their shortness: But it would not be fair to Mrs Hemans not to present our readers with one longer specimen—and to give a portion of her graceful narrative along with her pathetic descriptions. This story, of 'The Lady of the Castle,' is told, we think, with great force and sweetness: [prints the poem.] The following sketch of 'Joan of Arc in Rheims,' is in a loftier and more ambitious vein; but sustained with equal grace, and as touching in its solemn tenderness. [. . . Prints 7–32, 46–49, 55–87.] There are several strains of a more passionate character; especially in the two poetical epistles from Lady Arabella Stuart and Properzia Rossi. We shall venture to give a few lines from the former. [Explains the setting and quotes 125–199; . . .] There is a great sweetness in the following portion of a little poem of a "Girls' School": [prints *Evening Prayer* 13–36.]

There is a fine and stately solemnity in these lines on "The Lost Pleiad": [prints all but the first stanza.] The following, on "The Dying Improvisatore," have a rich lyrical cadence, and glow of deep feeling: [prints stanzas 5–7, 10–13.]

But we must stop here. There would be no end of our extracts, if we were to yield to the temptation of noting down every beautiful passage which arrests us in turning over the leaves of the volumes before us. We ought to recollect, too, that there are few to whom our pages are likely to come, who are not already familiar with their beauties; and, in fact, we have made these extracts, less with the presumptuous belief that we are introducing Mrs Hemans for the first time to the knowledge or admiration of our readers, than from a desire of illustrating, by means of them, the singular felicity in the choice and employment of her imagery, of which we have already spoken so much at large;—that fine accord she has established between the world of sense and of soul—that delicate blending of our deep inward emotions with their splendid symbols and emblems without.[9]

We have seen too much of the perishable nature of modern literary fame, to venture to predict to Mrs Hemans that hers will be immortal, or even of very long duration. Since the beginning of our critical career, we have seen a vast deal of beautiful poetry pass into oblivion, in spite of our feeble efforts to recall or retain it in remembrance. The tuneful quartos of Southey are already little better than lumber:—And the rich melodies of Keats and Shelley,—and the fantastical emphasis of Wordsworth,—and the plebeian pathos of Crabbe, are melting fast from the fields of our vision. The novels of Scott have put out his poetry. Even the splendid strains of Moore are fading into distance and dimness, except where they have been married to immortal music; and the blazing star of Byron himself is receding from its place of pride. We need say nothing of Milman, and Croly, and Atherstone, and Hood, and a legion of others, who, with no ordinary gifts of taste and fancy, have not so properly survived their fame, as been excluded by some hard fatality from what seemed their just inheritance. The two who have the longest withstood this rapid withering of the laurel, and with the least marks of decay on their branches, are Rogers and Campbell; neither of them, it may be remarked, voluminous writers, and both distinguished rather for the fine taste and consummate elegance of their writings, than for that fiery passion, and disdainful vehemence, which seemed for a time to be so much more in favour with the public.[10]

If taste and elegance, however, be titles to enduring fame, we might venture securely to promise that rich boon to the author before us; who adds to those great merits a tenderness and loftiness of feeling, and an ethereal purity of sentiment, which could only emanate from the soul of a woman. She must beware of becoming too voluminous; and must not venture again on anything so long as the "Forest Sanctuary." But, if the next generation inherits our taste for short poems, we are persuaded it will not readily allow her to be forgotten. For we do not hesitate to say, that she is, beyond all comparison, the most touching and accomplished writer of occasional verses that our literature has yet to boast of.

¹ Lady of fashion Marie de Rabutin-Chantal, Marquise de Sévigné (1626–96) was famous for her lively *Lettres* to her daughter and friends describing life in the court, in the city, in the country, and at home. Six of Jane Austen's novels were published between 1811 and 1818, none signed in her lifetime. Barbauld's *Hymns in Prose for Children* (1781) was translated into several European languages (Jeffrey does not mention her harshly reviewed *Eighteen Hundred and Eleven*, a critique of warfare, imperial conquest, and the moral corruptions of commerce). Jane Marcet was famous for her educational series: *Conversations on Chemistry, intended especially for the Female Sex* (1806; 15 subsequent editions), *Conversations on Natural Philosophy* (science for children, 1815), and her widely admired *Conversations on Political Economy* (1816; often reprinted).

² Best-selling Irish novelist Maria Edgeworth (1767–1829) published stories for children from 1801 into the 1820s; her volumes for adults include *Popular Tales* (1804) and *Tales of Fashionable Life* (1809). Dramatist and essayist Mary Russell Mitford's extremely popular *Our Village* sketches began to appear in 1824. Amelia Opie, also a poet and abolitionist, published a dozen works of fiction between 1790 and 1825.

³ Lady Rachel Russell (1636–1723) wrote several letters after her husband was executed for treason by Charles II. First published in 1773, they were widely admired, saw several editions, and led to the publication in 1817 of her earlier letters to her husband. Lady Mary Wortley Montagu (1689–1762), Fielding's cousin and at one time a close friend of Pope, was an essayist, poet, and letter writer, especially admired for her posthumously published *Embassy Letters*, about her experiences in Constantinople. Memoirist, travel writer, poet, and dramatist Lady Elizabeth Craven (1750–1828) was part of the late-18th-c. London intellectual circle that included Johnson, Walpole, Garrick, and Elizabeth Montagu; she wrote *A Journey Through the Crimea to Constantinople* (1789). Mary Tighe's *Psyche* (1811) remained very popular.

⁴ Staël's novel (1807) was an international success.

⁵ Marie-Sophie Risteau Cottin (1770–1807) was a prolific French sentimental novelist (see *The Domestic Affections* 217ff for a likely reference to her popular *Elizabeth* [1806]). Mme. de Souza (Botelho Mourao e Vasconcelios, Adelaide Marie Emile, Comtesse Flahaut, Marqueza de Sousa [?1761–1836]) wrote *Adèle de Sénage, ou lettres de Lord Sydenham* (1794). Mme. de Staal (1684–1750) was maid to the Duchesse du Maine, a difficult mistress whose contentious relations with the royal court got them both exiled and even sentenced to the Bastille; *Memoirs of Madame de Staal de Launay*, widely admired for its sparkling prose, was published in France 1755 (London edition, 1767), and often reprinted in the 19th c.

⁶ The elided paragraph involves a discussion of dead metaphor.

⁷ In the Preface to *Lyrical Ballads* (1800–1805), Wordsworth stated his intent to represent "the passions of men [. . .] incorporated with the beautiful and permanent forms of nature": a poet "considers man and the objects that surround him as acting and reacting upon each other, [. . .] finding every where objects that immediately excite in him sympathies." In his Preface of 1815, he insisted that the "appropriate business of poetry, [. . .] her appropriate employment, her privilege and her *duty*, is to treat of things not as they *are*, but as they *appear*: not as they exist in themselves, but as they *seem* to exist to the *senses*, and to the *passions*." Jeffrey's seeming echo complicates his famous antipathy to Wordsworth (his censure was so influential that as late as 1825 no bookseller in Edinburgh would carry Wordsworth's poetry). As with the other echoes (see n. 7), it may be that he misremembers even as he recalls the Wordsworthian source. Or can he admire this poetic if the agent is not Wordsworth? Or is he deliberately refusing Wordsworth credit, tweaking him with its better success in Hemans, Milton, and Shakespeare?

⁸ Cf. Preface to *Lyrical Ballads*: "all good poetry is the spontaneous overflow of powerful feelings."

⁹ The excerpt in *1839* concludes here.

¹⁰ Dead by 1829 were Keats (d. 1821), Shelley (d. 1822), and Byron (d. 1824). Keats and Shelley were coterie poets, though FH was among Shelley's enthusiastic readers (*CM* 2.193–94). Even among admirers, Wordsworth was regarded as having peaked long ago, though he was revered as a national treasure and would become Poet Laureate within a decade or so.

Southey published poetry in the 1790s that Jeffrey despised, and was now writing forgettable verse as Poet Laureate. Scott, who wrote most of his poetry in the first decade of the century, had turned to fiction. Of the other poets: Moore, a popular poet, lyricist, and satirist, published steadily from 1800 through the 1820s, as did Campbell; Crabbe (d. 1832) published from about 1780 to 1812; Hood began publishing in the 1820s as a belated Romantic-Keatsian, but by the end of the decade was moving into topical satire and comedy. Rogers published fairly regularly from the 1790s on; George Croly and Edwin Atherstone were minor figures; and FH's friend Milman published throughout the Regency and the 1820s.

---

## The Wordsworths, 1830–37

[By 1830, Wordsworth was writing little new poetry, but rather, collecting and revising previous pieces, and being persuaded by M. J. Jewsbury to enter the lucrative annuals market. Always irked by his slow sales compared to Byron's and the novelists', he appreciated attention and praise. Jewsbury, of whom he was very fond, was a close friend of his daughter Dora. Comments are excerpted from *The Letters of William and Dorothy Wordsworth: The Later Years, 1821–1850*, ed. Ernest de Selincourt, rev. by Alan G. Hill (Oxford UP, 1979).]

### *William Wordsworth to George Huntly Gordon,*[1] *ca. 1 July 1830*

Mrs Hemmans has been staying with us a fortnight, and one of her Sons also, a very interesting boy, 11 years of age.[2] She has taken lodgings upon the Banks of Windermere, and we expect her this afternoon to tea with two other of her Sons. We should have enjoyed Mrs Hemans company more had it not been for the deranged health both of my Sister and Daughter; which made us anxious and cast a cloud over our spirits.[3] She is a great Enthusiast both in Poetry and music, and enjoys this beautiful Country as much as any one can do who is new to such scenery.

### *William Wordsworth to Samuel Rogers,*[4] *30 July 1830*

We like Mrs Hemans much—her conversation is what might be expected from her Poetry, full of sensibility—and she enjoys the Country greatly.

### *Sarah Hutchinson to Edward Quillinan,*[5] *31 July 1830*

For one *long* fortnight we had Mrs Hemans and one of her boys—he was a sweet interesting creature—but she tho' a good natured person is so spoilt by the adulation of "*the world*" that her affection is perfectly unendurable. Don't say this to Miss Jewsbury who idolizes her. Mr W. *pretends* to like her very much—but I believe it is only because we do not; for she is the very opposite, her good-nature excepted, of anything he ever admired before either in *theory or practice*.

### *William Wordsworth to George Huntly Gordon, early August, 1830*

Mr H's Sister is [. . .] staying with us.[6] Her poetical genius is highly promising, and her modest and unassuming manners have recommended her much to the

Ladies of this family. Yester afternoon we had Mrs Hemans who favored us with music. She is restricted from singing by her medical advisers, but she plays upon the Piano with great feeling and taste. We meet her tomorrow also.—I could say much very much in praise of Mrs Hemans—but certainly, though I beg it may not be repeated from me—as she has been our Inmate, there is a draw-back. Her conversation, like that of many literary Ladies, is too elaborate and studied—and perhaps the simplicity of her character is impaired by the homage which has been paid her—both for her accomplishments and her Genius.

*William Wordsworth to Felicia Hemans, 30 April 1834*

My dear Mrs Hemans

My first duty is to thank you for your National Lyrics and the accompanying Letter.[7] [. . .] many of the Pieces had fallen in my way before they were collected; and had given me more or less pleasure—as all your productions do. [. . .] the pleasure is yet to come of perusing your Pieces in succession. I can only say that whenever I have peeped into the volume—I have been well recompensed. This morning I glanced my eye over the Pilgrim Song to the evening Star with great pleasure.[8]

And now my d^r Friend to a subject which I feel to be of much delicacy—You have submitted what you had intended as a Dedication for your Poems to me. I need scarcely say that as a *private letter* such expressions from such a quarter, could not have been rec^d by me but with pleasure of *no ordinary kind*, unchecked by any consideration but the fear that my writings were overrated by you, and my character thought better of than it deserved. But I must say that a *public* testimony in so high a strain of admiration is what I cannot but shrink from—be this modesty true or false, it is in me—you must bear with it, and make allowance for it. And therefore as you have submitted the whole to my judgement, I am emboldened to express a wish that you would instead of this Dedication in which your warm and kind heart has overpowered you, simply inscribe them to me, with such expression of respect or gratitude as would come within the limits of the rule which after what has been said above, will naturally suggest itself. Of course if the sheet has been struck off, I must hope that my shoulders may become a little more Atlantean than I now feel them to be.[9]

My Sister is not quite so well. She, Mrs W. and Dora all unite with me in best wishes and kindest remembrances to yourself and yours; and believe me d^r Mrs Hemans

to remain faithfully yours

*William Wordsworth to Felicia Hemans, September 1834*

My dear Mrs Hemans,

I [. . .] acknowledge the honour you have done me in prefixing my name to your volume of beautiful poems [*Scenes and Hymns*], and to thank you for the copy you have sent me with your own autograph. Where there is so much to admire, it is difficult to select; and therefore I shall content myself with naming only two or three pieces. And, first, let me particularise the piece that stands

second in the volume, *Flowers and Music in a Room of Sickness*. This was especially touching to me, on my poor sister's account, who has long been an invalid,
confined almost to her chamber. The feelings are sweetly touched throughout
this poem, and the imagery very beautiful; above all, in the passage where you
describe the colour of the petals of the wild rose.[10] This morning I have read the
stanzas upon *Elysium* with great pleasure.[11] You have admirably expanded the
thought of Chateaubriand. If we had not been disappointed in our expected
pleasure of seeing you here, I should have been tempted to speak of many other
passages and poems with which I have been delighted.

Your health, I hope, is by this time re-established. Your son Charles looks
uncommonly well, and we have had the pleasure of seeing him and his friends
several times; but as you are aware, we are much engaged with visitors at this
season of the year, so as not always to be able to follow our inclinations as to
whom we would wish to see. I cannot conclude without thanking you for your
sonnet upon a place so dear to me as Grasmere; it is worthy of the subject.[12]
With kindest remembrances, in which unite Mrs Wordsworth, my sister, and
Dora,

> I remain, dear Mrs Hemans,
> Your much obliged friend,

### Mary Wordsworth to Henry Crabbe Robinson, 1 November 1836[13]

Mrs Hemans's letters etc. [*CM*] we consider as a very flimsy Publication—and
not at all likely to support the opinion of those who have extolled her genius—I
must not say it disappoints me—from my personal knowledge, it is exactly what
I should have expected—But we have strong evidence that her mind was stead-
ied, and she became much more interesting, after she went to Dublin,—that is,
she discarded what to us seemed to be a lightness and affectation of manner. The
Mr Graves, who saw much of her in Dublin, to the last—quite reverence her.—
and you know they are sensible Persons not likely to be carried away by what is
superficial. Poor woman! she was sorely tried—and a beautiful trait in her character was, that she never uttered a complaint of her Husband.[14]

### William Wordsworth to Elizabeth Fisher,[15] 15 December 1837

I think highly of that Lady's [FH] genius—but her friends, and I had the
honor of being one of them—must acknowledge with regret, that her circumstances, tho' honorably to herself, put her upon writing too often and too
much—she is consequently diffuse; and felt herself under the necessity of *expanding* the thoughts of others, and hovering over their feelings, which has
prevented her own genius doing justice to itself, and diminished the value of her
productions accordingly. This is not said with a view to the withdrawing Mrs
H's works, but with a hope that it may be a caution for you to place those of the
elder Writers in your daughter's way, in preference to modern ones, however
great their merits. And in this implied recommendation, I do not speak without
allusion to my own.

[1] Walter Scott had employed Gordon as a secretary and in 1826 secured a position for him as secretary to S. R. Lushington, Secretary of the Treasury.

[2] The youngest, Charles.

[3] William's sister Dorothy had been afflicted by a series of debilitating illnesses from which she would never recover. His beloved daughter Dora (b. 1804) began to suffer from ill health in 1827.

[4] Rogers is most famous for *The Pleasures of Memory* (1792) and a collection of verse tales, *Italy* (1822–28). He would decline the Poet Laureateship when it was offered to him on Wordsworth's death in 1850.

[5] Sarah Hutchinson, the sister of William's wife, Mary, was a member of the household. Edward Quillinan was a neighbor and widower who later courted Dora, much to the Wordsworths' displeasure, though they would eventually consent to the marriage, in 1841.

[6] Both William Rowan Hamilton (professor of astronomy at Trinity College, Dublin) and his sister were guests; they both wrote poetry, for which they sought Wordsworth's advice.

[7] Referring to FH's letter of 1834, accompanying a gift of *National Lyrics and Songs for Music* (1834), in which she asks permission to dedicate *Scenes and Hymns of Life* to him.

[8] *Pilgrim's Song to the Evening Star* was among the "Miscellaneous Lyrics."

[9] A parody of Milton's depiction of the fallen angel Beëlzebub: "sage he stood / With Atlantean shoulders fit to bear / The weight of mightiest Monarchies" (*Paradise Lost* 2.305–7).

[10] "touch'd so tenderly, / As a pure ocean-shell, with faintest red, / Melting away to pearliness" (66–68).

[11] Reprinted from *The Siege of Valencia &c.*

[12] *A Remembrance of Grasmere* (a village near Rydal Mount where the Wordsworths lived for many years) would be published in *Poetical Remains* (1836), in a section titled *Records of the Spring of 1834*.

[13] FH died 16 May 1835. Mary is William's wife; Robinson (1775–1867) was a foreign correspondent for the *Times* during the Peninsular War (1808–9), and later a lawyer, a career from which he retired in 1828. He is remembered for his diaries (1867), which contain recollections of many writers, including Wordsworth.

[14] But see her letter to Rev. Samuel Butler, 7 November 1833. Poet Mary Howitt, also a friend, wrote in her journal (18 July 1827), "I have just now received a letter from Mrs. Hemans. She congratulates me, I can fancy, with a mournful reference to herself, in possessing in a husband and a kindred spirit and a friend" (qtd. in Trinder 20). Writer William Howitt encouraged his wife's literary endeavors; they coauthored *The Forest Minstrel* in 1823.

[15] Elizabeth Fisher's daughter Emmie had poetic aspirations; Wordsworth thought her a prodigy.

## Maria Jane Jewsbury

[Jewsbury (1800–33) was a sparkling poet, essayist and fiction-writer, and like FH a frequent contributor to the magazines and annuals. She was one of FH's closest friends. She had just begun to write for the new journal *The Athenæum* in 1830, and soon would become a major contributor. *The Three Histories* (London: F. Westley, 1830) was well reviewed. Texts are from the American edition (Boston: Perkins & Marvin, 1831).]

### The Three Histories *(1830)*

#### *The History of an Enthusiast*

[This is Jewsbury's revisionary version of the *Corinne* story. Julia Osborne gains fame, finds it hollow, and misses out on domestic bliss; instead of dying of a broken heart, she sets out, at the history's close, for a European adventure. The episode below, from her childhood, is based on an oft-repeated story about FDB, first reported by Chorley and Hughes: "One of her earliest tastes was a passion for Shakspeare, which she read, as her choicest recreation, at six years old; and in later days she would often refer to the hours of romance she had passed in a secret haunt of her own—a seat amongst the branches of an old apple-tree—where, revelling in the treasures of the cherished volume, she would become completely absorbed in the imaginative world it revealed to her" (*HM* 6–7). Without naming FDB, but alluding to this anecdote in a footnote, Jewsbury's vignette at once celebrates intellectual girlhood transgressions and satirizes a pervasive cultural anxiety about unsupervised girlhood reading, especially of Shakespeare (for which, see my essay in *Nineteenth-Century Contexts*). *The Family Shakespeare*, edited by Thomas and Henrietta Bowdler (whence "bowdlerized") was the preferred edition for family reading. Julia Osborne is being sought by her grandmother and Martin, a servant. That she addresses her exasperated Grandmother as "Nurse" suggests that she has also read *Romeo and Juliet*, and perhaps identified with Shakespeare's similarly named rebellious heroine.]

"Dear Miss Julia, love, why didn't you just answer when you heard us all calling out for you?"

"Because I did not hear you, nurse; I was up in the great apple tree—"

"A pretty place for a grand-daughter of mine, indeed! and pray—oh you naughty, naughty girl! —and pray what took you there?"

The child colored, and seemed ashamed to speak.

"So, so;—more mischief I perceive—why could not you wait till the apples were ripe?"

"The apples! O grandmamma, just as if I cared for *them!*"

"Don't speak so scornfully, if you please, of my golden pippins, the finest tree in the country; but tell me at once what you were doing there—and be so good, child, as to bring that hand from behind your back."

The child obeyed slowly, and with evident reluctance produced a book.

"Shakspeare, as I live! Well to be sure!"

"Mercy upon us, Miss! but heathen play-acting books are not for babes like you."

"And you have absolutely, and positively, and up in my golden-pippin apple tree, been reading this book?"

"Yes grandmamma,* Oh, don't take it from me dear, dear grandmamma! I will promise not to spoil, (sobbing,) not to spoil anything any more, and I will be *so* good [. . .] if only you will leave me this book, and let me read in the parlor—oh, do let me know what becomes of Macbeth at last!"

\* Fact of a child seven years old, a year younger than Julia

*The History of a Nonchalant*
(Part 3, "Egeria")

["Egeria" is the Nonchalant's pet name for his wife, taken from Numa's wife and counselor, who (as recounted in Ovid's *Metamorphoses*) was so bereft at his death, that she dissolved into tears and was changed into a fountain by the goddess Diana. Jewsbury cited FH as the basis of this portrait, and everyone agreed. Chorley summons it to gloss her character (*CM* 1.187–89); Gilfillan uses "Egeria" as a synonym for FH (*Tait's* 361, 363); Jane Williams quotes the whole description as "obviously true" for FH (*Literary Women* 479–80), as does W. M. Rossetti.]

Other women might be more commanding, more versatile, more acute; but I never saw one so exquisitely feminine. She was lovely without being beautiful; her movements were features; and if a blind man had been privileged to pass his hand over the silken length of hair, that when unbraided flowered around her like a veil, he would have been justified in expecting softness and a love of softness, beauty and a perception of beauty, to be distinctive traits of her mind. Nor would he have been deceived. Her birth, her education, but above all, the genius with which she was allied, combined to inspire a passion for the ethereal, the tender, the imaginative, the heroic—in one word, the beautiful. It was in her a faculty divine, and yet her daily life—it touched all things, but like a sunbeam, touched them with a "golden finger."[1] Anything abstract or scientific was unintelligible and distasteful to her; her knowledge was extensive and various, but true to the first principle of her nature, it was poetry that she sought in history, scenery, character, and religious belief—poetry that guided all her studies, governed all her thoughts, colored all her conversation. Her nature was at once simple and profound; there was no room in her mind for philosophy, or in her heart for ambition—one was filled by imagination, the other engrossed by tenderness. She had a passive temper, but decided tastes; any one might influence, but very few impressed her. Her strength and her weakness alike lay in her affections; these would sometimes make her weep at a word, at others imbue her with courage; so that she was alternately a "falcon-hearted dove," and "a reed shaken with the wind."[2] Her voice was a sad, sweet melody, and her spirits reminded me of an old poet's description of the orange-tree, with its "Golden lamps hid in a night of green," or of those Spanish gardens where the pomegranite grows beside the cypress.[3] Her gladness was like a burst of sunlight; and if in her depression she resembled night, it was night wearing her stars. I might describe, and describe forever, but I should never succeed in pourtraying Egeria; she was a muse, a grace, a variable child, a dependent woman,—the Italy of human beings.

[When she proposes to "exercise [. . .] her surpassing accomplishments to in-crease our pittance," the Nonchalant is "repelled with a vehemence amounting almost to anger": "live upon the money earned by a woman—that woman my wife—and that wife Egeria!—I could far sooner have died than permitted such a reversal of the order of nature, a desecration of my dignity and her softness."]

*"Literary Sketches No. 1: Felicia Hemans,"*
Athenæum *172 (12 February 1831): 104–5; unsigned*

[Founded as a weekly literary and artistic review in 1828, *The Athenæum, Journal of English and Foreign Literature, Science, and the Fine Arts* was just emerging into prominence in 1831, championed by the "Cambridge Apostles," university men (among them, Tennyson, Arthur Hallam, and R. M. Milnes) eager to reform the world through moral and spiritual regeneration. Early contributors included Coleridge, Leigh Hunt, and Charles Lamb, and works by Keats and Shelley appeared posthumously; in the 1830s Elizabeth Barrett was a major contributor. Jewsbury began writing for it in 1830 and by 1831 regularly supplied poems, reviews, and essays. It was through her that Chorley began his long association with the paper.]

Were there to be a feminine literary house of commons, Felicia Hemans might very worthily be called to fill the chair as the speaker—a representative of the whole body, as distinguished from the other estates of the intellectual realm. If she wrote, or rather published prose, for write it we know she does very charmingly, it would be characterised by the same qualities that mark her poetry, and by some that in poetry cannot well appear:—wit, for instance; but then it would be poetical wit, dealing chiefly in fanciful allusion and brilliant remark, but no puns, not even upon ideas. The wit of society is sparkling repartee, intel-lectual snap-dragon; poetical wit is essentially imaginative—spiritual rather than satiric—and female wit differs as much from a man's, as Cœur de Lion chopping the iron mace by a single blow of his straight ponderous sword, differed from Sultan Saladin severing the down pillow with his thin shining scimitar.[4] But to return to Mrs. Hemans. The remark that genius always gives its best first is by no means worthy of invariable credit. Inferior minds may, by throwing all their energies into a first effort, achieve more than they ever do afterwards;—but it is because, in that first effort, they overleaped and exhausted themselves. Ge-nius of a higher order generally developes gradually, passing through a regular gradation of bud, blossom, and fruit. If a first production evidence the sudden maturity of a Siberian summer, it is not improbable but the creative power may be as short-lived. The best writers have all been improving writers—so have the best painters. We have at his moment before our eyes a very interesting docu-ment in proof of our assertion—a MS. copy of various poems, the composition, and in the handwriting of Felicia Hemans, when *thirteen years old*. There is not a greater disparity between the text-hand of the child, and the formed, delicate, flowing autograph of the woman, than exists between their compositions. The oak is not in the acorn; and, except remarkable smoothness of versification, these poems contain nothing of the promise that has since been so splendidly fulfilled. The following is one of the prettiest of these juvenile productions:—[5]

### To the Muse

Goddess of the magic lay,
Ever let me own thy sway!
Thine the sweet enchanting art,
To charm and to correct the heart—
To bid the tear of pity flow,
Sacred to thy tale of woe;
Or raise the lovely smile of pleasure
With sportive animated measure!

O Goddess of the magic lay,
To thee my early vows I pay!
Still let me wander in thy train,
And pour the wild romantic strain:
Be mine to rove, by thee inspired,
In peaceful vales and scenes retired;
For in thy path, O heavenly maid!
The roses bloom that never fade.

That the childhood of our poetess was no common thing—that she had, from its dawn, gleams and visitings of the imagination that has since won for her such high fame—that from very early years she walked in the light of her own spirit, is true; but she has yet manifested more *progression* than any one who has written as much, and whose course we can as faithfully follow. Leaving her childhood wholly out of the question, and examining those works which have at intervals issued from the press during the last fifteen years, even they may be divided into two distinct styles—the classic and the romantic. Within the time specified, Mrs. Hemans has differed as materially from herself as from any other writer; and not in minor points merely, but in very essential ones. Up to the publication of the "Siege of Valencia," her poetry was correct, classical, and highly polished—but it wanted warmth; it partook more of the nature of statuary than of painting. She fettered her mind with facts and authorities, and drew upon her memory when she should have relied upon her imagination:—she did not possess too much knowledge, but she made too much use of it. She was diffident of herself, and, to quote her own admission, "loved to repose under the shadow of mighty names":[6]—Since then she has acquired the courage which leads to simplicity. Those were the days when she translated, and when her own poetry had somewhat the air of translation:—see the "Restoration of the Works of Art to Italy"—the "Tales and Historic Scenes"—"Modern Greece"—"The Greek Songs"—"The Last Constantine"—and "Dartmoor." But now this is no longer the case. The sun of feeling has risen upon her song—noon has followed morning—the Promethean touch has been given to the statue—the Memnon yields its music.[7] She writes from and to the heart, putting her memory to its fitting use—that of supplying materials for imagination to fashion and build with. It is ridiculous to compare poets who have no points in common—equally vain to settle their priority of rank: each has his own character and his own station without reference to others. There will always be a difference between the poetry of men and women—so let it be; we have two kinds of excellence instead of one; we have also the pleasure of contrast: we discover that power is the element of man's genius—beauty that of woman's;—and occasionally we reciprocate their respective influence, by discerning the beauty of power, and feeling the power of beauty.

Mrs. Hemans has written pieces that combine power and beauty in an equal degree:—"Cœur de Lion at the Bier of his Father"—"England's Dead"—"The Pilgrim Fathers"—"The Lady of Provence"—"The Vaudois Wife"[8]—and numbers of the same stamp, are "lumps of pure gold": poems full of heroism, full of strength, and full of spirit; but the most distinctive feature in the mind and poetry of Mrs. Hemans, is their bias toward the supernatural of thought. Most of her later poems breathe of midnight fancies and lone questionings—of a spirit that muses much and mournfully on the grave, not as for ever shrouding beloved objects from the living, but as a shrine whence high unearthly oracles may be won; and all the magnificence of this universal frame, the stars, the mountains, the deep forest, and the ever-sounding sea, are made ministrants to this form of imagination.

"The Address to a Departed Spirit"—"The Message to the Dead"—"The Spirit's Return,"[9] are express embodyings of this longing after visible signs of immortality—this turning inward and looking outward for proof that the dead dream in their long sleep, and dream of *us*; whilst incidental breathings of the same nature continually occur through her volumes.

As poetry, the productions thus characterized are exquisite; but we deeply regret the habit of thought they embody and display. With the dead we have nothing to do: we shall go to them, but they shall not return to us; and to invest anything like a wish for such return—anything like belief in its possibility—with the charms and subtleties of imagination, fancy, or feeling, is neither wise nor safe. The field of human feeling is large and varied; well has Mrs. Hemans availed herself of its resources! "Others," says an American critic, "have had more dramatic power, more eloquence, more manly strength, but no woman had ever so much true poetry in her heart." This is saying much; but only look in confirmation at the feelings she loves to pourtray—they are the purest, most profound, or, in other words, the most poetic of our nature:—look again at the characters she delights to honour—the wise, the virtuous, the heroic, the self-devoted, the single-hearted; those who have been faithful unto death in a noble cause; those who have triumphed over suffering and led on to holy deeds; those who have lived, and those who have died for others. PASSION is a poetical watch-word of the day;—unfortunately, it is also something worse—a species of literary Goule that preys upon good sense, good feeling, and good taste. Nothing now is considered to be said strongly that is said simply—every line must produce "effect"—every word must "tell"; in fact,

Who peppers the highest is surest to please.[10]

The human heart is to be treated like Lord Peter's coat, in the Tale of a Tub: authors need "mind nothing; so they do but tear away."[11] POWERFUL is another watchword, which palms off every delineation that is monstrous and absurd. Thus, language is powerful when epithets succeed each other as fast and heavily as the strokes of a blacksmith's hammer; ideas are powerful when, like Ossian's ghosts, they reveal themselves in mists and shadow; and characters and incidents are powerful when they are worthy of the Newgate Calendar.[12] Those who catered for the nursery in olden times had very correct notions on these points: Jack the Giant-killer is truly "powerful"; Blue Beard is fraught with "passion."

The admirable taste possessed by Mrs. Hemans has entirely preserved her from these, the besetting sins of our imaginative literature; she always writes like one who feels that the heart is a sacred thing, not rashly to be wounded; whilst she scorns to lower her own intellectual dignity by an ambitious straining after effect. Her matronly delicacy of thought, her chastened style of expression, her hallowed ideas of happiness as connected with home, and home-enjoyments;— to condense all in one emphatic word, her *womanliness* is to her intellectual qualities as the morning mist to the landscape, or the evening dew to the flower—that which enhances loveliness without diminishing lustre. To speak confidentially to our trusted friend the public, Mrs. Hemans throws herself into her poetry, and the said self is an English gentlewoman. Now this proves the exceeding good sense of Imagination, a faculty that Utilitarians are so apt to libel:[13] Imagination says, that a poetess ought to be ladylike, claiming acquaintance with the Graces no less than with the Muses; and if it were not so, Imagination would conceive he had a right to be sulky. We appeal to any one who is imaginative. If, after sighing away your soul over some poetic effusion of female genius, a personal introduction took place, and you found the fair author a dashing dragoon-kind of woman—one who could with ease rid her house of a couple of robbers—would you not be startled? Or, if she called upon you to listen to a discussion on Petrarch's love[14] in a voice that brayed upon your sense of hearing, would you not feel that nature had made a mistake? Without a doubt you would. Your understanding might in time be converted; you might bow at the very feet, and solicit the very hand, the proportions of which at first inspired terror, but your Imagination, a recreant to the last, would die maintaining that a poetess ought to be feminine. All that we know are so; and Mrs. Hemans especially. Her Italian extraction somewhat accounts for the passion which, even in childhood, she displayed for sculpture and melody;[15] but her taste for the beautiful, so fastidious, so universal, so unsleeping—(we are not discussing how far such a taste contributes to happiness, but in what way it modifies genius,)—is that, to which may mainly be attributed Mrs. Hemans's separation from all other sisters of the lyre. One or two might be named who excel her in some

things, but not one who equals her in *this* point. Beauty of sound, natural spectacle, form and colour, is to her a life and presence—the spirit that deifies existence—the dial that records time in sunbeams.

All who remember "The Voice of Spring"—"Bring Flowers"—"The Death-
song of the Nightingale"—the "Music of Yesterday"—"The Song of Night,"
and others of this class, will agree, that "the imperfection of language, the embarrassment of versification, all that is material and mechanical, disappears, and
the vision floats before us 'an aery stream.'"[16] They seem like some of Shelley's—
less written than dreamed.

We must adventure a general remark on the subject of poetry as connected or
unconnected with moral truth. It is not necessary that every poem should be a
homily in verse, or a sermon written for music; but it *is* necessary that the bias
of a poet's own mind should be towards the beneficial. It has been finely said,
that the intention of poetry, like that of christianity, is "to spiritualize our nature"; if so, every poet should emulate the birds that ministered to the prophet
in the wilderness, and bring us food from heaven. Such a poet may pourtray the
passions, the joys, the griefs, and the affections of earth—but he will not rest
among them. Like the angel who appeared to the Hebrew chief, he will touch
the offerings with his staff, and there will rise from them, a pure, a heavenly, an
aspiring flame. Great improvement has taken place in this respect; there is a
holier spirit abroad in our poetry of an imaginative nature; and, in common with
some other poets, Mrs. Hemans has given us many poems destined, we trust, in
better than a human sense, to "shine as the stars for ever":—"The Hebrew
Mother"—the "Cross in the Wilderness"—"The Trumpet"—"The Fountain of
Marah"—"The Penitent"—"The Graves of the Martyrs"—&c.[17] We look for
yet more like these, and entreat that we may not look in vain. To our minds Mrs.
Hemans always succeeds best when her "strain is of a higher" mood; when she
sings to us of "melancholy fear subdued by faith"; and, when, through the tender
gloom that habitually hangs over her poetry (twilight on a rose-bed) we have
glimpses of that future which alone can "make us less forlorn."[18] For this reason
the "Forest Sanctuary" is our first favourite. But

> Time is, our tedious *prose* should here have ending.

Had Felicia Hemans belonged to antiquity, it is probable that some of her
lyrics might have descended to us, and been considered now as perfect specimens
of song. That word reminds us that we have not mentioned one branch of
composition in which our poetess especially excels, and to which she appears
recently to have given particular attention—we mean song-writing. Our musical
readers are probably familiar with many so sweetly set to music by her sister. In
songs there should be *one* thought or *one* feeling flowing out in simple, natural,
melodious words. Mrs. Hemans's best, whilst full of melody, are remarkable for
their variety of subject; avoiding sentiment, they contrive to embody knowledge,
description, affection; and we hope she will continue this species of writing.
Good Mr. Printer's black spirit, and worthy Mr. Editor's angelic spirit, be so

good as make room for the following one of six, about to be published (if not already published) by Power[19]— [prints *The Lyre and Flower.*]

Long may Mr. Power's *Strand* be strewn with such gems![20] But to conclude at last: Mrs. Hemans often partakes, it is true, of the modern faults of diffuseness, over-ornament, and want of force; but, taken for all in all, and judged by her best productions, she is a permanent accession to the literature of her country; she has strengthened intellectual refinement, and beautified the cause of virtue. The superb creeping-plants of America often fling themselves across the arms of mighty rivers, uniting the opposite banks by a blooming arch: so should every poet do to truth and goodness—so has Felicia Hemans often done, and been, poetically speaking, a Bridge of Flowers.

[1] In poem XIV of *Memorials of a Tour of the Continent, 1820*, Wordsworth describes a sunlit landscape as "Touched by his golden finger" (16).

[2] Reacting to John the Baptist's inquiries about his spiritual authority, Jesus says to the multitude, "What went ye out into the wilderness to see? A reed shaken with the wind?" (Matthew 11.7); Hughes uses this last image to describe FH at the end of her life (*HM* 15). In Coleridge's *Zapolya* (1817), Glycine, who has saved her lover's life by shooting his would-be assassin with a poison arrow, is described as a "sword that leap'dst forth from a bed of roses," a "falcon-hearted dove" (Act 4). FH used the last phrase as her epigraph for *Marguerite of France* (*Blackwood's* 30 [October 1831]).

[3] Andrew Marvell, *Bermudas* (*Miscellaneous Poems* [1681]): the voyagers praise the God who "hangs in shades the orange bright, / Like golden lamps in a green night, / And does in the pom'granates close / Jewels more rich than Ormus shows" (17–20).

[4] Saladin (1137–93) was the famous opponent of Richard I in the Third Crusade (1190–92). Both leaders figure in FH's *The Troubadour and Richard Cœur de Lion* and Scott's novel, *The Talisman* (1825), which FH enjoyed.

[5] In *Poems* (1808), long out of print; this ode was not even reprinted in any of the selections of "Juvenile Poems" in the chief nineteenth-century editions.

[6] Cf. *Modern Greece*: "midst thy laurel shades the wanderer hears / The sound of mighty names" (XXII).

[7] Prometheus created man from clay and animated him with the divine spark. Memnon, son of the dawn goddess Eos, was slain in the Trojan War; it was fabled that when his statue in Thebes was struck by the rising sun, it produced music. Jewsbury's narrative of FH's career proved influential. It was followed by D. M. Moir in one of the first retrospects: "In her earlier works she follows the classic model as contradistinguished from the romantic, and they are inferior in that polish of style and almost gorgeous richness of language, in which her maturer compositions are set" (*Blackwood's* 38 [July 1835], 97). The headnote to "Selections from Juvenile Poems" in *1839* divides the career into "the *classical*" (*Restoration; Modern Greece; Tales*) and "the *romantic*, which commences with the 'Forest Sanctuary,' and includes 'Record of Woman,' together with nearly all her later efforts" (7.329). Jane Williams defines four stages: the "juvenile," the "classic," the "romantic," and the "mature style" (481–82).

[8] *Cœur de Lion at the Grave of his Father* (*NMM*, January 1825) was collected with *Lays of Many Lands* in *Forest Sanctuary* (1825). *The Vaudois Wife* was published in *Blackwood's* 24 (December 1828): 782–83, signed "F. H."; *The Lady of Provence* in *Blackwood's* 27 (February 1830): 372–75, signed "Mrs. Hemans." Both were collected in *Songs of the Affections* (1830).

[9] All are among *Songs of the Affections*. *To a Departed Spirit* first appeared in *LS* 1829: 189–92, and *Message to the Dead* in *Blackwood's* 24 (September 1828): 353, signed "F. H."

[10] Oliver Goldsmith (?1730–74), *Retaliation* (1774), referring to renowned actor David Garrick (1770–79): "Of praise a mere glutton, he swallow'd what came, / And the puff of a dunce,

he mistook it for fame; / Till his relish grown callous, almost to disease, / Who peppered the highest was surest to please" (109–12).

[11] In Jonathan Swift's satire *A Tale of the Tub* (1704), a father leaves his three sons a coat apiece, prohibiting alterations. All violate the edict, Peter (Roman Catholic) most elaborately. (FH and Jewsbury were Anglicans).

[12] Legendary Gaelic hero Ossian was the bardic "author" of James Macpherson's bogus translations (1760–63). *The Newgate Calendar, or the Malefactors' Bloody Register* (1774) reported crimes in eighteenth-century England (Newgate was a famous prison dating from the twelfth century). In 1826 or so, *The Newgate Calendar, Comprising interesting memoirs of the most notorious characters* and *The New Newgate Calendar* were published by Andrew Knapp and William Baldwin.

[13] Jeremy Bentham and John Stuart Mill, founders the Utilitarian Society (1823–26), argued that the value of an action is its usefulness in promoting (in Bentham's motto) "the greatest good for the greatest number."

[14] FH translated one of Petrarch's sonnets (from *Rime in Vita e Morte di Madonna Laura*) in her 1818 collection.

[15] FH's mother "was a descendant of a Venetian house, whose old name [was] Veniero," a family that included three Doges; in "the waning days of the Republic" (i.e., 1797), FDB's "grandfather held the humbler situation of Venetian Consul in Liverpool" (*CM* 1.10). Staël's *Corinne* is half-English, half-Italian. For the Italian aura, see "Egeria."

[16] *The Voice of Spring* (also admired by Baillie) is in *The Siege of Valencia &c* (1823); *The Nightingale's Death Song* (first published in *NMM*, September 1829) and *The Song of Night* (*Winter's Wreath* 1830, 141) are in the "Miscellaneous Poems" of *Songs of the Affections &c.* *Music of Yesterday* is in *The Forest Sanctuary &c*, 2d ed. (1829). The prose quotation is unidentified; its phrase "aery stream" may allude to Milton's *Il Penseroso*: "let some strange mysterious dream / Wave at his Wings in airy stream" (147–48).

[17] *The Trumpet* and *The Hebrew Mother* appeared in the annual *The Amulet* 1826 (1, 125), and were collected in *The Forest Sanctuary*, 2d ed. (1829), along with *The Cross in the Wilderness* (*Amulet* 1827, 123) and *The Graves of the Martyrs* (*NMM*, April 1827). *The Penitent* is either *The Penitent's Offering* (*Literary Magnet*, 1827) or *The Penitent's Return* (*Blackwood's* 29, January 1831: 130–31). *The Fountain of Marah* (*Amulet* 1827, 305) would be reprinted in *Hymns for Childhood* (1833). "Shine as the stars for ever" is from E. Perronet, *The Mitre* (1757): the "reward . . . reserved [in Heaven] for all such as turn many to righteousness, viz. to shine as the stars for ever and ever!" (2.1320).

[18] The "strain of a higher mood" loosely translates "Paulò major canamus" ("Let us sing of higher things"), the opening line of Virgil's fourth eclogue (used by Wordsworth as the epigraph for the 1807 version of the "Intimations" *Ode*). The other two quotations are from Wordsworth's "Prospectus" to *The Excursion* (15), and his sonnet "The world is too much with us" (12), in the 1807 *Poems*.

[19] This and five other songs, set to music by H. F. Chorley and James Zengheer Herrmann, were published by James Power. Power also brought out Thomas Moore's *Irish Melodies*, and Byron had hoped to publish songs with him. FH's six songs also appeared as "Words for Melodies," *NMM* December 1832. Power had published her *Welsh Melodies*, with musical arrangements by John Parry, in 1821. FH took music lessons from Herrmann, with a special study of Pergolesi's *Stabat mater* (*HM* 168).

[20] Power's business was located at 34 The Strand, London.

**Andrews Norton,** Cambridge, Mass., spring 1831,[1] to Hemans.
Poetry and suffering

My dear Mrs. Hemans
[. . .] thank you both for the poems and for the annuals which I received through Mr. Chorley. We shall keep these and the other volumes with which you have favored us as a legacy for our children, who will live in an age when [*MS torn*] [. . .] think better of the world for the reception it has given to your poetry. It implies a wider diffusion of delicate and elevated feelings than the general character of the literature of the day might authorize us to expect. And its whole influence is for good—unless it be, if you will allow me to make the exception, that the thrilling expression of suffering which it sometimes utters, belongs too exclusively to this world. [. . .] The dark picture of the evils of our present state drawn by such writers [as Byron] can be recognized as true only by one who regards himself as nothing more than a suffering creature of this world, not as an immortal spirit. Acutely as our present trials must be sometimes felt, especially by those of more sensitive minds, yet our feelings are rather to be borne with as much patience as we can [?manage], than indulged even in their most poetical and most powerful expression. [. . .]

Ever, my dear Mrs. Hemans,
your sincere friend,
Andrews Norton

[1] HL MS 42552. The letter was forwarded to FH c/o Major Browne, Kilkenny, Ireland, from Wavertree 26 June 1831. Andrews Norton (1786–1853), man of letters and Biblical scholar, in 1819 became Professor of Sacred Literature at Harvard Divinity School, then resigned the post in 1830 to devote himself to literary and theological pursuits. His most famous work would be *The Evidences of the Genuineness of the Gospels* (1837–44). He edited *Poems of Mrs Hemans* (Boston, 1826–28), the major U.S. edition of her works, and wrote numerous appreciations of her poetry for the reviews. His lengthy obituary for the *Christian Examiner* (January 1836) was generously excerpted in *1839* (7.299–328). Norton also had a long correspondence with Joanna Baillie and helped bring her work to U.S. attention.

---

## Grants in Aid

*Robert Peel to Felicia Hemans, 1835*[1]

[In 1831 Joanna Baillie expressed a wish to Andrews Norton that some sort of pension be granted to FH, in failing health, with three sons left to support, and not up to the "drudgery of periodical writing"; but Baillie worried that the involvement of FH's brother (Sir Thomas Henry Browne) in spying for the late king (George IV) on the queen's activities would taint consideration "by the people in power at the present" (*Letters* 925–26), chief among them Robert Peel (Tory M.P. from 1809; Prime Minister, November 1834–April 1835). After the newspapers reported FH's straits, Lord Sandon, M.P. for Liverpool, urged Peel to offer assistance (Lawrence 386 n), for which FH was thankful (letter, 10 February 1835). During his second ministry (1841–46), Peel would grant a pension to poet Thomas Hood, in poor health and dire financial straits at the end of his life.]

Whitehall Gardens
Feb. 7. 1835

Madam,

I have this moment heard from an authority which I fear I cannot question, that you are suffering from sickness, and from embar[r]assed pecuniary circumstances.

The position in which I am placed as Minister of the Crown, and the claims upon me in that capacity which high literary distinction establishes, will I trust entitle me to make a Communication which might otherwise from a stranger to you, appear somewhat abrupt, if not indelicate.

I hear that you have a son of about the age of 17, for whom you are anxious to provide, and I beg to assure you that if a Clerkship in a respectable public Department would be acceptable to you, I will place him with the greatest satisfaction in one of the first which becomes vacant.[2]

For the relief of your own immediate wants, I beg your acceptance of the inclosed sum of £100. You need have no difficulty in accepting it. It imposes no personal obligation; it is only the fulfilment of a public duty, which I feel incumbent on me as the King's Minister, to prevent the reproach which would justly attach to me, if I could permit a Lady so distinguished for literary exertions, which have aided the cause of virtue, and have conferred honour on her Country and her sex, to suffer from privations, which Official Station gives me the opportunity of relieving.

I have the Honour & c
Robert Peel

*Minutes of the Royal Literary Fund, 8 April 1835*[3]

Mr. Dilke, a member of the committee, mentioned to the meeting that Mrs. Felicia Hemans, an Authoress of high and deserved reputation, was now in Dublin in a state of sickness and distress, when it was unanimously "Resolved that the sum of fifty Pounds be voted to this Lady, and that Mr. Dilke be requested to ascertain the best method of conveying this testimony of the Society's sympathy for her situation."

[1] BL Add. MS 40413, ff.291–92.

[2] Sandon urged Peel to procure an appointment for Charles Hemans in the Navy Office; he was appointed to a clerkship in the Customs (Lawrence 407 n).

[3] BL Microfilm M1077/2b, Archives of the Royal Literary Fund 1790–1918 (qtd. Feldman, *KSJ* 174 and n. 64). Charles Wentworth Dilke (1789–1864), friend of Keats and Chorley, was owner and editor of the *Athenæum*.

# Death

~~~~~~~~~~

## L.E.L.

[Letitia Elizabeth Landon (1802–38) made the trials of love her poetic theme and, like Hemans, cherished Staël's *Corinne* as a self-image. She won fame in 1824 with *The Improvisatrice &c*, pieces previously published by "L.E.L." in the *Literary Gazette*, stirring much interest. In quick succession followed *The Troubadour* (1825), *The Golden Violet* (1826), and *The Venetian Bracelet* (1828), along with much verse in the annuals and magazines. At the height of her fame (fueled, like Byron's, by celebrity and notoriety, but with female liabilities), her income—£900 from *Improvisatrice* and *Troubadour* alone—exceeded FH's. Richard Bentley commissioned her to write "metrical versions" of Corinne's improvisations for Isabel Hill's translation of *Corinne* in his Standard Novels series (1833). Her *Stanzas* on FH appeared in *NMM* 44 (July 1835): 286–88, and were reprinted in *The Ladies' Wreath; A Selection from the Female Poetic Writers of England and America*, ed. Sarah J. Hale (Boston: March &c, and New York: D. Appleton, 1837), 138–41, and Laman Blanchard, *Life and Literary Remains of L.E.L.* (London: Henry Colburn, 1841), 145–48. I use the *NMM* text.]

### STANZAS ON THE DEATH OF MRS. HEMANS

*The rose—the glorious rose is gone.*
*—Lays of Many Lands*[1]

Bring flowers to crown the cup and lute,—
    Bring flowers,—the bride is near;
Bring flowers to soothe the captive's cell,
    Bring flowers to strew the bier!
Bring flowers!—thus said the lovely song;[2]
    And shall they not be brought
To her who linked the offering
    With feeling and with thought?

Bring flowers,—the perfumed, and the pure,—
    Those with the morning dew,           10
A sigh in every fragrant leaf,
    A tear on every hue.
So pure, so sweet thy life has been,
    So filling earth and air
With odours and with loveliness,
    Till common scenes grew fair.

Thy song around our daily path[3]
    Flung beauty born of dreams,
That shadows on the actual world
    The spirit's sunny gleams.           20

Mysterious influence, that to earth
    Brings down the heaven above,
And fills the universal heart
    With universal love.

Such gifts were thine,—as from the block,
    The unformed and the cold,
The sculptor calls to breathing life
    Some shape of perfect mould;[4]
So thou from common thoughts and things
    Didst call a charmed song,           30
Which on a sweet and swelling tide
    Bore the full soul along.

And thou from far and foreign lands
    Didst bring back many a tone,
And giving such new music still,
    A music of thine own.[5]
A lofty strain of generous thoughts,
    And yet subdued and sweet,—
An angel's song, who sings of earth,
    Whose cares are at his feet.          40

And yet thy song is sorrowful,
    Its beauty is not bloom;
The hopes of which it breathes, are hopes
    That look beyond the tomb.
Thy song is sorrowful as winds
    That wander o'er the plain,
And ask for summer's vanished flowers,
    And ask for them in vain.

Ah! dearly purchased is the gift,
    The gift of song like thine;          50
A fated doom is hers who stands
    The priestess of the shrine.
The crowd—they only see the crown,
    They only hear the hymn;—
They mark not that the cheek is pale,
    And that the eye is dim.

Wound to a pitch too exquisite,
    The soul's fine chords are wrung;
With misery and melody
    They are too highly strung.[6]          60
The heart is made too sensitive
    Life's daily pain to bear;

It beats in music, but it beats
    Beneath a deep despair.

It never meets the love it paints,
    The love for which it pines;
Too much of Heaven is in the faith
    That such a heart enshrines.
The meteor wreath the poet wears
    Must make a lonely lot;                70
It dazzles, only to divide
    From those who wear it not.

Didst thou not tremble at thy fame,
    And loathe its bitter prize,
While what to others triumph seemed
    To thee was sacrifice?[7]
Oh Flower brought from Paradise
    To this cold world of ours,
Shadows of beauty such as thine
    Recall thy native bowers.               80

Let others thank thee—'twas for them
    Thy soft leaves thou didst wreathe;
The red rose wastes itself in sighs
    Whose sweetness others breathe!
And they have thanked thee—many a lip
    Has asked of thine for words,
When thoughts, life's finer thoughts, have touched
    The spirit's inmost chords.

How many loved and honoured thee
    Who only knew thy name;             90
Which o'er the weary working world
    Like starry music came!
With what still hours of calm delight
    Thy songs and image blend;
I cannot choose but think thou wert
    An old familiar friend.

The charm that dwelt in songs of thine
    My inmost spirit moved;
And yet I feel as thou hadst been
    Not half enough beloved.            100
They say that thou wert faint, and worn
    With suffering and with care;
What music must have filled the soul
    That had so much to spare!

Oh, weary One! since thou art laid
   Within thy mother's breast—
The green, the quiet mother-earth—
   Thrice blessed be thy rest!
Thy heart is left within our hearts,
   Although life's pang is o'er;         110
But the quick tears are in my eyes,
   And I can write no more.

[1] "Mournfully, sing mournfully, / And die away, my heart! / The rose, the glorious rose is gone, / And I, too, will depart" (*The Nightingale's Death-Song* 1–4). This poem is not in *Lays of Many Lands* (in *The Forest Sanctuary* [1826, 1829]). It was first published in *NMM* 25 (September 1829), then in the "Miscellaneous Poems" of *Songs of the Affections* (1830).

[2] *Bring Flowers*, in *Forest Sanctuary* (1825).

[3] *Our Daily Paths*, in *Forest Sanctuary*, 2d ed. (1829).

[4] The general compliment involves a regendered allusion to the story of Pygmalion in Ovid's *Metamorphoses*, book 10.

[5] FH's genre of "national songs": *Welsh Melodies, Greek Songs, Songs of the Cid, Lays of Many Lands, National Lyrics, Songs of Spain.*

[6] The lines ring with puns: the participle *wound* also suggests the noun; *wrung*, by force of *chords*, implies the music "rung" (also the word within *strung*) from pain, while *chords* sounds "cords," the winding and stringing of which (Isobel Armstrong comments) "ends sound or strangles even while it produces it" ("A Music" 254).

[7] See, for example, *Woman and Fame, Corinne at the Capitol*, and *Properzia Rossi*.

---

## Elizabeth Barrett

[Poet, translator, and essayist Elizabeth Barrett (1806–61), although not famous at the time she wrote these stanzas, was at her death England's leading woman poet, more celebrated than her husband, Robert Browning, whom she married in 1846. The *Athenæum* urged her appointment as Poet Laureate after Wordsworth. Barrett had mixed feelings about FH's poetry (see also her letter to their mutual friend, Mary Russell Mitford). Landon died in North Africa, under mysterious circumstances, the same year Barrett published these stanzas in *NMM* 45 (1835): 82, signed "B." They were reprinted in *The Seraphim and Other Poems* (London: Saunders and Otley, 1838). Using the same stanza as L.E.L., Barrett's impatient reply is also a gentle parody.]

STANZAS ADDRESSED TO MISS LANDON,
AND SUGGESTED BY HER
"STANZAS ON THE DEATH OF MRS. HEMANS"

Thou bay-crown'd living one—who o'er
   The bay-crown'd dead art bowing,
And o'er the shadeless, moveless brow
   Thy human shadow throwing;
And o'er the sighless, songless lips
   The wail and music wedding—

Dropping o'er the tranquil eyes
    Tears not of *their* shedding:

Go! take thy music from the dead,
    Whose silentness is sweeter;            10
Reserve thy tears for living brows,
    For whom such tears are meeter;[1]
And leave the violets in the grass,
    To brighten where thou treadest,
No flowers for *her!* Oh! bring no flowers—
    Albeit "Bring flowers,"[2] thou saidest.

But bring not near her solemn corse[3]
    A type of human seeming;
Lay only dust's stern verity
    Upon her dust undreaming.            20
And while the calm perpetual stars
    Shall look upon it solely;
Her spherèd soul shall look on *them*,
    With eyes more bright and holy.

Nor mourn, oh living one, because
    *Her* part in life was mourning:
Would she have lost the poet's flame,
    For anguish of the burning?
The minstrel harp, for the strain'd string?
    The tripod,[4] for th' afflated          30
Woe? or the vision, for those tears
    Through which it shone dilated?

Perhaps she shudder'd while the world's
    Cold hand her brow was wreathing:
But wrong'd she ne'er that mystic breath
    Which breathed in all her breathing,—
Which drew from rocky earth and man
    Abstractions high and moving,—
Beauty, if not the beautiful,—
    And love, if not the loving.          40

Such visionings have paled in sight
    The *Saviour* she descrieth,
And little recks who wreath'd the brow
    That on His bosom lieth.
The whiteness of His innocence
    O'er all her garments flowing,
There learneth she that sweet "new song"
    She will not mourn in knowing.

Be blessed, crown'd and living one:
   And when thy dust decayeth,           50
May thine own England say for thee
   What now for her it sayeth,—
"Albeit softly in our ears
   Her silver song was ringing,
The footsteps of her parting soul
   Were softer than her singing."

[1] "More apt," but also punning on "meter."
[2] L.E.L.'s homage to FH's poem.
[3] An archaism for "corpse," to pun on "course."
[4] Vessel for the ritual fires of oracular communications (the "afflatus").

---

## Joanna Baillie

### To The Revd. Doctor Andrews Norton, 20 August 1835[1]

My dear Sir

[. . .] The melancholy expectation expressed in your letter regarding M^rs Heman was very soon fulfilled. She is now gone to the many great poets who have charmed the world in different countries & different ages and there is not one of them all whose Lyre emitted sweeter or more touching sounds than her own. I hope she will receive the honours due to her in her own country and in yours there can be no doubt that she will, for I rather think you took precedence of us in appreciating her as she deserves. I never had the good fortune to become personally acquainted with her, though letters & sometimes little friendly offices past between us, but I always hoped to become so, my own advanced age appearing to me the most probable obstacle to this gratification. Who would have thought of her going first! The uncertainties of life will never cure us of reckoning on future events in the ordinary way. It is grievous to think that her life—the latter years of it at least, have been unhappy as well as short. [. . .]

[1] Houghton Library MS Eng 944, 12. Cf. *Letters* 933 (which varies from my transcription). Baillie was almost 73 when she wrote this letter.

---

## William Wordsworth, *Extempore Effusion on the Death of James Hogg*[1]

### Prefatory Note

[. . .] Mrs. Hemans was unfortunate as a poetess in being obliged by circumstances to write for money, and that so frequently and so much, that she was compelled to look out for subjects wherever she could find them, and to write as expeditiously as possible. As a woman, she was to a considerable degree a spoilt child of the world. She had been early in life distinguished for talent, and poems of hers were published while she was a girl. She had also been handsome in her youth, but her education had been most unfortunate. She was totally ignorant of housewifery, and could as easily have managed the spear of Minerva as her needle. It was from observing these deficiencies, that, one day while she was under my roof, I *purposely* directed her attention to household economy, and told her I had purchased *Scales*, which I intended to present to a young lady as a wedding present; pointed out their utility (for her especial benefit), and said that no *ménage* ought to be without them.[2] Mrs. Hemans, not in the least suspecting my drift, reported this saying, in a letter to a friend at the time, as a proof of my simplicity. Being disposed to make large allowances for the faults of her education and the circumstances in which she was placed, I felt most kindly disposed towards her, and took her part upon all occasions, and I was not a little affected by learning that after she withdrew to Ireland, a long and severe sickness raised her spirit as it depressed her body. This I heard from her most intimate friends, and there is striking evidence of it in a poem written and published not long before her death.[3] These notices of Mrs. Hemans would be very unsatisfactory to her intimate friends, as indeed they are to myself, not so much for what is said, but what for brevity's sake is left unsaid. Let it suffice to add, there was much sympathy between us, and, if opportunity had been allowed me to see more of her, I should have loved and valued her accordingly; as it is, I remember her with true affection for her amiable qualities, and, above all, for her delicate and irreproachable conduct during her long separation from an unfeeling husband, whom she had been led to marry from the romantic notions of inexperienced youth. Upon this husband I never heard her cast the least reproach, nor did I ever hear her even name him, though she did not wholly forbear to touch upon her domestic position; but never so as that any fault could be found with her manner of adverting to it.

> When first, descending from the moorlands,
> I saw the Stream of Yarrow glide
> Along a bare and open valley,
> The Ettrick Shepherd was my guide.[4]
>
> When last along its banks I wandered,
> Through groves that had begun to shed
> Their golden leaves upon the pathways,
> My steps the Border-minstrel led.
>
> The mighty Minstrel breathes no longer,
> 'Mid mouldering ruins low he lies;
> And death upon the braes of Yarrow,[5]
> Has closed the Shepherd-poet's eyes:
>
> Nor has the rolling year twice measured,
> From sign to sign, its stedfast course,
> Since every mortal power of Coleridge
> Was frozen at its marvellous source;

10

The rapt One, of the godlike forehead,
The heaven-eyed creature sleeps in earth:
And Lamb, the frolic and the gentle,
Has vanished from his lonely hearth.                        20

Like clouds that rake the mountain-summits,
Or waves that own no curbing hand,
How fast has brother followed brother
From sunshine to the sunless land!

Yet I, whose lids from infant slumber
Were earlier raised,[6] remain to hear
A timid voice, that asks in whispers,
"Who next will drop and disappear?"

Our haughty life is crowned with darkness,
Like London with its own black wreath,                      30
On which with thee, O Crabbe! forth-looking,
I gazed from Hampstead's breezy heath.°      *(north of London)*

As if but yesterday departed,
Thou too art gone before; but why,
O'er ripe fruit, seasonably gathered,
Should frail survivors heave a sigh?

Mourn rather for that holy Spirit,
Sweet as the spring, as ocean deep;
For Her, who, ere her summer faded,
Has sunk into a breathless sleep.[7]                        40

No more of old romantic° sorrows,         *(the literary genre)*
For slaughtered Youth or love-lorn Maid!
With sharper grief is Yarrow smitten,
And Ettrick mourns with her their Poet dead.

---

[1] Previously published in the *Athenæum*, 12 December 1835, prompted by the news of Hogg's death on 21 November. Wordsworth added the lines on FH (37–40) and a long preface (its first part devoted chiefly to Scott) for the 5th edition of his collected *Poems* (1836–37).

[2] See FH's letter, July 1830, which Wordsworth may have read either in *Athenæum* (27 June 1835) or *CM*.

[3] *Despondency and Aspiration: A Lyric*, in *Blackwood's* 37 (May 1835): 793–95, signed "Mrs. Hemans." Jane Williams would print the poem entire at the close of *Literary Women*.

[4] The Yarrow flows through southeast Scotland. Poet, essayist, novelist, and editor James Hogg was born in Ettrick Forest and had worked as a shepherd; "the Ettrick Shepherd" was his famous monicker. Wordsworth commemorated his "first" visit, in 1814, in *Yarrow Visited*.

[5] Wordsworth revisited Yarrow in 1831, when Sir Walter Scott was his guide (*Yarrow Revisited*). Scott (b. 1771) died in 1832 and was buried at Dyrburgh Abbey. He established his fame with his anthology, *Minstrelsy of the Scottish Border* (1802–03), which included *The Braes o' Yarrow*, a traditional ballad about a fatal ambush at this site.

[6] Wordsworth was born in 1770, elder not only to Scott but also, with the exception of George Crabbe (1754–1832), the other writers he mourns: Samuel Taylor Coleridge (1772-1834), Charles Lamb (1775–1834), and Hemans (1793–1835).

[7] FH is unnamed as a concession to the decorum of "feminine" modesty, but her fame made the reference transparent.

# Nineteenth-Century Retrospects

—*◦◦◦*—

L.E.L.

*"On the Character of Mrs. Hemans's Writings,"*
New Monthly Magazine *44 (August 1835): 425–33*[1]

"Oh! mes amis, rapellez-vous quelquefois mes vers; mon ame y est empreinte."
"Mon ame y est empreinte."[2] Such is the secret of poetry. There cannot be a
greater error than to suppose that the poet does not feel what he writes. What
an extraordinary, I might say, impossible view, is this to take of an art more
connected with emotion than any of its sister sciences. What—the depths of the
heart are to be sounded, its mysteries unveiled, and its beatings numbered by
those whose own heart is made by this strange doctrine—a mere machine
wound up by the clock-work of rhythm! No; poetry is even more a passion than
a power, and nothing is so strongly impressed on composition as the character
of the writer. I should almost define poetry to be the necessity of feeling strongly
in the first instance, and the as strong necessity of confiding in the second.

It is curious to observe the intimate relation that subsists between the poet
and the public. "Distance lends enchantment to the view,"[3] and those who
would shrink from the avowing what and how much they feel to even the most
trusted friend, yet rely upon and crave for the sympathy of the many. [. . .] Fame,
which the Greeks idealized so nobly, is but the fulfilment of that desire for
sympathy which can never be brought home to the individual. [. . .] There is a
well of melancholy poetry in every human bosom. We have all mourned over the
destroyed illusion and the betrayed hope. [. . .] We have all stood beside the
grave, and asked of the long grass and ever-springing wild flowers why they
should have life, while that of the beloved has long since gone down to the dust.
[. . .]

[I]t was not my good fortune to know Mrs. Hemans personally; it was an
honour I should have estimated highly—a happiness that I should have enjoyed
so keenly. I never even met with an acquaintance of hers but once; that once,
however, was much. I knew Miss Jewsbury [. . .] She delighted in speaking of
Mrs. Hemans: she spoke of her with the appreciation of one fine mind compre-
hending another, and with the earnest affection of a woman and a friend. She
described her conversation as singularly fascinating—full of poetry, very felici-
tous in illustration by anecdote, happy, too, in quotation, and very rich in imagery: "[. . .] 'The Treasures of the Deep' would best describe it." She mentioned
a very striking simile to which a conversation on Mrs. Hemans's own poem of
"The Sceptic" had led:—"Like Sindbad, the sailor, we are often shipwrecked on
a strange shore. We despair; but hope comes when least expected. We pass
through the gloomy caverns of doubt into the free air and blessed sunshine of

conviction and belief." I asked her if she thought Mrs. Hemans a happy person; and she said, "No; her enjoyment is feverish, and she desponds. She is like a lamp whose oil is consumed by the very light which it yields." [. . .] [Of the "moral" character of] Mrs. Hemans's poetry [. . .] Nothing can be more pure, more feminine and exalted, than the spirit which pervades the whole: it is the intuitive sense of right, elevated and strengthened into a principle. It is a glorious and a beautiful memory to bequeath; but she who left it is little to be envied. Open the volumes which she has left, legacies from many various hours, and what a record of wasted feelings and disappointed hopes may be traced in their sad and sweet complainings! Yet Mrs. Hemans was spared some of the keenest mortifications of a literary career. She knew nothing of it as a profession which has to make its way through poverty, neglect, and obstacles: she lived apart in a small, affectionate circle of friends. The high road of life, with its crowds and contention—its heat, its noise, and its dust that rests on all—was for her happily at a distance; yet [. . .] Genius places a woman in an unnatural position; notoriety frightens away affection; and superiority has for its attendant fear not love. [. . .] In every page of Mrs. Hemans's writings is this sentiment impressed; what is the conclusion of "Corinne crowned at the Capitol"? [Quotes the last stanza of *Corinne at the Capitol*.] What is poetry, and what is a poetical career? The first is to have an organization of extreme sensibility, which the second exposes bareheaded to the rudest weather. The original impulse is irresistible—all professions are engrossing when once began; and acting with perpetual stimulus, nothing takes more complete possession of its follower than literature. But never can success repay its cost. The work appears—it lives in the light of popular applause; but truly might the writer exclaim—

> "It is my youth—it is my bloom—it is my glad free heart
> I cast away for thee—for thee—ill fated as thou art."[4]

If this be true even of one sex, how much more true of the other. Ah! Fame to a woman is indeed but a royal mourning in purple for happiness.

[1] Facing p. 425 is an engraving of Angus Fletcher's bust of FH as a classical poetess, her signature underneath. *1839* has an excerpt of this essay (7.291–96). For the full text, see McGann and Reiss 173–86.

[2] "Oh! my friends, remember my verses sometimes; my soul is there imprinted"; from *Dernier Chant de Corinne* in the Conclusion of Staël's *Corinne*. FH was haunted by this song (*CM* 1.228, 304; *HM* 160) and used the same quotation as her epigraph for *A Parting Song*.

[3] Thomas Campbell, *The Pleasures of Hope* (1799) 7.

[4] *The Chamois Hunter's Love* 17–18, in *NMM* 22 (April 1828): 312, and *Songs of the Affections* (1830), where the reading is "all reckless," not "ill fated." The hunter prefers the "high and haughty life, with rocks and storms at war," while the maiden who has left her home for love of him pines away in his hut, "with tremblings and with vigils lone."

## Felicia Hemans[1]

No more, no more—oh, never more returning[2]
    Will thy beloved presence gladden earth;
No more wilt thou with sad, yet anxious, yearning
    Cling to those hopes which have no mortal birth.
Thou art gone from us, and with thee departed
    How many lovely things have vanished too;
Deep thoughts that at thy will to being started,
    And feelings, teaching us our own were true.
Thou hast been round us, like a viewless spirit
    Known only by the music on the air;                                    10
The leaf or flowers which thou hast named inherit
    A beauty known but from thy breathing there,
For thou didst on them fling thy strong emotion,
    The likeness from itself the fond heart gave,
As planets from afar look down on ocean
    And give their own sweet image to the wave.

And thou didst bring from foreign lands their treasures,
    As floats thy various melody along;
We know the softness of Italian measures,
    And the grave cadence of Castilian song.[3]                            20
A general bond of union is the poet,
    By its immortal verse is language known,
And for the sake of song do others know it—
    One glorious poet makes the world his own.
And thou, how far thy gentle sway extended—
    The heart's sweet empire over land and sea;
Many a stranger and far flower was blended
    In the soft wreath that glory bound for thee.
The echoes of the Susquehanna's waters
    Paused in the pine-woods words of thine to hear,                       30
And to the wide Atlantic's younger daughters
    Thy name was lovely, and thy song was dear.[4]

Was not this purchased all too dearly?—never
    Can fame atone for all that fame hath cost.
We see the goal, but know not the endeavour,
    Nor what fond hopes have on the way been lost.
What do we know of the unquiet pillow
    By the worn cheek and tearful eyelid pressed,
When thoughts chase thoughts, like the tumultuous billow
    Whose very light and foam reveals unrest?                              40

We say, the song is sorrowful, but know not
    What may have left that sorrow on the song;
However mournful words may be, they show not
    The whole extent of wretchedness and wrong.
They cannot paint the long sad hours passed only
    In vain regrets o'er what we feel we are.
Alas, the kingdom of the lute is lonely—
    Cold is the worship coming from afar.[5]

Yet what is mind in woman, but revealing
    In sweet clear light the hidden world below,        50
By quicker fancies and a keener feeling
    Than those around, the cold and careless, know?
What is to feed such feeling, but to culture
    A soil whence pain will never more depart?
The fable of Prometheus and the vulture
    Reveals the poet's and the woman's heart.[6]
Unkindly are they judged, unkindly treated
    By careless tongues and by ungenerous words,
While cruel sneer, and hard reproach, repeated,
    Jar the fine music of the spirit's chords.        60
Wert thou not weary—thou whose soothing numbers°    *meters*
    Gave other lips the joy thine own had not?
Didst thou not welcome thankfully the slumbers
    Which closed around thy mourning human lot?

What on this earth could answer thy requiring,
    For earnest faith—for love, the deep and true,
The beautiful, which was thy soul's desiring,
    But only from thyself its being drew!
How is the warm and loving heart requited
    In this harsh world, where it awhile must dwell;        70
Its best affections wronged, betrayed and slighted—
    Such is the doom of those who love too well.[7]
Better the weary dove should close its pinion,
    Fold up its golden wings and be at peace;
Enter, oh ladye,[8] that serene dominion
    Where earthly cares and earthly sorrows cease.
Fame's troubled hour has cleared, and now replying,
    A thousand hearts their music ask of thine;
Sleep with a light, the lovely and undying,
    Around thy grave—a grave which is a shrine.        80

[1] From *Fisher's Drawing Room Scrapbook, 1838* (London: Fisher, 1837), an annual. On the facing page is an engraving of one of the portraits of FH by W. E. West painted in 1827, which Fisher inherited (*HM* 130). Republished in *The Zenana, and Minor Poems of L.E.L.* (London: Fisher, 1839).

[2] Cf. Properzia Rossi's lament for her lost ambitions (87, 93) and *The Dying Improvisatore* (17). P. B. Shelley mourns for Keats: "He will awake no more, oh, never more!" (*Adonais* 64).

[3] FH's translations of Italian and Spanish poetry, as well as her genre of "national songs."

[4] A reference to FH's popularity in the United States.

[5] A theme in L.E.L.'s essay on FH, inflected by FH's own poetry on the subject, Jewsbury's *Enthusiast*, Staël's *Corinne*, and Chorley's *Memorials*.

[6] For defying Jove, Prometheus is chained to a mountain, where a vulture daily devours his heart, which grows back every night. Contemporary versions of the fable include Byron's *Prometheus* (1816), P. B. Shelley's *Prometheus Unbound* (1820), and Mary Shelley's *Frankenstein; or, The Modern Prometheus* (1818; 1831).

[7] Othello asks to be remembered as "one that loved not wisely, but too well" (5.2.343).

[8] A medievalizing archaism often used in L.E.L.'s poetry—e.g., *The Proud Ladye*, in *The Troubadour* (1825).

## Henry F. Chorley

[Musician, music critic, journalist, reviewer for the *Athenæum*, and frequent contributor to the annuals, Henry Fothergill Chorley (1808–72) befriended FH at Wavertree in 1828. At this time, he and his sister were editing *The Winter's Wreath*, an annual to which they invited FH to contribute (they had two dozen poems from her over the next four years). Jewsbury introduced Chorley to the circle at the *Athenæum*, and he became one of its most prolific writers on a variety of subjects (including L.E.L.) for almost thirty years. Among his intimate friends were Mary Russell Mitford, Lady Blessington, the Brownings, Dickens, and Thackeray. See *Autobiography, Memoir and Letters*, ed. Henry G. Hewlett, 2 vols. (London: Richard Bentley and Son, 1873), and Leslie A. Marchand, *The Athenæum, a Mirror of Victorian Culture* (U of North Carolina P, 1941), 181–93.]

*"Personal Recollections of the Late Mrs. Hemans,"*
Athenæum 398 (13 June 1835): 452–54[1]

[. . .] When I first became acquainted with Mrs. Hemans, her fame was at its brightest, and her lyrics published in the different periodicals—her "Forest Sanctuary," and above all her "Records of Woman," (probably from the happy choice of its subject) had not only raised her name high in the estimation of all classes of readers, but had excited considerable curiosity, and I really believe genuine interest, as to the person and fortunes of the writer. She was, however, unknown, save to a small and select circle of friends. [. . .] [H]er claim to something more than the ephemeral reputation of a *young lady* writer, was admitted by stern critics [. . .] dating from the publication of her "Siege of Valencia,"—she had taken a permanent place in the republic of letters; and it was natural that the world, always preferring the peep behind the curtain, to the finest acted nature before it, should express great anxiety and solicitude to know "what she was like."

[. . .] [H]er residence at Wavertree, a pleasant village about three miles from Liverpool [in hopes] of education for her sons, and cultivated society for herself [was a "mistake" . . .]: Liverpool was then singularly deficient in good schools, and its society was too much broken up into small circles, too completely under the dominion of a money aristocracy, to offer much that was congenial to her own tastes and pursuits. She was too imaginative and fanciful to be thoroughly understood. [. . .] they found that the brilliant things which she threw out, the spontaneous overflowing[2] of her peculiar mind, "proved nothing"; and they did not perceive the elevation of thought, and the frequent religious feeling which also formed a part of her character. The less intelligent, who discovered that she did not enjoy dinners, balls, and concerts after their fashion—and there is no code so arbitrary as the statute of manners in a provincial town—who remarked one or two singularities in her dress, and were frightened by her allusions to things and feelings of which they knew nothing, kept aloof from her, with suspicion and uneasiness. [. . .] She had never learned the feignings and *prettinesses* of the world's manners; nor, on the other hand, did she find it agreeable always to sit upon her throne, as it were, with her book of magic upon her knee, and her conjuring wand in her outstretched arm. Her humour was sprightly and searching, as well as original: she could talk delicious nonsense, as well as inspired sense; and the utilitarian and the serious, who would fain have had a *moral* placarded and paraded upon every chance phrase of conversation, "wondered, and went their way."[3] At this time, she was sought out in her retreat by every species of literary homage, from every corner of England and America; gifts, offers of service, letters of introduction crowded upon her:—literary engagements were pressed upon her. [. . .]

The house which Mrs. Hemans occupied was too small to deserve the name; the third of a cluster or two close to a dusty road,—and yet too *townish* in appearance and situation to be called a cottage. It was set in a small court, and within was gloomy and comfortless; its parlours being little larger than closets:[4] and yet she threw something of her own spirit round her, even in so unpromising an abode,—and with her books, and her harp, and the flowers which sometimes half filled her little rooms, they presently assumed a habitable, almost an elegant appearance. [. . .] Scarcely had she settled herself at Wavertree, than she was besieged by visitors, to a number positively bewildering; a more heterogeneous company cannot be imagined. Many came merely to stare at the strange poetess,—others to pay proper neighbourly morning calls, and these were surprised to find that she was not ready with an answer, when the talk was of housekeeping and like matters. [. . .] I must not forget to allude to what Charles Lamb calls the "albumean persecution" which she was called upon to endure. People not only brought their own books, but those of "my sister and my sister's child," all anxious to have something written on purpose for themselves. One gentleman, a total stranger to her, beset her before (as the housewives say) "she was fairly settled," with a huge virgin folio splendidly bound: which he had brought on purpose "that she might open it with one of her exquisite poems."[5] On the whole, she bore her honours meekly, and for a while, in the natural kindliness of her heart, gave way to the current, wishing to oblige every one. Sometimes, however, her sense of the whimsical would break out; sometimes it was provoked by the thorough-going and coarse perseverance of the intrusions, against which it was difficult to guard. What could be done with persons who called thrice in one morning, and refused to take their final departure till they were told "when Mrs. Hemans *would be* at home"? It was on one of these occasions, that she commissioned a friend of hers, in a lively note, to procure her "a dragon to be kept in her court-yard." At another time (and that I well remember was a flagrant case,) her vexation worked itself off in a no less cheerful manner:—

"They had an album with them, absolutely an album! You had scarcely left me to my fate—oh! how you laughed the moment you were set free!—when the little woman with the inquisitorial eyes, informed me that the tall woman with the superior understanding—Heaven save the mark! was *ambitious* of possessing my autograph, and out "leaped in lightning forth" the album.[6] A most evangelical and edifying book it is truly; so I, out of pure spleen, mean to insert in it something as strongly savouring of the Pagan miscellany as I *dare*. Oh! the 'pleasures of fame'! Oh! that I were but a little girl in the top of the elm tree again! Your much enduring F. H."

## Memorials of Mrs. Hemans *(1836)*

["It is now twelve months ago," writes Chorley in his Advertisement, "since I collected and published, in the 'Athenæum,' a few sketches and remembrances of one whom I had known intimately during the later years of her life. The general interest excited by these papers—or rather by the vivacity and elegance of the letters which they contained—led me to contemplate their extension and republication" (1.v-vi). FH's family gave him most of the new materials for *CM*. After his own remuneration, the profits were "appropriated to the benefit of her children" (Hewlett 1.128, cf. letter to the editor of the *Athenæum*, 15 August 1839).]

### *["Introductory Remarks"]*

It was our divine Milton, who, wisely as forcibly, laid down the principle "that he who would not be frustrate of his hope to write well hereafter, in laudable things, ought himself to be a true poem, that is, a composition of the best and honourablest things."[7] Often as this golden wisdom has been neglected by our poets—often as passion, or frivolity, or—worst of all —a mean love of gain and worldly advancement—have spoiled and silenced the song, and, as it were, quenched the altar-fire of those whose voices would otherwise have been heard long after they were no more,[8] whose light might at once have led and warmed the hearts of future generations—in the many exceptions, no less than the few examples, Milton's precept holds good as a rule. The works of the *really* gifted (passing over those clever mechanists who can affect every form and feeling with equal ease and absence of sincerity) *must*, in some sort, mirror their lives: and he who reads with the mind and not merely with the senses, will find in them the weakness and the strength, the tastes and the antipathies of their writers clearly indicated—the tenor at least, if not the separate incidents, of their history, distinctly set forth. [1.1–2]

[I]n the pages which follow, I am making a contribution to the annals of English Poetry; and to that chapter in particular, which, besides its intrinsic interest, has a significance as illustrating the spirit of the age,—I mean the one which shall treat of the popularity and prevalence of female authorship.

With regard to its popularity, it would, indeed, be shameful if,—with the long list we possess of names, excellent in the literature of romance, art, criticism, nay, even in the exact sciences, whose paths it might be thought were too uninviting and arduous to be pursued with steadiness and success by female feet,—the contemptuous party-words formerly wielded in attack and defence were to be heard among us any more. If we are not prepared to admit that genius is of no sex[9]—to hold with some intemperate enthusiasts, who plead their *right* to take up the lion's skin and club, and, assuming the stern and peculiar cares of manhood, would (unwarned by the disastrous example of England's wisest king in the neat-herd's cot) condemn the poor lords of the creation to the small cares of housewifery[10]—we are willing—we are thankful to acknowledge, that in our graver and gayer hours, we have found help-mates, whose services, if not performed by them, must have remained unfulfilled. "If"—to quote one[11] who wrote eloquently in defence of, and apology for, her own sex—"we still secretly dread and dislike female talent, it is not for the reason generally supposed—because it may tend to obscure our own regal honours; but because it interferes with our implanted and imbibed ideas of domestic life and womanly duty."[12] But this prejudice (let us not inquire whether or not it may have been based upon experience) is fading rapidly away. With the increase of female authorship, a change has taken place in the position of the authors. Our gifted women must feel themselves less alone in the world than was formerly their case; they have therefore daily less and less cause to despise its ordinances—to claim toleration for eccentricity of habits as well as latitude of opinion; and thus they are winning day by day, in addition to the justice of head commanded by their high and varied powers, the justice of heart which is so eminently their due.

On all these grounds, a work which shall trace out the career of a poetess, may not be altogether uninteresting or unseasonable at the present time. That the subject of the following memorials deserves to rank high among the bright names[13] of English song will not be questioned; and I think that they will be found at once to throw a new light upon, and to harmonize with, the spirit of the writings which the world has so deservedly recognised. [1.6–9]

*[Hemans's Childhood Reading]*

She was early a reader of Shakespeare;[14] and, by way of securing shade and freedom from interruption, used to climb an apple tree, and there study his plays; nor had she long made familiar friendship with his "beings of the mind,"[15] before she was possessed with the temporary desire—so often born of an intense delight and appreciation—of personifying them. It is remarkable that her fancy led her to prefer the characters of Imogen and Beatrice; nor were her favourites without strong points of resemblance to herself—the one in its airy sentiment tempered with sweet and faithful affection—the other in its brilliant wit redeemed by high-mindedness, from sarcasm or vulgarity—so early were her tastes and personal feelings and mental gifts identified! [1.17–18]

She was never at school,—had she been sent to one, she might probably have run away,—and I am told that the only things she was ever regularly taught were French, English grammar, and the rudiments of Latin, communicated to her by a gentleman, who used to deplore, "that she was not a man to have borne away the highest honours at college!" [1.20]

### [Hemans's Sensitivity; Progress of Mind]

A man cannot far advance on his pilgrimage without his views becoming widened by that actual collision with life which a woman can rarely experience. [. . .] for one of the gentler sex, shielded as she is by her position in society—engrossed by affections which colour every object coming within their circle—there is always too great a danger of being too exclusive in her devotions [. . .] shrinking from all that jars upon her highly-wrought and sensitive feelings.

It would be difficult, were the whole range of our imaginative literature searched through, to discover a more perfect illustration of the above remarks than is to be found in the works of Mrs. Hemans, and in the progress of mind they register. That she did only a partial justice to her powers, must be admitted by all who ever held friendly intercourse with her: they will feel, too, that she was summoned away at the moment when she might, and must have risen higher than she had ever done before. Her first works are purely classical or purely romantic; their poems may be compared to antique groups of sculpture, or the mailed ornamental figures of the middle ages set in motion. As she advanced on her way, sadly learning the while the grave lessons which time and trial teach, her songs breathed more reality and less of romance; the too exclusive and feverish reverence for high intellectual or imaginative endowment, yielded to a calmness, and a cheerfulness, and a willingness more and more, not merely to speculate upon, but to partake of the "beauty in our daily paths."[16] Had she lived to bring these yet more fully to bear upon the stores of knowledge she had heaped up, she would have produced a work as far superior to any she has left us, as her own latest lyrics and scenes exceed the prize poems of her girlhood. [1.23–25]

### [Hemans Relinquishes a Cherished Relic of Byron]

The relic in question was a small lock of Lord Byron's hair; the brooch which contained the portion reserved for herself was one of her favourite ornaments till the Memoirs of the poet appeared. [. . .] after having heard those beautiful stanzas addressed to his sister by Lord Byron—which afterwards appeared in print—read aloud twice in manuscript, she repeated them to us, and even wrote them down with a surprising accuracy. On two lines, I recollect, she dwelt with particular emphasis,—

> There are yet two things in my destiny,
> A world to roam o'er, and a home with thee.[17]

Her anxiety to see the memoirs was extreme,—her disappointment at the extracts which appeared in the periodicals so great as to prevent her reading the work when published. "The book itself," says she, in one of her notes, "I do not mean to read; I feel as if it would be like entering a tavern, and I shall not cross the threshold." She found the poet whom she had long admired at a distance invested with a Mephistopheles-like character which pained and startled her; for the unworldly and imaginative life she had led, rendered her slow to admit and unwilling to tolerate the strange mixture of cruel mockery and better feeling, which breathe through so many of his letters; and the details of his continental wanderings shocked her fastidious sense as exceeding the widest limits within which one so passionate and so disdainful of law and usage might err and be forgiven. From this time forth she never wore the relic. [2.21–23]

[1] With some revisions, these anecdotes appear in *CM* (cf. 1.208–20).

[2] In Preface to *Lyrical Ballads* (1800), Wordsworth defined poetry as "the spontaneous overflow of powerful feelings."

[3] A light allusion to Jesus' deft evasion of the rhetorical plotting of the Pharisees, who "marvelled [. . .] and went their way" (Matthew 22.22).

[4] Small private rooms.

[5] A folio is an expensive volume of large pages, its sheets folded ("folio") just once before binding. An album is a souvenir book. Charles Lamb used the phrase Chorley quotes in a letter to Bryan Waller Procter 19 June 1829, and he published a collection of his *Album Verses* in 1839, among which is *What is an album?* (dated 7 September 1830): "'Tis a book kept by modern young ladies for show, /. . . / A medley of scraps, half verse and half prose, / And some things not very like either—God knows," and "with autographs plenty."

[6] Cf. Horatio Smith: "Fierce leap'd the lightning forth, as if with savage / Triumph" (*The Hurricane and the Menace*, 19–20, in *Comic Poems*).

[7] A famous sentence from *An Apology Against a Pamphlet Called "A Modest Confutation of the Animadversions Upon the Remonstrant against Smectymnuus"* (1642).

[8] Cf. Wordsworth: "The music in my heart I bore, / Long after it was heard no more" (*The Solitary Reaper* 31–32).

[9] An emerging subject in the 18th c.: "Souls are of no sex, any more than wit, genius, or any other of the intellectual faculties," argued the authors of *Biographium Fæmineum* (London, 1766). Such conviction was the foundation of Wollstonecraft's *Vindication of the Rights of Woman* (1792), and Lucy Aikin echoed the declaration directly in *Epistle III* of *Epistles on Women* (1810). The claim is also the theme of Staël's *Corinne*, but with the implied moral that a woman is ultimately governed by a "feminine" heart that will not allow genius without misery.

[10] By the 1820s, the advocacy of the "Rights of Woman" launched in the 1790s had fallen into disrepute, except among radicals. Chorley's cartoon-feminist suggests the stigma, even for this admirer of female intelligence. As a slave to Queen Omphale of Lydia, Hercules plied tasks such as weaving and spinning in the company of her women, while she wore his lion's skin and wielded his club. In a famous anecdote, King Alfred the Great (849–99), a scholar who promoted learning and literacy, took refuge in a peasant woman's hut after a defeat in battle, only to find himself berated for the uselessness of his learning and his inability to perform basic household tasks. Lords of creation: men were created to be "lords of the world" (*Paradise Lost* 1.32).

[11] Miss Jewsbury [Chorley]

[12] "Man does not secretly dread and dislike high intellect in woman, for the mean reason generally supposed—because it may tend to obscure his own regal honors; but because it interferes with his implanted and imbibed ideas of domestic life and womanly duty" (Jewsbury, *Enthusiast* 127).

[13] Cf. this phrase in FH's letter to Mary Russell Mitford, 23 March 1828.

[14] This paragraph was reprinted in the review of *CM* in *Athenæum* 462 (3 September 1836), 618, and its anecdote became famous.

[15] FH's *The Beings of the Mind*, about her affection for Shakespeare's characters, appeared in *NMM* 22 (June 1828): 555–56, signed "F. H." In a famous stanza of *Childe Harold's Pilgrimage IV* (1818), Byron writes: "The beings of the mind are not of clay; / Essentially immortal, they create / And multiply in us a brighter ray / And more beloved existence" (v).

[16] Alluding to *Our Daily Paths*.

[17] From *Stanzas* ("My Sister—my sweet Sister") 7–8, the closing couplet of the first stanza. The poem was written in August 1816, as a salvo in the public scandal of Byron's separation from Lady Byron, but at the request of his sister, not published. It appeared for the first time in 1831, in Thomas Moore's edition of Byron. It is likely that Murray shared the MS with F. H.

---

### Elizabeth Barrett to Mary Russell Mitford, 23 November 1842[1]

[. . .] M^r Chorley is very good [. . .] I like what you say of him & what his books say of him too. Is it not true that M^rs Hemans's friends took offence at his work respecting her?[2] I inferred so from the memoir written by her sister & could not make out <u>why</u>—for surely nothing could be more delicate, even hyper-delicate, than his manner of treating the subject. For my own part & as you & I my dearest friend are talking low together & nobody by to hear us, I will think aloud in my low talk that the sister's memoir touching as it is in many ways, & in its sisterhood & pure affection, always, is totally void of character, undescriptive of character, scentless, colorless .. with the taste of holy water. It partakes of the fault of the commemorated person .. of being too ladylike in proportion to its humanity. Is not that M^rs Hemans's own fault? I admire her genius—love her memory—respect her piety & high moral tone. But she always does seem to me a lady rather than a woman, & so, much rather than a poetess—her refinement, like the prisoner's iron .. enters into her soul.[3] She is polished all over to one smoothness & one level, & is monotonous in her best qualities. We say "How sweet & noble" & then we are silent & can say no more—perhaps, presently, we go to sleep, with angels in our dreams. We grow tired, not so much of hearing her called, as of calling her "the just."[4] Is <u>this</u> not just? Do you agree with me? Or can you read her poems one after another, & feel a vital difference in them, & no diminution of your own delight?—[5]

Well—<u>they</u> are monotonous music. But the sister's memoir according to my doxy, is monotonous, not being music. [. . .]

[1] *The Letters of Elizabeth Barrett Browning to Mary Russell Mitford 1836–1854*, ed. Meredith B. Raymond and Mary Rose Sullivan, 3 vols. (Winfield, Kans.: Wedgestone P, 1983), 2.88.

[2] See *HM* 2, and Lawrence 228, 334, 413–14.

[3] *The Book of Common Prayer*, "The Psalter," 105.

[4] In *Lives of the Noble Greeks and Romans*, Plutarch reports Aristides being banished from Athens because one of the magistrates, although he suffered no injury, had grown "tired hearing him everywhere called *the Just*" (trans. of A. H. Clough).

[5] Barrett later commented to Mitford that FH "was bound fast in satin riband" (*Letters* 2.425).

**George Gilfillan,** "Female Authors. No. I.—Mrs. Hemans,"
*Tait's Edinburgh Magazine*, n.s. 14 (June 1847): 359–63

[Eminent Scots critic Rev. George Gilfillan (1813–78) was a protégé of "Christopher North" (John Wilson) of *Blackwood's* fame. His *Gallery of Literary Portraits* appeared in *Tait's*, November and December 1845, and January and April 1846. In the ensuing three-part series, "Female Authors" (1847), "No. II" was Browning and "No. III" was Shelley. Founded in 1832 by Whig radical William Tait to oppose the sway of the Toryish *Blackwood's*, *Tait's* was looked down on by establishment readers. As the Wollstonecraftian tone of the essays on Browning and Shelley makes clear, its politics were liberal, and included polemics for improved education for women.]

Female authorship is, if not a great, certainly a singular fact. And if a singular fact in this century, what must it have been in the earlier ages of the world—when it existed as certainly as now, and was more than now a phenomenon, standing often insulated and alone? If, even in this age, *blues* are *black*-balled and homespun is still the "only wear," and music, grammar, and *gramarye* are the three elements, legitimately included and generally expected in the education of woman, in what light must the Aspasias and the Sapphos of the past have been regarded?[1] Probably as *lusus naturæ* [freak of nature] in whom a passionate attachment to literature was pardoned as a pleasant peccadillo, or agreeable insanity; just as a slight squint in the eye of a beauty, or even a far-off *faux pas* in her reputation, is still not unfrequently forgiven. But alas! in our age, the exception is likely soon to become the rule—the *lusus* the law; and, at all events, of female authorship, the least gallant of critics is compelled now to take cognizance; and without absolutely admitting this as *our* characteristic, we must confess the diffidence as well as the good-will wherewith we approach a subject where respect for truth and respect for the sex are sometimes apt to jostle and jar.

The works of British women have now taken up, not by courtesy but by right, a full and conspicuous place in our literature. They constitute an elegant library in themselves; and there is hardly a department in science, in philosophy, in morals, in politics, in the belles lettres, in fiction, or in the fine arts, but has been occupied, and ably occupied by a lady. This certainly proclaims a high state of cultivation on the part of the many which has thus flowered out into composition in the case of the few. It exhibits an extension and refinement of that element of female influence which, in the private intercourse of society, has been productive of such blessed effects—it mingles with the harsh tone of general literature, "as the lute pierceth through the cymbal's clash"[2]—it blends with it a vein of delicate discrimination, of mild charity, and of purity of morals—gives it a healthy and happy tone, the tone of the fireside; it is in the chamber of our literature a quiet and lovely presence; by its very gentleness, overawing as well as refining and beautifying it all. One principal characteristic of female writing in our age is its sterling sense. It is told of Coleridge, that he was accustomed, on important emergencies, to consult a female friend, placing implicit confidence in her first instructive suggestions. If she proceeded to add her reasons, he checked her immediately. "Leave these, madam, to me to find out."[3] We find this rare

and valuable sense—this short-hand reasoning—exemplified in our lady authors' producing, even in the absence of original genius, or of profound penetra-
tion, or of wide experience, a sense of perfect security, as we follow their gentle
guidance. Indeed, on all questions affecting proprieties, decorums, what we may
call the *ethics* of sentimentalism, minor as well as major morals, their verdict may
be considered oracular, and without appeal. But we dare not say that we consider
them entitled to speak with equal authority on those higher and deeper questions, where not instinct nor the heart, but severe and tried intellect is qualified
to return the responses. We remark, too, in the writings of females, a tone of
greater generosity than in those of men. They are more candid and amiable in
their judgments of authors and of books. Commend us to female critics. *They* are
not eternally consumed by the desire of being witty, astute, and severe, of carp-
ing at what they could not equal —of hewing down what they could or *would* not
have built up. The principle, *nil admirari* [nothing is to be admired], is none of
theirs; and whether it be that a sneer disfigures their beautiful lips, it is seldom
seen upon them. And in correspondence with this, it is curious that (in our
judgments, and we suspect theirs) the worst critics are persons who dislike the
sex, and whom the sex dislikes—musty, fusty old bachelors, such as Gifford,[4] or
certain pedantic prigs in the press of the present day. Ladies, on the other hand,
are seldom severe judges of anything, except each other's dress and deportment;
and in defect of profound principles, they are helped out by that fine instinctive
sense of theirs, which partakes of the genial nature, and verges upon genius
itself.

Passing from such preliminary remarks, we proceed to our theme. We have
selected Mrs. Hemans as our first specimen of Female Authors, not because we
consider her the best, but because we consider her by far the most feminine
writer of the age.[5] All the woman in her shines. You could not (unknowing of
the author) open a page of her writings without feeling this is written by a lady.
Her inspiration always pauses at the feminine point. It never "oversteps the
modesty of nature,"[6] nor the dignity and decorum of womanhood. She is no
Sibyl, tossed to and fro in the tempest of furious excitement, but ever a "deep,
majestical, and high-souled woman"[7]—the calm mistress of the highest and
stormiest of her emotions. The finest compliment we can pay her—perhaps the
finest compliment that it is possible to pay to woman, as a moral being—is to
compare her to "one of Shakspeare's women,"[8] and to say, had Imogen, or Isabella, or Cornelia become an authoress, she had so written.

Sometimes, indeed, Mrs. Hemans herself seems reduced, through the
warmth of her temperament, the facility and rapidity of her execution, and the
intensely lyrical tone of her genius, to dream that the shadow of the Pythoness[9]
is waving behind her, and controlling the motions of her song. To herself she
appears to be uttering oracular deliverance. Alas! "oracles speak,"[10] and her
poetry, as to all effective utterance of original truth, is silent. It is emotion only
that is audible to the sharpest ear that listens to her song. A bee wreathing round
you in the warm summer morn, her singing circle gives you as much new insight
into the universe as do the sweetest strains which have ever issued from this

"voice of spring."[11] We are reluctantly compelled, therefore, to deny her, in its highest sense, the name of poet—a word often abused, often misapplied in mere compliment or courtesy, but which ought ever to retain its stern and original signification. A *maker* she is not.[12] What dream of childhood has she ever, to any imagination, reborn? whose slumbers has she ever peopled with new and terrible visions? what new form or figure has she annexed, like a second shadow, to our own idiosyncrasy, to track us on our way for ever? to what mind has she given such a burning stamp of impression, as it feels eternity itself unable to efface? There is no such result from the poetry of Mrs. Hemans. She is less a maker than a *musician*, and her works appear rather to rise to the airs of the piano than that still sad music of humanity.[13] [. . .]

With what purpose does a lady, in whom perfect skill and practice have not altogether drowned enthusiasm, sit down to her harp, piano, or guitar? Not altogether for the purpose of display—not at all for that of instruction to her audience—but in a great measure that she may develop by a lawful form, the sensibilities of her own bosom. Thus sate Felicia Hemans before her lyre—and touching it with awful reverence, as though each string were a star, nor using it as the mere conductor to her overflowing thoughts, but regarding it as the soother and sustainer of her own high-wrought emotions—a graceful *alias* of herself. Spring, in its vague joyousness, has not a more appropriate voice in the note of the cuckoo than feminine sensibility had in the more varied but hardly profounder song of the authoress before us.

We wish not to be misunderstood. Mrs. Hemans had something more than the common belief of all poets in the existence of the beautiful. She was a genuine woman, and, therefore, the sequence (as we shall see speedily) is irresistible, a true Christian. [. . .] She was, as Lord Jeffrey well remarks, an admirable writer of *occasional* verses.[14] She has caught, in her poetry, passing words of her own mind—meditations of the sleepless night—transient glimpses of thought, visiting her in her serener hours—the "silver lining" of those cloudy feelings which preside over her darker[15]—and the impressions made upon her mind by the more remarkable events of her everyday life—and the more exciting passages of her reading. Her works are a versified *journal* of a quiet ideal, and beautiful life—the life at once of a woman and a poetess. [. . .] In many poets we see the germ of greatness, which might in happier circumstances, or in a more genial season, have been developed. But no such germ can the most microscopic survey discover in her, and we feel that at her death her beautiful but tiny task was done. Indeed, with such delicate organization, and such intense susceptiveness as hers, the elaboration, the long reach of thought, the slow *cumulative* advance, the deep-curbed, yet cherished ambition which a great work requires and implies, are, we fear, incompatible.

It follows, naturally from this, that her largest are her worst productions. They labour under the fatal defect of tedium. They are a surfeit of sweets. [. . .] Hence few, comparatively, have taken refuge in her "forest sanctuary," reluctant and rare the ears which have listened to her "Vespers of Palermo," her "Siege of Valencia," has stormed no hearts, and her "Sceptic" made, we fear, few converts.

But who has not wept over her "Graves of a Household," or hushed his heart to hear her "Treasures of the Deep," in which the old Sea himself seems to speak, or wished to take the left hand of the Hebrew child and lead him up, along with his mother, to the temple service; or thrilled and shouted in the gorge of "Mergarten" [*sic*], or trembled at the stroke of her "Hour of Death?"[16] Such poems are of the kind which win their way into every house, and every collection, and every heart. They secure for their authors a sweet garden plot of reputation, which is envied by none, and with which no one intermeddles. Thus flowers smile, unharmed, to the bolt which levels the pine beside them. Cataracts, in the course of ages, wear away their cliff of vantage, and so their glory suicidally perishes, while "one meek streamlet, only one," beautifies its narrow glen for ever[17]—tapers live while suns sink and disappear. Even a single sweet poem, flowing from a gentle mind in a happy hour, is as "ointment poured forth,"[18] and carries a humble name in fragrance far down into futurity, while the elaborate productions of loftier spirits rot upon the shelves. A Lucretius exhausts the riches of his magnificent mind in a stately poem, which is barely remembered, and never read. A Wolfe expresses the emotions of every heart at the recital of Sir John Moore's funeral in a few rude rhymes, and becomes immortal. A Shelley, dipping his pen in the bloody sweat of his lonely and agonized heart, traces voluminous lines of "red and burning" poetry, and his works are known only to some hardy explorers. A Michael Bruce transfers one spring joy of his dying frame, stirred by the note of the cuckoo, to a brief and tear-stained page; and henceforth the voice of the bird seems vocal with his name, and wherever, from the "engulphed navel" of the wood you hear its strange, nameless, tameless, wandering, unearthly voice, you think of the poet who sighed away his soul, and gathered his fame in its praise.[19] A Baillie constructs a work "before all ages,"[20] lavishes on it imagination that might suffice for a century of poets, and writes it in colours snatched from the sun; and it lies, on some recherché tables, like a foreign curiosity, to be seen, shown, and lifted, rather than to be read and pondered. A William Miller sings, one gloaming, his "Wee Willie Winkie,"[21] and the nurseries of an entire nation re-echo the simple strains, and every Scottish mother blesses, in one breath, her babe and his poet. We mention this, not entirely to approve, but in part to wonder at it. It is not just that one strain from a lute or a pan's-pipe should survive a thunder-psalm—that effusions should eclipse works.

Mrs. Hemans's poems are strictly effusions. And not a little of their charm springs from their unstudied and extempore character.[22] This, too, is in fine keeping with the sex of the writer. You are saved the ludicrous image of a double-dyed Blue, in papers and morning wrapper, sweating at some stupendous treatise or tragedy from morn to noon, and from noon to dewy eve[23] —you see a graceful and gifted woman, passing from the cares of her family, and the enjoyments of society, to inscribe on her tablets some fine thought or feeling, which had throughout the day existed as a still sunshine upon her countenance, or perhaps as a quiet unshed tear in her eye. In this case, the transition is so natural and graceful, from the duties or delights of the day to the employments of the desk, that there is as little pedantry in writing a poem as in writing a letter, and the authoress appears only the lady in *flower*. Indeed to recur to a former remark, Mrs. Hemans is distinguished above all others by her intense womanliness. And as her own character is so true to her sex, so her sympathies with her sex are very peculiar and profound. Of the joys and the sorrows, the difficulties and the duties, the trials and the temptations, the hopes and the fears, the proper sphere and mission of woman, and of those peculiar consolations which the "world cannot give nor take away"[24] that sustain her even when baffled, she has a true and thorough appreciation; and her "Records of Woman," and her "Songs of the Affections," are just audible beatings of the deep female heart. In our judgment, Mrs. Ellis's idea of Woman is trite, vulgar, and limited, compared with that of "Egeria," as Miss Jewsbury used fondly to denote her beloved friend.[25] [. . .]

Next to her pictures of the domestic affections stand Mrs. Hemans's pictures of nature. These are less minute than passionate, less sublime than beautiful, less studious than free, broad, and rapid sketches. [. . .] Her favourite season was the autumn [. . .] the fine firing of all the groves (not the "fading but the kindling of the leaf")[26] [. . .] [S]he loved the autumn principally for its correspondence with that fine melancholy which was the permanent atmosphere of her being. In one of her letters, speaking of an autumn day, she says, "the day was one of a kind I like, soft, still, and grey, such as makes the earth appear a 'pensive but a happy place.'"[27] [. . .]

In many points Mrs. Hemans reminds us of a poet [. . .] whom she passionately admired, namely, Shelley. Like him, dropping fragile, a reed shaken by the wind, a mighty wind,[28] in sooth, too powerful for the tremulous reed on which it discoursed its music; like him, the victim of exquisite nervous organization; like him, verse flowed for and from her, and the sweet sound often overpowered the meaning, kissing it, as it were, to death; like him, she was melancholy, but the sadness of both was musical, tearful, active, not stony, silent and motionless, still less misanthropical and disdainful; like him, she was gentle, playful, they could both run about their prison garden, and dally with the dark chains which, they knew, bound them till death. Mrs. Hemans, indeed, was not like Shelley, a vates;[29] she has never reached his heights, nor sounded his depths, yet they are, to our thought, so strikingly alike, as to seem brother and sister, in one beautiful, but delicate and dying family. Their very appearance must have been similar. How like must the girl, Felicia Dorothea Browne, with the mantling bloom of her cheeks, her hair of a rich golden brown, and the ever varying expressions of her brilliant eyes, have been to the noble boy Percy Bysshe Shelley, when he came first to Oxford, a fair-haired, bright-eyed enthusiast, on whose cheek and brow, and in whose eye was already beginning to burn a fire, which ultimately enwrapped his whole being in flames!

In Mrs. Hemans's melancholy, one "simple" was wanting, which was largely mixed in Shelley's, that of faithless despondency. Her spirit was cheered by faith. [. . .] Indeed, females may be called the natural guardians of morality and faith. [. . .] Their piety, too, is no fierce and foul polemic flame—it is that of the feelings—the quick instinctive sense of duty—the wonder-stricken soul and the loving heart —often it is not even a conscious emotion at all—but in Wordsworth's language—they lie in

> "Abraham's bosom all the year,
> And God is with them, when they know it not."[30]

In Mrs. Hemans's writings you find this pious tendency of her sex unsoiled by an atom of cant, or bigotry, or exclusiveness; and shaded only by so much pensiveness as attests its divinity and its depth: for as man's misery is said to spring from his greatness, so the gloom which often overhangs the earnest spirit arises from its more immediate proximity to the Infinite and the Eternal. And who would not be ready to sacrifice all the cheap sunshine of earthly success and satisfaction, for even a touch of a shadow so sublime?

After all, the nature of this poetess is more interesting than her genius, or than its finest productions. [. . .] If not, in a transcendent sense, a poet, her life was a poem. Poetry coloured all her existence with a golden light—poetry presided at her needlework—poetry mingled with her domestic and maternal duties—poetry sat down with her to her piano—poetry fluttered her hair and flushed her cheek in her mountain rambles—poetry quivered in her voice, which was a "sweet sad melody."[31] [. . .] Poetry performed for her a still tenderer ministry; it soothed the deep sorrows, on which we dare not enter, which shaded the tissue of her history—it mixed its richest cupful of the "joy of grief"[32] for her selected lips—it lapped her in a dream of beauty, through which the sad realities of life looked in, softened and mellowed in the medium. What could poetry have done more for her, except, indeed, by giving her that sight "as far as the incommunicable"[33]—that supreme vision which she gives so rarely, and which she bestows often as a curse, instead of a blessing? Mrs. Hemans, on the other hand, was too favourite a child of the Muse to receive any such Cassandra boon.[34] Poetry beautified her life, blunted and perfumed the thorns of her anguish, softened the pillow of her sickness, and combined with her firm and most feminine faith to shed a gleam of soft and tearful glory upon her death.

Thus lived, wrote, suffered, and died "Egeria." Without farther seeking to weigh the worth, or settle the future place of her works, let us be thankful to have had her among us, and that she did what she could, in her bright, sorely-tried, yet triumphant passage. She grew in beauty;[35] was blasted where she grew; rained around her poetry, like bright tears from her eyes; learned in suffering what she taught in song;[36] died, and all hearts to which she ever ministered delight, have obeyed the call of Wordsworth, to

> "Mourn rather for that holy spirit,
> Mild as the spring, as ocean deep;—
> For her who, ere her summer faded,
> Has sunk into a dreamless sleep."
>
> [*Extempore Effusion*]

[1] *Blues* are intellectual women. The "trivium," the lower three of the seven liberal arts curriculum for men in the Middle Ages, consisted of logic, rhetoric, and grammar (learning in general), this last evolving to refer more specifically to occult learning, magic, and necromancy; *gramarye* is an archaic term, revived for literary usage by Scott in *Minstrelsy of the Scottish Border* (1802). Sappho is the Greek lyric poet. Aspasia (fl. 440 b.c.) was a Greek courtesan celebrated for her beauty and talents, whose home was a center of literary and philosophical society. A lifelong companion of Pericles, she was the inspiration for Walter Savage Landor's series of imaginary letters, *Pericles and Aspasia* (1836).

[2] In Byron's *Sardanapalus*, Sardanapalus marvels at the transformation of his lover, the slave Myrrha, into a warrior, whose voice "clove through all the din, / As a lute's pierceth through the cymbal's clash" (3.1.394–95).

[3] When the wife of Coleridge's doctor objected to one of his opinions and offered to give her reasons, Coleridge replied, "No madam; don't, for God's sake . . . for if you do you will spoil the whole. A woman judges by her instinct, and not by reason. . . . I've more respect for your first impression than I should probably have for your argument" (footnote in Coleridge's *Table-Talk*, ed. Carl Woodring, 2 vols. [Princeton: Princeton UP, 1990], 1.315).

[4] William Gifford began his career with *The Baviad* (1794) and *The Maeviad* (1795), satires on the Della Cruscan poets of the 1790s, including Hannah Cowley and Mary Robinson. He moved on to editing the Tory *Anti-Jacobin Review* and the Tory *Quarterly Review*.

[5] "No. II" (September 1847) begins: "In selecting Mrs. Hemans as our first specimen of Female Authors, we did so avowedly, because she seemed to us the most feminine writer of the day. We now select Mrs. Browning for the opposite reason, that she is, or at least is said by many to be, the most masculine of our female writers"—that is, "hers is a high heroic nature."

[6] Hamlet instructs the players, "o'erstep not the modesty of nature" (3.2.19).

[7] Cf. "stately, beautiful and deep-souled woman" from *A Mother's Blessing*, by Thomas Aird (1802–76), a well known figure in Scottish literary circles. Gilfillan had reviewed one of his volumes of poetry in a recent issue of *Tait's*.

[8] Julian's description of Maddalo's (Byron's) daughter, in Shelley's *Julian and Maddalo* (592); by "Cornelia," Gilfillan means Cordelia.

[9] Priestess of Apollo at the oracle at Delphi; FH compares the Wife of Asdrubal to a pythia.

[10] From the Preface "To the Reader" of Chapman's sixteenth-century translation of *The Iliad*: "Heare ancient Oracles speake."

[11] *The Voice of Spring* is the closing poem of *Siege of Valencia &c* (first published in *NMM* 7 [April 1823]).

[12] "Poet" derives from the Greek word for "maker," in the sense of an original creator.

[13] Wordsworth describes himself in *Tintern Abbey* as "hearing oftentimes / The still, sad music of humanity" (90–91).

[14] Francis Jeffrey was Lord Advocate, 1830–34; Gilfillan refers to the rather qualified praise in the last sentence of his 1829 essay on FH, as well as to FH's verses on the deaths of George III and of Princess Charlotte.

[15] Lost in the woods, the Lady in Milton's *Comus* seeks confidence from the moonlight: "there does a sable cloud / Turn forth her silver lining on the night, / And casts a gleam over this tufted Grove" (223–25).

[16] Sarcastic comments about FH's longer works. *The Sceptic* (1820) urges Christian hope against the philosophy of hopelessness. *Song of the Battle of Morgarten* was published in *Siege &c*. *The Hour of Death* (first published in *NMM* 9 [January 1824]) and *The Hebrew Mother* are in the "Miscellaneous Pieces" of *Forest Sanctuary &c*, 2d ed. (1829).

[17] Wordsworth, *Glen-Almain; Or, The Narrow Glen*: "In this still place, where murmurs on / But one meek streamlet, only one" (3–4). FH liked this poem.

[18] *Song of Solomon*: "Because of the savour of thy good ointments, thy name is as ointment poured forth, therefore do the virgins love thee" (1.3).

[19] The chief work of Lucretius (1st c. b.c.) is the didactic six-book *De Rerum Naturae* (On the nature of things), the only known large-scale poem in dactylic hexameter from the era of the Roman Republic. Every schoolchild could recite Charles Wolfe's thirty-two-line dirge, *The*

*Burial of Sir John Moore At Corunna*; Moore was a hero of the Peninsular War, killed in 1809 while supervising the British retreat. He died at the Citadel, and was buried there. In the 1840s Shelley's popularity had yet to be established, although Gilfillan was fanning the flames. The phrase he quotes is from one of his most controversial poems, *The Revolt of Islam*, in which the Eagle, temporarily vanquished by the Snake, beholds his adversary rear "on high / His red and burning crest, radiant with victory" (I.xii). Michael Bruce is an eighteenth-century Scots poet.

[20] Jesus is "dominion and power before all ages and now" (Epistle of St. Jude, the Catholic Bible).

[21] A poem in *Whistle Binkie*, by the Scots poet (1782–1849) known as the "Laureate of the Nursery."

[22] Cf. FH's self-description in her letter to Lawrence (published in her *Recollections*) about her having wasted her mind in "mere desultory effusions."

[23] Milton briefly recounts the classical fable of the ejection from Heaven of the now Satanically confederate architect, Mulciber: "from Morn / To Noon he fell, from Noon to dewy Eve" (*Paradise Lost* 1.742–43).

[24] A version of John 14.27, in which Jesus promises that after his death the Holy Ghost will give peace such as the "world cannot give nor take away."

[25] See Jewsbury's *Nonchalant*. Sarah Stickney Ellis published several popular conduct manuals for women, championing their moral influence and their angelic mission to preserve home as a place of purity against the encroachments of the modern world. *The Women of England: Their Social Duties, and Domestic Habits* (1835) was a best-seller (16 editions in two years), followed by *The Wives of England: Their Relative Duties, Domestic Influence, and Social Obligations* (1843; dedicated to Queen Victoria) and *The Daughters of England: Their Position in Society, Character, and Responsibilities* (1845).

[26] FH admired this phrase from William Howitt's "Chapter on Woods" (*Book of the Seasons*): "'the fading of the leaf, which ought rather to be called the kindling of the leaf,'—how truly and how poetically was that said!" she told his wife, Mary (*CM* 1.239).

[27] Autumn 1831 (*CM* 2.241), quoting from Wordsworth's *Laodamia*: Protesilaus's ghost appeared to his widow as "Elysian beauty, melancholy grace, / Brought from a pensive though a happy place" (94–96).

[28] Cf. "a reed shaken with the wind" (Matthew 11.7).

[29] A prophet or oracle—one of Shelley's favorite (self-) descriptions of poetic power.

[30] In Wordsworth's sonnet, "'Tis a beauteous evening, calm and free," the poet says to a young girl (his daughter): "Thou liest in Abraham's bosom all the year; / . . . / God being with thee when we know it not" (12–14).

[31] Cf. *The Bird of Ebro*, in *Songs of Spain* (first published in *NMM* 40 [1834], 28): "Teach me the spell of thy melody. // Bird! is it wrong'd affection's pain, / Whence the sad sweetness flows through thy strain?" (6–8).

[32] A famous phrase from Scots poet Thomas Campbell's *The Pleasures of Hope* (1799): "On Nature's throbbing anguish pour relief / And teach impassioned souls the joy of grief" (1.181–82).

[33] A Shelleyan sense of poetic access: "incommunicable sight" (*The Revolt of Islam* 1.50); "incommunicable dream" (*Alastor* 39); "incommunicable woe" (*Julian and Maddalo* 343).

[34] Cassandra's gift of prophecy is cursed by her never being believed—the revenge of Apollo (god of poetry) for her rejection of his advances.

[35] Cf. Andrew Marvell, *The Match*: "one perfect Beauty grew" (15), and Shelley, *Revolt of Islam*: "gathering beauty as she grew" (I.xxii).

[36] The phrase from *Julian and Maddalo* that FH made her epigraph for *The Diver*: "Most wretched men / Are cradled into poetry by wrong, / They learn in suffering what they teach in song" (544–46).

**Jane Williams,** "Felicia Dorothea Hemans," *The Literary Women of England* (1861)

["This book owes its origin to a sort of accident," reports its Introduction: "Having undertaken to write a Critical and Biographical Essay on the subject of Mrs. Hemans and her poetry, I was consequently led to institute a comparison between her compositions and those of other English poetesses. The want of *a compendious work exclusively appropriated to a summary view of our literary countrywomen* being thus forced upon my attention, I was induced to enlarge my plan, and [. . .] take a brief survey of the general progress of female literature in England." Historian, poet, essayist, and biographer, Williams (1806–85) is best known for her still standard *History of Wales* (1869). Her "brief survey" treats ninety-one authors, beginning with the Anglo-Saxons and including Queen Catherine Parr, Lady Jane Grey, Queen Mary Tudor, Queen Mary Stuart, Queen Elizabeth, Mary Countess of Pembroke, Lady Mary Wroth, Anne Killegrew, Aphra Behn, Anne Countess of Winchelsea, Mary Robinson, Charlotte Smith, Hannah Cowley, Anna Seward, Mary Tighe, Hester Lynch Thrale, Jane Taylor, Anna Barbauld, Helen Maria Williams, Hannah More, Maria Jane Jewsbury, Letitia Landon, and Anne Grant. The 106-page, three-chapter treatment of FH is the longest in the volume's 564 pages, and the volume closes with the full text of FH's late poem *Despondency and Aspiration*, "in order to leave with the reader a favourable impression of the Literary Women of England" (560–64). The only other "poetesses" to merit even single chapters are More, Jewsbury, Landon, and Grant. Williams not only confirms and reinforces the canonical status of FH by midcentury but also spells out the vocabulary of her Victorian reception—childhood precocity, motherhood, the Bible, melancholy.]

*[Influence of Mrs. Browne and the Bible (319–92)]*

Happily for Felicia Browne, the singular combination in her mother's character of tenderness, intelligence, and judgment, encouraged confidence to the utmost; and while the gifted child poured out her thoughts and feelings, her difficulties and aspirations, she found habitually the sympathy of a maternal heart, and the kind guidance of a wise and pious counsellor. [. . .] In the life of Mrs. Browne true religion was exemplified. She seldom spoke upon the subject, unless by way of direct instruction; but her habitual look of care was set aside, and her fine countenance brightened with serene joy, as she daily read the Bible to her children, and tried to impress upon her little Felicia, whose thoughts were often wandering after birds' nests and new-blown primroses in the dingles, the heart-touching truths concerning a Divine Creator, Father, and Saviour. Among the earliest impressions which the gifted girl received from the Scriptures, or probably from any book, were the pastoral images of patriarchal life, the tents, the palm-trees, the fountains of the desert, the rocks, the reposing flocks, and the slow procession of the loaded camels. The effect produced upon ordinary children by pictorial illustrations is much fainter and slighter than that produced upon Felicia Browne was by words heard and read; for out of those words her mind made pictures, vivid and durable enough to serve in after years as the basis of accurate descriptions.

Her senses were acute, exact, and delicately fine; her temperament was sanguine, sensitive, and easily agitated, blending the liveliness, pathos, and pi-
quancy of Irish music; her intellect was of that rare kind which, discerning things
at a glance, and not by a process of reasoning, seizes on them and firmly grasps
them as its own for ever.

*[Love of Shakespeare and books (395–96)]*

Deeply impressed by Shakspeare's delineations of character, and more especially
of female character, she longed to be, or at least to personify, such of them as she
most admired. Imogen and Beatrice were her favourites, for she was drawn
towards them by the strong sympathy of conscious resemblance. Rosalind, an
amalgamation of the two, would probably have concentrated her preference had
the sorrows of that heroine equalled those of Imogen. In the midst of manifold
enjoyments, and in the fullness of their gratification, Felicia Browne recognised
the possession of a keen capacity for sorrow; and a lady having once impru-
dently said aloud of her, in her hearing, "That child is not made for happiness, her colour comes and goes too fast," the words shocked her spirits at the
time, and often recurred to her memory as prophetic, until events realized them.[1]
[. . .] Vaguely feeling that she had to fulfil some peculiar purpose in the world
by means of yet latent poetic ability, visions of future fame and future usefulness often floated through her fancy. She had a natural intolerance of all things
base, and harsh, and coarse. Beauty, sublimity, and refinement she sought in all
things, with a preference rather inclining towards minute details than extent
or vastness. Her pursuits were spontaneous growths of unsuggested interests. She loved books as she loved the fresh air and sunshine, and she read them
of her own accord and at her own free choice, for she had access to "an ample
library."

*[The romance of Captain Hemans (403)]*

[W]hile her mind was full of enthusiasm for Spain, its language, its literature,
its chivalry and patriotism, and while, to her imagination, all the world glistened
as a bright illusion, and human life as a romantic fiction, the young poetess first
became acquainted with Captain Hemans, of the 4th regiment of foot, who was
then on a visit in the neighbourhood. Struck with her extraordinary beauty, he
fell passionately in love with her. He was handsome, well-bred, a soldier, about
to embark for Spain to fight in the cause of freedom, and he was her declared
lover. She was fifteen; her mind invested him with every heroic and amiable
attribute, and her honest heart fervently returned his affection. The real incom-
patibility of their natures was plainly visible to the friends of both.

*[Her capacities of memory (406)]*

She read with extraordinary celerity, but with such concentrated attention,
that she accurately imaged the contents of books in her mind, and could repro-
duce them at will, and repeat whole pages of poetry by heart which she had read

but once. The rapid action and tenacious grasp of her memory were habitually as marvellous as in those vaunted instances where memory constitutes the only mental talent. On one occasion, at the request of an incredulous brother, she took up Heber's "Europe," a poem containing four hundred and twenty-four lines, which she had never seen before, and in the space of one hour and twenty minutes repeated the whole from beginning to end, "without a single mistake or a moment's hesitation." On another occasion, which subsequently excited observation, she listened twice to Lord Byron's "Stanzas to his Sister," which were read aloud from a manuscript, and immediately repeated them and wrote them down.[2]

### [Early married life (410–16)]

[A]t the age of eighteen, she became the wife of Captain Alfred Hemans, who had returned from the Spanish war and the Walcheren expedition an exacting valetudinarian.[3] By this marriage he meant to appropriate the heart and hand of a lovely and clever woman to administer henceforth exclusively to his comfort and satisfaction; and she gave herself, heart and soul, to a husband who was to be for life her chivalrous lover, to admire and pet her as her fond brothers did, and to delight and glory in her like her sister and her mother. [. . .] [T]hey took up their abode under the roof of Mrs. Browne. With devoted affection Mrs. Hemans fulfilled a mother's duties, pursuing simultaneously and with unabated assiduity her literary avocations, acquiring a knowledge of the Latin language, and improving her mind by the study of the best authors. [. . .] [In] the immethodical way in which Mrs. Hemans used to surround herself with books in different languages and on different subjects, while, nevertheless, the various stores of knowledge they supplied found clear and orderly arrangement in her mind[, . . .] the poetess was either pursuing and collecting the scattered parts of one series of ideas or tracing out parallels. Many volumes of extracts and transcribed passages show how industriously she worked.[4]

### [The Siege of Valencia (424)]

[In scene 2], the mind of Elmina, bent on one purpose, full of devices for its accomplishment, seeing and feeling nothing but the peril of her children, and the necessity of averting it, is unnaturally interrupted in its course by a tedious and vain attempt to divide the reader's sympathy with the old griefs of a fierce ecclesiastic. [. . .] In [Elmina], Mrs. Hemans seems to have embodied her idea of how she herself would have felt and acted under similar trials: there is in it such an intensity of life and love, such majesty, such tenderness, such sad reality, that the most vivid imagination must have failed in creating it without the concurrent wear and tear of a fervid heart. The terrible conflict of Elmina between maternal instinct on one side and conjugal love with chivalrous honour on the other, her temporary subjection to evil, her conscious loss of moral dignity under the crushing pressure of temptation, her vacillation, her repentant recognition of the purpose of affliction, her faith and heroic constancy when all is lost, forms

one of the finest word-pictures ever drawn by a woman's hand. For such originality the penalty must have been previously paid in tears.

### [Records of Woman *(440–41)*]

All these poems, founded on facts or recorded incidents, Mrs. Hemans has made
inalienably her own, not by a mere paraphrastic version, but by the absolute
fusion and complete recasting of material in amalgamation with ore of the richest kind from her own mines. In thus exemplifying the characteristics of women,
by instances of lofty self-sacrifice, tender devotion, attractive amiability, and
inextinguishable faithfulness, she has indeed coined and exhibited her very self.
"Arabella Stuart" offers an exquisite correlative, corrective, and counteractive of
Pope's "Epistle" in a similar subject treated by a feminine hand [*Eloisa to Abelard*]. The scenic accessories with which she adorns a story of lonely and
monotonous imprisonment, render every division a pausing place for enjoyment
and admiration.

> Misery still delights to trace
> Its semblance in another's case;
> [Cowper, *The Castaway* 59–60]

and "Properzia Rossi" tells but too plainly the recorder's own tale, while relating
the unrequited, ill-requited love of a woman of genius, who yearns for the affection of one, and sickens at the world's applause.

### [Hemans in Scotland, August 1829 (450–51)]

Mrs. Grant of Laggan [. . .] has traced a shadowy sketch of the English poetess's
passing image, which is worthy of note as a testimony of the general effect
produced by her appearance and manners. "I had a charming guest before I left
town to come here—no other than the very charming Mrs. Hemans, for whom
I have long felt something very like affection. She had two fine boys with her, the
objects visibly of very great tenderness, who seem equally attached to her. She is
entirely feminine; and her language has a charm like that of her verse—the same
ease and peculiar grace, with more vivacity. If affliction had not laid a heavy hand
upon her she would be playful: she has not the slightest tinge of affectation; and
is so refined, so gentle, that you must both love and respect her."[5]

### [Conclusion (494)]

The writings of Mrs. Hemans met with immediate and extensive popularity,
alike in the most distant and alienated colonial settlements and in the old home
of the British race. Their suitability to more than one condition of social life has
thus been manifested. Their writer died more than a quarter of a century ago,
and many of them have now been more than forty years before the public in
undiminished favour. These are good auguries. Perhaps when the century has
run its course, and a critical reviewer, like a gardener at the breaking up of
winter, examines the ground and sorts out surviving plants from those which

have perished in the frost of time, two-thirds of those produced by Mrs. Hemans will be found to possess perennial vitality.

[1] *CM* 1.13; Chorley comments on the indelible, painful impression this remark made on FDB. The sensation of prophecy is Williams's elaboration.

[2] *HM* (159) reports this feat of memory as occurring in 1828. FDB read with admiration Reginald Heber's war-poem *Europe* (1809) the year it was published; for the anecdote and quotation see *HM*, which reports that this performance was "the subject of a wager" (13–14).

[3] The Captain's concern for his health is understandable. In the abortive Walcherin expedition of 1809, undertaken to seize Antwerp from the French, about one-third of the 40,000 troops were devastated by malaria.

[4] Her commonplace books, one of which is held by the Houghton Library.

[5] Mrs. Grant's "Letters," vol. iii, p. 156 [Williams]

*Memoir and Correspondence of Mrs. Grant of Laggan*, ed. J. P. Grant, 3 vols. (London, 1844). Poet, essayist, and letter writer Anne [Macvicar] Grant (also with a chapter in *Literary Women*), was admired for her *Poems on Various Subjects* (1803), and had numerous friends in the Edinburgh literary world. In July 1829 (?) she wrote to a friend, "Mrs Hemans [. . .] is in person, mind, & manners the most charming person I ever met with, & that inclusive of her talents. She is feminine & natural, & very pretty. But she sings like a nightingale with a thorn at her breast—" (HL MS 42515).

---

**William Michael Rossetti**, "Prefatory Notice" to *Poetical Works of Mrs. Hemans*, 1878

[W. M. Rossetti (1829–1919), Dante Gabriel and Christina's brother, was a member of the original Pre-Raphaelite Brotherhood. His art criticism from the *Spectator* was collected as *Fine Art, Chiefly Contemporary* (1867); he wrote a "Memoir of Shelley" for *The Poetical Works of Percy Bysshe Shelley* (1870), a "Biographical Sketch" for *Poems of John Keats* (1872; expanded to *Life of John Keats* [1887]), a critical edition of Shelley's *Adonais* (1891), memoirs of his family (1895, 1904), and a study of Dante (1910). This "Notice" was first a "Critical Memoir" for *Poetical Works of Mrs. Hemans* (London: Ward & Locke, 1873), often republished as an authoritative biography and critical assessment.]

*[Introduction; lineage and childhood (11–13)]*

Sentiment without passion, and suffering without abjection—these, along with a deep religious sense, and with the gifts of a brilliant mind taking the poetical direction through eager sympathy and some genuine vocation, constitute the life of Mrs. Hemans.[1] Whatever may be the deservings of the poems in other respects, they do not fail to convey to the reader a certain impression of beauty, felt to be inherent as much in the personality of the authoress as in her writings: they show as being the outcome of a beautiful life, and in fact they are so. The impression which the reader will thus have received from perusing the poems is not only confirmed but intensified when he knows the events of the writer's life.

Felicia Dorothea Browne, born in Duke Street, Liverpool, on the 25th of September, 1793, was daughter of a merchant of considerable eminence, a native of Ireland, belonging to a branch of the Sligo family. Her mother, whose maiden name was Wagner, was partly Italian and partly German by extraction, her father having held the post of Consul at Liverpool for the Austrian and Tuscan Governments. The surname Wagner was in reality a corruption from the illustrious Venetian name Veniero, borne by three Doges, and by the commander of the fleet of the Republic at the great battle of Lepanto. Felicia was the fifth child in a family of seven, of whom one died in infancy; she was distinguished, almost from her cradle, by extreme beauty and precocious talents. "The full glow of that radiant beauty which was destined to fade so early" is one of the expressions used by the poetess's sister [*HM* 12] in describing the former at the age of fifteen. This reference to "early fading" appears to be intended to apply rather to the death of Mrs. Hemans when only in her forty-second year, and to the ravages of disease in the few years preceding, than to any loss of comeliness in mature womanhood. An engraved portrait of her by the American artist William E. West, one of three which he painted in 1827, shows us that Mrs. Hemans, at the age of thirty-four, was eminently pleasing and good-looking, with an air of amiability and sprightly gentleness, and of confiding candor which, while none the less perfectly womanly, might almost be termed childlike in its limpid depth. The features are correct and harmonious; the eyes full; and the contour amply and elegantly rounded. In height she was neither tall nor short. A sufficient wealth of naturally clustering hair, golden in early youth, but by this time of a rich auburn, shades the capacious but not over-developed forehead, and the lightly-pencilled eyebrows. The bust and form have the fulness of a mature period of life; and it would appear that Mrs. Hemans was somewhat short-necked and high-shouldered, partly detracting from delicacy of proportion, and of general aspect or impression on the eye. We would rather judge of her by this portrait (which her sister pronounces a good likeness) than by another engraved in Mr. Chorley's *Memorials*. This latter was executed in Dublin in 1831 by a young artist named Edward Robinson. It makes Mrs. Hemans look younger than in the earlier portrait by West, and may on that ground alone be surmised unfaithful; and, though younger, it also makes her heavier and less refined.

The childhood of Felicia Browne was probably rendered all the happier by a commercial reverse which befell her father before she was seven years of age. The family hereupon removed to Wales, and for nine years they lived [. . .] close to the sea and amid the mountains. This was the very scene for the poetically minded child to enjoy, and to have her powers nurtured by. [ . . .] Her mother, a most amiable and excellent woman, fully qualified to carry on her daughter's education, devoted the most careful attention to this object, and was repaid by an unswerving depth and constancy of love. A large library was kept in the house, and Felicia drew heavily upon its stores: a pretty picture is presented to the mind's eye, and would not be unworthy of realization by art, in the anecdote that it was her habit, at the age of six, to read Shakspeare while seated in the branches of an apple-tree.[2] Along with great rapidity of comprehension, she had a memory of surprising retentiveness, and would repeat whole pages of poetry after a single reading.

*[The mystery of the failed marriage (13–15)]*

Biographers have not permitted us to know distinctly whether or not the conjugal life of Mrs. Hemans was happy, or what Captain Hemans might possibly have found to say on the subject: at any rate, it was a short one, practically speaking. The wedded couple resided at first at Daventry in Northamptonshire, where the Captain was Adjutant to the County Militia: here they remained about a year, and here was born their son Arthur, the first of a family of five, all of whom were boys. They then went to live with Mrs. Hemans's own family at Bronwylfa; her mother was now at the head of the house, as her father, having resumed the mercantile career, had gone out to Quebec, where finally he died. In 1818 Captain Hemans resolved to go to the south of Europe "for the sake of his health"[3]—a very inconvenient motive, or a highly convenient one, according to circumstances: he had suffered much from the vicissitudes of a military life, especially during the retreat to Corunna, and afterwards through fever caught in the Walcheren expedition. He departed just before the birth of his fifth son; went to Rome; and there settled down. The parting proved to be a final one. It might have been fancied that even the shattered frame of a young officer who had survived Corunna and Walcheren would suffice for the effort of coming to Wales, England, or Ireland, at some time between 1818 and 1835, so as to rebehold a wife whom he had left in the bloom of youth and loveliness, and whose literary fame, for many years succeeding his departure, lent an ever-brightening lustre to the name of Hemans, and so as to get a glimpse of his five promising boys. But this was not to be: for some reason or other, not defined to us, even the charms of Bronwylfa, with a wife, five sons, and a resident mother-in-law, did not relax the tenacious grasp which Italy and Rome obtained on Captain Hemans. Or again it might have seemed conceivable that not only Captain Hemans but also his wife, the author of *Lays of Many Lands*, sensitive to the historical and romantic associations of such a country as Italy, would find it compatible with her liking as well as her duties to pay a visit to Rome, or possibly to make it her permanent dwelling-place. As to this, it may perhaps be inferred, in a general way, that the family affections of daughter and mother were more dominant and vivid in Mrs. Hemans than conjugal love; her intense feeling of the sacredness of home, which it would be both idle and perverse to contest, may have set before her, as more binding and imperative, the duties of service to her own mother, and of guidance to her own children, than the more equal, passionate, and in some sense self-indulgent relation between wife and husband. However, abandoning conjecture, it may be best here to transcribe the reticent hints of the subject which are given by the poetess's sister, Mrs. Hughes, in her Memoir, and which show that the *de facto* separation between Captain and Mrs. Hemans depended partly upon general considerations of family obligation, and partly upon special circumstances not clearly indicated, but apparently reflecting more or less on the marital deportment of the Captain. "It has been alleged, and with perfect truth, that the literary pursuits of Mrs. Hemans, and the education of her children, made it more eligible for her to remain under the maternal roof than to accompany her husband to Italy. It is, however, unfortunately but too well known that such were not the only reasons which led to this divided course. To dwell on this subject would be unnecessarily painful; yet it must be stated that nothing like a permanent separation was contemplated at the time, nor did it ever amount to more than a tacit conventional arrangement which offered no obstacle to the frequent interchange of correspondence, nor to a constant reference to their father in all things relating to the disposal of her boys. But years rolled on—seventeen years of absence, and consequently alienation; and, from this time to the hour of her death, Mrs. Hemans and her husband never met again." [*HM* 29–30]

With this incident of the lifelong separation between her husband and herself, anything of a romantic character in the occurrences of Mrs. Hemans's career comes to a close; although the coloring of high-toned romance in her mind and writings never died out, but to the last continued to permeate, enliven, and beautify, that other element and staple of her life, its sweet and earnest domesticity. Now we have only to contemplate the loving daughter, glad, as long as fate permitted, to escape being the head of a household, although invested with the matronly dignity proper to the motherhood of five boys. We see in her the not less deeply affectionate, tender, and vigilant mother; the admired and popular poetess, distinguished and soon burdened by applause; shortly afterwards the cureless invalid, marked out for an early death, towards which she progresses with a lingering but undeviating rapidity—calm in conscience, bright and cheerful in mind, full of faith and hope for eternity, and of the gentlest charities of life for her brief residue of time.

[The Siege of Valencia *(16–17)*]

In *The Siege of Valencia* the situation is in a high degree tragical—even terrible or harrowing: and there is this advantage,—no small one in the case of a writer such as Mrs. Hemans—that, while the framework is historical, and the crisis and passions of a genuinely heroic type, the immediate interest is personal or domestic. Mrs. Hemans may be credited with a good and unhacknied choice of subject in this drama, and with a well-concerted adaptation of it to her own more special powers: the writing is fairly sustained throughout, and there are passages both vigorous and moving. As the reader approaches the *dénouement*, and finds the authoress dealing death with an unsparing hand to the heroically patriotic Gonzalez and all his offspring, he may perhaps at first feel a little ruffled at noting that the only member of the family who has been found wanting in the fiery trial—wanting through an excess of maternal love—is also the only one saved alive: but in this also the authoress may be pronounced in the right. Reunion with her beloved ones in death would in fact have been mercy to Elmina, and would have left her undistinguished from the others, and untouched by any retribution; survival, mourning, and self-discipline, are the only chastisement in which a poetic justice, in its higher conception, could be expressed.

*[Hemans's character; her "female" poetry (21–24)]*

Mrs. Hemans, while sprightly, versatile, and conversible, was not the less of a very retiring disposition, shrinking from self-display, and the commonplaces of a public reputation. Her character was extremely guileless. Notwithstanding her exceeding sensitiveness—which extended not only to the affections and interests of life, but to such outer matters as the sound of the wind at night, the melancholy of the sea-shore, and in especial (though there was no reason for this in any personal occurrences) to the sadness of burials at sea—she was yet very free from mere ordinary nervous alarms. "My spirits," she once wrote, "are as variable as the lights and shadows now flitting with the winds over the high grass, and sometimes the tears gush into my eyes when I can scarcely define the cause. I put myself in mind of an Irish melody sometimes, with its quick and wild transitions from sadness to gayety." Her conversation was various and brilliant, with a total freedom from literary pretence. She had a strong perception of the ludicrous, but abstained from sarcasm or ill-nature, more especially as weapons against any who had injured or neglected her; and personal or invidious literary gossip was her aversion. She would not permit herself to be vexed at small things: but was wont to quote the saying of Madame l'Espinasse (applying it no doubt chiefly to the severance of her matrimonial ties) "Un grand chagrin tue tout le reste."[4] She had a keen dislike to any sort of coarseness in conversation or in books, and would often tear out peccant pages from volumes in her possession. Her accomplishments were considerable, and not merely superficial. She knew French, Italian, Spanish, Portuguese, and in mature life German, and was not unacquainted with Latin. She had some taste and facility not only in music [. . .] but likewise in drawing; and some of her sketches of localities have served for vignettes in the copyright edition of her complete works [*1839*]. Her poetry was often written with a readiness approaching improvisation: this she felt as in some degree a blemish, and towards the close of her life she regretted having often had to write in a haphazard way, so as to supply means for the education of her sons. Byron, Shelley, and Madame de Staël, were among the writers she was in the habit of quoting. Jealousy of contemporary female writers, prominent in the public eye, was unknown to her gentle and true-hearted nature: Miss Jewsbury (afterwards Mrs. Fletcher) was among her intimates, and she indulged herself in friendly correspondence with Miss Baillie, Miss Mitford, Mrs. Howitt, and others. The first-named of these ladies, Mrs. Fletcher (whose death preceded that of her friend by about a year), has, in her book named *The Three Histories*, described Mrs. Hemans under the name of Egeria; and as the faithfulness of the portrait, allowing for some degree of idealization, is attested by Mrs. Hughes, I am induced to repeat it here: [quotes Jewsbury's portrait of "Egeria."]

In Mrs. Hemans's poetry there is (as already observed) a large measure of beauty, and, along with this, very considerable skill. Aptitude and delicacy in versification, and a harmonious balance in the treatment of the subject, are very generally apparent: if we accept the key-note as right, we may with little misgiving acquiesce in what follows on to the close. Her skill, however, hardly rises into the loftier region of art: there is a gift, and culture added to the gift, but not a great native faculty working in splendid independence, or yet more splendid self-discipline. Her sources of inspiration being genuine, and the tone of her mind feminine in an intense degree, the product has no lack of sincerity; and yet it leaves a certain artificial impression, rather perhaps through a cloying flow of "right-minded" perceptions of moral and material beauty than through any other defect. "Balmy" it may be: but the atmosphere of her verse is by no means bracing. One might sum up the weak points in Mrs. Hemans's poetry by saying that it is not only "feminine" poetry (which under the circumstances can be no imputation, rather an encomium) but also "female" poetry: besides exhibiting the fineness and charm of womanhood, it has the monotone of mere sex. Mrs. Hemans has that love of good and horror of evil which characterize a scrupulous female mind; and which we may most rightly praise without concluding that they favor poetical robustness, or even perfection in literary form. She is a leader in that very modern phalanx of poets who persistently co-ordinate the impulse of sentiment with the guiding power of morals or religion. Everything must convey its "lesson," and is indeed set forth for the sake of its lesson: but must at the same time have the emotional gush of a spontaneous sentiment. The poet must not write because he has something of his own to say, but because he has something *right* to feel and say. Lamartine was a prophet in this line.[5] After allowing all proper deductions, however it may be gratefully acknowledged that Mrs. Hemans takes a very honorable rank among poetesses; and that there is in her writings much which both appeals, and deserves to appeal, to many gentle, sweet, pious, and refined souls, in virtue of its thorough possession of the same excellent gifts. According to the spiritual or emotional condition of her readers, it would be found that a poem by this authoress which to one reader would be graceful and tender would to another be touching, and to a third poignantly pathetic. The first we can suppose to be a man, and the third a woman; or the first a critic, the second a "poetical reader," and the third a sensitive nature, attuned to sympathy by suffering. [the conclusion]

[1] The Memoir of Mrs. Hemans, written by her sister Mrs. Hughes [. . .] is the best authority for the facts of the poet's life.—There are also the *Memorials* by Mr. Chorley in 2 vols., containing a good deal of Mrs. Hemans's correspondence (reproduced to a large extent by Mrs. Hughes) and mostly bearing on her literary career rather than the circumstances of her private life. The former of these accounts is pleasantly written, in a tone of deep affection, and admiration as well, which the reader will not be disposed to cavil. [WMR]

[2] See Jewsbury, *The History of an Enthusiast.*

[3] This is the tenor of the explanation in the "Memoir" in *Poetical Remains* by "Δ" ("Delta," David Macbeth Moir [1795–1851], a regular contributor to *Blackwood's*), *CM* and *HM*. Rossetti hints at an evasive official explanation. Hearing that Scots poet Allan Cunningham was planning a biographical sketch of her for the *Athenæum*, FH wrote to implore his discretion concerning her failed marriage—a heartbreak as well as an embarrassment to the poet known as "Mrs Hemans," the icon of domestic affection. See Marlon Ross for a discussion of the various narratives of this failure. My information about the letter to Cunningham comes from Paula Feldman.

[4] A great sorrow kills all the rest.

"No part of her character was more remarkable than her placid indifference to those trifling annoyances, about which the unoccupied and the narrow-minded are for ever 'disquieting themselves in vain.' She would often quote [these] words of Madame l'Espinasse" (*HM* 263). Julie-Jeanne-Éléanor de Lespinasse (1732–76), famed hostess of a progressive Paris salon, was a possible model for Staël's Corinne, said to have died in despair of winning the comte de Guibert's love. FH quotes from Letter 14 (15 August 1773) *Lettres à M. de Guibert* (1776).

[5] Across the decade that marks the height of FH's career, Alphonse de Lamartine was publishing religious-mystical poems: *Méditations poétiques* (1820), *Nouvelles Méditations poétiques* (1823), and *Harmonies poétiques et Religieuses* (1830).

# BIBLIOGRAPHY

## CHIEF LIFETIME PUBLICATIONS

Bracketed initials indicate unsigned authorship. Full information for publishers is given once only and thereafter abbreviated.

1808: *Poems by Felicia Dorothea Browne*. Liverpool and London: T. Cadell and W. Davies.
 [FDB], *England and Spain; or Valour and Patriotism*. Cadell & Davies.
1812: [FDB], *The Domestic Affections, and Other Poems*. Cadell & Davies.
1816: [FH], *The Restoration of the Works of Art to Italy: A Poem*. "By a Lady." Oxford: R. Pearson; London: J. Ebers. 2d ed., "By Felicia Hemans." London: John Murray.
1817: [FH], *Modern Greece, A Poem*. Murray.
1818: *Translations from Camoens, and Other Poets, With Original Poetry*. By the Author of "Modern Greece," and the "Restoration of the Words of Art to Italy." Murray; Oxford: J. Parker.
 "F.D.H., Brownwhyfla," *Stanzas on the Death of the Princess Charlotte*, *Blackwood's Edinburgh Magazine* 3 (April) 5–8. Rpt. *Translations*.
1819: *Tales, and Historic Scenes, in Verse*. By Felicia Hemans, Author of *The Restoration of the Works of Art to Italy*, *Modern Greece*, &c. &c. Murray.
 *The Meeting of Wallace and Bruce on the Banks of the Carron*, *Blackwood's Edinburgh Magazine* 5 (September): 686–88.
 *Wallace's Invocation to Bruce, A Poem*. Cadell & Davies; Edinburgh: W. Blackwood.
1820: *The Sceptic; A Poem*. By Mrs. Hemans, Author of *The Restoration of the Works of Art to Italy*; *Modern Greece*; *Tales and Historic Poems*; *Wallace's Invocation to Bruce*. Murray.
 *Stanzas to the Memory of the Late King*. By Mrs. Hemans, Author of *The Restoration of the Works of Art to Italy*; *Modern Greece*; *Tales and Historic Poems*; *Wallace's Invocation to Bruce*; *The Sceptic*; and *Translations from Camoens*. Murray.
1821: *Dartmoor: A Poem*. By Felicia D. Hemans. London: Royal Society of Literature.
 2d ed. *The Sceptic*, bound with *Stanzas to the Memory of the Late King*. Murray.
 2d ed. *Modern Greece*. Murray.
1822: *A Selection of Welsh Melodies, with Symphonies and Accompaniments by John Parry, and Characteristic Words by Mrs. Hemans*. London: J. Power.
1823: *The Siege of Valencia, A Dramatic Poem; The Last Constantine: With Other Poems*. Murray.
 [FH], *Vespers of Palermo: A Tragedy in Five Acts*. Murray.
1824: *Hymns for Childhood*. [Ed. Andrews Norton.] Boston: Hilliard, Gray, Little, and Wilkins.
 2d ed. *Tales, and Historic Scenes*. Murray.
1825: *The Forest Sanctuary; and Other Poems* (includes *Lays of Many Lands*). Murray.
1826: *The League of the Alps, The Siege of Valencia, The Vespers of Palermo, and Other Poems, by Mrs. Felicia Hemans*. [Ed. Andrews Norton.] Hilliard &c.
1827: *The Forest Sanctuary and Other Poems, by Mrs. Felicia Hemans*. [Ed. Andrews Norton.] Hilliard &c.

1827: *Forest Sanctuary &c*, bound with *League &c*, as *Poems, by Mrs. Hemans*. Hilliard &c.
   *Hymns on the Works of Nature, for the Use of Children*. [Ed. Andrews Norton.]
   Hilliard &c.
1828: *Records of Woman: With Others Poems*. Blackwood; Cadell; Hilliard. Pirated ed.,
   New York: W. B. Gilley.
   *Poetical Works*. New York: Evert Duyckinck; New Haven, Conn.: N. Whiting.
   October: 2d ed. *Records*. Blackwood.
1829: 2d ed. *The Forest Sanctuary, With Other Poems*. (Many new poems not in 1st ed.)
   Blackwood; Cadell.
1830: *Songs of the Affections, with Other Poems*. Blackwood; Cadell.
   3d ed. *Records*. Blackwood.
1833: 4th ed. *Records*. Blackwood; Cadell. (5th ed. 1837).
1834: *Hymns for Childhood*. Dublin: William Curry.
   *National Lyrics, and Songs for Music*. Curry; London: Simpkin & Marshall.
   *Scenes and Hymns of Life, with Other Religious Poems*. Blackwood; Cadell.
   *German Studies*. By Mrs. Hemans. No. I—"Scenes and Passages from the 'Tasso'
   of Goethe." *NMM* 40.157 (January): 1–8.
1835: 3d ed. *The Forest Sanctuary*. Blackwood.
   2d ed. *Songs of the Affections*. Blackwood; Cadell.
   *Songs of the Affections and Lays of Many Lands*. Philadelphia: H. F. Anners.


## The Periodicals

*Blackwood's Edinburgh Magazine*, founded in 1817 by William Blackwood (1776–1834) as
   a Tory-conservative rival to Francis Jeffrey's increasingly Whig-liberal monthly, the
   *Edinburgh Review*. Popularly called "Maga," it was generally anti-Catholic, anti-abo-
   lition, anti-democracy, anti-reform. In the hands of John Wilson ("Christopher
   North") and John Gibson Lockhart, it became infamous for its attacks (signed "Z.")
   on "The Cockney School" poets (Hazlitt, Hunt, Keats) and later, on Byron and Shelley. Even so, it was hospitable to a number of women writers, especially Baillie,
   L.E.L., and FH. *Stanzas on the Death of Princess Charlotte* marked FH's debut in
   1818; *Maga* published almost 200 poems over her career, including her last, *Sabbath
   Sonnet* (38 [July 1835]: 96–97).
*The New Monthly Magazine*, founded in 1814 by Henry Colburn and Frederic Shoberl
   (who would later edit *Forget Me Not*, one of the annuals) as an anti-Jacobin, anti-
   Painite, anti-Napoleon antidote to liberal publisher Sir Richard Phillips's *Monthly
   Magazine*. It emerged into literary importance after Thomas Campbell became editor
   in 1821; in his first volume he disclaimed interest in "directing, or deeply influencing
   political opinion." With handsome payment, he secured contributions from William
   Hazlitt, Mary Russell Mitford, Horace Smith, Countess Marguerite Blessington
   ("Conversations with Byron" was serialized in 1830–31), and FH, who contributed
   about 200 poems from 1823 to 1835.
*The Monthly Magazine and British Register*, a "new series" of the *Monthly Magazine* (1796–
   1825), liberal in tone and regarded as radical by the Tory establishment. From 1826–
   27, FH published 16 poems here, including *Casabianca* and *The Illuminated City*
   (both about the human cost of the Napoleonic wars).

NINETEENTH-CENTURY REMARKS, BIOGRAPHY, MEMOIRS,
REVIEWS, ASSESSMENTS

This list supplements the "Reception" excerpts, or offers fuller information about them.

*A Short Sketch of the Life of Mrs. Hemans; with Remarks on her Poetry; and Extract.* London: James Paul, 1835. Unsigned.

[Chorley, Henry Fothergill.] "Mrs. Hemans," *Athenæum* 395 (23 May 1835): 391–92 (obit.); excerpted *1839*, 7.296–99.

———. [H.F.C.] "Personal Recollections of the Late Mrs. Hemans." *Athenæum* 398 (13 June 1835): 452–54; 400 (27 June 1835): 493–95; 402 (11 July 1835): 527–30.

———. Review of *Poetical Remains. Athenæum* 437 (12 March 1836): 186–87.

———. *Memorials of Mrs. Hemans, with Illustrations of her Literary Character from her Private Correspondence.* 2 vols. London: Saunders and Otley, 1836. Reviewed in *Athenæum* 462 (3 September 1836): 618–20; and 463 (10 September): 646–48.

Delta or Δ. See Moir.

*Fraser's Magazine for Town and Country* 7 (May 1833): 591–601. "The Female Character."

Gaskell, Elizabeth. *Wives and Daughters.* 1864–66. Harmondsworth: Penguin, 1986.

Howitt, William. *Homes and Haunts of the Most Eminent British Poets.* 2 vols. London: Richard Bentley, 1843. 2.105–24.

[Hughes {later Owen}, Harriett Mary]. *Memoir of the Life and Writings of Felicia Hemans: By Her Sister.* In FH, *1839*, 1.1–315.

Lawrence, Mrs. [Rose D'Aguilar]. *The Last Autumn at a Favourite Residence, with other Poems; and Recollections of Mrs. Hemans.* Liverpool: G. and J. Robinson &c; London: John Murray, 1836. 287–419.

*Leisure Hour* 1 (1952): 72–76. "Felicia Hemans."

*London Literary Gazette* 335 (21 and 28 June 1823): 385–86 and 407–8. On *The Siege of Valencia &c.*

Moir, David Macbeth. [Delta or Δ, pseud.] Obituary essay. *Blackwood's* 38 (July 1835): 96–97. Excerpted in *1839*, 7.289–91.

*New European Magazine* 3 (1823) 120–23. "Contemporary Poets. No. I." On *Siege &c.*

Robinson, A[gnes] Mary F. "Felicia Hemans." *The English Poets: Selections with Critical Introductions by Various Writers.* Ed. T. H. Ward. 5 vols. London and New York: Macmillan, 1880. 4.334–35.

Rowton, Frederic. *The Female Poets of Great Britain, Chronologically Arranged: With Copious Selections and Critiial Remarks.* London: Longman, Brown, Green, and Longmans, 1848.

Scott, Walter. *The Journal of Sir Walter Scott, 1824–1832.* Edinburgh: David Douglas, 1891.

———. *Memoir of the Life of Sir Walter Scott.* Ed. J. G. Lockhart. Edinburgh: Robert Cadell, 1837.

Sigourney, Mrs. [Lydia H.]. "Essay on the Genius of Mrs. Hemans" and "Monody on Mrs. Hemans." *Memoir [. . .] By Her Sister.* New York: C. S. Francis; Boston: J. H. Francis, 1845. vii–xxvi.

Symons, Arthur. *The Romantic Movement in English Poetry.* New York: Dutton, 1909.

Tuckerman, H. T. "Mrs. Hemans." *Southern Literary Messenger* 7 (1841): 380–83.

Williams, Jane. "Felica Hemans." *The Literary Women of England Including [. . .] Sketches of the Poetesses to the Year 1850; With Extracts from their Works, and Critical Remarks* (London: Saunders, Otley, 1861). 389–494.

Major Posthumous Nineteenth-Century Editions

Many of these editions have biographical sketches and memoirs, as well as selections of critical commentary. They were frequently published in lavish volumes, and often purchased for gifts, honorary "presentation" items, or prizes. The list is chronological. Full information for publishers is given once only and thereafter abbreviated.

*Poetical Remains of the Late Mrs. Hemans.* Edinburgh: William Blackwood & Sons; London: Thomas Cadell, 1836. Edited with a biographical memoir by D. M. Moir.

*The Collected Works of Mrs. Hemans.* Dublin: W. Curry, 1836.

*The Poetical Works of Mrs. Felicia Hemans; Complete in One Volume.* Philadelphia: Grigg & Elliot, 1836. The first "complete" (and also inexpensive) edition, bound in boards; in this "Splendid Library Edition," FH is the only woman included in this series.

*[1839] The Works of Mrs. Hemans; with a Memoir of her Life, by her Sister.* 7 vols. Blackwood & Sons; Cadell, 1839. The first family-authorized edition; includes engravings of portraits of FH and sketches by FH, and review-excerpts, with most of Jeffrey's *Edinburgh Review* essay of 1829 (5.317–26). Vol. 7 excerpts appreciations by Delta (*Blackwood's*, July 1835), L.E.L. (*NMM*, August 1835), Chorley (*Athenæum*, May 1835), Norton's monograph for the *Christian Examiner* (January 1836). Blackwood & Sons held the copyright until the 1870s.

*Tales, and Historic Scenes, With Other Poems.* Blackwood & Sons, 1840. With an engraving of FH's sketch of Bronwylfa. Includes *The Restoration of the Works of Art to Italy*, *Modern Greece* (both with review-excerpts), *Translations*, *Stanzas on the Death of Princess Charlotte*, essays on Italian literature, and miscellaneous short poems.

*Early Blossoms; a Collection of Poems Written Between Eight and Fifteen Years of Age.* By Felicia Dorothea Browne; afterwards Mrs. Hemans. With a life of the Authoress. London: T. Allman, 1840. Rpt. 1846.

*The Sacred Poems of Mrs. Hemans and the Hebrew Melodies of Lord Byron.* New York: Mirror Library, 1844.

*Tales, and Historic Scenes.* Blackwood & Sons, 1851. To the original contents, adds *The Maremma, Belshazzar's Feast, The League of the Alps, The Last Constantine,* among others.

*Poems of Felicia Hemans: A New Edition, Chronologically Arranged, with Illustrative Notes and a Selection of Cotemporary Reviews.* Blackwood & Sons, 1852. With chronology, ten engravings, and appreciations from Delta, L.E.L., Chorley (*Athenæum* essays; *CM*), the *Eclectic Review* (1836), Norton's essay in the *Christian Examiner*. This edition was often reprinted. In 1872 it was issued in elaborate purple cloth, embossed in black and gold, with the pages gilt-edged; similarly in 1873 in green cloth.

*The Forest Sanctuary, De Chatillon, With Other Poems.* Blackwood & Sons, 1854.

*Poems.* Blackwood & Sons, 1865. 365-page selection, with simple gilt-embossing.

*The Poetical Works of Mrs. Hemans.* London: Frederick Warne, n.d. (ca. 1875). "Chandos Classic": the least expensive, least ornate production. "Imperial Edition": cloth-bound with gilt edges for 8$^{1}/_{2}$ s. "Lansdowne Edition": stamped cover and green gilt cloth edition for 3$^{1}/_{2}$ s. (a frequently reprinted, affordable luxury); or padded French morocco, red and gold, for 8s. "Albion Edition" (1891): cloth and gilt for 3$^{1}/_{2}$ s.; cloth, gilt, leather, with engraved frontispiece, 5s.; in French morocco red leather, or calf-boxed.

*The Poetical Works of Mrs. Felicia Hemans.* London and Edinburgh: Gall & Inglis, [1876].

Gilt-edged, tooled, gold-embossed, gilt-stamped, elaborate borders, color inks, 6 engravings.

*The Poetical Works of Mrs. Hemans*. Ed. William Michael Rossetti. London: Ward & Locke, 1873. Includes a fourteen-page "Critical Memoir" by Rossetti and illustrations. A less fancy edition was produced by Moxon in London, and J. B. Lippincott in Philadelphia, 1881.

### TWENTIETH-CENTURY EDITIONS

*The Poetical Works of Felicia Dorothea Hemans*. London: Humphrey Milford; Oxford and elsewhere: Oxford UP, 1914. Part of Oxford's "Standard Authors" series. Long out of print; lacks plays. Includes indices of titles and first lines; frontispiece portrait; and Wordsworth's *Extempore Effusion 29–40* as an epigraph (xvi).

Facsimiles of many lifetime volumes. Westport, Ct.: Garland P, 1978.

Facsimiles of *The Domestic Affections &c* (1995) and *Records of Woman &c* (1991). Poole, England; New York: Woodstock P.

*Records of Woman, With Other Poems*, ed. Paula Feldman. Lexington: U of Kentucky P, 1999.

### HEMANS IN TWENTIETH-CENTURY ANTHOLOGIES

This list is chronological, to show the evolving shapes and shifts of preference. Poem titles are abbreviated after the first instance.

*The Oxford Book of English Verse, 1250–1900*. Ed. Arthur Quiller-Couch. Oxford: Clarendon P, 1906. One short piece: *Dirge*.

*The Distaff Muse: An Anthology of Poetry Written by Women*. Ed. Clifford Bax and Meum Stewart. London: Hollis and Carter, 1949. *The Cliffs of Dover* and *The Homes of England* represent an "outmoded" "Age of Sensibility" that FH is taken to exemplify (59–62).

*Salt and Bitter and Good: Three Centuries of English and American Women Poets*. Ed. Cora Kaplan. New York and London: Paddington, 1975. Headnote and five poems: *The Landing of the Pilgrim Fathers in New England, Properzia Rossi, The Indian Woman's Death-Song, The Memorial Pillar, The Homes of England*.

*Women Romantic Poets, 1785–1832, an Anthology*. Ed. Jennifer Breen. London: J. M. Dent & Sons; Vermont: Charles E. Tuttle, 1992. Includes *Dirge* (cf. *Oxford Book of English Verse*) and *To Wordsworth*.

*The Norton Anthology of English Literature*. 6th ed. New York: Norton, 1993. *England's Dead, Pilgrim Fathers, Casabianca*. 7th ed. (1999) adds *Homes of England* and *A Spirit's Return*.

*Romanticism: An Anthology*. Ed. Duncan Wu. Oxford: Blackwell, 1994. Annotated. *Indian Woman's Death-Song, The Grave of a Poetess, Mozart's Requiem, The Land of Dreams, Nature's Farewell, Second Sight, Sickness Like Night*. 2d ed. (1998) drops *Mozart's Requiem*, adds *Properzia Rossi* and *Casabianca*.

*English Romantic Writers*. Ed. David Perkins. 2d ed. Fort Worth: Harcourt Brace, 1995. Annotated. *Homes of England, Casabianca, The Image in Lava, To Wordsworth, Woman and Fame, The Mirror in the Deserted Hall, Parting Words, The Return, A Spirit's Return, To the Blue Anemone*.

*Victorian Women Poets.* Ed. Angela Leighton & Margaret Reynolds. Oxford, U.K., and
    Cambridge, Mass.: Blackwell, 1995. Headnote and bibliography (Leighton). *The Last
    Song of Sappho, Corinne at the Capitol, To a Wandering Female Singer, Woman and
    Fame, Properzia Rossi, The Grave of a Poetess, Evening Prayer at a Girls' School, Image
    in Lava, Casabianca, Song of Emigration, The Chamois Hunter's Love, The Stranger's
    Heart, A Parting Song.*
*British Literature 1780–1830.* Ed. Anne K. Mellor & Richard Matlack. Fort Worth: Har-
    court Brace, 1996. Annotated. *The Widow of Crescentius, The Wife of Asdrubal, The
    Siege of Valencia, Pilgrim Fathers, The Graves of a Household, To the Poet Wordsworth,
    Casabianca, Evening Prayer at a Girls' School, The Bride of the Greek Isle, Properzia
    Rossi, The Indian City, Indian Woman's Death-Song, Joan of Arc, Madeline, The Me-
    morial Pillar, Homes of England, Image in Lava, Spirit's Return, The Two Homes,
    Corinne at the Capitol, Woman and Fame,* and a few excerpts from letters and
    journals.
*British Women Poets of the Romantic Era: An Anthology.* Ed. Paula R. Feldman. Baltimore:
    Johns Hopkins UP, 1997. Substantial headnote and annotations. *Epitaph on Mr.
    W——, a Celebrated Mineralogist, Epitaph on the Hammer of the Aforesaid Mineralogist,
    The Voice of Spring, The Messenger Bird, Bring Flowers, Troubadour Song, Graves of a
    Household, Pilgrim Fathers, The Monarch's Death-Bed, Gertrude, Casabianca, The
    Wings of the Dove, Image in Lava, The Coronation of Inez de Castro, Indian Woman's
    Death-Song, Arabella Stuart, The Dreamer, The Return, The Painter's Last Work—A
    Scene, I Dream of All Things Free.*
"The Romantics and Their Contemporaries." Ed. Susan J. Wolfson & Peter J. Manning.
    *Longman Anthology of British Literature.* New York: Addison-Wesley-Longman,
    1998. Headnote and annotations. *Wife of Asdrubal, The Last Banquet of Antony and
    Cleopatra, Bride of the Greek Isle, Properzia Rossi, Indian Woman's Death-Song, Joan of
    Arc, Graves of a Household, Homes of England, Corinne at the Capitol, Evening Prayer
    at a Girls' School, Casabianca, Woman and Fame,* excerpts from Jeffrey's review of 1829,
    and Wordsworth's *Extempore Effusion.*
*Women Romantic Poets: An Anthology.* Ed. Duncan Wu. Blackwell, 1998. Introduction,
    bibliography, annotated 100-p. selection: *Written on the Sea Shore, The Statue of the
    Dying Gladiator, To My Eldest Brother, with the British Army in Portugal, Last Banquet
    of Antony and Cleopatra, Stanzas to the Memory of the Late King, The Rock of Cader
    Idris, The Meeting of the Bards, The Voice of Spring, The Stranger in Louisiana, Ancient
    Greek Song of Exile,* all of *Records of Woman, Homes of England, To Wordsworth, The
    Spirit's Mysteries, The Illuminated City, Graves of a Household, Casabianca, To a De-
    parted Spirit, The Chamois Hunter's Love, The Return, Woman on the Field of Battle,
    The Beings of the Mind, Second Sight, Thoughts of an Italian Poet, Despondency and
    Aspiration.*

### Web Sites and On-Line Texts

These are appearing and being updated almost monthly. The best places to begin are the
hubs, which have links to specific authors. Reliable sites (some with facsimiles of first or
other lifetime editions) include

Hemans facsimile texts: http://www.lib.ucdavis.edu/English/BWRP/Works/HemaF
Hemans: http://www.cs.cmu.edu/~mmbt/women/hemans/biography.html
Romantic Circles: http://www.rc.umd.edu/reference/s-resource.html/#ww

University of Pennsylvania: http://www.english.upenn.edu/~mgamer/Romantic/
    index.html
Romanticism Unbound: http://www.iris.nyit.edu~dhogsett/romanticsunbound/
    writers.html

TWENTIETH-CENTURY STUDIES AND BIBLIOGRAPHIES

For full information on some items identified by editors' names only, see under editor, on
this list or the next ("Related Issues").

Albergotti, Charles Dantzler. *Byron, Hemans, and the Reviewers, 1807–1835: Two Routes
    to Fame.* Diss., U of South Carolina, 1995.
Anderson, John M. "The Triumph of Voice in Felicia Hemans's *The Forest Sanctuary.*"
    Melnyk & Sweet, eds., 55–73.
Armstrong, Isobel. "A Music of Thine Own: Woman's Poetry—an expressive tradition?"
    in her *Victorian Poetry: Poetry, Poetics and Politics* (1993). Rpt. *Victorian Women Poets*,
    ed. Leighton, 245–76.
———. "Natural and National Monuments—Felicia Hemans's 'The Image in Lava': A
    Note." Melnyk & Sweet, eds., 212–30.
———. "The Gush of the Feminine: How Can We Read Women's Poetry of the Ro-
    mantic Period?" Feldman & Kelley, eds., 13–32.
Behrendt, Stephen C. "'Certainly Not a Female Pen': Felicia Hemans's Early Public Re-
    ception." Melnyk & Sweet, eds., 95–114.
Clarke, Norma. *Ambitious Heights: Writing, Friendship, Love—The Jewsbury Sisters, Felicia
    Hemans, and Jane Welsh Carlyle.* London and New York: Routledge, 1990.
Cochran, Peter. "Fatal fluency, fruitless dower: The eminently marketable Felicia Hem-
    ans." *TLS* 4816 (21 July 1995): 13.
Edgar, Chad. "Felicia Hemans and the Shifting Field of Romanticism." Melnyk & Sweet,
    eds., 124–34.
Eubanks, Kevin. "Minerva's Veil: Hemans, Critics, and the Construction of Gender."
    *ERR* 8 (1997): 341–59. Bibliography includes key contemporary reviews.
Feldman, Paula R. "Endurance and Forgetting: What the Evidence Suggests." Linkin &
    Behrendt, eds., 15–21.
———. "The Poet and the Profits: Felicia Hemans and the Literary Marketplace." *KSJ* 46
    (1997): 148–76. I am indebted to this landmark article for much of my information
    about exact dates of publication, print runs, sales and payments.
Goslee, Nancy Moore. "Hemans's 'Red Indians': Reading Stereotypes." *Romanticism, Race,
    and Imperial Culture, 1780–1834.* Ed. Alan Richardson & Sonia Hofkosh. Blooming-
    ton: Indiana UP, 1996. 237–64.
Harding, Antony. "Felicia Hemans and the Effacement of Woman." Feldman & Kelley,
    eds., 138–149.
Hickok, Kathleen. *Representations of Women: Nineteenth-Century British Women's Poetry.*
    Westport, Conn.: Greenwood P, 1984.
Jack, Ian. *English Literature, 1815–1832.* Oxford: Clarendon P, 1963.
Kelly, Gary. "Death and the Matron: Felicia Hemans, Romantic Death, and the Founding
    of the Modern Liberal State." Melnyk & Sweet, eds., 196–211.
———. "Gender and Memory in Post-Revolutionary Women's Writing." *Memory and
    Memorials, 1789–1914*, ed. S. Shuttleworth, J. M. Labbe, & M. Campbell. New York
    and London: Routledge, 1998.

Kelly, Gary. *Women, Writing, and Revolution, 1790–1827*. Oxford: Clarendon P, 1993. 189–91.

Kennedy, Deborah. "Hemans, Wordsworth, and the 'Literary Lady.'" *Victorian Poetry* 35 (1997): 267–85.

Leighton, Angela. *Victorian Women Poets: Writing Against the Heart*. New York and London: Wheatsheaf/Harvester, 1992. 8–44.

———, ed. *Victorian Women Poets: A Critical Reader*. Oxford: Blackwell, 1996.

Lenckos, Frauke. "'The Spells of Home': Hemans, 'Heimat,' and the Cult of the Dead Poetess in Nineteenth-Century Germany." Melnyk & Sweet, eds., 135–51.

Lootens, Tricia. "Hemans and Home: Victorianism, Feminine 'Internal Enemies,' and the Domestication of National Identity." *PMLA* 109 (1994): 238–53. Rpt. Leighton, ed., 1–23.

[McGann, Jerome J.] "Literary History, Romanticism, and Felicia Hemans." *MLQ* 54.2 (1993) 215–35. Under McGann's name: Wilson & Haefner, eds., 210–227; *The Poetics of Sensibility: A Revolution in Literary Style*. Oxford: Clarendon P, 1996. 174–94 (see also 70–73, 160–64).

McGann, Jerome J., and Daniel Reiss. Introduction to *Letitia Elizabeth Landon*, esp. 20–23 and 29–30.

Mellor, Anne K. *Romanticism & Gender*. New York and London: Routledge, 1992. 123–43.

Melnyk, Julie. "Hemans's Later Poetry: Religion and the Vatic Poet." Melnyk & Sweet, eds., 74–92.

Melnyk, Julie, and Nanora Sweet, eds. *Felicia Hemans: Reimagining Poetry in the Nineteenth Century*. Houndsmill, U.K.: Macmillan, 2000.

Nicholson, Francis. "Correspondence between Mrs. Hemans and Matthew Nicholson." *Memoirs and Proceedings of the Manchester Literary and Philosophical Society* 54 (1910): 1–40. Important documents of the correspondence of FDB, her mother, and her sister with Nicholson; fascinating information about the young FDB and her first three volumes.

Reiman, Donald H. Introductions, ca. 1978, to the Garland Press facsimile reprints of Hemans's lifetime volumes.

Reynolds, Margaret. "The Woman Poet Sings Sappho's Last Song." Leighton, ed., 277–306.

Roberts, Adam. "Felicia Hemans, *Records of Woman*." *A Companion to Romanticism*. Ed. Duncan Wu. Oxford: Blackwood, 1998. 313–19.

Ross, Marlon B. *The Contours of Masculine Desire: Romanticism and the Rise of Women's Poetry*. New York and London: Oxford UP, 1989. 232–310.

———. "Now *Our* Hemans." Melnyk & Sweet, eds., x–xxvi.

Scott, Grant F. "The Fragile Image: Felicia Hemans and Romantic Ekphrasis." Melnyk & Sweet, eds., 36–54.

Stephenson, Glennis. "Poetic Construction: Mrs Hemans, L.E.L., and the Image of the Nineteenth-Century Woman Poet." *Reimagining Women: Representations of Women in Culture*. Ed. Shirley Neuman & Glennis Stephenson. Toronto: U of Toronto P, 1993. 61–73.

Sweet, Nanora. *The Bowl of Liberty: Felicia Hemans and the Romantic Mediterranean*. Diss., U of Michigan, 1993. Microfilm 9332173.

———. "Felicia Hemans." *Cambridge Bibliography of English Literature: The Nineteenth Century*, Ed. Joanne Shattock. Cambridge: Cambridge UP, 2000.

———. "Hemans's 'The Widow of Crescentius': Beauty, Sublimity, and the Woman Hero." Behrendt & Linken, eds., 101–5.

———. "History, Imperialism, and the Aesthetics of the Beautiful: Hemans and the Post-Napoleonic Moment." *At the Limits of Romanticism: Essays in Cultural, Feminist, and Materialist Criticism.* Ed. Mary A. Favret & Nicola J. Watson. Bloomington: Indiana UP, 1994. 170–84.

———. "Gender and Modernity in *The Abencerrage*: Hemans, Rushdie, and 'The Moor's Last Sigh.'" Melnyk & Sweet, eds., 181–95.

Sweet, Nanora, and Julie Melnyk. "Why Hemans *Now*?" Melynk & Sweet, eds., 1–15.

Taylor, Barbara D. "The Search for a Space: A Note on Felicia Hemans and the Royal Society of Literature." Melnyk & Sweet, eds., 115–23.

Trinder, Peter W. *Mrs Hemans.* Wales: U of Wales P, 1984.

Tucker, Herbert F. "House Arrest: The Domestication of English Poetry in the 1820s." *NLH* 25 (1994): 521–48.

Williamson, Michael T. "Impure Affections: Felicia Hemans's Elegiac Poetry and Contaminated Grief." Melnyk & Sweet, eds., 19–35.

Wolfson, Susan J. "Domestic Affections and the Spear of Minerva." Wilson & Haefner, eds., 128–66.

———. "Felicia Hemans and the Revolving Doors of Reception." Linkin & Behrendt, eds., 214–41.

———. "Gendering the Soul." Feldman & Kelley, eds., 33–68. Revised in *The Lessons of Romanticism.* Ed. Thomas Pfau & Robert Gleckner. Durham, N.C.: Duke UP, 1997. 349–75.

———. "Hemans and the Romance of Byron." Melnyk & Sweet, eds., 155–80.

———. "Men, Women, and 'Fame.'" Behrendt & Linken. 110–20.

———. "'The Mouth of Fame': Gender, Transgression and Romantic Celebrity." *Essays on Transgressive Reading: Reading over the Lines.* Ed. Georgia Johnston. New York, Ontario, Wales: Edwin Mellen, 1997. 1–34.

Wordsworth, Jonathan. Introductions to Woodstock facsimiles of *The Domestic Affections &c* (1995) and *Records of Woman &c* (1991). Rpt. *The Bright Work Grows: Women Writers of the Romantic Age.* Poole, U.K.; New York: Woodstock, 1997.

## Related Issues

Altick, Richard D. *The English Common Reader: A Social History of the Mass Reading Public, 1800–1900.* Chicago: U of Chicago P, 1957.

Baillie, Joanna. *The Collected Letters of Joanna Baillie.* 2 vols. Ed. Judith Bailey Slagle. London: Associated University Presses, 1999.

Behrendt, Stephen C., and Harriet Kramer Linken, eds. *Approaches to Teaching British Women Poets of the Romantic Period.* New York: MLA, 1997. Includes massive bibliography.

Bennett, Betty T., ed. *British War Poetry in the Age of Romanticism: 1793–1815.* New York: Garland, 1976.

Curran, Stuart. "The I Altered." *Romanticism and Feminism,* ed. Anne K. Mellor. Bloomington: Indiana UP, 1988. 185–207.

———. "Women Readers, Women Writers." *The Cambridge Companion to British Romanticism.* Ed. Stuart Curran. Cambridge: Cambridge UP, 1993. 177–95.

Davidoff, Leonore, and Catherine Hall. *Family Fortunes: Men and Women of the English Middle Class, 1780–1850.* Chicago: U of Chicago P, 1987.

Feldman, Paula R., ed. *British Women Poets of the Romantic Era.* Baltimore: Johns Hopkins UP, 1997.

Feldman, Paula R., and Theresa M. Kelley, eds. *Romantic Women: Voices and Counter-voices*. Hanover, N.H.: UP of New England, 1995.

Gilbert, Sandra M., and Susan Gubar. *The Madwoman in the Attic: The Woman Writer and the Nineteenth-Century Literary Imagination*. New Haven: Yale UP, 1979.

Greer, Germaine. *Slip-shod Sibyls: Rejection and the Woman Poet*. New York: Viking, 1995.

Haefner, Joel. "(De)Forming the Romantic Canon: The Case of Women Writers." *College Literature* 20.2 (1993): 44–57.

Hofkosh, Sonia. *Sexual Politics and the Romantic Author*. Cambridge: Cambridge UP, 1998.

Kelly, Gary. "Revolutionary and Romantic Feminism." *Revolution and English Romanticism*, ed. Keith Hanley and Raman Selden. New York: St. Martin's P, 1990. 107–30.

L.E.L. *Letitia Elizabeth Landon: Selected Writings*. Ed. Jerome J. McGann & Daniel Reiss. Canada: Broadview P, 1997.

Linken, Harriet Kramer. "Taking Stock of the British Romantics Marketplace: Teaching New Canons through New Editions." *Nineteenth-Century Contexts* 19 (1995): 111–23.

Linken, Harriet Kramer, and Stephen C. Behrendt, eds. *Romanticism and Women Poets: Opening the Doors of Reception*. Lexington: U of Kentucky P, 1999.

Lipking, Lawrence. *Abandoned Women and Poetic Tradition*. Chicago: U of Chicago P, 1988.

McGann, Jerome J. "Mary Robinson and the Myth of Sappho," *The Poetics of Sensibility: A Revolution in Literary Style*. Oxford: Clarendon P, 1996. 94–116.

Mellor, Anne K. "The Female Poet and the Poetess: Two Traditions of British Women's Poetry, 1780–1830." *Studies in Romanticism* 36 (summer 1997): 261–76.

Poovey, Mary. *The Proper Lady and the Woman Writer*. Chicago: U of Chicago P, 1984.

Prins, Yopie. *Victorian Sappho*. Princeton: Princeton UP, 1999.

Southey, Robert. *Chronicle of the Cid, from the Spanish*. London: Longman &c, 1808.

Staël, Germaine (Mme de). *Corinne, ou l'Italie*. 1807. Trans. and ed. Avriel H. Goldberger. New Brunswick: Rutgers UP, 1987.

Wilson, Carol Shiner, and Joel Haefner, eds. *Re-Visioning Romanticism: British Women Writers, 1776–1837*. Philadelphia: U of Pennsylvania P, 1994.

Wolfson, Susan J. *Women in the Curriculum: British Literature: Discipline Analysis*. Baltimore: National Center for Curriculum Transformation Resources on Women, 1997.

———. "Shakespeare and the Romantic Girl Reader." *NCC* 21 (1999) 191–234.

Wu, Duncan, ed. *Women Romantic Poets: An Anthology*. Oxford: Blackwell, 1997.

# INDEX OF TITLES

Inset songs in longer works are also listed.
For references to these works elsewhere, see General Index.

# GENERAL INDEX

References to FH's works are by short title (for the work itself, see the title index). I have not indexed merely incidental references, mythological names, items in the bibliography, most items in the chronology. Boldface indicates the main discussion of a subject with several entries.

GPSR Authorized Representative: Easy Access System Europe - Mustamäe tee
50, 10621 Tallinn, Estonia, gpsr.requests@easproject.com

www.ingramcontent.com/pod-product-compliance
Lightning Source LLC
Chambersburg PA
CBHW070923100726
47908CB00001B/79